T0135388

Domain-Specific Conceptual Modeling

Dimitris Karagiannis • Moonkun Lee •
Knut Hinkelmann • Wilfrid Utz

Editors

Domain-Specific Conceptual Modeling

Concepts, Methods and ADOxx Tools

Springer

Editors
Dimitris Karagiannis
Faculty of Computer Science
Research Group Knowledge Engineering
University of Vienna
Vienna, Austria

Moonkun Lee
College of Engineering
Chonbuk National University
Jeonju, Korea (Republic of)

Knut Hinkelmann
School of Business
University of Applied Sciences and Arts
Northwestern Switzerland
Olten, Switzerland

Wilfrid Utz
OMiLAB gGmbH
Berlin, Germany

ISBN 978-3-030-93549-8   ISBN 978-3-030-93547-4   (eBook)
https://doi.org/10.1007/978-3-030-93547-4

This Springer imprint is published by the registered company Springer Nature Switzerland AG
The registered company address is: Gewerbestrasse 11, 6330 Cham, Switzerland

A Note from the Editors of the Previous Volume "Domain-Specific Conceptual Modeling"

The predecessor volume *Domain-Specific Conceptual Modeling: Concepts, Methods and Tools* (henceforth called "volume I") published in 2016 represented at that time a novelty in the field of conceptual modeling. It collects the work of different international research groups, each focusing on a domain-specific modeling method, accompanied by proof of concept within its tool implementation based on ADOxx.

A detailed overview of the domain-specific conceptual modeling methods and tools, developed by members active in the OMiLAB Community of Practice showcased in volume I, is given in the chapter "The Purpose-Specificity Framework for Domain-Specific Conceptual Modelling" by Robert A. Buchmann.

The success and positive reception of the first volume among researchers, practitioners, as well as students eager to expand and strengthen their knowledge in conceptual modeling led to our suggestion to continue with a further publication. We are thankful to the scientific community that volume I motivated new researchers and that the new team of editors took our advice and presented these results in this book, showing that this field has continuity and plays a key role, especially in the digital age.

Guided by domain experts, the work of recently established research groups will continue to have an impact and benefit academia and industry, interested students, as well as members of the conceptual modeling community to embrace digital transformation initiatives and projects.

As editors of volume I, we are confident that the new volume will be received by the conceptual modeling community with at least the same outstanding response!

October 2021

Dimitris Karagiannis
Heinrich C. Mayr
John Mylopoulos

Preface

Following the goal of the previous volume, *Domain-Specific Conceptual Modeling: Concepts, Methods and Tools*, to "increase the visibility of domain-specific modelling," in this volume, the significance of the topic is once more demonstrated through new research and development approaches that are manifested in each of the chapters. These include novel modeling methods and tools that emphasize the recent results accomplished and the adequacy to assess specific aspects of a domain.

This successor volume, *Domain-Specific Conceptual Modeling: Concepts, Methods, and ADOxx Tools*, highlights again the work of researchers who have designed and deployed domain-specific modeling methods and tools in the context of the OMiLAB (www.omilab.org) Community of Practice.

Each chapter offers detailed instructions on how to build models in a particular domain, such as product-service engineering, enterprise engineering, digital business ecosystems, and enterprise modeling and capability management. Furthermore, they emphasize possible future developments and research directions in an open manner. All these achievements are enriched with case studies, related information, and tool implementation. The tools are based on the ADOxx metamodelling platform and are provided free of charge via OMiLAB.

The accomplishments are embedded in the OMiLAB approach, more specifically introducing the Agile Modelling Method Engineering (AMME) approach, the ADOxx (www.adoxx.org) platform for experimental realization, the Digital Innovation Environment (DiEn) powered by OMiLAB, and a synopsis on the results of the previous volume in the context of new developments.

We are confident that the theoretical foundation and collection of domain-specific modeling methods and tools presented in this volume will benefit experts and practitioners from academia and industry alike, including members of the conceptual modeling community as well as researchers, lecturers, and students.

A large scientific community was involved in creating this volume, and we would like to express our gratitude to each and every one for their contribution: First of all, we thank all the authors who submitted their work and provided their expertise in the field, and reviewers for their constructive and helpful feedback.

We are also thankful for the support received from the team at Springer led by Ralf Gerstner in the publication of the book!

We highly appreciate the efforts of all those involved!

OMiLAB NPO envisions an active global community for conceptual modeling that benefits from open artifacts. To this end, it acts as a facilitator to the development of scientific methods and technologies for all those who value models. In addition, it is a platform where participants can bring in ideas related to modeling and engage in the exploration process. Get in touch with us via info@omilab.org to get involved in the **OMiLAB Community of Practice**!

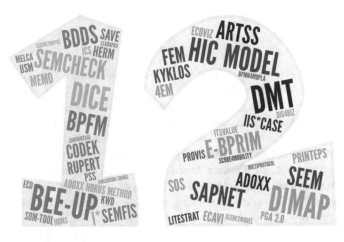

Fig. 1 ADOxx-based tools from volume I and volume II

Vienna, Austria   Dimitris Karagiannis
Jeonju, Korea (Republic of)   Moonkun Lee
Olten, Switzerland   Knut Hinkelmann
Berlin, Germany   Wilfrid Utz
October 2021

Contents

About the Editors

Dimitris Karagiannis holds a full professor position for Business Informatics at the University of Vienna since 1993, leading the Research Group Knowledge Engineering (www.dke.univie.ac.at). He received his PhD degree from the Technical University of Berlin in 1987. The same year he joined the Research Institute for Application-oriented Knowledge Processing in Ulm as division head for "Enterprise Information Systems." Prof. Karagiannis holds an honorary professorship from the Babes-Bolyai University in Cluj-Napoca, Romania. His research interests include metamodelling, knowledge engineering, business process management, enterprise architecture management, and artificial intelligence. The industrial application of his metamodelling research was demonstrated within the BOC Group (www.boc-group.com), a European software and consulting company founded in 1995. In parallel, scientific applications of his research are applied in the Open Models Laboratory—OMiLAB, http://www.omilab.org, an open collaborative environment for modeling method engineering, which he has established and is currently leading, located in Berlin.

Moonkun Lee holds a full professor position for Computer Science and Engineering at Jeonbuk National University (JBNU) in the Republic of Korea since 1996. He received a Bachelor's degree in Computer Science from Pennsylvania State University in the USA in 1989, and a Master's and Ph.D. degrees in Computer and Information Science from the University of Pennsylvania in the USA in 1992 and 1995, respectively. He worked at CCCC in the USA as Computer Scientist from 1992 to 1996 and developed SRE (Software Re/reverse-engineering Environment) applied to the modernization of legacy OS and SW of NSWC in US Navy to Ada. His main research interests are SW round-trip engineering, distributed real-time systems, formal methods, ontology, behavior engineering, etc. He published a number of research papers in journals and conferences, related to the family of *delta-Calculus*, including *dT-* and *dTP-Calculus*. He also developed a mathematical structure called *n:2-Lattice* to define the graphical notion of *behavior ontology*. Further, he published several books in Korean, among which most noticeable are *Formal Methods* (2017, JBNU Press) and *Theory of Multi-Paradigm Programming*

Languages (2021, JBNU Press). For the implementation of the calculus and the ontology, he developed the *SAVE* and the *PRISM* tools on the *ADOxx* metamodeling platform. In industrial applications, one of the most interesting research with SAVE was to prove the integrity of a new engine from a research center of Hyundai Motor Company in 2018 by generating more than 1 million safe cases of the engine states without any deadlock. Currently, he focuses on the specification, analysis, verification, and implementation of the CPS (Cyber-Physical Systems) for Smart City and Industry in SAVEon the ADOxx and the OLIVE with IoT devices in terms of probabilistic models for non-deterministic behavior of the AI applications.

Knut Hinkelmann is Professor for Information Systems and Head of the Master of Science in Business Information Systems at the FHNW University of Applied Sciences and Arts Northwestern Switzerland, where he also is head of the research group Intelligent Information Systems. He is Managing Director of OMiLAB NPO since 2020. Since 2015, he has been a Research Associate at the University of Pretoria (South Africa) and since 2017 he is an Adjunct Professor at the University of Camerino (Italy). His research interests are Enterprise Modeling and Artificial Intelligence. He has served as program chair of several international conferences and has published more than 130 publications. In 1988, he obtained a diploma in Computer Science from the University of Kaiserslautern and a Ph.D. in Natural Sciences from the Computer Science Department of the same university in 1995. From 1988 to 1990, he was a researcher at the Research Institute for Applied Knowledge Processing FAW in Ulm. From 1990 until 1998, he was a researcher and later Head of the Knowledge Management research group at the German Research Center for Artificial Intelligence, DFKI. From 1998 until 2000, he worked as product manager for Insiders Information Management GmbH. He was CEO of the KIBG GmbH from 1996 until 1998, and from 2006 until 2012 he was Scientific Advisor of STEAG & Partner AG.

Wilfrid Utz is one of the managing directors of OMiLAB NPO, the non-profit organization headquartered in Berlin supporting the conceptual modeling community organized around emerging topics with respect to domain-specific conceptual modeling. Wilfrid completed his PhD thesis in 2020 at the University of Vienna in the field of metamodel design and knowledge representation using conceptual structures. He has been involved in numerous international research and innovation projects and gained experience in the field of modeling method conceptualization, design, and implementation of modeling tools using the open ADOxx metamodeling platform (www.adoxx.org).

Part I
Background

Chapter 1
Conceptual Modelling Methods: The AMME Agile Engineering Approach

Dimitris Karagiannis

Abstract Current research in fields such as Business Process Management, Enterprise Architecture Management, Knowledge Management and Software Engineering raises a wide diversity of requirements for Conceptual Modelling, typically satisfied by Design Science artefacts such as modelling methods. When employed in the context of an Agile Enterprise, an underlying requirement for Conceptual Modelling *agility* emerges—manifested not only *on model content level* but also *on modelling method level*. Depending on the questions that must be answered and the systems that must be supported with modelling means, the need for agility may stem from the degree of domain-specificity, from gradual understanding of modelling possibilities, from evolving model-driven systems, etc. The hereby proposed Agile Modelling Method Engineering (AMME) approach thus becomes necessary to extend the traditional perspective of "modelling through standards"; consequently, the benefits of repeatability and wide adoption are traded for responsiveness to dynamic needs identified within an Agile Enterprise.

Keywords Agile Modelling Method Engineering · Metamodelling · Conceptual Modelling · Knowledge Management · Agile Enterprise

Reprinted from Informatics in Economy. IE 2016. Lecture Notes in Business Information Processing (Volume 273) by Gheorghe Cosmin Silaghi, Robert Andrei Buchmann, Catalin Boja. © Springer International Publishing AG 2018.

D. Karagiannis (✉)
Faculty of Computer Science, Research Group Knowledge Engineering, University of Vienna, Vienna, Austria
e-mail: dk@dke.univie.ac.at

1.1   Introduction

A diffuse notion of *Agile Enterprise* has emerged in the literature, as an umbrella term covering new challenges derived from increasingly dynamic needs that must be addressed by evolving and responsive enterprise functions. Agility is generally defined in relation with *change*: "comprehensive response to the business challenges of profiting from rapidly changing [. . .] global markets" [1]; "[the agile enterprise is] built on policies and processes that facilitate speed and change . . . " [2]. The requirement for agility is raised both from a technical perspective (e.g., considering the high dynamics of paradigms such as Industry 4.0 [3] or the Internet of Things [4]) and from a managerial perspective (e.g., Agile Manufacturing [5], Agile Knowledge Management [6]).

Consequently, specific challenges are also emerging for the paradigm of Conceptual Modelling, considering the evolving nature of modelling needs with respect to various functions within an Agile Enterprise. Modelling requirements reclaim flexibility and agility not only for model contents (already addressed in software engineering by the Agile Modelling approach [7]), but also for the adopted modelling language, modelling software and the encompassing modelling method (the relation between these will be established in Sect. 1.3). A methodology and a new modelling paradigm are therefore necessary to address the domain-specificity of the system to be modelled, as well as the evolution of case-specific modelling requirements, for which standards may be insufficiently flexible.

The fields of Business Process Management (BPM), Enterprise Architecture Management (EAM), Model-driven Software Engineering (MDSE) and Knowledge Management (KM)—selected here as representative practices within an Agile Enterprise—have traditionally relied on conceptual modelling standards for the benefits of repeatability and reusability across domains. However, in the pursuit of the "Agile Enterprise" status, the transformative effect of the Agile Manifesto [8] (originally advocated in the context of MDSE) must also be considered for the practice of modelling method engineering in general. Regardless whether a modelling method is subordinated to an Information Systems engineering method or to various management and decision-making practices, multiple factors may generate fluctuating requirements that should be addressed by agile conceptualisation methodologies.

In support of this underlying need for agility, the framework of Agile Modelling Method Engineering (AMME, initially outlined in [9]) is hereby proposed. In addition, a community-oriented research environment—the Open Models Initiative Laboratory (OMiLAB [10])—,where the framework has been applied in several projects, will be described. Two projects will be highlighted to emphasise the applicability of AMME: (1) a research-oriented project addressing KM and EAM concerns (the ComVantage method [11] and tool [12]) and (2) an educational project for teaching MDSE and BPM topics (the FCML method [13] deployed as the BEE-UP tool [14]).

The remainder of the paper is organised as follows: Section 1.2 will overview the key motivating factors for modelling method agility, illustrated for the selected fields of BPM, EAM, KM and MDSE. Section 1.3 will describe the key facets of modelling method agility and the AMME framework. Section 1.4 will share experience and results with applying AMME in projects that have been managed within the OMiLAB environment. The paper ends with a summary and an outlook to future challenges for further consolidating AMME as a method engineering paradigm.

1.2 Conceptual Modelling for the Agile Enterprise: A Selection

A selection of fields that are highly relevant for an Agile Enterprise are discussed here as application areas for Conceptual Modelling, in order to motivate the relevance of agile modelling methods with respect to their dynamic needs.

Conceptual Modelling for BPM is typically associated with popular languages such as BPMN [15], EPC [16], UML activity diagrams [17] or various flowcharting predecessors that have emerged along the history of Enterprise Modelling. Petri Nets [18] became a popular choice for formalisation concerns [19] (rather than a stakeholder-oriented language). Figure 1.1 suggests a semantic spectrum that may be subject to *evolving modelling requirements*: (1) at the "generic" end of the spectrum, UML activity diagrams may be used to describe any type of workflow (business processes, algorithms etc.), their domain-specificity being commonly left to human interpretation; (2) BPMN diagrams narrow down semantics by fixing several concept specialisations (e.g., manual task, automated task); (3) at the right end of the spectrum, AMME was employed to semantically enrich the Task concept with a "concept schema" comprising machine-readable properties (e.g., different types of times, costs) that are relevant for decision-making or for simulation mechanisms required by stakeholders. Other BPM scenarios benefitting from AMME include (1) notational heterogeneity—i.e., when multiple business process notations co-exist and a semantic integration is required [20]; (2) the extension of business process models with conceptual patterns for semantic evaluations [21]; (3) the customisation of processes for the specificity of product-service systems [22].

Conceptual Modelling for EAM also benefits from various standards—e.g., Archimate [23], IDEF [24], or frameworks having a rather ontological scope without necessarily imposing diagrammatic designs (e.g., Zachman's framework [25]). Typically, EAM employs multi-perspective methods with viewpoints that can be instantiated in various modelling views (see also ARIS [16, 26], BEN [27, 28] and MEMO [29, 30] where the multi-perspective nature is emphasised). These may also be subjected to modelling requirements that reclaim a gradual domain-specificity in the language or the method itself (as shown in the case of BPM); another common requirement is for semantic enablers to support decision-making

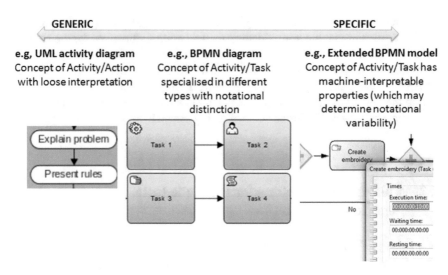

Fig. 1.1 A semantic spectrum for BPM concepts [13]

mechanisms (commonly pertaining to business-IT alignment challenges). For this, a minimal necessity is consistency management across viewpoints. Figure 1.2 shows a multi-view modelling tool for the SOM enterprise modelling method [31], where changes in one model are required to propagate in the others according to semantic overlapping and dependencies—AMME is called to extend the method with consistency-preservation mechanisms that are tightly coupled with the language vocabulary (different approaches to multi-view modelling may also be consulted in [32–35]).

Conceptual Modelling for KM is less reliant on standard modelling languages, at least when the focus is on management practices, rather than KM systems or knowledge representation. The KM community is particularly concerned with knowledge processes such as acquisition, externalisation and learning (also in the focus of an Agile KM approach) and several key processes have been systematised in Nonaka's seminal cycle of knowledge conversion [37]. Figure 1.3 shows how this cycle may be extended when employing Conceptual Modelling methods for knowledge representation. The following phases are hereby proposed: (1) *human-human socialisation* corresponds to Nonaka's traditional "socialisation" phase; (2) *externalisation in raw form* corresponds to Nonaka's traditional "externalisation" phase, if knowledge is captured in semi-structured content (to be managed with content management system); (3) *externalisation in diagrammatic-form* is enabled by modelling methods that enable knowledge acquisition through diagrammatic means (e.g., work procedures described in models rather than natural language); (4) *combination* corresponds to Nonaka's traditional "combination" phase, with additional opportunities for combining diagrammatic knowledge representations; (5) *internalisation at machine-level* is enabled if the models are further exposed as a knowledge base to model-driven systems; (6) *machine-to-human socialisation*

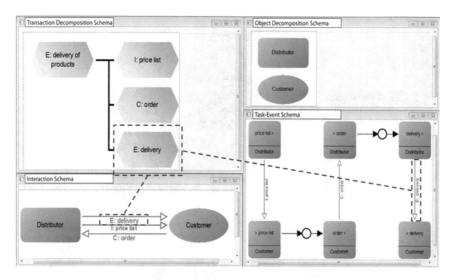

Fig. 1.2 Multi-view consistency challenges in Enterprise Modelling [36]

would (potentially) be a socialisation variant where the "shared doing" involves a human and a knowledge-driven system (e.g., robots). The challenge of AMME in this context is to facilitate the knowledge acquisition with modelling means and tool support that are adequate to the semantics deemed relevant for KM practices and systems. Other approaches to the interplay between KM and modelling practices, based on business process modelling as a facilitator, have been overviewed in [38].

Conceptual Modelling for MDSE typically relies on modelling languages tailored for software design and development—e.g., UML [17], ER [39]. A popular underlying ambition is that of code generation, a task that depends on a fixed and well-defined semantic space (hence an invariant modelling language amenable to standardisation). Agile Modelling [7] is employed as a matter of quickly adapting model contents and procedures rather than the governing language. AMME becomes relevant here by raising the level of abstraction for MDSE agility, as it allows the propagation of change requests to the language semantics and further to modelling functionality. This, of course, limits the "modelling is programming" [40] possibilities (e.g., code generation); instead, AMME is motivated by a "modelling is knowledge representation" perspective, with a model base that drives "model-aware" run-time systems that are parameterised with knowledge items (rather than generated). Figure 1.4 suggests an approach proposed by the ComVantage project, where app orchestrations are derived from app requirements captured in diagrammatic form, indicating the precedence of mobile app support along a business process [42].

BPM, EAM, KM and MDSE are several fields that, under the hereby discussed assumptions and driven by project-based requirements, have motivated the emergence of AMME. The literature reports on several other approaches related

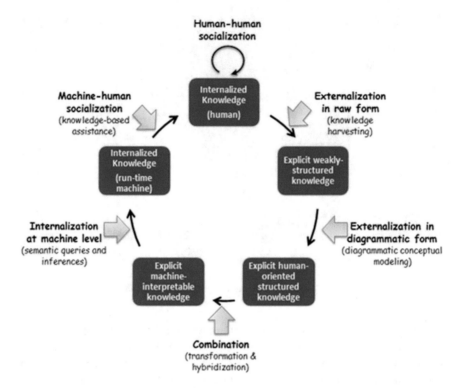

Fig. 1.3 An extended Knowledge Conversion cycle involving Conceptual Modelling

to AMME in certain aspects, however typically subordinated to MSDE goals and focusing on the domain and case specificity aspect rather than the agility of the modelling method artefact—e.g., the notion of "Situational Methods" for Information Systems Engineering [43, 44], the Domain-specific Modelling Language design methodology [45], extensibility mechanisms for standard languages [46]. Metamodelling environments such as [47–49] have significantly contributed to increasing the productivity of modelling tool implementation, thus providing candidate environments for the rapid prototyping support needed during an AMME deployment.

1.3 The AMME Framework

The notion of Agile Enterprise opens a wider scope for agility than the one advocated in agile software development and its conceptual dynamics must be captured in adequate conceptualisation and engineering processes. A classification of change drivers for an Agile Enterprise is proposed here, as illustrated in Fig. 1.5:

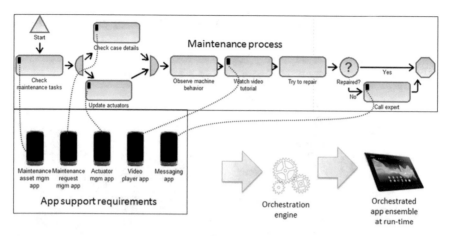

Fig. 1.4 Models for "model-aware information systems" (adapted from [41])

- *Changes in the business model and value proposition*—e.g., shifting the value proposition towards the servitisation of existing products, a deeper specialization of products reclaiming new domain-specific properties in design decisions;
- *Changes in management strategy*—e.g., shifting between different KM approaches or process improvement methods, reclaiming the inclusion of new properties in key performance indicators;
- *Changes in support technology and infrastructure*—e.g., migration to a bring-your-own-device strategy;
- *Digitisation of assets*—e.g., migration to new technological paradigms (Internet of Things, Industry 4.0);
- *Changes in the business context*—e.g., market changes, reconfigurations of virtual enterprises;
- *Self-initiated changes*—e.g., pro-active process re-engineering, adoption of a capability-driven Enterprise Architecture [50];
- *Normative changes*—e.g., changes pertaining to legal or certification compliance, evolution of already adopted standards.
- *Changes in the social eco-system*—e.g., changes in user behaviour, in interactions between users or between users and systems.

The enterprise performance, from an information and communication technology viewpoint, is primarily supported by (1) Enterprise Information Systems (EIS) employed at run-time (e.g., for enacting business processes and managing resources) and (2) an Enterprise Architecture (EA) supporting design-time decisions (e.g., business-IT alignment). Conceptual Modelling practices traditionally support both facets: they can enable the deployment of model-based EIS as part of some IS engineering method; they can also enable the accumulation of a Knowledge Base in conceptual model form. In both cases, modelling activities must be supported by a modelling method and adequate tooling—i.e., modelling software that supports communication, sense-making, the accumulation of knowledge assets or analytical system designs, etc.

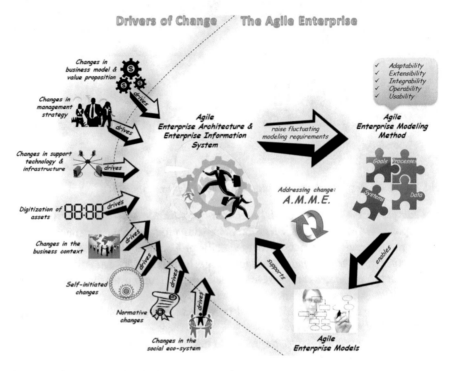

Fig. 1.5 The role of AMME in the Agile Enterprise

For this purpose, various model-based management and engineering practices typically employ available standards or well-established languages and methods. These bring inherent governance benefits (e.g., repeatability, compatibility)—however, the general assumption for adopting such methods is that modelling requirements are fixed and a standards-oriented modelling culture can be uniformly established within the enterprise and for its application domain. The hereby discussed AMME framework is motivated by the assumption that modelling requirements evolve due to one or more of several factors:

- users become gradually familiar with modelling possibilities;
- richer semantics become necessary, either for design-time (e.g., decision-support) or run-time use cases (e.g., model-driven systems);
- stakeholders gain gradual insight and common understanding of the application domain, of the properties that are relevant to the model abstractions.

Under these assumptions, the Agile Modelling Method Engineering (AMME) approach (providing several qualities suggested in Fig. 1.5) becomes necessary and the benefits of standards may be traded for other benefits—e.g., gradual domain-specific enrichment of the modelling language, in-house evolution of model-aware systems.

Agility, as understood by AMME from an internal perspective, has two basic manifestations: (1) *artefact agility* is enabled by the decomposition of a modelling method into building blocks that define the backlog items to be managed through agile engineering efforts; and (2) *methodological agility* manifests in the engineering process itself, taking the form of an incremental and iterative spiralling development.

Artefact agility is enabled by the definition of a modelling method. The artefact created by AMME was originally defined in [51] in terms of its building blocks (Fig. 1.6):

- A *modelling language* further decomposed in notation (graphical symbols corresponding to the language concepts), syntax (the language grammar and associated syntactic constraints) and semantics (language vocabulary, machine-readable properties of each concept, associated semantic constraints);
- *Mechanisms and algorithms* cover the model-based functionality to be made available in a modelling tool—either generic (applicable to models of any type), specific (applicable only to models of a specific type) or hybrid (applicable to a limited set of model types that fulfil specific requirements);
- A *modelling procedure* consists of the modelling activities to be performed in order to reach modelling goals; it may take the form of method documentation or may be supported by mechanisms aiming to improve user experience (e.g., by automating certain procedure steps).

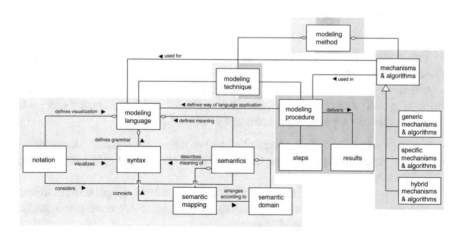

Fig. 1.6 The modelling method building blocks [51]

Methodological agility is enabled by an iterative engineering process at the core of the AMME framework and depicted in Fig. 1.7. This process is generically named the "Produce-Use" cycle, with two phases per iteration: (1) the *Produce* step will capture domain knowledge ("models of concepts"), formalise it and deploy it in a modelling tool; (2) the *Use* step will employ this modelling tool to capture case knowledge that instantiates the domain concepts ("models using concepts") while also evaluating acceptance and various quality criteria to feed back in the next iteration of the *Produce* phase.

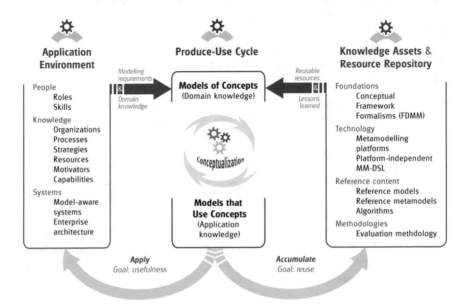

Fig. 1.7 The AMME Framework (adapted from [9])

This cycle may be conveniently specialised for different contexts and deployments. The assumption is that different instances will be necessary depending on the requirements to the conceptualization process. The "AMME Lifecycle" described below (Fig. 1.8) shows how a concrete instance of the conceptualization process is realized within the Open Models Laboratory (OMiLAB).

- *Create*: a mix of knowledge acquisition and requirements elicitation techniques;
- *Design*: practices for designing the modelling method building blocks depicted in Fig. 1.6;
- *Formalise*: refinements of the method design in terms of appropriate formalisms, to supporting implementations across various platforms by removing ambiguities from the method design specification;
- *Develop*: the modelling tool development phase, typically benefitting from rapid prototyping environments (e.g., [47]);
- *Deploy/Validate*: the packaging and deployment of the tool with improved user experience and an evaluation protocol that feeds back into the *Create* step of the next iteration.

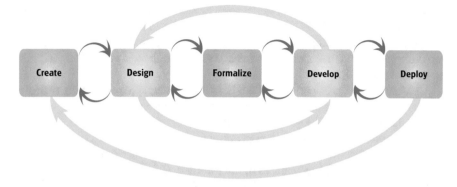

Fig. 1.8 The AMME lifecycle

Feedback loops occur both internally, between subsequent phases, and for the overall cycle, as each deployment collects change requests for the next method increments.

The Produce-Use cycle interacts, at the method "front-end", with (1) the enterprise environment by assimilating requirements and domain knowledge; and, at the method "back-end", with (2) an asset repository where lessons learned, method fragments and various reusable assets are accumulated for future deployments.

1.4 Project Experience and Results

1.4.1 The Open Models Initiative Laboratory

The Open Models Initiative Laboratory (OMiLAB) [10] is a research environment (both physical and virtual) that fosters a global community of researchers sharing a common understanding of the concept of *modelling method* and of models value. OMiLAB may be considered an instance deployment of AMME, providing specific enablers. A number of domain-specific or hybrid modelling methods and their deployments (tools) have been developed in projects of different kinds (1) *educational* (e.g., modelling tools for didactic purposes), (2) *research-oriented* (i.e., results of metamodelling tasks in research projects) and (3) *digitisation-oriented* (i.e., typically follow-up developments of research projects). A selection of such methods are presented in [52]—a first volume in a planned community-driven book series, reporting on projects that benefit from the OMiLAB enablers and its collaborative network.

Additionally, community-oriented events have established forums for dissemination or knowledge transfer between academic research, industry and education. The most prominent event is NEMO (Next-generation Enterprise Modelling)— an annual summer school [53] where the principles and framework of AMME have been initially articulated and students have received initial training with its application. Currently OMiLAB has European and Asian "collaboratories", as well as Associated Organisations fostering localised communities. An organisational structure and related management policies (e.g., for intellectual property rights) may be consulted in [54].

One key enabler provided by AMME is ADOxx—the rapid prototyping platform for developing and deploying modelling tools [47]. Its meta-metamodel provides built-in facilities for developing the building blocks of a modelling method—e.g., a design environment for the language grammar and vocabulary, a vector graphics language for dynamic notations, a scripting language for developing model-driven functionality. In addition, a richness of plug-ins and ancillary development services and reusable items are made available through the OMiLAB portal. Research is underway regarding MM-DSL, a platform-independent declarative language for modelling method definitions–an initial version was presented in [55].

1.4.2   The ComVantage Research Project

ComVantage, an FP7 European Project [56], proposed an IT architecture based on mobile app ensembles consuming Linked Enterprise Data shared among organisations, in support of collaborative business processes for various application areas (e.g., customised production, mobile maintenance) [57]. The run-time architecture was complemented with design-time support in the form of the evolving *ComVantage modelling method*, a process-centred enterprise modelling method tailored for the domain-specificity of the project application areas, for the goal of establishing a knowledge repository in diagrammatic form (hence supporting KM and EAM).

Various semantic lifting approaches were applied to unify heterogeneous data sources in a Linked Data cloud, from which front-end apps can retrieve them through protocols established by the Linked Data technological space [58]. An RDFizer mechanism was implemented to also expose the diagrammatic contents in Linked Data form [59, 60], thus contributing to the knowledge processes proposed in Fig. 1.3 and opening new opportunities of semantic lifting (as suggested in Fig. 1.9).

Consequently, requirements on client applications would inherently propagate to requirements for the modelling method, reclaiming an AMME approach to evolve it accordingly, and to ensure that a sufficient semantic space is available to clients.

By the end of the project, the modelling method reached a Zachman-style multi-viewpoint structure addressing various aspects (perspectives) and scopes (levels of domain-specificity) as reflected in Table 1.1. Multiple sources may be consulted for the method documentation [11, 61–63]. Details on the method's conceptual evolution with respect to AMME are available in [41]. The modelling tool is hosted by OMiLAB at [12].

Table 1.1 Viewpoints of the ComVantage method [33]

Scopes:	Aspects: Behavioural aspect		Structural aspect	
	Procedural views (procedural knowledge captured in the form of flowcharts with varying semantics and customised notation)	Collaborative views (the same kind of knowledge, expressed as interactions in order to highlight necessary interfaces)	Motivator views (structural descriptions of the commodities offered by the enterprise)	Participants views (structural descriptions of available or required resources, liable entities and their capabilities)
Business/Enterprise	Models that describe a business on its highest level of business process abstraction (e.g., abstract value creation processes)	Models that describe value exchanges between entities that participate in the business model or in an enterprise-level process	Models that describe the values that are created by the business or by each process in particular	Models that describe actors and roles involved in the business model, including their business capabilities
Requirements	Models that describe how work processes are mapped on requirements for different kinds of resources	Models that describe how different resources must interact based on their mappings on work processes	Models that describe required and available resources	
App execution	Models that describe how mobile apps must be "orchestrated" (chained) according to the flow of the process they must support	Models that describe how mobile apps must interact according to the flow of the process they must support	Models that describe mobile apps that are required and must be "orchestrated" to support a process	
App design	Models that describe the flow of interactions between a user and elements of an app's user interface	Models that describe a navigational map across required app features	Models that describe the features and data requirements for a mobile app	

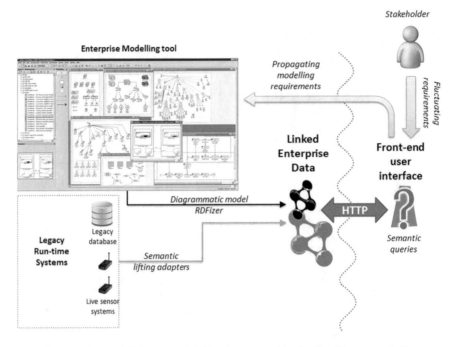

Fig. 1.9 Enterprise models for semantic lifting (as proposed by the ComVantage method)

1.4.3   The FCML/BEE-UP Educational Project

FCML (Fundamental Conceptual Modelling Languages) is a teaching-oriented modelling method providing a hybridisation of 5 well-known modelling languages: BPMN, EPC, ER, UML and Petri Nets. Their initials form the acronym BEE-UP which is the name of the modelling prototype made available through OMiLAB for teaching purposes, already adopted for teaching MDSE and BPM topics by several universities associated with the OMiLAB collaboration network. Details on the FCML method can be consulted in [13], only a brief overview is provided here.

FCML is not only a convenience tool that supports model types belonging to different languages. It also agilely assimilated semantic integration, extensions and functionality to address modelling requirements for various teaching scenarios subordinated to BPM (e.g., process path simulation, Petri Nets simulation) or MDSE (e.g., SQL code generation):

- In the "mechanisms" building block, all three types of mechanisms are exemplified: (1) *generic* (e.g., model queries or diagram exports in the form of RDF knowledge graphs), (2) *specific* (e.g., SQL generation from ER diagrams, Petri Nets simulation/stepping), (3) *hybrid* (applicable to different types of models complying to some well-formedness requirements—e.g., process path analysis

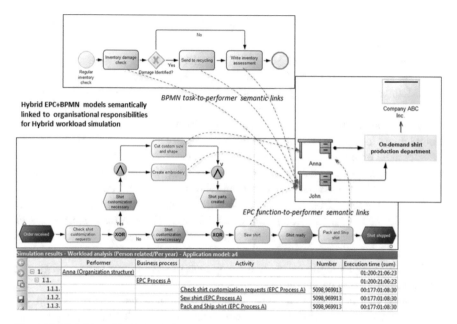

Fig. 1.10 Hybrid workload simulation mechanism on EPC and BPMN process models (adapted from [13])

for models that correctly use the basic workflow patterns, i.e., BPMN, EPC, UML activity diagrams—as suggested in Fig. 1.10);

- In the "language" building block, semantic extensions are applied to support these mechanisms: (1) at *language level* (e.g., an organigram model type to support workload simulations); (2) at *model type level*, (e.g., EPC extensions to support multiple variants of EPC recommended in the literature, depending on their goal and required rigor); (3) at *concept level* (e.g., user-editable and machine-readable properties such as costs, times, probabilities to support process path simulations, SQL-specific properties to support SQL code generation);
- The "modelling procedure" component is aligned accordingly to guide users in how to create models for the different scenarios.

FCML and its BEE-UP implementation enable a multi-purpose and multi-layered modelling approach, providing on one hand notational alternatives for BPM and, on the other hand, a complementary set of languages for teaching MDSE topics. The modelling tool is hosted by OMiLAB at [14].

1.5   Summary and Future Challenges

The relevance of Conceptual Modelling to selected fields of research and management practices—namely, Business Process Management, Enterprise Architecture Management, Knowledge Management (Systems) and Model-driven Software Engineering—was hereby discussed. A common underlying requirement for modelling method agility was highlighted and the AMME framework was proposed as a complement to standard methods, which are typically considered invariants in agile development practices. Thus, the work at hand raises the level of agility from that of software engineering to that of modelling method engineering—even in the case of MDSE, where agility is advocated here in relation to generic "conceptual model"-awareness concerns (rather than standard-driven code generation). Experiences and results accumulated through the Open Models Initiative Laboratory research environment validate the applicability of AMME. The current experience is based on several project-based deployments and further enablers must be developed, similarly to how the agile software development practices have been emerging as a community-driven paradigm.

Several key enablers that must further consolidate the AMME vision are suggested here as open challenges for which research is already under way: (1) an executable declarative modelling language for coding modelling method definitions in a platform-independent manner; (2) interoperability mechanisms at meta^{2}model level between the popular metamodelling platforms; (3) specialised issue tracking platforms considering the specific characteristics of modelling methods as Design Science artefacts.

References

1. Goldman, S., Naegel, R., Preiss, K.: Agile Competitors and Virtual Organizations: Strategies for Enriching the Customer. Wiley (1994)
2. The Business Dictionary: The Agile Enterprise definition. http://www.businessdictionary.com/definition/agile-enterprise.html.
3. Schwab, K.: The Fourth Industrial Revolution. Crown Business (2017)
4. Internet of Things Global Standard Initiative, http://www.itu.int/en/ITU-T/gsi/iot
5. Levy, M., Hazzan, O.: Agile Knowledge Management. In: Encyclopedia of Information Science and Technology, pp. 112-117, IGI Global (2008)
6. Gunasekaran, A.: Agile Manufacturing: the 21st century competitive strategy. Elsevier (2001)
7. Ambler, S. W.: Agile Modeling: Effective Practices for Extreme Programming and the Unified Process. Wiley (2002)
8. The Agile Manifesto, http://www.agilemanifesto.org.
9. Karagiannis, D.: Agile modelling method engineering. In: Karanikolas, N., Akoumianakis, D., Mara, N., Vergados, D., Michalis, X. (eds.) Proceedings of the 19th Panhellenic Conf. on Informatics, ACM, p 5-10 (2015)
10. The Open Models Initiative Laboratory portal. http://omilab.org.

11. Buchmann, R. A.: Modeling Product-Service Systems for the Internet of Things: the Com-Vantage Method. In: Karagiannis, D., Mayr, H. C., Mylopoulos, J. (eds.), Domain-specific Conceptual Modelling, pp. 417-437, Springer (2016)
12. The ComVantage project page in the OMiLAB portal. http://austria.omilab.org/psm/content/comvantage.
13. Karagiannis, D., Buchmann, R. A., Burzynski, P., Reimer, U., Walch, M.: Fundamental Conceptual Modeling Languages in OMiLAB. In: Karagiannis, D., Mayr, H. C., Mylopoulos, J. (eds.), Domain-specific Conceptual Modelling, pp. 3-30, Springer (2016)
14. The Bee-Up project page in the OMiLAB portal. http://austria.omilab.org/psm/content/bee-up/info.
15. Object Management Group, The official BPMN specification. http://www.bpmn.org.
16. Scheer, A. W.: ARIS. Vom Geschäftsprozess zum Anwendungssystem. Springer (2002)
17. Object Management Group, The official UML resource page. http://www.uml.org.
18. Petri, C. A., Reisig, W..: Petri net.Scholarpedia 3 (4): 6477. doi:https://doi.org/10.4249/scholarpedia.6477
19. van der Aalst W M P (1999) Formalization and verification of event-driven process chains. Information and Software Technology 41(10):639-650.
20. Prackwieser, C., Buchmann, R., Grossmann, W., Karagiannis, D.: Overcoming Heterogeneity in Business Process Modeling with Rule-Based Semantic Mappings. Int. Journal of Software Engineering and Knowledge Engineering 24(8):1131-1158 (2014)
21. Fill, H. G.: Semantic evaluation of business processes using SeMFIS, In: Karagiannis, D., Mayr, H. C., Mylopoulos, J. (eds.), Domain-specific Conceptual Modelling, pp. 149-170, Springer (2016)
22. Boucher, X., Medini, Kh., Fill, H. G.: Product-Service-System modeling method, In: Karagiannis, D., Mayr, H. C., Mylopoulos, J. (eds.), Domain-specific Conceptual Modelling pp. 455-484, Springer (2016)
23. The Open Group, ArchiMate® 2.1 Specification, http://www.opengroup.org/archimate.
24. IEEE, IEEE Standard for Functional Modeling Language – syntax and semantics of IDEF0, IEEE std. 1329.1-1998
25. Zachman, J.A.: A framework for information systems architecture. In: IBM Systems Journal 26 (3): 276-292 (1987)
26. Software AG, ARIS – the community page. http://www.ariscommunity.com.
27. Aier, S., Kurpjuweit, S., Saat, J., Winter, R.: Business Engineering Navigator: A "Business to IT" Approach to Enterprise Architecture Management. In: Bernard, S., Doucet, G., Gotze, J., Saha, P. (eds.) Coherency Management: Architecting the Enterprise for Alignment, Agility, and Assurance, pp.77-89, Author House (2009)
28. Winter, R.: Business Engineering Navigator. Springer (2011)
29. Frank, U.: Multi-Perspective Enterprise Modeling (MEMO) – Conceptual Framework and Modeling Languages. In: Proceedings of HICSS-35, pp. 1258-1267, IEEE (2002)
30. Bock, A., Frank, U.: Multi-perspective enterprise modeling – conceptual foundation and implementation with ADOxx. In: Karagiannis, D., Mayr, H. C., Mylopoulos, J. (eds.), Domain-specific Conceptual Modelling, pp. 241-268, Springer (2016)
31. Ferstl, O.K., Sinz, E. J.: Modelling of Business Systems Using SOM. In: Bernus, P., Mertins, K., Schmidt, G. J. (eds.) Handbook on Architectures of Information Systems, Springer, p. 347-367 (2006)
32. Karagiannis, D., Buchmann, R. A., Bork, D.: Managing consistency in multi-view enterprise models: an approach based on semantic queries. Paper 53, Proceedings of ECIS 2016, Association for Information Systems (2016)
33. Bork, D.: Using Conceptual Modelling for Designing Multi-view Modelling Tools. In: Proceedings of the AMCIS 2015, Association for Information Systems (2015)
34. Fertsl, O. K., Sinz, E. J., Bork, D.: Tool support for the Semantic Object Model. In: Karagiannis, D., Mayr, H. C., Mylopoulos, J. (eds.), Domain-specific Conceptual Modelling, pp. 291-312, Springer (2016)

35. Jeusfeld, M. A.: SemCheck: checking constraints for multi-perspective modeling languages. In: Karagiannis, D., Mayr, H. C., Mylopoulos, J. (eds.), pp. 31-54, Springer (2016)
36. The SOM project page in the OMiLAB portal: http://www.omilab.org/web/som.
37. Nonaka, I.: The Knowledge-Creating Company, Harvard Business Review 69, 96-104 (1991)
38. Karagiannis, D., Woitsch, R.: Knowledge Engineering in Business Process Management" In: vom Brocke, J., Rosemann, M. (eds.) Handbook on Business Process Management 2, Springer, pp. 623-648 (2015)
39. Chen, P.: The Entity-Relationship Model - Toward a Unified View of Data. In: ACM Transactions on Database Systems 1 (1): 9–36, ACM (1976)
40. Aquino,N., Vanderdonckt, J. I. Panach, J. I., Pastor, O.: Conceptual modelling of interaction. In: Embley, D. W., Thalheim, B. (eds.) Handbook of conceptual modeling: theory, practice and research challenges, pp.335-355, Springer (2011)
41. Ziegler, J., Graube, M., Pfeffer, J., Urbas, L.: Beyond App-Chaining: Mobile App Orchestration for Efficient Model Driven Software Generation, In: Cyganek,, B., Nolte, Th. (eds.) Proceedings of EFTA 2012, IEEE, pp.1-8 (2012)
42. Welke, R. J., Kumar, K.: Methodology engineering: a proposal for situation-specific methodology construction. In: Cotterman, W., Senn, J. (eds.) Challenges and strategies for research in systems development, pp. 257-269, Wiley (1992)
43. Henderson-Seller, B., Ralyte, J., Agerfalk, P., Rossi, M.: Situational Method Engineering, Springer (2014)
44. Frank, U: Domain-specific modelling languages: requirements analysis and design guidelines. In: Reinhartz-Berger, I., Sturm, A., Clark, T., Cohen, Sh., Betin, J. (eds.) Domain Engineering, pp. 133–157. Springer (2013)
45. Object Management Group, UML Superstructure Specification. http://www.omg.org/cgi-bin/doc?formal/05-07-04.
46. BOC GmbH, The ADOxx metamodelling platform – reference webpage. http://www.adoxx.org/live.
47. Kelly, S., Lyytinen, K., Rossi, M.: MetaEdit+ a fully configurable multi-user and multi-tool CASE and CAME environment. In: Bubenko, J., Krogstie, J., Pastor, O., Pernici, B., Rolland, C., Solvberg, A. (eds.) Seminal Contributions to Information Systems Engineering, pp. 109–129, Springer (2013)
48. Budinsky, F., Steinberg, D., Merks, E., Ellersick, R., Grose, T.J.: Eclipse Modeling Framework. In: The Eclipse Series. Addison Wesley (2004)
49. Buchmann, R. A., Karagiannis, D.: Agile Modelling Method Engineering: Lessons Learned in the ComVantage Project", In: Ralyte, J., Espana, S., Pastor, O. (eds.) Proceedings of PoEM 2015, LNBIP 235, Springer, p. 356-373 (2015)
50. Loucopoulos, P., Kavakli, E.: Capability-oriented enterprise knowledge modeling: the CODEK approach. In: Karagiannis, D., Mayr, H. C., Mylopoulos, J. (eds.), Domain-specific Conceptual Modelling, pp. 197-216, Springer (2016)
51. Karagiannis, D., Kühn, H.: Metamodelling Platforms. In: Bauknecht, K., Tjoa, A. M., Quirchmayer, G. (eds.) Proceedings of the Third International Conference EC-Web 2002 – DEXA 2002, LNCS 2455, Springer, p. 182 (2002)
52. Karagiannis, D., Mayr, H. C., Mylopoulos, J. (eds.): Domain-specific Conceptual Modelling, Springer (2016)
53. Next-generation Enterprise Modelling (NEMO) Summer School series – official website. http://nemo.omilab.org.
54. Gotzinger, D., Miron, E. T., Staffel, F.: OMiLAB: an open collaborative environment for modeling method engineering. In: Karagiannis, D., Mayr, H. C., Mylopoulos, J. (eds.), Domain-specific Conceptual Modelling, pp. 55-78, Springer (2016)
55. Visic, N., Fill, H.-G., Buchmann, R., Karagiannis, D.: A domain-specific language for modelling method definition: from requirements to grammar. In: Rolland C, Anagnostopoulos D, Loucopoulos P, Gonzalez-Perez C (eds.) Proceedings of RCIS 2015, IEEE, p 286-297 (2015)

56. ComVantage Consortium, Public project deliverables page, http://www.comvantage.eu/results-publications/public-deriverables.
57. Münch, T., Buchmann, R., Pfeffer, J., Ortiz, P., Christl, C., Hladik, J., Ziegler, J., Lazaro, O., Karagiannis, D., Urbas, L.: An Innovative Virtual Enterprise Approach to Agile Micro and SME-based Collaboration Networks, in: Camarinha-Matos, L. M., Scherer, R. J. (eds.) Proceedings of 14th IFIP Conference on Virtual Enterprises, Springer Heidelberg, p 121-128 (2013)
58. Heath, T., Bizer, C.: Linked Data: Evolving the Web into a Global Data Space (1st edition). Morgan & Claypool (2011)
59. Karagiannis, D., Buchmann, R. A.: Linked Open Models: extending Linked Open Data with conceptual model information. In: Information Systems 56, 174-197 (2016)
60. Buchmann, R. A., Karagiannis, D.: Enriching Linked Data with Semantics from Domain-specific Diagrammatic Models. Business and Information Systems Engineering 58(5):341-353, Springer (2016)
61. Buchmann R. A.: Conceptual modeling for mobile maintenance: The ComVantage Case. In: Proceedings of HICSS-47, p 3390-3399, IEEE (2014)
62. Buchmann, R. A., Karagiannis, D.: Modelling mobile app requirements for semantic traceability. In: Requirements Engineering, DOI https://doi.org/10.1007/s00766-015-0235-1 (2015)
63. Buchmann, R. A., Karagiannis, D.: Domain-specific Diagrammatic Modelling: a Source of Machine-Readable Semantics for the Internet of Things. In: Cluster Computing, DOI https://doi.org/10.1007/s10586-016-0695-1 (2016)

Chapter 2
Development of Conceptual Models and Realization of Modelling Tools Within the ADOxx Meta-Modelling Environment: A Living Paper

The OMiLAB Community

Abstract A community for a specific domain forms around common but specific artifacts found in that domain. For the domain of conceptual modelling, the ADOxx meta-modelling environment is such an artifact, having formed a community through projects, realized tools, and knowledge exchange. This chapter presents the development of conceptual models and their realization in the form of modelling tools using the ADOxx meta-modelling environment. First, it describes relevant concepts of conceptual models, the modelling layers, and modelling methods before introducing their formalization using the ADOxx environment. Second, additional implementation cases are depicted with examples, providing references and elaborating further details on the realization of conceptual models. This chapter is built as a so-called living paper meant to be further extended in the future by members of the OMiLAB community.

Keywords Conceptual models · Conceptual modelling · Model value · ADOxx · Meta-modelling · Modelling tools

2.1 Introduction

Research and development in a scientific field require sustainability of results and achievements for its community. For the field of computer science and more specifically information systems, such sustainability can be achieved among other things through the software the community has formed around. Such software can be used to observe, evaluate, and transport conserved knowledge between members

The OMiLAB Community (✉)
Community of Practice, OMiLAB NPO, Berlin, Germany
e-mail: info@omilab.org

of the community; it becomes a central part in working, discussing, and sharing of knowledge between participants creating and (re-)using parts of the software.

The observation that software artifacts for a specific domain form the community is underlined by prominent examples such as the Eclipse community for software development, the Mozilla community for web development, or the recently evolved Visual Studio Code community for advanced code editing. As such, the ADOxx community acts in the domain of conceptual modelling utilizing the environment of the ADOxx platform as a common denominator.

Throughout several years the ADOxx platform has been steadily employed in several European, national, and individual research projects (CloudSocket,[1] complAI,[2] DISRUPT,[3] and more[4]), used to create multiple tools[5] and as an integral part of the knowledge exchange on conceptual models with its community members. Educational activities have promoted its use, e.g., in the international NEMO Summer School[6] series.

This chapter is a result of the OMiLAB community with a specific version at the current date of publishing. However, we aim to support its further growth and extension with additional content, materials, etc., applying an approach similar to open-source software by creating a living paper. Every member of the OMiLAB community is invited to participate in enhancing and extending this text with own results and achievements. For further information and the latest version, visit https://www.omilab.org/activities/living-paper/develop+realize-within-adoxx/ (accessed July 2021).

In the remainder of the chapter, we will first introduce the essentials of conceptual modelling through the concepts used to both develop such models and realize the corresponding modelling tools in Sect. 2.2. Section 2.3 shows general application cases of models in an ADOxx-based modelling tool with examples, distinguishing different types of interactions. Section 2.4 wraps up the chapter with a conclusion.

2.2   Essentials

When developing conceptual models, it is important to consider the domain they are created for, what purpose they are for, and on what level in the modelling hierarchy they are positioned. Relevant levels of that hierarchy can be seen in Fig. 2.1. It also shows the relation between the levels and two parts of the ADOxx

---

[1] CloudSocket webpage: https://site.cloudsocket.eu/ (accessed 06.2021).

[2] ComplAI webpage: https://complai.innovation-laboratory.org/ (accessed 06.2021).

[3] DISRUPT webpage: http://www.disrupt-project.eu/ (accessed 06.2021).

[4] More projects using ADOxx can be found at https://www.adoxx.org/live/development-spaces (accessed 06.2021).

[5] Overview of modelling tools available at https://projects.omilab.org (accessed 06.2021).

[6] See https://nemo.omilab.org/ (accessed 06.2021) for more on the NEMO Summer School.

platform: the development tools and the modelling tools. On the model level, the main concern is depicting a system under study (the "original"), which can be either something that already exists (as-is as a descriptive model) or something that should exist (to-be as a prescriptive model). To be able to create models, a modelling language is required. The modelling language in turn can be depicted by a meta-model that is realized in a modelling tool.[7] These meta-models are developed beforehand with a specific language, in this case a meta-modelling language. Again, the meta-modelling language can be depicted through another model: the $meta^2$-model (meta-meta-model) which is realized in the development tools. The hierarchical approach assumes a language-oriented understanding of the models as introduced in [2] and further refined by [1].

While this approach could be further applied to allow customizable and adaptable $meta^x$-models, it must end at some point for practical reasons to create a runnable application. In case of the ADOxx platform, the highest implemented level is the $meta^2$-model, which uses a $meta^2$-modelling language that can be executed on a computer (a programming language). Thus, it provides a meta-modelling language that can be used to create own meta-models that are then realized as modelling tools.

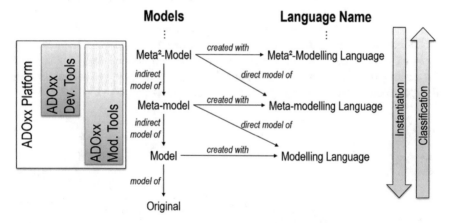

Fig. 2.1 Modelling hierarchy and language levels (adapted from [1])

When developing and realizing your own modelling language with the ADOxx platform, the purpose is generally to create a modelling tool which can be used for the creation of models with your modelling language; thus, the domain of conceptual modelling itself becomes relevant. In conceptual modelling there are three important concepts to specify a modelling language as depicted in Fig. 2.2: Concept, Characteristic, and Connector.

---

[7] While the focus of the ADOxx modelling tools is on the meta-model and model levels, they are influenced by the concepts existing on the $meta^2$-model level.

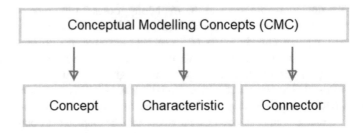

Fig. 2.2 Conceptual modelling concepts

The three Conceptual Modelling Concepts deal mainly with the structure of the modelling language by describing its elements. **Concepts** represent something that is relevant and worth to be modelled. **Characteristics** don't provide any substantial value by themselves, but instead are used to describe other things, providing relevant details. **Connectors** link or connect things, introducing a relation between them. The declaration of Concepts, Characteristics, and Connectors provides a conceptual blueprint of elements within the modelling language and consequently what can be used in models adhering to it.

According to [1], it is insufficient to only consider the general structure of a modelling language. Further aspects of the elements also need consideration: their semantics (meaning), their notation (visual representation), and their syntax (rules for creating models). Moreover, modelling languages by themselves are not the only thing of interest but also in relation to other concepts as shown in Fig. 2.3.

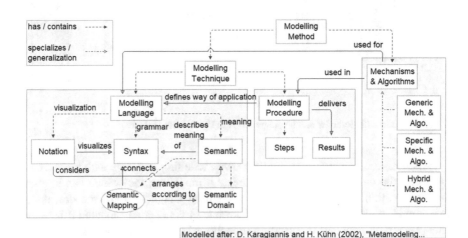

Modelled after: D. Karagiannis and H. Kühn (2002), "Metamodeling...

Fig. 2.3 Modelling language, technique, and method (based on [1])

Besides the modelling language itself, there is also a procedure on how the language is intended to be applied to achieve specific results, where the restrictiveness of the procedure can vary. Additionally, mechanisms and algorithms support the procedure in achieving those results by processing the available model data. All these parts together form the modelling method. These parts need to be considered together, since they influence each other: a step of the procedure could be enhanced, for example, by a mechanism, which in turn could require certain elements in the modelling language to be present or certain combinations of elements to be prohibited in a model.

We like to also mention that there is a process for the formalization on three different layers, although this is not the core issue of this chapter: definition, specification, and implementation (see also Fig. 2.4 [3, 4]).

A language which supports among other things the description of a modelling language, its purpose, procedure, and functionalities, allowing to capture its requirements, has been discussed in [5]. It is called CoChaCo, which builds on the ideas of Concept, Characteristic, and Connector and extends it with additional elements to allow the description of modelling methods.[8]

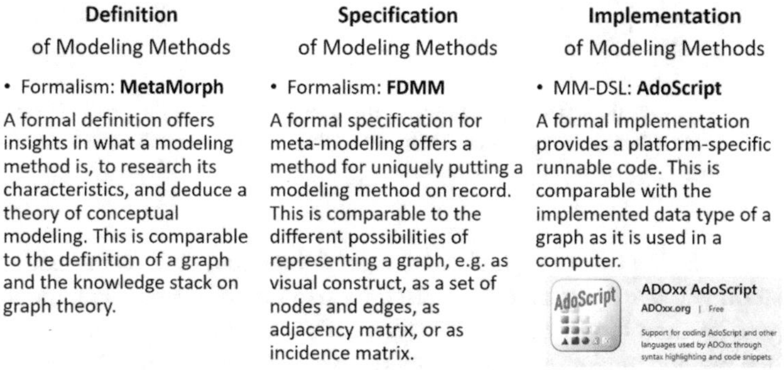

Definition of Modeling Methods	**Specification** of Modeling Methods	**Implementation** of Modeling Methods
• Formalism: **MetaMorph**	• Formalism: **FDMM**	• MM-DSL: **AdoScript**
A formal definition offers insights in what a modeling method is, to research its characteristics, and deduce a theory of conceptual modeling. This is comparable to the definition of a graph and the knowledge stack on graph theory.	A formal specification for meta-modelling offers a method for uniquely putting a modeling method on record. This is comparable to the different possibilities of representing a graph, e.g. as visual construct, as a set of nodes and edges, as adjacency matrix, or as incidence matrix.	A formal implementation provides a platform-specific runnable code. This is comparable with the implemented data type of a graph as it is used in a computer. ADOxx AdoScript ADOxx.org | Free Support for coding AdoScript and other languages used by ADOxx through syntax highlighting and code snippets

Fig. 2.4 Modeling methods—different layers of formalization

The CoChaCo language has also been used to describe the ADOxx platform, providing an overview of the concepts and functionalities (see Fig. 2.5).

---

[8] An implementation is available at https://www.omilab.org/cochaco (accessed 05.2021).

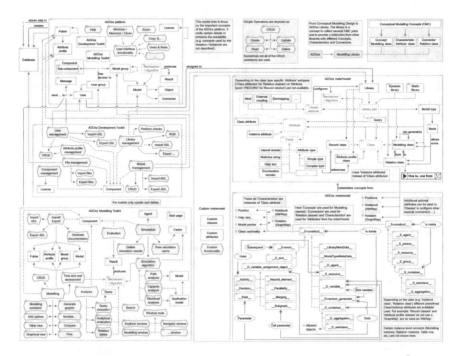

Fig. 2.5 Overview of the ADOxx platform components, functionalities, and meta(^{2})-model concepts (A more readable version can be found at https://www.omilab.org/adoxx/ (accessed September 2021))

The left side describes the platform's major components and functionalities, like the creation and management of models, the execution of queries, and the import/-export into specific format on model level but also the creation and management of modelling method implementations through so-called libraries and file management on meta-model level.

The right side of the image contains a description of the structural aspects of the ADOxx platform, describing its meta^2-model and a meta-model that is provided as a starting point. These are used to realize the necessary parts of a modelling language through instantiating the main concepts: modelling classes, relation classes, and attributes. For these the syntax, notation, and semantics can be further described, through the relationships between these concepts (syntax), through assignment of visualizations (notation), or through help texts for humans and code for the machine (semantic).

Mechanisms and algorithms can be implemented through code and activated through the platform. Pre-packaged and configurable functionalities provided by the platform can also be adapted and used. The procedure can be supported through the mechanisms, and tailored functionalities can guide the user through the different steps.[9] The tall element in the middle of Fig. 2.5 represents the own meta-model to be realized and the configuration of the other elements of the ADOxx platform in order to provide a modelling tool for the desired modelling method.

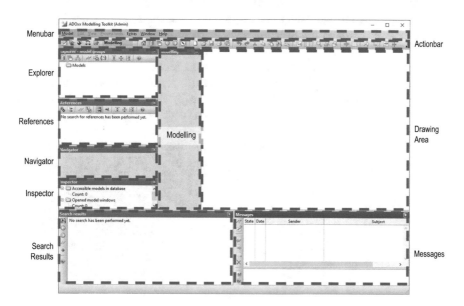

Fig. 2.6 Parts of the user interface of an ADOxx based modelling tool

Depending on the realization of one's own modelling method, different parts of the ADOxx platform's user interface are relevant in the resulting modelling tool. Figure 2.6 shows some of the different components that are available in the user interface of an ADOxx modelling tool. Some of these are generally the same in every implementation, like the Explorer showing the available models structured in folders. Some dynamically change based on the meta-model, like the Modelling bar showing the types of elements available for an opened model. Others have a default configuration that can be further customized, like adding new entries to the Menu bar or the Action bar.

An often-applied scenario for developing a modelling method and realizing a modelling tool with the ADOxx platform consists of using the following tools related to Fig. 2.7:

---

[9] Note that these are just some of the elements of the ADOxx platform used to realize a modelling method. There are other elements to handle additional details like the representation of attributes, cardinalities, or elements of the user interface.

1. CoChaCo[10] to design the modelling method by capturing the requirements for its elements, their allowed structure, the supported procedures, and the relevant functionalities.
2. The ADOxx Development Toolkit[11] to instantiate the elements of the modelling language through modelling classes, relation classes, and attributes. This can be achieved through the user interface or by directly writing ADOxx Library Language (ALL) code. This creates a configuration of the modelling language (the "library") that is interpreted by the ADOxx Modelling Toolkit.
3. Visual Studio Code with the ADOxx AdoScript extension[12] to write code for the configuration and the desired functionalities, e.g., using AdoScript to implement the functionalities or using GraphRep code to specify the notation.

Fig. 2.7 Three tools used for the development and realization of modelling methods

Depending on the requirements of the modelling method, different issues have to be considered for the implementation. The next section introduces some approaches for different kinds of requirements. For example, if simulation of models is required, then an approach can be found in Sect. 2.3.3.

For additional details on the conceptualization of modelling methods with the ADOxx platform, see [6, 7]. Some of the modelling tools realized with the ADOxx platform can also be found on the OMiLAB webpage.[13]

---

[10] Available from https://www.omilab.org/cochaco (accessed 05.2021).

[11] Available from https://www.adoxx.org (accessed 05.2021).

[12] Available from https://marketplace.visualstudio.com/items?itemName=ADOxxorg.adoxx-adoscript (accessed 05.2021) or in the VSC by searching for the extension "ADOxx AdoScript".

[13] Overview of modelling tools available at https://projects.omilab.org (accessed 06.2021).

2.3 Application Cases

The ADOxx platform supports different types of interactions with actors or agents for modelling and development of modelling methods. For one its modelling capabilities and models can be used for both the interaction with (a) human users and with (b) other systems, like other applications or web services. Additionally, the interactions can be motivated either to create models or to utilize models (e.g., execute, simulate alternatives, etc.), providing value to the user. The realization of these interactions can be done by the ADOxx platform itself, using external components like scripts, dynamically linked libraries, and web services or a mix of both. Implementing a specific interaction using exclusively functionality from the platform requires that all the relevant information can be found in the meta[2]-model, the meta-model, and the model themselves.

In this section we are showing some cases with different variations on the kinds of interactions depicted in Fig. 2.8 that go beyond the basic creation and use of models for communication between humans.

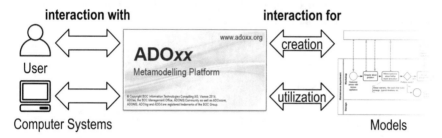

Fig. 2.8 Types of considered interactions between the ADOxx platform, users, other systems, and models

2.3.1 Dynamic, Interactive Notation

One possible interaction with the user is through dynamic notations, which change based on the current state of the model. This can go beyond the simple depiction of values entered by the user, additionally performing calculations and adding shapes and icons based on their results, showing or hiding specific details, or depicting external graphics. Furthermore, the notations can provide interactable points which allow the user to access functionalities directly through the drawing area. These kinds of functionalities are generally implemented for models of a specific modelling language and can help both creating models (e.g., by inserting new objects) and using models (e.g., by starting a simulation).

2.3.1.1 Petri Net Transitions with "Fire" Buttons

An example for this can be found in the realization of the Petri Net language in the Bee-Up modelling tool [8].[14] The implementation of the transitions dynamically evaluates whether they are ready to fire according to the execution semantics of Petri Nets, and if so, then a "Fire" indicator is visualized. The "Fire" indicator also serves as a button that can be clicked on, which fires the transition in the model and moves any tokens according to the specified net.

Both the dynamic notation and the result of using the interactive "Fire" button can be seen in Fig. 2.9. The model depicts a simple Petri Net of available molecules and their chemical reactions. The state of the net changes after certain transitions fire and rearrange the tokens, influencing the readiness of the transitions and thus the available "Fire" buttons.

While the example shows how such functionality can support the building of models, the implementation in Bee-Up also provides means to further use the models. It allows to specify so-called Effects for transitions through AdoScript code. These are triggered when the transition fires, allowing to use all the processing and interaction capabilities of the platform and further extend the interaction between the user, the model, and possibly other systems.

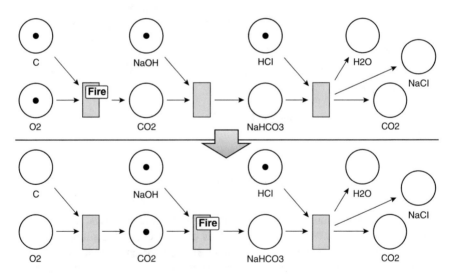

Fig. 2.9 Example for dynamic and interactive notation in Bee-Up Petri Nets (model based on example from [9])

---

[14] An implementation is available at https://bee-up.omilab.org/ (accessed 05.2021).

2.3.2   Conceptual Models in a Machine-Readable Format

Another form of interaction allows the use of models by providing them in a machine-readable format, based on established standards, file formats, etc. These can then be further processed by other applications or services. Depending on the desired level of specificity, these functionalities can either be implemented for models of a specific modelling language or on the meta^2-model level to be language independent. While the latter works for models of any language, it also means not reflecting specific semantics that a modelling language provides to the model when transforming the model into the desired format.

2.3.2.1   Use of Models in an RDF Format with a BPMS

An approach where the content of ADOxx models is exported in an RDF (Resource Description Framework) format is described in [10]. The exposed data from the models is linked with other sources of data and further enhanced using relevant reasoning axioms/rules. All these together provide a more complete view of the relevant part of the world as a knowledge base, which is used by a Business Process Management System (BPMS) frontend. Therefore, the interaction is here mainly with other systems, targeting to provide value from created models.

Figure 2.10 depicts a case of how this can be used. The left side shows parts of two connected models about the tasks and actors for the transportation of materials and the RDF graph these parts are transformed into. The right side shows parts of external data about parking lot locations that have also been transformed into an RDF graph. Both graphs are linked together and are further extended with results from reasoning axioms and GeoSPARQL annotations, providing geospatial context. The image depicts the links and annotations through dashed arrows. This enhanced RDF graph provides the knowledge base used by a BPMS frontend, where relevant information is shown to a logged-in user, like their active tasks and parking recommendations (not depicted).

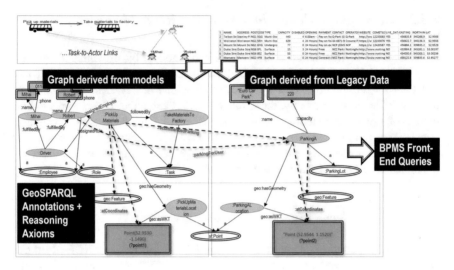

Fig. 2.10 Example case using models transformed into RDF with other RDF data and reasoning rules for a BPMS (based on [10])

A service enabling the transformation of ADOxx models to RDF is available on ADOxx.org.[15] It implements several transformation rules, both for models and meta-models. The rules themselves are realized on a meta-model independent level, relying on generic concepts like instances and relations linked to concepts of the meta-model. This allows the RDF transformation to be used for any meta-model and any model.

2.3.3 Simulation of Process Models

Implementations based on the ADOxx platform can also provide an interaction for creation and use of process models through simulation capabilities. They support the creation of models by allowing to compare the results from a simulation of an as-is model with data from the real world. Furthermore, to-be models can be created and compared with the as-is model through simulation. These kinds of functionalities may be implemented for a specific modelling language or on a more generic level of abstraction of the language, covering concepts of processes in general.

---

[15] RDF transformation service available at https://www.adoxx.org/live/rdf_details (accessed 05.2021).

ADOxx provides a configurable implementation for process model simulation for a specific abstraction of process modelling languages. It allows to perform a path analysis of process models, as well as a capacity analysis or workload analysis when paired with models describing the organizational or working environment the processes are executed in. A path analysis simulates the process model multiple times to find possible paths through the process, as well as their quantitative metrics (e.g., execution time, cycle time, etc.) and probabilities based on the performed simulations. The capacity analysis runs a simulation of process models and determines results for them in a specific environment, like how much time a specific performer would spend doing certain work. The workload analysis goes further and not only combines the process models with their environment but also considers waiting times, queues, and a calendar when simulating the work of performers. Considering the oscillation in starting the process, as well as individual workload of performers, this may lead to results showing unexpected or unhealthy accumulation of work.

2.3.3.1   Simulation of BPMN Models

The Bee-Up modelling tool [8][16] configures the simulation capabilities provided by the platform for the Business Process Model and Notation [11]. Together with an implementation for Working Environment Models, it allows for all three types of simulations provided by ADOxx.

Figure 2.11 shows an exemplary process model in BPMN, describing the repair of a home appliance consisting of several tasks: communication with the customer, determining the fault, obtaining spare parts, performing the repair, and disposing in case a repair is not performed, among others. It also contains a loop back if the repairs did not solve the problem. The path analysis has run 1000 simulations for the model and has found six different paths. The results for the two most likely paths are shown, with quantitative information like the expected execution time or cycle time for each path. The second path is also highlighted in the image.

---

[16] An implementation is available at https://bee-up.omilab.org/ (accessed 05.2021).

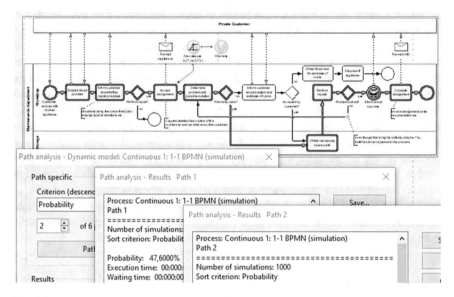

Fig. 2.11 Example BPMN process with results from a path analysis in Bee-Up

Assuming the model to represent the current state of the process, the results of the model simulation can be checked against reality. Based on those results, the process can be adapted, by either changing certain parameters or altering the structure of the flow, creating alternatives. Those alternatives can then be simulated to compare with the original model.

2.3.4 Model Adaptation Through Internet Resources

Interactions with resources found on the Internet can be beneficial for the creation of models: providing data to either create new parts of the model or adapt existing parts. Cases where the data is used for other purposes are possible as well, like for the validation of models. A benefit of using resources from the Internet is the possibility of retrieving the data at the time when it is needed and receiving a current version. The connection to the resources may be realized through simple HTTP requests. As such the interaction between the ADOxx platform generally happens with other webservers.

2.3.4.1 Displaying a Map Image as Part of a Model

A case where an image is retrieved from the Internet and used in a model is realized in the GeoLocation modelling implementation used as part of teaching ADOxx.[17] The implementation displays a map centered on a specific location as part of a model and allows placing additional elements on or around it. It works by providing a name for the location as an attribute of the model, which is then used to determine the latitude and longitude by calling a web service.[18] The latitude and longitude are then used to retrieve an image of the map portion from the Internet[19] and visualize it as the model background. Both services are available through simple HTTP calls, providing the result like a resource on the Internet.

Figure 2.12 shows an example where an empty model is created, where "Vienna" is specified as the name of the location. Afterwards the two-step functionality is executed. The first step retrieves all locations that fit the name "Vienna." Since there are several options available (in Austria, France, United States, etc.), it prompts the user to specify which option they want to use. Having selected the first one in Austria provides the latitude and longitude for that location, which is then used to retrieve the map image and set it as the background of the model.

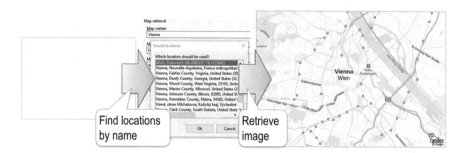

Fig. 2.12 Example of retrieving the location and visualizing a map image for Vienna as the model background

---

[17] For example: the OMiLAB ADOxx Crash Course from March, details can be found at https://www.omilab.org/activities/events/adoxxcrashcourse2021_march/ (accessed 05.2021).

[18] Using the OpenStreetMap Nominatim service. For more details see https://wiki.openstreetmap.org/wiki/Nominatim (accessed 05.2021).

[19] Using the Yandex Static Maps API. For more details see https://yandex.com/dev/maps/ (accessed 05.2021).

2.3.5 Integration with Cyber-Physical Systems

The ADOxx platform enables the integration with cyber-physical systems (CPS, e.g., robots), allowing additional capabilities for models when interacting with physical devices. Such models and CPS interactions can, for example, be used to control the behavior or to represent the current state of the CPS. While the main interaction is with other computer systems or agents, the models can also provide feedback to the user of the modelling environment. The realized integrations can be on varying levels of specificity in the modelling method: from a generic approach that allows to send any form of HTTP request to methods tied to interfaces of a specific CPS.

2.3.5.1 Controlling a Robot Through Petri Nets

A simple integration with CPS is possible in the Bee-Up modelling tool [8][20] on a very generic level. As mentioned in Sect. 2.3.1.1, a transition that fires can also trigger an "Effect." These effects are specified for each transition in the model using AdoScript code, which allows for a wide range of possibilities. One of them is to send HTTP requests[21] to an interface providing functionalities to control a robot. In this case the integration with CPS is not on the domain level of the modelling method, not in the semantics of the used modelling language elements, but instead realized as the implementation provides capabilities on a generic level.

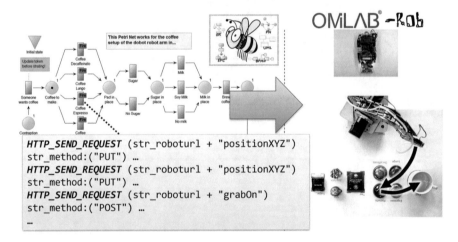

Fig. 2.13 Example of a Petri Net in Bee-Up which controls behavior of a robot arm

---

[20] An implementation is available at https://bee-up.omilab.org/ (accessed 05.2021).

[21] Using, for example, https://www.adoxx.org/live/extended-http-requests-details (accessed 05.2021).

An example for a model which controls the behavior of a robot arm can be seen in Fig. 2.13. The example[22] uses a scenario where a robot arm is used to collect the ingredients to make coffee. It consists of a Petri Net whose transitions contain the instructions to move a robot arm and the corresponding hardware which is part of OMiLAB.[23] The instructions entered as the "Effect" of a transition specify the requests that are sent to the HTTP interface provided by the robot arm. While the robot arm provides several simple instructions (move to position, grab on, let go), these are bundled together into more meaningful actions (use Ristretto coffee, add sugar, etc.) in the transitions.

2.4 Conclusion

Some basic concepts for developing conceptual modelling methods and realizing a modelling tool with ADOxx have been presented in this chapter, starting with the relevant levels of models (original, models, meta-models, and meta^2-models) and their relation to the ADOxx platform, through the basic concepts used in a modelling language (Concept, Characteristic, Connector) to the modelling method framework presenting additional aspects and elements that have to be considered besides a modelling language (modelling language, modelling procedure, mechanisms, and algorithms). Based on this a general introduction on the realization using the ADOxx platform was given. It touched the concepts, components, and tools employed to implement a modelling language, the necessary mechanisms and algorithms and to support the modelling procedure.

Afterwards the realization of different interactions between users, modelling tool, and other systems has been presented, considering cases focusing on interaction with the user (e.g., Sect. 2.3.1) or on interaction with other systems (e.g., Sect. 2.3.2). Additionally, the interactions can be motivated for the creation of models (e.g., Sect. 2.3.4), the use of models to gain additional value (e.g., Sect. 2.3.5), or both (e.g., Sect. 2.3.3).

Every reader is also invited to join the OMiLAB community at www.omilab.org, develop and realize new modelling methods, and participate in writing this living paper. Everybody interested in learning more about the details of realizing a modelling tool with the ADOxx platform is also invited to join one of the **freely available** ADOxx trainings.[24]

---

[22] The example scenario can be found on the Bee-Up page: https://bee-up.omilab.org/activities/bee-up/scenario-details/ (accessed 05.2021).

[23] See https://www.omilab.org/nodes/innovation.html (accessed 05.2021) for more information.

[24] More details available at https://www.omilab.org/adoxx (accessed 06.2021).

References

1. Karagiannis, D., Kühn, H.: Metamodelling platforms. In Proceedings of the Third International Conference EC-Web 2002, Aix-en-Provence (2002)
2. Strahringer, S.: Ein sprachbasierter Metamodellbegriff und seine Verallgemeinerung durch das Konzept des Metaisierungsprinzips. In Modellierung '98, Proceedings des GI-Workshops, Münster (1998)
3. Döller, V., Karagiannis, D.: Formalizing conceptual modeling methods with MetaMorph. In Enterprise, Business-Process and Information Systems Modeling. BPMDS 2021, EMMSAD 2021 (2021)
4. Fill, H.-G., Redmond, T., Karagiannis, D.: FDMM: a formalism for describing ADOxx meta models and models. In Proceedings of ICEIS 2012 - 14th International Conference on Enterprise Information Systems (2012)
5. Karagiannis, D., Burzynski, P., Utz, W., Buchmann, R.A.: A metamodeling approach to support the engineering of modeling method requirements. In 2019 IEEE 27th International Requirements Engineering Conference (RE), Jeju (2019)
6. Fill, H.-G., Karagiannis, D.: On the conceptualisation of modelling methods using the ADOxx meta modelling platform. Enterp. Model. Inf. Syst. Archit. Int. J. **8**(1), 4–25 (2013)
7. Karagiannis, D.: Agile modeling method engineering. In PCI '15: Proceedings of the 19th Panhellenic Conference on Informatics, Athens, Greece (2015).
8. Karagiannis, D., Buchmann, R.A., Burzynski, P., Reimer, U., Walch, M.: Fundamental conceptual modeling languages in OMiLAB. In: Domain-Specific Conceptual Modeling, p. 594. Springer International Publishing (2016)
9. Petri, C.A., Reisig, W.: Petri net (2008). http://www.scholarpedia.org/article/Petri_net. Accessed 05 2021.
10. Cinpoeru, M., Ghiran, A.-M., Buchmann, R.A., Karagiannis, D.: Model-driven context configuration in business process management systems: an approach based on knowledge graphs. In Perspectives in Business Informatics Research, Katowice (2019)
11. Business Process Model and Notation (2014) https://www.omg.org/spec/BPMN/2.0.2/. Accessed 05 2021.

Chapter 3
Challenging Digital Innovation Through the OMiLAB Community of Practice

Iulia Vaidian, Arkadiusz Jurczuk, Zbigniew Misiak, Michael Neidow, Martin Petry, and Martin Nemetz

Abstract Digitalization requires cyber-physical ecosystems to achieve the goals of its transformation process, which should be primarily driven by innovation. OMi-LAB (www.omilab.org) supports digital innovation within a community of practice and technical environment, based on a global network of physical laboratory nodes. The Digital Innovation Environment (DiEn) powered by OMiLAB located at industrial and academic organizations responds to digital transformation challenges. It facilitates the co-creation, design, and engineering of early prototypes. Digital innovation is challenged by the OMiLAB community of practice through tool-aided conceptual modelling and elevates model value in domain-specific scenarios and experiments.

Keywords Digital innovation environment · Digital engineer · Digital innovator · Conceptual modelling · Digital innovation · Community of practice

I. Vaidian (✉)
Research Group Knowledge Engineering, University of Vienna, Vienna, Austria
e-mail: iulia.vaidian@univie.ac.at

A. Jurczuk
Bialystock Technical University, Bialystock, Poland
e-mail: a.jurczuk@pb.edu.pl

Z. Misiak
BOC Poland, Warsaw, Poland
e-mail: Zbigniew.Misiak@boc-pl.com

M. Neidow
Hilti AG, Schaan, Liechtenstein
e-mail: michael.neidow@hilti.com

M. Petry
Hilti Befestigungstechnik AG, Buchs, Switzerland
e-mail: martin.petry@hilti.com

M. Nemetz
Hilti Entwicklungsgesellschaft mbH, Kaufering, Germany
e-mail: Martin.Nemetz@hilti.com

3.1 Introduction

OMiLAB stands for Open Models Initiative Laboratory and supports digital innovation within a community of practice and technical environment, based on a global network of physical laboratory nodes. Digitalization requires cyber-physical ecosystems to achieve the goals of its transformation process, which should be primarily driven by innovation. An Intelligent Agent, such as OMiLAB, has the methodology, technologies, and know-how to drive the shift in innovation, from mechanical solutions to digital solutions [1]. Digital innovation is understood as a fundamental and powerful concept, where products, processes, or business models are perceived as new, may require significant changes on the part of adopters, and are embodied in or enabled by IT [2].

As a nonprofit organization, OMiLAB acts as a facilitator to the development of scientific methods and technologies for all those who value semantic-rich models, a place where participants can bring in ideas related to conceptual modelling and engage in an exploration process. OMiLAB is both a physical and a virtual space, where the physical space contains equipment and software for the development of modelling methods and the virtual space is a platform, where information and tools of domain-specific modelling methods for academia and industry can be discovered and used for free [3].

OMiLAB follows a user-driven approach in exploring the value of models. It recognizes that there are useful models in widely different domains like information technology, biology, chemistry, or medicine, as well as various functional areas like procurement, marketing, logistics, and engineering [3]. The environment created by OMiLAB (see Fig. 3.1) encourages researchers and practitioners to conceptualize modelling methods that are novel and are valued with respect to requirements emerging from domain-specific or case-specific needs. It is important for stakeholders, and for the digital innovator and the digital engineer, which are emerging professional skills, to have a common space where their vision is supported by a conceptualization process and an ecosystem that allows them to operationalize their novel ideas [4]. In other words, OMiLAB challenges digital innovation and enables an environment where novel ideas can be tested and evaluated by the community and all those willing to put their know-how and expertise into practice. They are invited to explore the Digital Innovation Environment (DiEn) powered by OMiLAB, utilize its capabilities, and make the most out of its offering.

OMLAB® Ecosystem

Fig. 3.1 An organizational and technical view

The skill profile and role of the digital innovator and digital engineer are essential in a smart innovation environment, such as OMiLAB. The digital innovator must have the ability to understand what has become possible due to advances in technology and to have a vision of the organizational and societal needs, to create a valuable artifact with digital technology [2]. The challenge in recent years has been to develop this profile and the set of skills required to successfully conduct digital transformation projects. The framework and infrastructure of OMiLAB enable the consolidation and allow the execution of both digital design and engineering activities, to semantically bridge multiple layers of abstraction and specificity [5]. Conceptual modelling methods enable the design of semantically rich diagrammatic models that are both human-understandable and machine-processable while providing mechanisms for analyzing models and interacting with open digital environments. Further, conceptual models can be co-created through collaboration between digital engineers and other stakeholders. The models themselves can be used as a knowledge base of an organization, which supports a further utilization of the model value [6]. There is no barrier anymore that determines who can become a digital innovator and/or digital engineer. Those who understand what drives and where digital transformations are headed towards can effectively initiate and manage digital innovation [2].

This chapter explores the Digital Innovation Environment (DiEn) powered by OMiLAB, the three pillars that are at its core, as well as the technologies that enable the design and engineering of early prototypes for organizations pursuing digital transformation initiatives. The OMiLAB community of practice and its knowledge transfer assets are detailed, too. Moreover, two experience reports are covered, the academic approach of the Bialystok Technical University node and the industrial needs, presenting the Hilti node.

3.2   The OMiLAB Community of Practice

OMiLAB has a community open to individuals and organizations from all domains and functional areas that want to contribute or offer their content and technology for free or through open copyright licenses on a common platform. The only prerequisite for contribution is a focus on conceptual modelling. A fundamental aspect is model-driven value creation and its application and adoption in specific domains. Educational institutions, digital innovation hubs, and research and innovation organizations are the primary beneficiaries of the virtual and physical space of OMiLAB [3].

OMiLAB is present globally through a network of physical laboratory nodes, each aiming to establish themselves as open model communities with a specific focus and competence in the field. An OMiLAB node is one OMiLAB instance, established by a community member. Currently, there are 15 nodes (both at academic institutions and industrial sites), in 9 countries and 2 continents, and the network is continuously expanding (https://www.omilab.org/nodes). The Digital Innovation Environment supports the nodes and other stakeholders through its conceptual framework, the technical environment, and the physical infrastructure. Organizations with an academic background, as well as organizations with an industrial background, can ideate, test, and evaluate innovative concepts and respond to digital transformation challenges. Both academic and industrial members take a co-creative approach to brainstorm ideas together with the domain experts and stakeholders by means of design thinking. Moreover, the decision-making is supported by a knowledge-based approach using smart conceptual models. The proof-of-concept environment realizes early prototypes to be tested, and their feasibility is assessed using robots, IoT sensors, other cyber-physical systems (CPSs), or virtual services [7].

The OMiLAB community of practice conducts a variety of activities to bring the concept of the open model laboratory to a larger network of researchers and practitioners. Openness, knowledge-sharing, and dissemination are fundamental for the OMiLAB ecosystem and its collaboration network [5]. Who is interested in applying conceptual modelling in their domain will find the tools, documentation, and expertise at OMiLAB. Three characteristics of the community of practice are highlighted below [8].

3.2.1 Serving a Cause: Education

This characteristic aims to highlight the importance of conceptual modelling, semantics, and technologies for digital ecosystems. Education is one example of serving a cause. Interested students and/or practitioners are encouraged to develop their professional skills needed for the digital transformation initiatives conducted by companies across multiple branches of the industry with teaching materials designed for the digital engineer and the digital innovator. One instance of how OMiLAB supports education that is accessible to all interested stakeholders is through the NEMO Summer School Series (https://nemo.omilab.org/).

NEMO is the international educational platform of OMiLAB. It is a series of summer schools that focus on learning conceptual modelling, to innovate, design, and engineer digital ecosystems. The 2-week event takes place in the summer at the University of Vienna and combines lectures and practical sessions in multicultural groups of participants. The six topical pillars that the summer school is based on are conceptual modelling foundations, smart models for humans and machines, semantics and technologies for digital ecosystems, digital design thinking, enterprise digital twins, as well as cross-cutting issues. Working in and for a digitized organization where smart devices, digital artifacts, robots, data streams, and connectivity are ubiquitous, challenges regarding human resources, process lifecycle, business, or regulatory rules must be faced. Thus, NEMO provides a vertical overview across different application domains to prepare digital engineers and digital innovators for all dimensions of digitization. Renowned speakers and experts are giving lectures related to emerging research in digital transformation processes and conduct practice sessions with modelling tools, which were developed by the community and are freely available on the OMiLAB platform [9]. The results of a survey among NEMO Alumni show that participants appreciated being taught conceptual modelling in interesting application domains, such as Smart Cities, as well as gaining hands-on experience in the practical sessions by using the modelling tools for engaging case studies [4].

3.2.2 Sustained Mutual Relationships: Research

This characteristic of the OMiLAB Community of Practice has the objective to address the challenges that digital ecosystems are facing. By acting as a research partner and collaborating with multidisciplinary academic and industrial experts, OMiLAB aims to bridge the gap of these challenges with the creation and engineering of smart conceptual models as innovative solutions. OMiLAB is involved in multiple projects, and an example is given below, the DigiFoF project.

The European-funded project "DigiFoF: Digital Design Skills for Factories of the Future" proposes a network of training environments where HEIs (High Education Institutions), enterprises, and training institutions work together to develop skill profiles, training concepts, as well as materials for design aspects of the Factories of the Future (FoF). OMiLAB provides expertise in the project for the creation of laboratories and a smart environment for experimentation with FoF design [10]. Five laboratories (in France, Poland, Romania, Finland, and Italy) have been established in the context of this project with core competencies on industrial business model transformation, manufacturing systems and processes, and service operations management.

The work of the OMiLAB community is highlighted through publications, journals, conference proceedings, and books. Members share their results, achieved within the Digital Innovation Environment framework, as well as learnings from creating and engineering smart models for digital ecosystems. The knowledge transfer to a broader public in the form of dissemination is realized. An example for this endeavor is the OMiLAB Book Series, "Domain-Specific Conceptual Modelling: Concepts, Methods and Tools," that increases the visibility of domain-specific conceptual modelling, by presenting the work of thought leaders that have designed and deployed specific modelling methods. Both volumes consist of 25 modelling tools each realized on the ADOxx meta-modelling platform (www.adoxx.org) and provided via the OMiLAB platform (https://projects.omilab.org). Each chapter provides hands-on guidance on how to build models in a particular domain. The framework of the Digital Innovation Environment of OMiLAB is fundamental for the conceptualization and the use of modelling for specific domains and purposes [11].

3.2.3   Sharing Artifacts: Value-Added Services

The motivation to develop value-added services for and by the community is to propose solutions to be used by digital ecosystems and to support the digital transformation processes of organizations. An example is an open-source service for AI-based Domain-Specific Assessment, detailed below.

The AI-based Domain-Specific Assessment Service is one of the services offered by OMiLAB, which aims to increase the value contribution of an organization's enterprise architecture. It aims to bridge the gap between enterprise architects, CIOs, and stakeholders, as through this service information is gathered and combined dynamically: Users are involved directly in the design/assessment of the enterprise architecture, several data sources are combined, and smart analysis and recommendations based on logical rules provide insights, through a user-friendly visualization of the results. These insights come directly from the users and add value to future actions, as they are based on user-centric architectural knowledge. A service like this brings transparency by performing continuous assessments, storing data, and supporting decision-making with intelligent analytics [12].

3.3 Digital Innovation Environment (DiEn)

The Digital Innovation Environment (DiEn) powered by OMiLAB is based on three fundamental pillars (shown in Fig. 3.2): the **creation** of business ecosystems, **design** of smart conceptual models, and **engineering** of digital twins [6]. Open source and open community principles guide both the virtual and physical space of the laboratory, to foster cross-domain practice-oriented information science and design science research [4]. OMiLAB challenges digital innovation through DiEn, where innovation leads to digital transformation, and transformation paves the way for innovation. It supports organizations to face the rapid changes in their business and drive innovation to stay relevant in the age of digital evolution. Hence, digital innovation must become a core part of organizations [13].

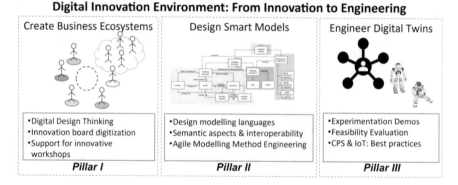

Fig. 3.2 The fundamental pillars of the Digital Innovation Environment

The OMiLAB ecosystem acknowledges the necessary capabilities that are required by digital innovation [14]: The service development capability is met by the multiple domain-specific modelling tools developed by the community (https:// projects.omilab.org) and the open-source software offering (e.g., AI-based Domain-Specific Assessment Service); the network management capability is facilitated by the strategy of knowledge transfer and the worldwide network of nodes; digital-related technical capabilities are fulfilled by the virtual and physical space of the laboratory, which provides their implementation of digitalization in organizations. Moreover, the toolkits available in OMiLAB for digital design thinking, digital twin modelling, integration, and engineering serve the technical environment that must respond fast to prototyping enablers, support evaluation, and interoperability. The conceptual models that are created within this environment support digital integration, as they decompose the insights from the business layer to the cyber-physical layer while preserving the semantic links across multiple perspectives. The smart models interact with other systems through a variety of connectivity options [5]. The capability to be agile, and adapt fast to changes in the surrounding environment, is met through the **Agile Modelling Method Engineering (AMME)** framework and lifecycle [15], which is employed throughout the three fundamental pillars of the laboratory. An in-depth description of the AMME framework, lifecycle, and usage to react to challenges in creating modelling methods is given within the second pillar, based on the smart conceptual models.

The OMiLAB ecosystem foresees five professional roles that are integrated across the three fundamental pillars, based on their skill profile. These roles are the digital innovator (first pillar), the modelling method engineer, the meta-model designer, the digital product designer (second pillar), and the digital engineer (third pillar). They are supported in their work by a variety of assets, both software and hardware, based on community efforts and available through the OMiLAB platform. For example, OMiPOB, which stands for OMiLAB Physical OBjects, provides the infrastructure, equipment, and know-how for experiments with cyber-physical systems (CPSs). OMiPOB focuses on the interaction between models and CPSs to execute specified use cases. Figure 3.3 shows graphically the three layers and their connection in the OMiPOB environment, described in relation to the three pillars in the next sections.

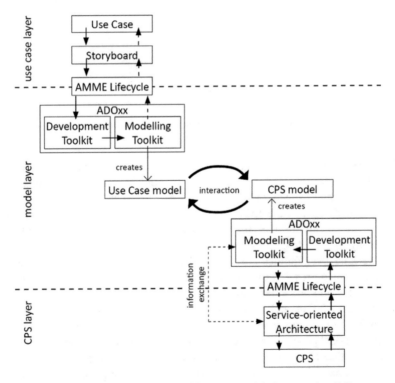

Fig. 3.3 OMiPOB: Graphical representation of the layers and their connection [16]

One way to use the environment of the physical objects is with robot experiments, known as OMiROB. Multiple-use cases have been successfully tested and evaluated within OMiROB, where CPSs are used in combination with knowledge engineering approaches, such as an ontology, a rule engine, speech recognition, and conceptual models. The term robot is understood in the OMiLAB environment as a machine that is controlled by a computer program and can fulfill certain tasks autonomously, like a humanoid robot, a car, or a robotic arm [16].

The applicability of the OMiLAB Digital Innovation Environment has been successfully demonstrated in European-funded projects [7]. For example, it supported the creation of novel business models for manufacturing SMEs that aim to use digital twin technology in the H2020 EU project Change2Twin [17], it supported the design of organizational models that can be used as a digital twin for the renovation process of building in the H2020 EU project BIMERR [18], and it studied the different interaction alternatives between information technology and robots in the Austrian FFG project complAI [19]. Depending on the project goals, each pillar can be independently employed; however, for more complex initiatives, a combination of activities across all pillars can be required [6].

The pillars and the semantic technologies for digital innovation and experimentation will be explored in more depth in the following sections. They stay at the disposal of all interested users of the Digital Innovation Environment by OMiLAB and aim to support them in the realization of their domain-specific scenarios. By combining these technologies, the OMiPOB and OMiROB environments, and know-how, everyone can challenge and make the next step towards digital innovation.

3.3.1 Create Business Ecosystems

The need for new and disruptive business ecosystems is rising due to the influences of globalization; continuous advances in cyber-physical systems and technology, IT and software; as well as the digital transformation of domain-specific products and services. The first fundamental pillar of DiEn, which is the **creation** pillar, led by the digital innovator, aims to settle this challenge. OMiLAB provides all the necessary means, from technology, software to documentation, for the digital innovator to create digital business models and business ecosystems through co-creation and problem-solving workshops supported by digital design thinking. The goal is to ideate these disruptive business models and to support their transformation, realized with technological and organizational changes [6].

The transfer of ideas from the physical world to the virtual world is facilitated by the Scene2Model tool, which breaks the limitations of the working environment and distributed teams. Digital innovators irrespective of time and place can collaborate in remote environments to create the next-generation business ecosystems and business models [6]. To show the advantages of this tool and the benefit of digitizing haptic figures into diagrammatic models that enable the instantiation, processing, and dissemination of the results, OMiLAB organizes design thinking workshops. In this context, the term "haptic figures" describes physical objects that are used to visualize and structure knowledge, like paper figures or sticky notes. Ontologies help to reuse existing knowledge and connect external knowledge to enhance the semantic context [20]. Design thinking workshops facilitate co-creation and knowledge exchange between domain experts and stakeholders. By using haptic figures, the visualization and conceptualization of the product/service/business model design approach are realized, and the connected digitized version helps to share the created knowledge [21].

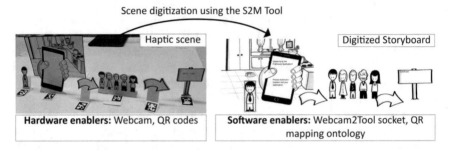

Fig. 3.4 Scene2Model—from haptic scene to digitized storyboard

The top layer in the OMiPOB environment (Fig. 3.3) that corresponds with the creation pillar represents the real world, such as the use case, the novel business model, or ecosystem, which are abstracted and transformed from real-world objects into smart models. The novel business models and the corresponding use cases should thereby not be captured only in lengthy textual description or in the head of workshop participants, but in digital conceptual models which can be shared and adapted in a refinement step using the Scene2Model tool in the OMiLAB environment. The physical storyboards, mostly created using paper figures from SAP Scenes [22], are enhanced with computer understandable tags, which are captured by a webcam and transferred to a model within the S2M modelling tool for further processing [20], as depicted in Fig. 3.4.

The OMiLAB network is constantly working on new technologies and tools to support digital transformation. Two new tools are being developed for the digital design thinking workspace, to extend its capabilities, namely, the Text2Model (T2M) and the Voice2Model (V2M). Besides Scene2Model (S2M), these two new tools are used in the first pillar of DiEn to enhance the creation of disruptive business ecosystems.

3.3.2 Design Smart Conceptual Models Within AMME

A digital business model uses a digital twin as a conceptual representation. The digital twin is built on smart models as interactive knowledge structures, thus leading to the second fundamental pillar of DiEn, the **design**. This transformation, from business ecosystems to digital twins, is represented in Fig. 3.5 and described further in this section of the chapter.

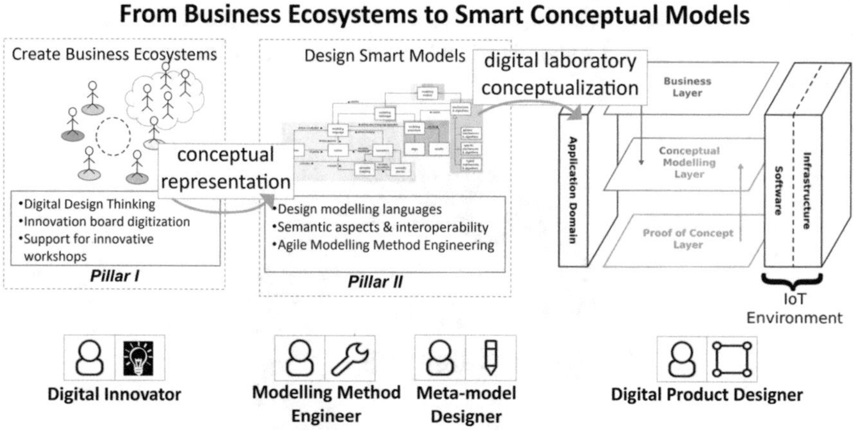

Fig. 3.5 From business ecosystems to smart conceptual models

A digital twin is a virtual representation of a physical asset that mirrors in real time the appearance and behavior of the physical environment with the added advantage of prediction, optimization, monitoring, controlling capabilities, and enhanced decision-making. Digital twins are enabled by significant technology upgrades, such as sensors, communication technologies, artificial intelligence, machine learning, advances in computational hardware, as well as cloud and edge computing [23]. There are three types of digital twins [24]: digital twin prototype (a digital model of an object that doesn't have yet a physical correspondent), digital twin instance (the virtual representation of the physical object focuses only on one of its aspects), and a digital twin aggregate (multiple digital twin instances are aggregated to complete the virtual representation of the physical object). The OMiLAB environment supports all these three categories, however focusing on the digital twin instance and aggregate.

The modelling method engineer, the meta-model designer, and the digital product designer collaborate and co-design smart models that provide adequate virtualization of reality, consider domain-specificity, and enable experimentation and evaluation of the novel business model [6]. The digital twin is a collection of smart models that correspond each to a certain part of the physical asset [25]. Hence the conceptual models comprise the interactions between the physical, virtual, and communication environment [26].

The digital twin brings value to the physical asset, by supporting informed decision-making through [23] real-time remote monitoring and control, increased efficiency and safety, predictive maintenance and scheduling, the possibility to perform what-if analysis, risk assessment, and better documentation and collaboration.

The creation of a modelling method is supported by **Agile Modelling Method Engineering (AMME)**, which offers a framework to create and adapt modelling methods in fast-changing environments [15]. The modelling method engineer is guided by the steps of the AMME lifecycle (Fig. 3.6) to build method artifacts, enable model value and maximize it while making fine adjustments, and design digital twins [4].

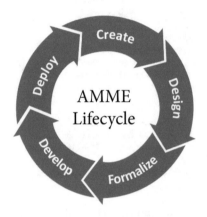

Fig. 3.6 AMME lifecycle [15]

Moreover, the meta-model designer tailors the modelling method to fit the required model artifact in a particular domain. In other words, he/she is responsible for the modelling language definition, including notation, syntax, and semantics [4].

One of the most important resources for the modelling method engineer and the meta-model designer is the ADOxx meta-modelling platform, which is used in the OMiLAB ecosystem for domain-specific modelling method implementation and modelling tool deployment, as it provides built-in functionalities that allow them to focus on the modelling language, modelling procedure, and on mechanisms and algorithms, without worrying about generic programming concerns [27]. OMiLAB meets both beginners and advanced developers' needs with ADOxx Crash Courses that guide them on the agile ADOxx development and deployment process, clarifying concepts in a hands-on manner and exploring the functionalities and capabilities of this platform.

The middle layer in the OMiPOB environment (Fig. 3.3) corresponds with the second pillar, namely, it focuses on modelling the created business model and contains conceptual models of the application scenario and the CPSs. It connects these to execute the modelled scenario in experiments. To connect these layers, as mentioned above, the requirement-oriented and agile properties of the AMME framework are thereby used to facilitate the creation of domain-specific conceptual modelling methods, which can be quickly adapted to change in the overall case [15]. The smart conceptual models are driven by artificial intelligence and aim to enable digital learning, digital reasoning, and digital self-correction. A set of rules is integrated into the models that use real historical data and convert it into actionable information (learning). The model knows what rule and when to apply it to reach the desired outcome (reasoning). AMME allows for this process to be iterative; hence, the models can adapt to the learning outcomes and reasoning (self-correction) [28].

For model realization, OMiLAB provides the bee-up tool [29], which is an ADOxx-based hybrid modelling tool consisting of five fundamental conceptual modelling languages, as it incorporates BPMN (Business Process Model and Notation), EPC (Event-driven Process Chains), ER (Entity-Relationship Models), UML (Unified Modelling Language), and PN (Petri Nets). The aim of the tool is, besides the creation of models, to provide functionality for elevated model value. As different modelling languages are incorporated in a single modelling tool, they can be used for different purposes and projects. Students, researchers, and practitioners that use bee-up observe that conceptual models can be automatically processed by machines to, e.g., generate RDF structures out of the models, manipulate the models through voice control, simulate process models, generate code, and execute the models [30]. For the bee-up tool, there exists an example of created teaching materials in form of the IMKER case study. It was created to guide the user through the majority of the tool's features and show its benefits and applicability [31].

The process of ideating, creating, and designing modelling methods and their meta-models is supported through CoChaCo. This is a tool-aided modelling method. It uses the core constructs, *Concept*, *Characteristic*, and *Connector*, to design an early-stage, platform-agnostic meta-model, whereas the *Purpose* and *Functionality* constructs depict the utilization of the later created (meta-)model. The tool offers features, such as compatibility-checking (this functionality is a prototype and available upon request), which reports the deviations between the designated meta-model and platform-specific constraints, as well as the possibility to export the models as RDF knowledge graphs to produce various model-driven artifacts. Thereby, CoChaCo offers the possibility to create meta-models independent of a specific framework, platform, or implementation, by concentrating solely on meta-modelling [32].

Lastly, the digital product designer must apply and test the method created in the selected domain [6]. The newly created modelling method and the corresponding modelling tool are used as "knowledge engines" for the digital product [4]. Stakeholders from industry, academia, and research institutions share their insights from pilot projects that integrate digital twins, as well as validation and usefulness results [23]. Hence, the activities performed in the Digital Innovation Environment of OMiLAB are open-source, and collaboration between different stakeholders is encouraged to develop and advance the technology enablers for digital twin, as well their physical-to-virtual and virtual-to-physical connection.

3.3.3 Engineer Digital Twins

The materialization of the digital laboratory is seen in the third fundamental pillar of DiEn, namely, the **engineering** of digital twins. The digital twins can be implemented as either cyber-physical systems or virtual services, to enable the experimentation and feasibility evaluation that is necessary for an enterprise to take the next step of digitalization, namely, the implementation. The digital engineer is the one that experiences and tests the digital twin in a laboratory [6]. The connection from physical-to-virtual is established by technologies that support the information flow from the physical asset to the digital twin, allowing the virtual counterpart to be constantly adjusted and maintaining/closing the differences between the two environments. The connection from virtual-to-physical holds information that may change the state of the physical object in case of optimization or what-if analysis performed on the digital twin; results show that the system's parameters should be adapted [28]. Figure 3.7 shows the connection between digital twins and cyber-physical systems.

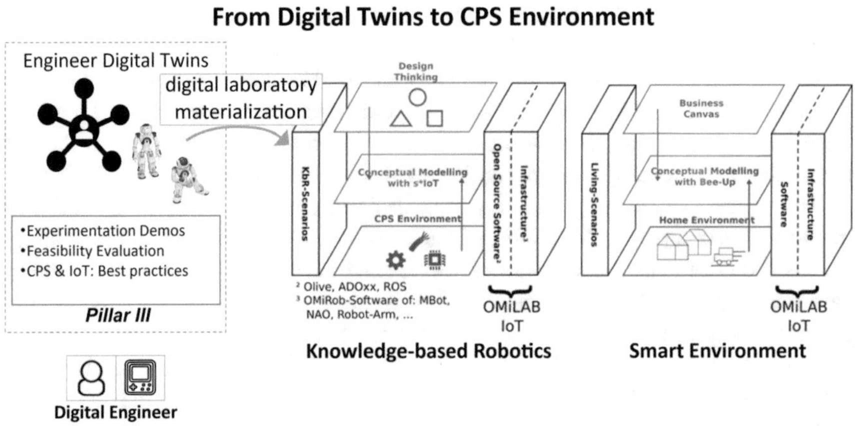

Fig. 3.7 From digital twins to CPS environment

The bottom layer in the OMiPOB environment (Fig. 3.3) contains the CPSs, which are placed in the physical laboratory, and their virtual representations can be accessed over the Internet or local connection protocols. The CPS is seen as a system-of-systems, where information systems (for social and technical information processing) cooperate with control systems (for physical processes control) [33]. In DiEn, both systems are supported by the smart conceptual models, designed in the second pillar. The CPSs movements and the flow of the use case are defined in these models. The execution is not one-way, but the feedback from the CPSs can also influence the models and their depicted flow. The models offer the users an intuitive and straightforward way to interact with the CPSs and therefore improve usability [16].

The CPS must adapt to the disruptive business models created by the digital innovator, and the new environments that thereby arise, as well as face high interoperability and open interfaces. Hence, the concept of cyber-physical ecosystems (CPES) has been introduced by researchers, for adaptive and open cyber-physical systems, with an approach of interacting with other systems [33]. One challenge identified in connection with CPS is in the design and development of methods. An interdisciplinary multi-view and multilevel modelling and development approach is required [33]. The domain-specific modelling approach and AMME principles pursued by the OMiLAB environment are integrated into CPS, handling the abovementioned challenge, by managing complexity and adaptivity. Moreover, one of the novelties of CPES is to perform integration and validation during runtime, moving away from the approach that the system cannot change after the design phase [33]. The modelling method defined and employed in the second pillar of DiEn must be suitable for various domains and engineering areas and allow adaptability to changing environments. Once again, the principle of abstraction, to reduce complexity in a domain for a specific purpose, is recognized as necessary in cyber-physical ecosystems.

For the engineering of a proof-of-concept prototype, OMiLAB provides OLIVE (OMiLAB Integrated Virtual Environment), which is a Microservice framework. Thereby, the functionality of a system (created with OLIVE) is composed of different services that run within their processes and communicate using standard network protocols, thus enabling technology transparency/independence [34]. OLIVE is connected to the ADOxx meta-modelling platform so that all ADOxx-based modelling tools can use OLIVE Microservice [7].

Figure 3.8 highlights the connection between the technologies used to create and deploy smart models and their role in the digital innovation and experimentation environment.

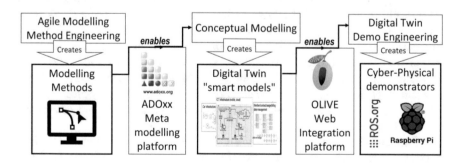

Fig. 3.8 Technologies applied in the digital innovation and experimentation environment [5]

Digital innovation is challenged within the OMiLAB environment, enabled by the three pillars described in Sect. 3.3. Particular use cases that emerged from DiEn are, for example, a specific modelling method to support the design of smart Product-Service-Systems (PSS), which can be used in the manufacturing sector to provide an overview of the PSS organizational scenarios and valuable decision support for designers [35] developed by the OMiLAB node in France. Furthermore, DiEn facilitates the simulation of real-life scenarios of assembly line automation. The OMiLAB node in Romania created a model for the automation of assembly lines assisted by a robotic arm and a mobile robot [36]. There are many more successful use cases created within the Digital Innovation Environment of OMiLAB, and they are accessible to the community but also serve as inspiration and motivation to other members and interested researchers to apply the fundamentals of DiEn in their scenarios.

3.4 Experience Reports

This section highlights two OMiLAB nodes, namely, the Bialystok University of Technology in Poland, which is an academic node, and the industrial node at Hilti in Germany. The first representation focuses on "how" the OMiLAB physical and virtual environment has been applied in an academic setting, whereas the second representation concentrates on "why" DiEn should be integrated in industrial settings as well.

3.4.1 An Academic Approach: The UNIBIAL Node

The activity of the OMiLAB node at the Faculty of Management Engineering of the Bialystok University of Technology (OMiLAB@UNIBIAL) was initiated within the project "DigiFoF: Digital Design Skills for Factories of the Future." Its setup is the result of close cooperation between Bialystok University of Technology and the Centre for the Promotion of Innovation and Development representing industrial enterprises associated with the Metal Processing Cluster. OMiLAB@UNIBIAL is an integral part of the research and didactic infrastructure of the Faculty of Management Engineering of the Bialystok University of Technology, which supports the education of students, mainly in logistics and management and production engineering fields.

Taking into account the idea of the Open Models Initiative Laboratory network, the key challenge of the UNIBIAL node is to stimulate the cooperation and exchange of experiences between academia and the business sector.

It aims to shape and develop the competencies of students, academics, and employees of local companies in process design and analysis. The main areas of knowledge developed by the UNIBIAL node are related to design thinking and business models (Business Model Canvas), business process management (BPM), and robotic process automation (RPA). The development of competencies of students and practitioners within the OMiLAB node is achieved through the use of problem-based learning and knowledge-based simulation. Furthermore, it is supported by the Digital Innovation Environment powered by OMiLAB, as well as a transfer of knowledge and experience from cooperating companies.

The application and usability of the framework and technologies provided by OMiLAB are illustrated by a use case, developed in cooperation with BOC Poland. The case is linked to the technological and environmental challenges, as well as the logistical problems of large cities. The presented case focuses on the management of a fleet of autonomous vehicles. This case aims to present a complex approach to business process design and analysis using a combination of storytelling and a scene to model as a design thinking technique and ADOxx as a meta-modelling tool.

The story is not a blueprint, but an inspiration for innovation and designing new businesses. Stories help identify and define the goals and needs of potential customers for whom a new product or service is designed. The main role of storytelling in innovation and process design is to [37]:

- Illustrate an idea
- Describe the context of product or services
- Describe the impact of a new design
- Support communication and understanding

To create a story and a scene, one can use a simple schema based on a rule of thumb. Knowing that a good story has at least one person, place, action, and motivation, the following scenario was formed.

Scenario:

As the owner of a fleet of dozens of autonomous cars, I want to offer a service to white-collar workers downtown – driving them to work in the morning and then picking them up from work. The service could also include an additional stop at a supermarket on the way back home. Given the growing parking problems and the possibility of eco-friendly, convenient travel to work without owning a car, I expect a high interest in such a service.

Based on the scenario, several scenes (using SAP Scenes) were prepared and then digitalized (see Fig. 3.9). Thereby, using the Scene2Model tool, a storyboard has been created.

Considering the aim of the core process, namely, delivering a value in this business model, the analytical problem can be formulated as follows: *Is it possible*

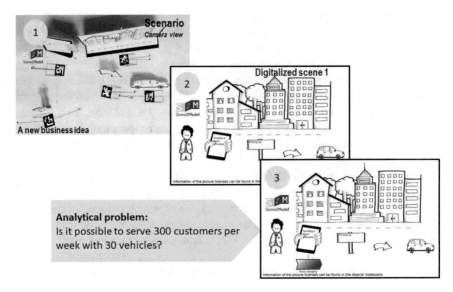

Fig. 3.9 Scene digitalization with Scene2Model (S2M) tool

to serve 300 white-collar workers per week with a fleet of 30 autonomous vehi-cles? It is assumed that a potential customer sends his/her home-office commute schedule. Based on this the availability of vehicles and the possibility of providing *Home2Work* service were assessed. To analyze and solve this business problem, knowledge-based simulation (KBS) instruments were used.

Knowledge-based simulation [7] makes it possible to combine business process diagrams (BPMN 2.0) depicting the flow of the process as well as its most important characteristics with the knowledge of experts about specific scenarios. This way it is possible to analyze complex scenarios with many variants.

The graphic (Fig. 3.10) shows a BPMN 2.0 diagram for the *Home2Work* service described above.

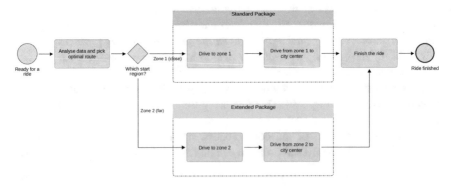

Fig. 3.10 BPMN diagram created for the scenario

To run KBS, tools developed within the BIMERR project [18] are used.

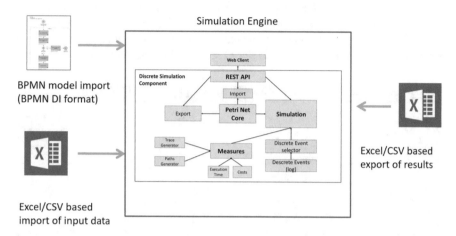

Fig. 3.11 Overview of KBS tool

As mentioned above, KBS takes as an input a BPMN diagram and an Excel file (see Fig. 3.11) with the configuration—in this case, the file contains information about the home-office commute schedules of the customers extended with additional input from experts. The file contains several sheets. The first one lists information about process starts based on customer schedules. The following sheets are filled by experts who, e.g., specify how long it takes to perform tasks in a process. This is visible in column C in Fig. 3.12.

Apart from providing specific values, it is also possible to use various statistical distributions to make the scenario closer to the real-life case (the example shown below uses Gaussian distribution with mean and variance provided in milliseconds).

Similarly, experts can override information about path probabilities from a diagram with their input. This allows running several simulations with one diagram and Excel files with, e.g., optimistic or pessimistic scenarios.

	A	B	C	D
1	Analyse data and pick optimal route	2025-09-24T07:00:00	60000@6000	default
2	Drive to zone 1	2025-09-24T07:00:00	900000@90000	default
3	Drive from zone 1 to city center	2025-09-24T07:00:00	900000@90000	default
4	Drive to zone 2	2025-09-24T07:00:00	1800000@360000	default
5	Drive from zone 2 to city center	2025-09-24T07:00:00	1800000@720000	default
6	Finish the ride	2025-09-24T07:00:00	default	default
7				
8				
9				
10				

C_START_EVENT | Start times | C_TASK | C_EXCLUSIVE_GATEWAY ⊕

Fig. 3.12 Example Excel file with information about task durations

Uploaded files are being processed by the KBS engine, which provides an open REST interface, and results are provided both in a graphical user interface and as a CSV log with additional data for further analysis (see Fig. 3.13). This way, outcomes can be analyzed by stakeholders with statistical skills, and they can easily see how their assumptions impact the possibility of serving 300 customers with 30 vehicles.

	A	B	C	D	E
1				Cars ch	Car stock
45	Run-44	Ready for a ride	2025-09-24T07:26:00.000	-1	1
46	Run-45	Ready for a ride	2025-09-24T07:27:00.000	-1	0
47	Run-23	Ride finished	2025-09-24T07:28:17.339	1	1
48	Run-26	Ride finished	2025-09-24T07:29:10.754	1	2
49	Run-7	Ride finished	2025-09-24T07:29:58.621	1	3
50	Run-11	Ride finished	2025-09-24T07:31:23.618	1	4
51	Run-9	Ride finished	2025-09-24T07:32:09.314	1	5
52	Run-3	Ride finished	2025-09-24T07:32:20.349	1	6
53	Run-22	Ride finished	2025-09-24T07:32:20.670	1	7
54	Run-29	Ride finished	2025-09-24T07:32:35.943	1	8
55	Run-18	Ride finished	2025-09-24T07:32:48.100	1	9

◀ ▶ | C_START_EVENT | C_TASK | C_END_EVENT | **Fleet planning** | C_EXCLUSIVE_GATE\ ... ⊕ ⋮ ◀

Fig. 3.13 Example results of the KBS showing fleet usage in a scenario

The presented use case illustrates the possibilities of using design thinking techniques (SAP Scene, Scene2Model) and ADOxx in combination with a KBS tool for process design and analysis. Solving a business problem requires basic knowledge and skills in storytelling and process modelling with BPMN. Therefore, this case can be used both in the didactic process and can be a contribution to further discussion and development in workshops aimed at practitioners and researchers.

3.4.2 The Industrial Needs: The Hilti Node

OMiLAB NPO and the Hilti Corporation are engaged in a partnership for several years, and the collaboration has been focused on mutual support during numerous NEMO Summer Schools [9]. Only recently, both corporations have emerged on the idea to start a jointly run OMiLAB node for verifying its purpose and applicability to solve business-related challenges. During the discussion phase for the OMiLAB installation at Hilti in Southern Germany, we have identified three main areas of interest for both the OMiLAB NPO and the Hilti Corporation to further investigate:

1. **To what extent can an OMiLAB node help both Hilti employees and interns to learn and apply structural problem-solving capabilities and thinking in meta-models in a virtual and globally distributed team setup?**

    Hilti's software team is distributed with its main locations in Malaysia, India, Germany, Switzerland, Liechtenstein, France, and the USA. The corresponding business colleagues are located in nine different hubs around the globe. Typically, with these many geographies, cultural backgrounds, and local business needs, it is a lengthy and iterative process to define products and services that serve the needs of Hilti customers globally. Consequently, we can observe several projects that undergo revisions and re-scoping as it is merely impossible to bring all stakeholders onto one (virtual) table or into one (virtual) lab discussing product and service ideas and their impacts on customers. With OMiLAB, we will undergo an exercise to use the simplest boxboard (Hilti-specific design thinking elements) miniatures on the *business canvas* to play through different scenarios and hence initiate discussions about their potential impacts. Instead of having these discussions—like today—during video conferences sharing sketches, we hope that the more interactive interplay with the boxboard miniatures will allow for a thorough analysis anticipating potential blockers typically leading to a later re-scoping of projects. We think the value of using boxboard miniatures on the business canvas will be visible as there is less of a need for deep technical understanding versus more focus on the customer problem that should be solved. Eventually, the usage of the business canvas will help in training structural problem-solving skills.

2. **How can OMiLAB support Hilti design and define processes for products and services in the area of Cyber-Physical Systems (CPS), in which inherently a huge number of possible product and/or service variants can be imagined?**

   Assuming we have our Hilti colleagues together with other members of the OMiLAB community in a virtual workshop, we aim to jointly work on the design and the definition of product and service variants and their continuous improvement. The aforementioned boxboard miniatures will be the starting point for the technical design of these products and services by applying modelling techniques. We hereby foresee that we will translate the steps simulated with the boxboard miniatures into computer-readable *conceptual models* allowing for (a) simulation of outcomes and (b) derivations of system and platform needs. An example of this could be products and services in the area of IoT, in which Hilti tools offer certain IoT capabilities. Variants of those can be found in diverse legal requirements that have to be complied with in different countries, system designs that take into consideration aspects such as latency, response time optimizations, dimension of micro- vs macro-services, and many others. We hope that with the application of the modelling layer as well as by bringing together experts in the virtual OMiLAB, we will be able to anticipate impacts of product and service variants much earlier compared to what we achieve nowadays with the approach of "classical" videoconferences.

3. **Is OMiLAB a common virtual ground, in which simulations of such products and/or services can be executed in an end-to-end manner resulting in a concise decision proposal before software development activities can start?**

   As a final step, we plan to bring the abovementioned conceptual models "to life" by applying the concept of *digital and physical twins*. We hereby plan to demo the different product and service variants for evaluating their practical implementation in an end-to-end fashion, meaning from production via distribution over usage by the customer to after-market service. We hope that these demos will allow for a more vivid and tangible discussion and decision-making for or against certain product and service variants. Considering the aforementioned re-scoping of projects, we foresee an opportunity to make more conscious decisions for the start of a product, service, or software development project and hence reduce the amount of necessary re-scoping.

3.5 Conclusion

In this chapter, the OMiLAB network is introduced, its goal and tools as a community of practice and environment aimed at increasing the value of conceptual models. The focus is thereby set on how tool-aided conceptual modelling can facilitate digital innovation within the Digital Innovation Environment. This environment, its application in an academic and in an industrial context, and different approaches on how knowledge can be transferred within the community were also discussed.

The fundamental pillars for creation, design, and engineer, as well as the semantic technologies for conceptual modelling of the OMiLAB environment, are adopted by communities, researchers, and industries from all over the world. Each node thereby has its area of expertise, where conceptual modelling is applied and gained knowledge is shared with other nodes.

As the use cases presented in this chapter show, the Digital Innovation Environment by OMiLAB supports the ideation, testing, and evaluation of novel ideas and early prototypes as innovative solutions for digital transformation initiatives. Domain experts and stakeholders work together and collaborate in a co-creative approach to develop these solutions and to support decision-makers with know-how from the proof-of-concept environment facilitated by OMiLAB. They are supported by software and hardware assets, based on open platforms and open interfaces.

OMiLAB is present in education and research through a diverse range of activities, brings value-added services through open-source software, and facilitates knowledge transfer between different participants. It aims and has the potential to support and drive digital transformation initiatives by stakeholders through the application of conceptual modelling. Digital innovation is challenged throughout the OMiLAB environment by its members and community. At the same time, it serves as motivation for all interested stakeholders to join and bring their expertise and know-how and expand the capabilities and functionalities of DiEn, as well as co-create and test new experiments to serve their domain-specific scenario and purpose.

References

1. Przybilla, L., Klinker, K., Lang, M., Schreieck, M., Wiesche, M., Krcmar, H.: Design thinking in digital innovation projects - exploring the effects of intangibility (IEEE, Ed.) IEEE Transactions on Engineering Management, pp. 1–15. doi:https://doi.org/10.1109/TEM.2020.3036818 (2020, 12 31)
2. Fichman, R.G., Dos Santos, B.L., Zheng, Z.: Digital innovation as a fundamental and powerful concept in the information systems curriculum. MIS Q. **38**(2), 329–353 (2014)
3. OMiLAB NPO. About Us. Retrieved 05 05, 2021, from www.omilab.org: https://www.omilab.org/about.html (2021a)
4. Bork, D., Buchmann, R.A., Karagiannis, D., Lee, M., Miron, E.-T.: An open platform for modeling method conceptualization: the OMiLAB digital ecosystem, pp. 673–679. CAIS. doi:https://doi.org/10.17705/1CAIS.04432 (2019)
5. Karagiannis, D., Buchmann, R.A., Boucher, X., Cavalieri, S., Florea, A., Kiritsis, D., Lee, M.: OMiLAB: a smart innovation environment for digital engineers. In: Camarinha-Matos, L., Afsarmanesh, H., Ortiz, A. (eds.) Boosting Collaborative Networks 4.0. PRO-VE 2020. IFIP Advances in Information and Communication Technology, vol. 598, pp. 273–282. Springer, Cham (2020). https://doi.org/10.1007/978-3-030-62412-5_23
6. OMiLAB Team. A Digital Innovation Environment powered by Open Models Laboratory. doi:https://doi.org/10.5281/ZENODO.3899990 (2020)
7. Woitsch, R.: Industrial digital environments in action: The OMiLAB innovation corner. In: Grabis, J., Bork, D. (eds.) The Practice of Enterprise Modeling. PoEM 2020. Lecture Notes in Business Information Processing, vol. 400, pp. 8–22. Springer, Cham (2020). https://doi.org/10.1007/978-3-030-63479-7_2
8. Wenger, E.: Communities of practice: learning, meaning and identity. Cambridge University Press (1998). https://doi.org/10.1017/CBO9780511803932
9. OMiLAB NPO. Retrieved 05 12, 2021, from nemo.omilab.org: https://nemo.omilab.org/ (2021c)
10. digifof.eu. Retrieved 05 13, 2021, from digifof.eu: https://www.digifof.eu/ (2021)
11. Karagiannis, D., Mayr, H.C., Mylopoulos, J. (eds.): Domain-specific conceptual modelling: concepts, methods and tools. Springer, Cham (2016). https://doi.org/10.1007/978-3-319-39417-6
12. OMiLAB NPO. Open EA User-Centric Assessment Service. Retrieved 05 13, 2021, from omilab.org: https://www.omilab.org/usercentricassessment/ (2021j)
13. Kaushik, K.: Beginner's Guide to Understanding Digital Innovation. Retrieved 06 15, 2021, from https://www.apty.io/:https://www.apty.io/blog/digital-innovation-guide (2020, 06 22)
14. Nasiri, M., Saunila, M., Ukko, J., Rantala, T., Rantanen, H.: Shaping digital innovation via digital-related capabilities. Information Systems Frontiers (2020, 11 12). doi:https://doi.org/10.1007/s10796-020-10089-2
15. Karagiannis, D.: Agile modeling method engineering. In: Proceedings of the 19th Panhellenic Conference on Informatics, pp. 5–10. ACM Press, Athens (2015). https://doi.org/10.1145/2801948.2802040
16. Karagiannis, D., Muck, C.: OMiLAB Physical Objects (2017)
17. Change2Twin. Retrieved 05 12, 2021, from www.change2twin.eu: https://www.change2twin.eu/about/ (2021)
18. BIMERR. Retrieved 05 12, 2021, from https://bimerr.eu/:https://bimerr.eu/ (2021)
19. complAI Project. Retrieved 05 12, 2021, from https://complai.innovation-laboratory.org/:https://complai.innovation-laboratory.org/ (2021)
20. Muck, C., Miron, E.-T., Karagiannis, D., Lee, M.: Supporting service design with storyboards and diagrammatic models: the Scene2Model tool. Proceedings of the Joint International Conference of Service Science and Innovation (ICSSI 2018) and Serviceology (ICServ 2018), (pp. 389–396). Taichung, Taiwan (2018)

21. OMiLAB NPO. Design Thinking. Retrieved 05 13, 2021, from www.omilab.org: https://www.omilab.org/nodes/design-thinking.html (2021i)
22. SAP SE. SAP Scenes. Retrieved 05 11, 2021, from https://experience.sap.com/:https://experience.sap.com/designservices/resource/scenes (2021)
23. Rasheed, A., San, O., Kvamsdal, T.: Digital twin: values, challenges and enablers from a modeling perspective. IEEE Access. **8**, 21980–22012 (2020). https://doi.org/10.1109/ACCESS.2020.2970143
24. Grieves, M., Vickers, J.: Digital twin: mitigating unpredictable, undesirable emergent behavior in complex systems. In: Kahlen, F., Flumerfelt, S., Alves, A. (eds.) Transdisciplinary Perspectives on Complex Systems, pp. 85–113. Springer, Cham (2017). https://doi.org/10.1007/978-3-319-38756-7_4
25. Kirchhof, J. C., Michael, J., Rumpe, B., Varga, S., Wortmann, A.: Model-driven digital twin construction: synthesizing the integration of cyber-physical systems with their information systems. Proceedings of the 23rd ACM/IEEE International Conference on Model Driven Engineering Languages and Systems. ACM (2020)
26. Wu, C., Zhou, Y., Pereira Pessoa, M.V., Peng, Q.: Conceptual digital twin modeling based on an integrated five-dimensional framework and TRIZ function model. Journal of Manufacturing Systems. **58**, 79–93 (2021). https://doi.org/10.1016/j.jmsy.2020.07.006
27. ADOxx.org. Retrieved 05 10, 2021, from adoxx.org: https://www.adoxx.org/live/home (2021a)
28. Rathore, M.M., Shah, S.A., Shukla, D., Bentafat, E., Bakiras, S.: The role of AI, machine learning, and big data in digital twinning: a systematic literature review, challenges and opportunities. IEEE Access. **9**, 32030–32052 (2021). https://doi.org/10.1109/ACCESS.2021.3060863
29. OMiLAB NPO. Bee-Up for Education. Retrieved 05 12, 2021, from https://bee-up.omilab.org/:https://bee-up.omilab.org/activities/bee-up/ (2021b)
30. Burzynski, P., & Karagiannis, D.: bee-up - a teaching tool for fundamental conceptual modelling. Modellierung 2020 Short, Workshop and Tools & Demo Papers. Vienna (2020)
31. Karagiannis, D., Burzynski, P., Miron, E.-T.: The "IMKER" case study - practice with the bee-up tool. doi:https://doi.org/10.5281/zenodo.345846 (2017)
32. Karagiannis, D., Burzynski, P., Utz, W., Buchmann, R.A.: A metamodeling approach to support the engineering of modeling method requirements. 2019 IEEE 27th International Requirements Engineering Conference (RE), pp. 199–210. IEEE, Jeju Island. doi:https://doi.org/10.1109/RE.2019.00030 (2019)
33. Bartelt, C., Rausch, A., Rehfeldt, K.: Quo vadis cyber-physical systems. Research areas of cyber-physical ecosystems. A position paper. CTSE2015: Proceedings of the 1st International Workshop on Control Theory for Software Engineering, pp. 22–25 doi:https://doi.org/10.1145/2804337.2804341 (2015)
34. ADOxx.org. Olive. Retrieved 05 12, 2021, from https://www.adoxx.org/:https://www.adoxx.org/live/olive (2021b).
35. Boucher, X., Medini, K., Fill, H.-G.: Product-service-system modeling method. In: Karagiannis, D., Mayr, H.C., Mylopoulos, J. (eds.) Domain-Specific Conceptual Modeling. Springer, Cham (2016). https://doi.org/10.1007/978-3-319-39417-6_21
36. Baltes, O.-I.: Automation of assembly lines assisted by a robotic arm and a mobile robot. Retrieved 05 26, 2021, from http://digifof.omilab.ulbsibiu.ro/:http://digifof.omilab.ulbsibiu.ro/psm/content/roboticarm/info (2021)
37. Quesenbery, W.: Storytelling for user experience: crafting stories for better design. Rosenfeld Media (2010)

Part II
Previous Volume: Synopsis

Chapter 4
The Purpose-Specificity Framework for Domain-Specific Conceptual Modeling

Robert Andrei Buchmann

Abstract The literature on domain-specific languages typically positions its discourse relative to a traditional dichotomy between *general-purpose* and *domain-specific*. This may be a sufficient distinction for end users, but modeling method engineers need a more refined frame—they are in the position to build artifacts (i.e., modeling methods) where boundaries of the modeling universe of discourse must be aligned with the method requirements (purpose). Therefore, instead of choosing on which side of the dichotomy their artifact belongs, it is more useful for methodologists to think about purpose and specificity as orthogonal dimensions. Modeling method engineers typically work on metamodeling platforms that enable fast prototyping of tools, allowing them to focus precisely on how to serve a purpose and which concepts or properties should be captured as first-class modeling citizens. These are fine-tuning design decisions that should benefit from adequate methodologies—during recent years the Agile Modeling Method Engineering (AMME) framework emerged not only to support such fine-tuning but also to enable the evolution of modeling methods in response to changing purposes or shifting specificity needs. To frame this principle, the chapter proposes a Purpose-Specificity framework where modeling methods may occupy a possibly shifting or expanding gamut of purposes and specificities—contributions to the first volume of this book series are briefly characterized through this lens. For practitioners, the chapter also points to an open tool that operationalizes this idea; for theory builders, a rhetorical analysis on the multidimensional value of models as Design Science artifacts is also derived.

Keywords Domain-specific conceptual modeling · Model purpose · Model value · Agile modeling method engineering · ADOxx · Design Science Research

R. A. Buchmann (✉)
Business Informatics Research Center, Babeș-Bolyai University, Cluj-Napoca, Romania
e-mail: robert.buchmann@econ.ubbcluj.ro

4.1 Introduction

Languages evolve—they expand as new terms are needed to concisely encode novel ideas, they adapt as depth of understanding evolves, and they specialize in jargons in order to support discourse of specialized scope and nuance. Curated dictionaries and standard grammar rules facilitate a certain level of unification allowing agents to communicate efficiently, to encode implicit information according to commonly agreed patterns. Sometimes the encoder will compress the information hoping that the receiver has sufficient knowledge to decode meanings that are only implied [1]; other times, the encoder needs to provide a sufficiently elaborated representation to eliminate ambiguity or reduce effort on the decoder's end. Natural evolution of languages tends to establish a balance of efforts on both sides [2], assuming a commonly agreed willingness in this respect; there may also be the case that the encoder warps the message to send duplicitous or ambiguous meaning or that the decoder applies such a strict validation that it will miss valuable information for syntactic compliance reasons. The latter category motivates ongoing research efforts for engineering knowledge representations that are machine-readable/interpretable— i.e., not relying on an approximate ability to "learn" from patterns detected in some unstructured knowledge expression, but allowing the non-ambiguous ingestion of a knowledge layer into smart systems, to support reasoning within a domain of discourse and to automate tasks based on it.

Domain-specific language engineering contributes to these efforts; more specifically, domain-specific conceptual modeling relies on the fact that domain concepts and their properties are distinguishable as explicit first-class modeling citizens, not only as ad hoc human interpretations of generic constructs. These first-class citizens bring to a modeling language assets such as built-in properties, fixed property values, and built-in constraints that capture patterns recurring in a bounded domain, serving explicit purposes. Depending on the depth of specificity, the built-in aspects may be superficial (strictly notational, e.g., a graphical variant to improve semantic transparency) or deep—manifesting in syntactic constraints and semantics, propagating to model-driven or model manipulation features that bridge the language to its purpose. There is, of course, a trade-off—the productivity or comprehension gain versus the reusability loss: the more a language ("jargon") is tailored for a context, the less fit it will be for other contexts. This is not a loss of quality but a trade-off of qualities—languages do not have to be designed with the ambition of being "the next standard" (i.e., aiming for global adoption); they may serve a narrow application area, even a single enterprise or a single model-driven system. If this is a worthy goal, it depends on whether technical and methodological support is available to make such a narrow-use language operational in the context of a method, and that method in the form of a tool—this is what metamodeling platforms and frameworks bring to the table, thus turning domain-specific conceptual modeling into an artifact-oriented research field. It is the intention of this book series to showcase the variety of modeling jargons that are thus enabled, in relation to a wide array of explicit purposes (classifications are available in the literature, see [3]), guided by recurring patterns and design decisions that may inform design theories in this field.

The goal of this chapter is to introduce the Purpose-Specificity framework and to characterize past contributions to this book series through the lens of this framework. The remainder of the chapter is structured as follows: Section 4.2 will advocate the relevance of the Purpose-Specificity framework starting from a specificity spectrum derived from modeling method requirements. Section 4.3 will apply this frame to characterize contributions to the first volume of this book series. Section 4.4 will apply rhetorical devices to provide a value perspective on domain-specific conceptual modeling as an artifact building field of Design Science Research. The chapter ends with concluding remarks.

4.2 Managing Specificity and Purpose

4.2.1 The Specificity Spectrum

Traditionally, *domain-specific* languages have been contrasted against *general-purpose* languages—we argue, however, that the subsumption relation, which can specialize concepts across any number of taxonomical levels, leads to a gradient of specificities determined by the level of detail that must be captured in first-class citizen constructs of a language. The field of Formal Concept Analysis [4] formalizes this gradient by making a distinction between the extension and intension of a concept, then using the intension to organize the concepts of a "formal context" (which may be proxied as a "domain of discourse") in a lattice (hence partial ordering of concepts).

To ground this idea to a concrete simple example from the world of diagrammatic modeling, in Fig. 4.1 we specialize the concept of Transition (from the strongly formalized Petri Nets language) by two means:

- *By subtyping*: a BPMN typed task as a specialization of an EPC non-typed task, which further specializes (for business administration) the highly abstract Petri Net transition; at the bottom of a hierarchy, the BPMN task is further specialized into tasks having app requirements attached to them (as prescribed by the domain-specific ComVantage method [5]).
- *By expanding the intension*: the BPMN task schema expanded first with RACI attributes (Responsible-Accountable-Consulted-Informed) and then further expanded with parameters necessary to interoperate with some Java class responsible for the automation of the task; similarly, on the opposite site, the Petri Nets transition is enriched with simulation-relevant parameters (e.g., prioritization).

The two means of subsuming are conceptually similar—they are distinguished by their operationalization: When subtyping, we imply that some additional properties distinguish the subtype, but we don't necessarily care to make those new properties explicit; when expanding the intension, we add new properties (possibly also fixing somfime to put an end to Be of their values) and by doing so we create a subtype that we don't necessarily care to label explicitly.

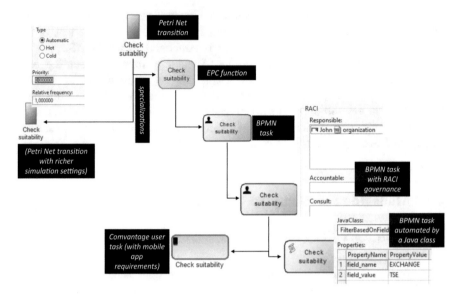

Fig. 4.1 Gradually deepening the specificity of a concept over different modeling languages

End users may perceive the newly added attributes as tool developer workarounds or as tool utilities to enable some required (interoperability) feature. Conceptually, however, more machine-readable properties imply more specific semantics and richer possibilities for constraints: the BPMN with RACI attributes may be considered a specialized "RACI-governed task" and the variant with Java parameters may be seen as a "Java-automated task," both being specializations relative to the BPMN task taxonomy. Only the Java-aware variant is justified by interoperability with an execution environment, and RACI is a common managerial approach that relies on enriching task descriptions with more refined responsibilities compared to what BPMN pools and lanes can express; and if those responsibilities fall on some automated Java service of agent, then why not treat it as just another level of specificity, assimilating in the modeling method or language some relations with the technological environment, not only with the organizational environment.

If domain-specific languages are supposed to improve productivity and adequacy to a particular context, why not go all the way and recognize agents/abstractions from a technological context? In the recent publications [6, 7], this idea is manifested not only as an annotation property but as modeling symbols that represent technological abstractions crossing the boundary from the technological environment to the modeling language. In terms of model-driven engineering, this also implies that a middleware compiler approach relying on intermediate serialization formats (e.g., XMI [8]) or heavy model rewriting may be replaced by an interpreter that can query technical parameters directly from a model(-as-a-service). Separation of concerns is, of course, sacrificed to some degree—depending on how much technical detail becomes configurable in the diagrammatic environment.

Conceptual modeling is about abstracting away details while keeping those that are relevant for the modeling purpose—however, the boundary between the two should be dictated by purpose and modeling method requirements; they will determine the desired level of decoupling between the modeling environment and the technological context in which it will operate.

4.2.2 The Need for Specificity

Information Systems research is significantly biased towards observing the use of artifacts (taken for granted) to the detriment of innovative artifact building and design-oriented research, an imbalance that has gained explicit attention during the recent years, see [9]. In terms of method or language engineering, it is not uncommon to hear (from someone who doesn't want to be bothered with the field of domain-specific modeling) the argument "whatever I want to model, I can already do it with language X." The choice for language X is dictated by personal preference, language (or tool) popularity, practices imposed by an organizational context, or simply a disinterest in switching the hat of language user with that of a language analyst/engineer.

However, what the above argument typically means is "whatever I will not be able to express with language X, I will find a way around to compensate." A simple quasi-experiment with Business Informatics students being asked to describe a cooking recipe in a BPMN tool led to the compensation solutions shown in the top part of Fig. 4.2: (a) squeezing information in verbose task labels; (b) attaching sticky notes; and (c) repurposing existing language concepts (typically pools and information resources). The adequacy of these solutions depends on purpose— the basic purpose of "communication and understanding" [10] may be sufficiently well served; any purpose where the machine needs to distinguish between concepts will be difficult to satisfy—e.g., obtaining a bill of materials (ingredients) via model queries over multiple cooking recipes. Solution (b) provides some level of structuring, but it still meets difficulties with how to attach ingredient quantities needed for each individual task, or in the case that we actually need to express both data objects and material ingredients in the same process diagram.

A pragmatic design-oriented solution (described in more detail in [11] and suggested by the bottom part of Fig. 4.2) is to deepen the specificity by recognizing the cooking ingredient as a first-hand modeling citizen (i.e., a concept of the relevant domain of discourse). Assuming that platforms for productively achieving this are available (i.e., metamodeling platforms), this may be further extended with a possibility to improve semantic transparency by adding (a) a preferred graphical symbol (that may even differentiate between instances of the same concept) and (b) the possibility to tailor a machine-readable relation where ingredient quantities can be attached (and reflected dynamically as an interactive ornament to the task notation). Are these aspects language or tool concerns? Does a language only comprise the root form of a word as prescribed by dictionaries, or all its purposeful variations, specializations, and contextual meanings? We hereby advocate a flexible positioning of this boundary in the field of domain-specific modeling research, in alignment with the generalized specificity spectrum suggested in the previous section.

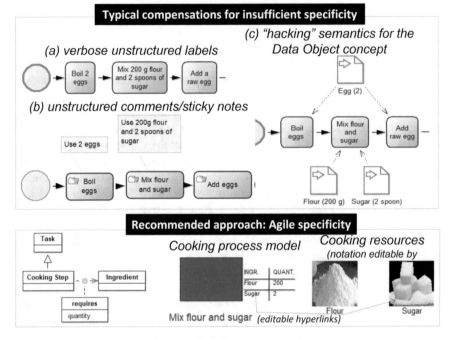

Fig. 4.2 Tackling specificity requirements: (**a**) verbose unstructured labels, (**b**) unstructured comments/sticky notes, (**c**) "hacking" semantics for the Data Object concept

One key challenge with enabling the flexible specialization is how to agilely deploy it in response to evolving requirements and purposes, so that:

- Artifact-in-use experimentation can easily switch between comparative design decisions (from an empirical IS research perspective)
- Tooling can be quickly prototyped for users who want to benefit in the short term from their preferred level of specificity (from a practitioner and artifact building research perspective)

In response to these needs, the Agile Modeling Method Engineering (AMME) framework [12] was introduced as an iterative agile methodology designed to facilitate the operationalization of modeling methods in tool form, typically in tandem with ADOxx [13]—the implementation platform employed for the prototypes presented in this book.

AMME is not strictly an implementation methodology; its engineering cycle starts with a requirements engineering phase for which model-based support was tailored—see the CoChaCo tool (Concept-Characteristic-Connector) [14] for describing and managing domain-specific modeling requirements in terms of both purpose and specificity. In doing so, CoChaCo is itself a domain-specific method for the requirements engineering domain—its key concepts are stakeholder, purpose/goal, functionality/backlog, and traceability relations to elements of an early-stage metamodel rudiment (basis for the actual metamodel design phase).

The detailed metamodel of CoChaCo and its role in the tooling chain supporting the AMME iterative cycle have been presented in [15]. The next subsection will overview it in support of this chapter's thesis for defusing the oversimplistic dichotomy between "general-purpose" and "domain-specific."

4.2.3 Mapping Specificity to Purposes

Modeling methods, like any Design Science artifact, are purposefully built for an identified problem captured in requirements that need to be elicited, represented, and traced to items to be created during later engineering activities. Due to the particular nature of modeling methods, it is useful to specialize the traditional requirements taxonomies—general categories are still applicable (e.g., functional, nonfunctional), but certain classes of requirements can be derived from how a modeling method is conceptualized in its building blocks. AMME resorts to the definition of a modeling method from [16], from which the following requirements categories can be derived, and have informed the design decisions of the CoChaCo method:

- Requirements on syntax
- Requirements on semantics
- Requirements on procedure
- Requirements on model-driven functionality ("mechanisms")

The decomposition may be further drilled down to treating various method aspects as artifacts in their own right—e.g., "notation" was isolated as an engineered artifact by the works of Moody [17]; later, "secondary notation" was separated from it in works such as [18, 19]; some scholars are more concerned with modeling grammars in relation to the "modeling scripts" [20] they can generate. Evaluation protocols designed specifically for such method facets have been proposed [21], while other quality evaluation approaches are rather holistic, treating a modeling language as a whole, in a "take all or leave all" approach [22].

This heterogeneity raises the need for a particular requirements engineering approach that maps purpose to specificity in a traceable manner, itself being a method that employs a purposeful conceptualization comprising relevant concepts: modeling stakeholders mapped to their purposes (business analysts, designers, developers, etc., expect different benefits from a modeling method), further mapped on modeling tool functionalities and further on the concepts, relationships, and attributes that can contribute to those functionalities. In Fig. 4.3 CoChaCo was used to capture modeling method requirements for a fragment of the ComVantage method [5] covering the three types of models sampled at the bottom of the figure.

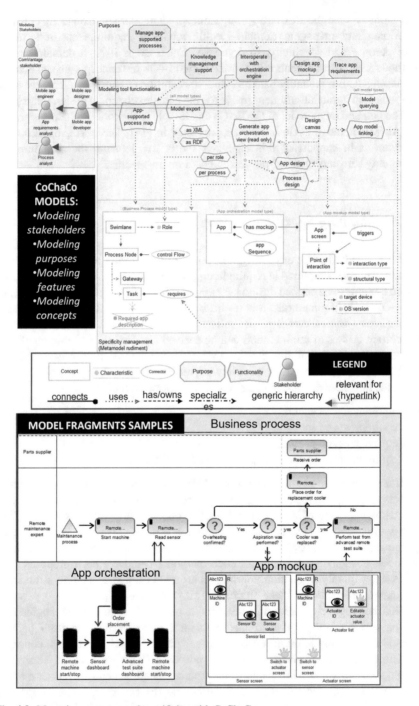

Fig. 4.3 Managing purposes and specificity with CoChaCo

The bottom part of the CoChaCo model, where the level of specificity is decided for each concept, shows a metamodel rudiment—a pool of concepts and properties directly relevant for identified purposes that may end up in the final metamodel (or not, notice the scrapped attribute for Task) and may take different forms, not necessarily as visual modeling elements (e.g., a "connector" may end up being a visual arrow, but also a visual containment or a hyperlink; a "concept" may become a model type containing things related to it, but also a modeling node; a "characteristic" may end up as a visual cue, an annotation property, both). Subtyping and intension schemas are also specified as early-stage metamodeling decisions, generally to ensure that nothing more and nothing less than what is relevant for identified "purposes" will be kept in the modeling language and that traceability is achieved during later evolution of the requirements.

Therefore, this is a hybrid tool for both knowledge acquisition and requirements modeling—the need for such a hybridization stems from the purpose-specificity interdependencies (i.e., something may get lost if tool requirements and the domain of discourse are elicited in separate engineering processes). CoChaCo, itself being a domain-specific language, tool, and method, was born out of recognizing recurring conceptualization and traceability efforts in metamodeling projects over the years, thus becoming a dedicated means for managing a potential purpose-specificity space to be further characterized in the next sections.

4.3   The Purpose-Specificity Framework

4.3.1   Purpose and Specificity as Dimensions

The position expressed in this chapter originates in knowledge representation frameworks (e.g., RDF) where conceptual models are supposed to be able to express anything ("resources") over any number of specialization layers—a more open-ended view compared to what users of BPMN, UML, ArchiMate, etc., expect when adopting an already agreed upon conceptualization and linguistic form (standards also provide certain mechanisms for shifting specificity, see UML stereotypes [23]).

Voelter's book on DSL engineering [24], although it also employs the *general-purpose vs. domain-specific* dichotomy, subtly recognizes it as an oversimplification by indicating examples of programming languages that are tweaked for certain tasks—e.g., PHP for Web sites, NodeJS for Internet of Things—or for different execution strategies—transpilers, compilers, etc. It is sufficient to look at how the JavaScript ecosystem is flooded by frameworks with their own dialects—not necessarily aiming to alleviate language shortcomings, but to enable richer abstractions and more productive development processes: e.g., the HTTP protocol is abstracted in simpler "fetching" operations, which in turn may be further abstracted in higher-level libraries. Coming back to modeling languages, the research field of DSML is to be blamed for a similar variety, which is analogously caused by a variety of purposes and specificities that may be seen as dimensions in an orthogonal framework depicted in Fig. 4.4 where some methods presented in the recent literature are positioned.

On the **purpose axis**, we may start from the fundamental purpose of supporting "understanding and communication" [10], to which further purposes may be added:

- Purposes pertaining to *design-time* model analysis (e.g., model-based reporting, reasoning, model transformations) or *design-time* interoperability (e.g., with ontologies serving to enrich the model content or to enforce ontological commitment); the figure points to the educational-purpose method for cooking recipes management presented in [11]; requirements management methods based on models would also fall in this category, e.g., [15].
- Pertaining to interoperability with an execution environment (any form of model-driven systems), i.e., *run-time* purposes that may include control, automation, code generation, etc.
- More refined classifications of modeling purposes can be consulted in [3], on which an open-ended *multi-purpose* quality may be granularly assessed.

On the **specificity axis**, we may consider the specificity spectrum suggested in Sect. 4.2.1 marked with several levels:

- *System-specific*—i.e., the modeling method relies on a language designed for a particular enterprise or model-driven system, with no chance of being reused outside that context (due to a unique combination of technologies or a proprietary internal system to which models need to interoperate); an example from the recent literature is [7], where models interoperate with an in-house ETL platform to achieve better productivity; the language can be reused across projects but not outside the organization since the in-house platform is not even a commercial product.
- *Technology-specific*—i.e., the modeling method relies on a language that assimilates abstractions from the technological environment where it has to operate, being agnostic of business sector or application domain but fairly reusable due to the general traction of those technological abstractions—e.g., [6] for business processes powered by REST APIs, [25] for processes relying on SPARQL endpoints, and [26] for model-driven PHP templating.
- *Field-specific*—i.e., the modeling method relies on a language that assimilates the discourse domain of a field of activity (industry, business sector, application domain); methods based on popular languages such as UML and BPMN typically serve software engineering and business process management, unless they are tailored for deeper specificity—e.g., [6] extends BPMN for REST API management, thus crossing the border to "technology-specific".
- *Formalism-specific*—i.e., the modeling method relies on a language whose concepts are derived from a highly abstract formalism (logics, set theory, algebras, etc.) that is applicable across multiple domains and technologies; Petri Nets and Entity-Relationship methods would fall in this category, unless they also include

technology-specific mechanisms (e.g., [27] is both highly abstract and includes SQL-specific datatypes).

Modeling tools/methods do not occupy a single spot on the specificity axis, since multiple levels of specificity may be combined in the same language—e.g., the MEMO metamodel depicted in [28] uses a less diverse subtyping of activities compared to BPMN, but a more diverse subtyping for human and IT resources. Evolution is also a factor which may shift the position of a language in time—e.g., the taxonomy of IT resources in an enterprise modeling language may evolve to capture modern enterprise technologies that did not exist at the initial specification of the language, something noticeable in methods having a long history—e.g., MEMO [29] or ADONIS [30].

Figure 4.4 also communicates that the conceptualizations underlying a modeling method are not always confined to one bracket. BEE-UP [31] implements a hybrid method that combines languages of a variety of specificity levels (UML, BPMN, EPC, ER, Petri Nets) extended with technology-specific properties in order to enable some run-time purposes (HTTP requests, RDF export, SQL generation). Similarly, ComVantage [5] covers a space including an ER subset, some business areas (e.g., mobile maintenance), and some technology-specific concepts (mobile apps, Internet of Things). CoChaCo [15] is a method addressing mainly requirements management for modeling methods but also includes some specific properties for the ADOxx metamodeling platform, where such methods can be implemented.

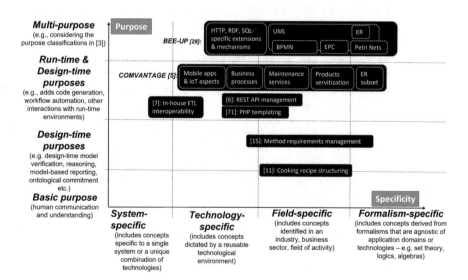

Fig. 4.4 Classifying modeling methods within the Purpose-Specificity framework

The next section surveys the modeling tools presented in the first volume of this book series and briefly characterizes them in terms of the two axes—the goal is to highlight the diversity of purposes and specificities for such artifacts in a very focused research community. We leave to future work the exercise of precisely outlining the specificity and purpose boundaries of each artifact.

4.3.2 Characterization of Modeling Tools

Table 4.1 lists the modeling tools presented in the previous volume of this book series, together with a brief characterization of the purpose and of the specificity levels suggested by their conceptualization and presentation.

The table leaves out one chapter that does not focus on a particular tool: the presentation of the OMiLAB pillars—its technological, innovation, and collaborative environments [60] (for which this book series constitutes a dissemination channel).

The majority of these modeling methods expand their purpose beyond the traditional support for communication and understanding. In numerous cases some level of interoperability is achieved using system-specific or technology-specific interfaces—the modeling environment becomes a knowledge workspace for a knowledge-based system or data management environment whose interfaces will influence the level of specificity. Interoperability is achieved either by a middleware that rewrites model content to fit it with the targeted interface, or the language itself assimilates attributes and concepts that are already present as interface abstractions. Design decisions for the boundary between the modeling language and external environments (execution environment, other modeling environments with which it interoperates) are rarely discussed in the DSL literature, most often obscured or expedited as tool implementation details although there is potential of theorizing on this boundary as a design artifact in its own right, having major impact on both:

- Method purpose: Are models a knowledge base, a dashboard for model-driven artifacts, a source of facts to be governed by an externally residing ontology?
- Method specificity: Should models abstract away their run-time environment, the same way domain-agnostic languages abstract away application domain? To what extent does domain specialization extend its productivity desideratum to environment specialization?

Design theories and empirical analyses of trade-offs still have a rich field to investigate—however these will remain superficial (i.e., on the level of "technology acceptance") if not backed by the artifact building experience and design insight that this book series aims to stimulate.

Table 4.1 Modeling methods/tools presented in the first volume

Tool/Chapter (and their authors)	Characterization of specificity	Characterization of purpose
BEE-UP [31] (Karagiannis, Buchmann, Burzynski, Reimer, Walch)	Incorporates several established languages of varying specificities—UML, BPMN, EPC, ER, Petri Nets (more recent versions, DMN) with semantic links between their elements. On one end of the specificity spectrum, it includes the formalized Petri Nets; on the other end of the spectrum, it lowers the specificity to the domains of Software Engineering and Business Process Management and some properties to enable technology-specific mechanisms (HTTP requests, RDF export, SQL generation)	It aims to be an out-of-the-box educational modeling toolkit. As it can be longitudinally observed in more recent versions, interoperability features are gradually added to expand its purpose from traditional ones (e.g., documentation, simulation) towards model-driven engineering—this turns it into a core asset for the OMiLAB digital innovation environment, the multi-abstraction installation introduced in [32]
ComVantage [5] (Buchmann)	Presented as a method for Product-Service Systems, it also integrates some industry-specific concepts from sectors that were involved in the ComVantage EU project [33]—mobile maintenance services, make-to-order clothing. Consequently, specificity ranges across multiple levels, from highly abstract Entity-Relationship constructs (a subset of ER) down to business-specific (Service Level Agreement) and technology-specific (Mobile user interface, Mobile-supported task)	The purpose covers both design-time Knowledge Management (as highlighted in [34]) and driving mobile app support for industry-specific processes at run-time [35]
DICE [36] (Grosmann, Moser)	Concepts are selected from statistical metadata modeling—e.g., observational units, datasets, variables, and a taxonomy of transformation tasks that may be arranged in a basic flowchart pipeline	The method provides a diagrammatic data ETL pipeline to support business intelligence; it also includes algorithms to perform certain data transformation tasks
MELCA [37] (Hawryszkiewycz, Prackwieser)	Captures concepts derived from the problem-solving and requirements elicitation practice of Design Thinking, therefore inspired by the design artifacts generated during such workshops. It therefore stays on the level of specificity of the Requirements Engineering domain, with concepts such as Role, Actor, Organizational unit, and Activity	The purpose is to support the ideation phase of Design Thinking in a multi-perspective manner, with plans to extend it towards other phases and traceability features

(continued)

Table 4.1 (continued)

Tool/Chapter (and their authors)	Characterization of specificity	Characterization of purpose
SemFIS [38] (Fill)	Extends traditional BPMN with Knowledge Representation constructs from OWL and RDF Schema, to support (Semantic Web-inspired) reasoning patterns. The primary beneficiary would be a hybrid of Process Analyst and Ontologist/Taxonomist roles—specificity is agilely shifted depending on the explicit concepts chosen as machine-readable annotation of BPMN elements	The method's main purpose is to support semantic evaluation of business processes with the help of Semantic Web reasoning patterns
Horus [39] (Schoknecht, Vetter, Fill, Oberweis)	Extends traditional business process modeling concepts with additional ones pertaining to project management—human resource requirements, KPIs, objects/entities, risks. The level of specificity is thus slightly lower than BPMN (i.e., more specialized for Project Management) and extended with elements of Enterprise Architecture	The method supports the management of projects concerned with business process engineering
PSS [40] (Boucher, Medini, Fill)	Captures concepts for describing Product-Service Systems (PSS) from both a structural and a performance perspective. The metamodel is built around the key concepts of Service, Product, Performer and Production Activity (for the structural view), Performance Indicator, Offer and performer Role (for the performance view). It comes close to a multi-perspective value modeling approach, specialized and refined for how value is delivered by a PSS	The purpose is to support decision-making regarding PSS design at different stages of maturing a PSS-based business model
MEMO4ADO [28] (Bock, Frank)	The conceptualization covers Enterprise Modeling from multiple perspectives—processes, goals, organization structures, and semantic bridges between these. The tool is a new implementation of the seminal MEMO [29]. It does not subtype process elements (e.g., task types, event types as in BPMN) but it does so with human and IT resources	Although MEMO itself has a wider scope, the reported implementation focuses on design-time enterprise model analysis across multiple perspectives. It also includes comprehension-enhancing features such as dynamic notation and constraint checks

SAVE [41] (Choe, Lee)	The conceptualization is derived from a process algebra, δ-calculus, for describing distributed behavior of processes in space and time. The work is demonstrated in a mobile Internet of Things context, since it manifests the characteristics of interactions in space-time, but the conceptualization itself does not assimilate any IoT-specific protocols or technologies; therefore it cannot be considered technology-specific	The purpose is to support simulations in space-time for distributed systems where the underlying process algebra is relevant (mobile IoT is employed as a showcase domain, but applicability is not limited to that)
BPFM [42] (Cognini, Corradini, Polini, Re)	Provides a decompositional approach to business process models inspired by feature modeling, with BPMN tasks and information resources subjected to decomposition and variability patterns. Business Process Management benefits primarily	Key functionality supports the generation of BPMN variants considering the variability options and constraints
LearnPad [43] (De Angelis, Pierantonio, Polini, Re, Thönssen, Woitsch)	The conceptualization extends BPMN and CMMN with aspects from the educational domain (learning concepts) and from Knowledge Management. Public administration is declared as the application domain, but the method seems appropriate for any learning processes in relation to knowledge assets and competency models	Focus of the presentation is on design-time benefits and showcase applications in the public administration domain. Some suggestions of interoperability features are given (semantic lifting for integration with ontologies, exporting of knowledge assets)
SOM [44] (Ferstl, Sinz, Bork)	The specificity is that of high-level Business Modeling—Transactions, Business Objects, Events, etc.—with processes being described mainly in terms of transactions (of goods/services) between Business Objects. It does not have the subtypes of BPMN; therefore, it is less specific	The purpose is to support multi-perspective and multi-granularity enterprise model analysis, with some functionality for maintaining cross-perspective consistency
OMiLAB i* [45] (Franch, Lopez, Cares, Colomer)	Captures a consolidated variant of the i* framework [46] for goal modeling. Requirements Engineering is the application domain	The reported purpose pertains to model analysis (goal satisfaction analysis) with the help of a forward evaluation algorithm

(continued)

Table 4.1 (continued)

Tool/Chapter (and their authors)	Characterization of specificity	Characterization of purpose
JCS [47] (Hara, Masuda)	Specializes control flow concepts with exception handling and contextual variability, for hospitality services and the communication involved during their delivery	The reported purpose pertains to design-time analysis for service re-engineering and service knowledge management ("serviceology"). Limited interoperability exists with a text-based file format from which communication with customers can be imported and sequenced
Knowledge Work Designer [48] (Hinkelmann)	Hybrid of BPMN, CMMN, and DMN to support diverse approaches to knowledge and decision structuring; therefore the business (management)-oriented specificity is determined by those standards	The purpose is to separate process logic from business logic at design time, primarily from a Knowledge Management perspective
RUPERT [49] (Johannsen, Fill)	Hybridizes a variety of established diagram types—SIPOC, Ishikawa, KPIs, etc.—to enable the design of multi-perspective Business Process Improvement approaches. A technology-specific interface with R is also included	The tool focuses mostly on design-time analysis, but it also includes interoperability with R for data management purposes
User Story Mapping [50] (Kiritsis, Milicic, Perdikakis)	Captures concepts relevant to Requirements Engineering (User, Backlog Item) and Knowledge Representation (Concept, Instance, Property). We consider the second category as being rather close to formalism-specificity, due to the established formal foundations underlying ontological constructs	Supports domain analysis employing user stories as the entry point. The main value proposition is visual guidance for the effort of domain knowledge capture and structuring. Future work suggests an extension with SWRL-based mechanisms
HERMxx [27] (Kramer, Thalheim)	Provides a higher-order enrichment to Entity-Relationship modeling. Although governed by a formalism, it also includes technology-specific (SQL) datatypes to support targeted code generation (HERM would be equally fit to generate noSQL schemas, but this particular implementation seems to adopt technological-specificity for demonstration purpose)	Besides design-time benefits, it generates SQL code out of a higher-order ER perspective

CODEK [51] (Loucopoulos, Kavakli)	Extends traditional enterprise architecture concepts with a novel concept of Capability distilled from a variety of fields where it was conceptualized in the past, from different viewpoints (teleological, social, etc.). Enterprise Architecture Management benefits primarily	The purpose is to support decision-making with conceptual analysis (e.g., model-based reports, graph searches over capability trees). It is a particular flavor of multi-perspective enterprise modeling where the different enterprise facets are integrated through semantic links to processes that have capability management as their core concern and capability structures as their key asset
HCM-L [52] (Mayr, Al Machot, Michael, Morak, Ranasinghe, Shekovstov, Steinberger)	Captures control flow concepts specialized as "behavioral units" with pre-conditions and post-conditions for daily human activities. This is extended with actors, goals, and contextual aspects of those activities (e.g., spatial context)	The purpose manifests primarily in design-time model verification, querying, and reasoning. Interaction with an external human behavior monitoring system is also envisioned, without detailing specifications about the interfacing which was work in progress at the time of publication (an RDF-based environment is suggested but abstracted away from the modeling language)
Secure Tropos [53] (Mouratidis, Argyropoulos, Shei)	Extends Tropos [54] with specificity pertaining to security engineering and privacy (e.g., Threat, Security Constraint)	The purpose is to provide, over the diagrammatic view, cross-referential computational analysis according to relevant indicators (satisfiability)
ADVISOR [55] (Reimann, Utz)	Captures concepts from the educational domain—e.g., learning sequences and assessment goals, knowledge states. Some of them specialize the typical process modeling concepts to describe in a step-wise manner educational activities	The purpose covers both design-time and run-time concerns, as the knowledge work is designed to interoperate with learning management systems, a knowledge state taxonomy, and a data marshalling environment
BD-DS [56] (Roussopoulos, Utz)	The conceptualization is inspired by both data modeling and service-oriented architecture, to support the design of data services. Both REST and SOAP variants are supported, as well as a diversity of data formats; therefore, it is targeted for a specific technological paradigm	The purpose is to design and deploy for execution data services for a variety of technological options (REST, SOAP, several data formats). Complex functionalities are provided to manage the deployment in an execution environment

(continued)

Table 4.1 (continued)

Tool/Chapter (and their authors)	Characterization of specificity	Characterization of purpose
Evaluation chains [57] (Wolff)	Captures goals and evaluations of how those goals are achieved in a dependency graph called "evaluation chain." Primary beneficiaries are decision-makers in the business administration domain, as the method relies mostly on managerial concepts	The purpose is to capture evaluation patterns in relation to their goals and to support the design of those patterns
Semcheck [58] (Jeusfeld)	It does not qualify as a modeling method, since it is an interoperability plug-in between two multi-purpose and multi-specificity knowledge capture platforms, ConceptBase [59] and ADOxx. The paper presents its applicability to enterprise models because of the inherent multi-perspective nature of such models, but ConceptBase is seen fit for any level of specificity (including the abstraction layers of metamodels and meta2models)	Taken by itself, SemCheck has the purpose of enabling constraint checking over semantically related models independent of the domain

It is also important to note that the survey summarized in Table 4.1 reflects only a snapshot of the investigated methods—hopefully their evolution will also be reported longitudinally, showing how a modeling tool branches out as purposes or specificity split. Figure 4.4 and Table 4.1 already showed that some methods expand either their purpose (e.g., ComVantage [5]) or their semantic coverage (e.g., BEE-UP [31]) over time. An additional axis of time may be added when considering *method agility*—i.e., when the modeling language, procedure, or mechanisms must evolve or branch out in response to changing requirements, or as some concepts become obsolete (e.g., information technology types).

The proposed Purpose-Specificity framework as depicted in Fig. 4.4 is a plane, i.e., limited to two dimensions that may be conveniently quantified to ensure some consistent ordering (e.g., considering the subsumption ordering as a proxy for specificity, a cardinality of granular use case as a proxy for purpose). Consequently, in the following we will employ the term "space" to suggest its potential extensions with additional dimensions—time has been suggested here; other dimensions may be derived from the literature, see [3]; in the next section, we make additional suggestions through the lens of value creation.

4.4 An Artifact Value Perspective

4.4.1 Generalizing the Purpose-Specificity Framework

If the Purpose-Specificity orthogonal system is seen as a frame for model value creation, then the multidimensional notion of value (from the value generation literature) may be adopted. Business model development frameworks have proposed diverse value components and dimensions—e.g., in Ojala's framework [61] we find *value proposition* (the artifact), *value network* (the contributors), *value delivery* (the deployment), and *value capture* (the revenue model). How these translate to the value of diagrammatic conceptual models is a challenge for future theorizing and conceptualizations—we may consider the following as a possible starting point and as candidate axes to a generalized version of the hereby discussed framework, i.e., to a Purpose-Specificity Space (see Fig. 4.5).

Value proposition represents what was already captured in the hereby proposed Purpose-Specificity framework—i.e., a modeling method is purposeful and employs adequately specific concepts to fulfil that purpose. Servitization may be considered as an extension to a modeling tool—e.g., to ensure on a subscription or consultancy basis that the modeling tool will shift purpose and specificity on commercial terms, as recently reported for a commercial product in [30].

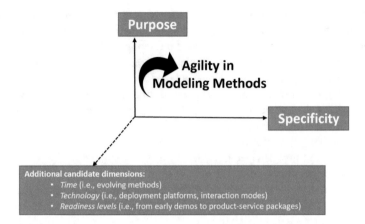

Fig. 4.5 Expanding the framework to a multidimensional space of model value

Value delivery refers to the means of delivering the value proposition. In the case of modeling methods, the most obvious interpretation is the technology used for method deployment—i.e., on one hand the metamodeling platform and on the other hand the means for deploying the resulting tool: as a mobile app, as an in-browser modeling-as-a-service tool, as a Web service allowing clients to consume model contents, as a read-only model visualization or annotation service, as a pen-and-paper method, etc. Recently the OLIVE Web integration framework [62] was introduced by OMiLAB to support a multitude of interoperability channels between an ADOxx-based modeling tool and technological environments—e.g., through HTTP interactions with IoT devices or Web services. An axis may therefore be added to express such technological variety for delivering the value of models, since the same modeling method may be deployed in numerous forms.

Value network comprises all roles contributing to the value proposition: The method engineer and the modeler are value co-creators—i.e., the modeler is the main source of domain knowledge and purpose, feeding into the AMME iterations as the method is evolved and refined. In addition we also have to consider the network effect of the OMiLAB community, as modeling tool sources are shared and possibly repurposed or expanded—see an example in [6] of branching out BEE-UP with technology-specific features for a REST API ecosystem. Based on this value aspect, an additional dimension of the Purpose-Specificity space would indicate community size, from modeling methods that involve only a project team for demonstration purposes, to modeling methods that organically grow from lessons learned longitudinally across multiple projects (the case of BEE-UP [31]).

Value capture in Ojala's framework relates to the revenue model. The community involved in the hereby surveyed methods (and also in the current book) follows the open science paradigm and does not have a commercial interest, although method engineering knowledge may be transferred to spin-offs or products of a higher Technological Readiness Level than the proofs-of-concept typically resulting from such design research efforts. Therefore one possible additional dimension could be the Technological Readiness Level on which a demonstrator is made available.

4.4.2 Modeling Methods and Design Science

In order to enable model value, modeling methods and their building blocks are purposeful artifacts created by design-oriented Information Systems research. Information Systems research generally takes two routes: (a) *design-oriented*, i.e., striving to propose (design and prototype) innovative artifacts that improve some aspect in a real or virtual organization, and (b) *behaviorist*, i.e., concerned with observing characteristics of IS artifacts taken for granted almost as natural phenomena, assuming that innovation is readily available to be picked and observed. This may be perceived as a distinction between:

- *Research for what we don't know* (observational)
- *Research for what we don't have* (design-oriented)

Recent works have called for a unified view to replace the dichotomous perception on these streams [63]. Why this should be a dichotomy is never explained—Design Science Research (DSR) [64] prescribes a hybrid engineering-evaluation cycle where both design decisions and empirical evaluation should form a feedback loop. Actual IS research seems, however, to favor approaches that are purely observational—potentially leading to an inflation of opinion-collecting journalism disguised as technology acceptance research recipes taking a "safe distance" from the design decisions and experimentation at the core of innovation.

One may argue that any research methodology is templated to some extent (especially when disseminated in papers); however, the behaviorist research recipes appear to have gained in the global IS community much wider traction compared to artifact/innovation building skills—a concern that was raised by mostly German-speaking academics in a memorandum more than 10 years ago [65]. The memorandum was met with swift response [66] indicating that seminal papers on design-oriented research show a strong recognition of this research stream in major journals of the IS community; it also invoked the journals' mission statements, reviewing principles and design-oriented expertise that confirm this recognition.

The quantity of research output for the two streams over the last decade tells, however, a different story—it is not in the scope of this book chapter to analyze those statistics (reserved for a stand-alone study; at this point we only refer to [9]); it is only a warning that a long-term effect of this imbalance is large-scale propagated bias in scientific policy-making: It is the personal experience of this chapter's author to receive the feedback "there's no such thing as a Design Science methodology" to a DSR project proposal or to participate in IS doctoral symposium lectures where Design Science is entirely omitted—while, at the same time, a brief SurveyMonkey questionnaire for collecting subjective opinion and popularity voting is showcased as scientific observation of phenomena. This strongly impacts debuting investigators as they are discouraged away from an entire stream of research, generating new scholarly frames of thought that are dangerously close to alchemy—i.e., IS artifacts perceived as magical black boxes to be poked with acceptance assessment recipes and socio-technical systems analysis where the "social" aspect occupies the entire discourse.

More recently (but perhaps rather late), the paper [67] formulated a useful set of recommendations about achieving balance between artifact and theory in DSR, revealing the value of conceptualization for early-stage theorizing. However, in the end it also leaves the impression that it is mandatory for any acceptable DSR publication to report threefold results: design-oriented, observational, and theory building, whereas behaviorist research may remain strictly observational— a (perhaps involuntary) suggestion towards a "path of least resistance" and a plausible explanation for the mass popularity of observational research, as junior design-oriented researchers are pushed to take their innovations out of academia, circumventing IS academic research entirely.

The field of domain-specific conceptual modeling (including here any related model-driven artifacts) is even more deeply affected, because of its inherently narrow scope limiting both the *generalization* and *projectability* desiderata formulated in [68]—it is depth-first design research, rather than breadth-first. It may be rejected as valid IS research, only to make its way back into IS research through a different door, as off-the-shelf products observable in action. A famous case in this respect is Robotic Process Automation, a flavor of domain- and technology-specific workflow modeling—barely present in IS journals as a research topic prior to 2018 while commercial products were already successful, decoupled for a while from the Business Process Management research field, reconciled more recently in a "catching up" manner but still lacking in terms of method engineering and design-oriented research.

Under such conditions, this book series aims to stimulate a network effect to increase visibility of domain-specific conceptual modeling artifact-oriented research and to foster a community that may consolidate this stream of research in all three keys aspects—design theories, empirical scrutiny, and innovative artifact building. Guidance is sparse, but not unavailable—besides the already mentioned [67], evaluation protocols or frameworks for different aspects of a modeling method emerged over recent years (see [17, 21, 22, 69, 70] and the generic but still useful tableau of evaluation criteria in [71]). Some prominent examples of artifact building methodologies that are specific to the field are [12, 72]. The OMiLAB community tries to be an ecosystem where such knowledge assets are complemented by tooling support to ease the way for new researchers who can see that digital innovation and transformation have, at their core, some form of conceptualization determined by explicit purpose and specificity.

4.5   Conclusions

This chapter scrutinized the notion of domain-specific conceptual modeling (methods) by applying rhetorical analysis—an approach which, according to [73], adds to logical reasoning rhetorical devices such as:

- *Kairos*, the argument of timeliness: with the help of available metamodeling platforms and dedicated engineering methodologies, domain-specific modeling becomes a generalized form of multi-purpose and multi-specificity low-code knowledge graph building, a goal gaining traction in recent years [74] which was however always at the heart of knowledge engineering.
- *Ethos*, the argument of credibility: there is a community of trusted expertise in the engineering of domain-specific languages, methods, and tools of diverse specificities and purposes; the community regularly makes and debates design propositions, long before they become available in some product subjected to a "technology acceptance" empirical recipe.
- Some degree of *pathos*, particularly in the plea for design-oriented IS research provided in Sect. 4.4.2 and for balancing the IS research streams.

The Purpose-Specificity framework (potentially generalizable to a "space") was introduced as an analysis frame that is richer and more open to theorizing than the traditional dichotomy between general-purpose and domain-specific. An exercise of applying this frame was performed while surveying contributions to the previous volume of this book series.

This will have to be revisited and refined—on one hand by expanding the framework with additional dimensions and on the other hand by including the new contributions collected in the current volume. Future work will consider longitudinal studies on evolving modeling method demonstrators and conceptualizations, as well as design theories that can be derived from both observed and first-hand method engineering efforts.

References

1. Kirby, S., Tamariz, M., Cornish, H., Smith, K.: Compression and communication in the cultural evolution of linguistic structure. Cognition. **141**, 87–102 (2015)
2. Saba, W.: Time to Put an End to BERTology, Available at: https://medium.com/ontologik/time-to-put-an-end-to-bertology-or-ml-dl-is-not-even-relevant-to-nlu-e5ba6fc53403 (2020)
3. Thalheim, B.: The theory of conceptual models, the theory of conceptual modelling and foundations of conceptual modelling. In: Handbook of Conceptual Modeling, pp. 543–477. Springer (2011)
4. Ganter, B., Stumme, G., Wille, R. (eds.): Formal Concept Analysis: Foundations and Applications, Lecture Notes in Artificial Intelligence, no. 3626. Springer (2005)
5. Buchmann, R.A.: Modeling product-service systems for the internet of things: the ComVantage method. In: Domain-Specific Conceptual Modeling, pp. 417–438. Springer (2016)

6. Chiș, A.: A modeling method for model-driven API management. Complex Systems Informatics and Modeling Quarterly. **25**, 1–18 (2020)

7. Deme, A., Buchmann, R.: A technology-specific modeling method for data ETL processes, in Proceedings of AMCIS 2021. 2. https://aisel.aisnet.org/amcis2021/sig_sand/sig_sand/2 (2021)

8. Object Management Group: The XMI Specification, Available at https://www.omg.org/spec/XMI/2.5.1/About-XMI/ (2015)

9. Goes, P.: Editor's comments: design science research in top information systems journals. MIS Q. **38**(1), iii–viii (2014)

10. Mylopoulos, J.: Conceptual modeling and Telos1. In Loucopoulos P, Zicari R. Conceptual Modeling, Databases, and Case: An Integrated View of Information Systems Development, pp. 49–68. Wiley (1992)

11. Buchmann, R.A., Ghiran A.: Engineering the Cooking Recipe Modelling Method: A Teaching Experience Report. In: CEUR-WS vol. 1999, paper 5 (2017)

12. Karagiannis, D.: Agile modeling method engineering, in Proceedings of PCI 2015, pp. 5–10. ACM (2015)

13. BOC GmbH. The ADOxx Metamodeling Platform, available at https://www.adoxx.org (2021)

14. OMiLAB. The CoChaCo Prototype, Available at https://www.omilab.org/activities/cochaco.html (2021)

15. Karagiannis, D., Burzynski, P., Utz, W., Buchmann, R.: A metamodeling approach to support the engineering of modeling method requirements. In: Proceedings of RE 2019, Jeju Island, pp. 199–210. IEEE Press (2019)

16. Karagiannis, D., Kühn, H.: Metamodelling platforms. In Proceedings of EC-Web 2002 – DEXA 2002, Aix-en-Provence, p. 182. Springer (2002)

17. Moody, D.: The "physics" of notations: toward a scientific basis for constructing visual notations in software engineering. IEEE Trans. Softw. Eng. **35**(6), 756–779 (2009)

18. Ghiran, A.M., Buchmann, R.A., Karagiannis, D.: Towards a framework of techniques for enabling semantics-driven secondary notation in conceptual models. Proc. RCIS, IEEE Press. doi:https://doi.org/10.1109/RCIS.2018.8406684 (2018)

19. Schrepfer, M., Wolf, J., Mendling, J., Reijers, H.A.: The impact of secondary notation on process model understanding, in Proceedings of PoEM 2009, pp. 161–175. Springer (2009)

20. Maes, A., Poels, G.: Evaluating quality of conceptual modelling scripts based on user perceptions. Data Knowl. Eng. **63**(3), 701–724 (2007)

21. Roelens, B., Bork, D.: A technique for evaluating and improving the semantic transparency of modeling language notations. Softw. Syst. Model. (2021). https://doi.org/10.1007/s10270-021-00895-w

22. Krogstie, J., Sindre, G., Jorgensen, H.: Process models representing knowledge for action: a revised quality framework. Eur. J. Inf. Syst. **15**(1), 91–102 (2006)

23. UML   Stereotypes,   Available   at   https://www.uml-diagrams.org/profile-diagrams.html#stereotype (2021)

24. Voelter, M.: DSL Engineering: Designing, Implementing and Using Domain-Specific Languages, CreateSpace (2013)

25. Harkai, A., Cinpoeru, M., Buchmann, R.A.: The What facet of the Zachman Framework – a Linked Data-driven interpretation, in Proceedings of Workshops at the CAISE 2018, pp. 197–208. Springer (2018)

26. Gog, C.I.: Agile development of PHP websites: a model-aware approach. Complex Syst. Inform. Model. Q. **25**, 19–31 (2020)

27. Kramer, F., Thalheim, B.: Holistic conceptual and logical database structure modeling with ADOxx. In: Domain-Specific Conceptual Modeling, pp. 269–290. Springer (2016)

28. Bock, A., Frank, U.: Multi-perspective enterprise modeling – conceptual foundation and implementation with ADOxx. In: Domain-Specific Conceptual Modeling, pp. 241–268. Springer (2016)

29. Frank, U.: The MEMO Meta-Metamodel. Research Report of the Institute for Business Informatics 9. University of Koblenz, Koblenz (1998)

30. Utz, W., Buchmann, R., Bork, D., Karagiannis, D.: A BPM lifecycle plug-in for modeling methods agility, in Proceedings of AMCIS 2020, Virtual Event, paper 2 (2020)
31. Karagiannis, D., Buchmann, R.A., Burzynski, P., Reimer, U., Walch, M.: Fundamental conceptual modeling languages in OMiLAB. In: Domain-Specific Conceptual Modeling, pp. 3–30. Springer (2016)
32. Karagiannis, D., Buchmann, R.A., Boucher, X., Cavalieri, S., Florea, A., Kiritsis, D., Lee, M.: OMiLAB: a smart innovation environment for digital engineers. Proceedings of PRO-VE 2020, pp. 273–282. Springer (2020)
33. Comvantage EU Project, Official Website, Available at http://comantage.eu (2014)
34. Karagiannis, D., Buchmann, R., Walch, M.: How can diagrammatic conceptual modelling support knowledge management? In Proceedings of ECIS 2017, pp. 1568–1583. Association for Information Systems (2017)
35. Buchmann, R. A., Karagiannis, D., Modelling mobile app requirements for semantic traceability, Requir. Eng. 22: 41–75 (2017)
36. Grossmann, W., Moser, C.: Big Data – Integration and Cleansing Environment for Business Analytics with DICE, pp. 103–126. Springer (2016)
37. Hawryszkiewycz, I.T., Prackwieser, C.: MELCA – customizing visualizations for Design Thinking. In: Domain-Specific Conceptual Modeling, pp. 383–398. Springer (2016)
38. Fill, H.G.: Semantic evaluation of business processes using SeMFIS. In: Domain-Specific Conceptual Modeling, pp. 149–170. Springer (2016)
39. Schoknecht, A., Vetter, A., Fill, H. G., Oberweis, A.: Using the Horus method for succeeding in business process engineering projects. In Domain-Specific Conceptual Modeling, pp. 127–148. Springer (2016)
40. Boucher, X., Medini, K., Fill, H.G.: Product-service system modeling method. In: Domain-Specific Conceptual Modeling, pp. 455–484. Springer (2016)
41. Choe, Y., Lee, M.: Algebraic method to model secure IoT. In: Domain-Specific Conceptual Modeling, pp. 335–356. Springer (2016)
42. Cognini, R., Corradini, F., Polini, A., Re, B.: Business process feature model: an approach to deal with variability of business processes. In Domain-Specific Conceptual Modeling, pp. 171–198. Springer (2016)
43. De Angelis, G., Pierantonio, A., Polini, A., Re, B., Thönssen, B., Woitsch, R.: Modeling for learning in public administrations – the Learn PAd approach. In: Domain-Specific Conceptual Modeling, pp. 575–594. Springer (2016)
44. Ferstl, O.K., Sinz, E.J., Bork, D.: Tool support for the Semantic Object Model. In: Domain-Specific Conceptual Modeling, pp. 291–312. Springer (2016)
45. Franch, X., Lopez, L., Cares, C., Colomer, D.: The i* Framework for Goal-Oriented Modeling, pp. 485–508. Springer (2016)
46. Yu, E.: Modelling strategic relationships for process reengineering. Ph.D. Dissertation. University of Toronto (1995)
47. Hara, Y., Masuda, H.: Global service enhancement for Japanese creative services based on the early/late binding concepts. In: Domain-Specific Conceptual Modeling, pp. 509–526. Springer (2016)
48. Hinkelmann, K.: Business process flexibility and decision-aware modeling – the Knowledge Work designer. In: Domain-Specific Conceptual Modeling, pp. 397–416. Springer (2016)
49. Johannsen, F., Fill, H.G.: Supporting business process improvement through a modeling tool. In: Domain-Specific Conceptual Modeling, pp. 217–240. Springer (2016)
50. Kiritsis, D., Milicic, A., Perdikakis, A.: User story mapping-based method for domain semantic modeling. In: Domain-Specific Conceptual Modeling, pp. 439–455. Springer (2016)
51. Loucopoulos, P., Kavakli, E.: Capability-oriented enterprise knowledge modeling: the CODEK approach. In: Domain-Specific Conceptual Modeling, pp. 197–216. Springer (2016)
52. Mayr, H.C., Al Machot, F., Michael, J., Morak, G., Ranasinghe, S., Shekhovtsov, V., Steinberger, C.: HCM-L: domain-specific modeling for active and assisted living. In: Domain-Specific Conceptual Modeling, pp. 527–554. Springer (2016)

53. Mouratidis, H., Argyropoulos, N., Shei, S.: Security requirements engineering for Cloud Computing: the Secure Tropos approach. In: Domain-Specific Conceptual Modeling, pp. 357–382. Springer (2016)
54. Bresciani, P., Perini, A., Giorgini, P., Giunchiglia, F., Mylopoulos, J.: Tropos: an agent-oriented software development methodology. Auton. Agent. Multi-Agent Syst. **8**(3), 203–236 (2004)
55. Reimann, P., Utz, W.: Modeling learning data for feedback and assessment. In: Domain-Specific Conceptual Modeling, pp. 555–574. Springer (2016)
56. Roussopoulos, N., Utz, W.: Design semantics on accessibility in unstructured data environments. In: Domain-Specific Conceptual Modeling, pp. 79–102. Springer (2016)
57. Wolff, F.: Evaluation chains for controlling the evolution of enterprise models. In: Domain-Specific Conceptual Modeling, pp. 313–334. Springer (2016)
58. Jeusfeld, M.A.: SemCheck: checking constraints for multi-perspective modeling languages. In: Domain-Specific Conceptual Modeling, pp. 31–54. Springer (2016)
59. Jeusfeld, M.A.: Metamodeling and method engineering with ConceptBase. In: Jeusfeld, M.A., Jarke, M., Mylopoulos, J. (eds.) Metamodelling for Method Engineering, pp. 89–168. MIT Press, Cambridge (2009)
60. Götzinger, D., Miron, E.T., Staffel, F.: OMiLAB: an open collaborative environment for modeling method engineering. In: Domain-Specific Conceptual Modeling, pp. 55–78. Springer (2016)
61. Ojala, A.: Business models and opportunity creation: how entrepreneurs create and develop business models under uncertainty. Inf. Syst. J. **26**(5), 451–476 (2016)
62. OMiLAB, OLIVE Microservice Framework, Available at https://www.adoxx.org/live/olive (2021)
63. Wieringa, R.J.: Design Science Methodology for Information Systems and Software Engineering. Springer (2014)
64. Goldkuhl, G.: Separation or unity? Behavioral science vs. design science, in AIS SIGPRAG Pre-ICIS 2016 Workshop on Practice-based design and innovation of digital artifacts (2016)
65. Osterle, H., Becker, J., Frank, U., Hess, T., Karagiannis, D., Krcmar, H., Loos, P., Mertens, P., Oberweis, A., Sinz, E.J.: Memorandum on design-oriented information systems research. Eur. J. Inf. Syst. **20**(1), 7–10 (2010)
66. Baskerville, R., Lyytinen, K., Sambamurthy, V., Straub, D.: A response to the design-oriented information systems research memorandum. European Journal of Information Systems. **20**(1), 11–15 (2011)
67. Baskerville, R., Baiyere, A., Gregor, S., Hevner, A., Rossi, M.: Design science research contributions: finding a balance between artifact and theory. J. Assoc. Inf. Syst. **19**(5), 358–376 (2018)
68. Baskerville, R., Pries-Heje, J.: Projectability in design science research. J Inf Technol Theory Appl. **20**(1), article 3 (2019)
69. Hahn, J., Kim, J.: Why are some diagrams easier to work with? Effects of diagrammatic representation on the cognitive integration process of systems analysis and design. ACM Trans. Comput. Hum. Interact. **6**(3), 181–213 (1999)
70. Malinova, M., Mendling, J.: Cognitive diagram understanding and task performance in systems analysis and design. MIS Q. **45**(4), 2101–2157 (2021)
71. Prat, N., Comyn-Wattiau, I., Akoka, J.: Artifact evaluation in Information Systems design science research – a holistic view, in Proceedings of PACIS 2014, Chengdu, China, paper 23 (2014)
72. Frank, U.: Domain-specific modelling languages: requirements analysis and design guidelines, in Domain Engineering, Springer, pp. 133–157 (2013)
73. Ramage, J.D., Bean, J.C., Johnson, J.: Writing Arguments: A Rhetoric with Readings. Pearson (2010)
74. Lopata, M.: The rise of NoCode Knowledge Graphs, Available at https://towardsdatascience.com/the-rise-of-no-code-knowledge-graphs-d0e8b7476dc6 (2020)

Part III
Enterprise Management

Chapter 5
Enterprise Modeling with 4EM:
Perspectives and Method

Birger Lantow, Kurt Sandkuhl, and Janis Stirna

Abstract Approaches and methods for enterprise modeling have been the subject of discussion and development in industry and academia during at least the last 30 years. Enterprise modeling supports organizations in coping with challenges related to dynamically changing business environments and the alignment of business goals and information systems to support these goals. For this purpose, different perspectives of an enterprise have to be taken into account—and, also, to be part of enterprise models, such as business goals, processes, products, services, business rules, and organization's structures. 4EM (for enterprise modeling) is an enterprise modeling method that offers a modeling language covering the different perspectives in conjunction with guidelines for the modeling process, strong stakeholder participation, and a project-based approach to conducting enterprise modeling.

Keywords 4EM · Enterprise modeling · Multi-perspective modeling · Participatory modeling

5.1 Introduction

Enterprise modeling (EM) is meant to support organizations in coping with a broad range of challenges including managing organizational change in dynamic business environments, aligning of business goals and information systems to support these goals, as well as explicating and consolidating business knowledge from diverse stakeholder groups, thus facilitating organizational learning. The role of enterprise modeling usually is to provide methods, tools, and practices for

B. Lantow · K. Sandkuhl (✉)
Universität Rostock, Rostock, Germany
e-mail: birger.lantow@uni-rostock.de; kurt.sandkuhl@uni-rostock.de

J. Stirna
Stockholm University, Stockholm, Sweden
e-mail: js@dsv.su.se

capturing and visualizing the current ("as-is") situation and to develop the future ("to-be") situation. In particular, a model of the current situation forms one of the fundaments for supporting future development of organizations. Without knowledge of the "as-is," a systematic design and development of future capabilities, products, or services is usually difficult, if not impossible. If an organization does not have existing models or their use is deemed impractical (e.g., they are severely out of date or the quality of models is below acceptable), new models need to be created.

In general terms, EM is addressing the "systematic analysis and modeling of processes, organization structures, products structures, IT-systems or any other perspective relevant for the modeling purpose" [1]. The variety and dynamics of methods, modeling languages, and tools supporting EM are visible not only in this book but also in the work on research roadmaps and future directions, originating both from the information systems community (see, e.g., [2]) and from scholars in industrial organization (e.g., [3]).

Enterprise modeling is related to a number of other modeling disciplines, such as conceptual modeling and business process modeling. As a discipline, conceptual modeling has established itself in dealing with the core aspects of modeling methods and tools. The relation between conceptual modeling and EM is twofold. First, EM methods are seen as conceptual modeling methods because they are based on the principles of conceptual modeling, such as EM languages, and are based on concepts and relationships. Second, EM addresses several perspectives of the enterprise, one of which is typically capturing and defining the organization's business concepts, information, and data, i.e., "things and phenomena" used in other perspectives of the enterprise model. Business process modeling and EM have the commonality that they both capture and visualize the relevant business processes with the actors involved and resources needed. However, in EM business processes are only one perspective of the enterprise model but not the predominant one like in business process modeling. EM can support different modeling purposes, which leads to a greater flexibility of the methods; some application areas of EM do not require detailed process modeling.

EM projects can have different purposes. Among the most prominent ones are [4, 5]:

- To develop the business. This entails, e.g., developing business vision and strategies, redesigning business operations, developing the supporting information systems, etc. Business development is one of the most common purposes of EM. It frequently involves change management—determining how to achieve visions and objectives from the current state in organizations. Business process orientation is a specific case of business development—the organization wants to restructure/redesign its business operations.
- To ensure the quality of the business operations. This purpose primarily focuses on two issues: (1) sharing knowledge about the business, its vision, and the way it operates and (2) ensuring the acceptance of business decisions through committing the stakeholders to the decisions made. A motivation to adopt EM is to ensure the quality of operations. Two important success factors for ensuring

quality are that stakeholders understand the business and that they accept/are committed to business decisions.

- To use EM as a problem-solving tool. EM is here only used for supporting the discussion among a group of stakeholders trying to analyze a specific problem at hand. In some cases, making an EM activity is helpful when capturing, delimiting, and analyzing the initial problem situation and deciding on a course of action. In such cases EM is mostly used as a problem-solving and communication tool. The enterprise model created during this type of modeling is used for documenting the discussion and the decisions made. The main characteristics of this purpose are that the company does not intend to use the models for further development work and that the modeling activity has been planned to be only a single iteration.

Approaches, methods, and tools for EM have been the subject of discussion and development in industry and academia during at least the last 30 years. Some of the many approaches proposed in this field are summarized in this book and also in [6]. This chapter focuses on one method, namely, "for enterprise modeling" (4EM), a representative of the Scandinavian strand of EM methods with its origins in the 1990s. This chapter presents the core components of 4EM (Sect. 5.2), discusses the underlying meta-model (Sect. 5.3), and introduces the ADOxx-based tool support using an application example (Sect. 5.4).

5.2   The 4EM Enterprise Modeling Method

4EM has its origin in the 1990s and has been developed on the basis of the method EKD—enterprise knowledge development [7, 8]. It has proven its value in many industrial projects[1] and is also used in IS education at a number of universities. This section gives an overview of the basic concepts of 4EM (Sect. 5.2.1) and the essential parts of the modeling method, the sub-models (Sect. 5.2.2). The full documentation is publicly available and includes four textbooks in three languages, as well as a freely available tool support (see Sect. 5.4).

5.2.1   Basic Components

4EM includes a modeling language for different perspectives of an enterprise that are also referred to as 4EM sub-models. However, the modeling language is only one component of the 4EM method. 4EM consists of three core elements, which

---

[1] See [7, 8] for examples of industrial projects.

can also be regarded as the basic principles of 4EM:

- A defined procedure for modeling using a fixed notation (defined procedure and notation). The notation is reflected in the modeling language.
- Performance of enterprise modeling in the form of a project with predetermined roles (project organization and roles).
- A participatory process to involve enterprise stakeholders and domain experts (stakeholder participation).

These three basic elements of 4EM are supported by appropriate tools and resources as illustrated in Fig. 5.1.

Fig. 5.1 Basic elements of the 4EM—framework

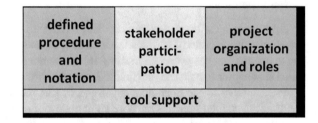

An important principle of the 4EM approach to modeling is its modular structure, providing self-contained, clearly defined procedures for each different aspect that needs to be modeled. However, how these different method procedures are combined can be decided based on the problem to be solved, i.e., 4EM offers a flexible method structure, which can be adapted as required. The individual components of the method and their respective notations define views or sub-models. Section 5.2.2 explains the differences between them.

From a 4EM perspective, it is not enough to merely define the procedure and notation as these do not provide a clear description of the purpose and content, an allocation of resources, or a definition of the decision-making and process structures. Understanding enterprise modeling as a project with a clear goal, timeframe, and resources facilitates practical implementation and helps to achieve the specified purpose. The 4EM principle of organizing enterprise modeling as a project includes recommendations for the project organization and required roles.

Stakeholder participation is another principle of 4EM that is reflected in both the procedure and notation and the project structure and roles. Moderated workshops and participatory modeling are techniques strongly recommended in 4EM for addressing complex modeling tasks involving broad and diverse stakeholder groups. Opportunities for involving domain experts and stakeholders should be used in both analyzing the current situation and designing changes and future situations.

Table 5.1 4EM method—reading recommendations

4EM core elements	Additional literature
Procedure and notation	Section 2.2 and Chap. 8 in the 4EM textbook [6]
Project structure and roles	Chap. 9 in the 4EM textbook [6] and Chap. 6 in textbook [9]
Stakeholder participation	Textbook on participatory modeling [9]
Tools and aids	Sect. 4 and Chap. 5 in the 4EM textbook [6] and Chap. 9 in textbook [9]

The 4EM tool support includes (1) traditional tools, such as the "plastic wall" and multi-touch tables for modeling used in case the main objective for modeling is to capture new knowledge, and (2) advanced computerized tools used for model documentation and analysis such as the 4EM Toolkit introduced in Sect. 5.4. The modeling instructions and incorporated checklists for each 4EM sub-model in Sect. 5.2.2 are applicable for both tool categories. The instructions and working guidelines also create an organizational framework for all persons involved in modeling, problem-solving, and knowledge sharing, because they not only define the meaning of the symbols, colors, formulations, etc., to be used but also indirectly define the interaction process. This aims to increase the productivity of the activities by preventing misunderstandings and conflicts.

Table 5.1 summarizes reading recommendations for the core elements of 4EM.

5.2.2 Sub-models and Perspectives

The modeling language of 4EM consists of seven sub-model types, each of them focusing on a specific aspect, or perspective, of the enterprise—goals, business rules, concepts, business processes, actors and resources, products and services, as well as information systems (IS) technical components. Table 5.2 shows a summary of the sub-models. The different sub-models are briefly presented in this section.

5.2.3 The Goals Model

The Goals Model (GM) focuses on describing the goals of the enterprise. It describes what the enterprise and its employees want to achieve, or to avoid, and when. The Goals Model usually clarifies questions, such as:

- Where should the organization be moving to in terms of the goals of the organization?
- What are the importance, criticality, and priorities of these goals?
- How are goals related to each other?
- Which problems hinder the achievement of these goals?

Table 5.2 Summary of sub-models in 4EM

	Goals Model (GM)	Business Rules Model (BRM)	Concepts Model (CM)	Business Process Model (BPM)	Actors and Resources Model (ARM)	Product/Service (P/S)	Technical Components Model (TCRM)
Focus	Vision and strategy	Policies and rules	Business ontology	Business operations	Organizational structure	Products and services	Information system needs
Issues to model	What does the organization want to achieve or to avoid and why?	What are the business rules, how do they support the organization's goals?	What are the things and "phenomena" addressed in other sub-models?	What are the business processes? How do they handle information and material?	Who are responsible for goals and process? How are the actors interrelated?	What product/service components exist? What are the core features?	What are the business requirements of the IS? How are they related to other models?
Components	Goal, problem, external constraint, opportunity	Business rule	Concept, attribute	Process, external proc., information set, material set	Actor, role, organizational unit, individual	Product, service, component, feature	IS goal, IS problem, IS requirement, IS component

The components of the GM are goal, opportunity, problem (threat and weakness), cause, and constraint. They are linked by binary relationships of the types supports and hinders. Goals are refined by goal operationalization relationships of types AND, OR, and AND/OR.

5.2.4 The Business Rules Model

The Business Rules Model (BRM) is used to define and maintain explicitly formulated business rules, consistent with the Goals Model. The Business Rules Model usually clarifies questions, such as:

- Which rules affect the organization's goals?
- Are there any policies stated?
- How is a business rule related to a goal?
- How can goals be supported by rules?

The component of the BRM is rule. Rules are linked by binary relationships of types supports and hinders as well as operationalization relationships of types AND, OR, and AND/OR. Business rules may be seen as the operationalization or limits of goals.

5.2.5 The Concepts Model

The Concepts Model (CM) is used to strictly define the "things" and "phenomena" that are mentioned in the other models. Enterprise concepts, attributes, and relationships are represented. Concepts are used to define more strictly expressions in the Goals Model as well as the content of information sets in the Business Process Model.

The Concepts Model usually clarifies questions, such as:

- What concepts are recognized in the enterprise (including their relationships to goals, activities, and processes, as well as actors)?
- How are they defined?
- What business rules and constraints monitor these objects and concepts?

The components of the CM are concepts and attributes. The relationship types are binary relationships, generalization/specialization, and aggregation. It follows the common notation of concepts modeling with concepts, relationships, and relationship cardinalities.

5.2.6   The Business Process Model

The Business Process Model (BPM) is used to define enterprise processes, the way they interact and the way they handle information as well as material. A business process is assumed to consume input in terms of information and/or material and produce output of information and/or material. In general, the BPM is similar to what is used in traditional data-flow diagram models.

The BPM usually clarifies questions, such as:

- Which business activities and processes are recognized in the organization, or should be there, to manage the organization in agreement with its goals?
- How should the business processes, tasks, etc., be performed (workflows, state transitions, or process models)?
- Which are their information needs?

The components of the BPM are process, external process, information set, and material set.

5.2.7   The Actors and Resources Model

The Actors and Resources Model (ARM) is used to describe how different actors and resources are related to each other and how they are related to components of the Goals Model and to components of the Business Process Model. For instance, an actor may be responsible for or is performing a particular process in the BPM, or the actor may be responsible for a particular goal in the GM.

The ARM usually clarifies questions, such as:

- Who is/should be performing which processes and tasks?
- How is the reporting and responsibility structure between actors defined?

The components of the ARM are role, non-human resource, organizational unit, and individual. The relationship types are binary relationships, generalization/specialization, and aggregation.

5.2.8   The Product/Service Model

The Product/Service Model (PSM) is used for describing the products and services of the enterprise along with their features and components. The sub-model was developed for EM projects with an explicit need to analyze and understand the effects of changes in processes, organization structures, or technical components on the products or services and vice versa, what effects changes in products and services have on other sub-models. The PSM describes essentially what is offered to the enterprise's customers in terms of (physical or digital) products and services, and what dependencies and inter-relations exist between these products and services. The components of PSM can be used to describe essential characteristics of products and services in terms of decomposition structure (i.e., products, components) and value proposition for the customer expressed in features. Through links to and from other 4EM sub-models, the PSM shows what processes and actors are involved in the value creation and administrative activities for the different processes and services. The components of the PSM are related to each other through unidirectional semantic links, of which the three main types are part_of, is_a, and requires.

Guiding questions for the model are:

- What are the products/services of an enterprise?
- What features do customers expect from products/services or does the enterprise want to offer?
- What products, services, or components are required for offering features?
- Who is responsible for features, products, components, or services?
- Which processes and business rules are related to products or services?
- What technical components and resources are required for products or services?

5.2.9 The Technical Components and Requirements Model

The Technical Components and Requirements Model (TCRM) becomes relevant when the purpose of EM is to aid in defining requirements for the development of an information system. Attention is focused on the information system that is needed to support the goals, processes, and actors of the enterprise. Initially one needs to develop a set of high-level requirements or goals, for the information system as a whole. Based on these, we attempt to structure the information system in a number of subsystems, or technical components. The TCRM is an initial attempt to define the overall structure and properties of the information system to support the business activities, as defined in the BPM.

The components of the TCRM are information system (IS) goal, IS problem, IS technical component, and IS requirement. IS requirements can be specialized into functional requirements and nonfunctional requirements. Similarly, to the GM, information system goals and problems are linked by binary relationships of types supports and hinders. IS goals are refined by goal operationalization relationships of types AND, OR, and AND/OR. IS components can have aggregation relationships between them (shown as a small square in Fig. 5.6). Between technical components and IS goals, binary relationships of types "supports," "has goal," and "has requirement" are also possible.

5.2.10   Inter-model Relationships

4EM distinguishes relationships with which the modeling components are related within the sub-model and relationships with components of other sub-models. The latter relationship type is called *inter-model relationship*, sometimes also called inter-model link.

The ability to trace decisions, components, and other aspects throughout the enterprise is dependent on the use and understanding of inter-model relationships. When developing a full enterprise model, these relationships between components of the different sub-models play an essential role, for instance, the clarity of the statements in the GM by defining the concepts more clearly in the CM. A link is then specified between the corresponding GM component and the concepts in the CM. In the same way, goals in the GM motivate particular processes in the BPM. The processes are needed to achieve the goals stated. A link therefore is defined between a goal and the related process. Inter-model links between models make the whole enterprise model traceable. They show, for instance, why certain processes and information system requirements have been introduced. Inter-model links are also used as a means to drive the modeling process forward in a modeling session by moving between perspectives.

5.3   Conceptualizing 4EM

This section presents the 4EM meta-model. The purpose of this section is to expose the meta-model in order to facilitate the adoption and use of the method. The meta-models are represented using the UML and can be seen as conceptual meta-models of the modeling language of 4EM. That is, they exclude aspects of implementation of the language in a modeling environment and management of models, such as sub-models, schemas, and views.

There are few underlying principles for reading the 4EM meta-model presented in this section. The enterprise model according to 4EM consists of seven sub-models; see Sect. 5.2. From a meta-modeling point of view, they all are part of the same model, but due to the size meta-models of each sub-model are presented separately. The 4EM sub-models contain several modeling constructs with similar names, for example, binary relationship "supports" is used in the GM to connect goals, and another relationship named "supports" is used in the BRM for modeling how one business rule supports another. However, this relationship should not be used for connection both goals and rules, which should be modeled by an inter-model relationship "goal motivates rule." To avoid ambiguity these relationships are modeled by different classes in the meta-model. To distinguish classes with similar names in the meta-model, their names include prefixes for the sub-model abbreviations to which they belong. Classes representing inter-model relationships are prefixed with "IM." We have also modeled relationship roles in cases where the same relationship can originate from a specific set of modeling components and can be connected to a specific set of components. Such class names are suffixed with "From" and "End," respectively.

For the sake of brevity, we have chosen not to show attributes of modeling components. For example, by default all 4EM components should have a short name representing the type of the components and number, e.g., "Goal 4," and a long name containing the textual expression of the component, e.g., "To be an attractive employer."

When presenting details of the meta-model in Sects. 5.3.1–5.3.7, we decided to add information about the ADOxx implementation in the figures. On the meta2 level, the ADOxx implementation of the 4EM Toolkit to some extent uses different concepts compared to the UML diagrams. The reasons mainly lie in implementation decisions that were made based on the ADOxx platform functionalities connected to the meta2 model of ADOxx [10]. Therefore, we provide a mapping in the UML diagrams. The following symbols for ADOxx meta2 concepts are used: (C) Class, (R) Relation Class, (A) Attribute, and (IR) Inter-model Relation. In the Goals Model meta-model (Fig. 5.3), to take an example, there is an ADOxx Class (C) for each GSMSymbolicRelationshipType. Binary relationships are mapped to a general ADOxx Relation Class (R), containing the relationship type as an Attribute (A). The 4EM Toolkit is based on a flat class hierarchy. Thus, abstract concepts without a visual symbol are not part of the model and not mapped consequently.

5.3.1   Meta-model of the Goals Model

The meta-model of the GM is shown in Fig. 5.2. In addition to its modeling components, goal, problem (with subtypes threat and weakness), opportunity, constraint, and cause, it shows the relationships available in the GM, more specifically, binary relationships of types "supports," "hinders," and "conflicts" as well as symbolic relationships of types "AND," "OR," and "AND/OR" used for expressing goal operationalization. GM also has one inter-model relationship "goal motivates," used to model that a goal motivates the inclusion in the model of a number of components in other sub-models. It is represented by class IMGoalMotivates.

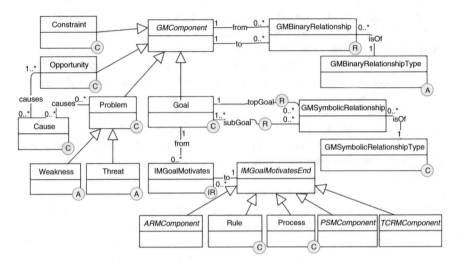

Fig. 5.2 Meta-model of 4EM Goals Model

5.3.2 Meta-model of the Business Rules Model

The meta-model of the BRM is shown in Fig. 5.3. The BRM's only component is business rule. Similarly to the goals in the GM, rules may be related to each other with binary relationships and with symbolic relationships of types "AND," "OR," and "AND/OR." Rules may have inter-model relationships of types "rule hinders goal," "rule directs use of an IS Component or a TCRM intentional component (IS goal or IS requirement)," and "rule triggers process." In Sandkuhl et al. (2014) we have specified the possibility to express rules in a semi-formal way according to a format of *WHEN [event] IF [preconditions on entities] THEN [process]*. This way of expressing rules is not represented in the meta-model and currently not supported by the tool.

5.3.3 Meta-model of the Business Process Model

The meta-model of the BPM is shown in Fig. 5.4. BPM components are process, external process, information set, and material set. Processes and external processes produce and consume information or material sets. Processes can be decomposed into sub-processes. In 4EM the sub-processes are then modeled in a separate model fragment linked to the "parent" process. This is not shown in the meta-model because its implementation varies depending on the modeling tool. Several inter-model relationships to BRM components are shown in meta-models of other sub-models, e.g., relationship Information and Material Sets "referring to" concepts is shown in the meta-model of the CM. In this figure we have included that the inter-model relationship process "motivates" the need for TCRM components.

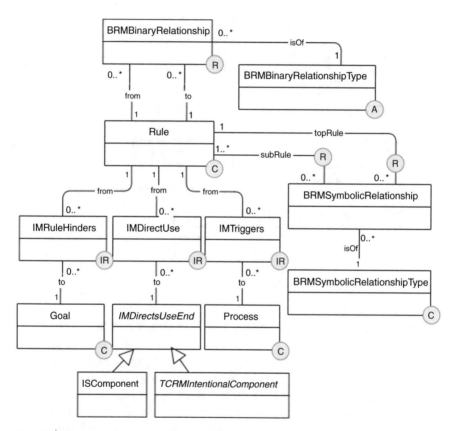

Fig. 5.3 Meta-model of 4EM Business Rules Model

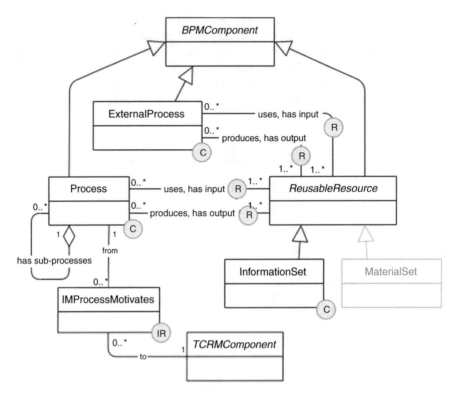

Fig. 5.4 Meta-model of 4EM Business Process Model

5.3.4 Meta-model of the Actors and Resources Model

The meta-model of the ARM is shown in Fig. 5.5. ARM components are individual, non-human resource, organizational unit, and role. A binary relationship of specific types may exist between these components to express responsibilities and dependencies between them. A special kind of relationship may be established between individual, non-human resource, and organizational unit and role in order to show who plays (or fulfills) the role. In addition, ARM components may also have generalization and aggregation relationships between them, represented by ARMSymbolicRelationship. Roles, individuals, and organizational units may be responsible for goals, processes, rules, and TCRM intentional components, modeled by class IMActorResponsibleFor.

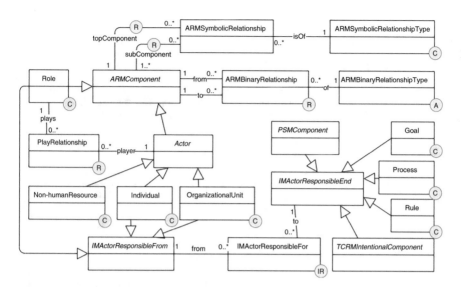

Fig. 5.5 Meta-model of 4EM Actors and Resources Model

5.3.5 Meta-model of the Concepts Model

The meta-model of the CM is shown in Fig. 5.6. CM components are concepts and attributes. They may be related with binary relationships with a custom name. Multiplicities of binary relationships are omitted from this meta-model for the sake of brevity. Concepts may also have generalization and aggregation relationships between them, represented by CMMSymbolicRelationship. One of the key purposes of the CM, besides defining the overall information structure of the problem domain, is to define terms that other models use. This is realized by inter-model relationship "refers_to" that allows components of other sub-models (goal, rule, information set, material set, or any component of TCRM, PSM, and ARM) to refer to a concept.

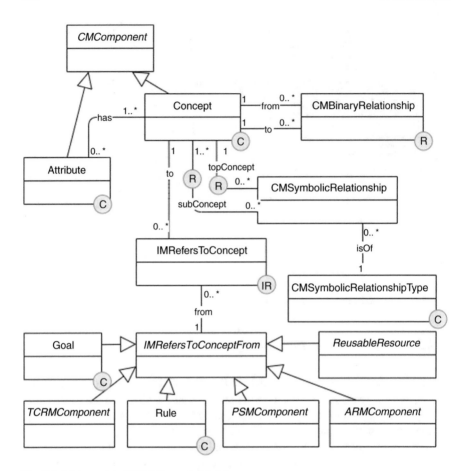

Fig. 5.6 Meta-model of 4EM Concepts Model

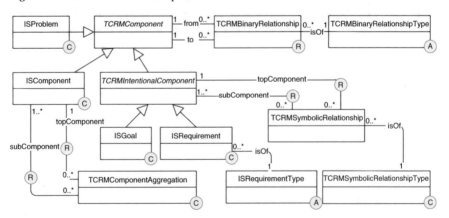

Fig. 5.7 Meta-model of 4EM Technical Components and Requirements Model

5.3.6 Meta-model of the Technical Components and Requirements Model

The meta-model of the TCRM is shown in Fig. 5.7. The TCRM components are information system (IS) problem, IS goal, IS requirement, and IS component. Binary relationships can exist between all TCRM components, and refinement relationships of types "AND," "OR," and "AND/OR" can exist between IS intentional elements of IS goal and IS requirement. IS requirements may have a requirement type specified, for example, functional or nonfunctional. The inter-model relationships to TCRM components are shown in meta-models of other sub-models, e.g., in the GM, goal "motivates" a TCRM component and in the ARM role "is responsible for" an IS goal.

5.3.7 Meta-model of the Product/Service Model

The meta-model of the PSM is shown in Fig. 5.8. PSM components are product/service (with the possibility to specialize into product or service), component, and feature. The relationships between the components of the PSM are symbolic for specifying aggregation and specialization, as well as "requires" to specify that the implementation of a feature requires a certain product, service, or component. All components of the PSM may also refer to processes or any TCRM component.

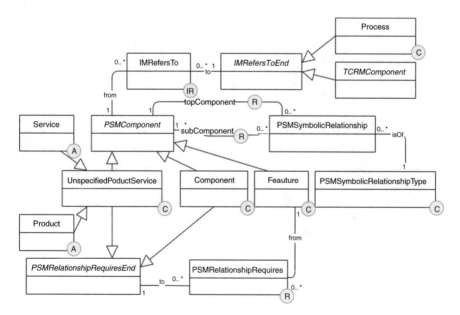

Fig. 5.8 Meta-model of 4EM Product/Service Model

5.4   Illustrating 4EM Use with the 4EM Toolkit

5.4.1   The 4EM Toolkit

To support the use of the 4EM method, the 4EM Modeling Toolkit has been developed based on the ADOxx platform. The toolkit implements the meta-model that is described in the previous section and provides a modeling environment with the visual notation that is recommended for expressing 4EM models [4]. The different sub-models can be modeled separately. Typical views that combine concepts of different sub-models like Goals and Rules Models are directly supported by the respective model types in the toolkit. General support of inter-model-relations is implemented by the inter-model-relation mechanism of ADOxx. This mechanism is also used to manage model complexity with the possibility to link decomposition models to single model elements. Furthermore, a 4EM General Model is provided by the toolkit that allows a visual model of arbitrary 4EM concepts and user-defined relations in order to ensure required flexibility. Besides the visual notation, rules and recommendation functionality for the creation of meta-model conform models are implemented.

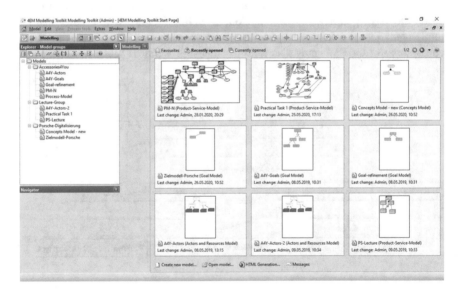

Fig. 5.9   User interface of the 4EM Toolkit

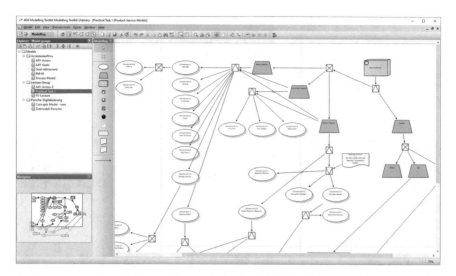

Fig. 5.10 The 4EM Toolkit with opened Product/Service sub-model

Figures 5.9 and 5.10 show screenshots of the user interface for the ADOxx-based 4EM Toolkit. Figure 5.9 shows different types of 4EM sub-models in the model overview pane. Figure 5.10 shows a Product/Service sub-model.

5.4.2 Illustrative Example

In the following we show the usage of 4EM and its sub-models based on the case of a small consulting company. All models are created using the 4EM Modeling Toolkit and show only a part of the original model. The starting point is the Goals Model (GM) depicted in Fig. 5.11. The top goal (G10) is refined into goals G1, G2, G3, and G4 by an AND relationship, which means that in order to achieve G10, all of the sub-goals need to be achieved. Similarly, goal G1 is refined into goals G1.1 and G1.2. Examples of binary relationships in the GM are "Weakness 1 hinders goal G2," "goal G5 supports goal G3," and "Threat 2 hinders Goal 4."

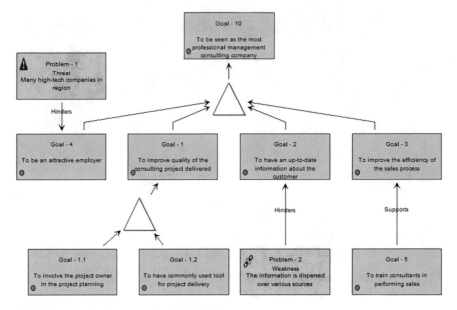

Fig. 5.11 Example fragment of a Goals Model

Business rules may be seen as the operationalization or limits of goals. For example, the Business Rules Model (BRM) in Fig. 5.12 shows how business rules can define more specific means for implementing goals.

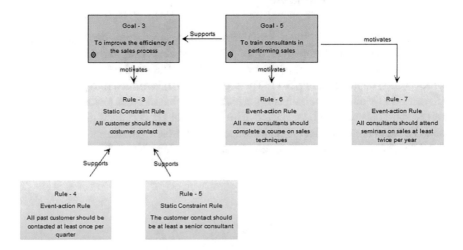

Fig. 5.12 Example fragment of a Business Rules Model

The components of the Concepts Model (CM) are concepts and attributes. The relationship types are binary relationships, generalization/specialization, and aggregation. Figure 5.13 shows a fragment of the CM of the consulting company. It follows the common notation of concepts modeling with concepts, relationships, and relationship cardinalities. Generalization/specialization is shown by circles; in this example Concept 5 "offering" is specialized to three concepts—Concepts 7 "Service," Concept 8 "Product," and Concept 9 "Customized offering."

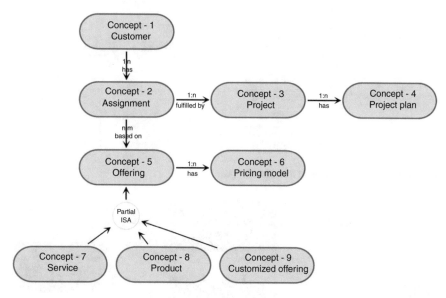

Fig. 5.13 Example fragment of a Concepts Model

Figure 5.14 shows a Business Process Model for preparing project after sales. It shows the flow of process information sets and one external process "customer."

Figure 5.15 shows a small Actors and Resources Model (ARM) of roles involved in the sales and project delivery processes.

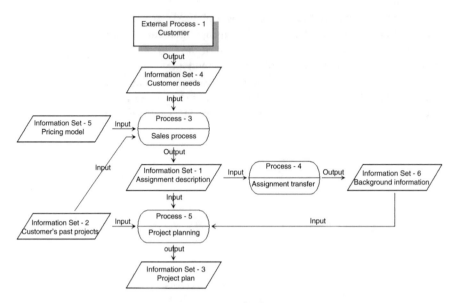

Fig. 5.14 Example fragment of a Business Process Model

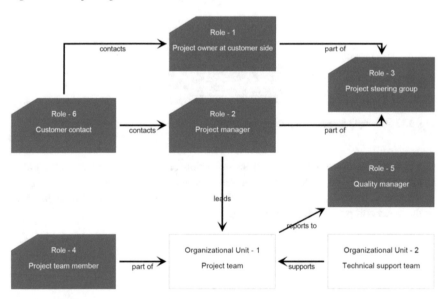

Fig. 5.15 Example fragment of a Actors and Resources Model

Figure 5.16 shows a fragment of a Technical Components and Requirements Model (TCRM) for a consultant portal (Technical component 1). It supports the IS Goal 1 "to support information sharing among consultants." The portal consists of several subsystems, of which three are shown in this model—time reporting system, project experience reports, and best practice subsystem. An IS Problem 9 documents that consultants prefer using their own IT environment.

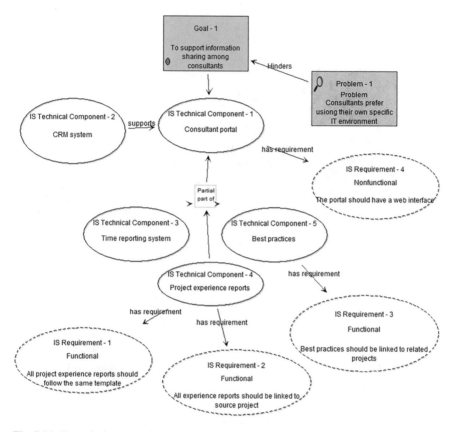

Fig. 5.16 Example fragment of a Technical Components and Requirements Model

Figure 5.17 shows the Product/Service Model (PSM) for the provided payroll services. While the Payroll Processing Service (Service 1) provides base function-ality, the Payroll Advisory Service (Service 2) offers on top of it the feature of risk and rework reduction (Feature 2) by checking for anomalies in the payroll data. The additional feature is bound to Component 2 and the use of the cloud platform (Component 3) for payroll processing.

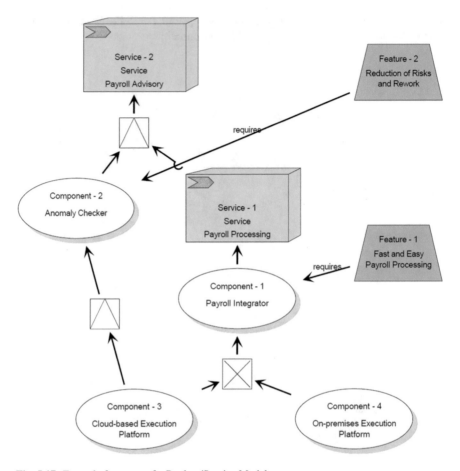

Fig. 5.17 Example fragment of a Product/Service Model

Figure 5.18 shows an example of several fragments of sub-models in a 4EM enterprise model and components that are linked between them with inter-model links based on the 4EM General Model component of the toolkit. This model depicts a part of an enterprise model aiming to improve project delivery (Goal G1). This goal is refined using AND decomposition into two sub-goals, namely, G1.1 "to involve the project owner in the project planning" and G1.2 "to have a commonly used tool for project delivery." This figure elaborates only on one of the sub-goals (G1.1) by specifying that it motivates Process 5 "project planning." This process has two information sets as input—"assignment description" and "customer's past project." These information sets are linked to corresponding concepts in the CM by inter-model links of type "refers to" in order to explain the information sets in more detail. In simple cases as in Figs. 5.12, 5.13, 5.14, 5.15, 5.16, 5.17, and 5.18, these kinds of connections might appear to be obvious. However, in real projects when the model complexity is much higher, they need to be documented to increase the overall clarity of the model. Here, inter-model relations can be modeled between separate sub-models to keep track of invisible dependencies.

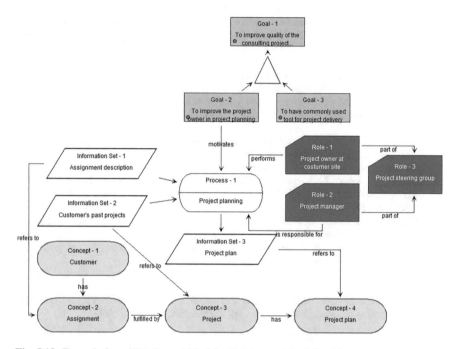

Fig. 5.18 Example for a 4EM General Model with inter-model relationships

5.5 Summary

The enterprise modeling method 4EM consists of a modeling language covering the different perspectives of an enterprise in conjunction with guidelines for the modeling process, the principle of strong stakeholder participation, and a project approach. In this chapter, our focus was on the modeling language with its meta-model and the tool support provided by the ADOxx-based 4EM Toolkit. A comparison of 4EM with other multi-perspective languages is part of the 4EM textbook [6].

Future work on modeling language and tool addresses the demand of 4EM users to extend the sub-models to cover other perspectives of an enterprise, e.g., the capabilities of an enterprise. For the 4EM Toolkit, the current work is focusing on additional assistive functions for the modeler, such as improvement of missing relationship detection or functions exploiting information captured in the attributes of different concepts.

Tool Download https://www.omilab.org/4em.

References

1. Vernadat, F.: Enterprise Modelling and Integration. Chapman & Hall (1996)
2. Sandkuhl, K., et al.: From expert discipline to common practice: a vision and research agenda for extending the reach of enterprise modeling. Bus. Inf. Syst. Eng. **60**(1), 69–80 (2018). https://doi.org/10.1007/s12599-017-0516-y
3. Vernadat, F.: Enterprise modelling: research review and outlook. Comput. Ind. **122**, 103265 (2020). https://doi.org/10.1016/j.compind.2020.103265
4. Persson, A., Stirna, J.: An explorative study into the influence of business goals on the practical use of Enterprise Modelling methods and tools, Tenth International Conference on Information Systems Development (ISD2001), Royal Holloway, University of London, 5–7 September 2001 (2001)
5. Bubenko, J.A. Jr, Persson, A., Stirna, J.: An intentional perspective on enterprise modeling, in C. Salinesi, S. Nurcan, C. Souveyet, J. Ralyté (eds.), An Intentional Perspective on Enterprise Modeling. Springer, ISBN 978-3-642-12543-0 (2010)
6. Sandkuhl, K., Stirna, J., Persson, A., Wißotzki, M.: Enterprise Modeling - Tackling Business Challenges with the 4EM Method. The Enterprise Engineering Series, Springer, ISBN 978–3–662-43724-7 (2014)
7. Bubenko, J.A. Jr, Stirna, J., Brash, D.: EKD User Guide, Department of Computer and Systems Sciences, Royal Institute of Technology, Stockholm (1998)
8. Loucopoulos, P., Kavakli, V., Prekas, N., Rolland, C., Grosz, G., Nurcan, S.: Using the EKD Approach: The Modelling Component. UMIST, Manchester (1997)
9. Stirna, J., Persson, A.: Enterprise Modeling – Facilitating the Process and the People. Springer, Cham (2018)
10. Fill, H.-G., Karagiannis, D.: On the conceptualisation of modelling methods using the ADOxx meta modelling platform. Enterp. Model. Inf. Syst. Archit. **8**(1), 4–25 (2013)

Chapter 6
PGA 2.0: A Modeling Technique for the Alignment of the Organizational Strategy and Processes

Ben Roelens (iD)

Abstract Successfully aligning a company's strategy with its processes is a major concern in practice. Indeed, almost half of the organizations are able to implement a mere 60% of its objectives. This problem has attracted attention in Strategic Management, Organization, and Conceptual Modeling literature. In previous research, we presented a first version of the Process-Goal Alignment (PGA) technique, which is a model-based approach for realizing strategic fit that was designed as the result of an iteration of Action Design Research (ADR). This chapter supplements the first PGA version by reflection and learning during a second cycle of ADR, which entails further development and application of the modeling technique in four real-life case studies. As such, this chapter formalizes the initial design in combination with the insights from the case studies, which results in PGA version 2.0. This also includes a description of the proof-of-concept version of the ADOxx modeling tool. Finally, we also present a brief outlook of future PGA research opportunities.

Keywords Organizational strategy · Process-goal alignment · Domain-specific modelling

6.1 Introduction

The alignment of the organizational strategy and processes is a topical issue for organizations. More particular, 46% of organizations can only implement 60% of their strategic objectives [13]. This challenge has attracted research attention in Strategic Management and Organization literature since the 1960s [19]. In line with the accelerating adoption of Information Technology (IT) in the 1990s, Henderson and Venkatraman developed the Strategic Alignment Model for organizational transformation via IT [14]. In their model, strategic fit is defined as *the interrelationships between the external and internal domain* [14]. While the external domain

B. Roelens (✉)
Faculty of Science, Open Universiteit, Heerlen, Netherlands
e-mail: ben.roelens@ou.nl

© The Author(s), under exclusive license to Springer Nature Switzerland AG 2022
D. Karagiannis et al. (eds.), *Domain-Specific Conceptual Modeling*,
https://doi.org/10.1007/978-3-030-93547-4_6

encompasses strategic decisions about an organization's position in competitive markets, the internal domain concerns an appropriate business infrastructure and processes. The concept of strategic fit was further developed by Maes in [18], who distinguishes between the strategic, infrastructural, and operational perspectives. As such, the infrastructural perspective can help overcome the conceptual gap that exists between the strategy and the processes of an organization [24]. A combined view on the external and internal domain is given by the business architecture, which represents *holistic, multidimensional business views of capabilities, end-to-end value delivery, information, and organizational structure, and the relationships among these business views and strategies, products, policies, initiatives, and stakeholders* [5].

In the Strategic Management and Organization fields, researchers mainly adopt a deductive approach for theory development by using quantitative methods to test propositions (e.g., see [19]). Additional insights to the theoretical basis can be provided by enterprise modeling methods, which provide a visual representation of relevant phenomena in a particular organization for means of understanding and communication by stakeholders [21]. More specifically, goal modeling approaches (e.g., iStar 2.0 [6]) can be used to capture the interactions and trade-offs between organizational objectives, thereby facilitating strategy formulation [17]. For the infrastructural perspective, value models (e.g., Value Delivery Modeling Language [22]) reflect the strategic choices made by a company by describing "what" a company must do to create value for itself and its environment, without committing to the required operational details [29]. Finally, process modeling can be used to describe *how businesses conduct their operations, by including elements as activities, events/states, and the control flow logic that constitute a business process* [27].

Different techniques have been developed to align the enterprise modeling methods operating at the strategic, infrastructural, and operational levels of the business architecture. As such, they provide a model-based approach to align the organizational strategy and processes (i.e., requirement 1). Depending on the way in which alignment is handled, the alignment techniques can be divided into four different categories: (i) top-down, (ii) bottom-up, (iii) hybrid, or (iv) integrative approaches (see Table 6.1).

Top-down alignment techniques employ transformation rules and construct mappings to help develop models at lower abstraction levels from models at higher abstraction levels. Bottom-up approaches annotate models with information of models found at higher abstraction levels, while hybrid techniques align the models that are used for the different business architecture perspectives by combining top-down and bottom-up approaches. A last subgroup achieves strategic fit in an integrative manner through the use of newly designed modeling languages, which include constructs that are relevant to two or all three of the strategy, infrastructure, and process perspectives of the business architecture.

Table 6.1 Overview of model-based alignment techniques

Category	Alignment approach	Reference examples
Top-down	Starting from goal models, alignment is realized by deriving value and process model structures through transformation rules and mapping corresponding constructs	[1, 3, 8, 10]
Bottom-up	Starting from process models, alignment is realized by deriving value and goal model structures through transformation rules and mapping corresponding constructs	[9, 11]
Hybrid	Techniques that combine the top-down and bottom-up alignment of enterprise modeling methods	[4, 12, 24]
Integrative	The design of a new DSML that combines elements from the strategic, infrastructural, and operational perspectives on the business architecture	[16, 35, 36]

A limitation of these techniques is the lack of integration with performance measurement, which prevents business stakeholders to set performance objectives and keep track of the actual performance within the business architecture (i.e., requirement 2). This mechanism is important to achieve strategic fit by *translating the vision and strategy into clear, understandable goals and measures*, as well as *by giving feedback on goal attainment and the drivers of those goals* [33]. Another drawback of existing alignment techniques is the use of models that were originally designed to elicit a complete set of detailed system requirements. The focus on completeness and formality does not facilitate a clear understanding of and communication about the content by the targeted business stakeholders, who are not familiar with this type of models (i.e., requirement 3) [2]. For a more detailed analysis of the existing alignment techniques, we refer the reader to [31].

Given the limitations of the existing model-based alignment approaches, Action Design Research (ADR) was employed to develop a more comprehensive alignment technique [34]. ADR is a type of Design Science Research [15] that explicitly recognizes that IT artifacts (e.g., enterprise modeling methods) are shaped during their development and application in real-life contexts [34]. As such, it provides a relevant methodology for aligning the organizational strategy and processes, which is a problem that still exists in today's practice [13].

The chapter is organized as follows. The substantiation of the ADR method is described in Sect. 6.2, while Sect. 6.3 describes the conceptualization of the PGA modeling method. Section 6.4 describes the proof-of-concept version of the ADOxx modeling tool and an illustrative example of the PGA modeling technique, as well as its evaluation by the end users during the real-life case studies. Finally, the findings of the chapter are summarized and future research opportunities are outlined in Sect. 6.5.

6.2   ADR Methodology

The ADR method consists of four stages, which will be further discussed in the remainder of this paragraph: (i) problem formulation; (ii) building, intervention, and evaluation; (iii) reflection and learning; and (iv) formalization of learning.

6.2.1   Problem Formulation

Three requirements (cf. Sect. 6.1) are important for the realization of strategic fit by means of a model-based alignment technique. To this end, we proposed an initial design of the PGA modeling method in [31]. This technique is a DSML that achieves strategic fit in an integrative manner as it enables to align models both in a top-down and bottom-up manner, without being dependent on a particular set of modeling languages for the business architecture perspectives (i.e., requirement 1). Furthermore, a measurement system enables to identify performance indicators, which quantify the organizational performance (i.e., requirement 2). The Analytic Hierarchy process (AHP) [32] supplements the performance measurement to create a heat map that enables the identification of business architecture elements that are crucial for the realization of strategic fit. This enables a clear communication with the targeted business stakeholders (i.e., requirement 3).

The initial PGA technique was developed and refined through three case studies in the context of a global IT solution provider. Although the case studies were executed independently, the use of a single organization hampers the external generalizability of the results. In this respect, the following research question is put forward:

How can the initial PGA modeling technique be further shaped by development and use in real-life organizational contexts?

6.2.2   Building, Intervention, and Evaluation

Four extra case studies were performed as part of the second iteration of ADR research (i.e., 2.1–2.4) to apply the initial PGA technique in different real-life organizational contexts. These case studies are a convenience sample as the organizations were chosen based on availability and existing issues with the realization of strategic fit. Case studies 2.2–2.4 were executed by a researcher, a PGA expert, and an end user in the respective private organizations. An exception is case study 2.1, in which the execution of the PGA modeling procedure was a collective effort of the researcher, the PGA expert, and nine board members of a public organization. Although the end users have varying profiles, they are closely related to the management layer of their organization. The PGA expert collected and processed the necessary input information in collaboration with the end user(s), including interview data and written documentation. A summary of the case study participant data can be found in Table 6.2.

Table 6.2 Case study participants

Case study	Sector	# End users	Profile
2.1	Public organization	9	Board members
2.2	Insurance company	1	Management trainee
2.3	Food company	1	Executive manager
2.4	Capital fund	1	Project analyst

The evaluation of the modeling method is based on the original questionnaire [31],[1] which is filled in by the end users after completing the PGA modeling procedure. This questionnaire assesses to what extent the technique is fulfilling the requirements, with respect to top-down and bottom-up alignment (i.e., requirement 1), performance measurement (i.e., requirement 2), and perceived usefulness and ease of use (i.e., underlying stakeholder acceptance with respect to requirement 3) [7]. Each item is measured on a 7-point Likert scale, ranging from strongly disagree (i.e., 1) to strongly agree (i.e., 7). This quantitative evaluation is supplemented by collecting qualitative feedback of the end users during the interview.

6.2.3 Reflection and Learning

The reflection and learning stage is performed in parallel with the first two ADR phases to reflect on how the technique can be improved in an iterative manner. During this phase, the insights with respect to the intervention and evaluation of the PGA technique were continuously discussed between the PGA expert and the researcher. These members of the ADR team collectively reflected on the design of the modeling method and suggested refinements to the modeling language and procedure.

6.2.4 Formalization of Learning

Formalization of learning includes the development of the situational learning into a generic solution for the addressed problem [34]. This chapter formalizes the results that were obtained during the second iteration of ADR research. This includes

---

[1] The evaluation form can be found via: https://doi.org/10.13140/RG.2.2.34080.92163.

combining the initial design with the insights from the case studies, which results in PGA version 2.0.

6.3 Method Conceptualization

6.3.1 Modeling Language

6.3.1.1 Syntax

To provide an integrative view on the business architecture, the PGA 2.0 meta-model (see Fig. 6.1) contains eight Elements that originate from the Value Chain [26], the Balanced Scorecard [20], and the Business Model Canvas [23]: Activity, Process, Competence, ValueProposition, FinancialStructure, InternalGoal, CustomerGoal, and FinancialGoal. These elements are connected by valueStream relations, which enable to build a hierarchical structure, which represents how value is created at the different business architecture levels. In this respect, insights from case study 2.2 and 2.3 enabled us to identify three new valueStream relations: from FinancialGoal to CustomerGoal, from CustomerGoal to InternalGoal, and from FinancialGoal to InternalGoal (see valueStream* in Fig. 6.1). These links between the strategic goals are also proposed by Kaplan and Norton in [20].

The performance measurement system of the business architecture elements is included in the Measure entity with attributes to specify its type, textual description, performance goal, allowed deviation percentage, and actual performance. The user is able to discriminate between three different types of indicators: positive (e.g., customer satisfaction: the higher the value, the more positive), negative (e.g., customer complaints: the higher the value, the more negative), or qualitative (e.g., perceived quality: either satisfied or unsatisfied). By combining the numeric performance goal with the allowed deviation percentage, it can be determined whether the actual performance is "bad," "as expected," or "excellent."

The input for the AHP mechanism is captured by a comparison matrix, which enables to choose a certain AHP scale value for the pairwise comparisons (i.e., between Element X_i and X_j) throughout the business architecture hierarchy. Besides this, a ratio needs to be calculated to verify whether the consistency of the chosen scale values is within an acceptable range (i.e., below 10% [32]). The resulting AHP importance is attached as an attribute to the valueStream relations in the business architecture hierarchy. The combination of the integrative view on the business architecture with the performance measurement system and the AHP mechanism will result in the creation of a heat map that that can be used to improve the realization of strategic fit (see Sect. 6.3.2).

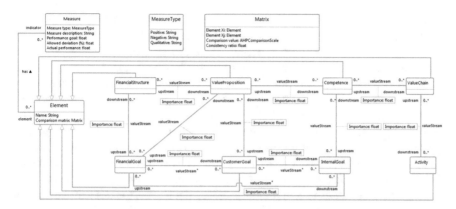

Fig. 6.1 Meta-model of PGA 2.0

6.3.1.2   Semantics and Notation

An overview of the semantics and notation of the PGA concepts is provided in Table 6.3. In line with the need for a more detailed analysis on the strategic level of the business architecture during case studies 2.2 and 2.3, PGA 2.0 further refines the definitions of the different types of goals based on the theoretical basis in the Conceptual Modeling [25] and Strategic Management [20] field.

Besides this, the intuitiveness of the original notation of the PGA technique was evaluated by a group of 139 students in [28] based on term association, notation association, and case study tasks. The analysis of the results eventually led to a new notation for five PGA meta-model concepts: Competence, ValueProposition, InternalGoal, CustomerGoal, and valueStream (see Table 6.3). This evaluation further increases the intuitive understanding and communication of PGA 2.0 model content by business stakeholders.

6.3.2   Modeling Procedure

Based on the second iteration of ADR case studies, the PGA modeling procedure is refined in four steps, for which separate interviews should be done: (i) development of the business architecture hierarchy, (ii) performing the AHP, (iii) execution of the performance measurement, and (iv) strategic fit improvement analysis.

6.3.2.1   Development of the Business Architecture Hierarchy

The first step is oriented toward the identification of relevant business architecture elements and their valueStream interrelationships. Depending on the context, the hierarchy can be built in a top-down (i.e., starting from strategic Goals) or bottom-up manner (i.e., starting from Activities and Processes). After the identification of a certain element, it is advised to explore more elements of the same type or add other elements that are connected through a valueStream relation in the meta-model. As such, the business architecture hierarchy is gradually built during the interview. This can also be visually reflected by a horizontal positioning of all elements of the same type in the resulting PGA model (e.g., see Fig. 6.4). This step in the modeling procedure can only be stopped if a minimal PGA cycle is completed. This means that at least one Activity or Process is connected to an organizational Goal via intermediate business architecture Elements and valueStream relations. This is related to the purpose of strategic fit, which aims at the alignment of the organizational strategy and processes. Once the business architecture elements are added, the hierarchy is completed by adding valueStream relations between them.

6.3.2.2 Performing the AHP

The goal of the second step in the modeling procedure is to set the importance attribute of the valueStream relations. To this end, we propose the original AHP procedure [32], which is based on pairwise comparisons between all elements that are connected to the same element on a higher level in the business architecture hierarchy. The pairwise comparisons are performed based on the AHP comparison scale, which ranges from 1 (i.e., X_i and X_j have an equal importance) to 9 (i.e., X_i has extreme importance compared to X_j), as well as the reciprocal values in case X_j is more important than X_i. Afterward, the pairwise comparisons are combined in a matrix, of which the normalized principal eigenvector represents the absolute priorities of the different elements. To calculate the importance attribute in the context of PGA, the priorities are rescaled relatively to the lowest value in the eigenvector. As such, we prevent that the priorities artificially diminish with the number of elements in the comparison. Based on the resulting values, the importance of a valueStream relation is classified as "high" (i.e., a priority higher than 4, visualized by three exclamation marks), "medium" (i.e., priority 3 or 4, visualized by two exclamation marks), or "low" (i.e., priority 1 or 2, visualized by one exclamation mark). In parallel with the calculation of the priorities, the consistency ratio verifies the consistency of the chosen scale values by the respondents. If this value is above 10%, the judgments of the respondents need to be revised [32].

Case study 2.1 enabled to refine the procedure for the application of AHP in a group of nine respondents. In this context, the AHP comparison values were individually determined upfront based on a new visualization of the AHP comparison scale for the end users (see Fig. 6.2).

Table 6.3 Semantics and notation of the PGA 2.0 modeling technique

PGA concept	Definition	Notation [28]
Activity	Work that is performed in a process by one or more actors, which are engaged in changing the state of one or more input resources or enterprise objects to create a single desired output [31]	
Process	A structured set of activities that use and/or consume resources to create the organizational competences [31]	
Competence	An integrated and holistic set of knowledge, skills, and abilities, related to a specific set of resources, which are coordinated through processes to realize the intended value proposition [31]	
Value-Proposition	Offered set of products and/or services that provide value to the customers and other partners and compete in the overall value network [31]	
Financial-Structure	Representation of the costs resulting from acquiring resources and the revenues in return for the offered value proposition [31]	
InternalGoal	Strategic objective that describes a desired state or development of the company to ensure that a company excels in processes, decisions, and actions to meet its customers' expectations [20, 25]	
CustomerGoal	Strategic objective that describes a desired state or development of the company to ensure that a customer is satisfied with the products and services the company provides [20, 25]	
FinancialGoal	Strategic objective that describes a desired state or development of the company to ensure that shareholders are satisfied with the future monetary performance of the company [20, 25]	
valueStream	Representation of the hierarchical structure, through which value is created at distinct levels in the business architecture [31]	
Measure	A quantitative or qualitative indicator that can be used to give a view on the state or progress of a business architecture element [31]	

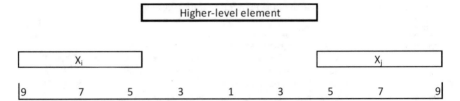

Fig. 6.2 End-user visualization of the AHP comparison scale

Afterward, the PGA expert collected all answers and analyzed whether a quantitative consensus was reached or whether further discussion was needed between the participants. Therefore, the following decision tree was developed (see Fig. 6.3). First, the percentage of respondents that attach a higher importance to one of the elements in the pairwise comparison (i.e., an approving value that is either higher or lower than 1) needs to be calculated. If this percentage is higher than 80% and the distance between the lowest and highest approving values is lower than 4, a quantitative consensus is reached by calculating the median value. Otherwise, the spread of 75% of the approving values needs to be lower than 2 to obtain a quantitative consensus by the median value. In all other cases, a group discussion is needed to reach a consensus about the AHP comparison values between the participants.

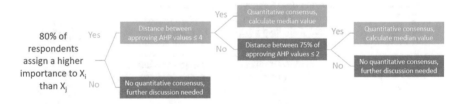

Fig. 6.3 Decision tree for AHP consensus between end users

Case study 2.3 provided insights that can be used to lower the learning curve of the AHP mechanism, as it was a challenge for the PGA expert to perform the AHP in collaboration with the end user. Therefore, it is advised to start with an Element, which is connected to the lowest number of downstream Elements in the business architecture hierarchy. This enables to make the participant familiar with the assignment of priorities, after which the more complicated comparisons can be performed. In case the number of pairwise comparisons is higher than 5, the consistency can be improved by making a qualitative ranking of the elements' importance first. Within this ranking, the end user should start with comparing the elements with the largest importance gaps, as the choice of a comparison value is easier in this case. Afterward, the respondent can continue with the elements that have a lower difference in importance.

6.3.2.3   Execution of the Performance Measurement

This step of the modeling procedure is oriented toward choosing appropriate performance Measures for each business architecture Element. Therefore, the PGA expert needs to collect information to specify a measure's type, textual description, performance goal, allowed deviation percentage, and actual performance. Based on the formulae developed in [31], it can be determined whether the actual performance of an Element is "bad" (i.e., visualized by a red border color), "as expected" (i.e., visualized by an orange border color), or "excellent" (i.e., visualized by a green border color in Fig. 6.4). This finalizes the construction of the business architecture heat map.

6.3.2.4   Strategic Fit Improvement Analysis

This step analyzes the business architecture heat map to identify operational improvements that achieve a better realization of the organizational goals. Within the PGA modeling method, this analysis is operationalized by the identification of a critical path, which starts from a Goal with a "bad" or "as expected" performance and continues via downstream valueStream relations that mostly have a "high" or "medium" importance and that connect business architecture elements of which the performance can be improved [31]. As such, a critical path provides input for a discussion with the end users about which operational improvements are relevant and could be possibly implemented in the organization.

6.4   Proof of Concept

6.4.1   Tool Prototype

The PGA 2.0 tool prototype is openly available through the PGA project space[2] within the Open Models Laboratory (OMiLAB). In this paragraph, we describe the PGA functionalities that are supported by the modeling tool. Illustrative screenshots in the context of the case study are added to Sect. 6.4.2.

The PGA meta-model is implemented as a set of classes and relationclasses in the ADOxx meta-modeling platform. The business architecture elements are defined as subtypes of an Element, which enable the inheritance of their common attributes. The valueStream relation is added as a recursive relationclass between two Elements as it enables its reuse throughout the business architecture hierarchy. Consequently, further constraints are needed to make the application of a valueStream relation

---

[2] Online link of the PGA project space: https://austria.omilab.org/psm/content/PGA/

consistent with the PGA meta-model. This is realized by specifying constraints to its "from" and "to" attributes in the external coupling component of ADOxx.

A second functionality of the tool prototype is the automation of the AHP (see screenshot in Fig. 6.5). To enable the specification of the AHP comparison values, each Element has a comparison matrix, which is a collection of attributes that are represented in a table-based structure. The AHP is further realized by adding ADO-Script files that read the necessary input information from the comparison matrix, realize a coupling with an external JAR file, and feed the calculated outcomes of the AHP back to the PGA model. This enables to fill in the importance attribute of the valueStream relations and the consistency ratio of the comparison matrix. Based on the classification of the importance attribute (i.e., "high," "medium," or "low"), a dynamic graphical representation enables to automatically adjust the notation of the valueStream relations. Besides this, users get a message to revise the AHP comparison values if the consistency ratio is above the threshold of 10%. Finally, the consistency between the comparison matrix and the ADOxx model is ensured when users delete or adjust content of the PGA model.

The performance measurement is implemented in the tool prototype by including the Measure attributes to the Element class (see screenshot in Fig. 6.6). This choice was made to incorporate this mechanism in a separate tab of a business architecture element. Based on the input values of the end user, a dynamic graphical representation automatically changes the border color of an Element for an "excellent," "as expected," or "bad" performance.

To facilitate the identification of a critical path during the strategic fit improvement analysis, a last functionality of the tool enables to remove the visualization of relations in the PGA model. This choice can be made for an individual valueStream or for a group of valueStream relations of which the importance attribute is below a user-defined threshold.

6.4.2 Case Study

This case study illustrates the use of the PGA modeling method and is based on case study 2.2. The choice for this case study is motivated by the balance between the size and complexity of the resulting PGA model, which makes it particularly useful for an illustration purpose. For reasons of anonymity, data that are specific to the organization are removed. The main purpose of this PGA application was to realize a further growth of lucrative B2B (i.e., business-to-business) contracts for the insurance company. This illustration is structured according to the four steps of the PGA 2.0 modeling procedure.

6.4.2.1   Development of the Business Architecture Hierarchy

Starting from the organizational goals, the business architecture hierarchy of the insurance company was built in a top-down manner. On the strategic level, two important objectives are "Increase revenues" (i.e., a FinancialGoal) and the "Increase of the B2B portfolio share" (i.e., a CustomerGoal). These objectives are supported by the Value Proposition, for which a distinction is made between "Offering insurance packages" and other "Customer services." Offering these two services is realized by three main Competences, including "Customer knowledge," "Product knowledge," and "Partnership development." These Competences are the result of the "Service execution," "Sales," and "Market research" processes. For these processes, critical Activities include "Personal advice," "Follow-up insurance files," "Attracting new customers," "Market analysis," "Compose insurance packages," and "Contracting agents." After the identification of the business architecture Elements, 19 valueStream relations were added between them (see Fig. 6.4).

6.4.2.2   Performing the AHP

Given the structure of the business architecture hierarchy, nine pairwise comparisons were needed to perform the AHP. In this respect, we focus on the comparisons between the three activities of "Marketing research." Given the AHP scale values that were chosen in Fig. 6.5, the rescaled PGA priorities for "Market analysis," "Compose insurance packages," and "Contracting agents" are, respectively, 1 (i.e., "low"), 2 (i.e., "low"), and 3 (i.e., "medium"). Given this classification, the corresponding PGA 2.0 notation is added in Fig. 6.4. The resulting consistency ratio is equal to 4.98%, which is acceptable given the threshold value of 10%.

6.4.2.3   Execution of the Performance Measurement

To complete the business architecture heat map, performance measurement data were added to the model. In this case study, positive and qualitative performance measures were used. Based on the numerical input data, seven elements are characterized by a "bad" performance, one element by an "as expected" performance, and eight elements by an "excellent" performance. An example of the performance measurement data for "Increase B2B portfolio share" is provided in Fig. 6.6. As the actual performance of this element (i.e., B2B ratio $= 30$) is below the lower acceptance level (i.e., $40 * (100\% - 12.5\%) = 35$), the performance is characterized as "bad" [31].

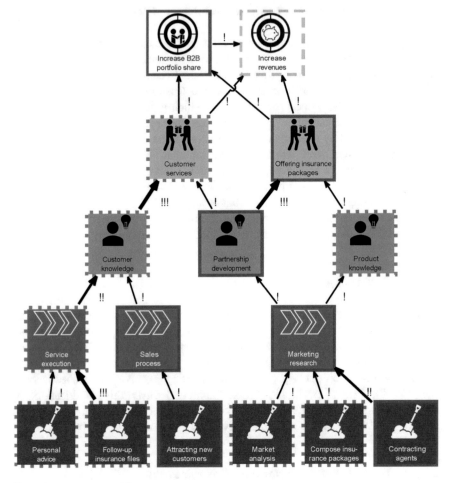

Fig. 6.4 Case study model

6.4.2.4 Strategic Fit Improvement Analysis

Given the business architecture heat map in Fig. 6.4, the following critical path can help identify operational improvements: "Increase revenues"–"Increase B2B portfolio share"–"Offering insurance packages"–"Partnership development"–"Market research"–"Contracting agents." In other words, increasing the number of lucrative B2B contracts can be realized by contracting more external agents. This can be explained as an increased number of sub-agents in a dispersed geographic area will lead to more B2B lead customers. In the longer term, more B2B customers will significantly increase the revenues of the insurance company.

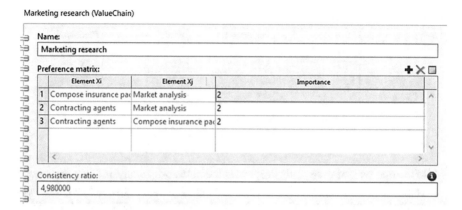

Marketing research (ValueChain)

Fig. 6.5 AHP example of the case study

Increase B2B portfolio share (CustomerGoal)

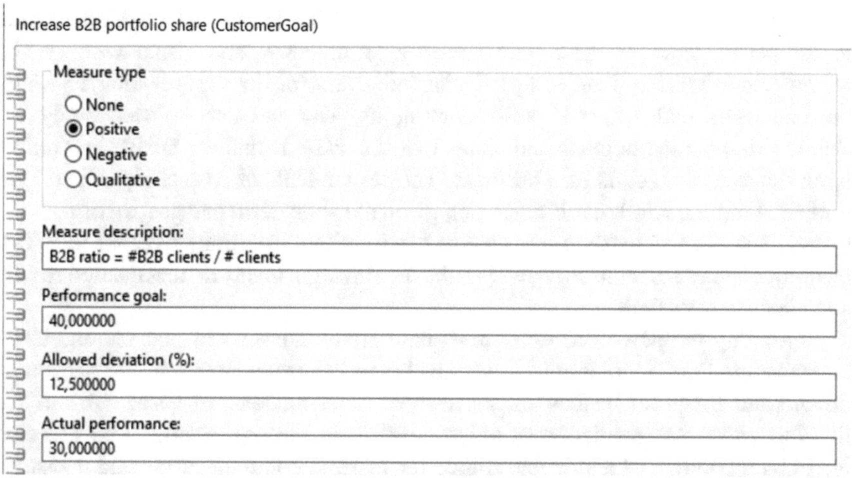

Fig. 6.6 Performance measurement example of the case study

6.4.3   Evaluation

Table 6.4 shows the results of the evaluation based on the questionnaire that was filled in by the end users after completing the PGA modeling procedure. The quantitative results show an average score of 5.09 for strategic fit, 4.81 for performance measurement, 5.23 for perceived usefulness, and 4.91 for perceived ease of use. In general, this means that the end users slightly agree that the PGA technique fulfills its design requirements.

The qualitative feedback that was collected during the evaluation interviews offers additional insights. With respect to strategic fit, the end users of case studies 2.2 and 2.4 have a slight preference to use the PGA method in a top-down approach,

Table 6.4 Case study evaluation results

Case study	Alignment	Performance measurement	Perceived usefulness	Perceived ease of use
2.1	5.35	5.25	4.92	4.28
2.2	5.5	4.5	5.38	4.67
2.3	5	4.5	5.38	5.50
2.4	4.5	5	5.25	5.17
Average	5.09	4.81	5.23	4.91

while the end user of case study 2.3 favors the bottom-up analysis. This preference corresponds with the approach that was followed during the case studies. Although the evaluation aims at the assessment of the application potential of the PGA technique, it is observed that the involved end users remained neutral with respect to the approach they have not experienced yet.

For the performance measurement, case study 2.1 learnt that PGA adds value to the performance of the organization by its objective and visual view on the business architecture. This was particularly relevant for this organization, in which the end users had different political opinions. The end user of case study 2.4 shared this positive opinion and states that the PGA technique enabled to reflect upon the success factors of a business. The respondents of case study 2.2 and 2.3 remained more neutral to this construct, given the short-term perspective of the case study. This is particularly applicable to the item that questions whether the PGA technique improves monitoring within the organization to ensure that desired results are achieved over time.

Regarding the perceived usefulness, case study 2.1 showed that the end users conceive the PGA modeling technique as being better applicable in the context of private and for-profit businesses. Nevertheless, respondents of cases 2.1 and 2.2 like the visual representation of value creation in the organization and perceive the PGA technique as a valuable source for internal communication and decision-making. This is confirmed by the end user in case study 2.3, who states that the PGA technique provides a good blueprint of how the organization is currently working.

Concerning the perceived ease of use, the PGA expert was confronted with multiple end users during the execution of the AHP in case study 2.1. As this provided a new challenge for the application of PGA, the expert and researcher developed a decision tree to reach AHP consensus between end users (see Fig. 6.3). Nevertheless, the qualitative feedback learnt that this AHP challenge largely explains the lower score given by the respondents. Although the PGA implementation is not perceived too difficult during the other case studies, the end users believe that an expert is needed to guide the respondent through the different steps of the PGA modeling procedure.

6.5 Conclusion

This chapter gives an answer to how the initial PGA modeling technique is further shaped by development and use in real-life organizational contexts. To this end, four case studies were performed in a second iteration of ADR research. The case studies were performed by a researcher, a PGA expert, and the respective end users of both public and private organizations. Based on a discussion between the PGA expert and the researcher about the intervention and evaluation, this chapter formalizes the suggested refinements to the modeling language and procedure, which results in PGA version 2.0.

The PGA modeling language was refined with respect to its strategic elements, which include the identification of new value stream relations between the organizational goals and a further specification of the semantics for financial, customer, and internal goal. Furthermore, previous research resulted in a more intuitive notation for five PGA meta-model elements. With respect to the modeling procedure, the case studies enabled to elaborate the step in which the AHP procedure is executed. This involves the development of a new end-user visualization of the AHP comparison scale, a decision tree to obtain AHP consensus between multiple respondents, and concrete guidance to lower the learning curve of the AHP mechanism.

Notwithstanding the two cycles of ADR research, an important issue for the PGA technique remains its long-term application in a practical organizational context. This would enable to analyze the actual impact of the proposed operational changes on the achievement of the organizational objectives, which provides an extra form of evidence besides the perceptions of the involved end users. Therefore, a prolonged PGA case study is an interesting opportunity for future research.

Besides this, a simulation mechanism could be a useful addition to PGA 2.0 as it enables to investigate the impact of process changes on the overall business performance. As such, we would be able to realize a modeling technique that combines a coherent view on both the organizational strategy and processes with a mechanism to analyze the impact of the simulated operational performance on indicators that reflect the overall business performance. Such a simulation mechanism would be a useful tool during a prolonged case study, as it provides a cost-effective, fast, and safe approach to evaluate different process alternatives. A first version of this simulation mechanism is presented in [30] and will be addressed by future PGA research.

Tool Download https://www.omilab.org/pga.

References

1. Andersson, B., Johannesson, P., Zdravkovic, J.: Aligning goals and services through goal and business modelling. Inf. Syst. e-Bus. Manag. **7**(2), 143–169 (2009)

2. Balabko, P., Wegmann, A.: Systemic classification of concern-based design methods in the context of enterprise architecture. Inf. Syst. Frontiers **8**(2), 115–131 (2006)
3. Bleistein, S.J., Cox, K., Verner, J., Phalp, K.T.: B-scp: a requirements analysis framework for validating strategic alignment of organizational it based on strategy, context, and process. Inf. Softw. Technol. **48**(9), 846–868 (2006)
4. Bouwman, H., Solaimani, S.: A framework for the alignment of business model and business processes. Bus. Process Manag. J. **18**(4), 655–679 (2012)
5. Business Architecture Guild: A Guide to the Business Architecture Body of Knowledge® (BIZBOK® Guide), Version 7.0. Tech. rep. (2018)
6. Dalpiaz, F., Franch, X., Horkoff, J.: iStar 2.0 Language Guide. arXiv:1605.07767. Tech. rep. (2016)
7. Davis, F.D.: Perceived usefulness, perceived ease of use, and user acceptance of information technology. MIS Q. **13**(3), 319–340 (1989)
8. de Kinderen, S., Gaaloul, K., Proper, H.A.: Bridging value modelling to archimate via transaction modelling. Softw. Syst. Model. **13**(3), 1043–1057 (2014)
9. Gordijn, J., Petit, M., Wieringa, R.: Understanding business strategies of networked value constellations using goal- and value modeling. In: 14th IEEE International Requirements Engineering Conference (RE'06), pp. 129–138 (2006)
10. Gordijn, J., Yu, E., Raadt, B.V.D.: E-service design using i* and e^3 value modeling. IEEE Softw. **23**(3), 26–33 (2006)
11. Grau, G., Franch, X., Maiden, N.A.: Prim: an i*-based process reengineering method for information systems specification. Inf. Softw. Technol. **50**(1), 76–100 (2008)
12. Guizzardi, R., Reis, A.N.: A method to align goals and business processes. In: Johannesson, P., Lee, M.L., Liddle, S.W., Opdahl, A.L., Pastor López, Ó. (eds.) Conceptual Modeling, pp. 79–93. Springer International Publishing, Cham (2015)
13. Harvard Business Review Analytic Services: Testing Organizational Boundaries to Improve Strategy Execution. Tech. rep. (2018)
14. Henderson, J.C., Venkatraman, H.: Strategic alignment: leveraging information technology for transforming organizations. IBM Syst. J. **32**(1), 4–16 (1993)
15. Hevner, A.R., March, S.T., Park, J., Ram, S.: Design science in information systems research. MIS Q. **28**(1), 6 (2004)
16. Horkoff, J., Barone, D., Jiang, L., Yu, E., Amyot, D., Borgida, A., Mylopoulos, J.: Strategic business modeling: representation and reasoning. Softw. Syst. Model. **13**(3), 1015–1041 (2014)
17. Horkoff, J., Aydemir, F.B., Cardoso, E., Li, T., Maté, A., Paja, E., Salnitri, M., Mylopoulos, J., Giorgini, P.: Goal-oriented requirements engineering: a systematic literature map. In: 2016 IEEE 24th International Requirements Engineering Conference (RE), pp. 106–115 (2016)
18. Huizingen, A., de Vries, E.J.: Information Management: Setting the Scene, 1st edn. Elsevier, Amsterdam (2007)
19. Jacobsen, D.I., Johnsen, Å.: Alignment of strategy and structure in local government. Public Money Manag. **40**(4), 276–284 (2020)
20. Kaplan, R., Norton, D.: Using the balanced scorecard as a strategic management system. Harv. Bus. Rev. **74**(1), 75–85 (1996)
21. Mylopoulos, J.: Conceptual modelling and Telos. In: Loucopoulos, P., Zicari, R. (eds.) Conceptual Modelling, Databases, and CASE: An Integrated View of Information System Development, pp. 49–68. Wiley, New York (1992)
22. OMG: Value Delivery Modeling Language (VDML) 1.1 (2018)
23. Osterwalder, A.: Business Model Generation: A Handbook for Visionaries, Game Changers, and Challengers. Wiley, Hoboken, NJ (2010)
24. Pijpers, V., Leenheer, P., Gordijn, J., Akkermans, H.: Using conceptual models to explore business-ICT alignment in networked value constellations. Requir. Eng. **17**(3), 203–226 (2012)
25. Popova, V., Sharpanskykh, A.: Formal modelling of organisational goals based on performance indicators. Data Knowl. Eng. **70**(4), 335–364 (2011)
26. Porter, M.: Competitive Advantage: Creating and Sustaining Superior Performance. The Free Press, New York, NY (1985)

27. Recker, J.C., Rosemann, M., Indulska, M., Green, P.: Business process modeling : a comparative analysis. J. Assoc. Inf. Syst. **10**(4), 333–363 (2009)
28. Roelens, B., Bork, D.: An evaluation of the intuitiveness of the PGA modeling language notation. In: Nurcan, S., Reinhartz-Berger, I., Soffer, P., Zdravkovic, J. (eds.) Enterprise, Business-Process and Information Systems Modeling, pp. 395–410. Springer International Publishing, Cham (2020)
29. Roelens, B., Poels, G.: Towards a strategy-oriented value modeling language: identifying strategic elements of the VDML meta-model. In: Ng, W., Storey, V.C., Trujillo, J.C. (eds.) Conceptual Modeling. Springer, Berlin (2013)
30. Roelens, B., Poels, G.: The design of a modeling technique to analyze the impact of process simulation throughout the business architecture. In: Pergl, R., Lock, R., Babkin, E., Molhanec, M. (eds.) Enterprise and Organizational Modeling and Simulation, pp. 37–52. Springer International Publishing, Cham (2017)
31. Roelens, B., Steenacker, W., Poels, G.: Strategic alignment: realizing strategic fit within the business architecture: the design of a process-goal alignment modeling and analysis technique. Softw. Syst. Model. **18**(1), 631–662 (2019)
32. Saaty, T.L.: How to make a decision: the analytic hierarchy process. Eur. J. Oper. Res. **48**(1), 9–26 (1990)
33. Schiemann, W.A.: Aligning performance management with organizational strategy, values, and goals. In: Smither, J.W., London, M. (eds.) Performance Management: Putting Research into Action. The Professional Practice Series, pp. 45–87. Jossey-Bass/Wiley, Hoboken, NJ (2009)
34. Sein, M.K., Henfridsson, O., Purao, S., Rossi, M., Lindgren, R.: Action design research. MIS Q. **35**(1), 37–56 (2011)
35. The Open Group: ArchiMate v3.0.1 Specification. Standard C179 (2017)
36. Zachman, J.A.: A framework for information systems architecture. IBM Syst. J. **26**(3), 276–292 (1987)

Chapter 7
The LiteStrat Modelling Method: Towards the Alignment of Strategy and Code

Oscar Pastor, Rene Noel, Ignacio Panach, and Marcela Ruiz

Abstract The integration of goals and business processes models in an MDE context has been widely studied. A specific kind of goals, the organisational goals, are addressed by business strategy. The increasing agility and effect over software systems development of the top-level strategic definitions drive the necessity of considering this domain knowledge into the software development process. However, most of the existing modelling frameworks that consider business strategy concepts are, justifiably, more complex than needed for this specific aim and lack a systematic modelling procedure, hindering their integration in an MDE context. In this chapter, we introduce LiteStrat, a lightweight organisational modelling method for business strategy. By selecting constructs and relationships from existing modelling frameworks, we designed a modelling language and a detailed modelling procedure. We implemented LiteStrat using the ADOxx framework, adapting the LiteStrat's conceptual metamodel to the ADOxx meta^{2}model. Through a lab demo supported by the tool prototype, we demonstrate the feasibility of the proposed method.

Keywords Model-driven development · Business strategy modelling · Organisational modelling

O. Pastor · R. Noel (✉)
PROS Research Centre, Universitat Politècnica de València, Valencia, Spain
e-mail: opastor@pros.upv.es; rnoel@pros.upv.es

I. Panach
Escola Tècnica Superior d'Enginyeria, Universitat de València, València, Spain
e-mail: joigpana@uv.es

M. Ruiz
Zürich University of Applied Sciences, Winterthur, Switzerland
e-mail: marcela.ruiz@zhaw.ch

7.1 Introduction

Model-Driven Engineering (MDE) requires the transformation of different abstraction level models to ensure that the knowledge of domain experts is considered into a model-driven software development process. As software development endeavours are triggered by business needs, a key knowledge domain is *business strategy*, which addresses the definition of the organisational goals and the courses of action to achieve them [11].

Strategic definitions belong to the highest abstraction level of knowledge in information systems engineering, setting the project scope from the perspective of the project planner [23] and contributing to understand the motivation, to guide the design, and to manage the change of business process models [16].

While goals are a well-known topic in information systems modelling, addressing strategy means to deal with multiple and interrelated definitions, as presented by Mintzberg et al. in the *5 Ps of strategy* [11]. Two of these definitions are *strategy as plan*, which considers the definition of a plan that defines the organisational goals and the courses of action to achieve them, and *strategy as ploy*, where specific goals and courses of action are designed to overcome external threats with a dynamic and competitive approach. While strategic planning as a big upfront effort is arguably an obsolete practice, nowadays a dynamic, adaptive, and agile approach to strategy is influencing management, enterprise architecture [21], and software development [15] areas.

As broad as defining what business strategy is, it is the possibility of conceptually modelling its different aspects. Agent-oriented and goal-oriented modelling frameworks such as i* [22] have supported the analysis of social agents dependencies and intentions, in order to explore different strategic configurations for the optimal satisfaction of their goals. Enterprise architecture frameworks have included strategic layers to describe business motivation elements [12, 17] (such as goals, objectives, strategies, and tactics) to support the strategic alignment of the whole organisation among its business, information, application, and technology layers.

While most of the concepts related to business strategy definitions have been covered by goal and enterprise architecture modelling frameworks [10], the integration of these frameworks in an MDE context is still a challenge in (at least) two different ways: (1) The complexity of existing modelling frameworks hinders the straightforward modelling of the business strategy definitions, and (2) the lack of a systematic modelling approach of the existing modelling frameworks hinders the transformation of business strategy into more concrete models (e.g. business process models).

The complexity of the existing modelling frameworks is needed because their purpose is different and broader than just representing the business strategy. Goal-oriented (GO) frameworks provide several types of goals and relationships among them to represent how actions contribute or harm the goals, or what softgoals that qualify these actions, for example. These modelling efforts support automated analysis of whether the goals are satisfied or not [6]. Enterprise architecture (EA) frameworks, such as ArchiMate [18], propose 74 constructs and relationships aiming to cover many organisational layers (business, information, application, and technology), from different viewpoints, to help reflect on and achieve the alignment of organisational strategy and technology. On the other hand, the *prescribed* business strategy definitions, thus, the results after the strategic analysis, can be expressed with a few concepts (such as strategy, tactic, goal, objective, policy, and program) that are mostly hierarchically related [11]. Hence, the complexity of the existing frameworks exceeds what is needed to solely capture the prescribed strategy.

The lack of a systematic way for representing business strategy is also inherited from the purpose of GO and EA frameworks. This modelling freedom is intended to provide flexibility to the analyst for applying these frameworks in different domains, by different stakeholders, and with different purposes. However, it hinders the mapping and/or transformation of models: For example, having different ways of modelling what the objectives of an organisational role are yields to a lack of repeatability in models [5] and, hence, to ambiguous integration points, impeding the design of model transformations and harming the overall quality of the combined modelling languages [7].

In this chapter, we introduce LiteStrat, a novel organisational modelling method that aims for describing business strategy, with low complexity and high emphasis on model integration. Also, we present its implementation under the ADOxx framework [13], as a means to support the agile evolution of the proposal. The contributions of the proposed method are:

- A low complexity language to model business strategy
- A systematic procedure to model business strategy
- A lab demo of the method, using an implementation based on the ADOxx framework

In Sect. 7.2, we describe the method by introducing its main aims, constructs, and modelling procedure, as well as how it differentiates from existing goal-oriented and enterprise architecture modelling frameworks. In Sect. 7.3, we present the conceptualisation of the method, including its metamodel, graphical representation, and naming conventions. In Sect. 7.4, we describe the implementation of LiteStrat in the ADOxx framework and illustrate its application through a working example. Finally, in Sect. 7.6, we present the conclusions and future work, after some discussion in Sect. 7.5.

7.2 Method Description

In this section, we introduce LiteStrat, a modelling method to represent the goals of an organisation and the strategy and structure to achieve these goals, in a systematic way and with a low syntactic and semantic complexity. It aims to provide a language and a procedure to capture and specify the business strategy in the context of meetings with top-level executives, whose domain knowledge and organisational authority enable them to answer the following questions:

- What is happening outside the organisation, and what opportunities or threats it sets to the organisational goals?
- How will the organisation act to take opportunities or mitigate the threats?
- How will the organisation measure the successful implementation of these actions?
- Who is responsible for implementing these actions?

The constructs needed to answer the above questions are certainly present in existing modelling frameworks, although these frameworks lack of systematicity and consider other constructs due to their wider scope and different purpose, as presented in Sect. 7.1. Hence, the design of the LiteStrat method is based on picking up elements from the existing modelling frameworks. In Sect. 7.2.1, we present the rationale for selecting constructs and relationships from the existent modelling frameworks, and in Sect. 7.2.2, we describe the resulting modelling language and procedure.

7.2.1 Related Initiatives

To answer the above questions, it is needed to integrate three business concerns: business motivation, business strategy, and organisation structure. As there are many definitions and interpretations of these concerns, LiteStrat embodies them with the following approaches:

- *Business motivation* explains why a business process must be performed, that is, the organisation's goals. From a business perspective, goals are decided by the leaders of the organisation after assessing the effect of external influences on the enterprise [12]. This is also the approach of LiteStrat.
- There are several definitions of *business strategy*, which vary in their scope and purpose [11]. LiteStrat approaches the business strategy as a plan of action towards the achievement of goals, but using an adaptive approach, where the organisational strategy is continuously adapting to its environment [1]. The business strategy considers both the analysis and the specification of the strategy; LiteStrat is focused on the specification of the strategy.
- *Organisation structure* aims for representing who undertakes organisation activities [18]. While organisation structure is treated separately in some EA modelling frameworks,[1] LiteStrat approaches consider into the strategical level following the business perspective *strategy sets structure and structure breeds behaviour* [2].

---

[1] https://www.omg.org/cgi-bin/doc?bmi/09-08-02.

The above-presented modelling concerns are currently supported by Enterprise Architecture (EA) frameworks such as Business Motivation Model (BMM) [12] and TOGAF [20] (and its modelling language, ArchiMate[18]) but are scattered in several perspectives, given the wider scope of these frameworks. Goal-oriented requirements engineering frameworks such as i* [22] also approach these questions but with an analytical and exploratory purpose.

A detailed comparison of the constructs and relations of LiteStrat with the previously mentioned frameworks is outside the scope of this chapter; we briefly summarise them and comment on their commonalities and differences with LiteStrat.

- BMM [12] allows to represent the business strategy with a business focus: It represents external influences, the assessment of these influences on the organisation, and the definition of the ends and means of the organisation in the context of these influences. LiteStrat shares to some point the purpose of BMM. The main differences between LiteStrat and BMM are:

  - BMM does not provides a systematic approach to the modelling procedure.
  - BMM does not consider the organisation structure in the strategy.
  - LiteStrat does not addresses business policy or resources needed for the strategy, as it is focused on goals and actions to achieve them.
  - LiteStrat does not consider the assessment criteria as it's considered part of the analysis of the strategy and not of the specification.
  - BMM has by far more constructs (17 constructs and 14 relationship types, while LiteStrat has 7 constructs and 3 relationship types).

- TOGAF [20] is an Enterprise Architecture framework by the Open Group, which is supported on the ArchiMate Modelling framework [18]. ArchiMate has been enriched to include business motivation by the Motivation Extension [17]. The Open Group has also been working on the Open Business Architecture [19], a three-part specification aiming to provide a common language to capture and interpret business strategy. LiteStrat differs from TOGAF/ArchiMate approach in its purpose: LiteStrat does not aim to represent the whole organisation architecture, but to support the elicitation and specification of business strategy in a specific context (short meetings). However, LiteStrat uses some of the constructs from the Motivation Extension of ArchiMate such as goal and objectives and also considers organisation structure. From OBA it also takes the approach (similar to BMM) to model the business strategy around an initial external influence.

- i* is an agent-oriented and goal-oriented modelling framework that allows modelling social dependencies among intentional, strategic agents to many applications, including organisation impact analysis. i* allows the specification of several intentional elements (goals, tasks, resources, and soft goals) and their relationships, which can have different configurations and dependencies among agents. LiteStrat exploits i*'s social dependency among agents to illustrate the assignation of responsibilities in the organisation. Also, LiteStrat uses the i*'s goal construct to represent the intention of an organisation unit and the refinement relationship between intentional constructs to represent that the source element is operationalised (thus, made more concrete or being implemented) by the target element. However, LiteStrat differs from i* on its purpose: while i* successfully supports the organisation impact analysis for the exploration of different strategies and business configurations, LiteStrat is only restricted to the specification of an already analysed and defined business strategy. This heavily constrains LiteStrat, but it also simplifies the modelling procedure and language.

7.2.2 The LiteStrat Method

The LiteStrat method consists on (1) a modelling language, (2) a modelling procedure, and (3) specific mechanisms and constraints, consistently with the three conceptual modelling method building blocks proposed in [8].

The **LiteStrat modelling language** has two main groups of constructs: (1) interacting entities and (2) intentional elements. Interacting entities consider actors, organisation units, and roles, which are described below:

- *Actors* are entities that behave regardless of the organisation under analysis; their behaviour cannot be controlled nor specifically defined, but they can *influence* (and can be influenced by) the organisation under analysis.
- *Organisation Units* represent the organisation under analysis and its subunits, which can be hierarchically related to allow modelling the organisational structure. Organisation units can have intentional elements and can influence actors and other organisation units.
- *Roles* are abstractions of well-defined behaviours in the organisation context, which belong to an organisation unit. In a similar way to organisation units, roles can have intentional elements.

The relations among these entities are the influence and containment:

- *Influence* describes an action or behaviour of the source element (actor or organisation unit) that affects the goals of the target element (an actor or organisation unit).
- *Containment* represents the belonging of an organisation unit or role to another organisation unit.

Concerning intentional elements, LiteStrat defines four constructs to describe the motivations of the organisation units and roles:

- *Goals* represent a high-level end of an organisation unit.
- *Strategies* represent a high-level action towards the achievement of a goal.
- *Tactics* represent more concrete actions towards the implementation of a strategy. Tactics involve the optimisation of existing business processes for a high-level quality attribute.

- *Objectives* represent quantifiable steps that allow verifying the successful implementation of a tactic.

It is worth noting that while the term *objective* could also be a synonym of goal, as it means *something that one wants to achieve*,[2] we selected this term given the business context[3] and previous conceptualisations in business motivation modelling [12], where an objective is defined as *a measurable, time-targeted step towards goals*. This is also the meaning that we adopt in our conceptualisation.

Regarding the relations among the before-listed constructs, there are two types of relations for these constructs, which are refinement and containment:

- *Refinement* represents that the source intentional element is operationalised or made more concrete by the target intentional element.
- *Assignment* represents the belonging of an intentional element to an organisation unit or role.

The **LiteStrat modelling procedure** considers four steps, in which the previously detailed constructs and relationships are meaningfully connected. The following steps must be performed for each external influence. If several external influences are affecting the organisation, they must be modelled in separate diagrams, but they are part of the same model:

- Step 1—External Influence Modelling: The procedure starts by identifying an external actor whose influence affects the organisation. The actor and the organisation under analysis are modelled. They are both connected by the influence relation, from the external actor to the organisation. Also, it is needed to analyse and model what would be the organisation goal or goals considering the influence. A SWOT analysis can be performed to identify these goals.
- Step 2—Strategy Modelling: After defining the organisation goal or goals and considering the SWOT analysis, the strategies to achieve the goals must be defined. The goals are connected to their respective strategies by a refinement relation. These strategies are defined at the highest organisation level. Then, each strategy is refined in one or many tactics. Each tactic involves the improvement of an existing business process and must be assigned (contained by) the organisation unit that is responsible for that business process. Strategies are connected to their tactics by a refinement relation.
- Step 3—Role and Responsibility Modelling: For each of the tactics, one or many objectives, thus, implementation indicators, must be defined. It is also needed to model the roles that will be responsible for achieving the objectives. All the objectives must be assigned (contained by) a role.
- Step 4—Reaction Modelling: Finally, the reaction of the organisation is the result of implementing the tactics. This reaction is modelled as influences; hence,

---

[2] https://dictionary.cambridge.org/es/diccionario/ingles/objective

[3] https://www.forbes.com/sites/mikalbelicove/2013/09/27/understanding-goals-strategies-objectives-and-tactics-in-the-age-of-social/

one organisation unit can influence another or influence an external actor. This external actor can be the one identified in Step 1 or a new one. At least one of the influences must go from the organisation or its units to an external actor.

The previously listed steps are presented sequentially; however, the procedure must be considered as iterative and incremental. LiteStrat supports incremental modelling by approaching to one external influence at a time in a single LiteStrat model; in case of simultaneous influences, the procedure is repeated from Step 1 for a new influence, in a new model. Hence, iterative modelling is considered both for every single model and the full set of LiteStrat models. This set of LiteStrat models is the result of the organisation modelling and serves as input for further requirements engineering processes, such as business process re-engineering.

Finally, regarding **LiteStrat mechanisms and constraints**, the correct execution of the modelling procedure will result in a subset of relations among the constructs which are valid and meaningful, while other possible combinations must be constrained. These valid relationships and constraints are further detailed in Sect. 7.3. From a high-level perspective, constraints can be grouped into four groups:

- The hierarchical nature of the intentional elements (e.g. a tactic cannot be refined by a goal, since a tactic is more concrete than a goal)
- The nature of the organisation structure (e.g. roles cannot contain organisation units)
- The correct assignment of intentional elements to organisation units and roles (e.g. a role cannot define a strategy)
- The input and output influences (there must be one influence from the external environment to the organisation and at least one from the organisation to the external environment)

7.3   Method Conceptualisation

In the following subsections, we present the LiteStrat metamodel, covering the concepts and relationships previously introduced in Sect. 7.2. Also, we detail the constraints needed to ensure the integrity of the LiteStrat models, according to the modelling guidelines described in Sect. 7.2. Also, we present the graphical representation and naming conventions for the LiteStrat concepts and relationships.

7.3.1   The LiteStrat Metamodel

The metamodel of LiteStrat is presented in Fig. 7.1. As shown, all the constructs and relations described in the Method Description section are straightforwardly represented. Besides the representation of constructs and relations as classes, the metamodel defines restrictions to the relationships among these classes, which are consistent with the modelling procedure in Sect. 7.2. Here we comment on the relationships among these constructs and how they support the modelling procedure:

- Actors and organisation units relate to each other only through influences. As actors are external entities beyond the knowledge of the organisation under analysis, their internal intentions cannot be accessed. This is presented in the metamodel as the absence of associations with the goal, strategy, tactic, and objective constructs.
- Organisation units can contain other organisation units (is-inside relationship). The organisation unit that is not inside any other organisation unit is the organisation under analysis. Also, organisation units can influence each other.
- The metamodel describes chained refinements that allow goals to only be refined to strategies, strategies to tactics, and tactics to objectives. The multiplicity of the refinement relationships means that strategic elements must be refined and strategies, tactics, and objectives must have a source refinement; thus, they cannot exist without the previous hierarchical level.

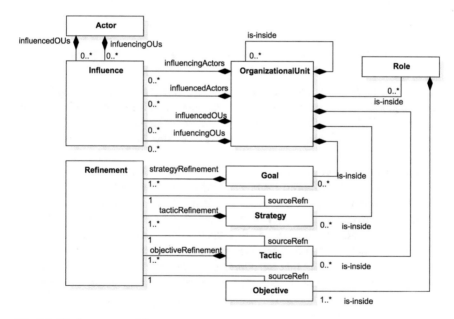

Fig. 7.1 LiteStrat metamodel

- The relations (and their multiplicity) from organisation units to the goal, strategy, and tactic concepts mean that all these elements can be contained by an organisation unit.
- Objectives cannot be refined, as they not are considered strategic elements, and can only be inside roles. The only relationships allowed to the role concept are their participation in organisation units and the assignation of objectives.

Table 7.1 Additional integrity constraints for LiteStrat

ID	Integrity constraint
IC1	The model must have at least one actor influencing an organisation unit
IC2	At least one organisation unit must have one or more goals associated
IC3	At least one organisation unit must have one or more strategies associated
IC4	At least one organisation unit must have one or more tactics inside
IC5	Tactics cannot be inside an organisation unit that is not inside other organisation unit
IC6	Roles cannot be inside an organisation unit that is not inside other organisation unit
IC7	At least one organisation unit must have one or more roles inside
IC8	At least one organisation unit must be inside other organisation unit
IC9	The model must have at least one actor being influenced by an organisation unit

Besides the constraints of the metamodel, there are integrity constraints (IC) that must be checked to completely validate that a LiteStrat model complies with the modelling guidelines. These constraints are presented in Table 7.1.

7.3.2 Graphical Representation and Naming Conventions

As detailed in Fig. 7.2, the graphical representation of LiteStrat provides one different graphical element for each class in the metamodel. Two main constructs for relationships (influence and refinement) have their constructs, too. A third relationship type, the *boundary*, represents the is-inside relationship between organisation units, roles, and intentional elements.

Regarding naming conventions, external actors, organisation units, and roles take their names from the real-world subjects, while refinement and is-inside relationships have no name. For the influence relationship and the intentional elements, the naming conventions are detailed in Table 7.2. For a more precise naming of tactics, we suggest considering a verb related to an optimisation (e.g. improve, reduce), the object related to a business process (product delivery process in the example in Table 7.2), and that the complement describes a quality characteristic. For objectives, we suggest that the object describes a key process indicator, the passive verb describes an optimisation, and a quantifier which allows the objective to be unequivocally verified.

While the current proposal symbols are mostly based on the i*, we think that the notation could be improved by a specific design process. We are currently addressing this issue with a user-centred approach, involving business users and students.

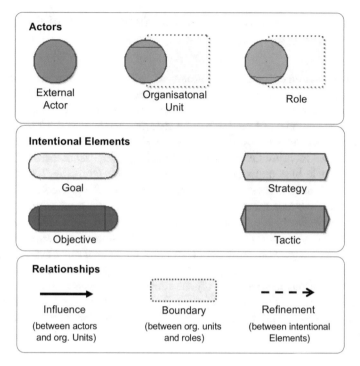

Fig. 7.2 LiteStrat graphical representation

Table 7.2 LiteStrat naming conventions

Construct	Naming convention	Example
Influence	(Actor) + verb + object + complement	Offers faster product delivery
Goal	Object + passive verb	Customers retained
Strategy	Verb + object + (complement)	Grow customer satisfaction
Tactic	Verb + object + (complement)	Reduce product delivery process time
Objective	Object + passive verb + quantifier	Product packing time reduced by 25%

7.4   Proof of Concept

In this section, we present a proof of concept of a LiteStrat supporting tool prototype, implemented on ADOxx. We describe the specific LiteStrat metamodel for ADOxx as well as some implementation considerations, a brief modelling example, and a comment about the advantages of the implementation that can be exploited to improve the modelling procedure and analysis with LiteStrat.

7.4.1 Implementation of a LiteStrat Supporting Tool Prototype on ADOxx

The implementation of the LiteStrat prototype is conceptually based on the ADOxx meta^{2}model introduced in [9] and technologically based on the ADOxx development toolkit version 1.5 [13]. From these two foundations, we adapted the conceptual metamodel of LiteStrat previously presented in Sect. 7.3.1 to the specific LiteStrat metamodel for ADOxx, presented in Fig. 7.3.

The ADOxx meta^{2}model classes from which the LiteStrat constructs inherit are coloured in pale blue and stereotyped as *metametamodel* in Fig. 7.3. As ADOxx *Relation* class only allows to define one construct as the source of the relation and another construct as the target of the relation, the implementation of the *Influence* and *Refinement* relations of the original LiteStrat metamodel need specific adaptations. Hence, we introduced two main abstractions: the *IntentionalElement* abstraction which generalises the goal, strategy, tactic, and objective constructs to allow them to be related by the same relation class (*Refinement*) and the *Influencer* abstraction, to group the actor and organisational unit constructs and to allow them to relate using the relationship (*Influence*). Both abstractions are coloured in yellow and are considered abstract classes, as they have no graphical representations in the prototype.

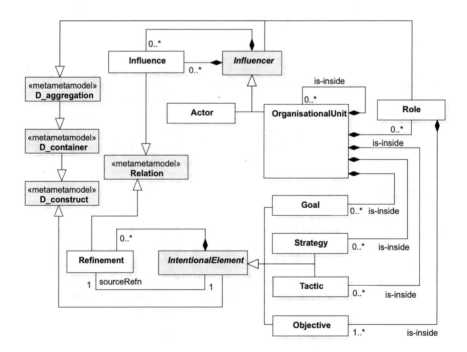

Fig. 7.3 LiteStrat metamodel adaptation for its implementation in ADOxx

Table 7.3 Additional integrity constraints for LiteStrat implementation in OMiLAB

ID	Additional integrity constraints
AIC1	Goals must not be refined from other elements, and must be refined only by strategies
AIC2	Strategies must only be refinements of goals and be only refined by tactics
AIC3	Tactics must only be refinements of strategies and be only refined by objectives
AIC4	Objectives must only be refinements of tactics and cannot be refined
AIC5	Strategies, tactics, and objectives must be refinements
AIC6	Actors cannot have elements inside of them nor be inside another element
AIC7	All Actors must be influenced by some organisational unit or influence an organisational unit
AIC8	Actors cannot be influenced by other actors or influence other actors
AIC9	All roles must have at least one objective
AIC10	All objectives must be inside roles
AIC11	Roles can only contain objectives

The adaptation of the LiteStrat metamodel allows to simplify the prototype from the perspective of the end user; otherwise, it would be needed to have different arrows to connect goals to strategies, strategies to tactics, and tactics to goals, as well as to connect actors to organisation units, organisation units to actors, and organisation units among them. However, some constraints from the original metamodel in Fig. 7.1 were lost and must be checked to preserve the integrity of the LiteStrat models. These additional constraints are detailed in Table 7.3 and, along with the original integrity constraints in Table 7.1, were implemented through a "Validate Model" menu option and using ADOxx scripting features.

In Fig. 7.4, we present a screenshot of the LiteStrat Supporting Tool prototype. This prototype is publicly available in ADOxx Developer Community website [14].

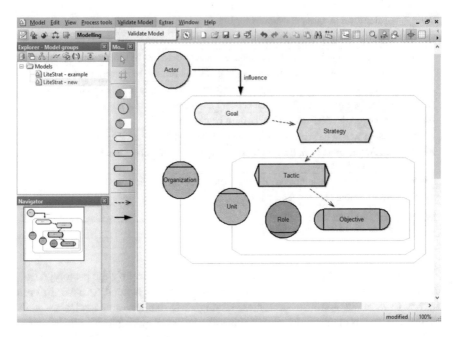

Fig. 7.4 Screenshot from the LiteStrat supporting tool prototype

7.4.2   Example of Application

To illustrate the application of the LiteStrat method and prototype, the following working example describes how the organisation under analysis defines a goal and the strategy to achieve it, given an external influence.

PCPart is the leader company in the computer component retail market in its local country. Recently, a new competitor named FastComp has entered the market, with a similar product offer, but with high focus in customer satisfaction value offer. PCPart acknowledges that its customers complain about long delivery times. PCPart is worried about losing its market leadership, and it intends to retain the market share that it already has. To achieve it, PCPart decides to improve the satisfaction of its customers in all ways possible. A specific course of action is to reduce the time of the product delivery process, which is managed by the Operations Area (Ops Area). To assess the successful implementation of the course of action, two key indicators are defined: to reduce the maximum delivery time by 25% and to reduce customer complaints with product delivery by 50%, which are assigned to the Logistics Manager and Post-Sale Manager, respectively. With this approach, PCPart aims to offer an improved delivery service to its customers.

By following the LiteStrat method presented in Sect. 7.2, we modelled the example following the four modelling steps: (1) the External actor influence, (2) the Organisation strategy, (3) responsibility assignment, and (4) the reaction of the organisation. The result is presented in Fig. 7.5.

The application of the modelling procedure detailed in Sect. 7.2 yields to the following modelling decisions:

- Step 1—External Influence Modelling: The competitor is modelled as an actor (*FastComp*) and its value offers as an influence (*high customer satisfaction value offer*) towards the organisation under analysis (*PCPart*). The main intention of the organisation given the external influence is modelled as a goal (*Market share retained*).
- Step 2—Strategy Modelling: The high-level action to achieve the goal is modelled as a strategy (*Improve customer satisfaction*) and the specific optimisation action as a tactic (*Improve the efficiency delivery process*).
- Step 3—Role and Responsibility Modelling: The indicators and responsibilities for a successful implementation of the tactic are modelled as objectives (*Maximum delivery time reduced by 25%* and *Customer delivery complaints reduced by 50%*) and roles (*Logistics Manager* and *Post-Sale Manager*), respectively.
- Step 4—Reaction Modelling: Finally, the organisation reaction towards the environment to achieve its goal is modelled as an influence (*improved delivery service* to an actor representing the customers (*Customer*).

7.5 Discussion

The proposed method aims to produce repeatable models, so it is possible to define several integration points with business process models. For example, since LiteStrat will always produce models in which organisational roles have assigned objectives from their organisational unit, it is possible to use the GoBis [16] technique to transform this relationship into a business process interaction between the role responsible for the objective and a superior role responsible for the unit, in which the actual value of the objective to be achieved is delivered. It is also possible to consider each LiteStrat diagram as the initial organisational modelling required for a business process purpose analysis, as proposed by De la Vara in [4]. Even though these or other integrations need to be formally designed, we believe that the well-defined modelling procedure and the simple and unambiguous language of LiteStrat are a good starting point.

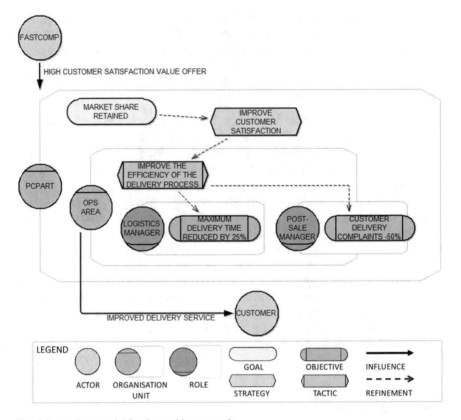

Fig. 7.5 LiteStrat model for the working example

However, while LiteStrat notation and procedure simplify modelling with respect to GO and EA frameworks, they also have limitations. Regarding EA modelling frameworks, LiteStrat clearly needs to be integrated with other modelling frameworks to support strategic alignment with business process and information systems layers. Comparing LiteStrat with GO frameworks, GO frameworks have a richer set of relationships, so they better support the analysis of different configurations of strategic elements for goal achievement, while LiteStrat is not focused on the analysis but in the specification.

Although further empirical research must be conducted, we think that the proposal could be easily adopted by business users, given its simplicity and experience reports using simplified versions of i* such as those reported by Carvallo and Franch in [3], where business stakeholders modelled the organisational context as part of a hybrid systems architecting method.

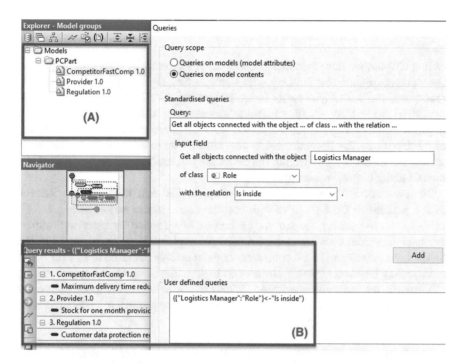

Fig. 7.6 ADOxx prototype features: (**a**) Model grouping and (**b**) Model querying

Regarding LiteStrat's application, while the example could seem simplistic, the strength of the LiteStrat method lies in putting together many models for different analyses, for example, for many external influences, or different tactics for the same strategy. The LiteStrat prototype implementation allows to fully exploit this strength, thanks to two features provided by the ADOxx development environment:

- The Model Group feature allows the creation of many LiteStrat models which are related to the same feature. For example, as depicted in Fig. 7.6a, three different models can serve to model simultaneous external events influencing PCPart, regarding new competitors (the example described in the previous subsection), changes in regulatory policies, and other influences by providers.
- The Analysis tools, in particular the Query feature, allow answering questions based on all the models from a group. In Fig. 7.6b, a query is shown to look for all the objectives that are assigned to the Logistics Manager role. These analyses are useful for further business process modelling.

These features allow to apply LiteStrat in real-world problems, providing complexity and scalability management and supporting the agile evolution of the method and the language [8].

7.6   Conclusions

In this chapter, we have introduced LiteStrat, an organisational modelling method for representing business strategy with a simple language, a systematic modelling procedure, and with focus on its future integration with business process models in a MDE context. By adapting LiteStrat's metamodel to ADOxx meta^{2}model, we implemented a prototype tool and performed a lab demo to illustrate the feasibility of the proposal. The implementation also allowed us to explore the feasibility of scaling the method, by managing the complexity of multiple strategies in different models under a single model group.

Future work is focused on two main topics. The first topic is the evolution of the method and the tool, through real-life case studies and experiments. We aim to explore whether the current method can be applied by users with different modelling skills and strategic knowledge, explore the expressiveness of the method, and discover if new constructs or perspectives could be useful for better representing business strategy. The second topic is the design and implementation of a transformation technique from LiteStrat to business process models, in order to take advantage of LiteStrat's well-defined modelling procedure to define precise integration points and mapping mechanisms.

Acknowledgments This project has the support of the Spanish Ministry of Science and Innovation through the DATAME project (ref: TIN2016-80811-P) and PROMETEO/2018/176 and co-financed with ERDF and the National Agency for Research and Development (ANID)/Scholarship Program/Doctorado Becas Chile/2020-72210494.

Tool Download https://www.omilab.org/litestrat

References

1. Boston Consulting Group: Your strategy needs a strategy | adaptive strategy. https://www.bcg.com/publications/collections/your-strategy-needs-strategy/adaptive (2021). Accessed 23 March 2021
2. Brodie, P.: Deciding your organization structure for 2021. https://www.forbes.com/sites/forbescoachescouncil/2021/01/04/deciding-your-organization-structure-for-2021/?sh=5be9a3b450a6 (2021). Accessed 04 March 2021
3. Carvallo, J.P., Franch, X.: On the use of i* for architecting hybrid systems: A method and an evaluation report. In: IFIP Working Conference on The Practice of Enterprise Modeling, pp. 38–53. Springer, Berlin (2009)
4. de la Vara, J.L., Sánchez, J., Pastor, Ó.: Business process modelling and purpose analysis for requirements analysis of information systems. In: International Conference on Advanced Information Systems Engineering, pp. 213–227. Springer, Berlin (2008)
5. Estrada, H., Rebollar, A.M., Pastor, O., Mylopoulos, J.: An empirical evaluation of the i* framework in a model-based software generation environment. In: Dubois, E., Pohl, K. (eds.) Advanced Information Systems Engineering, vol. 4001, pp. 513–527. Springer, Berlin (2006)

6. Franch, X., López, L., Cares, C., Colomer, D.: The i* framework for goal-oriented modeling. In: Domain-Specific Conceptual Modeling, pp. 485–506. Springer, Berlin (2016)
7. Giraldo-Velásquez, F.D., España Cubillo, S., Giraldo, W.J., Pastor López, O.: Evaluating the quality of a set of modelling languages used in combination: a method and a tool. Inf. Syst. **77**, 48–70 (2018)
8. Karagiannis, D.: Agile modeling method engineering. In: Proceedings of the 19th Panhellenic Conference on Informatics, pp. 5–10 (2015)
9. Karagiannis, D., Buchmann, R.A., Burzynski, P., Reimer, U., Walch, M.: Fundamental conceptual modeling languages in OMiLAB. In: Domain-Specific Conceptual Modeling, pp. 3–30. Springer, Berlin (2016)
10. Kitsios, F., Kamariotou, M.: Business strategy modelling based on enterprise architecture: a state of the art review. Busin. Proc. Manag. J. **25**, 606–624 (2019)
11. Mintzberg, H., Ghoshal, S., Lampel, J., Quinn, J.B.: The Strategy Process: Concepts, Contexts, Cases. Pearson Education, London (2003)
12. Objetc Management Group: Business Motivation Model Specification Version 1.3. https://www.omg.org/spec/BMM/About-BMM/
13. OMiLAB: The ADOxx metamodelling platform - adoxx.org. https://www.adoxx.org/live/home. Accessed 01 March 2021
14. OMiLAB: The ADOxx metamodelling platform - developer space - adoxx.org. https://www.adoxx.org/live/development-spaces. Accessed 01 March 2021
15. Richard, K., Leffingwell, D.: Safe 5.0 distilled: Achieving business agility with the scaled agile framework (2020)
16. Ruiz, M., Costal, D., España, S., Franch, X., Pastor, O.: Gobis: an integrated framework to analyse the goal and business process perspectives in information systems. Inf. Syst. **53**, 330–345 (2015). https://doi.org/10.1016/j.is.2015.03.007
17. The Open Group: Archimate® 2.1 specification - motivation extension. https://pubs.opengroup.org/architecture/archimate2-doc/chap10.html. Accessed 09 Nov 2020
18. The Open Group: The ArchiMate® enterprise architecture modeling language | the open group website. https://www.opengroup.org/archimate-forum/archimate-overview. Accessed 21 Dec 2020
19. The Open Group: The open group publications | standards - business architecture. https://publications.opengroup.org/standards/business-architecture. Accessed on 09 Nov 2020
20. The Open Group: The TOGAF® standard, version 9.2. https://publications.opengroup.org/c182. Accessed 09 Nov 2020
21. The Open Group: The Open Agile Architecture™standard. https://publications.opengroup.org/standards/c208. Accessed 21 Jan 2021
22. Yu, E.: Modeling strategic relationships for process reengineering. Soc. Model. Requir. Eng. **11**(2011), 66–87
23. Zachman, J.: A framework for information systems architecture. IBM Syst. J. **26**(3), 276–292 (1987)

Chapter 8
itsVALUE: Modelling and Analysing Value Streams for IT Services

Henning Dirk Richter, Birger Lantow, and Thomas Pröpper

Abstract In 2020, the new ITIL 4 standard was introduced. ITIL standardisation had and still has a big influence on how IT Service Management is seen and performed in practice. Thus, the new standard is expected to have a high impact as well. A key element of ITIL 4 is the strong focus on Stakeholder Value in the analysis of IT Services. Yet apart from ITIL, stakeholder orientation is a current trend in business analysis. *its*VALUE method and Modeller provide means to model and analyse value delivery in IT Services and thus can be used in Service Design. It combines "traditional" approaches to value stream analysis and service modelling and ads concepts and functionalities that meet the requirements of IT Service Management and ITIL 4. The resulting approach is unique in its combination of modelling and analysis capabilities and helps implement the advantages of value orientation in IT Service Management.

Keywords ITIL · Service modelling · Service value · Value stream modelling · Stakeholder value · Service blueprinting · IT Service Management

8.1 Introduction

A new era in the field of IT has begun, as services are the biggest and most dynamic market component of both industrial and developing countries [3]. Moreover, services are the most important goods for generating organisational value for both the company itself and its customers. Further, almost any current service is supported by IT components, and IT is developing as fast as never before in human history. Thus, companies can take advantage of enhancing their understanding and

H. D. Richter (✉) · B. Lantow
University of Rostock, Rostock, Germany
e-mail: henning.richter@uni-rostock.de; birger.lantow@uni-rostock.de

T. Pröpper
Prevolution GmbH & Co. KG, Hamburg, Germany
e-mail: t.proepper@prevolution.de

performance for IT Service Management. New techniques (e.g. cloud computing, machine learning, blockchain, etc.) enabled new opportunities for the value chains and value creation of companies. Thus, IT (especially IT Service Management) is one of the most important business drivers that companies should carefully consider nowadays to achieve competitive advantage. ITIL v3 is a well-known reference for best practices in IT Service Management. It describes processes, roles, and KPIs. Current trends like increasing market dynamics, the advent of agile software development, and the integration of products and services made a revision necessary. In 2020, ITIL 4 was released. It primarily focuses on enabling responding to new stakeholder demand quickly and simply. According to [3], a company's purpose is to create value for its stakeholders. Everything a company does must serve (directly or implicitly) creating value for its stakeholders. ITIL has a strong industrial background, and it is likely that many companies will adopt the new version in order to improve their IT Service Management capabilities. While ITIL 4 generally describes these capabilities and their integration, a concrete method or toolset for the integration of stakeholder value in service design is not provided. Even if an enterprise does not intend to implement ITIL 4, considering Stakeholder Value in IT Service Management can improve demand orientation.

A literature analysis [9] showed that there are approaches like IT Self-Service Blueprint[15] or VSD 4.0 [6, 7] that support modelling and analysis of IT Service delivery from a value and stakeholder-oriented perspective. However, these are either specialised on a certain use case (e.g. IT S-SB) or just miss some aspects and requirements of value delivery modelling that are important to ITIL v4. Furthermore, there are notations like Value Delivery Modelling Language[1] (VDML) and the Archimate Motivation Extension[2] that provide the necessary modelling concepts. Yet, there is no method support in terms of procedures and guidelines for the creation and usage of models. Usage of these notations for value-oriented IT Service Management would also imply a further operationalisation since they remain on a high abstraction level. "It's a Value Added Language You Employ" (*its*VALUE) has been developed to provide a method and a tool (the *its*VALUE Modeller) for modelling and analysing IT Service value delivery that can be generally applied to IT Services and that is built on proven concepts of Service-, Value, and Enterprise Modelling (references can be found in the sections discussing the method). Thus, it fills a gap in terms of missing tool, method, and notation support, for value-oriented design and analysis of IT Services.

The description of *its*VALUE in this chapter follows roughly the method framework suggested by Goldkuhl et al. [5]. According to them, a method consists of method components that can be arranged and combined based on the application context of the method. The framework defines the dependencies and conditions of component usage, and each component defines procedures, concepts, and a notation. Following this view on a method, the *its*VALUE framework and components and

---

[1] https://www.omg.org/spec/VDML/.

[2] https://pubs.opengroup.org/architecture/archimate3-doc/.

thus the process of *its*VALUE application are described in Sect. 8.2. The meta-model describing the complete notation and forming a base for the *its*VALUE Modeller implementation is presented in Sect. 8.3. An exemplary view and more detailed knowledge on modelling and analysing value delivery using the *its*VALUE Modeller can be obtained in Sect. 8.4. The last Sect. 8.5 describes the current state of the development and provides an outlook to next steps to foster *its*VALUE application.

8.2   The *its*VALUE Method

As mentioned in the introduction, *its*VALUE brings together and amends proven concepts of Service-, Value-, and Enterprise Modelling in order to support Value Stream analysis for IT Services, especially with a focus on ITIL v4 [3] because of its practical relevance. According to the ITIL 4 documentation [1, 3], *value* is a set of a perceived usefulness, importance, and benefits of something. This goes beyond "traditional" value stream analysis and value modelling, where the focus lies on value stream optimisation in terms of processing times and modelling the exchange of economic value. Furthermore, ITIL 4 recommends Service Blueprinting to model and understand the customer journey. The key features of Service Blueprints are customer actions and the physical evidence seen by the customer during the various stages of the service delivery. Service Blueprinting has some tradition as a modelling approach in Service Science (see, e.g. [4]). Service Blueprints allows everyone in the organisation to visualise an entire service process and its underlying business processes. It makes all points of customer contact and physical evidence explicit. This helps analyse the stakeholder perspective in a service setting. Yet, the "traditional" Service Blueprinting approach does not consider the complexity of IT Services. We developed *its*VALUE to provide a sound combination of new ideas and requirements for value-oriented IT Service Management based on ITIL 4 and the named "traditional" approaches. Thus, key elements of *its*VALUE are taken from VSA 4.0/VSM 4.0/VSD 4.0 [6, 7, 10, 11] and VSMN [8] as extensions of "traditional" value stream modelling that considers information processing and stakeholder perspectives, IT Self-Service Blueprint[15] as an approach that adds information technology to "traditional" Service Blueprints, and 4EM [14] as a participatory Enterprise Modelling method that supports the integration of stakeholders and provides concepts that allow to model context influence on value delivery.

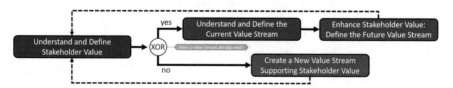

Fig. 8.1 *its*VALUE framework

The *its*VALUE method consists of four components that describe the steps to model, analyse, and (re-)design value streams of IT Services. Figure 8.1 shows the method framework, aligning the components in a process. Two alternatives are distinguished depending on whether there is already an existing value stream or not. As shown in the figure, we understand that the method has to follow an iterative approach in order to develop the required insight into the analysed value stream. We recommend also performing approximately four iterations of *its*VALUE, especially for an entirely new service.

*its*VALUE defines three model types that are used to collect and represent the resulting artefacts of the method components. Table 8.1 provides a brief overview. The generation of these models is described in the respective method components. Sections 8.2.1, 8.2.2, 8.2.3, and 8.2.4 introduce each component of *its*VALUE in detail.

Table 8.1 *its*VALUE model types

	Value Perception Model (VPM)	Stakeholder Value Map (SVM)	Value Stream Blueprint (VSB)
Purpose	Identify relevant stakeholders, their values, and value delivery perceptions of the value stream components (affecting objects)	Understand and define the relations between different Stakeholder values	Define and analyse AS-IS and TO-BE value streams. Identification of involved activities/processes, resources, and their relations. Mapping between value stream components (affecting objects) and Stakeholder values
Main concepts	Stakeholder, value, affecting objects (process, IT system, ...), values/affects relations	Value, problem, opportunity, cause, supports/hinders/contradicts relations	Activity/process, information flow, affecting objects (process, IT system, ...), interface, waste, requires/generates/affects relations
Method components	Understand and define Stakeholder value	Understand and define Stakeholder value	Understanding/defining/creating/improving value streams

8.2.1   Understand Stakeholder Value (SV)

The first phase of our major *its*VALUE approach model focuses on understanding and explicitly defining what each relevant stakeholder affected by a service actually values (see Fig. 8.2). Besides the customers, [2] lists employees, managers, suppliers, partners, the media, public, and much more as important stakeholders a company should also consider. It is recommended to explore and understand the needs of each relevant stakeholder to define what they value. Different approaches for assessing this information seem reasonable, depending on the relationship to a stakeholder. For instance, close customers or employees can be directly interviewed, whereas the public or media should be investigated by continuous monitoring of the own image. AXELOS [2] underlines that the closer the collaboration with a stakeholder is, the more affected they are. Thus, they should receive more attention in tracking their value perceptions.

The results of these investigations are modelled in the Value Perception Model. An example can be found in Sect. 8.4.1, Fig. 8.12. A Value Perception Model is is created for each relevant stakeholder. In these models, the stakeholder's value assumptions are placed around the stakeholder. Each modelled Stakeholder Value should be classified regarding its Relevance Factor (RF) and Current Performance Level (CPL):

- **Relevance Factor:** For the RF, we defined four rating values: *Mandatory*, *Moderate*, *High*, and *Outstanding*. Here, we adopted the idea of distinguishing between hygiene and success factors from [13]. A stakeholder value is considered as a hygiene factor if it causes dissatisfaction when missing while not providing much potential to increase satisfaction when delivered. Oppositely, we understand *Moderate*, *High*, and *Outstanding* Stakeholder Values as different levels of relevance for success factors: If success factors are provided, they increase satisfaction (depending on relevance) while causing not much dissatisfaction when missing.
- **Current Performance Level:** Current Performance Levels reflect the perceived performance of value delivery. If new value streams or value stream components like Processes, IT-Systems, or interfaces are designed, Current Performance Levels cannot be assessed. However, our method requires a CPL for each Stakeholder Value to perform a value stream analysis as later presented in Sect. 8.2.2.2. Thus, a default CPL should be defined for new Value Streams and new Value Stream components. For the CPL, we define the following rating values: *Poor*, *Moderate*, *High*, and *Outstanding*. We recommend to use *Moderate*

Fig. 8.2 *its*VALUE component: understand Stakeholder value

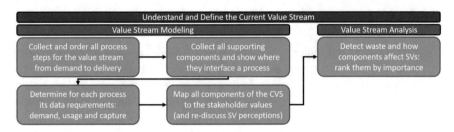

Fig. 8.3 *its*VALUE Approach model: define the current value stream

as the default value for the CPL, as this setting does not influence value stream analysis outcomes (cf. Sect. 8.2.2.2).

Once each relevant stakeholder's value perception is explicitly defined, the dependencies and relations among all Stakeholder Values should be investigated. We understand Stakeholder Value as a specialisation of business goals in the sense of [14]. Thus, delivering different values may cause mutual support, obstruction, or even contradiction. For example, an extra validation activity may reduce the risk within a Value Stream and thus provide value but also negatively influence value delivery in terms of short processing times. The results are reflected in the Stakeholder Value Map. Understanding how different Stakeholder Values affect each other can assist companies in detecting which Stakeholder Value are beneficial or problematical to other Stakeholder Values. Combined with the RF and CPL of a value, such an understanding can be useful for deciding which Stakeholder Values is more important than another when defining development actions (Fig. 8.3).

8.2.2   Understand and Model the Current Value Stream (CVS)

A Value Stream is a series of steps carried out by a company to create and deliver products or services to their consumers [1, 3]. When structuring a company's activities as Value Streams, a clear overview is created, showing what the company actually delivers. Services can be analysed for elements hindering the workflow and activities not adding any value. Such activities are commonly referred to as *"waste"* and should be eliminated. According to [1, 3], Value Streams focus on the end-to-end flow of activity from demand to value. Value Streams are not processes, but they can reference them. The processes are units of work (at different granularities or contexts). Value Streams use the information provided by stakeholders as inputs or other Value Streams and use resources of service providers and service consumers to generate outputs required to create outcomes demanded by the stakeholders. Key objectives are maximising value generation and minimising waste.

If a Value Stream already exists, it must be modelled, understood, and analysed before it can be improved. The second component of our *its*VALUE method deals with these issues. It is divided into two sub-components: first, the value stream modelling which is described in Sect. 8.2.2.1 and, second, the analysis described in Sect. 8.2.2.2. Though dividing both components, both are able to provide new insights into value stream performance.

8.2.2.1 Modelling and Connecting the CVS with the SVs

In the first step, any process or activity that is part of the Current Value Stream should be collected and ordered from the initial demand to the final delivery (cf. [6, 7]). We developed the Value Stream Blueprint for the visual representation of the value stream. It is described more precisely in Sect. 8.4.3. Basically, it is a combination of IT Self-Service Blueprint and Value Stream Model and Notation that can be used to model Value Streams.

After processes and activities have been collected, all additional components (e.g. storage media, IT systems, physical evidence, information, waiting times, etc.) should be collected and connected to the processes and activities they are used or required at. This step can also be carried out by using a Value Stream Blueprint. It combines steps 2 and 3 known from Value Stream Analysis 4.0 [6, 7].

Afterwards, required data for each process or activity should be defined (step 4 of Value Stream Analysis 4.0). Therefore, the following information of each desired or captured data should be defined: *desired (yes/no)*, *captured (yes/no)*, *used (yes/no)*, and *acquisition (automatically/manually)*. Collecting these information for each data of each process or action allows calculating Key Performance Indicators for value stream analysis (cf. Sect. 8.2.2.2).

Next, we advise mapping all components of the Current Value Stream to the Value Perception Models created earlier. The Value Perception Models describe Stakeholder Values belonging to their stakeholder. To map these Value Perception Models with all components that are part of the Current Value Stream, each component should be analysed with regard to its actual effects on any Stakeholder Value. This identification provides awareness and understanding of the Current Value Stream and Stakeholder Values. It is possible to detect hidden, indirect effects of components in the value stream on the value perceptions as well as new value perceptions. While new value perceptions should be added to the respective Value Perception Model, an indirect effect will be further investigated in the analysis step.

8.2.2.2 Analysing the CVS: Detection of Waste and Ranking

In this step, waste inside the Current Value Stream and potential improvement spots are detected (steps 5 and 6 from Value Stream Analysis 4.0 [6, 7]). Besides cycle time analysis from "traditional" value stream analysis, we distinguish between the analysis of data processing and the analysis of stakeholder perspectives. Generally, the analysis concentrates on value stream components that cause poor performance in value delivery (e.g. long idle times, increased effort, or general obstacles) and are thus considered wasteful or as producing "waste". *its*VALUE provides different mechanisms of waste detection. With regard to data processing, VSB allows identifying missed digitisation potentials and mismatches between information demand and provision. Furthermore, waste can be detected and analysed based on the mapping to Stakeholder Value Maps. Both analysis mechanisms are explained in the following. A third implemented mechanism for waste detection uses timing information to identify, for example, idle times. For reasons of brevity, it is not further described.

- **Data processing:** According to Meudt et al. [10, 11], data can generate waste regarding its usage, acquisition, processing, and storage. They originally derived the Digitisation Rate, Data Availability, and Data Usage Key Performance Indicators. These are calculated as described in Fig. 8.4. The required information for calculation is part of the Current Value Stream model (cf. Sect. 8.2.2.1). If the Digitisation Rate is lower than 1, the process has the potential to become more automatised and thus more efficient. If the Data Availability is not equal to 1, the process receives either not enough required or too much unnecessary data. If the Data Usage is lower than 1, the process captures unnecessary data. To conclude, with every Key Performance Indicator close or even equal to 1, a process produces very low or even no waste ([7, 11]).

- **Stakeholder perspectives:** ITIL 4 demands that each activity of a Value Stream should generate more value than it consumes. This originates from an economic perspective of value. Here, consumed value means costs that can be calculated for value delivery activities. Waste would be negative revenue from an activity. Especially in the service domain, there are also intangible, non-economic values like fun or simplicity delivered. Consequently, these values are generally not quantifiable in terms of costs and revenues. The VPMs mostly describe this "unquantifiable" type of value. Thus, *its*VALUE does not focus on the detection of negative revenues. Instead, we concentrate on the identification of the analysis and detection of waste based on RF, CPL, and dependencies in the Value Perception Models. We developed an algorithm detecting for each component of a Value Stream how it supports and hinders Stakeholder Values. With the Supporting Score and Hindering Score of such a component, we defined two new Key Performance Indicators addressing this issue: the Supporting Score (SS) and Hindering Score (HS) of a component. Not considering economic values, we are not dealing with a metric scale. A direct calculation of created value against the detected waste of negative influences on the delivery of certain Stakeholder Values is problematic. Therefore, interpretation of both is left to human analysis.

$$DR = \frac{\sum automatically\ acquired\ (and\ digitally\ captured)\ data}{\sum captured\ data}$$

$$DA = \frac{\sum captured\ data}{\sum desired\ data} \qquad\qquad DU = \frac{\sum used\ data}{\sum captured\ data}$$

Fig. 8.4 Calculating the DR, DA, and DU, according to [7, 11]

$$RF : \begin{cases} 3 & \textbf{if} \quad \textit{"Mandatory"} \\ 1 & \textbf{if} \quad \textit{"Moderate"} \\ 2 & \textbf{if} \quad \textit{"High"} \\ 3 & \textbf{if} \quad \textit{"Outstanding"} \end{cases} \quad CPL : \begin{cases} -3 & \textbf{if} \quad \textit{"Poor"} \\ 1 & \textbf{if} \quad \textit{"Moderate"} \\ 2 & \textbf{if} \quad \textit{"High"} \\ 3 & \textbf{if} \quad \textit{"Outstanding"} \end{cases} \quad IF : \begin{cases} \frac{1}{2} & \textbf{if} \quad \textit{"Low"} \\ 1 & \textbf{if} \quad \textit{"Moderate"} \\ \frac{3}{2} & \textbf{if} \quad \textit{"High"} \end{cases}$$

$$VW = RF \times CPL$$

Fig. 8.5 Variable assignments and calculating the Value Weight of a Stakeholder Value

The SS provides the created Stakeholder Value attributed to a Value Stream component, while the Hindering Score provides the waste attributed to that component. Thus, it is possible to identify components creating much value as well as components creating no value at all and also components that create waste by non-performance or hindering the creation of value. The calculation is based on the Value Weight (VW) as shown in Fig. 8.5. In addition to the ratings of the Value Perception Model, an influence factor (IF) of a component affecting service delivery can be specified for fine-tuning. Based on the VW, the SS (sum of positive Value Weights) and HS (sum of negative Value Weights) are calculated considering direct and indirect supports and hinder relations in the model. The weights assigned to the ratings "Mandatory", "Moderate", etc. are a first suggestion and need to be evaluated in the future.

- **Ranking of potential improvement spots:** The Key Performance Indicators previously described are used to identify potential improvement spots. Further, key Stakeholder Value can be identified as well, showing which Stakeholder Value or key components require enhancements the most. Those Stakeholder Values having a low CPL and high RF also embody a high potential for improvement. Therefore, the Supporting Score and Hindering Score of all affecting components can be considered as well. If they do not support those Stakeholder Values or even hinder them, they embody a high potential of improvement. This could reveal which specific development actions are required to directly enhance any Stakeholder Value. Moreover, we also recommend to consider the Stakeholder Value Map earlier created as well (see Sects. 8.2.1 and 8.4.2), as it might assist not missing out any problematically dependencies or relations between several Stakeholder Values. Understanding those relations might assist in identifying the best development actions to enhance as much Stakeholder Values as best as possible. Furthermore, the data processing Key Performance Indicators can be used to identify media breaches and other problems in the data supply.

8.2.3   Enhance Stakeholder Value: Define the Future Value Stream (FVS)

Once the Current Value Stream is understood and explicitly defined, one or multiple potential Future Value Streams can be developed. For this purpose, we derived our approach model (see Fig. 8.6) in reference to [10, 11, 14]. The Stakeholder

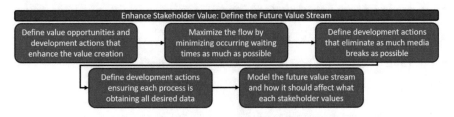

Fig. 8.6 *its*VALUE approach model: define the Future Value Stream

Value Map can be used to define further information like opportunities, problems, constraints, or causes to sharpen the general scope of improvement to be planned. Thus, opportunities regarding bad performing Stakeholder Values should be defined in the Stakeholder Value Map. Development actions explicitly affecting components that affect Stakeholder Value could be defined in the Value Perception Models.

Additionally, Value Stream Design 4.0 [10, 11] recommends maximising the flow of the Value Stream, especially by avoiding as much waiting times as possible. For information flows, avoiding media breaches seems to be the most important task. As media breaches require a manual processing of the information from one media to another, they immediately prevent a continuous and uninterrupted flow of information. The general solution to avoid media breaches is the development of machine-to-machine interfaces. The re-design of complex processes in the Value Stream should be done in a bottom-up approach. This ensures that combinations of sub-processes contain optimised components only. *Decomposition* of processes is possible in "It's a Value Added Language You Employ" to support this approach. For each process, development actions should be defined to satisfy each process needs regarding Digitisation Rate, Data Availability, and Data Usage. This also includes a thorough analysis of information demands and determining how required data and information are stored and accessed.

Lastly, the Future Value Stream is modelled. For *its*VALUE, this implies not just modelling the Value Stream Blueprint but also future versions of all Value Perception Models and the Stakeholder Value Map. After modelling the Future Value Stream, a new iteration of the *its*VALUE method is recommended to find unwanted side effects and iteratively refine them. However, we advise revising each service modelled with *its*VALUE on a regular basis, as [3] underlines the importance of achieving high business flexibility to be able to adapt to rapidly changing demands and requirements and to satisfy all stakeholder's needs and desires sustainably.

8.2.4   Create an Initial Value Stream Supporting Stakeholder Value

In Service Design, it might be possible that a new service has to be developed. This includes modelling a Future Value Stream and connected Value Perception Models and Stakeholder Value Maps. The first step of this method component is a combination of the first steps of the components "Understand Stakeholder Value" and "Enhance Stakeholder Value"—the definition of value opportunities and the collection of all processes required for the Value Stream. Each potential process of the new Value Stream should be immediately evaluated regarding its effects on the defined Stakeholder Values and its data processing Key Performance Indicators. If a process is considered as not beneficial to any Stakeholder Value or as hindering the continuous flow of the Value Stream, a company may drop that process or activity directly. This analysis is performed in the next steps.

The second step of this method component focuses on a similar domain like the second step of the "Enhance Stakeholder Value" component. Potential waiting time should be eliminated or at least minimised, as they embody waste by decreasing the efficiency and even potentially effectiveness of a Value Stream in the sense of [10]. The leaner and smarter a Value Stream is, the more efficient it performs (Fig. 8.7).

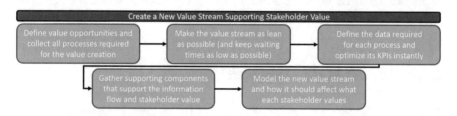

Fig. 8.7 *its*VALUE approach model: define a new value stream

The third step of this method component is a combination of the third step of "Understand Stakeholder Value" (define data requirements) and the fourth step of "Enhance Stakeholder Value" (development actions for data requirements). Once each required process or activity has been identified, the data and information requirements for each one of them should be defined to immediately achieve good Key Performance Indicator values (see Sect. 8.2.2.2).

For further refinement, the fourth step of this method component is a combination of the second step of "Understand Stakeholder Value" (identifying supporting components) and the third step of "Enhance Stakeholder Value" (development actions to avoid media breaches). Reasonable and effective (i.e. providing a supportive influence on Stakeholder Values) supporting components should be identified and connected to all processes or activities requiring or dealing with data.

Lastly, a combination of the fifth steps of "Understand Stakeholder Value" (mapping of the Value Stream components and Stakeholder Values) and "Enhance

Stakeholder Value" (modelling the future state) should be performed to explicitly define how each Stakeholder Value should perform and be affected with this new Value Stream. Like already argued at the end of Sect. 8.2.3, this should be checked by entering and performing a new iteration of *its*VALUE. Especially, a reconsideration of what highly relevant stakeholder values should be performed to ensure not missing out any forgotten or even new value perceptions that are important for the service and its value creation (like already argued at the end of Sect. 8.2.2).

8.3   Conceptualising *its*VALUE

This section presents the *its*VALUE meta-model. The purpose of this section is to expose the meta-model and in order to facilitate adoption and use of the method. The meta-models are represented using the UML standard and can be seen as conceptual meta-models of the modelling language of *its*VALUE. As described, the method adopts well-known and established concepts of existing approaches like 4EM and VSD 4.0 to assure understandability and to reduce learning effort. Thus, not all concepts will be described in detail. While Sect. 8.3.1 describes the abstract notation of our method based on the meta-model, Sect. 8.3.2 shows the visual notation of the meta-model's concepts.

8.3.1   The itsVALUE Meta-model

Figure 8.8 provides an overview of all *its*VALUE concepts. The most general is the abstract class *itsVALUE Object* providing each concept with a name. Besides the decomposition concepts, every concept carries a Description attribute. *Decomposition Objects* provide special semantics for decompositions within a visual model. *Decomposable Objects* can be decomposed in linked sub-models. These sub-models would then implement *Decomposition Objects* among other concepts to specify the decomposition. Concepts inheriting from *Linked Object* can be linked to identical instances in different models. Moreover, *Affecting Objects* (Value Stream Components) can influence Stakeholder Values and receive a Supporting Score and Hindering Score. Further, *Affecting Objects* can be related to other *Affecting Objects*. For instance, this provides the possibility to connect processes with supporting components of a Value Stream. *Activity/Processes* objects can be assigned to multiple Data Information objects providing all required data to calculate the Digitisation Rate, Data Availability, and Data Usage for a Process. Moreover, Processes and Events are *Time-Storing Objects* to explicitly track the time consumption of a Value Stream in the sense of [8]. In addition, *Typable Objects* can be further specified: Processes (not specified, information related, or material

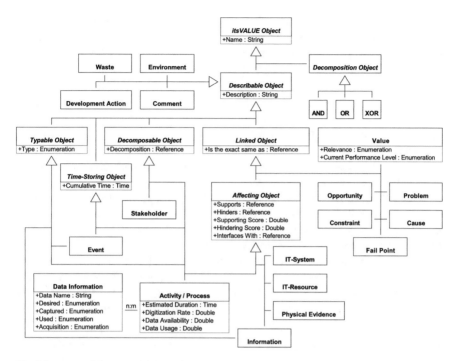

Fig. 8.8 *its*VALUE meta-model: concepts

related), Information (analog, digital input, or digital output), and Events (start, common, or end). Instances of the Value concept receive a RF and CPL.

Figure 8.9 shows the *its*VALUE relation concepts. The most general relation concept is the abstract *itsVALUE Relation* providing each relation with a name and description attribute. *Time-Containing Relations* provide explicit tracking of

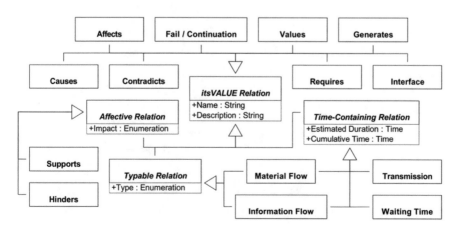

Fig. 8.9 *its*VALUE meta-model: relations

the time consumption of a Value Stream. Oppositely to the *Time-Storing Objects*, we intend to understand the Estimated Duration of a relation as a time buffer in the sense of [8]. By applying this property to relations, we do not have to introduce a separate buffer concept increasing the understandability and decreasing the complexity of "It's a Value Added Language You Employ". Some relation concepts inherit from *Typable Relation* providing them with a more precise specification: Material Flow (Push or Pull) and Information Flow (Product Information Flow or Process Information Flow). Those relation concepts inheriting from *Affective Relation* receive an Impact Factor. However, the relation concept *Affects* is not an *Affective Relation*. It just indicates that there is an influence that is not further specified but may be important for analysis.

Figure 8.10 shows the constraints for relation usage by specifying domains and ranges. For instance, any *itsVALUEObject* can be connected with any other *itsVALUEobject* with a relation of the class Affects. Oppositely, only *Activity/Processes* objects can require a specific Information.

Figure 8.11 presents an overview of *its*VALUE model types showing the concepts and relations that are provided by them. Many concepts and relations appear in multiple model types (e.g. Value is part of the Stakeholder Value Map and Value Perception Model). This underlines the importance of intermodel relations, especially for identical instances of the same object in multiple models. The concepts of *Development Action, Comment, AND, OR, XOR, and Affects-relation* are part of any model type of "It's a Value Added Language You Employ". We derived the Comment and Development Action from For Enterprise Modelling. According to [14], it is reasonable to provide users with the possibility to easily add further information they want to visualise in any model. The *Affects* relation is used for connecting *Development Actions or Comments* with any other object type.

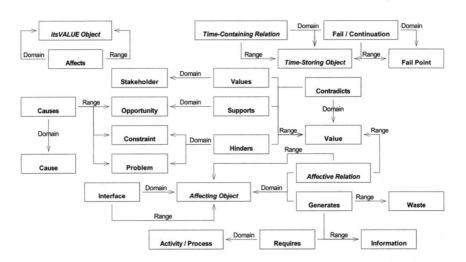

Fig. 8.10 *its*VALUE meta-model: relation domains and ranges

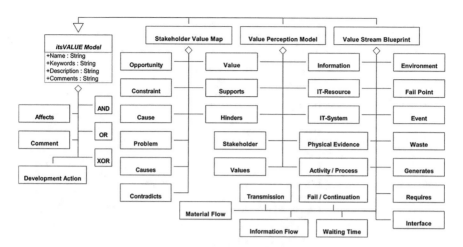

Fig. 8.11 *its*VALUE meta-model: model types

8.3.2   The itsVALUE Visual Notation

For drafting the visual representations of *its*VALUE notation elements, we stick very close to the visual representations of 4EM, BPMN, IT S-SB, and VSD 4.0, as we wanted to comply with the principles for cognitively effective visual notations by Moody [12]. These notations are familiar at least in parts to enterprise modelling experts. Thus, we support, e.g. the principle of *Cognitive Fit* of the visualisations. Table 8.2 provides an overview of the symbols used in *its*VALUE.

*its*VALUE complies with the *principle of semiotic clarity* [12], as we assigned each semantic construct an individual graphical representation. Further, we comply with the *principle of perceptual discriminability*, as every visual representation from Table 8.2 is clearly distinguishable from each other by providing a wide variety of colours and shapes. We aimed for this wide range of visual variables also to serve the *principle of visual expressiveness*. To follow the *principle of dual coding*, almost every concept contains visual text. Moreover, we added letters to small icons adding information to some instances. For Stakeholder Values, the circle in the lower left corner containing also an "R" indicates its RF and the square in the lower right containing a "P" for "Performance" its CPL by a specific colour (red, *Mandatory* or *Poor*; yellow, *Moderate*; green, *High*; blue, *Outstanding*). For *Affecting Objects*, a square containing a "S" indicates its Supporting Score by colour (Supporting Score = 0, yellow; Supporting Score > 0, green). Oppositely, a square containing a "H" indicates its Hindering Score by colour (Hindering Score < 0, red; Hindering Score = 0, yellow).

Further, *its*VALUE complies with the *principle of semantic transparency*, as the visual appearances suggest their meaning. For instance, stakeholders are represented by a group of three persons, information by letters, and relations like Supports with symbols indicating their influence ("+" indicating a positive influence). Elements

Table 8.2 Visual representations of the object and relation concept classes

Concept	Visualisation	Concept	Visualisation
Information	Analog / Digital In / Digital Out	Stakeholder	
Environment	An Environment	Value	A Value / With a description
Activity/process	An Activity / Process / Not Specified / 00:000:00:00:00 / 00:000:00:00:00	Opportunity	An Opportunity / With a description
(Information related)	An Activity / Process / Information Related / 00:000:00:00:00 / 00:000:00:00:00	Problem	A Problem / With a description
(Material related)	An Activity / Process / Material Related / 00:000:00:00:00 / 00:000:00:00:00	Constraint	A Constraint / With a description
Fail point	A Fail Point / With a description	Cause	A Cause / With a description
Physical evidence	A Physical Evidence / With a description	IT-system	An IT-System / With a description
Waste		IT-resource	An IT-Resource / With a description
Event (start/usual/end)		AND/OR/XOR	
Development action	A Development Action / With a description	Comment	A Comment / With a description
Fail/continuation	F/C	Affects	A
Transmission		Generates	G
Interface		Requires	R
Material flow (push)		Supports	+
Material flow (pull)		Hinders	-
(Product) information flow		Contradicts	#
(Process) information flow		Causes	!
Waiting time		Values	

inside the Value Stream Blueprint can be nested in order to express a relation (not explicitly part of the meta-model).

The *principle of cognitive integration* is supported by providing the possibility to explicitly define intermodel relations by linking objects across several models. For instance, this enables tracking whether an *Affecting Object* supports or hinders a Stakeholder Value. To address the *principle of complexity management*, we provide decomposition mechanisms for stakeholders and processes. However, such a mechanism is not applicable to the Stakeholder Value Map. We consider a decomposition of Stakeholder Values as not beneficial to effectively decrease a Stakeholder Value Map's complexity, as every single stakeholder may already have multiple Stakeholder Values that must be considered.

8.4   Modelling and Analysing with the *its*VALUE Modeller

This Section provides an insight into modelling and analysis of IT Service Value Streams using the *its*VALUE Modeller. First, the *its*VALUE sub-models are described together with exemplary models, and last, we provide an overview of the implemented analysis functionalities.

8.4.1   The Value Perception Model (VPM)

Value Perception Models provide stakeholder-centric views where each stakeholder has its own Value Perception Model. Figures 8.12, 8.13, and 8.14 provide exemplary Value Perception Models of the same fictional example. As Fig. 8.11 previously showed at the end of Sect. 8.3.1, a Value Perception Model consists of the following concepts and relations: Stakeholder, Value, *Affecting Objects* (Physical Evidence, IT-System, IT-Resource, Information, and Activity/Process), *Decomposition Objects* (AND, OR, and XOR), Development Action, Comment, Values, *Affective Relation* (Supports and Hinders), and Affects.

The core of every Value Perception Model is its stakeholder connected to all of its Stakeholder Values with the Values relation. Value Stream Components can be related to Stakeholder Values as *Affecting Objects* by using a Supports, Hinders, or general Affects relation. Furthermore, *Affecting Objects* can influence other *Affecting Objects* and thus implicitly via transitivity Stakeholder Values as well. Based on these relations, a stakeholder-specific Supporting Score (SS) and Hindering Score (HS) can be visualised for each *Affecting Object* showing how it influences those Stakeholder Values for that specific stakeholder. For this purpose, their Impact Factor as well as the Value Weight and CPL of the Stakeholder Values can be defined. For instance, in Fig. 8.14, the process "Orders Material" supports the Stakeholder Value "Receive Orders" belonging to a supplier. As this Stakeholder Value is mandatory to the supplier and performing well, the SS of the process

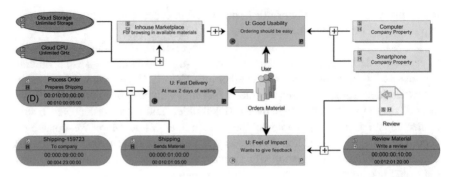

Fig. 8.12 Exemplary VPM of a user

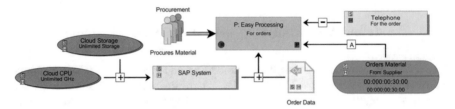

Fig. 8.13 Exemplary VPM of a procurement employee

Fig. 8.14 Exemplary VPM of a supplier

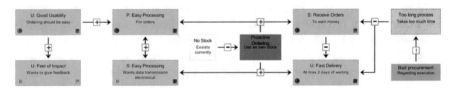

Fig. 8.15 Exemplary SVM for Figs. 8.12, 8.13, and 8.14

"Orders Material" is positive. Oppositely, the HS of the Physical Environment "Telephone" is negative. The Development Action, Comment, and *Decomposition Objects* are not part of the examples from Figs. 8.12, 8.13, and 8.14. To get an idea of their universal application in *its*VALUE, please consider the Value Stream Blueprint of Fig. 8.16 in Sect. 8.4.3.

8.4.2 The Stakeholder Value Map (SVM)

Figure 8.15 provides an exemplary Stakeholder Value Map containing all different Stakeholder Values of Figs. 8.12, 8.13, and 8.14. Thus, it continues the completely fictional example from Sect. 8.4.1. As Fig. 8.11 previously showed at the end of Sect. 8.3.1, a Stakeholder Value Map consists of the following object and relation concept classes: Value, Opportunity, Problem, Constraint, Cause, *Decomposition Objects* (AND, OR, and XOR), Development Action, Comment, *Affective Relation* (Supports and Hinders), Contradicts, Causes, and Affects.

The purpose of a Stakeholder Value Map is to explicitly define the dependencies between the several different value perceptions of all stakeholders involved. Furthermore, context information about influences on value delivery can be modelled using Opportunities, Problems, Constraints, and Causes. These concepts are adopted from the Goals Model of 4EM (cf. [14]). An Opportunity always supports Stakeholder Values, whereas Problems and Constraints always hinder Stakeholder Value. A Cause always causes something, and only Stakeholder Values can be Contradictory to each other. If a Stakeholder Value Map becomes too complex, it can be split up into several parts. For each part, specific clusters of Stakeholder Values can be focused independently from other clusters.

8.4.3 The Value Stream Blueprint (VSB)

Figure 8.16 provides an exemplary VSB continuing the example from Sects. 8.4.1 and 8.4.2. Additionally, Fig. 8.17 show an exemplary decomposition or sub VSB of the process "Process Order" from the main VSB of Fig. 8.16 (visually indicated by a "(D)" inside the process.). As Fig. 8.11 previously showed at the end of Sect. 8.3.1, a VSB consists of the following concepts and relations: Environment, *Affecting Objects* (Physical Evidence, IT-System, IT-Resource, Information, and Activity/Process), Fail Point, Event, Waste, *Decomposition Objects* (AND, OR, and XOR), Development Action, Comment, *Time-Containing Relation* (Transmission, Waiting Time, Material Flow, and Information Flow), Fail/Continuation, Interface, Requires, Generates, and Affects.

In contrast to the fixed layers of a "traditional" Service Blueprint, a VSB contains several horizontal lanes of Environments. This provides high flexibility in modelling, as the lanes can be chosen freely. Further, flows can easily switch between those environments (in contrast to other approaches like VSMN). Although environments can be defined freely, we recommend keeping at least the general order of a "traditional" Service Blueprint. The higher the environment is positioned in the model, the more visible it is to the customer or user.

To design the flow within the Value Stream, we adopted and amended the concepts of VSD 4.0. *Time-Containing Relations* carry a buffer as "estimated duration" and cumulative time that have passed in the Value Stream so far. Processes provide this timing information visually as well. Events just store them. Generally, a VSB always starts with a "Start" Event and ends with an "End" Event. Events always have to be linked to a Transmission indicating either the start, end, or switch of flow types inside a Value Stream. "Common" Events indicate such a switch from a material flow to an information flow or reverse. An Information Flow can be either a "Product" or "Process" Information Flow and a Material Flow either of the type "Push" or "Pull".

Furthermore, *Affecting Objects* can be linked by an Interface relation, indicating that one component uses the other. For a process, this shows which components are used by that particular process. For supporting components, this shows in what Processes they are actually used. For Information Flows, an Interface relation can

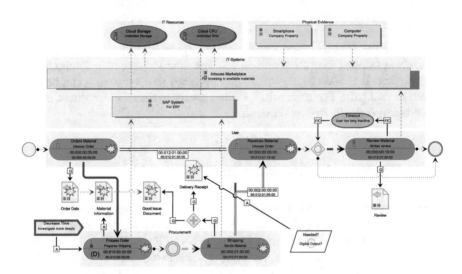

Fig. 8.16 Exemplary VSB for Figs. 8.12, 8.13, 8.14, and 8.15

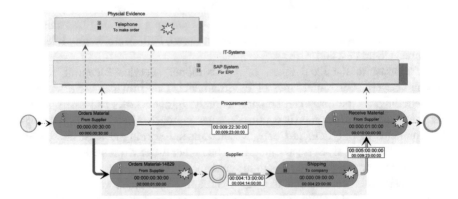

Fig. 8.17 Exemplary sub VSB for a process of Fig. 8.16

indicate whether there is a media breach by specifying the media types of outputs and inputs. Generally, waste can be assigned using the Generates relation applicable to any *Affecting Object*.

Process data requirements can be specified in the notebook of the process. This allows the calculation of data processing KPIs. Moreover, a Value Stream of an IT Service should consider Fail Points as suggested in the IT S-SB method. Usually, they are either connected to Processes, *Decomposition Objects*, or Events by the Fail/Continuation relation. Waiting Times can be specified for environments performing multiple Processes. These times indicate how long it takes to be able to continue the flow. As in the other sub-models, Development Actions or Comments can be defined and connected to any other component by the Affects relation. For complexity management, Processes can be decomposed in a sub VSB (like Fig. 8.17 does for Fig. 8.16).

8.4.4 VSB Analysis Functionality

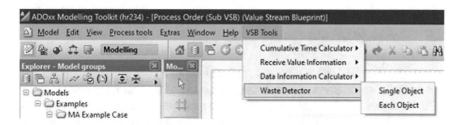

Fig. 8.18 Callable procedures in the upper menu bar

VSB analysis functionalities can be triggered manually through the upper menu bar of the *its*VALUE Modeller (cf. Fig. 8.18). All of them can be applied to either an object, a group of selected objects, or the entire model:

1. The "Cumulative Time Calculator" calculates and stores the cumulative time for *Time-Storing Objects* in a VSB. For Waiting Times, it further calculates its estimated duration. Waiting Times are generally considered as waste.
2. The "Receive Value Information" detects and stores all direct and implicit affections a component has to a Stakeholder Value. Moreover, it calculates and stores both the Supporting Score and Hindering Score of *Affecting Objects*. Therefore, these components are considered for any Value Perception Model they are part of. All Stakeholder Values that are supported or hindered are listed with references inside each *Affecting Object*. This allows to cumulate positive (Supporting Score) and negative (Hindering Score) value perceptions for Value Stream component.

3. The "Data Information Calculator" calculates and stores the Digitisation Rate, Data Availability, and Data Usage Key Performance Indicator for each Activity/Process.
4. The "Waste Detector" detects and places visual Waste indicators for each object of a VSB. It can detect "bad" KPIs indicating further potential for the improvement of data processing or value creation and media breaches in information Flows. Digitisation Rate, Data Availability, and Data Usage not equal to 1, Supporting Score equal to 0, and Hindering Score less than 0 are considered as "bad" KPIs.

Based on the analysis results, potential improvement spots can be identified in the Value Stream. The *its*VALUE Modeller allows further investigation of these spots with regard to the type of waste and possible side effects of changes. If, for example, a Value Stream component is subject to change, the mapping to the Stakeholder Value Maps identifies all involved stakeholders and their perceptions of the component. Positive and negative perceptions can be negotiated between stakeholders.

8.5 Conclusion and Outlook

*its*VALUE in combination with the Modeller supports comprehensive modelling and analysis of IT Service-related Value Streams. Based on its consideration of ITIL 4 concepts, it has the potential to support practitioners in adopting that standard. A first case study on a hardware purchasing service for the evaluation of *its*VALUE showed a great relevance of models and analysis results for Service Design according to the involved stakeholders (Service Users, Service Managers, Service Staff). Furthermore, a majority of case study participants showed interest in the future use of *its*VALUE method and Modeller. The feedback of this case study and future evaluations will help better adjust and refine the approach for practitioners. Having the Modeller freely available at OMiLAB assures access for and involvement of potential users. An important next step will be the development of a method guideline that fits the needs of practitioners. Furthermore, complexity handling needs to be evaluated in a more complex scenario compared to the first case study.

Tool Download https://www.omilab.org/itsvalue

References

1. AXELOS: ITIL 4 Managing Professional Create, Deliver and Support. The Stationery Office (2019)
2. AXELOS: ITIL 4 Managing Professional Drive Stakeholder Value. The Stationery Office (2019)

3. AXELOS: ITIL FOUNDATION, ITIL 4 Edition (GERMAN EDITION). The Stationery Office (2019)
4. Bitner, M., Ostrom, A., Morgan, F.: Service blueprinting: A practical technique for service innovation. California Manag. Rev. **50**(3), 66–94 (2008). https://doi.org/10.2307/41166446. https://www.scopus.com/inward/record.uri?eid=2-s2.0-46049090761&doi=10.2307%2f41166446&partnerID=40&md5=02729178b8138cb7f1e04fd8cddfba43
5. Goldkuhl, G., Lind, M., Seigerroth, U.: Method integration: the need for a learning perspective. IEE Proc. Softw. **145**(4), 113–118 (1998)
6. Hartmann, L., Meudt, T., Seifermann, S., Metternich, J.: Value stream design 4.0: Designing lean value streams in times of digitalization and industry 4.0 [wertstromdesign 4.0: Gestaltung schlanker wertstroeme im zeitalter von digitalisierung und industrie 4.0]. ZWF Zeitschrift fuer Wirtschaftlichen Fabrikbetrieb **113**(6), 393–397 (2018). https://doi.org/10.3139/104.111931. https://www.scopus.com/inward/record.uri?eid=2-s2.0-85051444239&doi=10.3139%2f104.111931&partnerID=40&md5=4596f892dd86aaad60f73c54a30ed4ca
7. Hartmann, L., Meudt, T., Seifermann, S., Metternich, J.: Value stream method 4.0: Holistic method to analyse and design value streams in the digital age. Procedia CIRP **78**, 249–254 (2018). Elsevier B.V. https://doi.org/10.1016/j.procir.2018.08.309. https://www.scopus.com/inward/record.uri?eid=2-s2.0-85059884535&doi=10.1016%2fj.procir.2018.08.309&partnerID=40&md5=5d9885f20f96369992f8130a7c5a3632
8. Heger, S., Valett, L., Thim, H., Schroeder, J., Gimpel, H.: Value Stream Model and Notation – Digitale Transformation von Wertstroemen, pp. 710–724. (2020). https://doi.org/10.30844/wi_2020_g2-heger
9. Henning, R., Lantow, B.: It-service value modeling: A systematic literature analysis. In: 12th Workshop on Business and IT Alignment (BITA 2021)). Accepted paper (2021)
10. Meudt, T., Leipoldt, C., Metternich, J.: Der neue blick auf verschwendungen im kontext von industrie 4.0: Detaillierte analyse von verschwendungen in informationslogistikprozessen. Zeitschrift für wirtschaftlichen Fabrikbetrieb **111**(11), 754–758 (2016)
11. Meudt, T., Metternich, J., Abele, E.: Value stream mapping 4.0: Holistic examination of value stream and information logistics in production. CIRP Ann. **66**(1), 413–416 (2017)
12. Moody, D.: The "physics" of notations: toward a scientific basis for constructing visual notations in software engineering. IEEE Trans. Softw. Eng. **35**(6), 756–779 (2009)
13. Nerdinger, F.W.: Teamarbeit, pp. 103–118. Springer, Berlin (2014). https://doi.org/10.1007/978-3-642-41130-4_8
14. Sandkuhl, K., Wißotzki, M., Stirna, J.: Begriffe im Umfeld der Unternehmensmodellierung, pp. 25–40. Springer, Berlin (2013). https://doi.org/10.1007/978-3-642-31093-5_3
15. Schoenwaelder, M., Szilagyi, T., Baer, F., Lantow, B., Sandkuhl, K.: It self-service blueprinting a visual notation for designing it self-services. pp. 88–99. CEUR-WS (2018). URL https://www.scopus.com/inward/record.uri?eid=2-s2.0-85062460565&partnerID=40&md5=1a33482b633b96402a025836576098a5

Part IV
Enterprise Information Systems

Chapter 9
Enterprise Construction Modeling Method

Marné De Vries and Jan L. G. Dietz

Abstract The design and engineering methodology for organizations (DEMO) is an established theory-based methodology for representing the organization domain of an enterprise in a concise way, using four aspect models. One of the aspect models, the Construction Model (CM), provides an overarching big picture to represent the essence of the construction of an enterprise. The CM hides complexity and hence facilitates the human need for simplicity to manage a problem situation intellectually. In this chapter, we introduce the Way of Thinking encapsulated in three theories that ground the four aspect models and provide a means for managing complexity. We discuss the aim of each aspect model and the Way of Working encapsulated in the Organizational Essence Revealing (OER) method to compose the four aspect models. We highlight the value of the CM and discuss a sub-method, the Enterprise Construction Modeling Method (ECMM), used to compose the CM. The CM metamodel is presented as the primary input for realizing a DEMO Modeling Tool (DMT), using the ADOxx platform. A fictitious enterprise, concerned with pet sitting services, is used to demonstrate the DMT features.

Keywords Enterprise modeling · Essence of organization · Design and engineering methodology of organizations · DEMO

9.1 Introduction

Modeling an enterprise is not a trivial task. The emerging discipline of enterprise engineering (EE) acknowledges the existence of several enterprise design domains [1]. De Vries [2] suggests that four main enterprise design domains exist, also

M. De Vries (✉)
Department of Industrial and Systems Engineering, University of Pretoria, Pretoria, South Africa
e-mail: Marne.devries@up.ac.za

J. L. G. Dietz
Delft University of Technology, Delft, The Netherlands
e-mail: jan.dietz@sapio.nl

called enterprise subsystems: (1) organization, (2) ICT, (3) infrastructure (including facilities), and (4) human skills and know-how. An organization system is conceived as a social system that includes human beings as system elements. Human beings form relationships due to their interactions and communications when they perform coordination acts and production acts [3]. Dietz and Mulder [3] argue that many existing organization systems are opaque to customers and even to employees, not knowing who is or should be responsible for certain acts. There is a need to provide both customers and employees with transparency about the business processes of the organization system. The designers of organization systems need to ensure that the new or re-designed organization system reflects the essence of the system [3].

9.1.1 Related Work

Understanding the essence of the system requires a conceptualization of the system. Adamo et al. [4] indicate that business process metamodels highlight different paradigms that exist for conceptualizing the organization system. They indicate that traditional metamodels are based on different paradigms, such as the *imperative paradigm* and *declarative paradigm*. The imperative paradigm assumes that the underlying system can be represented as a predictable set of activities with control-flow dependencies. Modeling languages that adopt the imperative paradigm include Business Process Modelling and Notation (BPMN), Event-driven Process Chains (EPCs), Unified Modeling Language Activity Models (UML2-AM), and Yet Another Workflow Language (YAWL). The declarative paradigm [5] is useful for knowledge-intensive systems where the control flow is not fully specified. Modeling languages that apply the declarative paradigm include the Case Management Model and Notation (CMMN) [6] and Declare [7]. According to [4], the *state-change paradigm*, when activities contribute toward multiple status changes, is under-represented in literature. Adamo et al. [4] also categorize metamodels on whether an *execution* dimension is included.

The next section applies a metamodel where the organization system is considered to be a discrete event automaton, operating in a linear time dimension [3]. The organization system is perceived as networks of social system that includes human beings as the elements of the system with three ways of mutual influence, called activating, restricting, and impeding. The Design and Engineering Methodology for Organization (DEMO) is a methodology with its own unique paradigm, but also aligned with the *imperative* paradigm and the *state-change* paradigm. One of the main objectives of DEMO is to depict the essence of the organization system, rather than the implementation-specific *execution* details.

9.1.2 Enterprise Ontology

Enterprise ontology is used as a notion to represent the essence of the organization system, adhering to five quality criteria: coherence, comprehensiveness, consistency, conciseness, and essence, collectively abbreviated as C_4E. A methodology, DEMO, develops the ontology of an enterprise in a systematic way, using four aspect models. DEMO is the result of scientific research from 1990 to 1994 at the University of Maastricht and from 1995 to 2009 at Delft University of Technology. Since 2010 the worldwide DEMO community pursued ongoing development. Courses in DEMO are also taught by the Enterprise Engineering Institute (www.ee-institute.org) and at several member institutes of the Ciao Network (www.ciaonetwork.org), as well as universities and polytechnic schools outside the network [3].

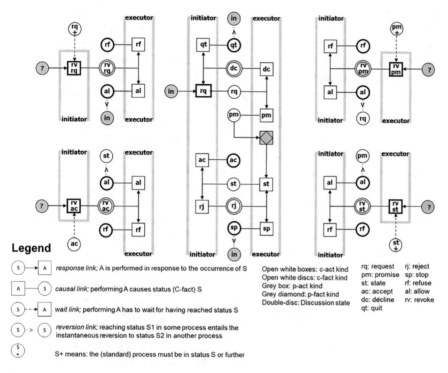

Fig. 9.1 Complete transaction pattern from [8]

The DEMO aspect models are based on a new paradigm, the CIAO (Communication, Information, Action, and Organization) paradigm, which emphasizes the role of communication in enterprises, i.e., the need of human beings to share their thoughts in order to collaborate. In addition to the CIAO paradigm, 11 enterprise engineering theories have been developed. They are the mental glasses through which enterprise engineers observe and understand enterprises [3]. Three of these theories, the PSI, ALPHA, and OMEGA theories, provide an effective means of hiding complexity when DEMO aspect models are used to represent the essence of the organization system, also called the ontological model of an enterprise [3].

The *Performance in Social Interaction* (PSI) theory provides a universal building block of enterprise organization [3], identifying transaction patterns, each involving two actor roles, a production act (and fact) and multiple coordination acts (and facts) that are performed in a particular sequence. Figure 9.1 depicts a generic transaction pattern that may exist between two actor roles, when the transaction pattern is initiated by an initiator, indicated by the gray-shaded disk, labeled "in" connected to the square labeled "rq."

In terms of the identified pattern presented in Fig. 9.1, Dietz and Mulder [3] indicated that a *complete* transaction pattern exists to represent the possible coordination acts (and facts) that describe the interactions between two actor roles for a particular transaction. Most of the transactions follow the *basic* transaction pattern (i.e., the happy flow), where two actor roles (i.e., *initiator* and *executor*) are in consent to each other's intentions when following four coordination acts in sequence, namely, *request*, *promise*, *state*, and *accept*. Yet, when the actor roles do not comply with each other's intentions, they follow a *standard* transaction pattern (depicted as the middle section in Fig. 9.1), which allows for a *decline act* (instead of a promise act) and a *reject act* (instead of an accept act). The *complete* transaction pattern extends the *standard* pattern with four revocation patterns that are visually depicted in Fig. 9.1 as four patterns that surround the middle section [3]. The complete transaction pattern addresses an actor role's need to revoke some of the coordination acts that were already performed. Once a *request act* was performed, the initiator may have second thoughts, requesting to revoke the initial *request act*. Likewise, the *promise* act, *state* act, and *accept* act may be revoked.

The *Abstraction Layers in Production for Holistic Analysis* (ALPHA) theory provides transaction layers for three sorts of production acts: original, informational, and documental [3]. Original production acts bring about original, new production facts, such as devising things, deciding, manufacturing, transporting, and observing. Informational production acts comprise remembering facts and deriving facts, i.e., not changing the state of a world. Documental production acts concern the signs that contain facts and include acts such as saving and transforming data. The distinct layers are called O-organization (O from original), I-organization (I from informational), and D-organization (D from documental). The ontological model of the O-organization of an enterprise is called its *essential model*.

The *Organizational Modules Emerging from General Arrangements* (OMEGA) theory states that different coordination structures exist when actor roles (ARs) at an enterprise coordinate their actions, namely, interaction, interstriction, and interimpediment [3]. The various coordination structures are further explained in Sect. 9.2.3.

In this chapter, we indicate that DEMO aspect models effectively hide complexity and hence facilitate the human need for simplicity to manage a problem situation intellectually, in applying the PSI, ALPHA, and OMEGA theories. In Sect. 9.2 we introduce the DEMO aspect models, focusing on one of its models, the CM. Section 9.3 presents a metamodel of the DEMO CM, as well as a demonstration case to explain the different concepts that form part of a CM. In Sect. 9.4 we present an implementation of the CM on ADOxx, called the DEMO Modeling Tool (DMT). Finally, in Sect. 9.5 we present conclusions and ideas for future research.

9.2   Method Description

Multiple modeling languages exist to represent a particular domain, such as the organization design domain [9]. Languages, other than DEMO, which also represent the organizational domain include EPCs (Event-driven Process Chains), BPMN (Business Process Modelling and Notation), and Petri nets [9]. Usually, an inherent trade-off exists between two qualities, machine analyzability (and therefore executability) and human-oriented understanding, when these languages are developed [9]. One of the qualities that is currently neglected by existing organization-domain languages is *complexity*. Organization systems are complex not only due to the large number of system elements that interact but also due to non-linearity, i.e., interaction between system elements that may lead to counterintuitive behaviors [10]. Another characteristic that is currently not accommodated in existing languages is a *consistent means* to hide the complexity of models. The PSI, ALPHA, and OMEGA theories provide additional means to hide complexity when four DEMO aspect models are used to represent the essence of enterprise operation.

DEMO aspect models are specified via a specification language, i.e., DEMOSL (DEMO Specification Language), and evolved to its recent version, DEMOSL 4.6.1 [11]. Although the existing specification still includes four aspect models, the descriptions and graphical representation of DEMOSL 4.6.1 models have changed. This chapter still refers to DEMOSL 3.7, since our prototype, the DMT (DEMO Modeling Tool), was based on DEMOSL 3.7. The DMT prototype focused on the CM.

We present the *language aspects* of DEMO, starting in Sect. 9.2.1 with DEMO's four aspect models, focusing on the CM. Then, in Sect. 9.2.2 we present some operations at a fictitious college, as a demonstration of the CM. Finally, Sect. 9.2.3 presents existing *modeling procedures* for composing DEMO aspect models but more specifically for composing a CM.

9.2.1   DEMO Aspect Models

The essential model of an enterprise is represented by four aspect models, illustrated in Fig. 9.2: Construction Model (CM), Process Model (PM), Action Model (AM), and Fact Model (FM) [8, 12].

The CM for a particular Scope of Interest (SoI) is the ontological model of its construction, representing actor roles and coordination structures among them [3]. The AM of an SoI is the ontological model of its operation, indicating rules that guide internal actor roles when they perform their work [3]. The PM of an SoI is the ontological model of the state space and the transition space of its *coordination world* and connects the CM and AM [3]. The FM of an SoI is the ontological model of the state space and the transition space of its *production world* and connects the CM and the AM. Connections between the models are depicted visually in Fig. 9.2 as horizontal and vertical separation lines. Figure 9.2 also indicates shaded sections that represent two different worlds, the *coordination* world (left) and the *production* world (right). DEMO's four aspect models are represented by different diagrams and tables, as shown in Fig. 9.2.

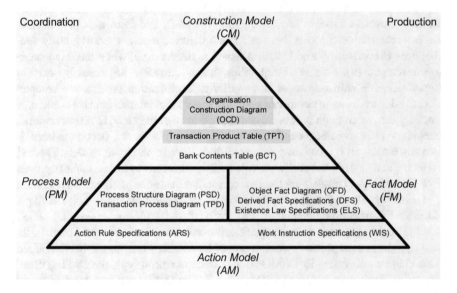

Fig. 9.2 DEMO aspect models with diagram types and tables, based on [8, 12]

The CM is the most concise model of the four DEMO aspect models and is useful to management, since it provides a bird's-eye view of coordination structures [3]. Figure 9.2 indicates that the CM is represented by an Organization Construction Diagram (OCD), a Transaction Product Table (TPT), and a Bank Contents Table (BCT). Both the TPT and BCT are cross-model tables, linking the CM to the FM. Also, both the TPT and BCT assist in validating the completeness of the OCD. Yet, the TPT does not require an explicit representation of the FM, whereas the BCT requires an explicit representation of the FM in terms of an Object Fact Diagram (OFD). Our prototype (DMT) only included the CM and not the FM. Therefore, in DMT, we only included the OCD and TPT [13] as representations of the CM, gray-shaded in Fig. 9.2.

In accordance with the PSI theory, the CM acknowledges that enterprise operations can be perceived as actor roles that perform multiple coordination acts and production acts. The coordination acts and production acts are performed in a particular sequence, called transaction patterns (see Fig. 9.1 for a complete transaction pattern). Instead of mapping out the detailed transaction patterns for each kind of transaction that takes place, the CM hides the detail of these consistent transaction patterns, hiding some of the complexity to enable human understanding. For instance, Fig. 9.3 includes an OCD for a fictitious enterprise. Every disk-diamond construct in Fig. 9.3 represents a transaction kind. The transaction kind *continuous pet service completion (TK01)* in Fig. 9.3 is a concise representation of the complete transaction pattern in Fig. 9.1.

In terms of the ALPHA theory, the CM abstracts from technological implementation and realization detail, only representing original transaction kinds, excluding the informational and documental transaction kinds [3]. For instance, in Fig. 9.3, an OCD for a fictitious enterprise only includes eight original transaction kinds where new facts are created in the production world. Informational and documental transaction kinds are intentionally excluded from the OCD. An example of an informational transaction kind that is intentionally omitted from the OCD is *information sharing of pet sitter availability*. An example of a documental transaction kind that is intentionally omitted on the OCD is *storage of pet sitter details*.

The OMEGA theory highlights different structures that exist between actor roles. These structures are visually depicted on the CM's OCD as solid-line connections and dotted-line connections (see Fig. 9.3 for an example). We elaborate on these structures in the next section.

9.2.2 The Demonstration Case

DEMOSL 3.7 and its associated CM focus on two structures of the OMEGA theory, the *interaction structure* and *interstriction structure*. The *interaction structure* determines for every transaction kind the initiating actor role and executing actor role and becomes the fundamental structure of business processes, indicated by solid-line connections in Fig. 9.3. In addition, it clarifies the areas of responsibilities for actor roles [3]. The *interstriction structure* indicates that some actor roles may have to inspect the history of transactions of other transaction kinds, since these historic facts need to be considered during decision acts [3], indicated by dotted-line connections in Fig. 9.3.

The universe of discourse for our demonstration case includes *some pet sitting operations* at a fictitious enterprise. The fictitious enterprise offers continuous pet sitting services. As an example, Client A receives a continuous pet service from the pet sitting enterprise for his/her dog for a continuous period, such as 3 weeks of pet care during the school holidays. As part of the continuous pet service, Client A's dog may also receive multiple pet services. In addition, pre-selected services are included in a 3-week continuous pet-care service, such as pet food supply (twice a day) and dog walking (once a day).

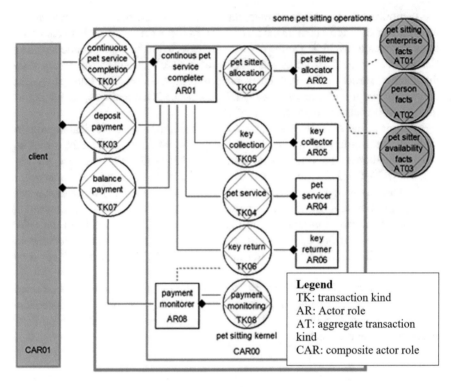

Fig. 9.3 The OCD for a pet sitting enterprise, based on [8]

First, we discuss the OCD in Fig. 9.3. **Bold** style indicates a particular type of construct, whereas *italics* refers to an instance of the construct (see Fig. 9.3).

Scope of Interest (SoI) indicates that the modeler analyzes a particular scope of operations, namely, *some pet sitting operations*. Given the SoI, Fig. 9.3 indicates that one **environmental actor role** is defined, indicated by the gray-shaded construct *client* that forms part of the environment. Within the SoI, multiple **transaction kinds (TKs)** are linked to different types of **actor roles** via **initiation links** or **executor links**. As an example, *continuous pet service completion (TK01)* is a **TK** that is initiated (via an **initiation link**) by the **environmental actor role** *client (CAR01)*. In accordance with [12], the *client (CAR01)* is by default also regarded to be a **composite actor role**, since the actor role is an initiating actor role for which we do not necessarily "know (or want to know) the details." Since *TK01* is linked to an **environmental actor role**, it is also called a **border transaction kind**. *TK01* is executed (via the **executor link**) by the **elementary actor role** named *continuous pet service completer (AR01)*.

All the other actor roles in Fig. 9.3 within the **SoI** are **elementary actor roles**, since each of them is only responsible for executing one **transaction kind**. A special case is where an **elementary actor role** is both the **initiator** and **executor** of a **transaction kind**, also called a **self-activating actor role**. Figure 9.3 exemplifies the **self-activating actor role** with *payment monitorer (AR08)*. Since **actor roles** need to use facts created and stored in transaction banks, an **information link** is used to indicate access to facts. As an example, Fig. 9.3 indicates that the *payment monitorer (AR08)* has an **information link** to **transaction kind** *key return (TK06)*, indicating that the *payment monitorer (AR08)* uses facts in the transaction bank of *key return (TK06)*. The rationale for accessing facts about *key return (TK06)* is that the payment monitorer has to ensure that a client's residential keys to his/her property have been returned, before the payment monitorer requests **TK** *balance payment (TK07)*.

It is also possible that **actor roles** within the **SoI** need to use facts that are created via **transaction kinds** that are outside the **SoI**. As an example, Fig. 9.3 indicates that **actor roles** within the **SoI** need to use facts that are created outside the SoI and stored in the transaction banks of **aggregate transaction kinds**, namely, *pet sitting enterprise facts* of *AT01* and *person facts* of *AT02*. Figure 9.3 also indicates that one particular **actor role**, namely, *pet sitter allocator (AR02)*, needs access to *pet sitter availability facts* of the **aggregate transaction kind** *AT03*.

Even though Fig. 9.3 only includes **elementary actor roles** within the **SoI**, it is possible to consolidate **elementary actor roles** within a **composite actor role**, where a composite actor role "is a network of transaction kinds and (elementary) actor roles" [12]. Figure 9.3 illustrates one **composite actor role** within the **SoI**, namely, *pet sitting kernel (CA00)*, that encapsulates a number of elementary transaction kinds and elementary actor roles.

The TPT for our fictitious enterprise provides a duplication of **transaction kinds** that are already included in the OCD, as indicated in the first two columns of Fig. 9.4. In addition, for every **transaction kind**, a **product kind** is defined in the third and fourth columns of Fig. 9.4. The **product kind** relates **product kinds** of the CM to corresponding **production-event types** in the FM. As an example, Fig. 9.4 indicates that a **transaction kind** *continuous pet service completion (TK01)* produces a **product kind** *[continuous pet service] is completed (PK01)* that is also called a **production-event type** on the FM. Thus, a **production-event type** in the FM is identical to a **product kind** in the CM [3].

Transaction Product Table			
transaction ID	transaction kind	product ID	product kind
TK01	continuous pet service completion	PK01	[continuous pet service] is completed
TK02	pet sitter allocation	PK02	the pet sitter of [continuous pet service] is allocated
TK03	deposit payment	PK03	the deposit of [continuous pet service] is paid
TK04	pet service	PK04	[pet service] is done
TK05	key collection	PK05	[continuous pet service] is key-collected
TK06	key return	PK06	[continous pet service] is key-returned
TK07	balance payment	PK07	the balance of [continous pet service] is paid
TK08	payment monitoring	PK08	payment monitoring for [month] is done

Fig. 9.4 The TPT for a pet sitting enterprise, based on [8]

DEMO as a methodology comprises a Way of Thinking (WoT), a Way of Modeling (WoM), and a Way of Working (WoW). In Sect. 9.1 we introduced some of the enterprise engineering theories that guide the WoT for DEMO. In Sect. 9.2.1 we introduced the four DEMO aspect models as a WoM, demonstrating one of the aspect models, the CM, in Sect. 9.2.2. Next, we introduce the OER method and as a WoW for DEMO aspect models in Sect. 9.2.3. Using the OER method as the main method, we introduce a sub-method, the Enterprise Construction Modeling Method (ECCM), to compose a CM.

9.2.3   Way of Working

The WoW to compose DEMO aspect models is called the *Organizational Essence Revealing* (OER) method. As indicated by Dietz and Mulder [3], two alternative options are available for composing DEMO models: (1) using a collaborative approach, involving employees that are or will be executing the organizational processes or (2) using documents and diagrams that provide an expression of existing organizational processes.

The OER method highlights five intellectual techniques that offer effective help in achieving essence and simplicity, summarized in the mnemonic called *sapiences*. The *sapiences*, highlighted in **bold**-style font, include: (1) **s**eparation of concerns, (2) use of **a**bstraction, (3) devising **p**roper concepts, (4) verification by **i**nstantiation, and (5) validation from **o**ntology [3].

The OER method includes four main steps for developing DEMO's four aspect models incrementally: (1) distinguishing performa-informa-forma; (2) identifying transaction kinds and actor roles; (3) composing the essential model, i.e., composing the four aspect models in a spiral way during multiple cycles; and (4) validating the essential model [3].

Even though the OER method suggests a spiral way of composing the four aspect models iteratively, some of the aspect models may also be useful to enhance other methodologies or models. As an example, the CM is useful to supplement agile software development methodologies, since agile developments, where scaling factors apply, need more advanced requirements: elicitation and management [14]. In addition, existing studies already indicated the possibility of combining the benefits of the CM with that of BPMN [13, 15].

The CM provides an overarching big-picture model to represent the organization design domain of an enterprise on a management level. Since the CM is a contribution in its own right with opportunities to combine it with other methodologies and languages, we present the Enterprise Construction Modeling Method (ECMM) as a sub-method within the OER method for composing a CM. As before, we refer to our fictitious enterprise case (and Fig. 9.3), using **bold**-style to indicate a type of construct, whereas *italics* refers to an instance of the construct.

Step 1: Distinguishing performa-informa-forma.

In the first step of the OER method, for an identified **Scope of Interest (SoI)**, the analyst has to classify existing operations as performa, informa, or forma acts or facts, extracting the performa acts/facts. The **SoI** is *some pet sitting operations* for which analysis is needed. The following fragment partially describes *some pet sitting operations* and solid underlining was used to highlight performa acts/facts, whereas dotted underlining highlights informa or forma acts/facts: "Clients currently perform requests for continuous pet sitting, usually for weekends and holidays, via WhatsApp messages or e-mail, also indicating a preference for a particular pet sitter."

Step 2: Identifying transaction kinds and actor roles.

During the next step, the performa fragments are used to identify and phrase appropriate **transaction kinds**, associated **product kinds**, and executing **actor roles**. Continuing with the example presented in Step 1, the phrase "requests for continuous pet sitting" is a performa fragment for which a **transaction kind** *continuous pet service completion (TK01)* can be phrased, associated with the **product kind** *[continuous pet service] is completed (PK01)* and an executing **actor role** *continuous pet service completer (AR01)*.

Step 3: Composing the essential model.

Once all **transaction kinds** have been identified for the **SoI**, the analyst compiles the CM, starting with the OCD. For the pet sitting demonstration case, the analyst will model the **SoI** *some pet sitting operations*, mapping out all the **elementary transaction kinds** *TK01 to TK08* within the boundary of the **SoI**.

Next, the analyst has to indicate a part of the interaction structure, i.e., for each **elementary transaction kind**, an executing **actor role** should be added, with an **executor link**. If the executing actor role is outside the **SoI**, it is called an **environmental actor role**. Also, if the environmental actor role is the executor of more than one **transaction kind**, it is called a **composite environmental actor role**. For the pet sitting enterprise, the *client (CAR01)* is considered to be a **composite environmental actor role**, since it is modeled outside the **SoI** and the client (CAR01) is an initiating actor role and we do not "know (or want to know) the details" of this actor role.

Next, the interaction structure should be completed, adding for each **elementary transaction kind** one or more **initiation links** to initiating **actor roles**. The analyst now needs to use his/her understanding about the concept of "operating cycle" to add initiation links. As an example, the **actor role** *continuous pet service completer (AR01)* is an initiator for multiple transaction kinds (*TK02 to TK07*), since these TKs are closely coupled with concluding an instance of *continuous pet service completion (TK01)*.

Finally, the analyst has to add the interstriction structure, indicating that **actor roles** need to access information created via multiple **transaction kinds**. As an example, the **actor role** *payment monitorer (AR08)* needs information access to facts created via TK06 (now also called a **transaction bank**), indicated via an **information link** between AR08 and TK06. Since some facts are created outside the **SoI**, the analyst should also indicate that these facts should be accessible to some of the actor roles. As an example, the **aggregate transaction kind** (i.e., also **an aggregate transaction bank**) *pet sitting enterprise facts (AT01)* should be accessible, indicated via an **information link**, to all actor roles within the **SoI**.

Step 4: Validating the essential model.

The purpose is to validate the CM with real human beings that will become authorized actor roles for the modeled transaction kinds. Since our DMT is based on DEMOSL 3.7, five validation activities apply, validating: (1) the existence of the transaction kind itself, (2) the interaction structure, (3) the interstriction structure, (4) the complete transaction pattern for every transaction kind, and (5) the completeness of information requirements.

Given the demonstration of a particular CM for a fictitious enterprise, Sect. 9.3 provides an abstraction of the CM concepts when we present a metamodel of the CM.

9.3 Method Conceptualization

The metamodel of the CM for DEMOSL 3.7 in [8] was extended by Mulder in [16].

Since the DMT was based on [8, 16], this section presents the CM metamodel in Fig. 9.5 using syntactic elements of an Object Fact Diagram (OFD), defined in [8]. The CM metamodel was also presented in [13].

9.3.1 Construction Model Metamodel

We use uppercase for entity types on the CM metamodel (i.e., Fig. 9.5) that are instantiated in a CM. Figure 9.5 indicates that multiple entity types exist: (1) TRANSACTION KIND (TK), (2) AGGREGATE TRANSACTION KIND (ATK), (3) COMPOSITE ACTOR ROLE (CAR), (4) ELEMENTARY ACTOR ROLE (EAR), (5) INDEPENDENT P-FACT KIND (IFK), and (6) FACT KIND (FK). We now discuss the attributes per entity type and the relationships between the entity types.

The TK has an attribute of "transaction sort." Although it is possible to identify three different sorts of a TK, i.e., original, informational, and documental, we focus on the original sort, since we want to produce the essential model of the enterprise. As indicated by a relationship in Fig. 9.5, an instance of a TK has exactly one instance of an IFK as its PK. An instance of TK may be contained in zero-to-many instances of ATK when it is executed by multiple actor roles. Furthermore, an instance of a TK may also be contained in zero-to-many instances of CARs. An instance of a CAR can also be a part of another instance of a CAR. Also, an instance of a CAR can be a specialization of an instance of an EAR.

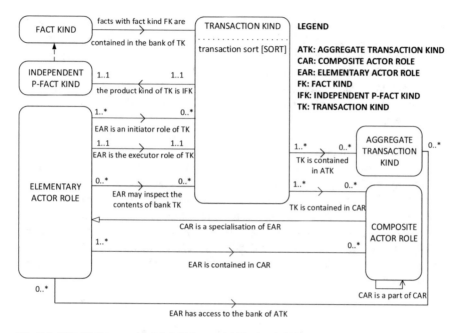

Fig. 9.5 DEMO Construction Model Metamodel Version 3.7 [8] with extensions of [16]

An instance of an EAR is contained in zero-to-many instances of CARs. An instance of an EAR has access to zero-to-many instances of ATKs. An instance of an EAR may inspect zero-to-many instances of TK's banks. An instance of an EAR is the executor role of exactly one instance of a TK and can be an initiator AR of zero-to-many instances of TKs.

An instance of an IFK is a specialization of an FK instance. In addition, an instance of an FK is contained in the bank of a particular instance of a TK.

The entity types are instantiated in the CM, using different graphical representations on the OCD and tabled items in the TPT. The next section delineates the notation standards that are used.

9.3.2   Construction Model Notation

As indicated in [8] and Fig. 9.6, multiple graphical representations exist for the OCD. Even though the notation standard of DEMOSL 3.7 allows for alternative representations for one construct (e.g., the self-activating actor role can be represented in different ways), Fig. 9.6 only includes those constructs that are used in our prototype, called DMT. The left-hand side of Fig. 9.6 represents the four main categories of constructs, discussed from top to bottom: (1) an actor role, represented by a quadrilateral; (2) transaction kind, indicated with a diamond disk;

(3) links, indicated by solid or dotted lines; and (4) a scope of interest, represented by a quadrilateral with a light-gray color and labeled "SoI." The different kinds of constructs can be used in various combinations, illustrated on the right-hand side of Fig. 9.6. The descriptions associated with each combination set provide an interpretation for the combination. For instance, the combination of actor role (ARi) connected via a solid link to transaction kind (TKj) indicates that ARi is the initiator role of TKj.

We also slightly adapted some of the legends to be aligned with the terminology used in [16]. As indicated as a note in Fig. 9.6, color-coding may be used to indicate a transaction's sort (original, informational, or documental). However, for our prototype (DMT), we have not implemented the color-coding, but assumed that all modeled TKs are of the original sort. As indicated by Dietz and Mulder [8], an alternative to color-coding is to indicate the transaction sort as part of the transaction kind identifier. Thus, instead of using *TK01* for the transaction kind *continuous pet service completion*, one could also indicate that the TK is of the original sort, e.g., *O-TK01*. Informational TKs would be indicated as O-TKj and documental transaction kinds would be indicated as D-TKj.

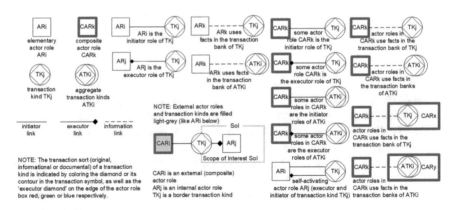

Fig. 9.6 DEMO construction model legend, based on DEMOSL Version 3.7 [8]

9.4 Proof of Concept

In this section, we present the main features of the DMT prototype, realized as an OMiLAB project which enables free download: https://austria.omilab.org/psm/content/demo.

Since DMT was developed within the ADOxx platform, various functionalities are automatically incorporated, such as the standard menu options (top section of Fig. 9.7). A *modeling* template (left-hand part of Fig. 9.7) provides access to all the graphical constructs presented in Fig. 9.6. When an OCD is composed, the modeler has to left-click on the construct in the template, dropping the construct by left-clicking within the modeling area on the right. The properties of each graphical construct can be updated via a *notebook*. In Fig. 9.7, the properties of the transaction kind *pet sitter allocation (TK02)* are displayed on the right-hand side. Using the notebook, the modeler provides a name and ID for the transaction kind, also adding a name and ID for the associated product kind.

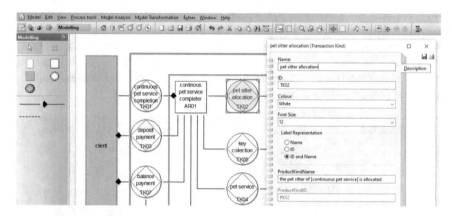

Fig. 9.7 DMT user interface

A DMT-specific menu item *model analysis* is available to the modeler, offering two features: (1) *generate TPT* or (2) *validate*. The *generate TPT* feature extracts properties captured on the OCD to generate a TPT, such as the one illustrated in Fig. 9.4. The *validate* feature ensures that the modeler adheres to the existence rules that are incorporated in the CM metamodel as depicted in Fig. 9.5. In Fig. 9.8 we illustrate the scenario where the modeler created an actor role *vet (AR09)*.

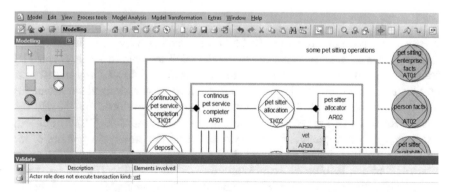

Fig. 9.8 DMT's validation feature

According to the CM metamodel (depicted in Fig. 9.5), every elementary actor role should be an executor actor role of exactly one transaction kind. Yet, actor role vet (AR09) is not the executor actor role of any transaction kind. This error is highlighted when the modeler uses the *validate* feature as illustrated at the bottom of Fig. 9.8.

A DMT-specific menu item *model transformation* is also available to the modeler to generate a BPMN diagram that is based on the standard transaction pattern, i.e., the middle section of Fig. 9.1. Based on our demonstration case, we demonstrate the transformation feature in Fig. 9.9, where the modeler selected the transaction kind *payment monitoring (TK08)*, generating a BPMN collaboration diagram, based on BPMN 2.0. Four different transformation scenarios were incorporated in the DMT prototype. The most complex scenario is presented in [15]. Follow-up research already highlighted the need to identify a more comprehensive set of transformation scenarios for future development of the DMT [17].

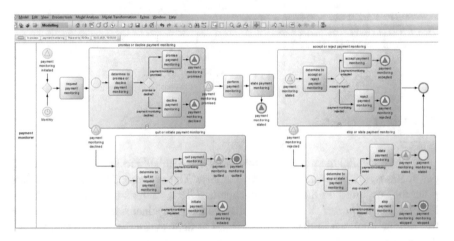

Fig. 9.9 DMT's transformation feature

The DMT has been evaluated empirically for its usability. Post-graduate participants received training on the DEMO aspect models, using a fictitious college demonstration case. Participants had to use the DMT to compose an OCD and TPT for the demonstration case, also experimenting with the OCD-BPMN transformation feature. Afterward, participants had to complete a standardized questionnaire, SUMI (Software Usability Measurement Inventory), developed by the Human Factors Research Group (HFRG) at the University College Cork [15]. The results draw a very positive picture, especially considering the prototypical nature of the DMT. The tool is evaluated positive in all five sub-categories and in the global scale: efficiency, affect, helpfulness, controllability, and learnability. The highest value was found in the category *affect* which measures the participant's emotional feeling mentally stimulated and pleasant versus the opposite: stressed and frustrated as a result of interacting with the tool. The results indicate that 31 out of 34 participants perceived the DMT as being *important* or *extremely important* for supporting their task [15].

9.5   Conclusion and Future Work

This chapter presented an Enterprise Construction Modeling Method (ECMM) as a sub-method within the OER method to represent the essence of enterprise construction using the Construction Model (CM). At the time of development, we used the DEMO Specification Language Version 3.7 as a baseline for developing an ADOxx-based DMT. The DMT has been evaluated empirically on its usability and performed well. Since the prototype only includes one of the four DEMO aspect models, an opportunity exists to also add the other three aspect models, i.e., the Action Model, the Fact Model, and the Process Model. In addition, the DEMO Specification Language has since evolved to Version 4.6.1 [11] and considerable changes would be needed to support DEMOSL 4.6.1. One of the main features, demonstrated by the DMT prototype, was the ability to semi-automate transformations from DEMO to BPMN. We used the phrase semi-automate, since the BPMN diagram that is generated from a selected transaction kind on the OCD may have to be further adapted by the modeler. As indicated in [17], a comprehensive set of transformation scenarios were identified to guide further development on DEMO-to-BPMN transformations. Further research should also investigate the possibility of using the transformed BPMN diagrams as representations of implementation. When activity durations and resource capacity constraints are added, simulations could be useful to predict the performance of a process, informing implementation decisions.

Acknowledgments We would like to thank Prof. Dimitris Karagiannis for initiating and supporting the DMT-tooling initiative, creating the research connection with Prof. Dominik Bork. We highly appreciate Prof. Dominik Bork's valuable experience and knowledge on the ADOxx platform, sharing his knowledge with Mr. Thomas Gray, assisting him hands-on in developing the DMT prototype, and contributing to multiple publications. Lastly, we are very grateful to Thomas Gray who spent many hours in developing and testing the DMT.

Tool Download https://www.omilab.org/dmt.

References

1. Hoogervorst, J.A.P.: Practicing Enterprise Governance and Enterprise Engineering - Applying the Employee-Centric Theory of Organization. Springer, Berlin (2018)
2. De Vries, M.: Towards consistent demarcation of enterprise design domains. In: De Cesare, S., Frank, U. (eds.) Advances in Conceptual Modeling, pp. 91–100. Springer (2017). https://doi.org/10.1007/978-3-319-70625-2_9
3. Dietz, J.L.G., Mulder, H.B.F.: Enterprise Ontology: A Human-Centric Approach to Understanding the Essence of Organisation. Springer International Publishing AG (2020)

4. Adamo, G., Ghidini, C., Di Francescomarion, C.: What's My Process Model Composed of? A Systematic Literature Review of Meta-Models in BPM. Report, Cornell University (2020)
5. De Giacomo, G., Dumas, M., Maggi, F., Montali, M.: Declarative process modeling in BPMN. In: Proceedings: Springer Lecture Notes in Computer Science. Vol. 9097, pp. 84–100. Stockholm (2015)
6. Object Management Group: Case Management Model and Notation Version 1.1, https://www.omg.org/spec/CMMN/About-CMMN/, last accessed 2021/15 June
7. Pesic, M., Schonenberg, H., Van der Aalst, W. M. P.: Declare: Full support for loosely-structured processes. In: 11th IEEE International Enterprise Distributed Object Computing Conference, EDOC 2007, p. 287 (2007)
8. Dietz, J.L.G., Mulder, M.A.T.: DEMOSL-3: DEMO specification language version 3.7. SAPIO (2017)
9. Karagiannis, D., Buchmann, R.A., Burzynski, P., Reimer, U., Walch, M.: Fundamental conceptual modeling languages in OMiLAB. In: Karagiannis, D., Mayer, H.C., Mylopoulos, J. (eds.) Domain Specific Conceptual Modeling: Concepts, Methods and Tools, pp. 1–30. Springer International Publishing, Cham (2016). https://doi.org/10.1007/978-3-319-39417-6_8
10. Giachetti, R.E.: Design of enterprise systems. CRC Press, Boca Raton, FL (2010)
11. Dietz, J.L.G.: The DEMO Specification Language v 4.6.1, https://demo.nl/demo/publications/, last accessed 2021/3 March
12. Perinforma, A.P.C.: The essence of organisation (3rd ed.). Sapio, www.sapio.nl (2017)
13. Gray, T., Bork, D., De Vries, M.: A new DEMO modelling tool that facilitates model transformations. In: Nurcan, S., Reinhardt-Berger, I., Soffer, P., Zdravkovic, J. (eds.) Enterprise, Business-Process and Information Systems Modeling. Vol. LNBIP 387, pp. 359–374. Springer Nature Switzerland, Cham (2020). doi: https://doi.org/10.1007/978-3-030-49418-6_25
14. De Vries, M.: DEMO and the story-card method: requirements elicitation for agile software development at scale. In: Buchmann, R., Kirikova, M. (eds.) 11th IFIP WG 8.1 Working Conference on the Practice of Enterprise Modelling. Springer (2018). doi:https://doi.org/10.1007/978-3-030-02302-7
15. Gray, T., De Vries, M.: Empirical evaluation of a new DEMO modelling tool that facilitates model transformations. In: Grossmann, G., Ram, S. (eds.) Advances in Conceptual Modeling. ER 2020. Lecture Notes in Computer Science. Vol. 12584, pp. 189–199. Springer, Cham (2020). https://doi.org/10.1007/978-3-030-65847-2_17
16. Mulder, M. A. T.: Towards a complete metamodel for DEMO CM. In: al., D. e. (ed.) OTM 2018 Workshops, LNCS 11231. pp. 97–106. (2019). https://doi.org/10.1007/978-3-030-11683-5_10
17. De Vries, M., Bork, D.: Identifying scenarios to guide transformations from DEMO to BPMN. In: Aveiro, D., Guizzardi, G., Pergl, R., Proper, H.A. (eds.) Advances in Enterprise Engineering XIV. EEWC 2020. Lecture Notes in Business Information Processing, pp. 92–110. Springer, Cham (2021). https://doi.org/10.1007/978-3-030-74196-9_6

Chapter 10
Tool Support for Fractal Enterprise Modeling

Ilia Bider, Erik Perjons, and Victoria Klyukina

Abstract This chapter discusses the authors' experience of building tool support for a modeling technique called Fractal Enterprise Model (FEM) using the ADOxx metamodeling environment. FEM is introduced as a means for helping the management to comprehend how their organization operates, giving a picture understandable for the management team. It depicts interconnections between the business processes in an enterprise and connects them to the assets they use and manage. Assets considered in the model could be tangible (buildings, heavy machinery, etc.) and intangible (reputation, business process definitions, etc.). First, the chapter presents FEM informally—as a text with examples—and formally, as a metamodel. Then, the authors present the requirements on a tool support for FEM and discuss how these requirements were fulfilled in a tool called the FEM toolkit developed with the help of ADOxx.

Keywords Enterprise modeling · Fractal Enterprise Model · FEM · ADOxx

10.1 Introduction

According to [1], modern organizations have become so complex that no one in the management of an organization fully understands how it *operates*. The paper also states that for enterprise architecture to be taken seriously, it should provide the business with models that the management *understands*. The two terms in italic

I. Bider (✉)
Department of Computer and Systems Sciences, Stockholm University, Stockholm, Sweden

Institute of Computer Science, University of Tartu, Tartu, Estonia
e-mail: ilia@dsv.su.se

E. Perjons · V. Klyukina
Department of Computer and Systems Sciences, Stockholm University, Stockholm, Sweden
e-mail: perjons@dsv.su.se; klyukina@dsv.su.se

from the above text constitute two requirements on the model that is needed for providing management with reliable information for decision making:

1. Providing a holistic view on how the organization operates
2. Being understandable for businesspeople, which might not have any technical or computer science background

To the two requirements as above, we can add a third requirement that is related to the fact that there might not exist a single person in an organization that has a holistic view on all organizational operations. Thus, it would be helpful if a modeling technique could guide the modeler through the organization and its operational activities with respect to what to look after and from whom to get information for building the model.

There is a multitude of modeling techniques; some of them are used in practice while others are used, mainly, in academia. Some of the techniques are widely popular, such as Business Process Modeling and Notation (BPMN) [2], others are used by a minority of business consultants, such as Viable System Model (VSM) [3].

Many of the existing techniques focus only on specific aspects of the company operations, e.g., goals [4] or business processes [2] . Thus, they do not satisfy the first requirement on providing a holistic view on the company's operations. Other techniques, like ArchiMate [5], come from the IT world, and they are doubly satisfying the second requirement of being understandable for businesspeople. In addition, they do not provide guidelines mentioned in the third requirement. In fact, one needs to understand the business quite well to be able to draw a set of ArchiMate diagrams that cover all parts of the business. Yet other techniques do not have good means of visualizing specifics of a given organization, e.g., VSM [3] . In addition, VSM's guidelines for investigating the business are rather vague, thus requiring a certain level of expertise from the modeler in order to build a model [6].

The factors listed above make the set of modeling techniques that satisfy all three requirements relatively small. As an example of modeling technique that in our view satisfies all requirements to a certain extent, we can name Integrated DEFinition Methods (IDEF0) [7] . However, in the last decades, it lost its popularity to more aggressively marketed modeling techniques like BPMN [2] and ArchiMate [5].

Based on the deliberation above, we can conclude that today, there are a room and practical needs for new modeling techniques that satisfy all three requirements discussed above. This chapter is devoted to one of such techniques, still under development, and especially to the tool support for it that is being developed using the ADOxx metamodeling environment [8].

The technique in question is called Fractal Enterprise Model (FEM) [9] . FEM has a form of a directed graph with two basic types of nodes *processes* and *assets*, where the arrows (edges) from assets to processes show which assets are used in which processes and arrows from processes to assets show which processes help to have specific assets in "healthy" and working order. The arrows are labeled with meta-tags that show in what way a given asset is used, e.g., as *workforce*, *reputation*, *infrastructure*, etc., or in what way a given process helps to have the given assets "in order," i.e., *acquire, maintain,* or *retire.* Besides processes and assets, the latest version of FEM includes two new types of nodes—*external pools* and *external actors* [10]. These are introduced to represent the environment outside the organization, e.g., markets or competitors, and connect it to the internal processes.

The rest of the chapter is structured in the following way. In Sect. 10.2, we give an informal overview of Fractal Enterprise Model. In Sect. 10.3, we discuss its semantics, metamodel, and requirements on tool support. In Sect. 10.4, we discuss the FEM toolkit and its usage in practical and research projects. Section 10.5 contains concluding remarks and plans for continuing development of the toolkit and the methodology of using FEM in practical projects.

10.2   Fractal Enterprise Model

10.2.1   Informal Overview

In this section, we give an informal overview of Fractal Enterprise Model (FEM) introduced in our earlier works, especially in [9], and in the extended form in [10]. The basic version of FEM includes three types of elements: business processes (more exactly, business process types), assets, and relations between them (see Fig. 10.1), in which a fragment of a model describing operational activities of a manufacturing company is presented.

The example is taken from [11]. The case considered in this paper concerns Robert Bosch GmbH Bamberg Plant that manufactures different lines of products for automotive industry, like spark plugs, fuel injection, and sensors. These products can be bought by companies, retailers, or end-consumers for their usage. The company uses different machines for producing the products, like laser machines and robots. In this paper, we refer to these machines as *sophisticated manufacturing equipment.*

The equipment requires maintenance, both periodical and emergency mainte-nance (i.e., when a machine stops working). The maintenance requires service technicians, machine process experts, and robots' providers (who are also partners in providing spare parts, advice on maintenance, etc.). To improve the effectiveness of maintenance, the company has developed *Diagnostic and Predictive Software* that helps to detect whether the equipment needs urgent maintenance and/or whether the periodic maintenance can be postponed, as the equipment is still in a good shape. To develop and support this software, the company has a special software development process and people engaged in it, which are called data scientists.

Returning to FEM, graphically, a process is represented in FEM by an oval, an asset is represented by a rectangle (box), while a relation between a process and an asset is represented by an arrow. We differentiate two types of relations in the fractal model. One type represents a relation of a process "using" an asset; in this case, the arrow points from the asset to the process and has a solid line. The other type represents a relation of a process changing the asset; in this case, the arrow points from the process to the asset and has a dashed line. These two types of relations allow tying up processes and assets in a directed graph.

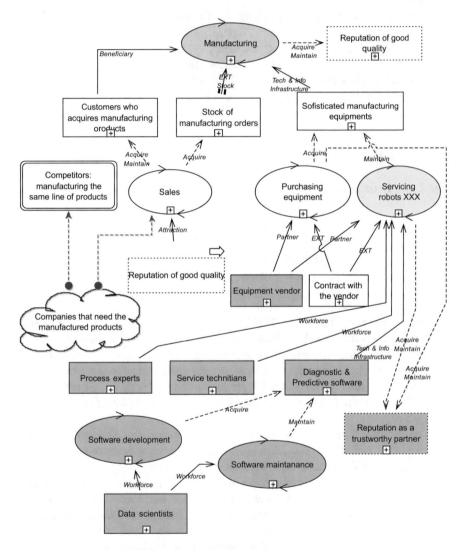

Fig. 10.1 A fragment of FEM for a manufacturing company

In FEM, a label inside an oval names the given process, and a label inside a rectangle names the given asset. Arrows are also labeled to show the type of relations between the processes and assets. A label on an arrow pointing from an asset to a process identifies the role the given asset plays in the process, for example, *workforce* or *infrastructure*. A label on an arrow pointing from a process to an asset identifies the way in which the process affects (i.e., changes) the asset. In FEM, an asset is considered as a pool of entities capable of playing a given role in a given process. Labels leading into assets from processes reflect the way the pool is affected, for example, label *acquire* identifies that the process can/should increase the pool size.

Note that the same asset can be used in multiple processes playing the same or different roles in them, which is reflected by labels on the corresponding arrows. It is also possible that the same asset plays multiple roles in the same process. In this case, several labels can be placed on the arrow between the asset and the process. Similarly, a process could affect multiple assets, each in the same or in different ways, which is represented by the corresponding labels on the arrows. Moreover, it is possible that a single process affects a single asset in multiple ways, which is represented by having two or more labels on the corresponding arrow.

Labels inside ovals (which represent processes) and rectangles (which represent assets) are not standardized. They can be set according to the terminology accepted in the given domain or be specific for a given organization. Labels on arrows (which represent the relations between processes and assets) are standardized. This is done by using a relatively limited set of abstract relations, such as *workforce* or *acquire*, which are clarified by the domain- and context-specific labels inside ovals and rectangles. Standardization improves the understandability of the models.

While there are several types of relations that show how an asset is used in a process (see example in Fig. 10.1), there are only three types of relations that describe how an asset is managed by a process—*acquire*, *maintain*, and *retire*.

Two new concepts were introduced to FEM in order to represent the business context of the organization and connect it to specific processes [10]. These are as follows:

- *External pool*, which is represented by a cloud shape; see Fig. 10.1. An external pool is a set of things or agents of a certain type. As an example, in Fig. 10.1, there is one such pool—a pool of *Companies that need the manufacturing products*. The label inside the external pool describes its content.
- *External actor*, which is represented by a rectangle with rounded corners. An external actor is an agent, like a company or person, acting outside the boundary of the organization. The label inside the external actor describes its nature. If the shade represents a set of external actors, the box has a double line (see Fig. 10.1), which has one external actor of this kind.

External pools and external actors may be related to each other and to other elements of the FEM diagram. Such a relation is shown by a dashed arrow that has a round dot start. More exactly:

- A business process may be connected to an external pool with an arrow directed from the pool to the process. In this case, the process needs to be an *acquire* process to one or more assets. The arrow shows that the process uses the external pool to create new elements in the asset for which this process serves as an acquire process; see an example of such relations in Fig. 10.1.

- An external actor may be connected to an external pool with an arrow directed from the pool to the external actor. In this case, the arrow shows that the external actor uses the external pool as bases for one of its own *acquire* processes; see an example of such relations in Fig. 10.1.
- A business process may be connected to an external pool with an arrow directed from the process to the pool. In this case the arrow shows that the process provides entities to the external pool (there are no related examples in Fig. 10.1).
- An external actor may be connected to an external pool with an arrow directed from the actor to the pool. In this case, the arrow shows that one of the actor's processes provides entities to the external pool (there are no examples of such relations in Fig. 10.1).
- Two pools can be connected to each other, which means that elements from one pool can move to another based on external condition (there are no examples of such relations in Fig. 10.1).

External pools and actors represent the context in which an organization operates, i.e., its external environment. External pools can be roughly associated with markets, e.g., a labor market, etc. External actors represent other organizations that are connected to the external pools. Dependent on the nature of the external pool, an external actor connected to it can be a competitor, provider, or collaborator. Note that an external organization can be an asset, e.g., partner or customer vs. an external actor. The difference reveals itself in how the external organization is connected to the internal processes; an external actor is always connected indirectly, i.e., via an external pool. If needed, an arrow that connects an external pool to some other element can be supplied with a label to clarify the condition on when or why the elements can be added to or withdrawn from the pool.

10.2.2   FEM Archetypes

To make the work of building a fractal model more systematic, a FEM modeler can use archetypes (or patterns) as fragments from which a particular model can be built. An archetype is a template defined as a fragment of a model where labels inside ovals (processes) and rectangles (assets) are omitted, but arrows are labeled. Instantiating an archetype means putting the fragment inside the model and labeling ovals and rectangles; it is also possible to add elements absent in the archetype or omit some elements that are present in the archetype.

FEM has two types of archetypes, process-assets archetypes and an asset-processes archetype. A process-assets archetype represents the kinds of assets that can be used in a given category of processes. There are several archetypes of this sort. Figure 10.2 presents a so-called generic process-assets archetype, which can be applied to any process. There are also specific process-assets archetypes [9], which will be discussed in the next section.

The asset-processes archetype shows the kinds of processes that are aimed at changing the given category of assets. There is only one such archetype, which is presented in Fig. 10.3.

The whole FEM graph can be built by alternative application of these two types of archetypes representing self-similar patterns on different scales, fractals. One usually starts with a *primary* process—a process that produces value for an external beneficiary—and continues down with finding assets needed for this process and then, finding *supporting* processes aimed at managing these assets. The term fractal in the name of our modeling technique points to the recursive nature of the model built with the help of alternating archetypes.

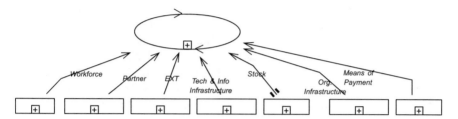

Fig. 10.2 A generic process-assets archetype

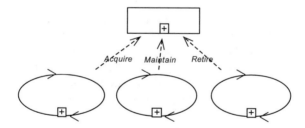

Fig. 10.3 Asset-processes archetype

10.2.3   Areas of FEM Application

As is explained in [9], the initial goal for FEM development was to find a way to identify if not all but at least the major part of the processes that exist in the enterprise. The result—FEM—however was much more powerful, and it was envisioned to be of help in multiple other areas. Though the initial goal has never been tested in a practical project, indirectly, it was used in some projects to identify not all processes in the company but all processes that were relevant for a particular purpose. Besides getting the relevant processes listed, using FEM helped to list relevant assets used in the processes, which was at least as helpful as listing the processes.

Paper [9] envisioned several additional areas of usage for FEM. In this chapter, however, we will not repeat this list, but discuss the areas for which FEM has been tested. One additional area of application will be considered in Sect. 10.4. Other suggestions for using FEM in practice can be found in [12].

10.2.3.1   Business Model Innovation

The idea of using FEM for industry-level Business Model Innovation (BMI) [13] was suggested in [14]. The industry-level BMI concerns creating new products and services for already existing or new markets. The idea of using FEM in BMI consists of finding a supporting process in the existing business that can be converted to a primary one in a new business. For example, a manufacturer can become a designer by converting a supporting process of designing products for own manufacturing into a primary process of designing products to be manufactured by others.

This idea was further developed to include patterns for the industry-level BMI, which is discussed in [11, 15]. Figure 10.1 is adapted from [11] and the example of BMI presented in it will be explained in more detail later in this chapter.

10.2.3.2   Arranging Process Documentation

When an organization has not adopted a uniform and standardized way of producing and storing process documentation, keeping track of and maintaining process documents can be a real challenge. There can be hundreds of documents and models created at different times for various purposes and related to different, but sometimes intersecting, parts of the business. In such a case, finding a document related to a specific process, or part of the business, can be a challenge.

FEM was tested as an organizing framework at a company that had more than a hundred of process documents. A simplified FEM of the company was built, and the existing documents were related to the nodes of this model. A test was conducted with the management of the company whether they can find a process document or attach a new document to a right node. Both tests gave positive results. For more on this project, see [16].

10.2.3.3   Structural Coupling

The concept of structural coupling comes from biological cybernetics, more specifically, from the works of Maturana and Varela, for example [17]. The idea of structural coupling is relatively simple; it suggests that a complex system adjusts its structure to the structure of the environment in which it operates. The adjustment comes from the constant interaction between the system and its environment. Moreover, during the system evolution in the given environment, some elements of the environment and interaction with them become more important than others. The latter leads to the system choosing to adjust to a limited number of environmental elements with which it becomes structurally coupled.

The concept of structural coupling can be successfully used in the organizational practice. For example, [18] suggests using structural coupling for defining and managing organizational identity, while [19] defines enterprise strategy as achieving a desirable position among the organization's structural couplings. Using these ideas, however, requires to find all structural couplings of an organization, which can be a difficult task, especially for unexperienced people. In [10], we suggested to use FEM of an organization to identify its structural couplings. The paper presents a set of rules of how to identify the elements of the model—assets, external pools, and eternal actors—as structural couplings. A structural coupling can be a customer (asset), a partner (asset), a competitor (external actor), or a market (external pool). For example, the company represented by FEM in Fig. 10.1 might be structurally coupled to the external pool *Companies that needs manufactured products* and/or the asset *Customers that acquire manufactured products* and/or the asset *Equipment vendor*. However, more information is needed to identify to which elements the company is actually structurally coupled.

10.3   Method Description

10.3.1   Metamodel and Semantics of FEM

A metamodel for FEM is presented in Fig. 10.4. In this metamodel, all associations represented by solid arrowheads are of *many-to-one* type, where *one* corresponds to the arrowhead. Arrows with a hollow arrowhead represent generalization. Classes *Asset*, *Process*, *Environmental relation*, *External relation*, and *Flow relation* have one attribute—*Label*—which appears inside the oval or rectangle for the first two and near the corresponding arrow for the rest. Also, for the first two classes *Label* cannot be NULL, while it can be NULL for the others.

The meanings of the *UsedInAs* relationships that appear in the metamodel in Fig. 10.4 and in the generic archetype of Fig. 10.2 are as follows:

1. *Workforce*—people trained and qualified for employment in the process, e.g., workers at the conveyor belt, physicians, and researchers.
2. *EXT*—process execution template. An EXT is an asset that governs or controls the process in some way. This can, for example, be a software development methodology accepted in a software vendor company; product design documentation for a manufacturer; technological process documentation, also for a product manufacturer; and description of the service delivery procedure, e.g., a process map for a service company. Note also that EXT does not need to be in a form of a procedure or algorithm. For example, a policy document on equal opportunities in recruitment of staff is regarded as an EXT for the recruitment process.

3. *Partner*—an agent, external to the given organization, who participates in the process. This, for example, can be a supplier of parts in a manufacturing process and a lab that completes medical tests on behalf of a hospital. Partners can be other enterprises or individuals, e.g., retired workers that can be hired in case there is a lack of a skilled workforce for a particular process instance.

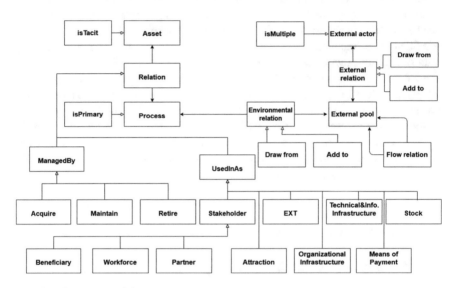

Fig. 10.4 FEM metamodel

4. *Stock*—a stock of materials or parts that are used in the process. This, for example, can be office products, e.g., paper, pens, printer and cartridges, in any office, or spare parts for a car repair shop. A stock needs to be represented in FEM only if the organization itself maintains the stock and does not directly get materials or parts from the supplier for each process instance. In the latter case, it is enough to represent a supplier as a partner. Note the stock does not need to be physical. For example, in Fig. 10.1, we have a stock of manufacturing orders. The main characteristic of *stock* that differs it from other assets is that each process instance depletes this asset by consuming one or more elements from it. Thus, the stock needs to be constantly refilled by some process. This is not the case with other assets. To show the special nature of the stock relation, its arrow has a different starting point—with two extra lines; see Fig. 10.1.

5. *Technical and Informational Infrastructure*—equipment required for executing the process. This, for example, can be a production line, computer, communication line, building, software system, and database.
6. *Organizational Infrastructure*—a unit of organization that participates in the process. This, for example, can be sales department and software development team.
7. *Means of Payment*—any kind of monetary fund that is needed to pay participating stakeholders, e.g., suppliers, if such payment is considered as part of the process.

The metamodel in Fig. 10.4 corresponds to the informal description of FEM in Sect. 10.2, but introduces several more concepts not fully explained in Sect. 10.2. In particular, it introduces a subclass of class *Process* called *Primary process*. As primary, we count processes that deliver value for which some of the enterprise's external stakeholders are ready to pay, e.g., customers of a private enterprise or a local government paying for services provided to the public. A primary process needs to have a special asset called *beneficiary* (see Fig. 10.1), in which the asset *customers* is connected with the primary process by an arrow labeled *beneficiary*. For the primary process, the generic archetype in Fig. 10.2 can be extended to become an archetype for the primary process presented in Fig. 10.5. This archetype "forces" the modeler to seek for who is a beneficiary of the process.

The relation *ManagedBy* (see the metamodel of Fig. 10.4) can be only of three types, which are as follows:

1. *Acquire*—a process that results in the enterprise acquiring new assets of a given type. The essence of this process depends on the type of asset, the type of the process(es) in which the asset is used, and the type of the enterprise. For a product-oriented enterprise, *acquiring* new customers (beneficiary) is done through marketing and sales processes. *Acquiring* skilled workforce is a task of a recruiting process. *Acquiring* a new *EXT* for a product-oriented enterprise is a task of new product and new technological process development.
2. *Maintain*—a process that helps keep existing assets in the right shape to be employable in the business process instances of a given type. For *beneficiary*, it could be a customer relationship management (CRM) process. For *workforce*, it could be training. For EXT, it could be product and process improvement. For *technical infrastructure*, it could be servicing.
3. *Retire*—a process that phases out assets that can no longer be used in the intended process. For *beneficiary*, it could be canceling a contract with a customer that is no longer profitable. For *EXT*, it could be phasing out a product that no longer satisfies the customer's needs. For *workforce*, it could be actual retirement.

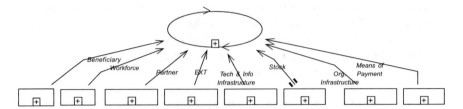

Fig. 10.5 Archetype for the primary process

In the metamodel of Fig. 10.4, three *UsedInAs* relations, namely, *beneficiary*, *workforce*, and *partner*, are grouped in a subclass called *stakeholders*. This is done because their management processes, especially *acquire*, require an asset called *attraction*, which is specific for stakeholders. For finding customers, for example, *attraction* could be an interesting value proposition, i.e., a statement of benefits that a customer will get by acquiring certain products and/or services. For recruiting staff, it could be salary and other benefits that an employee receives. For recruiting partners, it could be a lucrative exclusive contract.

An example of *attraction* for acquiring new customers is presented in Fig. 10.1— *Reputation of good quality*. This is a special type of assets which belong to the subclass *isTacit* in the metamodel of Fig. 10.4. The subclass means that the asset is intangible, and it exists only in the "heads" of a certain group of people. In Fig. 10.1, this asset has a dotted border to differentiate it from other types of assets. Having tacit assets allows to add to the model things that are not expressed as any physical or informational object. For example, an *EXT* of a process can be fully or partly tacit—existing only in the head of the process participants.

A special archetype can be introduced for processes that deal with acquiring stakeholders, which is presented in Fig. 10.6. It "forces" to look for *attraction* and also to find out from which external pool new elements will be acquired. In Fig. 10.1 this pool is labeled as *Companies that need the manufactured products*.

10.3.2   Requirements on Toolkit

A tool that supports drawing FEM diagram should have visual means to represent all FEM concepts so that a FEM diagram could be drawn using the tool while complying with the syntax of FEM expressed in the metamodel in Fig. 10.4. However, this is not enough; the toolkit also needs to facilitate creating diagrams in a consistent way and ensure that the results are understandable for the intended audience. As we stated in the Introduction, our goal is to explain to the management how their enterprise operates. Thus, the models produced with the toolkit should be understandable by nontechnical people. Below, we present requirements on the toolkit that would make it fit to the goal discussed above:

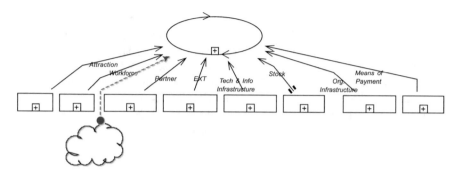

Fig. 10.6 Archetype for acquiring stakeholders

1. As has been discussed in Sect. 10.2, one way of building a FEM is by applying archetypes to processes and assets that have already found their place in the model. It should be possible to invoke an archetype for any process or asset to facilitate building the model a bit further. Expanding a node according to an archetype will initiate seeking for information to insert labels in the elements that the invocation has produced (see also requirement 3 in Introduction).

2. A model can become quite complex, especially, when the same process or asset is used in multiple relations or there are many processes and assets in the organization that need to be depicted. There is a need to introduce the same model element, e.g., an asset, several times without losing the information about the sameness. For example, an ERP system can serve as *technical and informational infrastructure* in many processes. When there are too many elements in the model, it should be possible to split the model in several pieces making the same elements (e.g., the ERP system) to become a mechanism for tying the models together. Thus, there is a need to have a navigation between models so that it is easy to find other models that have in them some model element, e.g., a process or asset.

3. Quite often, a modeler needs to use a different level of granularity when creating an enterprise model. For a high-level overview, the granularity will be coarse, while when one needs a detailed overview of a particular part of the business, a fine level of granularity is required. To make the connection between the models on different granularity levels, there needs to be a way to relate a concept/model element of a higher level to a fragment of the diagram on the low level, i.e., the level with higher granularity. For example, a business process that is depicted as one element in one model may need to be related to an interconnected set of subprocesses in a more detailed model.

4. In a specific modeling project, there often is a need to differentiate elements from the same class, e.g., asset. For example, in a FEM, one might need to differentiate assets that have a tight connection to a physical location, e.g., a warehouse, from the assets for which physical location does not matter, as they can be accessed from anywhere, e.g., electronic documents or IT systems. There is a need to have means to make the difference highlighted visually. These means should be easily adjusted to the needs of a specific project. It also should be possible to add textual explanation to elements of the model, easily accessible by the intended audience.

10.4 Proof of Concept

10.4.1 FEM Toolkit

The FEM toolkit [20] was developed using the ADOxx modeling environment [8], and now it is in its version 0.7. The overall layout when drawing a model with the help of the toolkit is presented in Fig. 10.7. The right-hand side presents a model under development. The column in the middle presents all modeling elements that can be picked and dropped in the modeling area to the right. The left-hand side has two areas. The area at the top shows the names of all models grouped in model groups. A model name in red color shows that the model has been changed, but not saved, while a model name in blue color shows that the model has been changed and saved in the current modeling session. The area at the bottom, *Navigator*, enables zooming parts of the model visible in the modeling area.

A FEM is built by adding processes, assets, pools, and external actors and connecting them with arrows that represent relations between them. The toolkit ensures syntactic correctness by not allowing drawing relations that are against the metamodel in Fig. 10.4. This is an improvement in comparison with drawing FEM with a general diagram drawing tool, or even a specific tool that is not designed to support FEM. In fact, before creating our toolkit, we used to employ InsightMaker [21]—a tool designed to support system dynamics modeling. The main problem when using it, especially, by novices, e.g., students, was the modeler tending not to observe the standardized set of labels on the arrows.

Besides ensuring syntactic correctness, the FEM toolkit also implements features that fulfill the requirements discussed in the previous section. These are described in the following subsections.

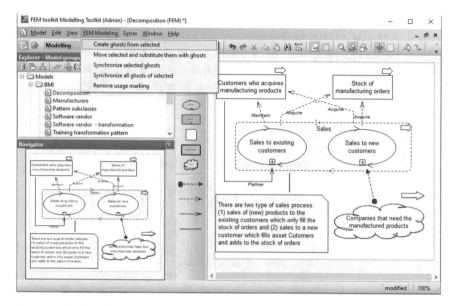

Fig. 10.7 FEM toolkit—general overview

10.4.1.1 Archetypes

The archetype function is invoked by a modeler via clicking on a "plus" sign placed at the bottom of each process and asset in the model. A menu that lists the relations from the generic process-assets archetype from Fig. 10.2 or from the asset-processes archetype from Fig. 10.3 appears; see the upper part of Fig. 10.8. Then, the modeler can adjust archetype by removing relations in which he/she is not currently interested from the list. After clicking on *Choose*, new model elements are added to the model and connected to the current one by chosen relations; see the bottom part of Fig. 10.8. Other process-assets archetypes can be implemented in the same manner as the generic one shown in Fig. 10.8, but it has not been done yet.

10.4.1.2 Ghost Feature

To solve the problem of multiple instances of the same model element, we have introduced the concept of *ghost*, which has been borrowed from *InsightMaker* [21]. A ghost is a copy of an element that already exists in the model. The ghost in InsightMaker is differentiated by a lighter background color compared to the original element. The ghost is accompanied by a simple navigation mechanism that allows to find an original which the ghost duplicates. We have extended this concept in three ways:

- More clear *visual difference* between the ghost and the original element, not totally relying on the background color. An example of a ghost is already presented in Fig. 10.1, which has a ghost for asset *Reputation of good quality*. The ghost has a thick arrow above the shape that represents the modeling element; clicking on the arrow will move the focus to the original modeling element.

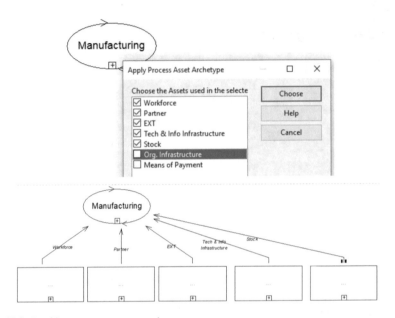

Fig. 10.8 Invoking a process-assets archetype

- Usage in multiple models, i.e., allow the ghost to be placed in a different model than the original. In Fig. 10.9, we have a number of ghosts of the elements that appear in Fig. 10.1. In addition to an arrow over the ghost shape, a special color scheme is used in Fig. 10.9, ghost having a lighter background color. To create ghosts, a modeler selects a number of elements in the current model and choose an item in the pull-down menu called *Create ghosts from selected*; see Fig. 10.7. A new window appears, which allows to select in which model the modeler wants to create ghosts. Default is the current model (see Fig. 10.10). Note that the ghost menu in Fig. 10.7 also allows to move the originals to another place and substitute them with ghosts, as well as some other functions (which are not described here).

Note that Fig. 10.9 represents a case of business model innovation in the manufacturing business presented in Fig. 10.1. As follows from Fig. 10.1, the node *Diagnostic and Predictive Software* requires quite a complex structure underneath that needs to be in place in order for the software to be used in practice. As this structure involves considerable costs, the management decided to explore a possibility to convert these costs into profit by licensing the software to other manufacturers that used the same equipment, including their own competitors. Figure 10.9 shows how the new business could be set in operation. Ghosts in this picture show how the new business could benefit from the usage of assets that the company already has. This example demonstrates how the ghost feature can be used for connecting a model of organization "as-is" to a model of organization "to-be." For more details on this case, see [11]. The background colors in Figs. 10.1 and 10.9 will be explained in Sect. 10.4.1.4.

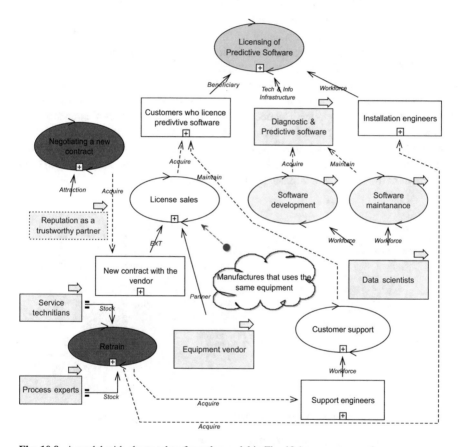

Fig. 10.9 A model with ghosts taken from the model in Fig. 10.1

- Extended navigation—allow to find all ghosts of the given element starting from a ghost or the original. This is done after choosing an element and using a popup menu attached to it. In it, the modeler can choose to find all occurrences in the current model or in all models. The relevant elements will be highlighted by a special kind of borders; see Fig. 10.11. If the modeler chooses to show occurrences in all models, a window that lists all relevant models appears, and it can be used for navigation; see Fig. 10.11.

10.4.1.3 Decomposition

We use nestling together with the ghost functionality for presenting the decomposition. This is illustrated in Fig. 10.7, which represents the decomposition of process *Sales* from Fig. 10.1. The decomposed process is presented as a special type of ghosts—group ghost—and it has two new processes inside it. All FEM elements provide an attribute that qualifies them for being a group or not. By changing the attribute value, the appearance of the selected element automatically changes, e.g., from a solid border line to a dashed border line and light background color. The group attribute exists independently of the ghost feature; thus, any element can become a group. However, for decomposition, choosing the ghost group is essential as it facilitates easy finding of the original element.

To show the connection between the new processes in Fig. 10.7 and other elements of the model from Fig. 10.1, ghosts of the connected elements are presented in the new model. The decomposition in this example is of specialization type, but other types can be depicted in the same way, e.g., by more tightly connecting the elements inside the group, which will be illustrated in Sect. 10.4.2. The ghost navigation means facilitating easy movement from the undecomposed element to the model that depicts the decomposition and back.

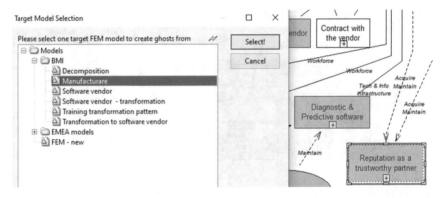

Fig. 10.10 Selecting a model to place the ghosts

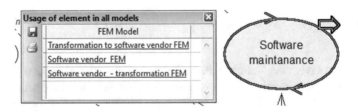

Fig. 10.11 Finding all occurrences of the current shape

10.4.1.4 Subclassing

Subclassing is a way of differentiating elements of the model that belong to the same class in the metamodel; see requirement 4 in Sect. 10.3.2. Visually, elements of subclasses are differentiated by their background color. Technically, subclassing is introduced in the toolkit by a special type of models called *FEM subclassing*. Such a model consists of a number of subclasses that use the same shapes as the nodes of the ordinary FEM, e.g., oval—for a process, rectangle—for an asset, etc. Each subclass has a dedicated background color and a label that describes what this color represents. There can be at the maximum one subclassing model in a modeling group.

As an example, consider a FEM subclassing model in Fig. 10.12 that is defined for the modeling group that includes models in Figs. 10.1 and 10.9. The example concerns a Business Model Innovation (BMI) case from [11], where a product manufacturer considers starting a new business of developing and licensing diagnostic and predictive software for complex equipment.

A FEM subclassing model presented in Fig. 10.12 is designed for the usage of FEM for BMI. It differentiates four types of processes: (1) a current primary process, beige; (2) a supporting process that can be transformed into a new primary process, yellow; (3) a process that can be used in a new business as is, blue; and (4) a temporal transformation process, which is needed for creating a new business, but will be disbanded after that, red. Processes of the first two subclasses appear in Fig. 10.1; processes of the third subclass appear both in Fig. 10.1—current business—and in Fig. 10.9, transformed business. Processes of the fourth subclass appear only in Fig. 10.9. There is one subclass of assets in Fig. 10.12, existing assets that can be used in a new business, blue—as is or changed through the transformation processes. These assets are presented in both Figs. 10.1 and 10.9.

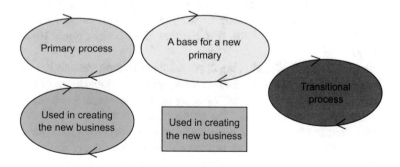

Fig. 10.12 An example for FEM subclassing model

Assigning a subclass to a model element is done by a special menu; see Fig. 10.13. Note that the subclassing allows to define a different background color for ghosts—normally lighter than the main background color. This can be seen in Fig. 10.9, in which there are a number of ghosts that originated from Fig. 10.1.

10.4.1.5 Notes

As was discussed in requirement 3 from Sect. 10.3.2, there is a need to add textual explanations in the model. This can be done in two ways. Firstly, each element has a set of properties, one of which is the textual *Description*. However, this method has a drawback—to show the description one needs to open the property sheet. A second method is adding notes and connecting them to particular elements as shown in Fig. 10.7.

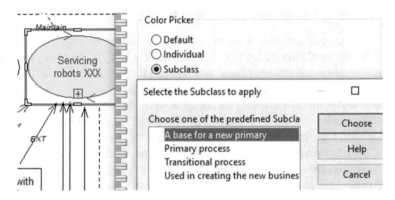

Fig. 10.13 Assigning a subclass to a shape

10.4.2 Example of Usage: Identifying Areas for Improvement

The first version of the FEM toolkit was used in a project identifying areas for improvement completed by the authors in 2019–2020. This project has initiated adding to the toolkit some of the new features discussed in Sect. 10.4.1, e.g., subclassing.

The project aimed at investigating opportunities for improvement in an EMEA (i.e., Europe, Middle East and Africa) branch of an international high-tech business concern. The concern provides test measurement products and related services to other high-tech organizations. The project started with a request from the department director of the internal Business Support and Services (BSS) department whose prime responsibility is sales support and managing supply chain activities. The BSS department is entrusted with the task of relieving sales and service departments from administrative work. Thereby, these departments could concentrate on their core businesses, i.e., increasing sales and providing efficient high-quality calibration and repair of products. As a result, BSS completes the activities in business processes that belong to other departments, while having no total responsibility for these processes. The staff of the BSS department is distributed across several European countries residing in sales and services headquarters of these countries.

The background of the request that triggered the project is the exposure of the EMEA branch to a significant economic decline that requires adjustment of the operational cost. Several alternatives to achieve cost reduction were considered, such as changing responsibility structure or relocating the staff to a lower-wage country. Our task has been to suggest a set of alternatives for organizational changes based on modeling of operational activities of the BSS department.

Building FEM for the department business activities was part of the project. FEM was found very useful to understand the whole business in general and especially the role played by BSS, which was quite difficult to grasp in the beginning. A simplified FEM of the whole EMEA is presented in Fig. 10.14. In this figure, border color is used to define who is responsible for the process: red, BSS; purple, another department of EMEA; and black, a third party.

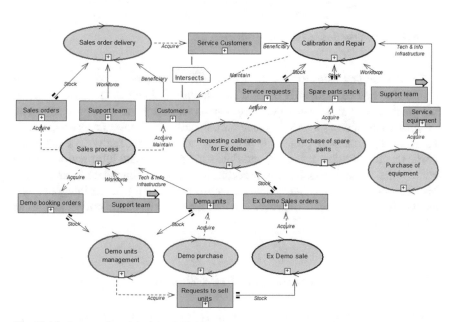

Fig. 10.14 A general model of the EMEA business

The processes in Fig. 10.14 were decomposed in separate diagrams to get more details on BSS engagement. As an example, Fig. 10.15 shows a simplified diagram of the decomposition of *Sales order delivery*.

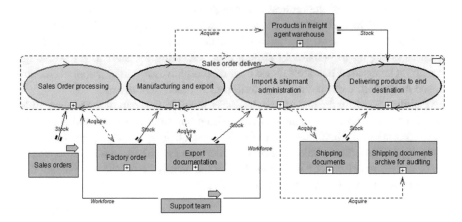

Fig. 10.15 Decomposition of *Sales order delivery*

Besides helping us to understand the overall business and BSS engagement in it, FEM has helped to identify areas with potential for improvement. Two patterns that point to such areas were identified. One is when a process/subprocess has no physical connection to a certain place on the earth; this allows to move the team that handles it to a more preferable place, e.g., a low-wage country. The other one is when a process/subprocess uses multiple software tools and information sources and requires the team to manually move information from one place to another. In this situation, integrating the systems or substituting them with an integrated one could make a considerable improvement. For more details on the project and usage of FEM in it, see [22].

10.4.3   Other Projects with the FEM Toolkit

The team that completed the project described in Sect. 10.4.2 included FEM experts. Recently, two other projects were completed, which employed FEM and FEM toolkit, where the project teams did not include FEM experts; some help from FEM experts, however, was provided.

The first project [23] was completed by Steven Leego at Tartu Water Utility company. The project aimed at designing a new digitalization strategy at a company with an outdated IT system park, as well as creating more detailed requirements for completing the first step of the strategy. FEM was successfully used in the following tasks:

1. Understanding how the company operates in general, especially in a situation where a domain is new for the business analysts engaged in the project.
2. Gathering detailed information related to each of the 14 departments. FEM was used as a guiding tool to find the gaps between the details obtained in the first round of interviews and formulate questions for the next rounds.
3. Producing a set of detailed diagrams of the business "as-is" for each department, which served as an informational basis for decisions on what needs to be changed.
4. Producing detailed diagrams of the business "to-be" for each department. These diagrams showed the changes to be introduced via a new strategy. They were also linked to the "as-is" diagrams, to show the difference. The "to-be" diagrams were also used as an informational basis for creating requirements on new IT systems and for initial market investigation.
5. For communicating changes to be introduced to the internal stakeholders.

As Steven has experience as business analyst from similar projects, his opinion on the usefulness of FEM reflects a comparative strength of the tool in the tasks listed above. Using FEM allowed him to use the time allocated for the project more effectively, especially regarding the first task on the list.

The first project was completed by a person with experience of system analysis, but without experience of FEM. In contrast to this project, the second project was completed by two MS students, Erik Falenius and August Carlsson, from Stockholm University as their MS thesis work. Neither of the students had any business analysis experience, and they did not have any knowledge of FEM before the project started. Nevertheless, they managed to obtain practically important results with minimum guidance from their supervisor (the first author). FEM structure and archetypes were used in the project to guide gathering and analyzing the information; this "guiding" property of FEM played the major role in their success.

The project's practical goal was to suggest improvements for a so-called sourcing process in an international concern. The sourcing project aimed at signing long-term purchasing contracts for all branches of the concern. By creating FEM model of the process and its context, the students could find several problems in it; the major one was not reusing information obtained in the previous instances of the process. The management of the concern agreed that the suggested improvements made sense and could be implemented. As a side effect of discussions held using FEM, internal business analysts became interested in the technique and wanted to use it in other projects.

10.5   Conclusion

This chapter started with formulating a goal of giving the management a model that explains how the organization operates in an, for the management, understandable way. We suggested that our Fractal Enterprise Model (FEM) could satisfy this goal. Furthermore, we presented the latest version of FEM, both informally and formally—as a metamodel—and then proceeded with discussing a toolkit to support building FEMs.

We consider creating a toolkit as an essential step in promoting FEM as a practical solution to the problem defined in Sect. 10.1. As has been discussed in the chapter, supporting building a single model does not satisfy the needs of the modeler. A modeler, usually, needs to create a package of diagrams, each filling its own purpose. Some diagram needs to present an overall picture; thus, the granularity of the model will be coarse. Others need to present the details of certain parts of the business; thus, their granularity should be finer. Some models will present the current state of the business, others will suggest changes. What is more, the models that constitute the package need to be connected, so that the user of the package can easily go from a general picture to a detailed one, or from a model "as-is" to the model "to-be." Also, the toolkit should help visualize particularities of a specific modeling project in a standardized way without substantially extending the toolkit.

By experimenting with the ADOxx environment, we have succeeded in implementing the toolkit that satisfies the requirements. The metamodeling environment was of great help here, as it allowed to test hypotheses, quickly modify the toolkit when some feature showed to be inconvenient, and get us to the point when the toolkit started to be useful in practice. The toolkit has already been tested in several practical projects, and it is also used in master of science level courses to introduce FEM to the students. Our plans include both further development and dissemination of the toolkit among the practitioners via webinars and tutorials.

Acknowledgments The authors are very grateful to the ADOxx team for providing them with the environment for experimentation that allowed the creation of a toolkit using the minimum of resources. They are also much in debt to Dominik Bork who implemented the first version of the FEM toolkit and continues to support their efforts. The authors are also grateful to their students and colleagues Steven Leego, Erik Falenius, and August Carlsson who independently tested the FEM toolkit in practical projects. The first author's work was partly supported by the Estonian Research Council (grant PRG1226).

Tool Download: https://www.omilab.org/fem

References

1. Hoverstadt, P.: Why business should take Enterprise architecture seriously. In: Gøtze, J., Jensen-Waud, A. (eds.) Beyond alignment, Systems, vol. 3, pp. 55–166. College Publishing, London (2013)
2. OMG: Business Process Model and Notation (BPMN), Version 2.0.2, Object Management Group (OMG), Document formal/2013-12-09, December 2013. In: OMG. Available at: http://www.omg.org/spec/BPMN/2.0.2/PDF. Accessed 2013
3. Beer, S.: The Heart of Enterprise. Wiley, Chichester (1979)
4. OMG: Business Motivation Model, Version 1.2, Object Management Group (OMG), Document formal/2014-05-01, May 2014. Available at: http://www.omg.org/spec/BMM/1.2/PDF
5. The open group: ArchiMate® 3.0.1 Specification. In: The Open Group. Available at: https://publications.opengroup.org/standards/archimate/specifications/c179. Accessed 2020

6. Hoverstadt, P.: The viable system model. In: Systems Approaches to Managing Change: A Practical Guide, pp. 87–133. Springer, London (2010)
7. NIST: Integration definition for function modeling (IDEF0), Draft Federal Information Processing Standards, Publication 183, 1993. In: IDEF. Available at: https://www.idef.com/idefo-function_modeling_method/. Accessed 1993
8. ADOxx.org: ADOxx. Available at: https://www.adoxx.org. Accessed 2017
9. Bider, I., Perjons, E., Elias, M., Johannesson, P.: A fractal enterprise model and its application for business development. SoSyM. **16**(3), 663–689 (2017)
10. Bider, I.: Structural coupling, strategy and fractal Enterprise Modeling. In: Research Challenges in Information Science. RCIS 2020, LNBIP 385, pp. 95–111. Springer (2020)
11. Bider, I., Lodhi, A.: Moving from manufacturing to software business: A business model transformation pattern. In: Enterprise Information Systems. ICEIS 2019, LNBIP 378, pp. 514–530. Springer (2020)
12. Bider, I., Chalak, A.: Evaluating usefulness of a fractal Enterprise model experience report. In: Enterprise, Business-Process and Information Systems Modeling. BPMDS 2019, EMMSAD 2019, LNBIP, vol. 352, pp. 359–373 (2019)
13. Giesen, E., Berman, S.J., Bell, R., Blitz, A.: Three ways to successfully innovate your business model. Strategy & Leadership. **35**(6), 27–33 (2007)
14. Bider, I., Perjons, E.: Using a fractal enterprise model for business model innovation. In: BPMDS 2017 RADAR, CEUR, vol. 1859, pp. 20–29. (2017)
15. Bider, I., Perjons, E.: Defining transformational patterns for business model innovation. In: Perspectives in business informatics research: 17th international conference, BIR 2018, Stockholm, Sweden. LNBIP. **330**, 81–95 (2018)
16. Josefsson, M., Widman, K., Bider, I.: Using the process-assets framework for creating a holistic view over process documentation. In: Enterprise, Business-Process and Information Systems Modeling, LNBIP, vol. 214, pp. 169–183. Springer, Stockholm (2015)
17. Maturana, H.: Autopoiesis, structural coupling & cognition. Cybern Hum knowing. **9**(3–4), 5–34 (2002)
18. Hoverstadt, P.: Defining Identity by Structural Coupling in VSM Practice. UK Systems Society, Oxford (2010)
19. Hoverstadt, P., Loh, L.: Patterns of Strategy. Taylor & Francis, London (2017)
20. FEM toolkit. Available at: https://www.fractalmodel.org/fem-toolkit/. Accessed 27 Feb 2021
21. Give Team: Insightmaker. Available at: http://insightmaker.com/. Accessed 2014
22. Klyukina, V., Bider, I., Perjons, E.: Does fractal enterprise model fit operational decision making? In: Proceedings of the 23rd International Conference on Enterprise Information System (ICEIS) 2021, vol. 2, pp. 613–624 (2021)
23. Leego, S., Bider, I.: Using fractal enterprise model in technology-driven organisational change projects: A case of a water utility company. In: 23rd IEEE Conference on Business Informatics, CBI 2021, vol. 2, pp. 107–116 (2021)

Chapter 11
The Integration of Risk Aspects into Business Process Management: The *e*-BPRIM Modeling Method

Elyes Lamine, Rafika Thabet, Amadou Sienou, and Hervé Pingaud

Abstract Risk consideration in enterprise engineering is gaining attention since the business environment is becoming more and more competitive, complex, and unpredictable. Risk-aware Business Process Management (R-BPM) is a recently emerged management paradigm, which assists organizations in addressing this concern. R-BPM strives to integrate two traditionally isolated areas: risk management and business process management. This chapter will present recent achievements of our long-term research devoted to this field. It consists in developing an integrated process-risk management methodological framework, named BPRIM, and its related multi-view modeling method, called *e*-BPRIM, which promotes and supports risk-aware process management with ADOBPRIM, a computer-assisted modeling environment based on ADOXX. A case study related to the management of the COVID-19 pandemic in France shall illustrate the usage of the *e*-BPRIM method with the ADOBPRIM modeling environment.

Keywords Risk-aware Business Process Management · Meta-modeling · Multi-view modeling method · Modeling tool · ADOBPRIM · COVID-19 pandemic

E. Lamine (✉) · R. Thabet
Toulouse University, ISIS, Institut National Universitaire Champollion, Castres, France

Toulouse University, IMT Mines Albi, Department of Industrial Engineering, Albi, France
e-mail: elyes.lamine@univ-jfc.fr; elyes.lamine@mines-albi.fr; rafika.thabet@inp-toulouse.fr

A. Sienou
abamix GmbH, Stuttgart, Germany
e-mail: sienou@abamix.com

H. Pingaud
Toulouse University, CNRS-LGC, Institut National Universitaire Champollion, Albi, France
e-mail: herve.pingaud@univ-jfc.fr

11.1   Introduction

Various dramatic events, which happened in the previous decade such as the 2008 financial crisis and the present COVID-19 sanitary situation, have brought our societies to their knees, increasing therefore awareness of risk management practices in different organizations.

According to ISO 31000: 2018 [8], Enterprise Risk Management (ERM) is a set of coordinated activities, which aim at directing and controlling an organization regarding risk. Several risk management methods have been developed to support the establishment of governance practices by identifying potential threats to business objectives and assessing their organizational level impacts. Actually the ALARM method [29] is commonly used in the health sector, while the OCTAVE method [1] well known in the defense sector and the CORAS method [5] in cybersecurity. These methods usually focus on three main elements: (a) risk identification, (b) assessment of risk criticality, and (c) definition of treatments for the identified risks.

These methods are generally based on a vertical approach and do not take into account, both, the organization as a whole and the context of the risk situation and its relationship to the business processes. This is indeed a narrow study of risk. Motivated by these observations, several researchers explored new perspectives to cope with the limits. A particular approach, which consists of embedding risk models into business process models, has been driven by the Risk-aware Business Process Management (R-BPM) paradigm, striving to integrate the two traditionally isolated areas of Enterprise Risk Management and Business Process Management (BPM)—which is a set of methods, techniques, and tools to identify, discover, analyze, redesign, execute, and monitor business processes in order to optimize their performance [3]. The goal of R-BPM is to support risk and business managers in the decision-making process at different organizational levels. Risk consideration is promoted by the R-BPM in the early stages of business processes management and enables robust and efficient business processes within risky situations.

Despite the significant benefits that can arise from the use of R-BPM, it suffers from a lack of solid scientific foundations as well as tools, compared to what is published individually with regard to BPM or ERM. Indeed, studies emphasize either a specific domain of applications (finance, IT, etc.) or specific stages of the life cycle (design time, assessment, etc.). In addition, R-BPM methods are generally limited to the proposal of new graphical notations toward the enrichment of process models with risk models. However, and as Pr. Karagiannis rightly points out [11], modeling languages are only one building block of a modeling method. Actually, a modeling method also encompasses a modeling procedure and modeling algorithms. The modeling procedure consists of a sequence of steps, which the user needs to follow in order to create valid models. The modeling algorithms process the knowledge captured in the conceptual models. R-BPM needs to be extended, exactly with this vision of modeling method in order to improve its result, mainly integrated modeling of risks and processes at different stages of their life cycles.

Our research contributes to the promotion of R-BPM by bridging this gap with two elements: (i) by establishing the foundations of a R-BPM methodology called BPRIM (Business Process-Risk management—Integrated Method), which is digitized as *e*-BPRIM framework, and (ii) by designing a dedicated tool, named ADOBPRIM, which supports the efficient application of the *e*-BPRIM modeling method.

This chapter presents recent achievements of this ongoing long-term research devoted to model-driven enterprise engineering through integrated consideration of risk and process management. Based on an agile development method, *e*-BPRIM provides insights and value-driven models able to support risk and process managers in their duties. The multi-view modeling language and the integrated management method are the backbone of the *e*-BPRIM approach, which also provides mechanisms and algorithms to verify and evaluate risk models.

The remainder of this chapter will provide first, in Sect. 11.2, an overview of BPRIM according to related work that was carried out on R-BPM paradigm. Then, in Sect. 11.3, the emphasis is on the presentation of the conceptualization of *e*-BPRIM method and its dedicated tool, namely, ADOBPRIM, which is realized with the ADOxx meta-modeling platform. Section 11.4 shall introduce a case study from the healthcare domain related to the COVID-19 health crisis management to illustrate the use of this new R-BPM modeling method before concluding in Sect. 11.5 while providing outlines for future work.

11.2   Method Description

11.2.1   Background and Related Work

Risk-aware business process management is an emerged management paradigm which strives to support risk managers and business managers at different life cycle phases and levels of the organization. It promotes risks consideration in early stages of business processes management and enables a robust and efficient business process management in an uncertain and highly dynamic environment [12, 22].

Earlier research published in [16] have also shown that risk is an inherent property of any business process and needs therefore to be integrated into business process at the model level. Based on a risk taxonomy defined in the Entity-Relationship model, the authors proposed four interrelated model types, namely, Risk Structure model, Risk Goal model, Risk State model, and Event-Driven Process Chain model extended with risks. These models support the visualization of risk components in the context of business processes. This provided the foundation for building a framework [13] in order to ensure a holistic business view of risk management in Enterprise systems. The proposed framework reuses concepts defined in value-focused process engineering and establishes a clear relationship between risks, business goals, and business activities.

Since the last decade, the research community of R-BPM growths in number and results as shown by Jakoubi et al. [9] and Suriadi et al. [21], who provided a comprehensive and systematic overview of state of the art.

A key limitation of this area, which is slowing down a wide adoption of R-BPM, was the lack of a methodological framework enabling an effective and a successful implementation in Enterprise systems. Furthermore, we found that, with the exception of the work of Pittl et al. [15] and Weiss and Winkelmann [31], only very few of these approaches are supported by engineering tools.

As an afterword, three main questions need to be answered in order to establish sound foundations for R-BPM as a new paradigm:

1. How to couple both life cycles, ERM and BPM, in order to define the life cycle of R-BPM?
2. What are the relationships between the concepts used by ERM and those used by BPM in order to define a common domain specific conceptual language that will support R-BPM?
3. How to support R-BPM with a software tool in order to ensure efficiency and effectiveness?

11.2.2 BPRIM: *Business Process-Risk Management—Integrated Method*

Aware of the beneficial contributions of R-BPM and its limitations, we have conducted several works in the previous decade to contribute to the research in R-BPM discipline by first setting the foundations of the BPRIM (Business Process-Risk management—Integrated Method) methodology. It addressed the first two research questions [12, 19]. Then, *e*-BPRIM framework was created as an endorsement of the BPRIM methodology which, among other components, added a multi-view modeling tool and addressed our third research question.

The BPRIM cornerstone was to integrate models from two disciplines which is not a new approach. It is well-known and used in the community of Enterprise Engineering (EE) consisting of bringing together heterogeneous knowledge to design or redesign business entities [28]. These knowledge are clarified by models belonging to different fields which are designed by several stakeholders with different modeling skills and practices. EE usually resorts to modeling framework which structures and guides the modeling process by specifying the relative positioning of models, the overlapping areas, and the mechanisms to go from one to another [27]. In addition, it promotes one or several modeling languages which incorporate fundamental concepts of the investigated domain, commonly specified through a meta-model.

Therefore, and according to the principles of Enterprise Engineering, BPRIM framework proposed a synchronization of the life cycles of Business process management focusing primarily on the design stage and risk management into a single process model, named BPRIM life cycle, which guides process owners and risk managers through their usual tasks. As shown in Fig. 11.1, the BPRIM life cycle consists in coupling steps of process management with those of risk management drawing upon an integration approach. This approach is based on the principle of the black box seeking to build relationships between the outputs and the inputs of the different steps belonging to the two cycles.

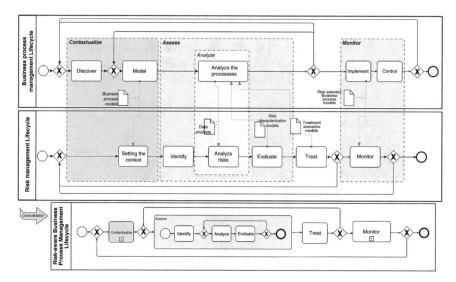

Fig. 11.1 BPRIM life cycle

Accordingly, BPRIM life cycle is an iterative cycle consisting in four phases. It is started by a **contextualization phase** aiming at setting up the context of the joint management of risks and processes. It can be triggered by a decision affecting a significant change in the context such as the implementation of a new delivery service, and which requires a proper vision of how the current organization effectively works. The outputs of this phase will then be gradually enriched by new insights about risks and their interactions with the organization's processes. These usual tasks of identifying, analyzing, and evaluating risks with process consideration are carried through the **assessment phase** of this BPRIM cycle. The outcome leads to risk prioritization and fosters the development of risk treatment alternatives, which will be conducted in the **treatment phase**. This later can lead to a reframing—meaning going back to the contextualization phase—which would require the implementation of risk handling actions. The BPRIM **Monitor phase** aims to ensure that decisions regarding treatment options have been taken according to predefined instructions, allowing the appreciation of the effectiveness of risk management policies. It is therefore a control phase, which could provide guidance for refinement of the models or the transition to the implementation phase, as depicted in Fig. 11.1 by the cycle loop following the monitor sub-activity. This is also the case for risks that have not been anticipated yet.

The information exchanged between these phases are embedded in a wide range of BPRIM models. These models are compliant to the BPRIM conceptual model which puts forward a conceptual unification of risks and processes into a common meta-model allowing to comprehensively address the semantics of R-BPM artefacts. The BPRIM conceptual model was based, on the one hand, on the business process meta-model proposed in the ISO 19440:2007 standard, which specifies the characteristics of the core constructs necessary for computer-supported modeling of enterprises (e.g. Process, Activity, Event) [7], and, on the other hand, on our proposition of a risk meta-model [12, 20], which is based on the study of the internal structure of risks. This one conceptualizes risks with regard to the causal and the consequence perspectives and for which the concepts of risk event, risk factor, and

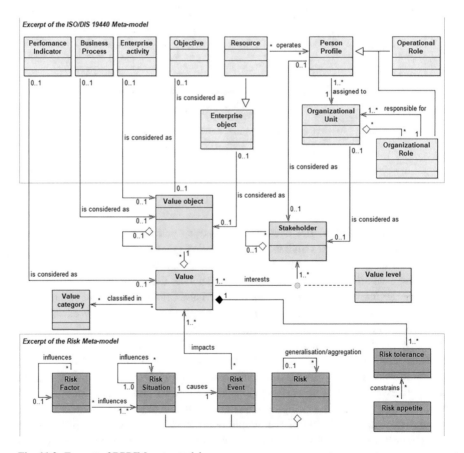

Fig. 11.2 Excerpt of BPRIM meta-model

risk situation have been introduced and linked together. Thus, the conceptual model embraces the three usual meanings of the word "risk."

Furthermore, in the context of BPM, a business process is a means, which is designed in order to coordinate value creation. Managing business processes requires a deep understanding of the relationship between value creation and the value itself. On the other hand, Enterprise Risk Management (ERM) is a systematic approach, which aims at managing variations of value levels in order to keep them in an area of acceptance. Although in practice the two management approaches are used independently from each other, they are by nature complementary: BPM improves decisions in value creation activities, whereas ERM looks for the preservation of these values.

Hence, the link between these two meta-models is then underpinned on the concept of **Value** which is a broad concept that has been highly debated in various studies and in many different fields [17, 18]. In this work, it designates the assessment of the tangible or intangible benefits of an asset by a given stakeholder. Namely, a value describes the interest of a stakeholder for a given object. It may be evaluated in terms of level of value. An excerpt of the BPRIM conceptual model is displayed in Fig. 11.2. The detailed description of these new concepts settled out in the BPRIM metamodel is given in Table 11.1.

The BPRIM conceptual model was used then to define the abstract syntax of BPRIM notation specific to the R-BPM domain, allowing the description of risk situations from the common perspective of risk and process experts. Graphic representations have also been proposed as a concrete syntax of this language and which reuses several eEPC element constructs and extends them with additional

Table 11.1 Excerpt of BPRIM meta-model concepts

Concept	Description
Value	The expression of the interest of a stakeholder for an object. Value is perceived by a stakeholder as an asset which may be affected by a risk event
Value object	An object which can be assessed by a stakeholder as valuable
Value level	Qualitative or quantitative evaluation of a value object by a stakeholder
Value category	Classification of value objects. This classification might be based on the role of the objects within the business process, e.g., input, control, resource, or output. Sample value categories are appraisal value, use value, societal value, and economic and financial value
Stakeholder	Organizational entity with an expressed value in relation to risk. This could be a person, a group, or organization affected by or likely to influence the risk
Risk factor	A set of conditions that favor the onset of a risk situation
Risk situation	Concept representing a feared or desired situation which can cause a risk event
Risk event	Concept that represents an instantaneous fact resulting from a hazardous event set
Risk	The possibility of a situation affecting an asset. Risk is a polysemous concept which encompasses three forms of interpretation: event, situation, and context. A risk is able to modify the level associated to a value interpreted by a set of stakeholders. A risk may cause, for example, performance, quality, or compliance variations. The possibility of a risk event affecting an asset

graphic symbols. This language will be further detailed in the following sections of this chapter.

These three preliminary promising findings, namely, BPRIM life cycle, BPRIM conceptual model, and BPRIM notation, led us to follow up on this work by performing a second stage firstly consisting of assessing the potential of the BPRIM framework in the field, in order to strengthen its foundations, and, secondly, by designing a dedicated modeling environment as supporting tool and methods for this new practice in order to facilitate its use and appropriation. The results of this second stage gave birth to *e*-BPRIM which digitized and enriched the basic concepts introduced by the BPRIM framework, notably by:

- Specifying multiple *e*-BPRIM points of view according to BPRIM conceptual model to clarify the expected models for each step in the BPRIM life cycle;
- Designing navigation techniques in the ADOBPRIM tool to ensure consistency between these points of view following an *e*-BPRIM modeling procedure that will be demonstrated using a case study;
- Defining several algorithms for model verification, and advanced risk management features, supported both by *e*-BPRIM on the theorical side and ADOBPRIM on the practical one.

The content of *e*-BPRIM includes the first step of an IT engineering project, i.e., the result of a requirement analysis extracted from the BPRIM theory, so as to be able to specify and develop ADOBPRIM in conformity with the underpinned theory. Then, many design choices have been made to get the expected R-BPM domain specific modeling language.

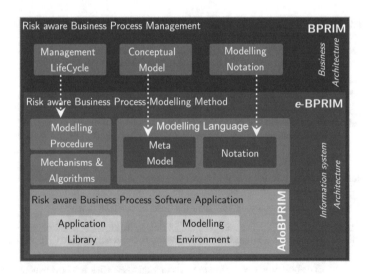

Fig. 11.3 An overview of *e*-BPRIM method

As shown in Fig. 11.3, all these improvements have been then implemented in the ADOXX environment to create the ADOBPRIM tool which is the dedicated support to *e*-BPRIM framework. The next section will present and discuss their conceptualization.

11.3 *e*-BPRIM and ADOBPRIM Conceptualization

As depicted in Fig. 11.3, the scope of *e*-BPRIM method matches up with the information system layer and fits into the business architecture which has been defined by the BPRIM framework. Consequently, to conceptualize and implement this, we went for the Design Science Research methodology (DSRM) which is well-known and frequently applied in information systems research [6, 14]. Pragmatically, and given that we were attempting to set up a modeling method, the conceptualization of the *e*-BPRIM modeling method generally is drawn upon the Agile Modeling Method Engineering (AMME) life cycle [10] which is compliant with DSRM. This later comprises five core phases, each of which focusing on selected aspects of modeling method conceptualization:

- **Creation** phase concerns the knowledge acquisition and requirements specification that capture and represent the modeling requirements.
- **Design** phase specifies the meta-model, modeling language, modeling procedure, and algorithms and mechanisms.
- **Formalize** phase aims to describe the outcome of the previous phase in non-ambiguous representations with the purpose of sharing results within a scientific community.
- **Develop** phase produces a concrete modeling tool.
- **Deploy** phase concerns the deployment of the modeling tool.

In this section, we will focus exclusively on presenting how we addressed the design and develop AMME phases to design our *e*-BPRIM modeling method and develop the corresponding modeling tool, called ADOBPRIM. A comprehensive presentation on how we addressed all AMME phases can be found in great detail in [23, 25, 26].

11.3.1 *e*-BPRIM *Multi-view Modeling Method Design*

This phase chiefly consists of rigorously defining the *e*-BPRIM modeling procedure, its modeling language, and several mechanisms and algorithms providing functionalities to use and evaluate models, which form, according to [11], the main components of a modeling method.

11.3.1.1   *e*-BPRIM Multi-view Modeling Procedure

As a matter of course, BPRIM life cycle gave a layout of the *e*-BPRIM modeling procedure, and for which particular attention was paid to setting out the different models to be established at each phase, as well as the sequence and the timing of their uses. The successive models of the complete modeling procedure are illustrated on Fig. 11.4. Each view corresponds to a viewpoint which focuses only on certain aspects of risk and/or process while abstracting away irrelevant detail. The upper viewpoints are related to the organizational and informational aspects, while the lower ones are more dedicated to the business dynamic aspect.

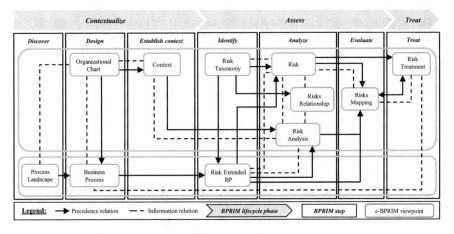

Fig. 11.4 *e*-BPRIM multi-view modeling procedure

Accordingly, the *contextualization* phase starts with a "Discover" step leading to establish a "Process Landscape" view which specifies the value-added processes of the system under study. Next, the "Organizational Chart" view is defined in the "Design" step which aims to identify roles and expectations, thereby establishing a greater understanding of the organization's structure. In addition, this definition serves to define the "Business Process" views, then enabling the establishment of the "Context" view.

The *Assess* phase gets going with an "Identify" step aiming to create firstly the "Risk Taxonomy" view which defines and classifies potential risks according to various criteria and secondly to generate the "Risk-extended Business Process" views which assign previously identified risks to individual activities of the business process views. After, the "Analyze" step starts with an individual risk analysis. It consists of elaborating three views: (1) a "Risk Analysis" view which underlines risk causes and consequences, risk analysis by risk level calculation, and qualitative/quantitative risk evaluation, (2) a "Risk" view which generates an overview of a given risk within its environment capturing all existing relationships between risk and other *e*-BPRIM concepts, and (3) a "Risk Relationship" view which describes all relationships between identified risks. In the "Evaluate" step, the dynamic risk characteristics are summarized in a "Risks Mapping" view. The latter is defined by a two-dimensional risk matrix showing the risk level of each analyzed risk.

The *Treat* phase aims to identify the most critical risks and to treat these risks by defining control mechanisms in "Risk Treatment" views. Once control mechanisms are defined, process changes and improvements may be implied, thereby closing one walk-through of the *e*-BPRIM modeling procedure.

Another important consideration to emphasize in this modeling procedure is the setting of two viewpoint relation types: The first one, named "Precedence relation," describes the sequential order to use *e*-BPRIM viewpoints, and the second one, named "Information relation," indicates that two viewpoints share information. These relations inevitably lead to overlaps between viewpoints concepts which have been extensively studied for designing navigation techniques in the ADOBPRIM tool.

11.3.1.2   *e*-BPRIM Modeling Language

As shown in Fig. 11.4, eleven interdependent viewpoints are identified in the *e*-BPRIM modeling procedure. Each viewpoint is defined by a subset of concepts necessary to address concerns framed by this point of view. All these concepts constitute the abstract syntax of the *e*-BPRIM modeling language which is defined by the meta-model, depicted in Fig. 11.5. This latter derived from the BPRIM conceptual model provides the language concepts and the rules for combining them.

A graphical representation is then associated with each *e*-BPRIM meta-model concept and whose union forms the concrete syntax of the *e*-BPRIM modeling language, namely, its notation. It also needs to be noted that the *e*-BPRIM concrete syntax is based on the BPRIM notation.

Figure 11.5 visualizes the meta-model of the eleven *e*-BPRIM viewpoints extended with the notation of each *e*-BPRIM meta-model concept. The figure also outlines the various *e*-BPRIM viewpoint relationships where we could differentiate four kinds: (1) *Syntactic overlap* which describes a relationship when a meta-model concept is represented in two different viewpoints by the same notation; (2) *Semantic overlap* which arises when a meta-model concept is represented in two different viewpoints by different notations but the semantics of the two concepts overlap; (3) *Refinement/Abstraction overlap* which describes a relationship between viewpoints where one viewpoint is an abstract representation of the other; and (4) *Association overlap* which describes a relationship where an association viewpoint is used to combine several concepts belonging to other viewpoints. This relation either binds the viewpoints together or constrains the shared semantics.

A comprehensive description of each *e*-BPRIM viewpoint relationship is elaborated in great detail in [23, 26].

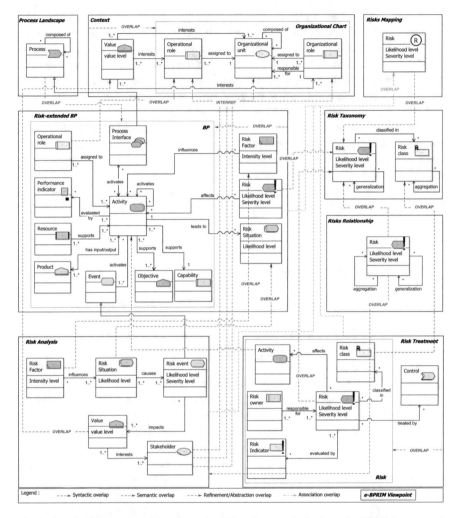

Fig. 11.5 *e*-BPRIM meta-model and notation inferred, respectively, from the BPRIM conceptual model and modeling notation

11.3.1.3 *e*-BPRIM Algorithms and Mechanisms

Based on the *e*-BPRIM modeling procedure and viewpoints, several mechanisms and algorithms have been identified, notably:

- **Multi-view consistency:** aiming to keep consistency between *e*-BPRIM viewpoints and for which multi-view modeling operations on *e*-BPRIM views are introduced, as shown in Fig. 11.6:

  1. Decomposition: With this operation, a new view is considered as a more abstract representation of a given view.
  2. Extension: With this operation, a new view is created by extending an existing view with additional syntactic concepts.

3. Reuse: With this operation, a new view is created by reusing one or several syntactic and/or semantic concepts from one or more existing views.
4. Merging: With this operation, a new view is created by combining some syntactic concepts of two of more existing views. The provided view can also add new syntactic concepts specific to the viewpoint of the new created view.
5. Synthesis: With this operation, a new view is created by gathering the information of several views and then generating a synthesis view.
6. Synchronization: This operation ensures the propagation of any modifications (i.e., create, edit, or delete) performed on an overlapping concept in one view to be propagated in semantically equivalent operations that need to be automatically performed on all other views. An extract of this synchronization algorithm is presented by Algorithm 1 which describes how consistency is ensured in all *e*-BPRIM views after any instance value modification.

Algorithm 1 Synchronization after modify instance value

---

input   : *event*: event which triggered when an view object is edited
           $V\_e - BPRIM$: All *e*-BPRIM views
Output : All $V_{e-BPRIM}$ automatically synchronized
begin
  if TypeOfEvent (*event*) = '*Modify*' **then**
      $Object_{Id}$ ←SearchModifiedObjectId($V_{e-BPRIM}$)
      $Affected\_V_{e-BPRIM}$ ←SearchAffectedViews($V_{e-BPRIM}$,$Object_{Id}$)
      foreach *View in Affected_$V_{e-BPRIM}$* **do**
          $SynchList$ ← FindRelatedObjectIDs (*View*,$Object_{Id}$)
          foreach *Id in SynchList* **do**
           | UpdateValue (*Id*)
          end
      end
  end
end

- **Model checking:** refers to several verification functionalities which are specified on different levels, ranging from *cardinality checks* as syntactical checks (checking whether all constraints of the BPRIM modeling language are satisfied) to source-target validation. The objective of this mechanism is to ensure the accuracy of diagrams created by checking their structure according to several defined syntactic and semantic rules.
- **Risk assessment:** The risk analysis view is analyzed and evaluated using a risk assessment matrix. The latter is a classical method to conduct qualitative risk assessment. The objective of this mechanism is to automatically produce a risk matrix in order to visualize the different risk levels. An extract of this assessment algorithm is presented by Algorithm 2 which describes how risk criticality is calculated in the risk analysis view and added in the risk mapping view.

In addition to these algorithms and mechanisms, we are currently working toward integrating new risk assessment techniques, particularly the Bow-tie method [2]. Indeed, the latter is a risk analysis and management technique that has been readily adopted into routine practice in many high-reliability industries such as

---

Algorithm 2 Assessment of a risk analysis view

---

input   : *event*: event which triggered when a risk analysis view is analyzed and evaluated
              V_{RA}: Risk analysis view
Output : Risk likelihood and severity automatically calculated and added in the risk mapping view
begin
   if TypeOfEvent (*event*) = '*Analyze*' **then**
      $RFList \leftarrow$ SearchRiskFactorObjects (V_{RA})
      $RSList \leftarrow$ SearchRiskSituationObjects (V_{RA})
      $REObject \leftarrow$ SearchRiskEventObject (V_{RA})
      $REObject_{Likelihood} \leftarrow$ PropagateLikelihoodCalculation (*RFList, RSList,*
      REObject)
      $Analyzed_{View} \leftarrow$ True
   end
   if TypeOfEvent (*event*) = '*Evaluate*' AND $Analyzed_{View}$ **then**
      $REObject_{Severity} \leftarrow$ GetSeverityValue (*REObject*)
      $REObject_{Criticality} \leftarrow$ CriticalityCalculation ($REObject_{Likelihood},$
      $REObject_{Severity}$)
      SetRiskEventInRiskMapping ($REObject_{Criticality}$)
   end
end

---

engineering, aviation, and emergency services. The Bow-tie method provides a readily understood visualization of the relationships between the causes of business upsets and the escalation of such events. This method also visualizes control mechanisms preventing the event from occurring and the preparedness measures in place to limit the business impact.

We also plan to provide other risk mapping views toward a dashboard of the risk evolution over time. This shall allow the risk manager to have better visibility of the evolution of the probability of occurrence, the severity, and the impact of risks over time.

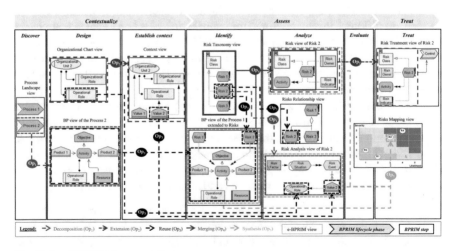

Fig. 11.6 *e*-BPRIM views operations

11.3.2 ADOBPRIM *Multi-view Modeling Tool Development*

In order to develop our *e*-BPRIM multi-view modeling tool, called ADOBPRIM, we reverted to meta-modeling platforms, which strongly support the implementation of a domain-specific conceptual modeling method (DSMM). Therefore, the ADOxx meta-modeling platform was deemed the most appropriate solution according to our needs and to a certain criterion. Indeed, ADOxx provides a user-friendly integrated environment for the definition and implementation of modeling languages. It integrates a set of tools that meet the most frequent needs in terms of meta-modeling and programming development. A comparative analysis of ADOxx and other meta-modeling platforms can be found in [12, 23, 24, 30].

The first step in the conception of the ADOBPRIM tool was the definition of the *e*-BPRIM meta-model concepts in ADOxx using the ADOxx Library Language (ALL). Therefore, the concepts of viewpoints, classes, relations between classes, and class attributes of the *e*-BPRIM meta-model are implemented, respectively, in ADOxx as model-types, classes, relation-classes, and attributes.

Almost simultaneously, *e*-BPRIM concrete syntax was created in ADOxx by using the GRAPHREP language which allowed us to define the graphical representation of each *e*-BPRIM meta-model concept. For example, the implementation of the "Event" concept notation, with the GRAPHREP language, is given in the top left side of Fig. 11.7.

The next phase consisted of setting up in the ADOBPRIM operating rules for a valid handling and use of *e*-BPRIM viewpoints and views respecting the *e*-BPRIM modeling procedure, as defined in Sect. 11.3.1.1. These rules were developed using the ADOScript language. The result of the implementation is given in the middle of Fig. 11.7. We also used the ADOScript language to implement the *e*-BPRIM algorithms and mechanisms that we have briefly presented in Sect. 11.3.1.3. For instance, the implementation of the Synchronized Algorithm with the ADOScript language is given in the left side of Fig. 11.7.

Figure 11.7 gives an overview of the realized ADOBPRIM modeling tool. The ADOBPRIM viewpoints in ADOxx mapped to specific phases and steps of the *e*-BPRIM modeling procedure. By this structure, the ADOBPRIM tool guides the user in choosing the right model type according to the currently engaged *e*-BPRIM modeling procedure step.

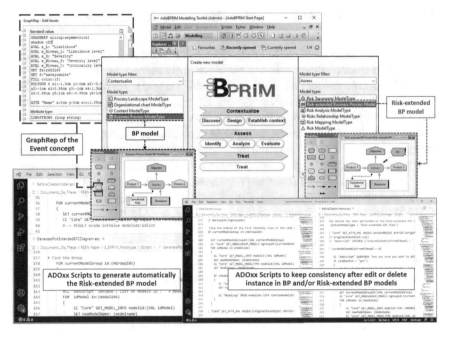

Fig. 11.7 Overview of the ADOBPRIM modeling tool. GraphRep of the "Event" concept (top left), modeling procedure (middle), and some ADOXX Scripts (bottom)

The ADOBPRIM modeling tool has been developed as a project within the Open Models Laboratory, a worldwide community of modelers and modeling method developers [4]. A free download and further information on ADOBPRIM are available through the corresponding project page.[1]

11.4 Case Study: The Crisis Management of the COVID-19 Pandemic

The content of this section is more than just a case study since it has been inspired by a real-life common experience shared by people around the world: the COVID-19 pandemic crisis.

End of 2019, and beginning of 2020, the COVID-19 virus began to spread from Asia over most of the other continents of the planet. February 2020, European governments became aware of the possible critical impact of this virus in terms of public health. Hence, they deployed systems to deal with the situation, which rapidly

---

[1] *e*-BPRIM project space within OMiLAB [online]: https://austria.omilab.org/psm/content/BPRIM, last visited: 24.03.2021.

degraded toward a generalized crisis. The force, the speed, and the damage caused in terms of people hospitalized and deaths quickly convinced a major part of the world, under the urgent request of the WHO, to take a first series of measures striving to limit the spread (the famous barrier gesture), but also to organize contaminated patient flows to hospitals while tracking the possible congestion in intensive care units for respiratory assistance over the country.

The motivation for considering this subject as a case study needs to be clarified. It is, first of all, a wide phenomenon with multiple facets. (1) Many nations have experienced this long period quite differently, from the first times of the low signals coming from China to the growing number of people affected by the virus, rising to a critical level that nobody could reasonably challenge. (2) Addressing a representation of the way the crisis has been managed is a difficult task. Each one in his/her own political culture has decided to struggle against the virus with a particular posture in a local ecosystem. Therefore, the craft of modeling must prove its ability to draw a kind of frontier between parts which are universal, when countries have more or less to face the same situations, on the one hand, and parts which are really particular to a given country, on the other hand.

Second, since the COVID-19 pandemic is a crisis, it is intrinsically a period of uncertainties where unpredicted events occur. A crisis management is founded on sound principles of risk management. The ability to explain what has happened, what will be the consequences, and how to mitigate them, as well as to estimate what could be the near future, has become a worldwide concern. As researchers involved in risk management modeling, we cannot make a shortcut of such a reality which impacts our private and professional daily life. Thus, this actual modeling practice should be considered as both, our modest contribution to the global problem and an act of solidarity with those who are trying to eradicate the virus from the earth as quickly as possible.

Insofar as the COVID-19 pandemic is considered as a crisis, i.e., an evolving situation subject to a complex risk chain, this use case offers us the possibility to demonstrate the capacity of our approach to capture and explain the dynamics of many inter-related risks. So, our aim is mainly to show the ability of BPRIM and its digitization by *e*-BPRIM to practically face such a challenge. As we target to make a real integration between business process management and risk management, an ambivalence has to be respected in accordance with two times in the *e*-BPRIM life cycle, i.e., (1) the risk management related to regular business process execution during the "contextualization" phase and (2) the business process refinements allowing to mitigate potential risks at the end, in the "Treatment" phase.

The complexity due to the multinational characteristics of this crisis and the diversity of situations to be considered as well as the weight of uncertainty are the main barriers, which need to be tackled while designing models. It is therefore obvious that the challenge is big; but the learning value of models is also high. We are confident that the *e*-BPRIM language and ADOBPRIM software will efficiently help us master these. The purpose of this section is therefore to demonstrate the use of this framework for modeling the COVID-19 crisis while addressing three goals:

1. Analyze the system and clarify our understanding of the COVID-19 pandemic in relation to the citizen's perception of the risk of contamination. This also includes the individual level of engagement with regard to respecting directives issued by government authorities.
2. Explain why it was not always possible to do what was requested because of many troubles, especially within supply chains.
3. Check the difficulties encountered by the implementation of public policies in the complex environment.

Scientifically, the purpose of this case study is to demonstrate the capabilities of ADOBPRIM to draw 13 diagrams, which together form BPRIM models. Actually, ADOBPRIM highly contributes with navigation features between the points of views. The capability of the method to guide the modeler toward the right diagram at the right time using the *e*-BPRIM procedure as a controller also needs to be underlined. The usage of the modeling procedure depicted in Fig. 11.4 shall demonstrate this. Model reuse as well as consistency between model objects that was shared by different diagrams is also a considerable outcome.

11.4.1   *e*-BPRIM *Approach to Analyzing the* COVID-19 *Pandemic Management Process in France*

A complete representation of elements, which explain the COVID-19 crisis situation, would be too ambitious. Hence the emphasis will be only on some aspects relating to the beginning and to the first wave of the pandemic. This section shall demonstrate the usage of the *e*-BPRIM procedure (Fig. 11.4) to adequately create the set of required diagrams in order to face this scenario of the COVID-19 pandemic. The subsection is structured according to the following first three phases of the BPRIM life cycle, contextualization of risks, assessment of risk, and treatment of risks, always in the context of business processes.

11.4.1.1   Contextualization: How a Normal Situation Degraded Rapidly

According to the *e*-BPRIM procedure, the business process map is the first view, which needs to be defined in order to establish the context for risk management. For this case study, the national management of the COVID-19 pandemic consists of five processes, which are mapped in Fig. 11.8.

The very first process encapsulates a set of activities to "protect against the spread of an active virus." It was the first tangible sign of change for the population, which was requested to actively consider protective measures. The process "restrict living conditions" relates to several lockdown stages with restriction of personal freedom of citizens, especially forbidding any activity, which is able to lead to groupings of persons while giving some latencies to essential activities to make sure that the country is still running at a low speed. People worried about social and economic impacts of lockdowns, at that time. The next process took shape as everyone understood that the fight against this virus would last several months. The crisis will be long and the end of the crisis would only go through the hope of a massive vaccination campaign, subject to effectiveness of vaccines that were not available on the market at this very beginning. This process is called "living with the virus and fighting."

The next step of the *e*-BPRIM procedure consists of setting up the context. To this end, the focus will be on one of the responses to the prime massive dissemination wave and more specifically on the business process "BP Model about the barrier gestures," which relates to barrier gestures as a subprocess of "protect against the spread of an active virus." The process is depicted in the central part of Fig. 11.8 and describes how a healthy person can protect himself:

1. Wear a mask to limit bilateral transfer through respiratory interfaces: the mouth and nose.
2. Limit indirect transfers from objects in the environment through hygiene hands and sneezing.
3. Impose a minimum distance to people in order to prevent direct transfers from each other.

In this view, the health condition of a person depends on objects around activities. The risk is proven if an unsuspicious individual begins to show symptoms of contamination and has a positive screening test. In case of contamination, all persons with whom this person has been interacting recently should be identified and tested as "contact cases." The referral of the infected person to the healthcare system will depend on the deterioration of the respiratory capacities. The person may be subject to an obligation asking him/her to remain isolated at home. An alternative decision may be to proceed to hospital admission if severe ailments are detected.

The bottom part of Fig. 11.8 outlines a decision-making process associated with the "wear a mask" activity. In fact, for this to be effective, it is necessary to have a mask that conforms to filtering requirements such that the particles expelled by the respiratory were trapped. The tension noted in early spring 2020 over the shortage of such masks focuses on a supply chain process including purchasing, storing, and distributing operations that has not been well performing in France. This was partly due to the fact that strategic stocks made for national defense purposes against chemical and biological attacks have been destroyed for a long time and not stocked up again. We will try to develop this particular situation as a new fragment of our model using the risk as an entry point.

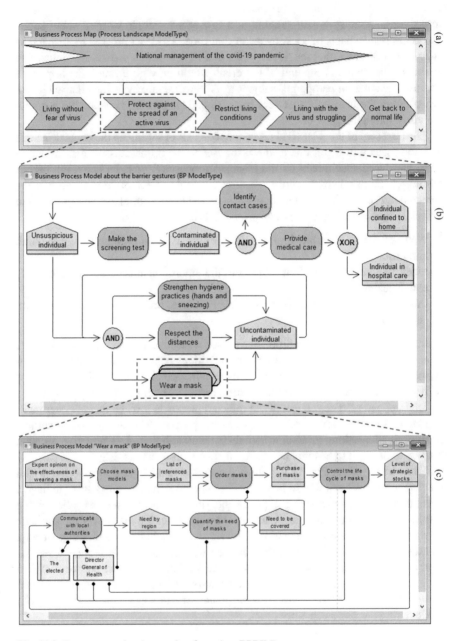

Fig. 11.8 Process mapping (screenshot from ADOBPRIM)

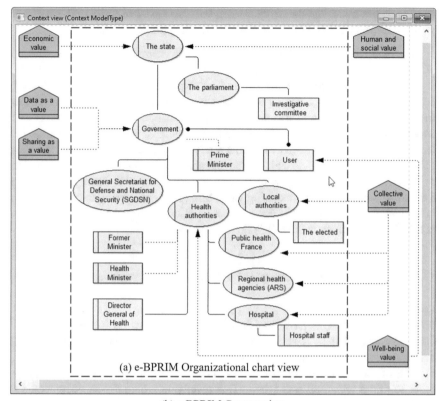

(b) e-BPRIM Context view

Fig. 11.9 Values and actors involved in crisis response (screenshot from ADOBPRIM)

At this stage of the *e*-BPRIM procedure, actors are identified as stakeholders. For example, the purchasing process first consists in choosing the mask references by mobilizing heath expert opinions. Then, it also needs data from local authorities to estimate the quantities to order. The part framed in blue dotted lines in Fig. 11.9 is an organizational chart listing the actors involved in the scope of our study. This view is based on three concepts:

1. An organizational unit is an institution making decisions within a range of responsibilities and skills. The crisis has concerned different levels, ranging from the highest state authorities to local representatives of territories and health organizations. These are represented by the oval graphic objects.
2. The organizational role (yellow rectangle) is a person who is legally responsible for the decisions made. The representatives of the authority are the prime minister and two successive ministers of health.
3. The operational role (pink rectangle) means an active person who is committed to the right progress of operations. It is the director general of the organization

of care, the users, and the medical staff, but also a control entity in the form of a parliamentary committee in charge of examining public policies.

As already mentioned in Sect. 11.2.2, the BPRIM framework defines the concept of value as an asset, which can be impacted by risks. Stakeholders' decisions strive to achieve a balance between the effort of value preservation and the potential loss due to lack of protection measures. Accordingly, we have chosen, within a broad framework, six values which cannot be neglected if one wants to keep the system under control: (a) individual welfare value; (b) collective value for a population in a territory; (c) human and social value that tends to federate citizens around the Head of State; (d) economic value which is the mainstay for having an acceptable standard of living; (e) data value because observability and information quality are essential for decision-making; and (f) sharing value that gives consistency to everyone's act in the context of multiple and necessary collaboration. These values are represented in the Fig. 11.9, which is the *e*-BPRIM context view.

11.4.1.2 Assessment: Entering into a Space of Risk Consciousness

During the "contextualization" phase of the BPRIM life cycle, a set of four models divided into three stages have been designed in order to set up the case study. Now the next phase, named "Assess," will reuse this knowledge in order to initiate risk management within the modeling process.

First of all, risks identification is conducted within a brainstorming session in order to find a set of adverse events. This results on a list of risks documented in the form of a taxonomy. Figure 11.10 suggests an exposure of the studied system to 16 different risks. The risk space is quite big; by consequence, BPRIM offers the opportunity to classify them for a better perception.

Figure 11.10 illustrates four risk classes: (1) viral risk relating to health risks, (2) logistical risk relating to the availability of qualified materials and equipment, (3) social risks dealing with the behavior of individuals and groups, and (4) political risk including societal risks and cultural risks, i.e., the capacity and the desire of citizens to respect directives and laws. This political risk also includes a class of economic risk, which will be out-scoped in this chapter. Note that this part of the model reveals the systemic nature of the pandemic.

Larger risk sets are also included. The health risk is obviously essential, but its effects, like the treatments proposed to control it, have created a waterfall of exposure to other types of risks. Consequently, the political decision becomes a very difficult exercise where one must consider firstly antagonistic effects and secondly learning outcomes from the past.

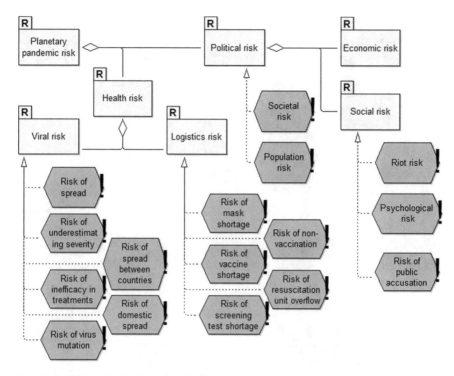

Fig. 11.10 Risks affecting the system during crisis

The next step in this phase consists of crossing knowledge between the defined activities in the business process views and potential risks identified in the taxonomy view. The result is a risk-aware business process view, as shown in Fig. 11.11. Four risks listed in the above nomenclature are associated with business processes:

1. The risks of mask shortage and spread are related to the "wearing a mask" activity.
2. The risk of spread also relates to two other activities, "strengthen hygiene measures" and "Respect distances."
3. The risk of ineffective treatment relates to the healthcare of any infected individual.
4. The risk of "underestimating the severity" applies to the identification of infected individuals, as well as to the management of his/her contact cases.

Similarly to the business processes of the "contextualization" scoping phase, which were described using two models, the extension of these processes to include risks also involves two representations. Figure 11.12 complements Fig. 11.11 as it is intended to be more analytical since its purpose is the quantitative identification of risks. Both are designed with a part of the *e*-BPRIM language specific to business

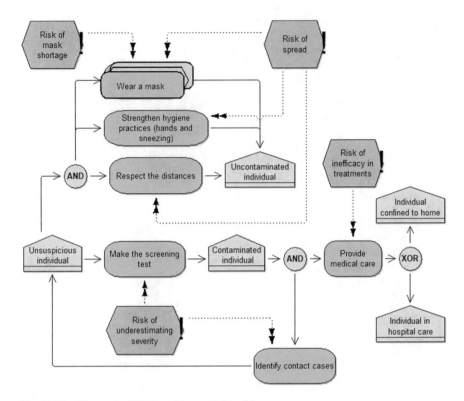

Fig. 11.11 "Wear a mask" BP model extended to risks

process extended to risk viewpoint. Hence, new constructs are used, which are superimposed on the business process elements of Fig. 11.12.

Indeed, four of the five activities explaining the work are carried out in order to have a sufficient quantity of mask. All are attached to a new risk knowledge: Risk factors are declared. These factors are sometimes linked by a logical operator (Or/And). For example, the lack of contact with local authorities is a factor of risk associated to the activity of communication between them. With regard to these risk factors, and always for a given activity, one or more risky situations indicate that a degraded mode of activity's progress could possibly emerge. This will become real if the risk factors are obvious. Once again, logical operators are used when several situations are considered.

Comparison between Fig. 11.11 and Fig. 11.12 shows at a glance the intensity of the risks surrounding the business process. Thus, eight risk factors are introduced, and six risk situations are declared.

After this step, and as a first draft is available about what risk could happened, the characterization of risk becomes the new subject of concern. The objective is to draw a risk map in the form of a two-dimensional diagram: a likelihood (frequency of occurrence) and severity (the level of damage on assets). Each risk will have a

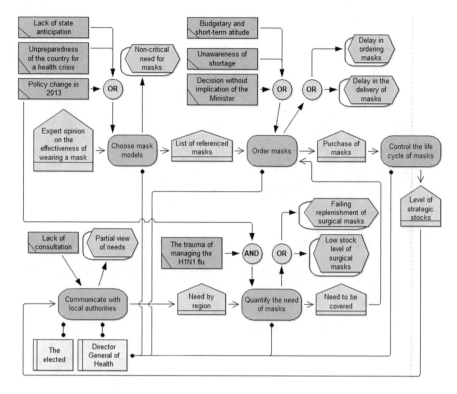

Fig. 11.12 Mask shortage BP model extended to risk

quantitative significance as it will become a point inside this diagram. Two forms of knowledge have to be mixed to reach this result: a risk analysis view as shown in Fig. 11.13 and a risk view depicted in Fig. 11.14.

For this purpose, one risk analysis view should be designed for each risk. Its utility is to connect the space of the causes of risk and the space of the consequences of risk. This could be perceived as a different way to address the featuring of risk to fill the risk map. The *e*-BPRIM language creates dependencies between risk factors and risk situations, foreshadowing the occurrence of the risk event.

The left part of the Fig. 11.13 must be considered as a tree (multi-graph) allowing to develop a frequency calculation (e.g., as a likelihood value), according to an embedded algorithm that is not so far from the Bayesian network theory. The risk of mask shortage induces consequences which have been framed in the context diagram.

If the next question asked is defining the impacts of the risk, i.e., its severity, the right-hand side is an answer which evokes the values exposed to damage. This part of the model therefore raises awareness among stakeholders. For example, the risk of mask shortages could undermine the welfare value of the healthcare system user. Figure 11.13 keeps track of the existence of a risk during the execution of the business process.

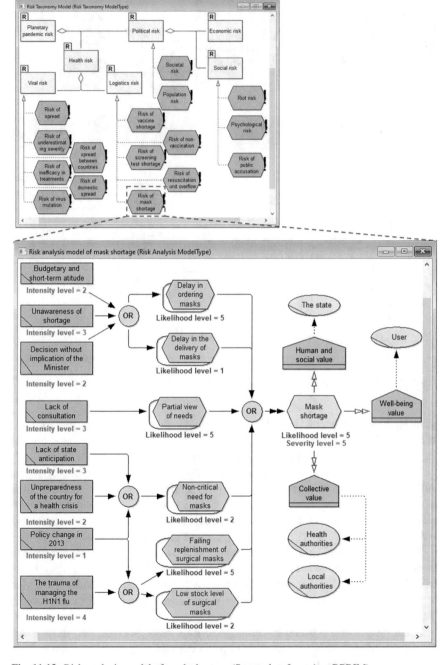

Fig. 11.13 Risk analysis model of mask shortage (Screenshot from ADOBPRIM)

It is somewhat like a memory of the activities which have been considered implicitly during the design of risk treatment view (see Fig. 11.17). This reminder conforms to the risk taxonomy. Talking about the risk of mask shortage therefore only makes sense in reference to the four activities that described protection by wearing a mask, detailed in Figs. 11.11 and 11.12. This is indeed a logistical risk. But the risk taxonomy, which is a tree structure, obeys the classification criteria at the source of a hierarchical design of risks and risk classes. However, experience has shown that all the criteria which can be applied to build a taxonomy can sometimes turn out to be conflicting. Only a subset among them is put into practice to find the chosen classification.

Therefore, it seemed useful to us not to lose knowledge about dependencies that would exist between risks, but are not members of the same pathway starting from the root in the taxonomy. Figure 11.15 is an example where the risks of vaccine shortage and non-vaccination, both annotated as being logistical risks, also turn out to be strong components of the risk of low efficiency of treatments, which has been classified as a viral risk. Even if logistical risk and viral risk are brought together at a higher hierarchical level under the same umbrella of health risks, without this model of the relationship between risks, this relationship would be too much implicit. But it goes without saying that the existence of such models induces a constraint field in the algorithms for calculating risk characteristics.

Fig. 11.14 Risk dependency
to activities

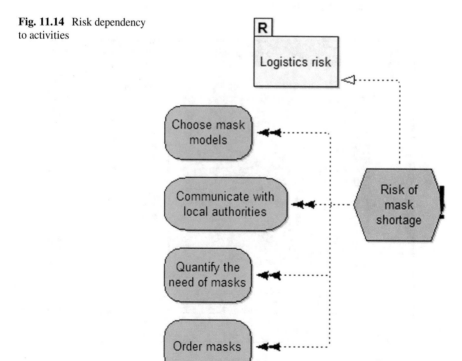

Fig. 11.15 Gathering risks
coming from different classes

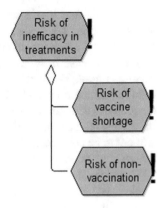

This Assess phase will produce a risk map that we have already mentioned above. Figure 11.16 describes this mapping based on a two-dimensional matrix representation where each element of the matrix has a color attribute. This set of three colors (green, orange, red) is a modeling artifact aimed at preparing the mitigation phase. Green points to the minor risks which will not be controlled. Red will force the implementation of control measures. Orange will delimit a middle space and calls for decision-making because the issue of risk control must be discussed on a case-by-case basis.

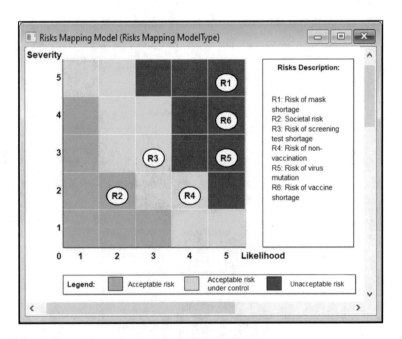

Fig. 11.16 Risk map (Screenshot from ADOBPRIM)

The risk map, shown in Fig. 11.16, is therefore indicative of the risk appetite of the stakeholders in charge of the reliability of the system. These are all organizational roles that must participate in the search for consensus. Thus, the discretization of the axes and the color chosen initially for the cells are configuration elements of this ADOBPRIM model, in order to reflect these profiles of the appetite of decision-makers according to their psychology of risk management.

11.4.1.3 Treatment: The Path from Analysis to Action

As required by the dynamics of risk treatment, the last phase of e-BPRIM modeling method will deal with risk treatment measures. These are preventive control measures, and/or curative control measures, and/or insurance measures. These measures are new activities that could change the business process model. By analogy, organizational engineering relating to risks is found to be similar to the one relating to quality procedures when performing continuous improvement. Any modification should be noted by declaring this corresponding mitigation measure. Their execution shall have an effect and move the risk from one point to another onto the risk map. Obviously, the goal is to get this risk from a red or orange cell into a green one in the perfect case of an efficient control. But at the same time, you have to specify which native business processes are going to be changed by these new ways of doing things. This first requirement is the subject of the right part of Fig. 11.17, while the perimeter of the initial model that will be changed is described on the left part of the same figure. Someway, the well-known "As-Is" and "To-Be" models are used in a different philosophy there.

Obviously, the revisited new business process model can be a starting point for the BPRIM life cycle, i.e., launching a new iteration for model design from its beginning. As a result, depending on developments and the context, the exercise

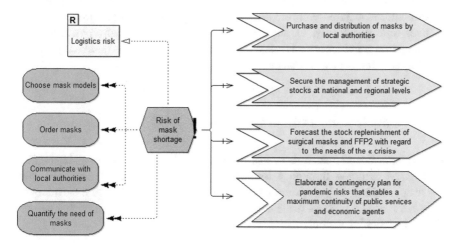

Fig. 11.17 Mitigate risk of mask shortage

will be rolled again with its battery of changes, and a new version of all models has to be set up. We should keep in mind that risk management and business process management are both based on sequences of progress that aim to keep control simultaneously on value added and value preserved. That's what BPRIM is able to perform and ADOBPRIM is promoting so easily through model-based engineering. The implementation of this case study using ADOBPRIM can be consulted online while following this link: https://austria.omilab.org/psm/content/BPRIM/info?view=casestudies.

11.4.2   *Experimental Feedback*

Let us refer to the three goals which motivate this case study design as detailed in the beginning of this section. Here are some results on which we want to put the emphasis on:

- We have proven the capability of ADOBPRIM to support the representation of the COVID-19 pandemic using a set of model's views. Even if this work focused on a sub-perimeter, the power of the *e*-BPRIM language, the range of available concepts, and the adequacy of the modeling procedure provide insights of what could be performed at a larger scale if an extension of the work was desired.
- Clearly, when business process modeling is applied to this crisis situation, the idea of adding knowledge about risks to it in a progressive approach is both straightforward and very efficient. It is a key factor that explains our ability to tackle this challenge. The multiple dimensions that have to be considered facing the complexity of the risk space have been captured inside the multiple views we have proposed. Browsing among these views is obviously the best way to understand the overall crisis logically and incrementally.
- Public policies are depicted in our case study, leading to explicitly address the difficulty associated with the decision-making problems that have to be faced over time. Especially, the need to balance between the many possibilities of mitigation activities is shown, and so, it will help to protect, as far as it is possible, different kinds of assets that could be impacted.

11.5   Conclusions and Perspectives

This chapter covers recent results of our research based on a deep understanding of R-BPM acquired through a long-term research. Hereby, we adopted a top-down approach while going through multiple steps: understanding first the interplay between risk and process management, then formulating research challenge, and finally envisioning the progress to be made.

BPRIM is a R-BPM architecture, which was continuously refined since 2008 in order to reach the current level of maturity toward the integration of BPM and ERM. We were aware of how ambitious our approach was, while highly elaborated with risk management most accurate knowledge. Accordingly, the COVID-19 experience described in the case study could be considered as a crash test. The proof of concept is now available.

Following this methodological achievement, it was then necessary to adopt a digitization approach in order to facilitate its use and appropriation. The crucial decision was to make it using model-driven engineering principles. The design was facilitated by the reuse of the BPRIM conceptual model and the related first intention about the associated notations. Then, a very tight specification of what was the purpose about digital tools and how to conceive them was thought in the *e*-BPRIM IT-based conceptual framework. The birth of ADOBPRIM was quite achievable starting from the knowledge we had at that time. The ADOxx environment was perfectly adapted to this last part of the creative process, making our DSML accessible online.

The future development of this work shall cover two major subjects:

- Dissemination of the first release of ADOBPRIM in order to collect users' feedbacks (i.e., risk managers), to test the assumptions and build a community of practitioners promoting knowledge sharing. ADOBPRIM needs to evolve toward an open tool.
- Research and development of mechanisms and algorithms regarding, on the one hand, risk mapping models, which will provide facilities to execute quantitative risk assessment as usually done by practitioners and, on the other hand, risk monitoring with the aim of assessing the effectiveness of the risk mitigation activities and alerting the risk manager when the risk situation would likely happen.

Tool Download https://www.omilab.org/ebprim.

References

1. Alberts, C.J., Behrens, S.G., Pethia, R.D., Wilson, W.R.: Operationally Critical Threat, Asset, and Vulnerability Evaluation (OCTAVE) Framework, Version 1.0. Tech. rep., Carnegie Mellon University, Software Engineering Institute (1999)
2. Culwick, M., Merry, A., Clarke, D., Taraporewalla, K., Gibbs, N.: Bow-tie diagrams for risk management in anaesthesia. Anaesth. Intensive Care **44**(6), 712–718 (2016)
3. Dumas, M., La Rosa, M., Mendling, J., Reijers, H.A.: Fundamentals of Business Process Management. Springer, Berlin (2018). http://link.springer.com/10.1007/978-3-662-56509-4
4. Fill, H.G., Karagiannis, D.: On the conceptualisation of modelling methods using the ADOxx meta modelling platform. Enterp. Model. Inf. Syst. Archit. **8**(1), 4–25 (2013)
5. Fredriksen, R., Kristiansen, M., Gran, B.A., Stølen, K., Opperud, T.A., Dimitrakos, T.: The CORAS Framework for a Model-Based Risk Management Process. LNCS 2434, pp. 94–105. Springer, Berlin (2002)

6. Geerts, G.L.: A design science research methodology and its application to accounting information systems research. Int. J. Account. Inf. Syst. **12**(2), 142–151 (2011)
7. ISO: 19440:2007 Enterprise integration – Constructs for enterprise modelling (2007)
8. ISO: 31000:2018 Risk management – Guidelines (2018)
9. Jakoubi, S., Tjoa, S., Goluch, S., Kitzler, G.: Risk-aware business process management–establishing the link between business and security. In: Xhafa, F., Barolli, L., Papajorgji, P. (eds) Complex Intelligent Systems and Their Applications. Springer Optimization and Its Applications, pp. 1–26. Springer, New York (2010)
10. Karagiannis, D.: Agile modeling method engineering. In: Proceedings of the 19th Panhellenic Conference on Informatics, pp. 5–10. ACM, New York (2015)
11. Karagiannis, D., Kühn, H.: Metamodelling platforms. In: Proceedings of E-Commerce and Web Technologies, Third International Conference, EC-Web 2002, Aix-en-Provence, 2–6 Sept 2002, p. 182 (2002)
12. Lamine, E., Thabet, R., Sienou, A., Bork, D., Fontanili, F., Pingaud, H.: BPRIM: an integrated framework for business process management and risk management. Comput. Ind. **117**, 103199 (2020)
13. Neiger, D., Churilov, L., zur Muehlen, M., Rosemann, M.: Integrating risks in business process models with value focused process engineering. In: Proceedings of the ECIS, pp. 1606–1615 (2006)
14. Peffers, K., Tuunanen, T., Rothenberger, M.A., Chatterjee, S.: A design science research methodology for information systems research. J. Manag. Inf. Syst. **24**(3), 45–77 (2007)
15. Pittl, B., Fill, H.G., Honegger, G.: Enabling risk-aware enterprise modeling using semantic annotations and visual rules. In: Proceedings of the 25th European Conference on Information Systems (ECIS), AIS (2017)
16. Rosemann, M., Muehlen, Mz.: Integrating risks in business process models. In: ACIS 2005 Proceedings (2005)
17. Sanchez-Fernandez, R., Iniesta-Bonillo, M.A.: The concept of perceived value: a systematic review of the research. Mark. Theory **7**(4), 427–451 (2007)
18. Sidorchuk, R.: The concept of "Value" in the theory of marketing. Asian Soc. Sci. **11**(9), 320 (2015)
19. Sienou, A.: Proposition d'un cadre méthodologique pour le management intégré des risques et des processus d'entreprise. PhD thesis, Institut National Polytechnique de Toulouse (2009)
20. Sienou, A., Lamine, E., Pingaud, H., Karduck, A.: Aspects of the BPRIM language for risk driven process engineering. In: Meersman, R., Herrero, P., Dillon, T. (eds.) On the Move to Meaningful Internet Systems: OTM 2009 Workshops, vol. 5872, pp. 172–183. Springer, Berlin (2009)
21. Suriadi, S., Weiß, B., Winkelmann, A., ter Hofstede, A.H.M., Adams, M., Conforti, R., Fidge, C., Rosa, M.L., Ouyang, C., Rosemann, M., Pika, A., Wynn, M.: Current research in risk-aware business process management - overview, comparison and gap analysis. Commun. Assoc. Inf. Syst. **34**(1), 52 (2014)
22. ter Hofstede, A.: Risk-Aware Business Process Management (2011). http://yawlfoundation.org/risk/
23. Thabet, R.: Ingénierie dirigée par les modèles d'un pilotage robuste de la prise en charge médicamenteuse. PhD thesis, Institut National Polytechnique de Toulouse et Institut Supérieur de l'informatique et des technologies de la communication de Hammam Sousse (2020)
24. Thabet, R., Lamine, E., Boufaied, A., Korbaa, O., Pingaud, H.: Towards a risk-aware business process modelling tool using the ADOxx platform. In: International Conference on Advanced Information Systems Engineering, pp. 235–248. Springer, Berlin (2018)
25. Thabet, R., Lamine, E., Boufaied, A., Bork, D., Korbaa, O., Pingaud, H.: Formal specification, implementation, and evaluation of the AdoBPRIM approach. In: Americas Conference on Information Systems (AMCIS) (2020)
26. Thabet, R., Bork, D., Boufaied, A., Lamine, E., Korbaa, O., Pingaud, H.: Risk-aware business process management using multi-view modeling: method and tool. Requir. Eng. (2021). https://doi.org/10.1007/s00766-021-00348-2

27. Vallespir, B., Ducq, Y.: Enterprise modelling: from early languages to models transformation. Int. J. Prod. Res. **56**(8), 2878–2896 (2018)
28. Vernadat, F.: Enterprise modeling in the context of enterprise engineering: state of the art and outlook. Int. J. Prod. Manag. Eng. **2**(2), 57–73 (2014)
29. Vincent, C., Taylor-Adams, S., Chapman, E.J., Hewett, D., Prior, S., Strange, P., Tizzard, A.: How to investigate and analyse clinical incidents: clinical risk unit and association of litigation and risk management protocol. BMJ **320**(7237), 777–781 (2000)
30. Visic, N.: Language-oriented modeling method engineering. PhD thesis, University of Vienna (2016)
31. Weiss, B., Winkelmann, A.: Developing a process-oriented notation for modeling operational risks-a conceptual metamodel approach to operational risk management in knowledge intensive business processes within the financial industry. In: 2011 44th Hawaii International Conference on System Sciences (HICSS), pp. 1–10. IEEE, Piscataway (2011)

Chapter 12
Modeling the Phenomenon of Capability Change: The KYKLOS Method

Georgios Koutsopoulos, Martin Henkel, and Janis Stirna

Abstract The dynamic environments where modern businesses operate in are a source of continuous change. As a result, change has emerged as an indispensable aspect of business management and analysis. The notion of capability is an essential element in business designs; therefore, business transformation is associated with monitoring and analyzing changing capabilities. Enterprise modeling can facilitate these tasks, and even though a plethora of capability modeling approaches exists, there is a lack of a method specialized for modeling capability change. The KYKLOS method, which is introduced in this chapter as a means to address the abovementioned challenge, is the result of an ongoing Design Science project aiming to provide methodological and tool support for businesses whose capabilities undergo changes or need to do so in the future. Its purpose is not only to capture the information types that are essential to the complex capability change phenomenon but also to guide the transition of capabilities. It is complemented by a homonymous tool developed using the ADOxx metamodeling platform.

Keywords Capability · Enterprise modeling · Change management · Organizational transformation

12.1 Introduction

Environmental dynamism constantly gains ground as a driving force for enterprise transformation. Furthermore, the degree of dynamism in business environments is increasing to a level where the environment's pace of change has surpassed and is significantly higher than the one of the organizations' and this distance can only be amplified [1]. The effects of this dynamism can appear in the form of needed changes, opportunities, or threats for an organization [2]. Thus, change is no longer

G. Koutsopoulos (✉) · M. Henkel · J. Stirna
Department of Computer and Systems Sciences, Stockholm University, Stockholm, Sweden
e-mail: georgios@dsv.su.se; martinh@dsv.su.se; js@dsv.su.se

© The Author(s), under exclusive license to Springer Nature Switzerland AG 2022   265
D. Karagiannis et al. (eds.), *Domain-Specific Conceptual Modeling*,
https://doi.org/10.1007/978-3-030-93547-4_12

an exception or a rarity in organizations. On the contrary, it can be considered as the new constant for contemporary business management. This means that there is a need to understand not only organizations but also organizational change [1].

Flexibility and adaptability are necessary traits for any organization aiming for continuity and they significantly affect business strategy. Change has an inextricable link with strategy [3], which concerns the necessary plans, decisions, and activities for achieving the business's goals [4]. A valuable activity that is also part of strategy is the analysis of change, especially while considering that an organization's response to environmental dynamism is by changing what it is capable of.

Capability thinking allows perceiving an organization as a set of capabilities. Being at the core of capability management, capability thinking can improve flexibility and productivity, especially when considering digital organizations [5]. Capability, as a concept, is the focal point of the actual business activities and also of information system (IS) development, so that the business is supported via the design and analysis of its capabilities.

Capability, as a concept, is also associated with strategy. The existing strategy of an organization dictates the development and ownership of capabilities, and, in return, the existing capabilities dictate the organization's strategy [3]. Organizational change and improvement, through the lens of capability management, are perceived as capability change and improvement [3]. Correspondingly, the value of change analysis is transferred to capability change analysis. The term capability change refers not only to the introduction of new capability but also to the modification or retirement of an existing one. Several capability modeling approaches exist; however, to the best of our knowledge, none is specialized in changing capabilities [6].

This chapter reports on the latest iteration of a Design Science Research (DSR) [7] project that aims to provide methodological and tool support for organizations that undergo changes or need to, via the improvement of capability modeling in dynamic contexts. The method's goal is to capture, elicit, document, and communicate all the concepts which are relevant to the complex phenomenon of capability change in order to facilitate and guide the transition of an organization's business capabilities.

The project was initiated by exploring the domain of capability modeling and identifying existing concepts relevant to capability change [6], followed by eliciting a set of requirements by combining literature sources with a case study [8], exploring the dimensions of capability and change [9], and finally introducing a conceptual metamodel [10] and its expansion [11] as the foundation for a modeling language and method. The method and a supporting tool are introduced in this chapter.

The rest of the chapter is structured as follows. Section 12.2 introduces the KYKLOS method developed for modeling capability change and its aims, semantics, and justification, along with related research. Section 12.3 elaborates on the conceptualization of the method. Section 12.4 presents the homonymous tool developed in ADOxx to support the method and a real-life case study where the method and tool have been applied. Section 12.5 provides concluding remarks and potentials for future developments of the presented method.

12.2 KYKLOS Method Description

This section introduces the method and its goals and requirements, along with background and related research of the project.

12.2.1 Goals and Requirements

The objective of this book is to present a collection of domain-specific modeling languages and supporting tools implemented in the ADOxx environment. The domain specificity, as referred by Karagiannis et al. in [12], addressed by KYKLOS, is that of capability change, independently of a specific industry or field. This section summarizes the requirements for the KYKLOS method, which have been elicited before we started the implementation of the method in the ADOxx environment. In [8] we summarized the goals and requirements for KYKLOS from an earlier literature study [6] and investigated a use case within the healthcare sector. The literature analysis was guided by the prism of three functionality areas needed for change management, namely, observation, decision-making, and delivery of change. The resulting goals model, made in 4EM notation, followed this structure, that is, the top-level goals 2, 3, and 4 represent the three functionality areas, respectively (see Fig. 12.1).

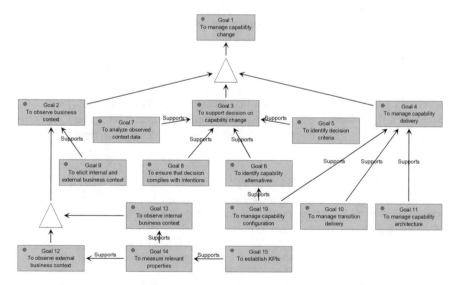

Fig. 12.1 A fraction of a 4EM Goals Model representing top goals for the KYKLOS method

The three goals at this level are refined into a number of sub-goals that need to be addressed by KYKLOS. More specifically, *observation* is to be addressed by the need to observe external (goal 12) and internal (goal 13) context changes, including measuring relevant context data (goal 14) and establishing key performance indicators (KPIs) (goal 15). Observation (goal 2) also requires support for eliciting internal and external context (goal 9). *Decision support* is supported by goals 5–8. They depict the need to provide methodological support for the analysis of context data and the identification of decision criteria and capability alternatives and ensure that the decision complies with intention elements. *Delivery* is supported by goals 10, 11, and 19. They state that support is needed for depicting management of transition delivery, capability architecture, and capability configuration accordingly. The latter goal also supports decision support and goal 6 because it helps identifying alternatives. Capability configuration is needed to represent what resources and behaviors are needed to implement a certain change decision. The complete elaboration and refinement of the goals outlined in this paragraph is available in [8].

The initial study on goals and requirements led to the development of the initial version of the KYKLOS metamodel. This was further analyzed and used as a framework for an investigation of expert opinions and broad requirements for method support for capability change reported in [11]. In addition to the goals mentioned above, we have also taken into account the relation of the KYKLOS with modeling methods that address similar or complementary modeling aspects, namely, 4EM [13] and CDD [5]. The guiding principle of development of the KYKLOS method is not to develop a monolith method for modeling all aspects of an organization but to focus on modeling the capability change and integrating other methods. Table 12.1 summarizes additional requirements for integration with other relevant methods.

The above requirements are put in the internal design of the KYKLOS method; however, it is also possible to integrate other methods that provide input to or works on the output of the method. For example, PESTLE (Political, Economic, Sociological, Technological, Legal and Environmental) analysis may be used as the input for defining the context of a capability. Another example is the method that

Table 12.1 Additional requirements stemming from alignment with other methods

• *Goal modeling as a self-contained component.* Intentional aspects of capability change should be possible to model with existing goal modeling methods, for example, 4EM
• *Context modeling as a self-contained component.* It should be possible to use existing context models to describe the capability context, for example, CDD context modeling
• *Capability representation aligned with existing notions of capability.* Most notably the KYKLOS capability concept could be aligned with CDD
• *Process models as complement.* It should be possible to refine the behavior of capability configurations with process models
• *Actor and resource modeling as a starting point.* It should be possible to use other models for identifying needed resources for a capability, for example, the 4EM actors and resource model

identifies needed changes and their pace, which is possible to use for planning while conducting change management projects. Likewise, the output of the methods in terms of alternative capability designs may be the input to further decision analysis.

12.2.2   Introduction of the KYKLOS Method

The KYKLOS method is aimed at supporting the change of organizations. As such, it may be used by managers who need to deliberate and decide on alternative paths to changes to address changes in the environment. KYKLOS also caters to changes stemming from internal requirements, such as the need to improve the quality of products and services. Since the method contains a visual notation, it is also suitable for collaborative work with a wider audience, for example, with subject matter experts that may be internal or external to the organization. Regarding the visual notation of KYKLOS, effort was made to ensure a short learning curve in order for it to be user-friendly to non-experts.

The method consists of key *concepts*, a *notation*, and a modeling *procedure*. Central to the method is the concept of *capability*, as it represents something that an organization can achieve (the concept is further defined in Sect. 12.3.1). The concepts of *context* and *intention* are used for capturing the origins of the need to change—either in the form of external push (context) or internal pull (intention). The entities being changed are described as capability *resources* and *behavior*. To manage the changes and alternatives for performing changes, resources and behaviors are grouped into capability *configurations*. Essentially, a capability configuration is a set of resources (such as workforce and tools) and behavior (such as work procedures) that can be used to produce the capability's outcome. The KYKLOS notation contains graphical elements to be used to visualize the concepts. Both the concepts and the notation are described in Sect. 12.3.1.

The KYKLOS modeling procedure contains phases and activities aimed at supporting the use of the concepts and notation. The procedure outlines a certain sequence of activities in general, such as first defining the context and intention of the capability under study. It consists of several procedure phases that may be used iteratively to refine a model of the desired change. As pointed out earlier, the KYKLOS method is designed in such a way that other types of modeling approaches may be incorporated or used with it, for example, goal modeling can be used for elaborating the overall vision of the business case on a macro level and the intention elements for the specific case of change. The modeling procedure is further described in Sect. 12.3.2.

The modeling tool support of KYKLOS consists of an implementation using the ADOxx platform. The tool uses symbols for the main concepts (capability, context, intention, configuration, etc.). It also includes several dynamic features that aid the user to construct the model. For example, the tool can assist the user in adding new capability configurations in an interactive way. The tool is further described in Sect. 12.4.

12.2.3 Background and Related Research

This section provides a brief presentation of the areas that have driven this research project, which are capability modeling and organizational change, and of the related work existing in the literature.

The widely researched phenomenon of organizational change bears importance for the area of business informatics which focuses on the role of ISs in the changes [14]. The terms change, adaptation, and transformation are sometimes used interchangeably or express different scopes [15]. Organizational change is driven by (i) rational adaptation, (ii) strategic decision-making, or (iii) a combination of the aforementioned with organizational inertia [16]. A commonly neglected element is the causality of change which should be implemented in any method aiming to address the complexity of organizational change [16].

Enterprise modeling (EM), as a discipline, aims to elicit, capture, document, and communicate this complexity. It concerns the process of capturing several organizational aspects which are considered relevant for a specific modeling objective, e.g., processes, goals, concepts, or business rules [13]. Consequently, an enterprise model often consists of a set of integrated sub-models, with each model's focus being a specific aspect. Capability is one such aspect.

Regarding capabilities, various definitions exist. Taking into consideration that there is no consensus in the literature, the concept is defined in this project as a set of resources and behaviors, with a configuration that bears the ability and capacity to enable the potential to create value by fulfilling a goal within a context [17]. Capability is associated with essential business concepts, e.g., goal, process, resource, actor, and context [5, 18]. A fact that emphasizes the significance of capability is that it is often perceived as the missing link for business/IT transformation, since it serves as a baseline for strategic planning, change management, and impact analysis [19].

Capability modeling is an ongoing research area. A systematic mapping of capability modeling, designing, and developing methods has been performed by Koç [20]. The findings include (i) a resource-based view and dynamic environments being the main sources of motivation for including the notion of capability, (ii) the scarcity of methodological support for capability management, and (iii) the limited usage of enterprise models. Koç et al. [21] additionally reviewed the literature on context modeling, which is a significant element of capability management, and the lack of methodological support for context modeling was identified and addressed [22].

Capability has also been included in enterprise architecture. An analysis of how capability is employed in business architecture, enterprise architecture, enterprise modeling, and business analysis frameworks by Zdravkovic et al. [23, 24] stated that capability is utilized to represent the ability to achieve a specific result in all the frameworks that were studied, even though there are differences derived from the difference in the purpose of each framework, for example, focusing on capabilities' strategic viewpoint, as in [25], leads to their association with goals.

The adaptation of capabilities has been studied in the context of business services, business process variants, and delivery adjustments. Delivering capability adjustments aims to change the way a capability is realized, in response to changes in the context and the capability's performance while avoiding to redesign the capability and possibly underlying IS [26]. One approach toward the description of adaptability of capabilities has been suggested in [27], where the issue is addressed through the introduction of a framework including the dimensions and related aspects for the analysis and evaluation of an organization's adaptability. The three dimensions the framework consists of are (i) complexity of the environment, (ii) managerial profiling, and (iii) artifact-integrated components.

Finally, capability has been utilized in modeling approaches of various types like stand-alone approaches, e.g., Capability-Driven Development (CDD) [5], CODEK [28], and Value Delivery Modeling Language (VDML) [29]; enterprise architecture frameworks, e.g., NATO Architecture Framework (NAF) [30], Department of Defense Architecture Framework (DoDAF) [31], Ministry of Defence Architecture Framework (MODAF) [32], and ArchiMate [33]; and existing methods' extensions, e.g., i* [34] and capability maps [35]. An analysis of the majority of the capability metamodels in the literature exists in [6].

12.3   Method Conceptualization

This section presents the semantics, notation, and modeling procedure of KYKLOS.

12.3.1   Concepts in KYKLOS

The method consists of concepts whose relevance to capability change has been identified in earlier work [10, 11]. The metamodel in Fig. 12.2 is a fragment of the conceptual model that has been previously published within the KYKLOS project and is the basis for the modeling language of the method presented in this chapter. The main concept is capability. It is assessed via one or more KPIs, which are expressing one or more monitored factors. Each monitored factor is part of a context. The capability also fulfills one or more intention elements, which can be fulfilled by more than one capability. Capability results in at least one outcome and has at least one configuration, which can belong to one capability only. Configuration consists of component elements, in particular resource and behavior elements, which are its specializations. Process is a specialization of behavior element and resources are part of a resource pool, which may consist of zero to many resources.

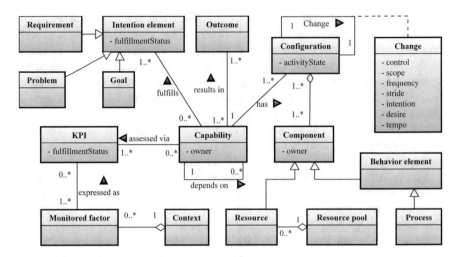

Fig. 12.2 The KYKLOS method metamodel

The modeling language includes the aforementioned concepts. Table 12.2 describes the concepts and the notation symbols that are associated with each concept.

12.3.2 The KYKLOS Modeling Procedure

The KYKLOS method can be used to both analyze existing proposals for change and to design new proposals for change. It also supports analyzing the options for delivering the change. This is done by being aware of three areas: (1) the environment in which the capability functions (*observation* of context and intentions), (2) its internal structure (*decisions* on capability configurations), and (3) the potential changes that may be done (*delivery* of configuration changes). The modeling procedure of the KYKLOS method supports knowledge capturing, documentation, and analysis of these three areas.

The KYKLOS modeling procedure is divided into four phases—one foundational phase for initial analysis and then one phase for each of the three areas—observation of context, decision alternatives, and delivery of change. The KYKLOS modeling procedure focuses on the last two phases and uses as input other models developed with other methods for the first two phases. For example, an organization's intentions can be modeled with some of the existing goal modeling methods, such as 4EM Goals Model. Table 12.3 and Fig. 12.3 provide an overview of the phases.

Table 12.2 The KYKLOS method concepts and their notation

Concept	Description	Notation
Capability	A set of resources and behaviors, whose configuration bears the ability and capacity to enable the potential to create value by fulfilling a goal within a context	(symbol)
Configuration	The set of resources that comprise the capability along with the behavior elements that deliver it. A capability may have several different configurations but only one may be active at any given moment in time	(symbol)
Resource	Any human, infrastructure, knowledge, equipment, financial, or reputation asset that can be used by an organization to enable the capability's realization. It can be allocated to one or more capability configurations, based on its capacity	(symbol)
Resource pool	The complete set of an organization's available resources	Container
Context	All the factors that form the setting in which a capability exists are relevant to its performance and within which the capability is perceived	Container
Outcome	The result of the capability's realization. Comparing it to KPIs and intention elements can provide insight on whether a capability change is necessary or not	(symbol)
KPI (key performance indicator)	A preset measurable value that expresses an important aspect of the context that a capability depends on to reach the desired outcome. Used to assess the efficiency of the capability's realization when compared with outcome values	(symbol)
Monitored factor	A context factor that has been identified and associated with a capability's performance and is being observed in relation to the capability. It is usually expressed as a KPI	(symbol)
Intention element	An abstract element that includes all the concepts that refer to the intentions governing the capability, for example, goals, problems, or requirements	(symbol)
Goal	A desirable state that an organization aims to achieve. It is a type of intention element	(symbol)
Problem	An undesirable condition that an organization aims to avoid or tackle. It is a type of intention element	(symbol)
Requirement	A necessary state that an organization has to fulfill. It is a type of intention element	(symbol)
Behavior element	An abstract element that describes a structured set of activities whose execution delivers the value of the capability, for example, a process, service, activity, or task	N/A
Process	A behavior element that consists of activities aiming to fulfill a certain goal	(symbol)
Change	Change represents the transition from one configuration to another. It can be described using several change properties. A capability change is finalized when a configuration's activity state is modified	(symbol)

Table 12.3 Overview of the modeling procedure phases

Phase	Main actions	Model elements used
0 foundation	Describe the base for the analysis in terms of an identified capability	Capability, outcome
1 observation of context and intentions	Analyze the internal and external context in which the capability must function. Identify needs for change	Context, monitored factor, KPIs, intention
2 decision alternatives	Analyze the alternatives for capability configurations that address the need for change, including needed resources and behavior	Configuration, resource, behavior
3 delivery of change	Understand what needs to be done in order to deliver the change in the form of a transition from current to a future capability configuration	Change, change properties

The procedure can be iterative, since the change has a potential impact on the capability and its outcome; therefore, the foundation phase may be triggered and the procedure may continue if needed. Each of the phases is elaborated in the following sections.

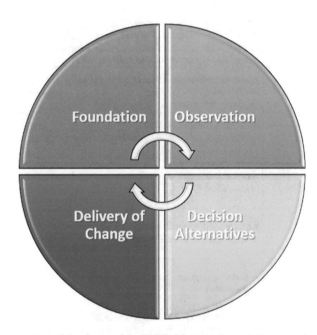

Fig. 12.3 An overview of the phases of the KYKLOS method's modeling procedure

12.3.2.1   Phase 0: Foundation

The target with the *foundation phase* is to identify the capabilities that should be further analyzed. Note that even a newly started company has some form of capability or an idea for a capability. As the analysis work begins, it may already be clear which capability should be studied in an organization. If this is not the case, there are several ways to identify capabilities and select one that should be analyzed in depth. For example, in [36] it is suggested that capabilities may be identified based on goals, processes, or concepts. Another way that is put forward in [37] is to focus on an organization's main capabilities, that is, those that are providing value to external customers by producing goods or services. The identified capability is then put in the KYKLOS model, along with its outcome.

The driving question for this phase is: Which capability's potential changes should we analyze?

The results of this phase are: an identified *capability*, its name, and a short description of what it does (its *outcome*). The capability and the outcome are put in the KYKLOS model.

12.3.2.2   Phase 1: Observation

In the *observation phase*, the internal intention and external context of the identified capability are analyzed. The external context consists of observable entities that have an effect on the capability and that are not controllable by the organization. This may be defined by extracting opportunities and threats from a SWOT analysis or by performing a wider PESTLE analysis. Existing context modeling approaches such as [38] may be used to refine the context into measurable items. The analysis of the internal intentions focuses on the organization's intentions/goals that constrain or guide the capability being analyzed. To perform this analysis, a goal model may be used, for example, a 4EM Goals Model [13]. During the analysis, the desire or need to change the capability is documented in the KYKLOS model as intentions that are not fulfilled (such as new efficiency criteria) or external context entities (such as a change in legislation) that are hindering the capability.

The guiding questions for this phase are: What external factors are relevant to the capability? What internal goals should be fulfilled by the capability?

The results of this phase are: The context is described using a set of *monitored factors* in the context and associated *KPIs*. The intention with the capability under study is described by a set of *intention elements*. The important results are also the identified KPIs and intention elements that are currently not fulfilled by the capability. The fulfilled, unfulfilled, or unknown fulfillment status of these elements is visualized differently using lines and symbols, solid green line and⊚ dotted red line and⊛/or dashed black line, respectively.

12.3.2.3   Phase 2: Decision Alternatives

The phase for elaborating *decision alternatives* aims to examine the capability configuration and to elaborate possible changes to it. A capability configuration consists of resources and behavior that makes a capability achieve its goals. Note that a capability can have several configurations that fulfill the same goal, for example, scanning tickets for an attendance of an event can be done by a machine (a resource) or by human work (another resource). A configuration's detailed behavior may be documented by, for instance, a process model.

To start with, the *active configuration* is examined as it represents the as-is state of the capability. The resources being used are documented in the KYKLOS model, as well as the behavior in terms of identified processes. Resources can be both tangible, such as money and goods, and intangible, such as goodwill [39]. Next, one or several *alternative configurations* that meet the changes of internal intentions or external contexts are identified, including their resources. This is a design task and thus needs to be done by domain experts together with modeling experts. During the design the KYKLOS model can be used as a tool for visualizing the configurations as they are designed.

An important part of this phase is the differentiation between the required and available resources and behaviors. While a configuration consists of required resources and behaviors, the state of the configuration is active only when these resources are available. The tool has been developed in a way to support this by visualizing the configuration as a container where the contained components are considered available.

In this phase, an additional task can be performed. Documenting the owners of the capability and the configurations' components enables the tool to visualize the internally and externally owned components and motivate consideration of organizational boundaries in terms of resources that imply additional costs.

The guiding questions for the phase are: What resources does the current capability consist of? What alternative capability configurations can meet new internal goals and external contexts? Which resources do we need to obtain in order for the new configurations to work? Which of these resources are available?

The results of this phase are: a set of capability *configurations*, their required and available *resources*, and *behavior* in terms of processes.

12.3.2.4   Phase 3: Delivery of Change

The purpose of the phase for *delivery of change* is to elaborate how the new capability configuration can be achieved. The active configuration documented in the previous phase represents the as-is state, and the newly designed configurations represent to-be states. Thus, there is a need to describe the actual change—the transition between configurations. This is done by adding one or several *changes* to the KYKLOS model, as an association between configurations. Note that changes

Table 12.4 Properties of change

Property	Dichotomies	Description
1. Control	Emergent—planned	A planned change occurs due to planned deliberate and conscious actions, while an emergent change is due to the fact that the organization is self-organizing
2. Scope	Adaptation—transformation	An adaptation is an adjustment of the existing capability, while transformation is a relatively deeper change in a capability or a new capability
3. Frequency	Continuous—discontinuous	Frequency is about how often a similar change needs to occur. For example, a continuous change is needed to follow consumer trends
4. Stride	Incremental—revolutionary	When incremental, the change can be implemented in a series of small steps. A revolutionary change entails a relatively larger change performed at once
5. Time	Long—short	Time is about the relative duration to implement a change
6. Tempo	Slow—quick	Tempo is related to time and deals with the speed with which change actions succeed each other
7. Desire	Desirable—undesirable	Desire refers to a change being welcomed to an organization or not, for example, as an identified opportunity or threat
8. Intention	Intentional—unintentional	Intention refers to a deliberate and conscious change that an organization aimed for, regardless of planning and desire

may be added between two to-be configurations as well—indicating a sequence of future changes.

Changes may be designed with different properties—for example, some are slow in tempo, others fast. Hence, there is a need to design the property of the changes in terms of *change properties*. Here, we apply the eight properties as defined in our previous work [9] (see Table 12.4). In essence, the eight properties are dichotomies that may be used to gain a clearer understanding of how the change should be delivered. For example, the magnitude of the change may be indicated by noting that the change *stride* is *revolutionary* and that the *time* for performing the change (relative to other changes in the model) is *short*.

The guiding questions for this phase are: What transitions between capability configurations can be done? What properties does the change itself have? For example, is it required to be fast or slow, etc.?

The results of this phase are: a set of *changes* in the form of relationships between capability configurations. Each change is documented by identifying its *change properties*.

A noteworthy fact is that the capability's active configuration is associated with the existing context and intentions that have been observed. This means that the contextual and intention elements that exist in the model are only relevant to the configuration that is currently active. Any delivered change that leads to a new active configuration can trigger a new observation phase, if, for example, the purpose is to continuously monitor the capability. In practice, the context and intention elements are updated, starting a new modeling iteration.

12.4 Proof of Concept

This section presents a proof-of-concept implementation of the KYKLOS method and its application in a real-life case study.

12.4.1 The KYKLOS Tool

The KYKLOS 1.0 tool is a prototype implementation of the KYKLOS method in the ADOxx metamodeling platform [40], which is provided by the Open Models Laboratory (OMiLAB). The platform provides graphical visualization of the method's elements along with complementing mechanisms and algorithms to enrich not only the experience of the modeling method's user but also automation of calculations and procedures that utilize the data input to provide visual results, in terms of dynamic model objects. All the previously presented concepts have been implemented as modeling classes, relation classes, and attributes according to the ADOxx metamodel, and the automated procedures have been implemented using ADOxx's script language AdoScript and query language AQL. The two main areas of the tool are the modeling toolkit and the modeling area, as shown in Fig. 12.4.

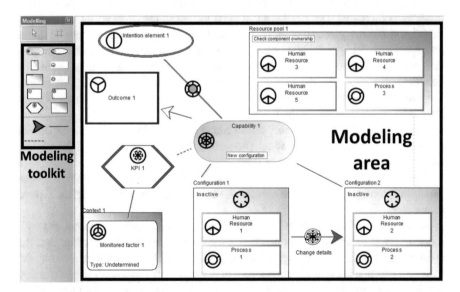

Fig. 12.4 The main areas of the KYKLOS 1.0 tool

The ADOxx metamodel provides a variety of alternatives for the implementation of the method. For example, Aggregation class in the ADOxx metamodel is a specialization of Container class and this has been valuable for modeling of UML aggregations, for example, context consists of monitored factor is implemented as a context object associated with monitored factor objects with an "Is Inside" relation class of the ADOXX metamodel. Visually this is depicted as objects enclosed in a container object instead of the traditional connecting lines. In a different example, the platform allows for dynamic configuration of visualized relationships. Two such cases are the Transition and Status relation classes that depict the states of change and capability, respectively. The former includes all the dimensions of change and the latter the capability state, as successfully fulfilling a goal or avoiding a problem or not. Finally, the AdoScript algorithms allow a dynamic visualization of objects, for example, a configuration documents its required resources and the allocation or removal of resource objects to a configuration object can change its state to active or inactive, respectively.

12.4.2   The Case Study

The tool is demonstrated in a case study conducted in the small urban city of Veria, in northern Greece. The organization, namely, Veria Arts Centre, is responsible for planning and implementing the cultural policy of the Municipality of Veria. Its responsibilities include producing and managing cultural events like film and music festivals, art education like music and dance education, and managing culture-related institutions like museums and libraries.

The following sections will describe the changes as an application of the KYKLOS method, while explaining the causes of change and the modification of the capability's configuration according to the abovementioned method phases.

12.4.2.1   Methodology

The goal of the study was to apply the KYKLOS method to provide analysis and support for the organization's capability's change planning. Guided face-to-face interviews have been used to collect the required data for every step of the application of the method. Convenience and purposive sampling [41] was the employed sampling strategy and resulted in the participation of all the managers and heads of the departments of the organization. In particular, apart from (i) the Centre's president, who is an elected politician, the participants' roles were (ii) CEO, (iii) CMO/COO, (iv) CFO, (v) CIO, and (vi) CTO. As a result, six 1-hour individual interviews and one 1-hour group interview were conducted, during which every participant provided insight from their own perspective. The collected data were organized and used for the application of the method and the development of the model in the tool.

12.4.2.2 Phase 0: Foundation

Veria Arts Centre has four main capabilities, which are (i) producing and (ii) organizing art festivals, (iii) providing art education, and (iv) managing culture-related institutions. Despite the fact that the conditions that will be described in the following sections and are affecting the organization have affected all the capabilities, the study focused only on the *organization of art festivals*, because it was the one whose analysis interested mostly the Centre and also for feasibility reasons.

The organization is part of the municipality; however, it is a public legal entity governed by private law. This means that its funding is a combination of municipality funds and self-funding. This results to a hybrid legal status where the Centre operates as a private organization that has to comply with the public agencies' regulations.

Various minor changes have been applied to the capability over the years, but in this study, we focused on two ongoing major changes and the planning for a desired change—in particular, the transition from its original version to a lean one and the transition from the lean version to a digital. Finally, the planned change is a combination of the beneficial lean and digital attributes.

The capability's scope is goal fulfillment in comparison to problem avoidance; it is value-producing and owned by a single organization, the Centre. Modeling the capability change is initiated by establishing the foundation, which means that the capability exists to provide an outcome, in particular, education entertainment, as shown in Fig. 12.5.

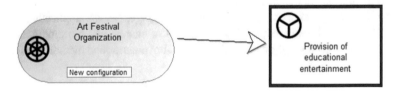

Fig. 12.5 The capability and its main outcome, modeled in KYKLOS 1.0

12.4.2.3 Phase 1: Observation

Regarding the transition from the original state to the lean version, there have been context factors that affected it. The Greek government-debt crisis has long-term ongoing effects, especially on the public sector, and the first change that was forcefully imposed on the capability is one of these effects. Consecutive budget cuts led to significant limitations to the available resources. This was practically applied through a legislation that did not require the dismissal of existing employees but essentially mitigated the ability to replace any retiring employees. Furthermore, any replacement is burdened by a restriction about expert employees that leads to their replacement by less knowledgeable human resources.

While the Centre is still under the effects of the ongoing transition to the lean version, the COVID-19 pandemic crisis made another emergent change necessary and led to a digital version. The cultural events and festivals have traditionally been held exclusively physically, a condition that is forbidden due to the social distancing regulations that were applied in Greece to tackle the pandemic. Veria Arts Centre had to comply with the emergent regulations and still invent new variations of the festival organization capability to fulfill the same goals and produce the same value to the audience. A weak spot that has been identified in the capability is the lack of data collection processes, which would enable the evaluation of the success of a festival, taking into consideration that all the festival activities are performed physically and the vast majority of events are outdoors with free attendance.

While predicting a transition's effects during planning is significantly limited, the scope can be clear. The two crises resulted in undesired and emergent changes and two configurations of the capability. Both have advantages and disadvantages, and Veria Arts Centre's aim is to combine the advantages into a new configuration when the COVID-19 pandemic is over. As far as the lean configuration is concerned, while it is viable to deliver the capability with a small yet efficient resource set, there is no need to revert back to the initial normal configuration. Regarding the digital configuration, an expanded audience has been achieved by the digital configuration and it should be preserved after the pandemic crisis.

It is important to note that the digital is the active version; therefore, the context and intention elements that are modeled are the ones related to the digital version. A fragment of the monitored factors and KPIs relevant to the as-is state of the capability has been modeled as shown in Fig. 12.6. The COVID-19 legislation and budget reduction, as part of the Greek context, are expressed as KPIs and associated with the capability, while the intention is depicted as a goal intention element. The pandemic indicators are fulfilled, the employee replacement is ongoing and can't be measured by the organization at the moment, and the goal is unfulfilled, a fact which motivates the planned change.

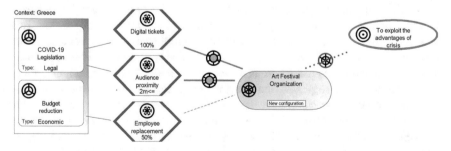

Fig. 12.6 Context and intention elements associated with the capability, as modeled in KYKLOS 1.0

12.4.2.4 Phase 2: Decision Alternatives

Normal configuration: The initial normal configuration of the capability usually involves its production capability, which means that the collaborations with external producers of art and culture events are continuous. The required resources for the realization of the capability are fundamentally the appropriate infrastructures like the three stages that the Centre owns and manages and the stages' maintenance staff. The stages also require staff for the festival equipment like light and sound operators. The operators' expertise is also an essential resource. Of course, there are necessary financial resources, not only for the aforementioned resources but also for the promotion of the festival with both physical and digital campaigns. Finally, reputation is an essential special resource because all the external collaborations and the success of all the promotional campaigns depend on it. Figure 12.7 depicts this configuration in KYKLOS 1.0. It is inactive because the active configuration is currently the digital one.

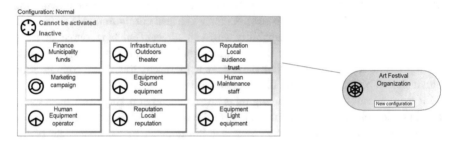

Fig. 12.7 The capability and its initial configuration in KYKLOS 1.0

A noteworthy fact is the blue color on the right side of the component objects, which indicates that the component is owned by the same owner as the capability. A red right side would indicate an external ownership.

Lean configuration: The essential impact of this change is gradually reducing the available human resources, in terms of quality and quantity. Regarding quantity, there were not enough people, even for performing the necessary tasks. This was addressed through a negotiation between employees and management that resulted in adopting a flexible work schedule. In this way, a level of flexibility was reached, which allowed using human resources optimally, so that the actual number of delivered events surpassed the previous one, despite the reduced resources. Regarding quality, the change resulted in missing several areas of expertise due to the retirement of experts. This was solved by spending finances on training the remaining employees or by collaborating with external organizations. The choice depended on whether the specific area of expertise was needed frequently or not. For example, if an expert on specific sound equipment operation is needed twice a year, contracting is selected, and, if an expert is needed to operate the lighting console of the Centre's own stage several times in a month, training is selected.

Digital configuration: Prior to applying the change, it was unanimously decided that the digital configuration cannot deliver the same quality as the normal, so the replacement of physical events with digital ones has to be a temporary solution. The digital configuration is advantageous in terms of reduced required resources. Physical infrastructures and their maintenance are not required along with less equipment and operators. In addition, promoting a digital event does not require physical means like posters and flyers, which in fact reduces the overall cost. Producing a home-based event is sometimes cheaper too, so the collaborations with external producers and artists also result in reduced costs. Another requirement concerns the collection of accurate data for the evaluation of an event's success. For the digital configuration, the digital platform that hosts the event and its promotion is an essential resource. A valuable solution with minimum cost has been identified in the social media. A noteworthy fact is that the digital events attracted a higher number of audience, since the usual physical restrictions for attending on a local level do not apply. This also results in increasing Veria Arts Centre's reputation because the digital event is attended nationwide.

New normal configuration: A potential hybrid configuration is by having parallel physical and digital events via streaming services. The data collection potential also bears value. Initially, the establishment of success criteria for events is possible. Furthermore, the usage of the collected data from digital participation can provide a criterion for evaluating if the expansion of a physical event's radius will have a positive impact. This can lead to an expansion of marketing campaigns so that a wider area and its residents are treated as "local" and invited to a physical event. The cost of a hybrid digital and physical marketing campaign, which is a process, is reduced in comparison to an exclusively physical and its gain has the potential to outweigh the cost. The plan involves that all the aforementioned digital traits will be implemented in a mobile app with the ability to handle all the functions required for digital and physical events like tickets, reservations, program, and rating. This fact indicates a dependency on a mobile app development capability. Regarding the lean traits of the capability, they are planned to remain unchanged unless the legislation changes and allows more flexibility.

12.4.2.5 Phase 3: Delivery of Change

Normal to lean: The identified imposed change from the normal version of the capability to a lean one is modeled as a transition from the normal to the lean configuration. The domain experts provided information about the properties of the transition. These have been identified as:

State: Active, *Tempo:* Slow, *Frequency:* Continuous, *Desire:* Undesirable, *Stride:* Incremental, *Scope:* Adaptation, *Control:* Emergent, *Intention:* Unintended

Lean to digital: Similarly, the second change is a transition from the lean to the digital configuration. It has the following properties:

State: Active, *Tempo:* Fast, *Frequency:* Continuous, *Desire:* Undesirable, *Stride:* Revolutionary, *Scope:* Adaptation, *Control:* Emergent, *Intention:* Unintended

Figure 12.8 depicts the transition.

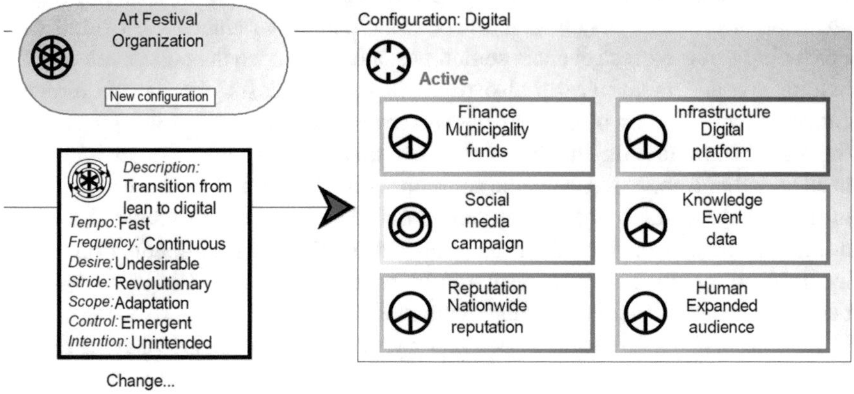

Fig. 12.8 The transition to the digital configuration, modeled in KYKLOS 1.0

Digital to new normal: The final change in the model is the planned and desired one from the digital to the new normal and is modeled as a transition between the respective configurations. The properties of the transition are:

State: Inactive, *Tempo:* Average, *Frequency:* Continuous, *Desire:* Desirable, *Stride:* Incremental, *Scope:* Adaptation, *Control:* Planned, *Intention:* Intended

12.4.2.6 Veria Arts Centre's Capability Change Model

The entire model of the Veria Arts Centre case study is presented in this section, in particular, in Fig. 12.9.

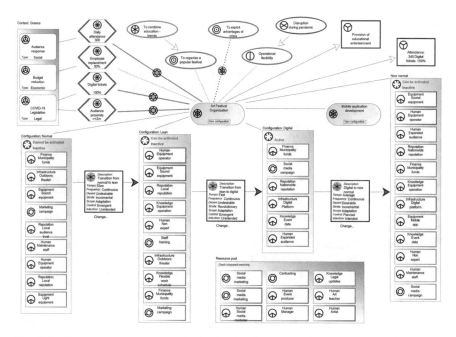

Fig. 12.9 The Veria Arts Centre capability change model, created using the KYKLOS method and tool

12.5   Conclusion

The purpose of the KYKLOS method and the KYKLOS 1.0 supporting tool is to capture all the elements that are relevant to the phenomenon of capability change and support its analysis. In this chapter, we introduced the first version of the complete KYKLOS method and its implementation using the ADOxx metamodeling platform. The method and tool have been applied on a case study performed in Veria Arts Centre and its capability to organize art festivals, which is undergoing changes due to external and internal motivation.

We hope that this chapter demonstrates the applicability of KYKLOS and stimulates its broader adoption by experts and practitioners, both from academia and industry, along with all the other members of the conceptual modeling community. In the future, we plan to improve KYKLOS as a method and as a tool, in terms of providing automated functionalities and connectivity with external sources of data to facilitate and guide the transition of changing capabilities.

Acknowledgments The authors would like to express their gratitude to all the Veria Arts Centre participants for their involvement in the case study presented in this chapter.

Tool Download: https://www.omilab.org/kyklos

References

1. Burke, W.W.: Organization Change: Theory and Practice. Sage Publications (2017)
2. van Gils, B., Proper, H.A.: Enterprise modelling in the age of digital transformation. In: Buchmann, R.A., Karagiannis, D., Kirikova, M. (eds.) The Practice of Enterprise Modeling, pp. 257–273. Springer International Publishing, Cham (2018). https://doi.org/10.1007/978-3-030-02302-7_16
3. Hoverstadt, P., Loh, L.: Patterns of Strategy. Routledge, London (2017)
4. Cunliffe, A.L.: Organization Theory. SAGE, London (2008)
5. Sandkuhl, K., Stirna, J.: Capability Management in Digital Enterprises. Springer, Cham (2018). https://doi.org/10.1007/978-3-319-90424-5
6. Koutsopoulos, G., Henkel, M., Stirna, J.: An analysis of capability meta-models for expressing dynamic business transformation. Softw. Syst. Model. **20**, 147–174 (2021). https://doi.org/10.1007/s10270-020-00843-0
7. Johannesson, P., Perjons, E.: An Introduction to Design Science. Springer, Cham (2014). https://doi.org/10.1007/978-3-319-10632-8
8. Koutsopoulos, G., Henkel, M., Stirna, J.: Requirements for observing, deciding, and delivering capability change. In: Gordijn, J., Guédria, W., Proper, H.A. (eds.) The Practice of Enterprise Modeling, pp. 20–35. Springer, Cham (2019). https://doi.org/10.1007/978-3-030-35151-9_2
9. Koutsopoulos, G., Henkel, M., Stirna, J.: Modeling the dichotomies of organizational change: A state-based capability typology. In: Feltus, C., Johannesson, P., Proper, H.A. (eds.) Proceedings of the PoEM 2019 Forum, pp. 26–39. CEUR-WS.org, Luxembourg (2020)
10. Koutsopoulos, G., Henkel, M., Stirna, J.: Conceptualizing capability change. In: Nurcan, S., Reinhartz-Berger, I., Soffer, P., Zdravkovic, J. (eds.) Enterprise, Business-process and Information Systems Modeling, pp. 269–283. Springer International Publishing, Cham (2020). https://doi.org/10.1007/978-3-030-49418-6_18
11. Koutsopoulos, G., Henkel, M., Stirna, J.: Improvements on capability modeling by implementing expert knowledge about organizational change. In: Grabis, J., Bork, D. (eds.) The Practice of Enterprise Modeling, pp. 171–185. Springer International Publishing, Cham (2020). https://doi.org/10.1007/978-3-030-63479-7_12
12. Karagiannis, D., Buchmann, R.A., Burzynski, P., Reimer, U., Walch, M.: Fundamental conceptual modeling languages in OMiLAB. In: Karagiannis, D., Mayr, H.C., Mylopoulos, J. (eds.) Domain-Specific Conceptual Modeling, pp. 3–30. Springer International Publishing, Cham (2016). https://doi.org/10.1007/978-3-319-39417-6_1
13. Sandkuhl, K., Stirna, J., Persson, A., Wißotzki, M.: Enterprise Modeling: Tackling Business Challenges with the 4EM method. Springer, Berlin (2014). https://doi.org/10.1007/978-3-662-43725-4
14. Proper, H.A., Winter, R., Aier, S., de Kinderen, S.: Architectural Coordination of Enterprise Transformation. Springer International Publishing, Cham (2017). https://doi.org/10.1007/978-3-319-69584-6
15. Maes, G., Van Hootegem, G.: Toward a dynamic description of the attributes of organizational change. In: (Rami) Shani, A.B., Woodman, R.W., Pasmore, W.A. (eds.) Research in Organizational Change and Development, pp. 191–231. Emerald Group Publishing Limited (2011). https://doi.org/10.1108/S0897-3016(2011)0000019009
16. Zimmermann, N.: Dynamics of Drivers of Organizational Change. Gabler, Wiesbaden (2011). https://doi.org/10.1007/978-3-8349-6811-1
17. Koutsopoulos, G.: Managing Capability Change in Organizations: Foundations for a Modeling Approach, http://urn.kb.se/resolve?urn=urn:nbn:se:su:diva-185231 (2020)
18. Wißotzki, M.: Exploring the nature of capability research. In: El-Sheikh, E., Zimmermann, A., Jain, L.C. (eds.) Emerging Trends in the Evolution of Service-oriented and Enterprise Architectures, pp. 179–200. Springer International Publishing, Cham (2016). https://doi.org/10.1007/978-3-319-40564-3_10

19. Ulrich, W., Rosen, M.: The business capability map: The "Rosetta stone" of business/IT alignment. Cutter Consortium, Enterprise Architecture, vol. 14 (2011)
20. Koç, H.: Methods in designing and developing capabilities: A systematic mapping study. In: Ralyté, J., España, S., Pastor, Ó. (eds.) The Practice of Enterprise Modeling, pp. 209–222. Springer International Publishing, Cham (2015). https://doi.org/10.1007/978-3-319-25897-3_14
21. Koç, H., Hennig, E., Jastram, S., Starke, C.: State of the art in context modelling – A systematic literature review. In: Iliadis, L., Papazoglou, M., Pohl, K. (eds.) Advanced Information Systems Engineering Workshops, pp. 53–64. Springer International Publishing, Cham (2014). https://doi.org/10.1007/978-3-319-07869-4_5
22. Koç, H.: A Capability-based Context Modelling Method to Enhance Digital Service Flexibility. https://doi.org/10.18453/ROSDOK_ID00002538 (2017)
23. Zdravkovic, J., Stirna, J., Grabis, J.: A comparative analysis of using the capability notion for congruent business and information systems engineering. Complex Syst. Inform. Model. Q. **1–20** (2017). https://doi.org/10.7250/csimq.2017-10.01
24. Zdravkovic, J., Stirna, J., Grabis, J.: Capability consideration in business and enterprise architecture frameworks. In: Sandkuhl, K., Stirna, J. (eds.) Capability Management in Digital Enterprises, pp. 41–56. Springer International Publishing, Cham (2018). https://doi.org/10.1007/978-3-319-90424-5_3
25. Loucopoulos, P., Kavakli, E.: Capability modeling with application on large-scale sports events. In: AMCIS 2016 Proceedings, pp. 1–10. Association for Information Systems, San Diego (2016)
26. Grabis, J., Kampars, J.: Design of capability delivery adjustments. In: Krogstie, J., Mouratidis, H., Su, J. (eds.) Advanced Information Systems Engineering Workshops, pp. 52–62. Springer International Publishing, Cham (2016). https://doi.org/10.1007/978-3-319-39564-7_5
27. Petrevska Nechkoska, R., Poels, G., Zdravkovic, J.: Enterprise adaptability using a capability-oriented methodology and tool support. In: Proceedings of the 2nd International Workshop on Practicing Open Enterprise Modelling within OMiLAB (PrOse) co-located with 11th IFIP WG 8.1 Working Conference on the Practice of Enterprise Modelling (PoEM 2018), Vienna, Austria, October 31, 2018. pp. 61–72 (2018)
28. Loucopoulos, P., Kavakli, E.: Capability oriented enterprise knowledge modeling: The CODEK approach. In: Karagiannis, D., Mayr, H.C., Mylopoulos, J. (eds.) Domain-Specific Conceptual Modeling, pp. 197–215. Springer International Publishing, Cham (2016). https://doi.org/10.1007/978-3-319-39417-6_9
29. Object Management Group (OMG): Value Delivery Modeling Language v.1.1. https://www.omg.org/spec/VDML/1.1 (2018)
30. NATO: NATO Architecture Framework v.4. https://www.nato.int/nato_static_fl2014/assets/pdf/pdf_2018_08/20180801_180801-ac322-d_2018_0002_naf_final.pdf (2018)
31. USA Department of Defense: Department of Defense Architecture Framework 2.02. https://dodcio.defense.gov/Library/DoD-Architecture-Framework/ (2009)
32. UK Ministry of Defence: Ministry of Defence Architecture Framework V1.2.004. https://www.gov.uk/guidance/mod-architecture-framework (2010)
33. The Open Group: Archimate 3.0.1. Specification. https://publications.opengroup.org/i162 (2017)
34. Danesh, M.H., Yu, E.: Modeling Enterprise capabilities with i*: Reasoning on alternatives. In: Iliadis, L., Papazoglou, M., Pohl, K. (eds.) Advanced Information Systems Engineering Workshops, pp. 112–123. Springer International Publishing, Cham (2014). https://doi.org/10.1007/978-3-319-07869-4_10
35. Beimborn, D., Martin, S.F., Homann, U.: Capability-oriented modeling of the firm. Presented at the IPSI Conference, Amalfi, Italy January (2005)
36. Henkel, M., Zdravkovic, J., Valverde, F., Pastor, O.: Capability design with CDD. In: Sandkuhl, K., Stirna, J. (eds.) Capability Management in Digital Enterprises, pp. 101–116. Springer International Publishing, Cham (2018). https://doi.org/10.1007/978-3-319-90424-5_6

37. Henkel, M., Bider, I., Perjons, E.: Capability-based business model transformation. In: Iliadis, L., Papazoglou, M., Pohl, K. (eds.) Advanced Information Systems Engineering Workshops, pp. 88–99. Springer International Publishing, Cham (2014). https://doi.org/10.1007/978-3-319-07869-4_8

38. Koç, H., Sandkuhl, K.: Context modelling in capability management. In: Sandkuhl, K., Stirna, J. (eds.) Capability Management in Digital Enterprises, pp. 117–138. Springer International Publishing, Cham (2018). https://doi.org/10.1007/978-3-319-90424-5_7

39. Henkel, M., Johannesson, P., Perjons, E.: An approach for E-service design using enterprise models. Int. J. Inf. Syst. Model Des. **2**, 1–23 (2011). https://doi.org/10.4018/jismd.2011010101

40. OMiLAB: The ADOxx Metamodelling Platform. https://www.adoxx.org/live/home. Accessed 26 June 2018

41. Denscombe, M.: The Good Research Guide: For Small-scale Social Research Projects. McGraw-Hill/Open University Press, Maidenhead (2011)

Chapter 13
A Security Assessment Platform for Stochastic Petri Net (SPN) Modelling in the Internet of Things (IoT) Ecosystem

Zacharenia Garofalaki, Dimitrios Kallergis, and Christos Douligeris

Abstract An Internet of Things (IoT)-based service includes several devices and applications. A service's security depends on the vulnerabilities of its individual components. Thus, because a security assessment is of high importance, it starts to be conducted in the design phase of the service's model. The Stochastic Petri net (SPN) modelling method can sufficiently depict the complexity and the unpredictability in terms of the time and the sequence of the events in an IoT service. Therefore, the SPN model can form the appropriate basis of a security assessment method. In this chapter, we propose an ADOxx-based modelling tool, the SAPnet, which includes the ontology toolkit for SPN modelling enriched with the tools that enable the necessary security assessment. SAPnet provides a modeler-friendly interface for the composition and updating of the security vulnerabilities list that affects the model, as well as fast and accurate results regarding the security metrics of the model, at any point of the design phase. The functionalities of SAPnet are tested in the security assessment of iBuC, an IoT-based novel transportation service. More specifically, we evaluate the security of iBuC's fleet management in two customised real-life scenarios. We observed that SAPnet provides fast and accurate results and visual aids to the modeler during the design and security assessment process.

Keywords Internet of Things (IoT) · Stochastic Petri net (SPN) · Security assessment · Intelligent transportation services

Z. Garofalaki (✉)
Department of Informatics and Computer Engineering, University of West Attica, Egaleo, Greece

Department of Informatics, University of Piraeus, Piraeus, Greece
e-mail: z.garofalaki@uniwa.gr

D. Kallergis
Department of Informatics and Computer Engineering, University of West Attica, Egaleo, Greece
e-mail: d.kallergis@uniwa.gr

C. Douligeris
Department of Informatics, University of Piraeus, Piraeus, Greece
e-mail: cdoulig@unipi.gr

© The Author(s), under exclusive license to Springer Nature Switzerland AG 2022
D. Karagiannis et al. (eds.), *Domain-Specific Conceptual Modeling*,
https://doi.org/10.1007/978-3-030-93547-4_13

289

13.1 Introduction

In the Internet of Things (IoT) era, the transportation solutions incorporate smart services to improve the quality of the offered services in terms of availability and interoperability. One of the benefits of implementing a smart service is the acceleration of the decision-making process. In this vein, IoT technological and operational features [1], such as the secure data sharing with extra-domain third-party services, are exploited. However, such features may change the original schema of the operations by adding more factors to the decision-making of an IoT-based transportation service and may affect some of its key processes, such as the fleet management.

Since the security of the fleet management processes is crucial for the wider acceptance and deployment of an IoT-based transportation service, and an IoT-based service incorporates several devices and applications, the overall system/service security depends on the weaknesses of the service's individual components. When integrating a third-party service's data, these extra-domain services and their relevant weaknesses become additional security factors for the IoT-based transportation service.

The third-party data integration feature introduces events that cannot be fully and timely predicted. Nevertheless, the lack of a thorough time-sequence for the events and the inherent complexity of an IoT service can be sufficiently depicted by employing the Stochastic Petri net (SPN) modelling method [2]. The SPN formalism allows the modelling of the activities' duration and the delay between events by using tokens and the firing settings of the transitions [3, 4]. Thus, the adoption of the SPN model can form the basis of an IoT service security assessment method [5] at the service's design phase.

Recent studies on fleet management mainly focus on itinerary planning and smart resource allocation. In these studies [6, 7], the access on real-time information regarding the environmental conditions, the traffic conditions and the weather conditions is considered as a factor of efficiency, effectiveness and quality improvement. However, the fact is that information about these conditions may be provided by an extra-domain service, while the integration of such extra-domain data also modifies the fleet management process. Furthermore, although the security threats for IoT-based transportation systems have attracted the interest of the research community [8], previous works do not conduct a security assessment of the fleet management to examine how the third-party data integration affects the security of the service.

In this chapter, we introduce SAPnet, an ADOxx-based modelling tool that includes the ontology toolkit for SPN modelling enriched with the tools that enable the security evaluation of a model. SAPnet provides (a) a modeler-friendly interface for the composition and the updating of the security vulnerabilities list that affects the model and (b) fast and accurate results regarding the security metric of the model, at any point of the design phase. SAPnet's functionalities are then tested in the security assessment of a previously proposed IoT-based novel transportation service, namely, the iBuC [1]. More specifically, we evaluate the security of iBuC's fleet management in two customised real-life scenarios. In the first scenario, we consider that the service exchanges data with the Public Transport System (PTS) and in the second one that the service exchanges data with a Weather Forecasting System (WFS). Based on the two scenarios, we study how the fleet management and the security of the iBuC service are affected by the nature of the integrated information. We, also, evaluate how SAPnet facilitates and expedites the security assessment process.

This chapter includes (*a*) the introduction of the security assessment method for an IoT-based service based on the service's SPN model and the Common Vulnerabilities List (CVE) of the participating components; (*b*) the presentation of the meta-model, the semantics and the algorithms composing the SAPnet ADOxx-based modelling tool; and (*c*) the proof of concept for SAPnet, evaluating the security of the stochastic model of a novel IoT-based transportation service, under two real-life scenarios.

This chapter is organised as follows: Sect. 13.2 introduces the main concepts of the modelling and the security assessment method, as well as the related work, Section 13.3 analyses SAPnet's meta-model, semantics and algorithms, while Sect. 13.4 illustrates the security assessment of an IoT-based Intelligent Transportation service, both theoretically and assisted by the SAPnet tool. Section 13.5 concludes the chapter and describes a future work path.

13.2 Method Description

13.2.1 Modeling an IoT-Based Service

The data sharing process using IoT-based third-party services is a feature which aims to achieve an information- and service-centric operation [9]. This feature maximises the usability of the data produced and benefits the collaborating sides in terms of the decision-making, the control and the quality of the offered service. However, this data integration may affect the operation not only of each service, but of the included processes as well, because new data are added in the decision-making process and the third-party is operating as an additional actor.

A service's dynamic behaviour can be depicted by using various modelling methods. However, in the case of an IoT-based service with the integration of a third-party service's data, the events may not be timely sequential, and we cannot rely on static modelling methods, making the stochastic approach mandatory. The SPN formalism models the activities' duration and the delay between events [2]. This is accomplished by using tokens and transition firing settings. The SPN states are also the states of the service's actors, allowing SPN to assess the security of the service based on the actor's security state.

13.2.2   Security Assessment Method

The security issues depend on the weaknesses of the service key enablers. The weaknesses (e.g., in the access control, the authentication or the information exposure) are expressed by the vulnerabilities of each hardware or software component. A weakness describes the errors, the faults and the bugs of a service without restrictions to a specific component, product or vendor. A weakness may lead to several vulnerabilities; the vulnerabilities of a service depend on the specific components, the software, the hardware and the architectural design of the service.

13.2.2.1   Weaknesses and Vulnerabilities of the Service

As a first step for the service assessment process, we develop a list of weaknesses using the Architectural Concepts list provided by the Massachusetts Institute of Technology Research & Engineering (MITRE) database [10]. Throughout this list, we choose an indicative vulnerability for every weakness, based on the following two criteria: (*a*) the relevance between a vulnerability and the service components and (*b*) the impact of a vulnerability on the service's data integrity and privacy, depicted by the vulnerability's security score [11]. These criteria allow the selection of a list, where every vulnerability is the most significant for the service under assessment.

The relevance of a vulnerability is defined by the logical association of the vulnerability with the service states. The relevance criterion helps to select the group of vulnerabilities that are inherent in the software and in the hardware which are included in the service. Within this group of relevant vulnerabilities, some have a greater impact, due to the frequency of their exploitability. The use of the Common Vulnerability Scoring System (CVSS) base score [11] shows the level of the impact for the specific entity (i.e., software, hardware component and OS, among others) that suffers from the vulnerability. The CVSS base score represents the vulnerability severity in a 0 to 10 scale, where 10 is the most critical value. The impact criterion limits the group of relevant vulnerabilities to the most critical relevant vulnerabilities.

13.2.2.2   Calculation of the Security Metric

The second step is the calculation procedure, which starts with the calculation of the *frequency of occurrences* (R_n) of every vulnerability. If R_n is calculated based on the Petri net model of a system or service, then R_n is given by:

$$R_n = \frac{K}{\Sigma_{n=1}^{m} A},$$

(13.1)

where K is the number of the identified vulnerabilities and A is the number of the Petri net model's states that are affected by each one of these vulnerabilities [12].

The *severity of every weakness* (W_n) is estimated by:

$$W_n = \Sigma_{i=1}^{k} \frac{V_i}{K \cdot CR \cdot IR \cdot AR}, \tag{13.2}$$

where V_i is the CVSS base score of each vulnerability i and CR, IR and AR are the Environmental Metrics of every vulnerability. The severity is affected by the values of the Environmental Metrics, which are modified as a result of mitigating a vulnerability. The Confidentiality Requirement (CR), Integrity Requirement (IR) and Availability Requirement (AR) metrics may take the values 1.0, 0.5, 1.0 or 1.51 [11].

The *vulnerability risk* (P_n) is given by:

$$P_n = \frac{R_n}{\Sigma_{i=1}^{m} R_i}, \tag{13.3}$$

where the R_n is calculated using Eq. 13.1 and R_i is the sum of all the weaknesses' R_n that are associated with the service.

The final step is the calculation of the *security metric SM(0)*:

$$SM(0) = \Sigma_{n=1}^{m}(P_n \cdot W_n), \tag{13.4}$$

where P_n is the risk result of Eq. 13.3 for the number m of the vulnerabilities and W_n is calculated using Eq. 13.2. If *SM(0)* has a high value, then the service is in a critical security state. The security metric *SM(0)*, which is the sum of the vulnerabilities associated with the service components, is always higher than the metric *SM(t)* of the service after the mitigation of those vulnerabilities.

13.2.3 Related Work

Significant efforts have been devoted to developing intelligent and sustainable transportation systems. Various innovative applications have been proposed in the fields of fleet management, itinerary planning and smart resource allocation. Aazam and Fernando [6] and Tilocca et al. [7] discuss factors, such as environmental, traffic and weather conditions and the improvement of quality on road transit services, while Remy et al. [13] propose the architecture and the decision-making operations within a vehicle booking system with itinerary planning, which is based on road cartography and weather conditions.

Communications security aspects in the transportation ecosystem are also crucial. Stellios et al. [14] study IoT-enabled attacks through assessing attack paths and conclude that the success of the attack relies on (a) the physical proximity of the IoT device to the target, (b) the exploitation of its communication interfaces (physical or network) and (c) the extension of the functionality provided by the IoT device.

The modelling of an IoT-based service using domain-specific modelling languages tackles the challenges of depicting the behaviour of distributed, heterogeneous and interconnected nodes. On these grounds, Mavropoulos et al. [15] present a tool named Apparatus for domain-specific modelling and security analysis [16] of an IoT-based service, while [17] proposes a code generation framework using a respective modelling language, namely, the ThingML, which provides the semantics for modelling the software components and generates programming code from the model. The Hierarchical Attack Representation Model (HARM) is used in [18] to model an IoT-based network. The HARM assessment is based on the security metrics for the respective vulnerabilities, as they are provided by the National Vulnerability Database (NVD) [11]. This assessment is conducted for different time instances and, therefore, takes under consideration the mobility of the nodes. In [19], the security metrics are classified in two categories, the host- and the network-based. The former category is studied based on the probability of attack success, while the latter category is studied based on the proximity of the attacker to one or more assets.

An IoT-based service security analysis is proposed in [20] using a stochastic modelling approach through Petri net (PNs). Yamaguchi and Tanaka [21] model a well-known malware infection using PNs and evaluate a mitigation method. Furthermore, the literature also utilises PNs to adopt mechanisms for orchestrating IoT-based services [22]. The IoT service deployment cannot underestimate issues, such as changes in IoT entities/IoT environment, and, hence, cannot fully rely on static models. Fortino et al. [23] denote that IoT operational representations in meta-models can enable verification and simulation in various fields, such as in security.

13.3   Method Conceptualisation

Petri net (PN) is a domain-specific modelling language with minimal semantics. The method itself and the models produced can depict the dynamic changes of a system with simplicity. The core elements of the PN notation are the *Places*, the *Transitions*, the *Arcs* and the *Tokens*, used to depict the states, the changes or actions, the state-to-state flow and the marks, respectively. The Transitions are fired if the previous state contains a Token. A fired Transition moves the Token from one state to the next. The assessment of (a) the reachability of all Places, (b) the risk for deadlock and (c) the liveness of the Transitions can ensure the validity of a PN model [3].

An extension of Petri net is the Stochastic Petri net (SPN) formalism. The SPN is strongly related to the mathematical Markov process. As opposed to the PN, in the SPN the duration of activities and the delay between events are depicted [2]. This is accomplished with the *Tokens* and the firing settings of the *Transitions*. This SPN feature is important while modelling real-time processes or systems, where the time consumed per state affects all the following system states.

When the main issue is the study of the security level of a system or a service, the use of SPN can be helpful because of the clear depiction of the system states and the transition from one state to the next. The security level of the system can increase if the vulnerabilities in every state are addressed or mitigated [24]. Also, the clear system-state modelling can indicate which states must be improved security-wise. These characteristics promote the SPN modelling as a valuable designing tool for an IoT service.

13.3.1 SAPnet Meta-Model and Semantics

The Bee-Up hybrid modelling tool [4], supported by the ADOxx $^\text{r}$ meta^2-modelling platform, provides a library with the Petri net semantics. The SAPnet extends the Petri net Dynamic Library (Fig. 13.1), mainly by two meta-model elements: (*a*) the CVSS class and (*b*) the Security Assessment class. The SAPnet's meta-model is shown in Fig. 13.1a, and the semantics CVSS (PN) and Security Assessment (PN) of the respective classes are shown in Fig. 13.1b.

The new classes are elements of the *PN-element* abstract class. This allows the modeler to utilise real-time data from the model, such as the model's list of Places, during the security assessment process. Therefore, the assessment process is facilitated and accelerated, and the results are more accurate and continuously updated. The new classes and the algorithms that each class includes are described in detail as follows.

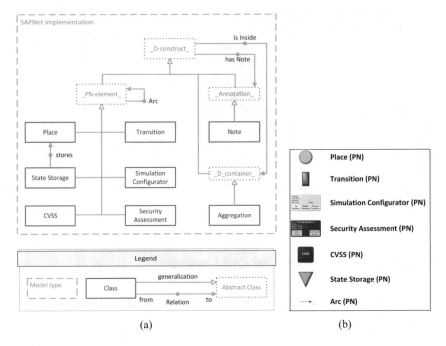

Fig. 13.1 SAPnet implementation

13.3.2 Features and Algorithms

13.3.2.1 CVSS Class

The CVSS class provides a modeler-friendly interface for the construction of the vulnerability list per model. This assisted list construction interface includes the following options:

- **The modeler may enter manually each vulnerability**

  In this case, the modeler is guided with messages and field restrictions, so that the list will only contain vulnerabilities having a valid CVSS base score (i.e., greater than 0 and less or equal to 10). However, the modeler may enter a vulnerability without any countermeasures and, hence, with no CVSS temporal score. In this case, the class's code will assume that the CVSS temporal score is equal to the CVSS base score for the specific CVE_ID.

  After entering the values for a vulnerability, the modeler calls the *csv2table* attribute (Algorithm 1). The *csv2table* contains the programming code for the validation checks of the new vulnerability record already submitted. Additionally, the *csv2table's* code compares the new record against all records already stored and prevents duplicates.

Algorithm 1 CSV2TABLE attribute

Input:	$CVE\_ID \in \mathbb{N}^*$
	$CVSS\_Base \in \mathbb{R}^+$
	$CVSS\_Temporal \in \mathbb{R}^+$
Output:	new record [CVE_ID, $CVSS\_Base$, $CVSS\_Temporal$] in $CVE\_choices$ table

1: **if** $CVSS\_Temporal$ = null **then**
2:     $CVSS\_Temporal \leftarrow CVSS\_Base$
3: **for each** $CVE\_ID \in CVE\_choices[]$ **do**
4:     **if** CVE_ID does not exist **then**
5:         **create** new record [CVE_ID, $CVSS\_Base$, $CVSS\_Temporal$]

- **The modeler may load a predefined list**

  This option, which is provided by the *Load_CVE_List* attribute (Algorithm 2), allows the list to be imported from a comma-delimited file saved in the path:

  ```
  "%ProgramFiles%/BOC/ADOxx15_EN_SA"
  ```

  The contents of the file must include at least one vulnerability in order to be considered valid. Each vulnerability is one line in the file's contents, with the ID, the base and the temporal score of the vulnerability separated by a special character, e.g., "CVE-2017-7214; 9.8; 9.1." If the comma-delimited file exists and it is not empty, the contents will be processed line-by-line and will be used to import the list.

Algorithm 2 LOAD_CVE_LIST attribute

Input:	$LFILE$ name of comma-delimited file
Output:	new records [CVE_ID, $CVSS\_Base$, $CVSS\_Temporal$] in $CVE\_choices$ table

1: **for each** line $\in LFILE$ **do**
2:     **create** new record [CVE_ID, $CVSS\_Base$, $CVSS\_Temporal$]

- **Changing and storing during and after the creation phase**

  The previous two features may occur more than once for every model's design. The modeler can revise a previously created list either manually for every record of the list or by importing a new list from a file. Also, the modeler may decide to start creation of the list from scratch. For that reason, an option for clearing the list is provided by the *Clear_CVE_List* attribute's code (Algorithm 3). The attribute's code contains checks for the list's contents. If the list is not empty, the *Clear_CVE_List* clears the contents after a confirmation message with the ok-cancel possible choices is given to the modeler. The modeler has the option to store the list for later use in an external comma-delimited file. This feature is provided by the *Save_CVE_List* attribute's code (Algorithm 4). This export feature is additional to the storing of the list for its use for the security assessment. The latter storing process is supported by the *cvss2table* record class.

Algorithm 3 CLEAR_CVE_LIST attribute

Input: records [*CVE_ID*, *CVSS_Base*, *CVSS_Temporal*] in *CVE_choices* table
1: **for each** record ∈ *CVE_choices[]* **do**
2:     **delete** record [*CVE_ID*, *CVSS_Base*, *CVSS_Temporal*]

Algorithm 4 SAVE_CVE_LIST attribute

Input: records [*CVE_ID*, *CVSS_Base*, *CVSS_Temporal*] in *CVE_choices* table
Output: *LFILE* name of comma-delimited file
1: **for each** record ∈ *CVE_choices[]* **do**
2:     **create** new *LFILE* line *"CVE_ID;CVSS_Base;CVSS_Temporal"*

The creation of a valid and clear vulnerabilities list is an important step of the security assessment process. Using the CVSS class, this creation process is still a complex time-consuming process for the modeler. However, the CVSS facilitates (*a*) the validity checks for the list's records and, for the record's values, (*b*) the revision and adjustment of the list's contents and (*c*) the import/export of the list from the ADOxx platform to other software and vice versa.

13.3.2.2   Security Assessment Class

The Security Assessment class supports the assessment process mechanism and provides real-time and updated information regarding the active model and the assessment's results. The modeler's aim is to make an association between the chosen vulnerabilities and the Places (i.e., the states) of the model that are affected by these vulnerabilities. This association is essential to the security assessment's calculations. This class supports the modeler with the following features:

- **Loading, modifying and storing options are available**
  Although this class aims at assisting the evaluation of the model's security, the modeler is once again given the ability to manipulate the contents of the vulnerabilities list before the evaluation. A new list can be loaded from a comma-delimited file with the *Load CVE List* attribute (Algorithm 5) and manually modified or cleared of contents with the *Clear CVE List* attribute (Algorithm 6), and it can be stored in an external comma-delimited file for later use with the *Save CVE List* attribute (Algorithm 7).

Algorithm 5 LOAD CVE LIST attribute

Input: *LFILE* name of comma-delimited file
Output: new records [*CVE_ID, CVSS_Base, CVSS_Temporal*] in *CVE_choices* table
             sm0_tag value on MODEL SM(0) attribute
             smt_tag value on MODEL SM(T) attribute

1: **for each** line ∈ *LFILE* **do**
2:    **create** new record [*CVE_ID, CVSS_Base, CVSS_Temporal*]
3: **update** *sm0_tag* ← null, *smt_tag* ← null

Algorithm 6 CLEAR CVE LIST attribute

Input: records in *CVE_choices* table

1: **for each** record ∈ *CVE_choices[ ]* **do**
2:    **delete** record

Algorithm 7 SAVE CVE LIST attribute

Input: records in *CVE_choices* table
Output: *LFILE* name of comma-delimited file

1: **for each** record ∈ *CVE_choices[ ]* **do**
2:    **create** new *LFILE* line "*CVE_ID;CVSS_Base;CVSS_Temporal;NofStates;Rn;Pn*"
3: **create** new *LFILE* line "*SM(0);SM(t)*"

- **Association of vulnerabilities and model states**

  The *Affected States* attribute (Algorithm 8) provides the modeler with a wizard to facilitate the association of the vulnerabilities with the current model's states. The attribute's code calls the modeler to (*a*) choose one CVE_ID from his list and (*b*) choose one or more states currently existing in the model that are affected by the vulnerability already chosen. At the third step of this wizard, the modeler gets a verification screen message regarding his choices. If the associations are confirmed, the vulnerabilities list is updated with the number of states affected per vulnerability (i.e., list's column titled "NofStates").

Algorithm 8 AFFECTED_STATES attribute

Input: *selCVE* ∈ *listCVE*
             selNOS ∈ *listPLACES*
Output: *listCVE* ⊂ *CVE_choices[CVE_ID]*
             listPLACES ⊂ Places (PN) in model
             value for [*NofStates*] in *CVE_choices* table

1: **for each** *selNOS* ∈ *listPLACES* **do**
2:    *csNOS* ← **count** *selNOS*
3: **for each** *CVE_ID* ∈ *CVE_choices[ ]* **do**
4:    **if** *CVE_ID* = *selCVE* **then**
5:       **update** record [*NofStates*] ← *csNOS*

- **Assessment process**

    The core of the assessment process is provided by the *SM(0)* and *SM(t)* attributes (Algorithm 9). Both attributes include the code needed to implement the process described previously in this chapter, and they result in the *SM(0)* and *SM(t)* security metrics, respectively. The mathematical procedure is performed based on the modeler's choices regarding the vulnerabilities and the affected model states. Therefore, these attributes should be the last ones to be used by the modeler to complete the security assessment of the model.

Algorithm 9 SM(0) and SM(T) attributes

Input:	records [*CVE_ID*, *CVSS_Base*, *CVSS_Temporal*, *NofStates*] in *CVE_choices* table
Output:	*CVE_choices* table
	sm0_tag on "MODEL SM(0)" attribute
	smt_tag on "MODEL SM(T)" attribute

1: **if** *SM(0)* **then**
2:     **for each** record ∈ *CVE_choices[]* **do**
3:         **compute** R_n, P_n and *SM(0)* values
4:         **update** record [*Rn*, *Pn*, *SM(0)*] ← (R_n, P_n, *SM(0)*)
5:     **update** *sm0_tag* ← *SM(0)*
6: **else if** *SM(t)* **then**
7:     **for each** record ∈ *CVE_choices[]* **do**
8:         **compute** R_n, P_n and *SM(t)* values
9:         **update** record [*Rn*, *Pn*, *SM(t)*] ← (R_n, P_n, *SM(t)*)
10:     **update** *smt_tag* ← *SM(t)*

The Security Assessment class complements the CVSS class and provides the modeler with a valid toolset for the assessment of the model in terms of security. This class allows the modeler (*a*) to modify partly or completely the list, at any point of the design process, (*b*) to easily and quickly select the number of model states which are affected by every vulnerability under study and (*c*) to calculate the security metrics of the model quickly and accurately for the chosen vulnerabilities. These features are not only faster and with greater accuracy, but they can also be updated equally fast and correctly after any change is made on the model itself.

13.4 Proof of Concept: The SAPnet Tool

In this section, the security assessment method is applied (*a*) utilising the mathematical model and the equations previously presented and (*b*) utilising the SAPnet tool. The fleet management of the iBuC IoT-based service in two real-life scenarios is used as a case study. The iBuC's fleet management under both scenarios is modelled based on the SPN formalism, and the two models are then assessed in terms of security.

13.4.1   An IoT-Based Service: The iBuC Paradigm

In this subsection, we present the fleet management of an IoT-based Intelligent Transportation System (ITS), the intelligent Bus on Campus (iBuC) [1]. iBuC is the service of a Personal Rapid Transit (PRT) system [25] which can be used in a local road network, such as a University campus. The service offers transportation between campus points and from any campus point to the public transport nodes which are in the campus perimeter.

The actors in the fleet management process of the iBuC service are (*a*) the autonomous vehicle (AV) fleet; (*b*) the Control Unit (CU) of the service that gathers the fleet's data (e.g., the vehicle's position, direction and speed, the number of passengers on board and the pending passengers' requests) and supports the decision-making process [26]; (*c*) the client application, which is accessible via smartphone devices and the web and offers a user interface for placing and monitoring itinerary requests; and (*d*) the third-party services.

The fleet management process is initiated upon a consumer's request. Upon receiving the request, the CU evaluates if the consumer is authorised to access the service; in such a case, the Decision Support System (DSS) module of iBuC is activated. The DSS has three main tasks: the first is to select a meeting place for the Consumer and the AV within the campus area; the second is to pick the closest available AV to service the request; the third is to locate the closest free parking space after the vehicle request is fulfilled.

The iBuC service shares information with third-party services, and the decision-making for the iBuC's fleet management is adjusted to the incoming information accordingly.

The iBuC's fleet management is implemented considering two scenarios: in the first scenario, we integrate the service data from a Public Transportation System (PTS), and in the second scenario, we integrate the data from a Weather Forecasting Service (WFS).

The modelling of the iBuC service under the two scenarios shows that the fleet management process changes depending on the nature of the integrated third-party data. This differentiation may also affect various aspects of the service, such as the security. These changes of the service will be assessed in the following sections.

13.4.1.1   The iBuC-PTS Scenario

In the case of the iBuC-Public Transport Service (iBuC-PTS), the iBuC's shared information can assist in the prediction of the number of attendants in the public transport nodes which are in the campus perimeter, and it can also be used by the PTS for adaptive route scheduling. For that purpose, the iBuC's CU sends real-time data regarding the fleet's status to the PTS service.

The incoming PTS itinerary information is used in the fleet management process to reduce the waiting time on the public transport nodes and to simultaneously increase the number of on-time passengers per PTS route. When the incoming information indicates that a PTS vehicle approximates a public node (PN) at the campus perimeter, the CU activates all the AVs to perform a full route through all the boarding nodes (BNs) within the campus and terminates the route at the nearest to the PN campus destination node (DN).

The Petri net model in Fig. 13.2 shows the fleet management of the iBuC-PTS service.

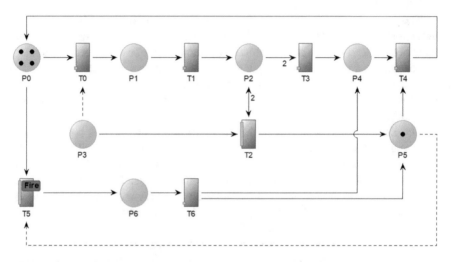

Fig. 13.2 iBuC-PTS fleet management model

For an in-depth analysis of the model, the meaning of the states (i.e., P0 to P6) and transitions (i.e., T0 to T6) is shown in Table 13.1. The tokens in state P0 represent the number of the fleet's AVs, and the token in state P3 shows that a Consumer's request is placed. The T5, T6 transitions and the P5, P6 states represent the data integration of the PTS to the iBuC service and the full-service process by the fleet in the case of incoming PTS itinerary information.

13.4.1.2   The iBuC-WFS Scenario

In the case of the iBuC-Weather Forecasting Service (iBuC-WFS), real-time environmental metrics within the campus, which can assist in the microclimate monitoring to manage the fleet under special weather conditions, are used. In this vein, the CU sends real-time environmental information which is gathered by the AV sensors.

A WFS incoming alert for extreme weather phenomena is used in the fleet management to complete any ongoing routes and, then, to suspend the service, if considered necessary.

Table 13.1 States and transitions of the fleet management

States		Transitions	
P0	Fleet is idle	T0	CU checks the request's validity and the fleet's availability
			CU sends service data to AV
			(*a*) Boarding node (BN)
P1	AV is activated	T1	(*b*) Appointment time (AT)
			(*c*) Destination node (DN)
			(*d*) Re-routing data
P2	AV is located at BN	T2	Consumer embarks on AV
P3	Consumer's request is placed	T3	AV travels from BN to DN
P4	AV is located at DN	T4	Consumer disembarks, AV receives parking data
P5	PTS incoming information	T5	CU checks the fleet's availability
	AV is activated for a		CU sends service data to AV
P6	full-route service (all	T6	(*a*) Full-route service (all BNs)
	BNs)		(*b*) DN pre-defined

The fleet management, as assisted by the WFS data integration, is shown in Fig. 13.3, where the T5 transition and the P5 state represent the data integration of the WFS and the iBuC service's suspension in the case of WFS incoming alerts.

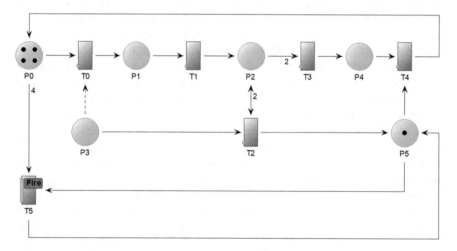

Fig. 13.3 iBuC-WFS fleet management model

13.4.2   Security Evaluation of the iBuC's Fleet Management Process

13.4.2.1   Theoretical Approach

The security issues of the iBuC service are dependent on the weaknesses of the CU, the AV fleet and the consumers (i.e., their smart device, or the service's passenger application). CU inherits the vulnerabilities of the operating system, of the hardware and of the software of its subsystems. Moreover, since the AVs are equipped with sensors, microcontrollers, communication interfaces and transceivers to achieve autonomous navigation by utilising obstacle-avoidance capabilities, these devices and the supporting software may have their own vulnerabilities. The consumer uses a device to interact with the iBuC's components; thus, the vulnerabilities of this device should also be considered. The final selection of iBuC's relevant vulnerabilities is made taking into account the vulnerabilities of all the aforementioned components.

The iBuC-PTS service's fleet management has more PN states and transitions compared to the iBuC-WFS counterpart. For this reason, the security assessment process is conducted separately for the iBuC-PTS and the iBuC-WFS models.

The security assessment focuses on the most relative and highly affective weaknesses, as reported by the CVSS. For each weakness, we choose the most critical and relevant vulnerability, based on the CVE list [10]. In CVE, each vulnerability is represented by the CVE-ID, and it has metrics which reflect the exploitability and the impact of the vulnerability [11], as shown in Table 13.2.

NIST [11] provides references to advisories, solutions and tools if those are available, for every CVE. By applying the patches or fixes for the vulnerabilities, the CVSS base score changes to the CVSS temporal score. In case that no patch or fix exists, the CVSS temporal score is equal to the CVSS base score. Table 13.3 shows the CVE list under study and the security evaluation for the iBuC-PTS and the iBuC-WFS models before and after the mitigation of their vulnerabilities.

A cross-reference is applied between the list of weaknesses and the states of the two models, based on the components involved in every state. It should be noted that the difference of the sums for the affected states in the two models is caused by the vulnerabilities of state P6, which is an extra state only in the iBuC-PTS model.

The number of states (i.e., the values in Table 13.3, in columns "A") is used in calculating the security metric $SM(0)$ for the iBuC service for all the weaknesses. The calculation process is described by Eqs. (13.1)–(13.4). $SM(t)$ represents the iBuC's security metric after the mitigation, considering the CVSS temporal score of the mitigated vulnerabilities.

Even though the $SM(0)$ metrics of the two models differ, this deviation is small. This happens because the fleet management transitions and not the states are the ones mainly affected. Hence, the dynamic adaptation of the iBuC to the third-party service affects the security only if new states arise.

Table 13.2 CVE list for the iBuC service

CVE	Description	CVSS	
		Base	Temporal
CVE-2017-7214	Information exposure	9.8	9.1
CVE-2018-4878	(Resource) use after free	9.8	9.1
CVE-2018-8174	Failure to constrain operations	7.5	7.3
CVE-2017-0199	Access control (authorization) issues	7.8	6.6
CVE-2018-7600	Improper input validation	9.8	8.5
CVE-2018-12942	OS command injection	8.8	8.1
CVE-2018-14643	Improper authentication	9.8	8.8
CVE-2018-10635	Missing critical function authentication	9.8	7.9
CVE-2016-6829	Use of hard-coded credentials	9.8	8.7
CVE-2016-5788	Improper authorisation	10,0	8.3
CVE-2016-5062	Incorrect resource transfer	9.8	8.3
CVE-2016-8209	Improper check	7.5	6.6
CVE-2017-5239	Inadequate encryption strength	7.5	7.1
CVE-2017-17717	Broken cryptographic algorithm	9.8	9.3
CVE-2017-7901	Use of insufficiently random values	8.6	7.6
CVE-2017-18146	Improper crypto verification	9.8	8.5
CVE-2016-5069	Insufficient session expiration	9.8	9.1
CVE-2016-7124	Deserialization of untrusted data	9.8	8.5
CVE-2018-12689	LDAP injection	9.8	9.3

After the mitigation, the security metric $SM(t)$ for the iBuC-PTS decreases to 8.15 compared to the metric $SM(0)$ before the mitigation, which has the value of 9.14. The same happens to the $SM(t)$ for the iBuC-WFS, which decreases to 8.09 compared to the $SM(0)$ value of 9.09. Nonetheless, in both cases $SM(t)$ has a smaller value than $SM(0)$, indicating that the security level of the service improves. However, the difference of the $SM(t)$ value in the two cases arises due to the additional states on the iBuC-PTS model, but also due to the different degree of mitigation of the vulnerabilities that affect these additional states. Hence, the dynamic adaptation of the iBuC to the third-party service affects security if these states are associated with critical vulnerabilities.

13.4.2.2 Assessment Process on SAPnet

The same assessment process for the two models, the iBuC-PTS and the iBuC-WFS fleet management, is performed utilising SAPnet. SAPnet is used for the creation of the two models as described using the SPN formalism. Additionally, the *CVSS (PN)* and the *Security Assessment (PN)* are placed on the drawing area of both models to be activated and made available for use (Fig. 13.4).

Table 13.3 iBuC's affected states and security metrics

CVE	Affected states	iBuC-PTS					iBuC-WFS				
		A	Rn	Pn	SM(0)	SM(t)	A	Rn	Pn	SM(0)	SM(t)
CVE-2017-7214	P0,P1,P2,P3, P4,P5,P6	7	0.14	0.04	0.34	0.32	6	0.17	0.03	0.32	0.29
CVE-2018-4878	P1,P2,P3,P5	4	0.25	0.06	0.60	0.56	4	0.25	0.05	0.47	0.44
CVE-2018-8174	P0,P1,P3 ,P5,P6	5	0.20	0.05	0.37	0.36	4	0.25	0.05	0.36	0.35
CVE-2017-0199	P0,P1,P3, P5,P6	5	0.20	0.05	0.38	0.32	4	0.25	0.05	0.38	0.32
CVE-2018-7600	P0,P1,P3, P5,P6	5	0.20	0.05	0.48	0.42	4	0.25	0.05	0.47	0.41
CVE-2018-12942	P0,P1,P2,P3 ,P4,P5,P6	7	0.14	0.04	0.31	0.28	6	0.17	0.03	0.28	0.26
CVE-2018-14643	P0,P1,P2,P4, P5,P6	6	0.17	0.04	0.40	0.36	5	0.20	0.04	0.38	0.34
CVE-2018-10635	P0,P1,P2,P4, P5,P6	6	0.17	0.04	0.40	0.32	5	0.20	0.04	0.38	0.31
CVE-2016-6829	P0,P1,P2,P4, P5,P6	6	0.17	0.04	0.40	0.36	5	0.20	0.04	0.38	0.34
CVE-2016-5788	P1,P5,P6	3	0.33	0.08	0.82	0.68	2	0.50	0.10	0.97	0.80
CVE-2016-5062	P0,P1,P3, P5,P6	5	0.20	0.05	0.48	0.41	4	0.25	0.05	0.47	0.40
CVE-2016-8209	P1,P5,P6	3	0.33	0.08	0.61	0.54	2	0.50	0.10	0.73	0.64
CVE-2017-5239	P0,P1,P3,P6	4	0.25	0.06	0.46	0.44	3	0.33	0.06	0.48	0.46
CVE-2017-17717	P0,P1,P3, P5,P6	5	0.20	0.05	0.48	0.46	4	0.25	0.05	0.47	0.45
CVE-2017-7901	P1,P5,P6	3	0.33	0.08	0.70	0.62	2	0.50	0.10	0.83	0.74
CVE-2017-18146	P1,P2,P3,P5	4	0.25	0.06	0.60	0.52	4	0.25	0.05	0.47	0.41
CVE-2016-5069	P0,P1,P2, P4,P6	5	0.20	0.05	0.48	0.45	4	0.25	0.05	0.47	0.44
CVE-2016-7124	P0,P1,P2,P4, P5,P6	6	0.17	0.04	0.40	0.35	5	0.20	0.04	0.38	0.33
CVE-2018-12689	P0,P1,P2,P4, P5,P6	6	0.17	0.04	0.40	0.38	5	0.20	0.04	0.38	0.36
TOTALS					9.14	8.15				9.09	8.09

For comparison reasons, the vulnerabilities list under study is kept the same as the one used in the theoretical approach. The list has already been constructed during the theoretical assessment and stored in a comma-delimited file. SAPnet supports the option of importing a list directly from a file, an option which is provided by the *CVSS* class. Figure 13.5 shows the steps taken to import the list.

The next step is the association for every record of the vulnerabilities list with the number of the model states that are affected by the corresponding vulnerability. As discussed in the theoretical approach of the assessment, the percentage of the affected model states overall is a factor of the security metric of the model. The *Security Assessment* class allows the modeler to update the vulnerabilities list with the number of affected states per vulnerability, in the *NofStates* field. The update of the *NofStates* field can be done manually or with the help of a wizard provided by the *Security Assessment* class (Fig. 13.6).

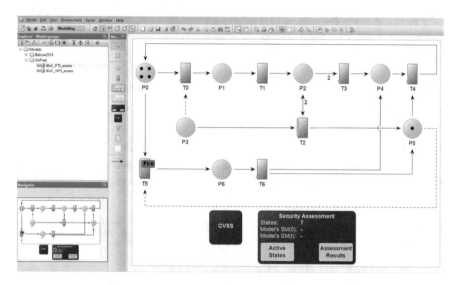

Fig. 13.4 The *CVSS* and the *Security Assessment* classes placed in the drawing area

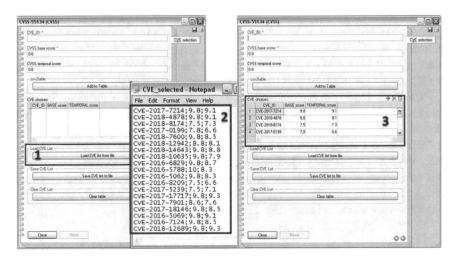

Fig. 13.5 Importing a list of vulnerabilities with the *CVSS* class

The core of the security assessment process, which results in the calculation of the security metrics for the model, is performed by the code of the attributes *SM(0)* and *SM(t)* of the Assessment SM(0) and the Assessment SM(t) buttons in the *Security Assessment* class's environment, respectively. The calculation of the metrics is fast and accurate even in the case of a complex model or of an exhaustive list of vulnerabilities. Additionally, the outcome of the assessment is visible to the modeler in the drawing area, thanks to the design of the *Security Assessment* class

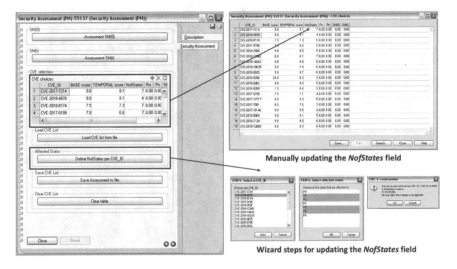

Fig. 13.6 Updating the *NofStates* field of the vulnerabilities' list

(Fig. 13.7). This feature allows the modeler to have a visual monitoring of the results while changing, updating or redrawing the model under study.

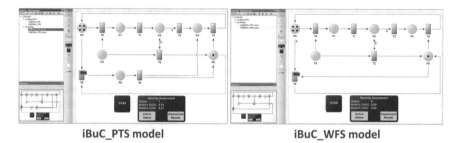

iBuC_PTS model   iBuC_WFS model

Fig. 13.7 The two models and the security metrics values on the drawing area

13.5 Conclusion

An IoT-based service includes several devices and applications, while its security depends on the vulnerabilities of these participating components. The complexity of such a service can be sufficiently depicted by the SPN modelling method [2]. The SPN formalism allows the modeling of the activities' duration and of the delay between events by using tokens and transition firing settings. Moreover, the SPN model can be used as the basis of the security assessment method for the IoT service [5, 12].

In this chapter, we developed an ADOxx-based modelling tool, the SAPnet, which includes the ontology toolkit for SPN modeling of the service states and transitions. SAPnet enables the security evaluation based on the service's SPN model. SAPnet extends the Petri net Dynamic Library so that the modeler is able to (*a*) create a selective vulnerabilities list for each model and (*b*) evaluate the security of the model based on the aforementioned list and the Common Vulnerabilities Scoring System (CVSS).

SAPnet provides a modeler-friendly interface for the creation of the model's CVE list. The tool supports the modeler with import, export, storing and migrating options for the creation of the list, which is usually a time-consuming process. These features not only expedite the composition of the list but, also, any updates in the case of a model change.

In addition, the security assessment method for the IoT service is embedded in SAPnet. The modeler can easily create a correlation between the states and the CVE list of the IoT service model and, then, apply the assessment method to accurately calculate the service security metric. On these grounds, SAPnet allows the modeler to quickly re-evaluate the security metric for any possible change of (*a*) the model's states or (*b*) the list of vulnerabilities under study.

The logical association between the vulnerabilities and the states is based on the fact that one or more actors are involved in every state. The vulnerabilities of an actor also affect the states the actor participates in; therefore, those vulnerabilities are associated with the states. We aim to provide an additional feature in the future for the depiction of the actors and the corresponding model states. This feature will facilitate the modeler to make the association between the states and the vulnerabilities.

There are cases where a sequence of two or more separate vulnerabilities are linked together and the impact of one is facilitating the operations of another. This vulnerability chaining may result in a higher impact than the maximum impact of any individual vulnerability included. As a future work, we consider to include functions and classes on SAPnet so that the modeler will be able to define possible vulnerability chaining in the model.

Tool Download https://www.omilab.org/sapnet

References

1. Garofalaki, Z., Kallergis, D., Katsikogiannis, G., Ellinas, I., Douligeris, C.: Transport services within the IoT ecosystem using localisation parameters. In: IEEE International Symposium on Signal Processing and Information Technology (ISSPIT), pp. 87–92. IEEE (2016)
2. Yu, Z., Zhou, L., Ma, Z., El-Meligy, M.A.: Trustworthiness modeling and analysis of cyber-physical manufacturing systems. IEEE Access **5**, 26076–26085 (2017)
3. Karagiannis, D., Buchmann, R.A., Burzynski, P., Reimer, U., Walch, M.: Fundamental Conceptual Modeling Languages in OMiLAB, pp. 3–30. Springer (2016)
4. Karagiannis, D., Burzynski, P., Miron, E.-T.: The Imker Case Study - Practice with the Bee-Up Tool (2017). https://doi.org/10.5281/zenodo.345846
5. Garofalaki, Z., Kallergis, D.: On the security of an IoT-based intelligent transportation service. In: 4th South-East Europe Design Automation, Computer Engineering, Computer Networks and Social Media Conference (SEEDA-CECNSM), pp. 1–5. IEEE (2019)
6. Aazam, M., Fernando, X.: Fog assisted driver behavior monitoring for intelligent transportation system. In: IEEE 86th Vehicular Technology Conference (VTC-Fall), pp. 1–5. IEEE (2017)
7. Tilocca, P., Farris, S., Angius, S., Argiolas, R., Obino, A., Secchi, S., Mozzoni, S., Barabino, B.: Managing data and rethinking applications in an innovative mid-sized bus fleet. Transp. Res. Procedia **25**, 1899–1919 (2017)
8. Kenyon, T.: Transportation Cyber-Physical Systems Security and Privacy. In: Transportation Cyber-Physical Systems, pp. 115–151. Elsevier (2018)
9. Höller, J., Tsiatsis, V., Mulligan, C., Karnouskos, S., Avesand, S., Boyle, D.: From Machine-to-Machine to the Internet of Things - Introduction to a New Age of Intelligence. Academic Press (2014)
10. MITRE Corporation: Common Vulnerabilities and Exposures: The Standard for Information Security Vulnerability Names (2007). https://cve.mitre.org
11. National Institute of Standards and Technology (NIST): National Vulnerability Database (NVD) (2019). https://nvd.nist.gov/
12. Khamparia, A., Pandey, B.: Threat driven modeling framework using petri nets for e-learning system. SpringerPlus **5**(446), 1–16 (2016)
13. Rémy, G., Mehar, S., Sophy, T., Senouci, S.-M., Jan, F., Gourhant, Y.: Green fleet management architecture: Application to economic itinerary planning. In: IEEE Globecom Workshops, pp. 369–373. IEEE (2012)

14. Stellios, I., Kotzanikolaou, P., Psarakis, M., Alcaraz, C., Lopez, J.: A survey of IoT-enabled cyberattacks: Assessing attack paths to critical infrastructures and services. IEEE Commun. Surv. Tutorials **20**(4), 3453–3495 (2018)
15. Mavropoulos, O., Mouratidis, H., Fish, A., Panaousis, E.: Apparatus: A framework for security analysis in internet of things systems. Ad Hoc Networks **92**, 101743 (2019)
16. Mavropoulos, O., Mouratidis, H., Fish, A., Panaousis, E.: ASTo: A tool for security analysis of IoT systems. In: IEEE 15th International Conference on Software Engineering Research, Management and Applications (SERA), pp. 395–400. IEEE (2017)
17. Harrand, N., Fleurey, F., Morin, B., Husa, K.E.: ThingML: A language and code generation framework for heterogeneous targets. In: Proceedings of the ACM/IEEE 19th International Conference on Model Driven Engineering Languages and Systems, MODELS '16, (New York, NY, USA), pp. 125–135. Association for Computing Machinery (2016)
18. Samandari, A., Ge, M., Hong, J.B., Kim, D.S.: Evaluating the security of IoT networks with mobile devices. In: IEEE 23rd Pacific Rim International Symposium on Dependable Computing (PRDC), pp. 171–180. IEEE (2018)
19. Enoch, S.Y., Hong, J.B., Ge, M., Kim, D.S.: Composite metrics for network security analysis. CoRR (2020)
20. Ahmadon, M.A.B., Yamaguchi, S., Saon, S., et al.: On service security analysis for event log of IoT system based on data Petri Net. In: IEEE International Symposium on Consumer Electronics (ISCE), pp. 4–8. IEEE (2017)
21. Yamaguchi, S., Tanaka, H.: Modeling of infection phenomenon and evaluation of mitigation methods for IoT malware mirai by agent-oriented Petri Net PN^2. In: IEEE International Conference on Consumer Electronics-Taiwan (ICCE-TW), pp. 1–2. IEEE (2018)
22. Ahmadon, M.A.B., Yamaguchi, S.: On service orchestration of cyber physical system and its verification based on Petri Net. In: IEEE 5th Global Conference on Consumer Electronics, pp. 1–4. IEEE (2016)
23. Fortino, G., Russo, W., Savaglio, C., Viroli, M., Zhou, M.: Opportunistic cyberphysical services: A novel paradigm for the future Internet of Things. In: IEEE 4th World Forum on Internet of Things (WF-IoT), pp. 488–492. IEEE (2018)
24. Ping, P., Xuan, Z., Xinyue, M.: Research on security test for application software based on SPN. Procedia Engineering **174**, 1140–1147 (2017)
25. Daszczuk, W.B., Mieścicki, J., Grabski, W.: Distributed algorithm for empty vehicles management in personal rapid transit (PRT) network. J. Adv. Transp. **50**(4), 608–629 (2016)
26. Garofalaki, Z., Kallergis, D., Katsikogiannis, G., Ellinas, I., Douligeris, C.: A DSS model for IoT-based intelligent transportation systems. In IEEE International Symposium on Signal Processing and Information Technology (ISSPIT), pp. 276–281. IEEE (2017)

Part V
Business Ecosystems and Services

Chapter 14
A Modeling Tool for Exploring Business Ecosystems in a (Pre-)conceptual Phase

Florian Schierlinger-Brandmayr, Birgit Moesl, Philipp Url,
Wolfgang Vorraber, and Siegfried Vössner

Abstract When modeling real-world activities involving social, economic, and technical aspects, conceptual modeling is a necessary prerequisite to set the stage and define the system boundaries. This can become a very difficult task, however, especially when all the relevant actors, shareholders, and stakeholders together with their intrinsic and extrinsic motivations are not known. One of the methodological challenges in this is to provide a unified framework for collecting as many relevant perspectives and pieces of information as possible for creating a fully comprehensive representation that is both insightful and readily understood. Another challenge is to transform these findings into standardized and re-usable information which can serve as input for other modeling tools downstream in the tool chain. In this chapter, we will present both a methodology based on value networks and a modeling tool (*EcoViz*), which is intended to address these issues and can also be used directly before the typical conceptual modeling starts in the course of a "pre-conceptual phase." We will also show how the identified interactions can be used for an insightful qualitative analysis and exploration of socio-technical ecosystems. To demonstrate how and where *EcoViz* can be applied, we will show four real-world cases from different domains.

Keywords Modeling · Conceptual modeling · Pre-conceptual modeling · Socio-technical system · Business ecosystem · Ecosystem analysis and design · Modeling tool

14.1 Introduction

Conceptual modeling along with its tools and frameworks has grown into a mature and widely accepted method in the context of mapping real-world activities to

F. Schierlinger-Brandmayr · B. Moesl · P. Url · W. Vorraber · S. Vössner (✉)
Institute of Engineering and Business Informatics, Graz University of Technology, Graz, Austria
e-mail: florian.schierlinger-brandmayr@tugraz.at; birgit.moesl@tugraz.at; philipp.url@tugraz.at; wolfgang.vorraber@tugraz.at; voessner@tugraz.at

D. Karagiannis et al. (eds.), *Domain-Specific Conceptual Modeling*,
https://doi.org/10.1007/978-3-030-93547-4_14

processes supported by automated services in the area of business informatics. With OMiLAB [1], a powerful platform is available that allows tool chains across different levels of detail and domains.

While the actors involved together with their goals and motivations are in many cases a given input for conceptual modeling, there are often situations where not all relevant activities and their logical connection and interdependence are clear at the beginning of the conceptual modeling phase. While a classic situation analysis can handle many of these information deficits, things become significantly more complicated when dealing with socio-technical systems in which not all relevant actors, shareholders, and stakeholders together with their intrinsic and extrinsic motivations are known. There are several approaches for tackling this problem, mostly from a social science perspective as in [2] or as outlined in [3]. Research in the area of stakeholder theory focuses particularly on the identification of stakeholders and the analysis of various properties of identified stakeholders such as power and interest [4, 5], whereas research in the area of value networks puts emphasis on the value exchange relations and their influences on business model and strategic aspects [6–8]. These socio-technical systems form networks of individuals and organizations with individual needs connected with value exchange relations between each other. We understand the viable forms of these networks as business ecosystems and thereby follow the definition of a business ecosystem of Moore [9] (p.26) as "[a]n economic community supported by a foundation of interacting organizations and individuals - the organisms of the business world. This economic community produces goods and services of value to customers, who are themselves members of the ecosystem. The member organisms also include suppliers, lead producers, competitors, and other stakeholders. Over time, they co-evolve their capabilities and roles, and tend to align themselves with the directions set by one or more central companies."

One of the methodological challenges here is to provide a unified framework for collecting as many relevant perspectives and pieces of information as possible and creating a fully comprehensive representation that is both insightful and readily understood. Another challenge is to create an information base from all of this, which provides standardized interfaces using modeling standards such as the Unified Modeling Language (UML) to other modeling tools for allowing the use of the relevant information by others.

With *EcoViz*, we provide a modeling tool which is intended to be used directly before the typical conceptual modeling starts—in the "pre-conceptual phase"—for business modeling and requirements engineering. Its main purpose is to provide the relevant components and their relationships as inputs for other modeling frameworks down the tool chain. The secondary use, which has proved to be sometimes equally as important as the main purpose, is to provide a structured and holistic basis for performing a qualitative analysis and exploration of business ecosystems [10, 11]. Here the benefit lies mostly in understanding the dynamics of interactions and value exchanges between players in a business ecosystem—both for tangible and intangible assets according to concepts used in value networks [12].

While the proposed technique has been successfully applied in various analog and digital formats across many domains and in different levels of detail, the biggest impact can be expected when implemented as a digital tool, embedded in a platform and connected to other apps.

We will outline the conceptual foundations of *EcoViz* and its key functionalities in the following paragraphs. To demonstrate the areas in which it can be applied, we have chosen use cases from different domains representing also different granularities of a system perspective:

- Ecosystem analysis for new business areas (technical equipment manufacturer),
- Dynamics of stakeholder interaction (service design in health care),
- Data privacy and legal aspects (surveillance operations via drones),
- Process interaction and use case analysis (public safety operations).

These cases will be modeled using *EcoViz* for illustrating the method and all tool functionalities.

14.2 Method Description

In practical modeling, the biggest challenge often lies right at the beginning, before the actual modeling starts. This is, when the modelers are facing a real-world situation which they are supposed to understand and for which they must create a mental abstraction good enough for producing a valid model thereof, what is done in the so-called conceptual phase. Here the basic primitive building blocks of such models are chosen including the relevant entities representing actors, stakeholders, their interaction, and other relevant mechanisms and processes affecting the real-world system. The reason why this is so challenging lies in the fact that real-world scenarios include a sheer endless multitude of potentially important levels of detail and an altogether endless magnitude of entities and interactions when it comes to selecting either the right scope or the system boundaries. Usually this step is done using pre-existing knowledge or experience, which is a good pragmatic approach and works well in moderately complicated settings. In more complex settings, where, for example, social and technical systems interact in previously not observed patterns or where aspects of these systems have unexpectedly become so important that they have a predominating influence on the system behavior, this approach is no longer sufficient. In such situations, pre-conceptual modeling is needed as a pre-processor to conceptual modeling. The basic assumption here (in agreement with Socrates) is "to know that we don't know" or to quote the former US secretary of defense, Donald Rumsfeld: "There are known knowns ... But there are also unknown unknowns." A frequently successful way to tackle this problem or at least to increase the chances for getting a better understanding of the real-world situation that is to be modeled is to start a system exploration by studying historic artifacts (records, user stories, etc.) and seeking live interaction with the people who appear to be relevant in the respective setting. This is usually done in process exploration

workshops where all relevant people are summoned and share all their knowledge
and perspectives. But where to start? Which people should be invited?

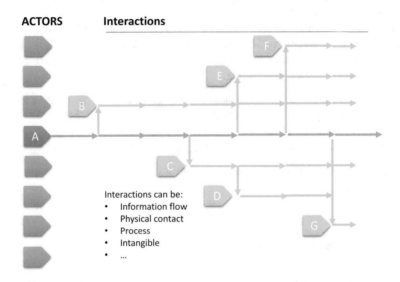

Fig. 14.1 An iterative approach to explore stakeholders and actors starting with one key actor (A)

In such situations, an importance-based process exploration technique is applied.
It starts by selecting an initial point, which could be, e.g., a person which seems
to be relevant in the scenario (see Fig. 14.1 where the initial point is labeled
"A"). Ideally, this point represents the start of a core process in the system
to be modeled. From here on, we follow this process thread until it touches
another process/resource/entity or actor (labeled "B" in Fig. 14.1). Starting from
here, a second exploratory thread spawns—and so on and so forth. Following
this procedure, we will be able to identify a sufficient collection of actors and
entities while also unveiling (some of) the most relevant interactions and processes
(including the support processes) to continue the system exploration. This collected
information forms the basis for a subsequent series of expert interviews or focus
groups in which the interaction of system entities and corresponding dynamics
is analyzed. All the collected information will then be made available for further
analysis by using a standardized notation supported by a digital tool, thus enabling
a holistic understanding of the entire system and enabling a joint discussion with
the identified key players and other affected people.

Such discussions usually take place in one or more workshops. In interactive
sessions, missing aspects are added, and a shared common view is created by this
means. In complex problems, which are difficult to comprehend fully, in particular,
the standardized notation designed to reduce unnecessary complexity is very helpful. Throughout this phase, *EcoViz* is used mostly interactively, always providing
a clear and tidy look at the entire model throughout the exploration, reflection,

and consolidation steps. While most meetings in pre-conceptual modeling are being held in person, *EcoViz* can also be used in virtual meetings for providing a central document when some or all participants join from different locations electronically—as, for example, during the Covid-19 pandemic.

Whereas this tool can be applied for exploring systems with a high degree of uncertainty and many unknowns, it is also very suitable in a contrary setting, where much existing knowledge and experience are available. Here it is often used to complement to existing tools in order to sort and analyze socio-techno-economic aspects in more detail. As described in [11], the tool can be used, for example, to refine and analyze ecosystems in the context of business model innovation including sustainability aspects.

Finally, it is important to mention that *EcoViz* integrates as one of the early tools into the conceptual modeling tool chain downstream by offering ways to export its entities, relations, and exchanged values.

14.3   Method Conceptualization

The V^2 notation used in the presented tool builds on the notation of Biem and Caswell [13], which synthesizes and extends concepts of e3 e-business modeling [6], c3-value method [8], and Allee's [7, 14] concept of intangibles [13]. The following section describes the V^2 notation structured around dedicated layers (see Fig. 14.2) which have been developed in the course of various research projects over the past decade [10–12, 15, 16].

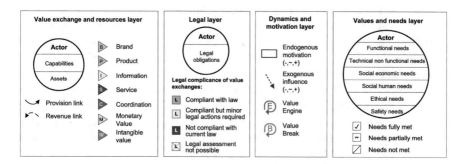

Fig. 14.2   The analysis layers of *EcoViz* (figure from [11] based on [10, 12, 13, 15])

- **Value exchange and resources layer** [11, 12]: The value exchange and resources layer [11, 12] provides insights into the actors that participate in an ecosystem and the values they exchange from a resource-based perspective [17]. This layer builds on the notation of Biem and Caswell [13] and enhances it in selected aspects. Accordingly, the main building blocks consist of tripartite circles which represent **actors** [18] and directed arcs which represent **value exchanges** between actors [13].

- Actors represent economic entities (e.g., organizations, business units, persons), which participate in an ecosystem. They are described by specifying their designation, capabilities (dynamic activities and processes that are contributed to the network by the actor), and assets (tangible and intangible things which facilitate the value generation of the actor) [13].
  Depending on the types and the numbers of actors involved, the clustering of actors with similar properties and semantics could become necessary for the sake of clarity. This kind of visual structuring can be realized with frames around groups of actors, dedicated labeling, or coloring.
- Value exchanges represent the transfer of various types of values between actors [13]. The value exchange concept between actors defined by [13] builds on [6] and [19] and specifies various types of value such as "product," "brand," "service," "coordination," and "information" [13]. These types are complemented in V^2[12] by the value exchange types "monetary value" and "intangible value" as defined in [6]. Value exchanges in the direction of the end customer are termed provision links and are represented by solid lines, whereas revenue links are represented by dotted lines and indicate values received by actors in return for value provisions [11, 12].

• **Legal layer** [10, 11]: The explicit consideration of legal aspects during ecosystem planning and exploration phases is particularly important to ensure legal compliance of the resulting business ecosystem. The legal layer [10, 11, 20] of the presented modeling tool provides functionality for representing the legal obligations of the actors and to illustrate the level of legal compliance of the value exchanges. The value exchange and resources layer provides the basis for this layer by identifying the actors and value exchanges within the network. Legal obligations are summarized for each actor of the ecosystem in the corresponding actor symbol. Both legal obligations within an actor and value exchanges between actors are assessed according to the four legal compliance levels defined in Table 14.1. The legal layer of the tool can be used to explore legal compliance of planned ecosystems by illustrating complex legal network settings. It can also be used to assess the legal compliance of existing ecosystems or compliance of anticipated changes in existing ecosystems. A combination of the legal layer with the underlying value exchange and resources layer provides a shared view on the ecosystem from a legal and resource-based perspective and thereby facilitates cooperation in interdisciplinary teams [10, 11].

• **Dynamics and motivation layer** [11, 12, 15]: The dynamics and motivation layer [11, 12, 15] supports the analysis of value exchange relations and related dynamics of value generation in ecosystems. Positive dynamics in ecosystems may arise if loops of positive value-generating activities and value exchanges reinforce each other to form "value engines" and in the case of negative dynamics to form "value breaks." Anticipation of positive and negative value-generating feedback loops is based on the motivation theory by Vroom [21] and Porter and Lawler [22] by analyzing internal and external influences on the motivation of actors to contribute to value generation in the ecosystem. Endogenous motivation

Table 14.1 Compliance levels of value exchanges as defined in [10, 11, 20]

Symbol	Existing ecosystem	Planned ecosystem
L	The value exchange is compliant with legal regulations	The value exchange is compliant with legal regulations
L	The value exchange needs special attention (e.g., due to anticipated changes of legal regulations in the near future)	Minor actions (e.g., notification of the data protection board about planned data exchanges between actors) need to be done to be compliant with existing legal regulations
L	The value exchange is not compliant with existing law. Action required	The planned value exchange is not compliant with existing legal regulations, and an amendment of these regulations would be required to permit the value exchange
L	Legal assessment not possible at this project stage	Legal assessment not possible at this project stage

Table 14.2 Levels of endogenous motivation and exogenous influences as defined in [12]

Level	Endogenous motivation	Exogenous influence
Defensive (−)	The agent performs the value activity only if it is not conflicting with his own goals. Employees give the least attention to the value network task	The external force discourages the value activity
Neutral (~)	The agent performs the value activity collaboratively in a timely manner. Tasks of the value activity have lower priority than personal tasks	The external force neither endorses, facilitates, nor discourages the activity
Active (+)	The agent performs and pursues value activity and collaboration actively. Tasks have either a higher than or equal priority than personal tasks	The external force actively encourages and facilitates the activity (e.g., special reward programs, management inquiries about project progress or performance)

and exogenous influences on actors and their related value exchanges within an ecosystem serve as means to approximate these influences (see Table 14.2). Endogenous motivation describes the level of motivation of employees or persons within an economic entity (actor) to execute value-generating activities. As described in [12], endogenous motivation is based on the "expectancy theory" of Vroom [21] and determined by individual evaluation of the expected outcome for the person who performs the value-generating activity. Exogenous influence describes the external force on the actor which could foster or restrain the value-generating activities within an actor. As described in [12] (p.360), " [...] this concept is based on Kelman's [23] external influences on the compliance of a person and on Porter and Lawler's [22] extrinsic rewards as a consequence of the agent's performance" [11, 12, 15].

- **Values and needs layer** [11]: The values and needs layer [11] aims to particularly focus on sustainability aspects [24] of an ecosystem in the sense of the
triple bottom line concept [25] which aims to create win-win-win situations
for companies, customers, and the environment [26]. Hence, the values and
needs layer also explicitly includes social and environmental dimensions of
ecosystem analysis in addition to economic aspects. It thereby builds on the
"values" concept of Breuer and Lüdeke-Freund [27] who differentiate the purely
economic-focused concept of "value" from the "values" concept which also
explicitly considers social and environmental dimensions of values and needs
of actors. This is also represented in the definition of the notion "values" which
"refers to what a person or group of people consider important in life" [28] (p.
2). The explicit representation and consideration of actors' needs and values
as defined in Table 14.3 in this layer are intended to facilitate the creation of
sustainable ecosystems [11].

The insights gained with the analysis of the needs of actors provide the foundation to identify satisfiers [33] for these needs to ultimately create sustainable

Table 14.3 Values and needs of actors for sustainable ecosystem analysis as defined in [11]

Actor needs	Description
Functional needs	Needs for a specific functionality to, e.g., support in getting a job or a process done. According to Partsch [29], functional requirements define functional aspects of a system or what a system or process should be able to accomplish
Non-functional needs	Non-functional needs represent the human side of needs and can further be classified into:
Technical non-functional needs (TNFN)	Technical non-functional needs of actors which need to be fulfilled by the system or service such as handling and design of the user interface and quality requirements to determine the quality of the system (based on Rupp [30])
Social economic needs (SEN)	Needs of customers (actors) in terms of how customers (actors) want to be perceived by others in economic terms, e.g., bragging and feeling better than others (based on the concept of social jobs in [31])
Social human needs (SHN)	Needs of customers (actors) in terms of doing good to others or the environment. This aspect covers all three dimensions of a sustainable development including environmental societal and economic aspects, which need to be arranged in a livable, equitable, and viable way to create sustainable business models [32] (based on [24]). This aspect is thus focused more on a person's external environment in a societal, economic, and ecological sense
Ethical needs (EN)	The need to comply with an individual's (actor's) ethics theory [32]. In contrast to the aspect of social human needs, ethical needs are more person centric and focused on a person's ethical theory. For example, the ethical need for privacy is represented by the fact that an employee wants to know and determine what information about himself or herself is communicated to others (e.g., current location of employee in a plant)
Safety needs (SN)	The need for preserving the customer's (actor's) need for safety when using the service (e.g., work and consumer safety)

and viable business ecosystems. The levels of matching between the needs and satisfiers can be rated as fully, partially, or not met (see Fig. 14.2), analog to the concept described by Gordijn et al. [34] primarily for economic contexts [11].

14.4   Proof of Concept

This section introduces the implemented proof of concept, termed *EcoViz*, based on [35]. *EcoViz* is intended for exploring, modeling, and analyzing business ecosystems in a (pre-)conceptual phase. It implements the V^2 notation and enables the user an interactive, dynamic modeling and analysis process. It enhances the paper-based method conceptualization of the V^2 notation by offering the user an easy-to-use multi-layer view for exploring different aspects of ecosystems. Furthermore, it places itself in the tool chain of (pre-)conceptual modeling tools by offering export functionalities of the generated ecosystem models.

The core functionalities of *EcoViz* are demonstrated in Sect. 14.4.1. Section 14.4.2 shows practical case studies where the introduced method conceptualization and the *EcoViz* implementation have been used.

14.4.1   Tool Functionalities

The following subsections will introduce the main functionalities provided by *EcoViz*. The sections focus on the essential functionalities to enable a quick and easy modeling start for users. The theoretical background of the implemented notation is outlined in Sect. 14.3.

14.4.1.1   EcoViz Environment

EcoViz (see Fig. 14.3) offers the user a model canvas (1) as well as an element toolbar (2). Furthermore, standard functionality is provided via the ADOxx modeling environment [36]. These are among others the model explorer (3), a navigator (4), a standard toolbar (5), as well as a menu bar (6) with standard and individual functionality offered by *EcoViz*. The items displayed in the main window can be customized by the user in the ADOxx environment.

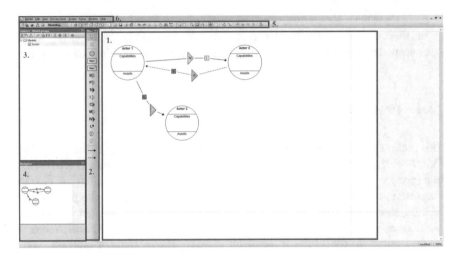

Fig. 14.3 The modeling environment

14.4.1.2 Main Elements

The main insertion workflow in *EcoViz* is done by the user selecting proper elements
which are offered by the notation in the element toolbar and adding them to
the model canvas. All elements, containing actors, labels, text fields, and links,
can be selected (mouse click on the element in the element toolbar) and inserted
properly (mouse click on the model canvas). Depending on the selected element
type, different inserting schemes have to be followed:

- To insert an actor, the user selects the actor element in the element toolbar and can
  then insert as many actors until the insertion process is stopped via a right mouse
  click (see Fig. 14.4). The actor element is a generic element which is offered just
  once in the element toolbar. *EcoViz* offers the functionality to switch the actor
  layer (see Sect. 14.4.1.7), so the appearance of the actor changes and attributes
  are shown according to the selected layer. For further details, please refer to the
  corresponding layer sections (Sects. 14.4.1.3, 14.4.1.4, 14.4.1.6).
- To insert links, the user first selects the type of link in the element toolbar and then
  the link source and the link destination on the model canvas (see Fig. 14.5). Links
  are unique, and there is thus only one link of the same type with the same source
  and destination. Links can be further described by adding textual descriptions
  using the attribute notebook for the link (double-click on link).
- To insert a value exchange or legal label, the user should select the desired label
  in the element toolbar and then select the link on the model canvas on which the
  label should be dropped.
- The insertion process for text fields and other annotation elements is basically
  equivalent to the insertion of actors.

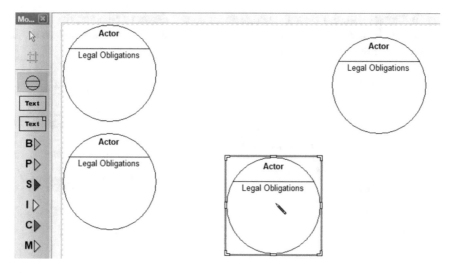

Fig. 14.4 Adding an actor element

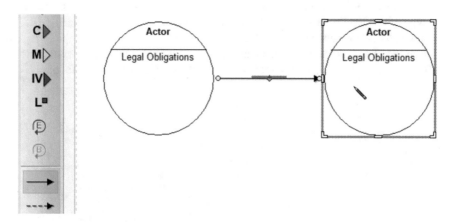

Fig. 14.5 Inserting a link

14.4.1.3 Value Exchange and Resources Layer

The user can drop value exchange labels directly onto connecting links between actors (see Fig. 14.6). Once dropped on the link, the labels can still be shifted among the link's arc, and they can also be deleted (attribute notebook). Labels have to be inserted directly onto specific links. The insertion of a label to the model canvas and the subsequent dropping of it onto a link afterward are not possible.

To interact with the value exchange and resources layer of an actor, the user can double-click on the name of the actor to fill in the name, capabilities, and assets of this actor via the attribute notebook.

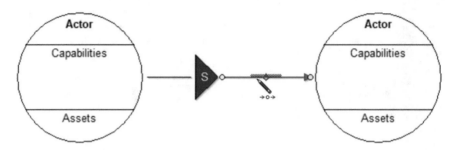

Fig. 14.6 Value exchange label: Dropping a value exchange label on a link

14.4.1.4 Legal Layer

The user can drop legal labels directly onto connecting links between actors. As these labels are following the scheme described in Sect. 14.3, the user can change the type of the legal label via its context menu (right mouse click on it, see Fig. 14.7) or in the attribute notebook of the relation.

To interact with the legal actor, the user can double-click on the name of the actor to fill in the name and legal obligations of the actor via the attribute notebook.

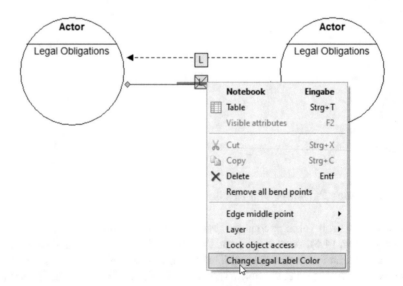

Fig. 14.7 Legal label: Changing the legal compliance level

14.4.1.5   Dynamics and Motivation Layer

To model the dynamics and motivational aspects, the user can use the corresponding elements:

- The value engines and breaks can be inserted as any other element and do not have further functionality.
- The endogenous motivation element is a text field which in addition allows the user to change the level of motivation a certain stakeholder offers. This can be achieved by a mouse click on the motivational level of the corresponding element.
- The exogenous influence can be inserted for each actor by ticking the checkbox in the attribute notebook of the corresponding actor. The level of influence can be altered by a mouse click on the exogenous influence link.

14.4.1.6   Values and Needs Layer

The user can directly interact with the inserted values and needs layer of an actor. The needs as well as the actor description can be filled by the user via the attribute notebook which can be opened with a double-click on the actor's name. Furthermore, the grade of fulfillment of the certain needs can be set via a mouse click on the corresponding actor's need fields (see Fig. 14.8).

Fig. 14.8   Actor values and needs: Changing the fulfillment grade of actor needs

14.4.1.7   Layer Switching

One of the main advantages *EcoViz* offers is the possibility for switching between different views on ecosystems. Once different layers are modeled with their corresponding elements, the user can switch between the actor layers that are shown and also show/hide different label layers. This leads to a highly interactive modeling and analysis possibility which further enhances the understanding of ecosystems. The actor layer switching as well as showing/hiding layer elements can be done via an external script in the drop-down menu bar (see Fig. 14.9).

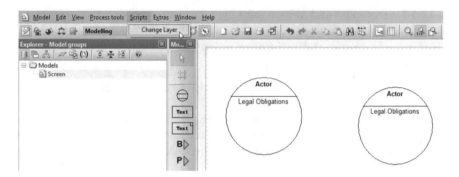

Fig. 14.9 Changing the viewpoint (layer) on the modeled ecosystem

14.4.1.8   Export/Import

EcoViz offers the ADOxx standard functionality to export the models in various graphical formats. To overcome barriers to different modeling and analysis tools, *EcoViz* offers the possibility to export models in a XML-based standard format of the ADOxx environment. This should ensure that further modeling tools can use the results from the ecosystem modeling and enable a different view on the generated data. The structured export can serve as a basis for further quantitative analysis.

14.4.2   Case Studies

This subsection describes the application of the *EcoViz* tool in the context of four different case studies. The first case study concerns a 3D printer manufacturer aiming to enter the medical industry with a new product. *EcoViz* is used here to identify and analyze this new business ecosystem. The second case study describes the application of *EcoViz* in the context of a research project, in which a medical 3D printing center shall be integrated in a hospital. The third case study focuses on legal aspects when using unmanned aerial vehicles (drones) by authorities for search and rescue missions in alpine regions. The last case study, which was a workshop on mission-critical communications in Public Protection and Disaster Relief, demonstrates the use of the *EcoViz* methodology both on paper and as a digital tool for analysis and documentation.

14.4.2.1   New Business Model for a 3D Printer Manufacturer

This case study describes the application of *EcoViz* in the exploration phase in the industry domain.

A 3D printer manufacturer, whose current customers are original equipment manufacturers (OEMs), tier 1 suppliers, and SMEs of various industries, wants to enter the medical industry market with a new product, a 3D printer for medical applications. The target of the case study was to support the development of a business model for this market. To support this, *EcoViz* was applied for the purpose of a detailed stakeholder analysis. The required data was gathered in a workshop with the CEO and the Head of Research & Development of our industry partner [37].

Application of *EcoViz*—value exchange and resources layer: The target of the application of *EcoViz* was the identification of all stakeholders and the long-term stakeholder values in the context of the new business. For this purpose, a simplified version of the ecosystem [13] was prepared with the help of *EcoViz*, using initial data from a stakeholder map [4], that was created in a previous workshop. This ecosystem was printed in a large format to be suitable for usage in the workshop. During the workshop, the values exchanged between the stakeholders were identified together with our industry partner. This was achieved by simply asking our industry partner to provide free-text answers to the question: What is exchanged between the actors on the chart? After the workshop, the ecosystem was digitized with *EcoViz* [37].

This digitized version is visible in Fig. 14.10. It includes all the identified actors and the values exchanged between them for the new medical business ecosystem of our industry partner. For illustration purposes, the values exchanged between the manufacturer and the key employees are highlighted. The values provided by our industry partner to its key employees are shown on the solid line. The dotted line conveys the values provided from the key employees to our industry partner [37].

The application of *EcoViz* was rated very positively by our industry partner. This partner stated that it would reuse the *EcoViz* tool in the own company. This would be done in particular for the purpose of developing cooperation, for activities that are related to sales, and also for evaluating new business areas [37].

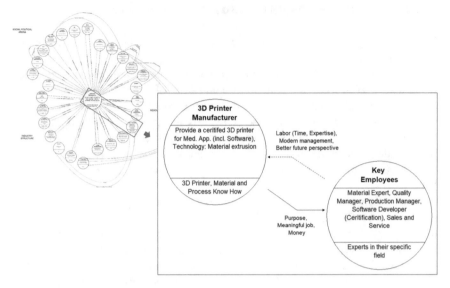

Fig. 14.10 Output of *EcoViz*: The ecosystem of a 3D printer manufacturer's medical business ecosystem [37]

14.4.2.2   Operation of a 3D Printing Center at Point of Care

This case study describes the application of *EcoViz* in health care. The *EcoViz* tool was applied in the reflexion phase in the context of the CAMed[1] research project. One target of this research project is the integration of a 3D printing center at the point of care to produce patient-specific medical products in the clinic [38].

Application of *EcoViz*—dynamics and motivation layer: The target of the application of *EcoViz* was to analyze the operation of the recently established 3D printing research center at the clinic. With the help of *EcoViz*, value engines and value brakes at current state of the operation are to be identified. The required data for analysis was gathered in semi-structured interviews. As an illustration for the interviewees, a simplified ecosystem of the 3D printing center at the point of care was created in advance with *EcoViz* (see Fig. 14.11). Based on this ecosystem, stakeholders were selected and interviewed for their opinions regarding exogenous influences and endogenous motivations of the actors of the ecosystem [39].

This analysis helped to reveal related dynamics of value generation in the ecosystem of the 3D printing research center. For example, Fig. 14.12 illustrates a value engine in the value exchange of the 3D printing research center and the scientific partners [39].

---

[1] CAMed (COMET K-Project 871132), which is funded by the Federal Ministry Republic of Austria Climate Action, Environment, Energy, Mobility, Innovation and Technology (BMK) and the Federal Ministry Republic of Austria Digital and Economic Affairs (BMDW) and the Styrian Business Promotion Agency (SFG)

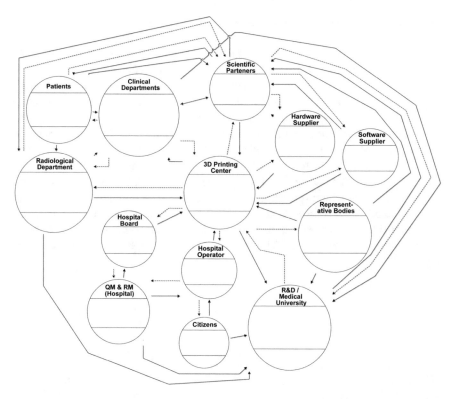

Fig. 14.11 Output of *EcoViz*: The simplified ecosystem of a 3D printing center at point of care [39]

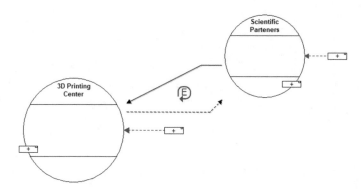

Fig. 14.12 Output of *EcoViz*: Example dynamics and motivation—3D printing center at point of care [39]

14.4.2.3 Using UAVs in PPDR Missions: Legal Aspects

In the project SmartScout[2], the use of unmanned aerial vehicles (UAVs) for Public Protection and Disaster Relief (PPDR) missions was investigated. One use case in the project was alpine search and rescue missions. Two different payloads were tested for this purpose, a thermal infrared and an optical camera. Particular attention was paid to legal aspects in the project, because it is essential to take various legal regulations into consideration in this context. One issue is to distinguish between private use and the use by the police. While a private person is allowed to do everything which is not forbidden by law, police forces are only allowed to do, to what they are empowered to. Furthermore, there are laws for the drone itself (aviation laws) and the information it collects (data protection laws) which have to be considered. A legal assessment was thus carried out using *EcoViz* and focusing on the legal layer. This was continuously updated throughout the project period in order to obtain more insights. The result of the legal assessment is illustrated in Fig. 14.13 [20].

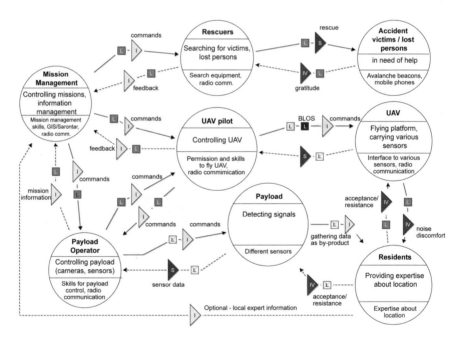

Fig. 14.13 Legal assessment combined with value exchange relations of the planned information service [20]

[2] Austrian security research program KIRAS, Federal Ministry of Transport, Innovation and Technology (bmvit), grant number 854769

Regulations regarding UAVs are constantly changing, and with *EcoViz*, the model can be easily updated by adapting the status of law compliance.

14.4.2.4   Using Mission-Critical Videos for PPDR: Workshop

During the Public Safety Communication Europe (PSCE) conference in Paris, December 2019, a workshop was held addressing the topic of "Mission Critical Videos for PPDR (Public Protection and Disaster Relief)—Benefits and Challenges." New possibilities are arising with the advance of technology, and these are opening up new ways of interaction that practitioners and first responders can use in exchanging information by using videos from, e.g., smartphones and drones.

The workshop had the aims of investigating ways of using mission-critical videos for practitioners, exploring different viewpoints and needs, and also discussing the emerging ethical issues. Participants were from police departments, emergency medical services, infrastructure provider, etc. from different European countries and also the United States. Groups of five to six participants were formed to work on the question of mission-critical videos, and they were accompanied by facilitators.

To find a common ground, the pre-conceptual modeling tool was used in a workshop setting. First, every team agreed on a specific use case, identified the important stakeholders, and wrote them on paper cards. For the workshop setting, paper cards were prepared for the stakeholders as well as a large sheet of paper for putting these all into relation with each other. Different colored pens were used to draw the relations for describing the exchange and the mode between the different stakeholders. No digital tool was used for the workshop.

Figure 14.14 shows the result of one group for a use case labeled "Construction Collapse" where inter-emergency services are called in to deal with a construction collapse. It is important to point out that due to the extremely operative environment, the decision was made to start initially with the analog version of *EcoViz* by using flip charts and pens and printed shapes from *EcoViz* and later transfer the results in digital form. The group identified 15 different stakeholders, among others, robot/drone operator, citizens (on scene), ROG (responders on ground), EMS (emergency medical services), ROG Fire, 911 dispatch, and media. One interesting aspect when using the tool was that it is important that the participants have a basic domain knowledge and a familiarity with the application area. Moreover, it is also important that the participants are aware of different meanings and wordings in different countries. Another point for intensive discussion was the transmission mode for provision and revenue links between the stakeholders: PTT (push to talk), video, data, and voice (phone). The group illustrated the modes by colors, and they partly categorized the links by type, e.g., live stream and coordination. The tool enabled a structured discussion and provided important insights.

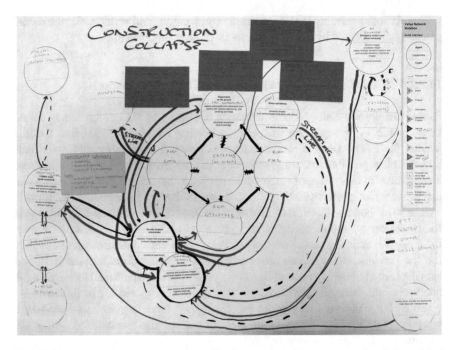

Fig. 14.14 Phase 1: *EcoViz*—methodology (flip chart version): The ecosystem for mission-critical video

After the workshop, the elaborated ecosystem was transferred into the digital tool, as shown in Fig. 14.15, and could now be easily enriched with observations from the workshop.

14.5 Conclusion

EcoViz is based on a conceptual framework for mapping ecosystems, which was developed over many years. Its digital version was originally developed as a browser-based application [35] and later ported to the ADOxx platform. In many applications, *EcoViz* has proved to be a valuable tool in very early stages of (pre-)conceptual modeling at different levels of pre-existing information about the system.

- Systems with no or little pre-existing information, knowledge, or experience: For exploring systems where neither relevant actors, shareholders, nor stakeholders are known.
- Systems with some pre-existing information, knowledge, or experience: For putting existing information together and identifying and collecting complementary information.

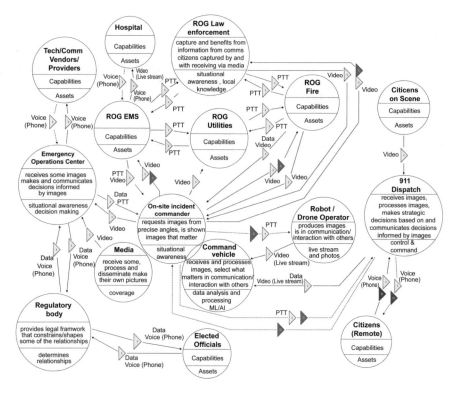

Fig. 14.15 Phase 2: *EcoViz*—methodology (digital version): The ecosystem for mission-critical video

- Systems with a lot of available information, knowledge, or experience: For visualizing and analyzing complex system settings as well as interactions and thereby providing a basis for further exploration, communication, and discussion.

As described by Täuscher and Abdelkafi [40] (p.161) in the context of business model innovation, visualization has various positive effects on cognitive processes, for example, by "[...] freeing up the working memory for other thinking processes [41] and [... it] structures the information [...] to enhance the representation of relationships [42]." Visualization also facilitates communication within interdisciplinary teams [10], which is particularly supported by the layers concept of *EcoViz* that, for example, supports a unified view on legal and economic aspects of an ecosystem.

The layer-structured design of *EcoViz* allows switching between different layers and therefore allowing a focus on distinct aspects of the different layers. It supports the phase of structuring, analyzing, and gaining insights and knowledge and fosters communication. With *EcoViz*, complex issues can be presented in the context of other aspects, e.g., legal issues in the context of value exchanges or resources. On the one hand, it provides a good overview, and on the other hand, it offers detailed insights related to different contexts, which allow a more holistic view to be made of the investigated system.

EcoViz also supports the generation of workshop templates which can be simplified versions of an ecosystem with only little information. Templates of this kind serve as a starting point for discussions and foster the creative generation of the ecosystem, especially when printed on paper in a large format (see Fig. 14.14 or [37]).

We have demonstrated the use of *EcoViz* on four different use cases from different scenarios. Practical experience has shown that *EcoViz* can also be very useful in the context of business model innovation [37]. We are currently using this tool in many domains and situations. Hence, we are continuously incorporating feedback and new findings and capabilities.

Acknowledgments The authors would like to thank all the colleagues involved for valuable discussions, contributions, and feedback from application projects, Monika Büscher and her team for contributions to the workshop format, and especially Matthias Kargl for his support in porting *EcoViz* to the ADOxx world.

Tool Download https://www.omilab.org/ecoviz

References

1. OMiLAB gGmbH: omilab.org. https://www.omilab.org/index.html, accessed 18.09.2021
2. Newton, K., Mason, R.O., Mitroff, I.I.: Challenging strategic planning assumptions – theory, cases and techniques. J. Oper. Res. Soc. **33**(4), 390 (1982). https://doi.org/10.2307/2581649
3. Clarkson, M.B.: In: Clarkson, M. (ed.) The Corporation and Its Stakeholders, pp. 243–274. University of Toronto Press, Toronto (1998). https://doi.org/10.3138/9781442673496-013
4. Fassin, Y.: The stakeholder model refined. J. Bus. Ethics **84**(1), 113 (2009). https://doi.org/10.1007/s10551-008-9677-4
5. Ackermann, F., Eden, C.: Stakeholders Matter: Techniques for their identification and management. Department of Management Science, University of Strathclyde (2001)
6. Gordijn, J., Akkermans, H., van Vliet, H.: In: Conceptual Modeling for E-Business and the Web, pp. 40–51. Springer, Berlin, Heidelberg (2000). https://doi.org/10.1007/3-540-45394-6_5
7. Allee, V.: Value-creating networks: organizational issues and challenges. Learn. Organ. **16**(6), 427 (2009). https://doi.org/10.1108/09696470910993918
8. Weigand, H., Johannesson, P., Andersson, B., Bergholtz, M., Edirisuriya, A., Llayperuma, T.: Strategic analysis using value modelling—a c3 approach. In: Prooceedings of the 40th Hawaii International Conference on System Sciences (2007)
9. Moore, J.F.: The Death of Competition: Leadership and Strategy in the Age of Business Ecosystems, 1st edn. HarperCollins Publishers, New York (1997)
10. Vorraber, W., Lichtenegger, G., Brugger, J., Gojmerac, I., Egly, M., Panzenböck, K., Exner, E., Aschbacher, H., Christian, M., Voessner, S.: Designing information systems to facilitate civil-military cooperation in disaster management. Int. J. Distrib. Syst. Tech. (IJDST) **7**(4), 22 (2016). https://doi.org/10.4018/IJDST.2016100102
11. Vorraber, W., Müller, M.: A networked analysis and engineering framework for new business models. Sustainability **11**(21), 1 (2019). https://doi.org/10.3390/su11216018

12. Vorraber, W., Vössner, S.: Modeling endogenous motivation and exogenous influences in value networks of information service systems. JCIT **6**(8), 356 (2011)
13. Biem, A., Caswell, N.: A value network model for strategic analysis. In: Proceedings of the 41st Annual Hawaii International Conference on System Sciences, pp. 1–7. IEEE (2008). https://doi.org/10.1109/hicss.2008.43
14. Allee, V.: The Future of Knowledge: Increasing Prosperity Through Value Networks. Butterworth-Heinemann (2003)
15. Vorraber, W., Müller, M., Voessner, S., Slany, W.: Analyzing and managing complex software ecosystems: A framework to understand value in information systems. IEEE Software **36**(3), 55 (2019). https://doi.org/10.1109/MS.2018.290100810
16. Lichtenegger, G., Vorraber, W., Gojmerac, I., Sporer, A., Brugger, J., Exner, E., Aschbacher, H., Christian, M., Voessner, S.: Identification of information gaps in civil-military cooperation in disaster management. In: 2015 2nd International Conference on Information and Communication Technologies for Disaster Management (ICT-DM), pp. 122–129. IEEE (2015). https://doi.org/10.1109/ict-dm.2015.7402030
17. Wernerfelt, B.: A resource-based view of the firm. Strateg. Manag. J. **5**(2), 171 (1984). https://doi.org/10.1017/cbo9781316466872
18. Hakansson, H., Johanson, J.: A Model of Industrial Networks, pp. 28–34. Routledge, London and New York (1992)
19. Normann, R., Ramírez, R.: From value chain to value constellation: designing interactive strategy. Harv. Bus. Rev. **71**(4), 65–77 (1993)
20. Vorraber, W., Neubacher, D., Moesl, B., Brugger, J., Stadlmeier, S., Voessner, S.: Uctm - an ambidextrous service innovation framework - a bottom-up approach to combine human- and technology-centered service design. Systems **7**(2) (2019).   https://doi.org/10.3390/systems7020023
21. Vroom, V.H.: Work and Motivation. Wiley, Hoboken, NJ, USA (1964)
22. Porter, L.W., Lawler, E.E.: Managerial Attitudes and Performance, vol. 23, 1st edn. Richard D. Irwin, Homewood, IL (1968). https://doi.org/10.2307/2521994
23. Kelman, H.C.: Processes of opinion change. Public Opin. Q. **25**(1), 57 (1961)
24. United Nations World Commission on Environment and Development: Report of the world commission on environment and development: Our common future. Tech. rep., United Nations, New York, NY, USA (1987)
25. Joyce, A., Paquin, R.L.: The triple layered business model canvas: A tool to design more sustainable business models. J. Clean. Prod. **135**, 1474 (2016).   https://doi.org/10.1016/j.jclepro.2016.06.067
26. Elkington, J.: Towards the sustainable corporation: Win-win-win business strategies for sustainable development. Calif. Manag. Rev. **36**(2), 90 (1994). https://doi.org/10.2307/41165746
27. Breuer, H., Lüdeke-Freund, F.: Values-based network and business model innovation. Int. J. Innov. Manag. **21**(3), 1 (2017). https://doi.org/10.1142/s1363919617500281
28. Friedman, B., Kahn, P.H., Borning, A., Huldtgren, A.: In: Early Engagement and New Technologies: Opening Up the Laboratory, pp. 55–95. Springer Netherlands (2013). https://doi.org/10.1007/978-94-007-7844-3_4
29. Partsch, H.A.: Requirements-Engineering Systematisch. Springer DE (2010)
30. Rupp, C.: Requirements Engineering und -Management. Carl Hanser Verlag München Wien (2009)
31. Osterwalder, A., Pigneur, Y., Bernarda, G., Smith, A.: Value Proposition Design: How to Create Products and Services Customers Want. Wiley (2014)
32. Pavie, X., Scholten, V., Carthy, D.: Responsible Innovation - From Concept to practice. World Scientific Publishing (2014)
33. Max-Neef, M., Dlizalde, A., Hopenhayn, M.: Human Scale Development: Conception, Application and Further Reflections. Apex Press (1991)
34. Gordijn, J., Yu, E., Van Der Raadt, B.: E-service design using i* and e3 value modeling. IEEE Software **23**(3), 26 (2006)

35. Schierlinger-Brandmayr, F.: Engineering of a toolkit to support ecosystem analysis and design. Master's thesis, Graz University of Technology, Rechbauerstraße 12, 8010 Graz, Austria (2019)
36. BOC Asset Management GmbH: adoxx.org. https://www.adoxx.org/live/home, accessed 18.09.2021
37. Ali Shah, S.: Url, P.: Vorraber, W.: Janics, T.: Katschnig, M.: Transformation towards sustainable business models in production. Technical Journal **14**(2), 224 (2020). https://doi.org/10.31803/tg-20200525204041
38. Medical University of Graz: CAMed - Clinical additive manufacturing for medical applications. https://www.medunigraz.at/en/camed/, accessed 23.03.2021
39. Rosenzopf, T.: Development of a decision support system for the implementation of a 3d printing centre at point of care. Master's thesis, Graz University of Technology, Rechbauerstraße 12, 8010 Graz, Austria (2021)
40. Täuscher, K., Abdelkafi, N.: Visual tools for business model innovation: Recommendations from a cognitive perspective. Creat. Innov. Manag. **26**(2), 160 (2017). https://doi.org/10.1111/caim.12208
41. Hegarty, M.: The cognitive science of visual-spatial displays: Implications for design. Top. Cogn. Sci. **3**(3), 446 (2011)
42. Larkin, J.H., Simon, H.A.: Why a diagram is (sometimes) worth ten thousand words. Cognitive Science **11**(1), 65 (1987)

Chapter 15
A Capability-Based Method for Modeling Resilient Data Ecosystems

Jānis Grabis, Līva Deksne, Evita Roponena, and Janis Stirna

Abstract Modern information systems rely on data analytics and use various data sources to steer information processing and process execution activities. Capability-driven development is a method for the design and delivery of this kind of information systems. This chapter elaborates a method extension for capability-based modeling of data ecosystems for the purpose of ensuring their resilience. The ecosystem perspective is adopted because there is a need to understand the interactions among the various parties involved in capability delivery. The ecosystem model allows to analyze the impact on reliability and other properties of data providers on capability delivery resilience. The meta-model is elaborated together with a set of rules for analyzing the ecosystem model. The model is perceived as a property graph, and the network theory is used for the analysis. The ADOxx meta-modeling platform is used to implement the modeling tool, which is integrated with a graph database, where the model analysis is performed. The method and the tool are demonstrated using an example of a winter road maintenance ecosystem.

Keywords Capability management · Resilience · Ecosystem modeling · Property graph

15.1 Introduction

Modern information systems increasingly rely on data analytics and use various data sources to steer information processing and process execution. The capability-driven development (CDD) method [1] has emerged as one of the methods suited for

J. Grabis (✉) · L. Deksne · E. Roponena
Management Information Technology, Riga Technical University, Riga, Latvia
e-mail: grabis@rtu.lv; liva.deksne@rtu.lv; evita.roponena@rtu.lv

J. Stirna
Department of Computer and Systems Sciences, Stockholm University, Kista, Sweden
e-mail: js@dsv.su.se

the development of data-driven adaptive information systems. From the perspective of CDD, and in the context of this chapter, capability is defined as an ability and capacity to deliver business services in a certain operational context in volatile environments. Capabilities are defined by business goals, application context, and IS functional services, thus linking business and IS layers. The capability-driven approach uses enterprise modeling techniques to capture the impact of contextual information on business service execution and to adapt the capability delivery according to business performance and context. Components of enterprise model like goals, business process, and concepts serve as an input to the CDD design stage. Capability is considered as the ability to deliver a business function in the enterprise models, while CDD uses the capability concept to facilitate delivery of values or services of a company [2], linking them with context elements and measurable properties. Contextualization patterns are used in CDD to form an application based on the capabilities represented in enterprise models, thus connecting IS components and contexts with business design [3]. As business contexts change, the CDD method enables to adjust application by changing and adding new capabilities and changing the delivery of contexts, thus providing rapid change interrelation between business design and IS components. The models developed are used to configure information systems supporting capability delivery [4].

A comprehensive literature review of notion "IS Capability" has been made by [1] and this is summarized as follows: *IS capability generally refers to the ability for an organization to redesign processes, facilitate information management, and fulfill knowledge sharing needs among many other benefits.* Also, its role on studies under Innovation, Turbulence (Organization Change), and Competitive Advantage domains is pointed out, and classification into four major IS components has been created based on capability context—IS infrastructure, business and IS development, network, IS management—thus determining the elements that define IS capability. Study [5] highlights the differences in capabilities' meaning and interpretation, as well as summarizes as follows: *most views on capability agree that possessing a capability means having competence and ability and also having the right resources in adequate amount, to do something.* Capability models typically contain aspects such as the organization's goals and KPIs, business service and process descriptions, specifications of contextual properties for which the capability is designed, as well as what needs to be changed in terms of services or processes if the context changes during capability delivery. The models reveal complex relationships among decision-making needs and data availability that influence capability delivery. A key challenge is that a significant part of context data is provided by external parties. While the CDD method focuses on capability design and delivery from the perspective of a single organization, its extension toward ecosystem modeling [6] takes into account data and information interdependencies in an inter-organizational setting. The data ecosystem is a complex network of organizations that exchange and use data, information, and knowledge [2]. From the capability perspective, the organizations participating in an ecosystem engage in reciprocal relationships to deliver the required business capabilities. Business ecosystems often lack a strong central coordinating unit, and, as a result, data interdependencies are volatile and obscure in the ecosystem. Therefore, understanding of the ecosystem, presumably by means of modeling, is essential to ensure resilience and long-term viability of data and information flows.

The ecosystem perspective of CDD was explored in a project designing secure and resilient services to deal with the challenges associated with the COVID-19 crisis.[1] This research has confirmed that resilience or the ability to quickly restore normal operations of services [7] is one of the crucial aspects of information systems development. In order to assess the resilience of an ecosystem, the data ecosystem should be discovered and analyzed. That can be achieved by extending the capability modeling with concepts representing the ecosystem perspective and elaboration of resilience evaluation methods. The evaluation methods should be supported by modeling and analysis tools.

The objective of this chapter is to elaborate methods and tools for analyzing resilient data ecosystems on the basis of capability models. The chapter extends the previous work on CDD by explicitly representing data and information dependencies among the parties involved in capability delivery and analyzing the overall characteristics of the ecosystem. Additionally, a modeling tool is developed as a part of the OMiLAB initiative [8] to facilitate wide dissemination and uptake of the modeling methods and tools.

The capability-based data ecosystem modeling method presented in this chapter captures domain-specific aspects of data ecosystem modeling. This includes representation of relevant data items, parties involved in the ecosystem, as well as means for analyzing data interdependencies and relationships among the parties. The modeling and analysis tool is developed using the ADOxx meta-modeling platform [9]. Its application is demonstrated using an example from a winter road maintenance use case.

The rest of the chapter is organized as follows. Section 15.2 discusses background and related work to data ecosystem modeling. The data ecosystem metamodel and its analysis methods are introduced in Sect. 15.3. The tool implementation is reported in Sect. 15.4. Section 15.5 briefly presents conclusions and issues for further development.

15.2   Background

Due to the rapid increase of data availability, variety, and importance, organizations have realized that individually they are not able to capture the value of data to the full extent and, hence, a collaborative approach is needed [10]. The review of current research on data ecosystems [11] has concluded that there are substantial gaps in literature on ecosystem modeling. The models cover only a small fragment of ecosystems, there is no common conceptualization, and there are few ecosystem

---

[1] https://artss.rtu.lv/

health assessment models. A preliminary data ecosystem meta-model [12] proposes to explicitly model actors, roles, relationships, and resources. It is of value to create a repository to resources in a relatively closed ecosystem; however, it would not be able to conveniently and efficiently address distributed environments and links with business services. The enterprise architecture ecosystem model [13] helps organizations to undertake large-scale digitalization projects. It focuses on overarching digital transformation influences, actors, and collaborations and is intended for the strategic level analysis. In order to analyze risk governance and regulatory ecosystems, ecosystem and organizational capabilities are distinguished [14]. This allows the identification of the impact on the viability of the ecosystem on individual organizations. Data exchange facilitators and inhibitors are important to instill vitality in ecosystems. The role of open data and knowledge is modeled and analyzed in [15]. The latter two papers have used the CDD method as a basis for studying ecosystems. The advantage of using the CDD method is its ability to support the integration of strategic level with operational level modeling, as well as explicit representation of data value chain.

The key concepts of the CDD meta-model [16] are shown Fig. 15.1. Goals are business objectives that the capability allows to achieve. They are measured by key performance indicators (KPIs). The capability is designed for delivery in a specific context as defined using context elements. The context elements express factors affecting the capability delivery. The context elements take values from a context range and jointly define a context set (not shown in Fig. 15.1) describing the area for which the capability is suitable. The service element specifies a capability delivery solution. The capability model does not model the whole delivery solution but only focuses on the context-dependent and adaptive features. The delivery solution is designed and implemented following the engineering process specific for a given organization and technological platform. In order to ensure that the capability is delivered as expected in the different contextual situations, adjustments are used to adapt capability delivery. They take the context data and KPIs as input and evaluate the potential changes in the capability delivery. Adjustments are also used to implement complex context-dependent decision-making logics. The capability designs are aimed to be reusable across organizations. The reusable components are represented by patterns. The patterns provide solutions to capability design and delivery problems observed in similar contexts. The data processing functionality is provided by the context platform [17]. Measurable properties having various structural, spatial, and temporal properties can be merged in the context platform [18] in order to form values for context elements.

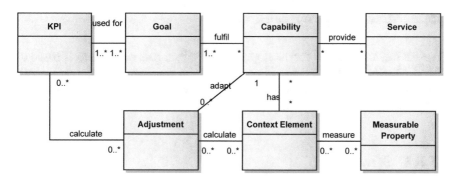

Fig. 15.1 Key concepts of the capability-driven development

The initial focus of CDD on the capability design of a single organization was extended to distinguish between open and proprietary data in [15]. The ecosystem perspective of the CDD method is furthered in a project on development of advanced methods for resilient and secure services referred to as ARTSS. The purpose of ecosystem modeling is to map the diverse actors and their involvement and contributions to the capability delivery. The ARTSS method supports the design of capability delivery services to show service adaptation according to the contextual situation in order to achieve the desired performance. The capability models enable to clearly identify relations among stakeholders, their goals, and information needs. This facilitates the emergence of collaboration clusters unifying the members of the ecosystem to understand and promote their mutual interests.

The ecosystem model is used to analyze the interactions among the organizations and their information flows. The aspect of resilience is one of the focal points of the analysis. It should be a measurable network design feature [19]. Considering design of resilient systems, the study reported in [20] suggested starting from a goal framework to achieve diversity (variety of actors), efficiency (productivity and resource utilization), adaptability (transparency and flexibility), and cohesion (alignment of actors and their capabilities), which then need to be realized by the goals and objectives specific to a business domain. Haque et al. [21] present a comprehensive cyber resilience framework for industrial control systems by decomposing "resilience" into a hierarchy of several sub-metrics. Their resilience framework can serve as a platform for a multi-criteria decision aid and help technical experts in identifying the gap in the study of network resilience. The resiliency measures are often derived from the network theory [22]. The data ecosystem analysis from the network perspective has commonalities with supply chain management [23]. The networks have different levels of resilience depending on domain [24]. The resilience is determined by an underlying degree distribution, short characteristic path length, and a high clustering coefficient.

15.3   Method Conceptualization

The ARTSS meta-model for development of resilient data ecosystems is based on the CDD meta-model [1, 16]. It is extended with concepts representing the data exchange ecosystem and attributes needed for the characterization of resilience of data objects.

15.3.1   Meta-model

Various organizations have capabilities to provide their business services. An ecosystem is a complex network of organizations collaborating and interacting during the capability delivery. There are various types of interactions depending on the role an organization assumes in an ecosystem [25]. This research focuses on data and information exchange as a type of interactions. The ARTSS meta-model (Fig. 15.2) assumes that organizations referred as to parties operate in the ecosystem. They possess capabilities to achieve their business goals, and successful capability delivery depends on other parties in the ecosystem. Thus, the evolution of the ecosystem contributes to the development of capabilities, which spurs further evolvement of the ecosystem.

Although there are various types of participants involved in ecosystems, only providers and consumers are distinguished in the context of this chapter. The ecosystem brings together parties on a premise that the consumers need specific assets to deliver capabilities, and that the providers possess these assets and are willing to share them under certain conditions. The asset is a resource contributing to the delivery of capabilities. In a data ecosystem, the key assets are data and their processing abilities. Therefore, the foundational elements of the CDD method, namely, measurable property, context element, and adjustment, are considered as assets. The assets are made available for the capability delivery as services. The services are software components providing a specified component in response to the consumer request. The capability delivery information system is developed as a composition of the services. It consists of both traditional services and adaptive and data services. The capability model concerns the adaptive and data services, while the traditional services responsible for generic business services (e.g., sales order creation) are outside the scope of this method and are modeled and developed using the organization's internal development and engineering processes.

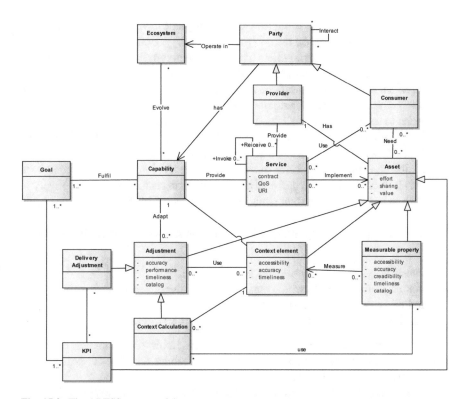

Fig. 15.2 The ARTSS meta-model

The assets have attributes *effort*, sharing conditions, and *value*. Effort represents the perceived development effort of the asset if it is not available in the ecosystem. Value represents the expected return of using the asset for its consumer. Effort and value are measured in relative units similarly as in the case of estimation of agile development projects [26]. Sharing conditions describe the degree of sharing of the asset ranging from the open access to closed proprietary asset.

The services have attributes *contract*, *QoS*, and *URI*. Contract specifies the usage conditions set by the provider to the consumer. That includes authentication, usage limits, and fees. QoS defines the provider's promise to the consumer to ensure specific latency, reliability, availability, and other relevant attributes. URI is the address for the service endpoint using the Uniform Resource Identifiers.

The capability delivery is data driven, i.e., the capability development environment is actively observed and the capability delivery is adapted according to these observations to ensure efficient operations. The context elements are used to describe the relevant environment factors affecting the capability delivery. The context elements assume either categorical or continuous values.

The context is measured using measurable properties, which are actual observations of some phenomena. In the ecosystem model, general measurable properties are represented. The actual providers of measurements are listed in a catalog, which is maintained in the ecosystem for each measurable property. The catalog specifies measurement source system, endpoint (e.g., URI address of a sensor), location, and specific quality attributes. During the analysis of the ecosystem model, the catalog is queried to determine the available sources of the required measurable properties.

The adaptation of capability delivery and context processing is specified using adjustments, which are expressed as algorithmic recommendations. The context calculation adjustment transforms measurable properties into context elements with clear business meaning. The delivery adjustment changes the capability delivery in response to changing contextual situations, and it uses KPIs to steer the capability delivery toward its goals.

The measurable property is characterized by the following data quality attributes [27]:

1. Accessibility—the ability of users to access data
2. Accuracy—the extent to which data are correct, reliable, and certified
3. Credibility—perceived trustworthiness of data
4. Timeliness—the extent to which the age of data is appropriate for the task at hand

In the ecosystem model, the attributes of measurable properties are evaluated using qualitative assessment, and specific quality characteristics of measurement sources are accumulated in the catalog.

The context element has similar attributes: *accessibility*, *accuracy*, and *timeliness*. The values of these attributes are derived from the attributes of measurable properties depending on the type of calculations performed. The adjustment also has attributes accuracy and timeliness as well as performance. These attributes characterize the ability of the adjustment to improve the capability delivery performance.

15.3.2 Ecosystem Modeling

The ARTSS meta-model is used to model a data ecosystem. In the modeling process, a capability model and an ecosystem view are distinguished. The capability model is created by a modeler who used the ARTSS meta-model, and the ecosystem view is generated from the capability model to highlight parties in the ecosystem and their interactions. A fragment of the capability model for a winter road maintenance case is shown in Fig. 15.3 (the case is further elaborated in Sect. 15.4). The model provides the capability view of the ecosystem. The focal point of this view are the capabilities provided by the organizations involved in the ecosystem. In this case, the road condition monitoring capability is shown. It concerns the organization's ability to determine the current road conditions, for example, *bare*, *partly covered*, and *covered*. The model shows the road condition monitoring capability provided by the road monitoring service (among other services not shown here), which in turn invokes the smart sign management service. Depending on the road monitoring results, appropriate warnings are displayed on the smart roadside information boards. The type of warning is determined using the Select warning adjustment that derives its recommendations according to the Driving condition context element measured by the roadside weather stations. These weather stations provide several measurements including a qualitative evaluation, such as *snow*, *icy road*, *water on icy road*, *slush on road*, and *freezing rain*. The model shows the parties using or providing specific services or assets. The municipality has road monitoring capability, the IT company provides monitoring solutions, and the road management company provides the road monitoring tools.

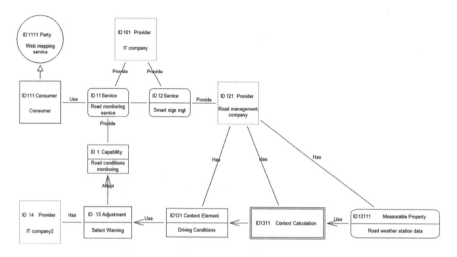

Fig. 15.3 A fragment of the capability model

From the ecosystem perspective, the main concerns are the interactions among the parties and their roles in the ecosystem. The capability model is processed and analyzed to obtain different views and properties of the ecosystem. For the purpose of the analysis, the ARTSS model is perceived as a property graph (the notation for describing the graph is available in [28]). The property graph of the aforementioned capability model is shown in Fig. 15.4. It consists of nodes n (set of nodes $\mathcal{N}$) and relationships (edges) r (set of relationships $\mathcal{R}$). Node labels $\mathcal{L}$ shown in the box attached to the node correspond to the concepts of the ARTSS meta-model:

$$\mathcal{L} = \{\text{Capability, Measurbale Property, Context Element, Adjustment}, \dots\}$$

and the relationship types $\mathcal{T}$ correspond to the associations in the ARTSS meta-model:

$$\mathcal{T} = \{\text{Evolve, Has, Provide}, \dots\}.$$

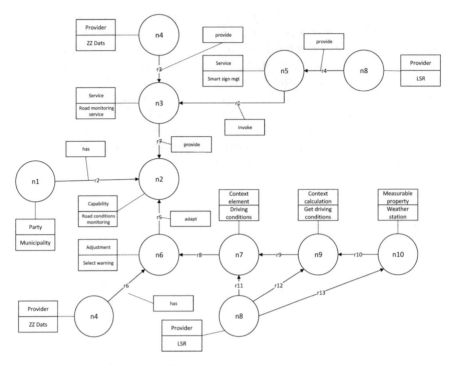

Fig. 15.4 A fragment of the capability model represented as property graph

The nodes have properties represented as key-value pairs and a set of the property keys is denoted as $\mathcal{K}$. Every node has a property representing its name and other properties as specified in the meta-model. A set of the property values is denoted as $\mathcal{V}$. There is a function λ that maps nodes to their labels (i.e., determines the type of the node). The function τ maps relationships to their types.

A chain of relationships among the classes forms a path from one object to another. The path consists of nodes and relationships to be traversed to reach one node from another, and it stands as a proxy for describing the interaction in the capability model. There are several sets of paths that are of interest in the ecosystem model, namely:

P1. Measurable property to capability
P2. Consumer to provider
P3. Party to consumer
P4. Asset to consumer
P5. Consumer to capability

These paths are used in the analysis of the ecosystem. The set of paths $\mathcal{P}_1$ formally is evaluated as

$$\mathcal{P}_1 = \left\{ n_i r_i \ldots r_j n_j | \lambda\,(n_i) = \text{MeasurableProperty},\ \lambda\,(n_j) = \text{Capability} \right\},$$

where $n_i r_i$. refers to the node and relationship attachment and the three dots denote that any nodes and relationships can be traversed from the starting node to the end node. The $\mathcal{P}_2$ path is determined as

$$\mathcal{P}_2 = \left\{ n_i r_i \ldots r_j n_j | \lambda\,(n_i) = \text{Consumer},\ \lambda\,(n_j) = \text{Provider} \right\}.$$

The other sets of paths are determined in a similar manner.

The ecosystem view is derived by inferring interactions among the parties in the ecosystem from the capability-based model. The ecosystem view is a graph consisting of the ecosystem parties as nodes and the interactions among the parties as relationships. In the graph, the interactions are represented as ecosystem relationship types $\mathcal{T}_\mathcal{E}$. There is an open set of interactions of interest to analysts of the ecosystem. The following interactions are currently considered:

I1. Measurable property provider—a provider of measurable properties for the capability delivery. The path traversed is Party > Capability > Context Element < Measurable Property < Provider.
I2. Adjustment provider—a provider of adjustments to the capability party. The path traversed is Party > Capability < Adjustment < Provider.
I3. Service provider—a provider of services to the capability party. The path traversed is Party > Capability < Service < Provider.
I4. Capability enabler—a provider that makes available assets needed by a party to deliver its capability. The path traversed is Party > Capability < Asset < Provider.
I5. Service consumer—links service providers and consumers. The path traversed is Consumer > Service < Provider.
I6. Joint service—a service which requires collaboration of multiple providers. The path traversed is Provider > Service < Provider.
I7. Shared goals—goals common to multiple parties in the ecosystem. The path traversed is Party > Capability > Goal < Capability < Party.
I8. Shared capability—a capability possessed by multiple parties in the ecosystem. The path traversed is Party > Capability < Party.
I9. External adjustment—the adjustment provided to ecosystem parties not directly involved in capability delivery. The path traversed is Provider > Adjustment > Service < Consumer.

Formally, the measurable property provider interaction I1 is identified by applying the following rule:

$$\mathcal{R} \cup \{r_i\},\ \mathcal{T}\,(r_i) = \text{I2},\ \text{src}\,(r_i) = n_j,\ \text{tgt}\,(r_i) = n_k,\ \text{path}\,(n_j, n_k) \in \mathcal{P}_2,$$

where scr() is a function that determines the source of the relationship, tgt() is a function that determines the target of the relationship, and path() is a function that determines the path between two nodes. The rule creates a I1 type of relationship between two parties if a measurable property by a provider is used in a capability by a party. Other interactions are defined in a similar manner.

The rules defined are applied to the capability model and the ecosystem view is created (Fig. 15.5). It clearly identifies all the parties involved in the data ecosystem and their interactions. For example, party P1 has a measurable property needed by P2. The ecosystem view is further used in the ecosystem model analysis.

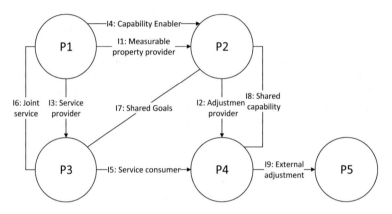

Fig. 15.5 The ecosystem view of the ARTSS capability model

15.3.3 Model Analysis

The model analysis is performed to comprehend the interactions in the ecosystem and to evaluate its resilience. The model analysis is performed in several stages (Fig. 15.6). The capability model is created using the ARTSS extension of the CDD method and it shows ownership and service provisioning relationships of assets and services, respectively. The ecosystem view is derived to highlight the interactions among the parties in the ecosystem. The capability model and its ecosystem view are analyzed to evaluate the properties of the data ecosystem. The ecosystem model can be used to create capability models and to set up capability delivery solutions for individual parties in the ecosystem, though this aspect is beyond the scope of this chapter.

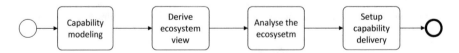

Fig. 15.6 The ARTSS model analysis activities

The ecosystem model is analyzed to evaluate resilience and other properties of the ecosystem. From the resilience perspective, there is a specific concern on the impact of losing some of the services or assets on the overall resilience of the ecosystem and capability delivery. Three types of measures are used to evaluate resilience:

1. The impact of node deletion
2. The degree of substitution
3. The centrality of parties

The node deletion (i.e., an asset or service becomes unavailable) affects another node if there is a path between the nodes that is determined by the indicator

$$\pi_{n_i n_i} . \pi_{n_i n_i} = \begin{cases} 1, \text{ if path } (n_i, n_j) \in \mathcal{P} \\ 0, \text{ otherwise} \end{cases}.$$

For example, if the measurable property of weather station data is lost, then assets like Select warning adjustment are affected. The overall ecosystem resilience is evaluated by the number of consumers ($CNSA$) and capabilities ($CPBA$) affected by the deletion of selected nodes. These measures are calculated using Eqs. (15.1) and (15.2), respectively:

$$CNSA = \sum_i \sum_j \pi_{n_i n_j}, \forall \lambda (n_i) \in \{Service, Asset\}, \lambda (n_j) \in \{Consumer\}$$

(15.1)

$$CPBA = \sum_i \sum_j \pi_{n_i n_j}, \forall \lambda (n_i) \in \{Service, Asset\}, \lambda (n_j) \in \{Capability\}$$

(15.2)

The resilience of a specific service or capability is evaluated as a count of services or assets disabled due to the node deletion. The former (service count) is used during the capability delivery. The latter (asset count) is used during the capability design if specific implementations of assets are not known.

The degree of substitution (DS) is specified as the number of providers for an asset or service:

$$DS(i) = \sum_j \sigma_{n_i n_j}, \forall \lambda (n_{ij}) \in \{Provider\},$$

where $\lambda(n_i) \in \{Service, Asset\}$ and $\sigma_{n_i n_i} = \begin{cases} 1, \text{ if } |path (n_i, n_j)| = 1 \\ 0, \text{ otherwise} \end{cases}$. The expression specifies that for a given service or asset, all directly connected providers are counted.

The centrality of parties is determined by its outgoing degree (NC):

$$NC(i) = \sum_j (\text{src} (r_j) = i), \forall \tau (r_j) \in \mathcal{T}_E,$$

where $\lambda(n_i) \in \{Party, Provider, Consumer\}$. The expression specifies that for a given party all originating associations of type $\mathcal{T}_\mathcal{E}$ are counted.

The centrality indicates the parties that potentially have the most significant impact on the ecosystem. It is calculated for specific types of interactions.

15.4 Proof of Concept

The ARTSS meta-model is implemented using the ADOxx meta-modeling platform. A modeling tool referred to as ARTSS@ADOxx has been created (Fig. 15.7). Its purpose is to support the creation of capability models and their ecosystem views. The graph representation of the model is created and stored in the database for analysis purposes. The XMI export facilities of the ADOxx platform are used to export the model. Currently, the Neo4j[2] graph database is used. The ADOxx interactions with the Neo4j database via a service were implemented in Python Flask.[3] The resilience analysis queries are invoked from ADOxx. The queries implementing the analysis rules described in Sect. 15.3.3 are handled by the Flask service, and the queries are executed in the graph database by invoking its API. The querying results (graph visualizations) are sent back to the user via a browser.

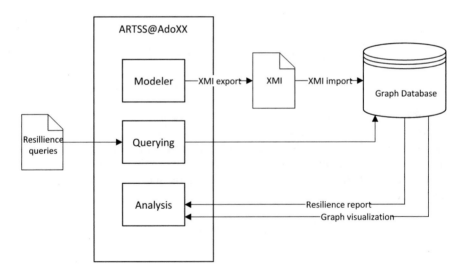

Fig. 15.7 The components of the data ecosystem modeling and analysis tool ARTSS@ADOxx

---

[2] https://neo4j.com/

[3] https://flask.palletsprojects.com/en/2.0.x/

15.4.1   ARTSS@ADOxx Tool

The modeling tool is created using the ADOxx Development Toolkit. The meta-model's classes and their relationships as well as visual notation used are specified in the toolkit and the modeling environment application is generated (Fig. 15.8). The generated modeling environment is used to create the ARTSS models and perform an ecosystem analysis.

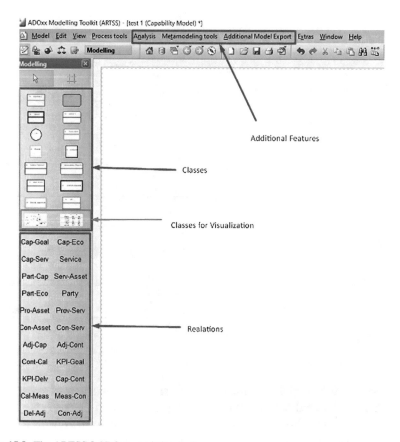

Fig. 15.8   The ARTSS@ADOxx modeling tool

The notation used to represent the concepts of the ARTSS meta-model as it looks in the modeling tool is shown in Table 15.1. It is based on the notation of the CDD method with additional elements introduced to represent the ecosystem. The class attributes are accessible and writable for each class in their notebook. The user can change the class name (type "short string") and ID (type "integer") in the class notebook. The attributes (type "long string") are also accessible and writable for each class in their notebook. To provide a user-friendly modeling interface, a changeable representation of the relations was created to generate different relation

Table 15.1 The toolbox of the ARTSS@ADOxx modeling tool

Class representation	Class name
	Capability
	Asset
	Party
	Provider
	Context Element
	Adjustment
	Delivery Adjustment
	Goal
	Service
	Ecosystem
	Consumer
	Measurable Property
	Context Calculation
	KPI

appearance in toolbox and the drawing area. Default representations of the relations are abbreviated as relation names, for example, "Adj-Cap" represents relation Adjustment to Capability. When two classes are connected in the drawing area, the user can change the attribute "Representation" from 0 or default representation to 1 in the relation notebook to get representation as in the meta-model.

The modeling environment includes standard features of the ADOxx Modeling Toolkit. The specific features added to the ARTSS@ADOxx tool are the generation of the ecosystem view of the capability model and the execution of analytical queries to evaluate the results, as well as visualization of these results in the modeling tool. These features are accessible from the toolbar.

The specific features of the ARTSS@ADOxx tool are developed using the AdoScript scripting language.[4] AdoScript allows to access various ADOxx func-

---

[4] https://www.adoxx.org/AdoScriptDoc/index.html

tionalities and automate some of the processes. Analytical queries can be launched from ARTSS@ADOxx. To execute the analytical query, a user can choose a predefined query from the list box. The modeling tool processes the request and sends it to the Python Flask service which establishes a connection with Neo4j database, processes the request, and generates the resulting graph using the code fragment in Fig. 15.9 based on Neo4j-generated GraphML file. Both the Neo4j database and the Python Flask service are located in an Ubuntu VM so that the user does not need to install additional features to the ARTSS@ADOxx tool.

```
def generate_plot():
    adoxx_request = api_id()
    adoxx_request_name = adoxx_request[0]['name']
    adoxx_request_query = adoxx_request[0]['neo4j_query']

    neo4j_results = session.run(adoxx_request_query)

    picture = neo4j_path + adoxx_request_name + '.graphml'
    query_neo4j = nx.read_graphml(picture)

    if nx.is_empty(query_neo4j):
        final_res = "The relations does not exists for this query"
    else:
        f = plt.figure(figsize=(8, 5), dpi=300)
        pos = nx.spring_layout(query_neo4j)
        nx.draw(query_neo4j, pos, node_size=1000,
node_color='lightgreen')
        node_labels = nx.get_node_attributes(query_neo4j, 'name')
        nx.draw_networkx_labels(query_neo4j, pos, labels=node_la-
bels)

        f.savefig(image_path + adoxx_request_name + '.jpg')
        final_res = render_template('home.html', user_im-
age=adoxx_request_name + '.jpg')

    return final res
```

Fig. 15.9 The Python code fragment for code generation

The tool analysis features are tested on static graph based on the properties from Fig. 15.10 using predefined queries described in Sect. 15.3.2 and stored in the Python Flask service as a dictionary using the Neo4j query language Cypher.[5] A query example of the GraphML file generation for interaction I1 or measurable

---

[5] https://neo4j.com/developer/cypher/

property provider is shown in Fig. 15.10. The following example executes the
Neo4j query written after clause WITH which matches the relations using the path
of "Providers—Measurable properties—Context element—Capability—Provider"
and returns the fitting classes and relationships. Afterward the call for the Neo4j
GraphML export procedure is made and the file is stored in the VM for further
usage.

```
WITH "MATCH (a:Provider)-[b]->(c:MeasurableProperty)-
[d]->(e:ContextElement)-[f:adapt]->(g:Capability)<-
[h:consumes]-(i:Provider) RETURN a,b,c,d,e,f,g,h,i" as
query
CALL apoc.export.graphml.query(query,'i1.graphml', {})
YIELD file, nodes, relationships, properties, source,
data
RETURN file, nodes, relationships, properties, source,
data;
```

Fig. 15.10 Neo4j query for I1 execution

Neo4j provides an opportunity to not only execute queries and export result into
files but also to visualize data as a graph (Fig. 15.11). The graphs created by the
ARTSS prototype visualize the relationships between classes in the ecosystem and
enable further analysis of, for example, a node's degree centrality to determine the
most important class in the ecosystem.

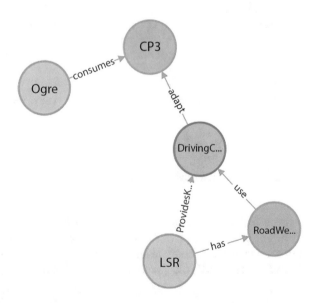

Fig. 15.11 Neo4j-generated graph for I1 interaction

Currently, the prototype allows the user to access graphs generated by the Python Flask service using the code in Fig. 15.9. Python library NetworkX is used to visualize the GraphML file. Figure 15.12 shows the generated graph for interaction I1 using the Flask service. Compared to the Neo4j-generated graph, the Python-generated graph includes only one relationship which leads from a specific node to another specific node. It is explained with the absence of these types of relations in the Neo4j-generated GraphML file.

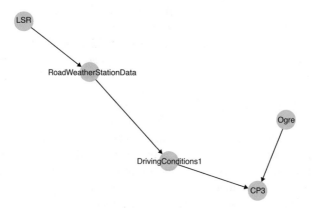

Fig. 15.12 Generated graph for I1 interaction using Python

The analysis outputs are retrieved by the Web browser and are downloadable from it. The visualizations can be uploaded to ARTSS@ADOxx in two ways: by choosing one of the visualization classes in the toolbox or by generating a class using the function "Analysis" from the menu bar. The file is to be uploaded in the visualization class notebook where the user can choose the image in three formats, namely, BMP, JPEG, and PNG.

In forthcoming releases, it is planned to improve the proposed prototype with additional features such as XMI file transformation in a suitable graph database format and XMI file import into the Neo4j database; to create a query catalog, which can be updated to add new queries or modify the existing ones; to execute queries directly from the Neo4j environment; and to improve numerical analysis result generation and displaying.

15.4.2 Case Study

The ARTSS modeling method is applied to model a winter road maintenance problem, broadly outlined in [29]. The case is characterized by the need for timely reaction to changes in road conditions due to snow or icing. The delayed action might cause traffic accidents with severe consequences. There are many parties involved and integrated solutions are needed for efficient response [30]. The ecosystem approach has been suggested for tackling these issues [31] and a capability-based proposal has been elaborated in [15].

The capability model is developed jointly with the organizational parties involved in the winter road maintenance in Latvia. The study was initiated due to the need to develop road clearing and work monitoring capabilities for a municipality, which is responsible for roads and driving conditions in its territory, and a road maintenance provider. An IT consulting company is also involved as a service provider to both the municipality and the road maintenance provider. Other parties were interviewed for their role in the winter road maintenance activities.

It was identified that road clearing, road condition monitoring, road mainte-nance controlling, environment monitoring, road maintenance analytics, and road maintenance accounting are the required capabilities. The parties involved in the ecosystem are organizations responsible for road maintenance, road maintenance providers, an IT consulting company providing the integrated decision support and resource planning system, national traffic authority, as well as providers of data used for measurements of the current state of driving conditions and performance. There are many measurement providers including weather forecasting companies, fleet data providers, road users, operators of traffic camera networks, and others. In order to make decisions about road maintenance, the main factors to consider are weather, road and driving conditions, as well as public perception and environmental impact factors. It is important to observe that weather stations and cameras for road monitoring are operated by different parties. While their data are comprehensive, they are limited to certain sections of major roads in the network. In case of insufficient coverage, nonconventional data sources such as data from the fleet of road maintenance vehicles and crowd-sourced data can also be used.

The capability models are created for all aforementioned capabilities. The fragment of the capability model is shown in Fig. 15.13. It shows the road condition monitoring and road clearing capabilities. The main attention is devoted to the road condition monitoring capability, which is needed by both the municipality and the road maintenance company (identified as LRM). The capability enables the organizations to determine the need for road clearing and to trigger work orders as well as warnings. The model presents that the road conditions can be determined by conventional means using roadside weather stations ID 24 Context Element: Road conditions provided by the LSR standing for the road infrastructure governance organization. Alternatively, raw video data can be used, ID 29 Context Calculation, to determine road conditions by image processing. There are many alternative providers of the video data albeit with different coverage and reliability. The services implementing the capability delivery are provided by the IT company (referred in the model as ZZ Dats).

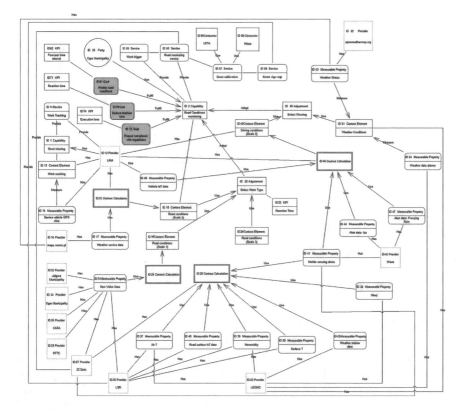

Fig. 15.13 A fragment of the winter road maintenance capability

The ecosystem view (Fig. 15.14) is generated according to the capability model. Specific types of interactions can be visualized. The ecosystem view shows all parties involved in the ecosystem as either providers or consumers as nodes in the graph. The interaction types are represented as edges. It shows that the municipality as a responsible road maintenance company has to interact with many different organizations. These organizations provide either assets or services necessary for the capability delivery. The road maintenance company interacts with fewer parties since it uses a smaller set of assets and services. The road information system Waze is both a capability enabler to RMC since it provides warnings about extraordinary circumstance of the road and a consumer of external adjustments as it also broadcasts warnings received from the IT consulting company.

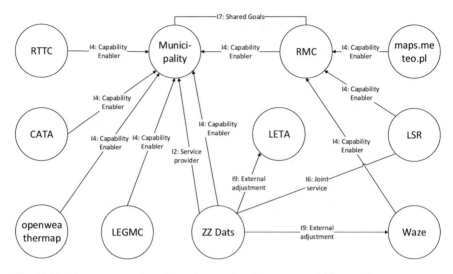

Fig. 15.14 The ecosystem view of the winter road maintenance capability model

The degree of substitution is determined for some of the measurable properties. It is 0 for the surface temperature measurable property provided only by the LSR, while the air temperature measurable property has a larger degree of substitution. It is 1 as shown in Fig. 15.14 though 5 in the complete ecosystem model (not shown), and in the case of common measurable properties, not all providers are shown but only those actually engaged by any party in the ecosystem. The IT consulting company and the LSR have the highest centrality. The prominence of the IT consulting company is determined because of its leading role in the case study development, while the LSR provides assets and services without easily obtainable alternatives.

15.5 Conclusion

The chapter has extended the previous work on CDD to model data ecosystems and to analyze their properties. The ecosystem model represents parties having capabilities and the consumers and providers of the services and the assets needed for capability delivery. The capability delivery assets are data and data processing objects considered in CDD and include measurable properties, context elements, and adjustments. The assets and service ownership associations allow to infer relationships in the ecosystem, which are not easily identifiable by analyzing the capability model alone.

The ARTSS CDD method provides an approach for designing a data ecosystem that ensures connection between business objectives and system components. As the modeled ecosystem has many parties, the possibilities for structuring and integrating their assets not only open the potential to increase the value of their existing data in a meaningful way but also to apply model analysis methods in order to determine the influence of each participant in certain context creation. Flexibility and adaptation to changes are defined as two of the main abilities of using capability context [1], and the defined KPIs enable control mechanism for capability delivery. However, this control mechanism defines the achieved goals, but does not define the overall management aspects related to the control and maintenance of the ecosystem. A strategic approach is needed to identify automated management options in the event of changes in ecosystem parties, in contexts, or in business objectives.

The capability model is abstracted as a property graph. The graph can be analyzed using the network theory methods to determine the current state of resilience of the ecosystem model. The modeling tool is implemented using the ADOxx platform to facilitate uptake of the modeling method. The ADOxx meta-modeling platform is a great tool to develop a graphical modeling toolkit for various tasks including capability modeling. It is also easily integrated with additional services. This platform combined with Python Flask service and Neo4j graph database was used to create the ARTSS@ADOxx tool prototype. The created ADOxx modeling tool is used as a user interface where the user can create a model and invoke queries. Neo4j graph database is used to store models for analysis purposes; it is accessed via the Python Flask service. Currently, the prototype provides features such as capability modeling, model export, ecosystem analysis using queries, and ecosystem graph visualization. Additional functionality will be added in the future including model import to the database, creation of a catalog of queries, and the numeric result representation. The ADOxx platform is integrated with tools for graph analysis to take advantage of the state-of-the-art analytical features.

The ecosystem model is used to analyze interactions in the ecosystem. The chapter defines an initial set of queries for graph analysis. This set can be extended according to the needs of analysis. The capability model representation as a property graph enables to use powerful features of graph analytics and graph databases to study the ecosystem.

Future research directions include the ecosystem model life-cycle management and the design and delivery of capabilities for individual parties on the basis of the ecosystem model. The analytical features of the method and the tool should also be enhanced. The ecosystem assets have several attributes, which can be used for in-depth analysis. Using these attributes, one can construct analytical queries to evaluate the expected level of data accuracy or trustworthiness.

Acknowledgment This research is funded in parts by the Ministry of Education and Science, Republic of Latvia, project ARTSS, project No. VPP-COVID-2020/1-0009.

Tool Download: https://www.omilab.org/artss

References

1. Sandkuhl, K., Stirna, J.: Capability Management in Digital Enterprises. Springer, Cham (2018)
2. Oliveira, M. I. S., Lóscio, B. F.: What is a data ecosystem? In: ACM International Conference Proceeding Series (2018)
3. Stirna, J., Grabis, J., Henkel, M., Zdravkovic, J.: Capability driven development – An approach to support evolving organizations. In: Sandkuhl, K., Seigerroth, U., Stirna, J. (eds.) The Practice of Enterprise Modeling. PoEM 2012. Lecture Notes in Business Information Processing, vol. 134. Springer, Heidelberg (2012). https://doi.org/10.1007/978-3-642-34549-4_9
4. Grabis, J., Kampars, J.: Capability management in the cloud. In: Sandkuhl, K., Stirna, J. (eds.) Capability Management in Digital Enterprises, pp. 175–188. Springer, Cham (2018)
5. Baiyere, A., Salmela, H.: Towards a Unified View of Information System (IS) Capability. In: PACIS 2014 Proceedings. p. 329. Available: http://aisel.aisnet.org/pacis2014/329 (2014)
6. Grabis, J., Stirna, J., Zdravkovic, J.: A capability based method for development of resilient digital services. In: Selected Papers of ICEIS 2020, Springer LNBIP (2020)
7. Bhamra, R., Dani, S., Burnard, K.: Resilience: The concept, a literature review and future directions. Int. J. Prod. Res. 49(18), 5375–5393 (2011)
8. Karagiannis, D.: Agile modeling method engineering. In: ACM International Conference Proceeding Series, pp. 5 (2015)
9. Karagiannis, D., Mayr, H.C., Mylopoulos, J.: Domain-specific Conceptual Modeling: Concepts, Methods and Tools, pp. 1–594. Springer, Cham (2016)
10. Ubaldi, B.: Open government data: Towards empirical analysis of open government data initiatives. In: OECD Working Papers on Public Governance (2013)
11. Oliveira, M.I.S., de Fátima Barros Lima, G., Lóscio, B.F.: Investigations about data ecosystems: A systematic mapping study. Knowl. Inf. Syst. 61, 589–630 (2019)
12. Oliveira, M.I.S., Oliveira, L.E.R.A., Batista, M.G.R., Loscio, B.F.: Towards a meta-model for data ecosystems. In: 19th Annual International Conference on Digital Government Research: Governance in the Data Age, DG.O 2018, ACM Int. Conf. Proceeding Ser., a72 (2018)
13. Burmeister, F., Drews, P., Schirmer, I.: An ecosystem architecture meta-model for supporting ultra-large scale digital transformations. In: 25th Am. Conf. Inf. Syst. AMCIS 2019. July (2019).
14. Feltus, C., Grandry, E., Fontaine, F.-X.: Capability-driven design of business service ecosystem to support risk governance in regulatory ecosystems. Complex Syst. Inform. Model Q. 10, 75–99 (2017)
15. Kampars, J., Zdravkovic, J., Stirna, J., Grabis, J.: Extending organizational capabilities with open data to support sustainable and dynamic business ecosystems. Softw. Syst. Model. 19(2), 371–398 (2020)
16. Berziša, S., et al.: Capability driven development: An approach to designing digital enterprises. Bus. Inf. Syst. Eng. 57, 1 (2015)
17. Grabis, J., Kampars, J., Mota, T.: Context processing for adaptive capability delivery. In: Sandkuhl, K., Stirna, J. (eds.) Capability Management in Digital Enterprises, pp. 189–207. Springer, Cham (2018)
18. Kampars, J., Grabis, J.: Near real-time big-data processing for data driven applications. In: Proceedings - 2017 International Conference on Big Data Innovations and Applications, Innovate-Data 2017. pp. 35–42 (2018)
19. Fiksel, J.: Designing resilient, sustainable systems. Environ. Sci. Technol. 37(23), 5330–5339 (2003)
20. Bodeau, D., Graubart, R.: Cyber Resiliency Design Principles. United States: The MITRE Corporation; 2017. Jan, pp. 1–90. Technical report, Report No: 17-0103 (2017)
21. Haque, M. A., Kamdem De Teyou, G., Shetty, S., Krishnappa, B.: Cyber resilience framework for industrial control systems: Concepts, metrics, and insights. In Proc. of IEEE International Conference on Intelligence and Security Informatics Conference, ISI, IEEE (2018)

22. Newman, M.: Networks: An Introduction in Networks: An Introduction, pp. 1–784. Oxford University Press, Oxford (2010)
23. Perera, S., Bell, M.G.H., Bliemer, M.C.J.: Network science approach to modelling the topology and robustness of supply chain networks: A review and perspective. Appl. Netw. Sci. 2(33), 1–25 (2017)
24. Mari, S.I., Lee, Y.H., Memon, M.S.: Complex network theory-based approach for designing resilient supply chain networks. Int. J. Logist. Syst. Manag. 21(3), 365–384 (2015)
25. Tsai, C. H., Zdravkovic, J.: A survey of roles and responsibilities in digital business ecosystems. PoEM'20 Forum: 13th IFIP WG 8.1 Working Conference on the Practice of Enterprise Modelling, Forum, CEUR Workshop Proceedings 2793, November 25–27, 2020, Riga, Latvia, pp 44–53 (2020)
26. Leffingwell, D.: Agile Software Requirements: Lean Requirements Practices for Teams, Programs, and the Enterprise. Addison-Wesley, Upper Saddle River, NJ (2011)
27. Batini, C., Cappiello, C., Francalanci, C., Maurion, A.: Methodologies for data quality assessment and improvement. ACM Comput. Surv. 41, 3 (2009)
28. Francis, N., Green A., Guagliardo, P., Libkin, L., Lindaaker, T., Marsault, V., Plantikow, S., Rydberg, M., Selmer, P., Taylor, A.: Cypher: An evolving query language for property graphs. SIGMOD '18: Proceedings of the 2018 International Conference on Management of Data, May 2018, pp. 1433–1445 (2018)
29. Dey, K.C., Mishra, A., Chowdhury, M.: Potential of intelligent transportation systems in mitigating adverse weather impacts on road mobility: A review. IEEE Trans. Intell. Transp. Syst. 16, 1107–1119 (2015)
30. Hinkka, V., Pilli-Sihvola, E., Mantsinen, H., Leviakangas, P., Aapaoja, A., Hautala, R.: Integrated winter road maintenance management - new directions for cold regions research. Cold Reg. Sci. Technol. 121, 108–117 (2016)
31. Pilli-Sihvola, E., Aapaoja, A., Leviäkangas, P., Kinnunen, T., Hautala, R., Takahashi, N.: Evolving winter road maintenance ecosystems in Finland and Hokkaido, Japan. IET Intell. Transp. Syst. 9(6), 633–638 (2015)

Chapter 16
Space of Services Method (SoS)

Vjeran Strahonja, Zlatko Stapić, and Martina Tomičić Furjan

Abstract The Space of Services (SoS) method was developed with the idea of completing a set of methods and techniques for designing services and digital transformation in different contexts. The method allows positioning services in four quadrants and in relation to other services and finally improvement and adding value to it. Services are multidimensional in nature. The dimensions of services, which are also design components, include various functional and structural elements of the service, but also the system of service delivery, users and the market. SoS is trying to overcome the complexity of simultaneous consideration of different design dimensions by reducing the number of dimensions that we observe at the same time to pairs. The method was implemented on ADOxx platform.

Keywords Service design method · Service design dimension · Four-quadrant analysis

16.1 Introduction

Modern society and economy are based on services. Services and the service sector are dominant in GDP and the number of employees in developed countries. It is therefore understandable that service development is based on the scientific methods of service sciences and the engineering approach to service engineering.

Service science is a relatively new scientific discipline, interdisciplinary in nature. The theoretical structure of service science is largely taken from other scientific disciplines. However, over the past 30 years, its own theoretical structure of this discipline has been developed. Based on methodological research and practical experience, numerous methods, techniques and tools have been developed.

V. Strahonja (✉) · Z. Stapić · M. T. Furjan
Faculty of Organization and Informatics, University of Zagreb, Zagreb, Croatia
e-mail: vjeran.strahonja@foi.unizg.hr; zstapic@foi.unizg.hr; mtomicic@foi.unizg.hr

© The Author(s), under exclusive license to Springer Nature Switzerland AG 2022
D. Karagiannis et al. (eds.), *Domain-Specific Conceptual Modeling*,
https://doi.org/10.1007/978-3-030-93547-4_16

Service design (SD) is defined as applying design methods and principles to the design of services. Holmid and Evenson [1] define it as a part of Service Science, Management and Engineering (SSME). Moritz [2] gives a good introduction to SD from a practical point of view.

The methods of SSME as a whole, and thus the methods of service design, have been largely taken over from other fields, such as information systems development and software engineering. There are also more and more original methods of service science and engineering that are taken over and shared by other professions.

Examples of such common methods are methods of modeling user experience, user behaviour or communication of different systems and participants, which are used in the development of new or improvement of existing services and information systems, or digital transformation, because it is an umbrella term used today for comprehensive business transformation by applying existing and upcoming technologies.

A good taxonomy of service design methods and tools is presented in a paper by Alves and Nunes [3]. The authors analysed different sources of information on tools and methods related to SD. They pointed out 164 tools and methods used in SD and classified them by frequency.

Mendel [4] gives a taxonomy of models used in the design process.

Mager [5] outlines the evolution of SD from its origin within Interaction Design to its mature state of development in terms of growing complexity, technological development and collaborative nature of service projects.

The sources of service design methods are twofold. On the one hand, these are methodological research in the field of service science, but also other disciplines, such as marketing and management, the results of which then specialize in the practical solution for a certain class of problems. Examples of such methods are Experience Prototyping (Buchenau and Suri, [6]), Personas (Pruitt and Adlin, [7]) or the Narrative Storyboard (Greenberg et al., [8]). Haritaipan [9] collected, described, illustrated by examples and analysed 112 tangible tools aimed at supporting designers' practice and creativity. Almost 90% of the tools are made as a low-tech, easily to use cards. The author identified two main courses for supporting creativity with tangible tools: (1) providing inspiration and (2) calling designers for action.

On the other hand, many methods and tools have been developed or improved by the industry. After their successful application, their authors, consulting companies or various organizations create from them "packages" of theories, methods, tools and instructions for their application. Examples of such an approach are Method-bank [10], Service Design Tools [11] and Design Council—Design methods [12]. Rubino et al. [13], from Booreiland, a Dutch design and strategy studio, prepared a creative card deck toolbox of 75 tools for creative thinking at different stages of any process or situation where new ideas are desired.

16.2   Method Description

The Space of Services (SoS) method has been developed with the idea of completing a set of methods and techniques for designing services and digital transformation in different contexts. The method allows positioning and adding value to some service in relation to other services and finally improvement and adding value to it.

16.2.1   Dimensions of the Service Design

SoS is complementary to the usual service design methods that include structural and functional aspects as well as interaction with the user.

Services are multidimensional, and some of the dimensions are service structure, service facility, location of provision, user participation, work intensity, availability, scalability, etc. Dimensions are also components of design, i.e. what we specify, model and evaluate in the design process. Simultaneous consideration of different design dimensions, some of which are contradictory, is certainly a complex problem. SoS is trying to overcome the complexity by reducing the number of dimensions that we observe at the same time to pairs.

Part of the development of the SoS method was a research of service design elements and their interrelationships, which also represent potential dimensions for SoS. In doing so, the design of the service is considered through the elements characteristic of the four basic areas of service design (service itself, service delivery system, user and market) and the elements of their interconnections, as shown in Fig. 16.1.

Fig. 16.1 Elements of the service design

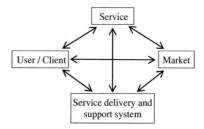

Dimensions in SoS are components of the service design. That's all we model, specify and evaluate during the design process.

There is no single taxonomy or ontology of service design elements, but there is more relevant research and work in this area. Thus, Evenson et al. [14] define the following elements of service design:

- Design objects (signs, products, actions, thought)
- Interactions (person-to-person, person-to-machine, machine-to-machine)

- Mediators of interactions (physical evidence, technologies, interpersonal communications)

The basic issue in the development of the SoS method is the definition of dimensions and the expression and metrics of each individual dimension.

Figure 16.2 shows some of the dimensions of the service structure.

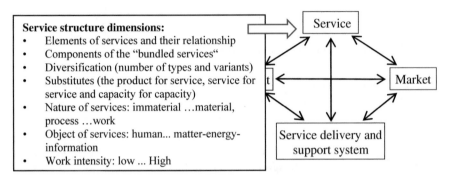

Service structure dimensions:
- Elements of services and their relationship
- Components of the "bundled services"
- Diversification (number of types and variants)
- Substitutes (the product for service, service for service and capacity for capacity)
- Nature of services: immaterial …material, process …work
- Object of services: human… matter-energy-information
- Work intensity: low … High

Fig. 16.2 Dimensions of the service structure

Each of the four design elements of the service has its own design dimensions, but the design dimensions also have their interrelationships. Thus, some dimensions of the Service-User relationship are shown in Fig. 16.3.

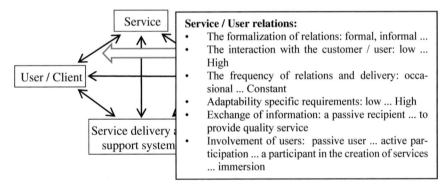

Service / User relations:
- The formalization of relations: formal, informal …
- The interaction with the customer / user: low … High
- The frequency of relations and delivery: occasional … Constant
- Adaptability specific requirements: low … High
- Exchange of information: a passive recipient … to provide quality service
- Involvement of users: passive user … active participation … a participant in the creation of services … immersion

Fig. 16.3 Dimensions of the Service-User relationship

Different dimensions differ in the type of expression and metrics:

(a) Quantitative statement of dimension (Metrics)—Measurable value. Some of them can be easily measured, and others are complex, for example, a weighted sum or polynomial, whose variables are measurable quantities. The state of the service according to that dimension can be absolutely positioned on a scale for a particular dimension.

(b) Qualitative statement of dimension—It is applied when the phenomenon can be qualitatively researched and described by statements that are non-numerical or mixed numerically and non-numerically. Qualitative data are collected using first-hand observation, questionnaires and interviews, focus groups and analysis of records of various phenomena, documents and other artefacts. Services are relatively (topologically) positioned on the scale.

(c) Complex decision, based on quantitative and qualitative data—It is possible to apply one of the structured techniques for organizing and analysing complex decisions, for example, the Analytical Hierarchy Process (AHP). The method seeks to accurately quantify the weights of decision criteria. Individual experts estimate the relative magnitudes of factors through pairwise comparisons, using questionnaires.

(d) Model—Representation of a service that reflects some of its structural, qualitative and/or quantitative properties, behaviour, etc. Individual dimensions (aspects) of services can be modeled. An example is the service delivery process as a dimension. Certain service properties, represented by the service delivery process model, are reduced and presented on the dimension axis of the four-quadrant (4Q) analysis, a method that will be described in more detail in the next chapter.

The model of input variables that describe a space of service (in our case two dimensions of that space) can be stochastic or deterministic. The model of a phenomenon should describe that phenomenon as accurately as possible, or its aspects of concern. The stochastic model recognizes the random nature of the input variables. The deterministic model is based on input variables that can be measured or calculated and on the relationship between output and input. The inputs in the stochastic model are basically random variables, and thus the outputs are estimates of the model characteristics for a given set of inputs. The stochastic model provides a distribution of relevant results for the distribution of scenarios. Therefore, we can look at the deterministic model as a simplified case of the stochastic model for one input data scenario.

The Likert scale [15] is often used to determine the value of a particular dimension. This is the sum of responses on several Likert statements. So far, a five-level Likert scale has been used in SoS where applicable (Strongly disagree; Disagree; Neither agree nor disagree; Agree; Strongly agree). Apart from Likert, Borg, K-factor, Guttman, rating and other scales can be used.

So far, several dozen dimensions have been identified in these four basic areas of service design and their interrelationships. Some dimensions can be assessed qualitatively or quantitatively, while others cannot. For example, in Fig. 16.2, the dimensions of *Elements of services and their relationship* and *Components of the "bundled services"* cannot be shown by a scale, but by structural models. Eventually, the properties of these models can be qualitatively described (e.g. invariant structure, modular structure, modular adaptive structure, etc.). At the same time, the *Diversification* (number of types and variants) can be expressed numerically. *Substitutes* can also be expressed in several categories (no substitutes, product for service, service for service and capacity for capacity, etc.). It is similar with the dimensions *Nature of services*, *Object of services* and *Work intensity*.

In conclusion, for each dimension, it is necessary to determine whether it is suitable for the application of quantitative analysis methods, qualitative analysis, complex decision methods or modeling. This research is still ongoing.

From previous research, it is evident that two or more methods can be applied to some dimensions, depending on the context. For example, *Flexibility* can be rated on a scale of 1 to 5, but flexibility as a complex term can be broken down into components (evaluation criteria) and then determined by some multi-criteria decision-making method.

Detailed definition of design dimensions, as well as the method of their determination, is the subject of ongoing research.

16.2.2 Four-Quadrant (4Q) Analysis

SoS is a method based on a graphical representation of phenomena in four quadrants (4Q) of the coordinate system. Such methods have been used in various scientific and professional fields for decades, primarily as analytical and diagnostic, but also as design methods.

The basis of the method is that the phenomenon to be analysed is positioned in one of the four quadrants using diagnostic questions. In the simplest case, one criterion (qualitative or quantitative indicator) is sufficient for positioning on the x and y axes, i.e. determining the position within one of the four quadrants.

In more complex cases, some metrics or decision methods (decision tree/decision table, multi-criteria decision methods, etc.) are used to determine the value of coordinates, and the result may carry some uncertainty/uncertainty. If the assessment is performed from several indicators/criteria, they can be weighted. A weighted calculation is used to determine the overall value of each item on the x and y axes, which allows positioning on the graph.

The simplest 4Q method is Quadrant Mapping (QM), where the phenomenon is just located in one or more quadrants, depending on the fulfilment of the conditions. Very similar are the matrices and decision tables where the satisfaction of conditions is examined with respect to the conditions that apply to individual rows and columns.

This technique exists in many variants, which are often adapted to a specific purpose. Thus, Dan Wengrod [16] uses Solution Quadrant Mapping (SQM) as graphical tools for design sprints in marketing analysis. One axis of the 4Q graph shows the team's perception of product uniqueness in the marketplace. The second shows the team's perception of how customers value their products, services or attributes. SQM is intended for teamwork and "ask the experts" discussions.

Gartner Magic Quadrant (GMQ) [17] is the method used by research and advisory company Gartner for positioning technology players within a specific market. Such representations are used for different technologies. One axis shows the Completeness of Vision, and the other shows the Ability to Execute. Quadrants I to IV show Leaders, Challengers, Niche Players and Visionaries (Fig. 16.4).

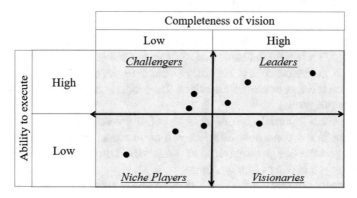

Fig. 16.4 Gartner Magic Quadrant

According to Gartner, "by applying a graphical treatment and a uniform set of evaluation criteria, a Magic Quadrant helps you quickly ascertain how well technology providers are executing their stated visions and how well they are performing against Gartner's market view".

It is essentially a QM graph. Individual phenomena are represented by points and are positioned within four quadrants, with their topological relations being more important than absolute positioning, which would be based on some precise metric. This point is a feature of the phenomenon.

It can be concluded that the SoS method maps phenomena within four quadrants (QM), but it is also possible to position the phenomenon and present it within the quadrant. The presentation of the phenomenon can be a point, as with GMQ. The point is the feature of the phenomenon. However, the phenomenon can also be described by the area where it is probably located, so the feature may have a different geometry.

The SoS method and associated tools can be applied at different stages of the service development or innovation (improvement) cycle, according to incremental and agile approaches.

The process or procedure of SoS application is not prescriptively determined. For example, a process pattern developed by Wengrod [16] for applying SQM can be used: "Begin the SQM by drawing the 2x2 and describing each of the axis. Then give the team five to ten minutes to silently note suggestions for relevant products, services or attributes and post them on the top of the board. Once they have completed posting their ideas, follow up with any previously submitted ideas or post these at the beginning to get the activity moving. Give the team time to silently review, arrange the post-its into groupings and eliminate any duplicates. Once the post-its are on board and arranged, it's time to vote. But instead of the usual voting ...".

16.3   Method Conceptualization

This chapter contains a conceptualization of the method. The metamodel contains classes, which represent the basic structural concepts that describe SoS.

The SoS model describes properties essential to the design or improvement of one or more services or multiple services. The model is actually composed of a set of Aspects (diagrams).

An Aspect is a partial view of an object of observation, in our case, a service. The Aspect in the context of SoS is a two-dimensional graphical representation. Depending on the design dimensions of the service it displays, it can be 4QD, or a graph displayed in one to four quadrants.

One Aspect can display the state values of one or more services at one time, or at different times (old state–new state).

The concept of Dimension has already been described. A set of dimensions is defined for each model, which is a subset of service design dimensions. The set of dimensions should be representative of the problem being described, that is, the purpose of the analysis.

As already stated, each instance of the Aspect displays two instances of Dimensions explicitly and may implicitly display a third dimension, as different states (invariants) that the service may have within two explicit dimensions.

A Feature shows the status and changes in the status of the service on one diagram (Aspect). A Feature is an object that stores its geometric representation on a diagram, which is typically a point, line or polygon, as well as attribute data (Fig. 16.5).

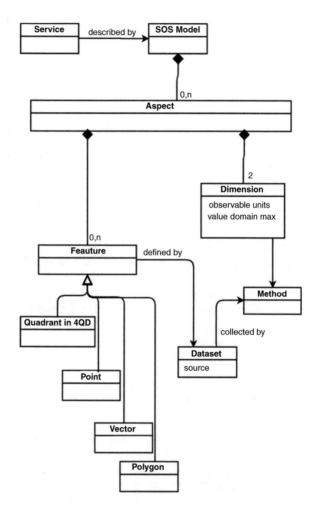

Fig. 16.5 SoS metamodel

As we described in the previous section, SoS maps services within four quadrants (QM). Positioning is possible by a point, or area where the phenomenon is likely to be located. As shown in the Fig. 16.6, the Feature of the service can be one or more quadrants (Q1 to Q4), a point or more points (P1 to P4) or some geometric shape (F1).

Fig. 16.6 SoS Feature

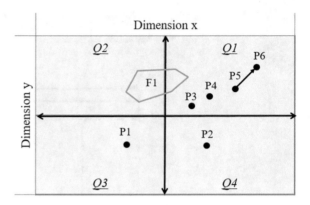

It has already been mentioned that the model of input variables that describe a space of service (in our case two dimensions of that space) can be stochastic or deterministic.

SoS can display the status of one or more services at one time, or changes in status, in time t and t + 1, as presented by P5 and P6. Changing the position of a point represents a change in the value of the service, in the Dimensions x and y, i.e. in the given Aspect.

16.4   Proof of Concept

The modern methods of research and engineering design in different areas, including service science and engineering, presuppose computer support by tools. In previous research and development of the SoS method, a spreadsheet was used for this purpose. Dimensions are rows and columns of the table, and values are entered in the fields of the table. A 4Q diagram was generated from the table for each aspect of the service. In this chapter, we introduce a novel toolkit that supports the implementation of the SoS method.

The SoS method is supported by SoS Modeling Toolkit developed by means of the ADOxx platform [18, 19]. The proof of concept prototype currently assists in modeling of one model type, namely, the aspect of two-dimensional diagram with quadrant features as well as evaluation and positioning of individual services through defined aspects. However, it is designed to be easily extended with other features of two- or more dimensional diagram aspect (such as point, vector, polygon, etc.), as well as with other aspects. Modeling toolkit and supporting library can be freely downloaded from the toolkit's home page.

16.4.1   Toolkit Implementation

Space of Services Modeling Toolkit is based on Space of Services Library which defines the metamodel information along with all attributes, relations and scripts defining the view and behaviour of individual elements as well as of the toolkit in general. The library extends and build on the ADOxx 1.5 Experimentation Library (adostd.abl) available in the ADOxx Development Toolkit. The metamodel classes included in the solution and example of attributes for one class are presented in Fig. 16.7.

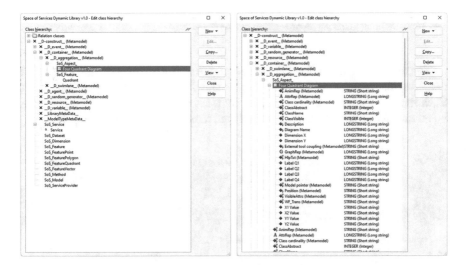

Fig. 16.7   Implementation of base metamodel classes and attributes

However, not all classes contribute to the visual elements of the toolkit. The *Four Quadrant Diagram* and *Service* are included in the *Modi* as add-ons to be displayed as model elements, and for those, among others, the *GraphRep* attributes are defined as well. The portion of the code to display coordinate system is presented in Fig. 16.8. Some of the model classes are defined as subclasses of _*D_aggregation_* construct in order to make them containers that would eventually contain other model elements, namely, features, which will contain the representations of one or more individual and services.

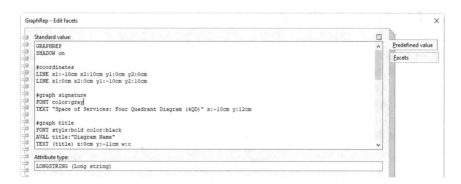

Fig. 16.8 Defining graphical representation of a model element

The model elements that are defined in the four-quadrant diagram model type are related to diagram definition and services evaluation and positioning (see Fig. 16.9). Each model element is further defined by a set of attributes in the NOTEBOOK notation. An example of properties displayed in notebook is given in Fig. 16.10.

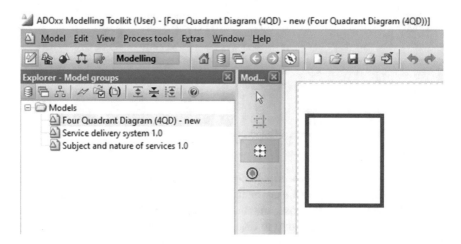

Fig. 16.9 Model elements in 4QD model type

Fig. 16.10 Four-quadrant diagram notebook

The model definition is supported by AdoScripts (asc files) which are defined in Visual Studio Code and executed on predefined events, such as model opening, closing or elements definition. The most important roles of the scripts include the dynamic change of attributes in relation to aspect definition as well as automatic positioning of the defined service in the corresponding quadrant related to horizontal and vertical evaluation results (an example is given in Fig. 16.11).

```
1   #Store information of current object
2   SET nCurrentClassID:(classid)
3   SET nCurrentObjID:(objid)
4
5   CC "Core" GET_CLASS_ID classname:"Service"
6   SET nServiceClassID:(classid)
7
8   CC "Core" GET_CLASS_ID classname:"Four Quadrant Diagram"
9   SET nDiagramClassID:(classid)
10
11  IF (nCurrentClassID = nServiceClassID) {
12      #CC "AdoScript" INFOBOX "Service added"
13
14      CC "Core" GET_ATTR_VAL objid:(nDiagramClassID) attrname:"X1 Value"
15      SET sX1Value:(val)
16      CC "Core" GET_ATTR_VAL objid:(nDiagramClassID) attrname:"X2 Value"
17      SET sX2Value:(val)
```

Fig. 16.11 Portion of AdoScript for service positioning

An example of toolkit in action when evaluating service in accordance to previously defined aspects and its dimensions is given in Fig. 16.12.

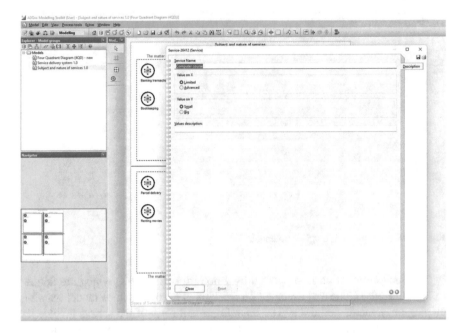

Fig. 16.12 Toolkit in action

16.4.2 Case Study

The application of the method is illustrated by several examples that follow.

Figure 16.13 shows two dimensions: *Nature of services*, which can be *Tangible* or *Intangible*, and Subject of services, which can be *Matter/Energy/Information* or *Human (living) being*. Examples of services are shown in four quadrants.

		Subject of services	
		The matter / energy / information	Human being
Nature of services	Intangible	• banking transactions • bookkeeping	• theatre performance • computer course
	Tangible	• parcel delivery • renting movies	• dental treatment • haircut and beauty

Fig. 16.13 Aspect: Subject and Nature of Service

This case analyses how to apply the SoS method and tool to improve the Parcel delivery service, with the aim to add value. In our case, this would mean that the service from the third quadrant (Tangible on Material) is extended to other quadrants, by adding some features, changing the delivery system and the like.

The material package delivery service can gain value if we add intangible ingredients (second quadrant), for example, a parcel tracking system in the form of a cloud computing application, which can be used from a computer or mobile device.

The transition to the fourth quadrant is possible if, in addition to the delivery of material packages, the delivery of living beings is also possible, for example, medical transport of patients or cargo transport of animals. This requires an appropriate service delivery system, for example, life capsules with all the necessary equipment, adapted to intermodal transport. In order to move the service to the first quadrant, an advanced telemedicine system or monitoring of the living being transported is necessary.

Figure 16.14 shows a use of toolkit with an example of a defined diagram and services for *Aspect: Subject and Nature of Services*, positioned in 4Q.

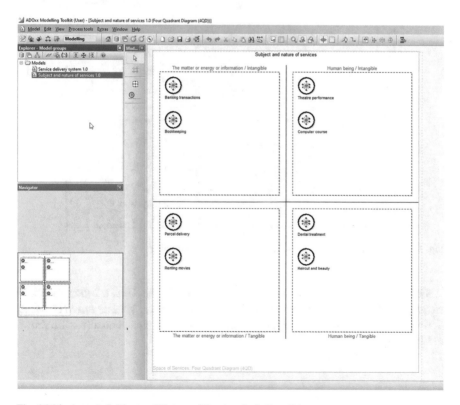

Fig. 16.14 Aspect: Subject and Nature of Services in SoS toolkit

In the example given, the lowest value added is in the third quadrant and the highest is in the first quadrant. That is not the rule, but it can be a useful convention. Also, in this example, we have positioned the service properties in one or more quadrants. This is the simplest application of the method. A more advanced application of the method is to position the service absolutely on the x and y axes, i.e. to position different services deterministically or stochastically, and to compare them.

Figure 16.15 shows the positioning of service *Complex transport and delivery, Aspect: Nature and Subject of services*, within 4Q, with coordinates showing the topology of services: Local parcel delivery $(-2;-2)$; Intermodal parcel delivery $(-1;-1)$; Tracking System $(-1;1)$; Animal transport $(1;-2)$; Human medical transport $(1;-2)$; Parcel real-time monitoring $(-1;1)$; Vital function real-time monitoring $(1;1)$; and Tele-diagnostics $(2;2)$.

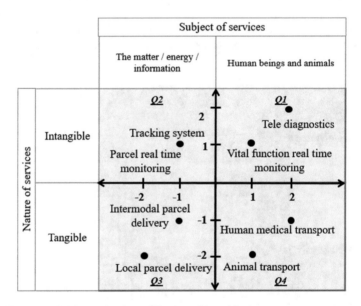

Fig. 16.15 Aspect: Subject and Nature of Service with positioning

Given the nature of the services, quadrants 1 to 4 for the *Aspect: Interaction with customer/Intensity of Work* are called *Professional service, Volume based services, Service factory and Service Shop*. Examples of services for each quadrant are shown in Fig. 16.16.

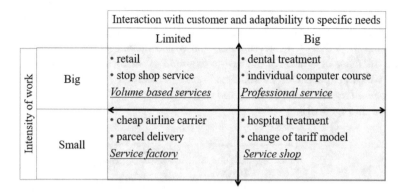

		Interaction with customer and adaptability to specific needs	
		Limited	Big
Intensity of work	Big	• retail • stop shop service *Volume based services*	• dental treatment • individual computer course *Professional service*
	Small	• cheap airline carrier • parcel delivery *Service factory*	• hospital treatment • change of tariff model *Service shop*

Fig. 16.16 Aspect: Interaction with customer/Intensity of Work

Figure 16.17 shows a use of toolkit with an example of a defined diagram and services for *Aspect: Interaction with customer/Intensity of Work*, positioned in 4Q.

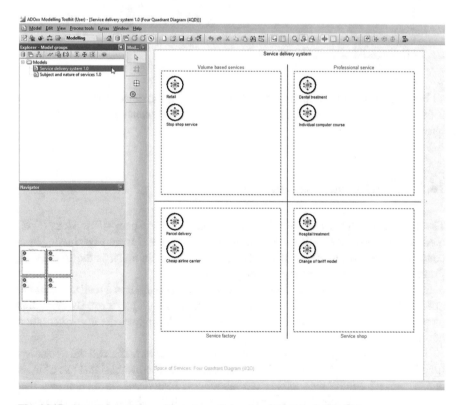

Fig. 16.17 Aspect: Interaction with customer/Intensity of Work in SoS toolkit

A typical example of SoS application is adding value to an existing service. For example, if we wanted to expand the service of a cheap airline (*Q3, Service factory*) by adding the value of the service in *Q2*, it would mean that we have to add value in the intensity of work, following the example of airlines of higher price range. In *Q1* we can expand with personalized services offered by small business aircraft. *Professional services* can be observed in another aspect, *Choice/Offer of Services*, as shown in Fig. 16.18.

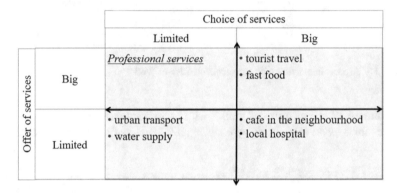

Fig. 16.18 Aspect: Choice/Offer of Services

Finally, it should be emphasized that the benefit for the objectives of the analysis is the only rule in the choice of aspects of services, i.e. dimensions that are mutually observed.

16.5   Conclusion and Outlook

The chapter presented the theoretical background of the Space of Services (SoS) method. The basic concepts on which the method is based were explained. These concepts were also elements of the metamodel. The metamodel is the foundation for making a SoS tool that supports the method.

A special challenge at the research presented in this chapter is a realization of the SoS support by the ADOxx development and configuration platform. By using this platform, a prototype tool has been made so far, which supports the implementation of the SoS method.

This prototype requires a lot of development in order to realize all the necessary functionalities and achieve a visualization that satisfies the professional use of tools in "industrial" conditions, outside the laboratory. Experience to date shows that a lot of effort is required to achieve the functionality and visualization provided by the spreadsheet. However, considering that the ADOxx platform provides a metamodeling support of modeling method requirements and development, which the spreadsheet does not cover. In addition, there are a number of methods and tools offered by the OMiLAB community, based on ADOxx, which allow modeling of individual dimensions of services. All this suggests that past and future efforts to support SoS with a tool based on the ADOxx platform are justified.

The research did not deal with defining the process pattern of application of the SoS method. SoS can be applied in methodological frameworks and processes designed to solve complex problems in teams involving multiple stakeholders, using a participatory approach. It can be combined and complemented with methods and tools of strategic decision-making, such as Complexity Maps (Qualitative and Quantitative) and Mess Maps^{TM}, which have so far been confirmed in laboratory conditions [20].

Tool Download: https://www.omilab.org/sos

References

1. Holmid, S., Evenson, S.: Bringing service design to service sciences, management and engineering. In: Service Science, Management and Engineering Education for the 21st Century, pp. 341–345. Springer, Boston, MA (2008)
2. Moritz, S.: Service Design: Practical Access to an Evolving Field. Köln International School of Design, Cologne (2005)
3. Alves, R., Nunes, N.J.: Towards a taxonomy of service design methods and tools. In: International Conference on Exploring Services Science, pp. 215–229. Springer, Berlin (2013)
4. Mendel, J.: A taxonomy of models used in the design process. Interactions. **19**(1), 81–85 (2012)
5. Mager, B.: Service Design: A Review. Köln International School of Design, Cologne (2004)
6. Buchenau, M., Suri, J. F.: Experience prototyping. In Proceedings of the 3rd Conference on Designing Interactive Systems: Processes, Practices, Methods, and Techniques, pp. 424–433. (2000)
7. Pruitt, J., Adlin, T.: The Persona Lifecycle: Keeping People in Mind Throughout Product Design. Elsevier, Burlington (2010)
8. Greenberg, S., Carpendale, S., Marquardt, N., Buxton, B.: The narrative storyboard: Telling a story about use and context over time. Interactions. **19**(1), 64–69 (2012)
9. Haritaipan, L.: Towards the creation of creativity tools for real-practice: A review of 112 design tools in the market. Des J. **22**(4), 529–539 (2019)
10. Methodbank. http://www.methodbank.com/.
11. Service Design Tools (sdt). http://www.servicedesigntools.org/
12. Design Council - Design Methods. http://www.designcouncil.org.uk/about-design/how-designers-work/design-methods/
13. Rubino, S. C., Hazenber, W., Huisman, M.: 75 Tools for Creative Thinking. http://75toolsforcreativethinking.com (2012)
14. Evenson, S., Holmlid, S., Kieliszewski, C., Mager, B.: Bringing design to service science [w:] In: Hefley B., Murphy B.(red.): Service Science, Management and Engineering Education for the 21st Century (2008)
15. Chimi, C. J., Russell, D. L.: The Likert scale: a proposal for improvement using quasi-continuous variables. In: Information Systems Education Conference, Washington, DC, pp. 1–10. (2009)
16. Dan Wengrod. 27.02.2019. https://sprintstories.com/solution-quadrant-mapping-a-map-alternative-for-design-sprints-41a18674da51

17. Gartner Magic Quadrant (GMQ) https://www.gartner.com/en/research/methodologies/magic-quadrants-research
18. Fill, H.G., Karagiannis, D.: On the conceptualisation of modeling methods using the ADOxx metamodeling platform. Enterp. Model. Inf. Syst. Architect. **8**(1), 4–25 (2013)
19. Karagiannis, D., Burzynski, P., Utz, W., Buchmann, R. A.: A metamodeling approach to support the engineering of modeling method requirements. In: 2019 IEEE 27th International Requirements Engineering Conference (RE), pp. 199–210. (2019)
20. Suoheimo, M. E., Miettinen, S. A.: Complexity Mapping and Mess Mapping Tools for Decision-Making in Transportation and Maas Development. In: Proceedings of the DMI, Academic Design Management Conference, pp. 1176–1188. (2018)

Chapter 17
Design and Engineering of Product-Service Systems (PSS): The SEEM Methodology and Modeling Toolkit

Fabiana Pirola, Giuditta Pezzotta, Danial Mohammadi Amlashi, and Sergio Cavalieri

Abstract Servitization is a global trend in the manufacturing industry that requires a challenging and complex transformation. In this context, engineering and design Product-Service Systems (PSS), capturing both product and service perspectives and balancing customer satisfaction and internal efficiency, are becoming more and more essential. To this purpose, the SEEM (SErvice Engineering Methodology) methodology is proposed, and the SEEM Modeling toolkit supporting its implementation is presented. Lastly, this chapter describes the methodology and the tool implementations in a case study on an Italian manufacturing company.

Keywords Product-Service System (PSS) · Service engineering methodology · SEEM tool

17.1 Introduction

Success stories such as Rolls-Royce, Alstom, Ericsson, Thales, ABB, IBM, and Xerox have highlighted the opportunity to exploit a "servitization" strategy in manufacturing [1]. Servitization is described as the integration of traditional product-based offerings with value-added services, defined in the literature as Product-Service Systems (PSS) [2, 3].

Although it is evident that selling product-service solutions fosters closer relationships with customers and generates higher and more stable revenue streams

F. Pirola (✉) · G. Pezzotta · S. Cavalieri
Department of Management, Information and Production Engineering, University of Bergamo, Bergamo, Italy
e-mail: fabiana.pirola@unibg.it; giuditta.pezzotta@unibg.it; sergio.cavalieri@unibg.it

D. M. Amlashi
Research Group Knowledge Engineering, University of Vienna, Vienna, Austria
e-mail: danial.mohammadi.amlashi@univie.ac.at

© The Author(s), under exclusive license to Springer Nature Switzerland AG 2022
D. Karagiannis et al. (eds.), *Domain-Specific Conceptual Modeling*,
https://doi.org/10.1007/978-3-030-93547-4_17

than pure product offerings, the literature points to several cases of failure where the solutions are not properly developed [4]. Above all, manufacturing firms generally do not think systematically about the solution as an overall, because historically, while product design has a focal role in business development, services have only a marginal role and are typically defined, not engineered, only after the product has been released on the market and managed either by the aftersales or marketing departments.

In this perspective, the definition of methodologies and tools for engineering Product-Service Systems has been discussed in the literature for about 20 years. Although different methodologies and methods have been developed over these years to support companies in systematically engineering their solutions, many of them are still on paper and require a computer-based tool to be largely adopted. This can help companies correctly use the theorized engineering processes and create a repository of knowledge and projects already developed.

In addition, companies still encounter difficulties in formulating a PSS value proposition that primarily focuses on fulfilling customer needs. In particular, there is still a lack of modeling methods and computer-based tools that support the PSS design and engineering taking customer satisfaction as a starting point but also looking at the internal efficiency of the service delivery processes.

In this chapter, the SEEM Modeling Toolkit implementing the SEEM (SErvice Engineering Methodology) methodology [5] developed in the ADOxx platform is described to fill the gaps. The SEEM methodology is focused on the engineering and re-engineering of the PSS offering and specifically on the modeling of the service delivery process within the PSS solution, balancing customer satisfaction and internal efficiency. This methodology is composed of four steps, and in each step, one or more methods are suggested.

To this purpose, the following section describes the SEEM methodology highlighting its main perspectives and the model requirements, Sect. 17.3 presents the model conceptualization, and Sect. 17.4 describes the SEEM Modeling toolkit implementation in a case study on an Italian manufacturing company. Then, Sect. 17.5 concludes the chapter with some remarks and further developments.

17.2   The SErvice Engineering Methodology (SEEM): Perspectives and Modeling Requirements

SEEM aims to support companies shifting from a traditional product-based service offering toward a more advanced PSS value proposition. In particular, SEEM supports companies in engineering and re-engineering their PSS while balancing the value perceived by customers with the service delivery processes' internal efficiency and productivity. The SEEM methodology, shown in Fig. 17.1, is divided into two main areas:

- **Customer area**: The analysis of customer needs, representing the starting point to design new product-services, and the re-arrangement of the company service portfolio.
- **Company area**: It deals with the design and assessment of the service delivery process to support the definition of a service delivery process considering the company's external and internal performance.

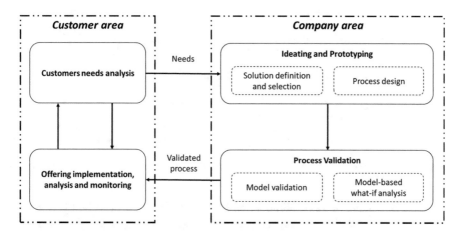

Fig. 17.1 The SErvice Engineering Methodology (SEEM) [5]

As shown in Fig. 17.1, the first two phases belong to the customer area, while the remaining two address the company area. These four phases have been used as guideline in the development of the conceptual model and the metamodel described in the following section. In particular, the development of these two models has been led by the three main perspectives at the basis of the SEEM methodology, namely:

- *Customer perspective* aims at modeling the main characteristics of the customers in terms of demographics, needs, values, issues, and so on, also considering the offering already available on the market. This perspective is the starting point based on which the company can conceptualize a new PSS solution.
- *Solution perspective* defines the combination of products and services (namely, solution) offered to customers to satisfy their needs. This dimension also comprises the main resources (both tangible and intangible) needed to deliver the solution.
- *Process perspective* aims at modeling the service delivery process of the identified solution, taking into consideration the internal activities and decisions carried out by the company to provide the solution to customers and highlighting the activities made in direct contact with the customers. This perspective is useful to evaluate internal performance and ensure a balance between company efficiency and customer satisfaction, with the final aim to provide successful and profitable PSS solutions.

Figure 17.2 shows these three main perspectives along with the main elements and their relationships.

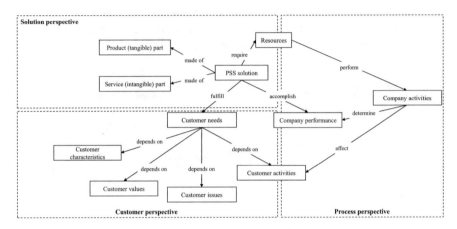

Fig. 17.2 The SEEM Perspective Views

In the remainder of this section, the SEEM phases are described highlighting the links with the three abovementioned perspectives and the models suggested in each of them.

17.2.1 Phase 1: Customer Needs Analysis

Focusing on the *customer perspective*, the main objective of the customer analysis is the representation of the customers' needs (expressed or not expressed), defined through feedback and complaints analysis (if an offer already exists), market research, interviews, focus groups, or more innovative tools such as sentiment analysis. Thus, the purpose of this phase is to obtain a clear understanding of the customers' needs and requirements in terms of products, services, and expected performance. This analysis can also lead to the segmentation of customers in several homogeneous classes in terms of main needs. In this phase, the modeling type **Persona Model (PM)**, coming from design thinking theory, is proposed as a model to collect and present information about customers. This model is based on Personas, fictional people describing the prototypical users of a product or service in terms of demographics and main values or needs. These Personas are the company reference point when engineering and defining the service offering [6].

In addition, especially in the case of PSS re-engineering, the **Customer Journey Model (CJM)** is suggested to highlight all the customer's decision-making moments and all the interactions between the customer and company.

17.2.2 Phase 2: Ideating and Prototyping

Starting from the customer's needs defined in the previous phase and represented in the PM, the process prototyping phase includes the generation of the PSS concepts, their evaluation, the selection of the concept to be added to the value proposition, and, finally, the delivery process's design. This phase covers both the PSS *solution perspective* and the *process perspective*.

17.2.2.1 Phase 2.1: Solution Definition and Selection

The *solution perspective* is implemented through the model **Product Service Concept Tree (PSCT)** [7], which is based on the principles of design thinking and functional design. This model aims to support customer needs analysis, defining the relationship between customer needs, the PSS solutions to be provided to the customers, and the provider's resources. The PSCT Model is presented in Fig. 17.3 as a tree consisting of four hierarchically arranged levels:

- *Needs* (N): Elements that customers consider essential or desirable.
- *Wishes* (W): How customers wish to satisfy their needs x.
- *Solutions* (S): Possible solutions (product, services, or a bundle of them) that the company can identify to fulfil customers' wishes and needs x.
- *Resources* (R): What are the main human/software resources and/or products and related features necessary to implement a solution?

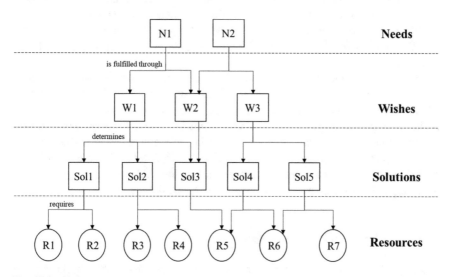

Fig. 17.3 Product Service Concept Tree (PSCT)

The solutions, defined in the PSCT, are evaluated using the Engineering Value Assessment (EVA) [8], a multi-criteria decision-making approach supporting the selection of the most suitable solution(s) to be added to the company offering.

The EVA method [9] systematically considers both customer value and provider value in the evaluation. It proposes a comprehensive set of value criteria for the assessment, which can be generalized and reused for PSS across industrial domains. It also considers all relevant "ilities" for engineering systems and value aspects such as knowledge-, emotion- and experience-related dimensions from a customer's perspective. At the same time, the provider value evaluation proposed in the EVA method is not limited to the provision of the best value for customers with the most limited amount of investments but also aspects related to the long-term survival and profitability of the enterprise.

The EVA method is composed of two different steps. The first step uses as input the list of PSS solutions identified, thanks to the PSCT for a high-level evaluation of the concepts. The output of this phase is the selection of solutions with higher customer and provider values. It could also entail a refinement and/or a combination of the solutions into new PSS solutions with high customer value and provider value. Then, these selected PSS solutions are assessed in more detail in the second step to come out with the final selection of PSS solutions to be designed and implemented into the company. Two exhaustive sets of evaluation criteria (one for the provider and one for the customer point of view) are also proposed at each step. To perform the assessment, the EVA leverages on a mixture of existing methods either already used in PSS engineering or belonging to other fields. In particular, step 1 uses the Weighted Pugh Matrix, while step 2 uses the TOPSIS method. At the end of each step, EVA foresees the adoption of the Importance-Performance Analysis (IPA) matrix to combine the evaluation scores of the two actors involved [9].

This phase represents one of the most critical aspects for manufacturing companies that tend to develop services without analyzing the most appropriate solution in detail.

Once selected, the PSS solution should be designed in detail, considering both the product and service components. Product and service design activities will follow separate paths by staying connected, thanks to the work done in these preliminary phases. In particular, if a new product design is foreseen, it will follow the traditional approaches already available in most companies using the widely spread product design methods and tools (e.g., CAD tool). Instead, the SEEM methodology concentrates on the service part of the PSS, providing guidance in the design, engineering, and validation of the service delivery process.

17.2.2.2 Phase 2.2: Process Design

Since the PSS solution should be customer centered, the starting point of this phase is the customer journey analysis to understand how the customer will use the designed solution. Thus, with the focus on the *process perspective*, the **Customer Journey Model** related to the specific PSS solution is the model used in this phase.

After this, the focus moves to the internal company process. The detailed service design consists of the definition of possible alternative delivery processes. In the re-engineering case, this phase involves mapping, first, the existing process (if any) and identifying possible alternatives for improvement. The models proposed to describe the service delivery process are the **BPMN2.0** and the **Service Blueprinting** approach. In particular, the pools in BPMN2.0 should correspond to the resources identified in the PSCT. The activities in the customer pool should reflect those in the CJM of the PSS solution. At this stage, in order to balance the customer perspective with the internal process, the CJM can be modified to allow a better service delivery.

Referring to process modeling, the SEEM integrates the BPMN2.0 with the Service Blueprinting [10, 11] structure for simultaneously depicting the service delivery process, the points of customer contact, and the physical evidence of the service delivery from the customer's point of view. Indeed, the activities composing the process are classified into four categories: (i) customer's activities (performed by the customer), (ii) front-end activities (performed by the company interacting with the customer), (iii) back-end activities (performed by the company, but hidden from customer view), and (iv) support activities (general management activities performed by the company to support several processes) (Fig. 17.4).

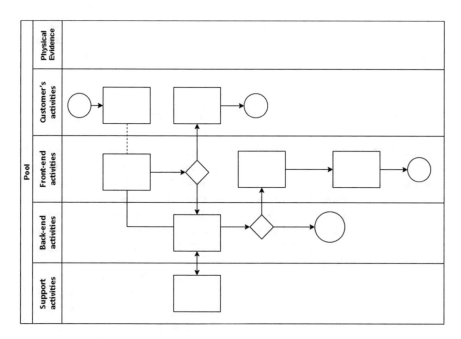

Fig. 17.4 Service Blueprinting architecture

17.2.3   Phase 3: Process Validation

Keeping the focus on the *process perspective*, process validation assesses qualitatively and quantitatively the performance of the service delivery processes previously designed, identifying possible alternatives, as well as identifying the most suitable process and its best resource configuration. To this end, starting from the static model developed in the BPMN2.0, SEEM adopts a process simulation approach (e.g., discrete event simulation, agent-based simulation, hybrid approaches), since it allows for the dynamic analysis of a system (the service process, in our case) under different conditions and scenarios.

17.2.4   Phase 4: Offering Implementation, Analysis, and Monitoring

Once the solution has been designed in terms of product and service components, the new PSS solution can be added to the company portfolio. In this phase, KPIs are defined to monitor performance, to have an effective and efficient value proposition with close market fit. The analysis carried out in this phase to understand how the solutions are performing on the market and if there are possible competitors/alternatives can then be used to start a new design or re-engineering process.

17.3   SEEM Conceptualization and Metamodel

In this section, the metamodel derived during the conceptualization of the SEEM methodology is introduced. The conceptualization process concerns the identification of concepts, characteristics, and connectors of the SEEM methodology to establish a formal representation and to enable the transfer toward model processing capabilities and interactions applying metamodeling techniques. As such, the conceptualization process is driven by methodological steps and derives, based on design decisions, the required specifications of a coherent and adequate metamodel definition, which will act as a blueprint for implementing tool support.

As a guiding framework, the Generic Metamodelling Framework introduced by Karagiannis/Kühn in [12] (Metamodelling Platform) is applied. The purpose of the framework is to classify the requirements of the methodology into requirements related to the (a) *structural aspects* (modelling language as syntax, notation, and semantic) and (b) *behavioral aspects* (mechanisms and algorithms that operate upon this structure and provide model value to the user). A metamodeling approach has been selected for this purpose to enable an agile engineering of concepts (extension, adaptation); mechanisms and algorithms are defined on the abstract constructs of the metamodel where concrete instances inherit the behavior defined.

This adds value to the methodology as a formal representation is established as input for later implementation and deployment phases of a tool environment for the SEEM methodology considered, at this stage, as a proof-of-concept implementation utilizing available functionalities of the ADOxx Metamodelling Platform. Implementation results and their evaluation are presented in the following section, utilizing a case study in the domain of automation sector.

The conceptualization results are presented in the following, using UML class diagram notation to represent the structural aspects of the metamodel, extended with functionality annotations (marked in green) as requirements of the conceptual structure and input for the tool implementation.

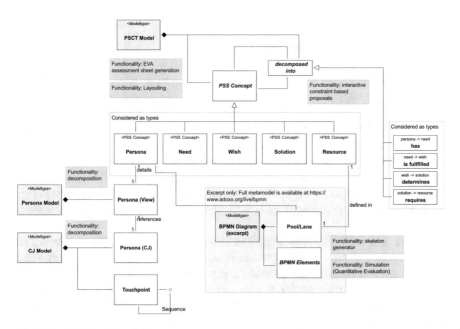

Fig. 17.5   SEEM metamodel

The SEEM metamodel consists of four model types supporting phases 1–3 of the SEEM methodology.

17.3.1   Phase 1: Customer Need Analysis

Model structure: Utilizing the *Persona model* as a container to identify different viewpoints of involved stakeholders. Each persona is defined using the "Persona (View)" element considering attributes to describe the specific persona (image, age, name, role, slogan, a list of wishes). The structure of the model type is in the form of a list, assuming that each instantiation of the model type results in a set of personas which describe the needs of the organization.

In addition the "Customer Journey Model (CJM)" is defined that utilizes the list of personas as an input and allows the descriptive design of touchpoints in the sequence of their occurrence.

Model processing functionality: For the persona concept, a decomposition functionality is defined. This functionality generates the first layer of the PSCT tree (persona as a virtual persona object and wishes derived from the structure) as well as the skeleton for the customer journey modeling (virtual persona object derived from the Persona model).

17.3.2   Phase 2: Ideating and Prototyping

Model structure: The ideation and prototyping phase is considered the core element of the SEEM methodology and its conceptualization. The metamodel considers a hierarchical tree structure that is defined on an abstract level ("PSS Concept" and "decomposed into") contained in the model type "PSCT Model." The tree representation enables a structural analysis of contained elements.

The structured design approach utilizes the BPMN metamodel as a foundation. The metamodel is based on the standard specification by OMG (BPMN 2.0), and only relevant concepts for the model processing functionality are considered in Fig. 17.5. The full metamodel applicable for SEEM is available at https://www.adoxx. org/live/bpmn/.

Model processing functionality: The design decision on PSCT level is based on the capabilities of metamodeling techniques. As the abstract constructs (class and relation) are concretized from a semantic perspective, they inherit on one hand the tree-based model representation format and are extended by constraint evaluation rules that support the ideation process. This means that the modeler is guided in the process of decomposition based on the initial input from Phase 1.

Evaluation: Assessment templates are embedded in the constructs to provide possibilities for a distributed and collaborative evaluation of ideas based on the PSCT representation.

Utilizing rule-based mapping techniques, the PSCT tree structure is resolved into a process representation skeleton as "Resources" in the tree are mapped to pools/lanes in BPMN, representing actor responsibilities in the process notation.

17.3.3   Phase 3: Process Validation

Model structure: The validation phase in SEEM is concerned with the evaluation of the process design of Phase 2. Available structural elements are considered on BPMN 2.0 level, more specifically the available conceptualization for process simulation using BPMN 2.0. This concerns extension for quantitative facets during process design.

Model processing functionality: Simulation algorithms are available as building blocks that operate upon an annotated graph structure (typing) and quantitative facets of nodes and edges.

The outcome of the conceptualization shows that the SEEM modelling method is established by defining a small set of semantic primitives (specifically for the PSCT model) that are concretized during their use (dynamic typing). This approach is considered relevant for the SEEM methodology in order to provide domain-specific extensions on type level without losing processing capabilities.

The above conceptual metamodel has been transformed into a prototype implementation utilizing the ADOxx Metamodelling Platform, resulting in the SEEM Modelling Toolkit presented in the following using a real case study.

17.4 SEEM Modeling Toolkit: Proof of Concept

The SEEM Modelling Toolkit is used as computer-based tool in a case study aiming at supporting an Italian company in the selection, design, and engineering of new PSS solutions. This section has the objectives of describing the SEEM Modelling Toolkit with an application in a real case and to show the tool's main features and validate its potentiality, feasibility, and ease of use in real-world settings.

The company in study is an Italian producer of automation systems for residential use, namely, automation systems and related accessories (e.g., remote controls, photocells, flagship light), for gates and garages. Historically, the company has always been strongly product-oriented, and its service offering is limited to support installers and final users through an external call center. Given the possibilities offered by technological advancement and the global trend toward servitization, the company is willing to move toward PSS provision to increase its revenue and customer loyalty.

To support the company in its journey toward servitization, the first two phases of the SEEM methodology have been applied and implemented using the SEEM Modelling Toolkit, namely, customer needs analysis and ideating and prototyping.

17.4.1 Phase 1: Customer Needs Analysis

The first phase of the methodology is the analysis of the customers and the actual service offering. As mentioned in the "The SErvice Engineering Methodology (SEEM): Perspectives and Modeling Requirements" section, this phase adopts traditional models coming from design thinking to support PSS designers in describing and analyzing the main company customers (i.e., Persona Model and the Customer Journey Model). The information needed in this phase generally comes from company unstructured knowledge, brainstorming, interviews with customers, focus groups, etc. Thus, the main added value of the SEEM Modelling Toolkit is the provision of a computer-based tool supporting the adoption and visualizing of these models in a unique environment and enhancing the development of common knowledge in the scope of PSS engineering. In particular, the Persona Model summarizes the main characteristics of the customer analyzed, such as picture, name, age, role, company, slogan, and needs. The Persona model can generate the following models ensuring a guided and improved design experience.

In the case study, interviews with company managers were allowed to gather all the information related to the market and its customers. The company has the following three main kinds of customers who sell the products to final consumers:

- *Wholesalers of electrical* equipment: This is the most important customer in terms of sales volumes since it accounts for about 60% of the company's turnover. The company sells its products to wholesalers, who, in turn, sell to "small" installers who sell and install the products to the final users. The installers are mainly generic electricians who carry out about five to six interventions of this type per year.
- *Professional installers:* It accounts for 30% of the company turnover and addresses professional installers specialized in automation, who carry out a higher number of interventions per year.
- *OEM:* It guarantees 10% of the turnover and is characterized by the direct sale to manufacturers of civil and industrial doors and gates.

The market addressed by the company has the following criticalities that hamper the introduction of services: (i) The value chain is quite long with several intermediaries, and, then, the final user is difficult to reach; (ii) final users consider the product as a commodity and focus more on the price rather than on its functionalities and added services; and (iii) generic installers are not prone to innovation, leading to failure when new technologies and services are proposed to them.

Given the market characteristics, the focus of the analysis has been the generic installer, namely, generic electricians who sell and install the product into the final customer (i.e., the customer house). Thus, the aim is to identify the services that can be offered to the installers and the product to increase the market share and the related revenues.

To this purpose, the Persona Model of the generic installer has been built using the SEEM Modelling Toolkit. A brainstorming session involving company employees with deep knowledge on products and customers led to defining the main characteristics of the customers that are summarized in Fig. 17.6. Obviously, the Persona Model reports only the most useful customer elements for the design purposes, but more information related to the main issues and values of the customer have been gathered during the analysis. The typical customer is a 50-year-old electrician who owns a small company that provides several installation and maintenance services of the house electrical system (Fig. 17.6). His main expertise is mainly in the electrical field, and he has very little or no competence in software, and, for this reason, he is averse to any technological innovation in the field of software. The analysis of the customer allows to identify its main needs that are:

- *Easiness to install*: Since he is not specialized in automation (on average, he carries out 5–6 installation per year), but he is a generic electrician dealing with all the electrical systems of a house, his main need is to have a product which is easy to install. He does not want to encounter problems during installation that will force him to contact the service support center of the company asking for support and waste time.
- *Reliability of the product*: Since this kind of customer generally owns a micro-company with one or two technicians, he considers more profitable the new installation instead of repairing already installed automation. This activity can require a long time and huge effort to identify causes and fix the problem.

Fig. 17.6 Persona Model of the installer

Name:

Giovanni

Age:

50

Role:

Installer

Company:

GINST

"I'm an electrician, not a software engineer"

Needs:

- Easiness to install
- Reliability of the product

To better understand the characteristics of the customer, its Customer Journey Model has also been defined in this phase to highlight its main activities, decisions, and contact points with the company. This helped the company define possible PSS solution in the following phase.

17.4.2 Phase 2: Ideating and Prototyping

Based on the Persona Model, the following phases of the SEEM methodology have been applied, namely, the Product Service Concept Tree. Starting from the main characteristics of the customer identified in the previous phase (e.g., needs, issues, values) and summarized in the Persona model, the PSCT supports the designer in identifying possible PSS solutions to be offered to the installers, the selection of the most convenient PSS solution(s) to be proposed, and the design of the delivery process of the identified PSS solution(s).

In the SEEM Modelling Toolkit, clicking on the button "Generate First Layer of PSCT" in the notebook window of the Persona Model (shown in Fig. 17.7), it is possible to automatically generate the first layer of the PSCT, namely, the need layer. Then, from the need level, the lower levels can be created in the PSCT model adding new boxes and defining their type (i.e., need, whish, solution, resource). When connecting the different boxes in the PSTC, the PSCT model automatically generates the relationships between the elements. In this way, a persona *has* a need, the need *is fulfilled through* a wish, and the wish *determines* a solution which *requires* a resource (Fig. 17.8).

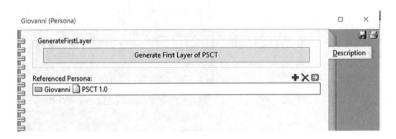

Fig. 17.7 PSCT generation

Fig. 17.8 Relationship in the
PSCT

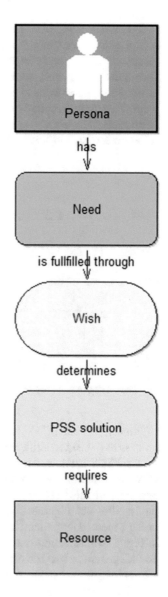

The PSCT (Fig. 17.9) has been implemented through a brainstorming session with the main company decision-makers: R&D manager, division manager, sales manager, product marketing managers, product manager, training and service manager, and business area manager. These people have direct contact with customers or have high knowledge of the products and the technologies available to improve them. The brainstorming session lasted about 4 h. After identifying the whishes (represented in yellow ovals) that allow to fulfil the customer's needs, the PSS solutions reported in Table 17.1 have been devised (represented in orange boxes).

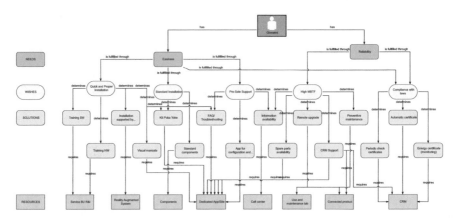

Fig. 17.9 The Product Service Concept Tree

Finally, for each PSS solution, the main resources involved in its service delivery process have been identified and represented in blue boxes.

The PSCT is allowed to define several possible PSS solutions, but it is important to assess them based on multiple criteria and select the best solution able, from one side, to fulfil customer needs and, from the other side, to ensure company profitability and alignment with its long-term strategy. To this purpose, the first step of EVA method (explained in Sect. 17.2) has been partially implemented. As shown in Fig. 17.10, selecting one solution generated in the PSCT, the SEEM Modeling Toolkit generates two Excel files, one from the provider and one from the customer viewpoints, each of them containing the list of predefined criteria for the assessment [9]. Then, all the people involved in the PSS design process have to fill out the Excel files generated for each solution of the PSCT, providing their assessment. All the first-step evaluations are summarized by the PSS designer who is also responsible of carrying out the second step (not implemented in the SEEM modeling toolkit yet) to define the solution that should be designed in detail.

Table 17.1 PSS solutions

PSS solutions	Description
Training software/hardware	To ensure quick and legally compliant installation, it entails documentation and courses that allow respecting the type of product in terms of the law (with a study of the impact curves)
Installation with augmented reality	Use of augmented reality trough smartphone to support installation
Visual manuals	Provision of visual manuals with drawings explaining the installation phases; these could be provided through an app to reduce printing costs and make constant updates
YouTube tutorial	A QR code placed on the product linked to YouTube content to view videos. This solution can be seen as an intermediate between manuals and augmented reality
Customized kit configurator	Possibility to configure the product and the installation kit via an app, reducing the complexity of the installation and the number of calls due to installation problems. In addition, the configurator would allow the installer to have a "shopping list" based on the solution chosen to buy everything from the wholesaler
App for configuration and quotation	Product configurator offered through an app to customize the product and get a quotation
Installers list	The installer can become a "recommended installer" by the company and be included in a list freely accessible by end users
Accreditation programs	Training and events to get known and trained in products and then be included in the "recommended installer" list
Automatic certificate	Checklist that allows the installers to automatically generate a certificate assuring that the installation complies with the local regulation
Safety procedures for installers	Courses and events that allow developing knowledge in this field
FAQ/troubleshooting	Dedicated area in the website/app where the installer can find answers to frequently asked questions
Maintenance supported by augmented reality	The maintenance of the automation system is performed through augmented reality which ensures a more effective and efficient intervention
Free assistance in pre-series	Offer a period of free service to the pre-series product, which would also allow the company to improve the knowledge about the behavior of the new product and its main problems
Preventive maintenance programs	Possibility of creating contracts between the installer and the end user for scheduled maintenance

Thus, the two steps of the EVA method have been carried, and the 14 solutions identified in the PSCT have been assessed. To this purpose, two single interviews (one per step) with the main decision-makers have been carried out. Each interview has been assisted by one of the authors acting as a facilitator. In the first-step interviews, the facilitator provided a general description of the overall method, its steps, and the categories for the high-level assessment to create a shared understanding among the participants. For the second step of the EVA method,

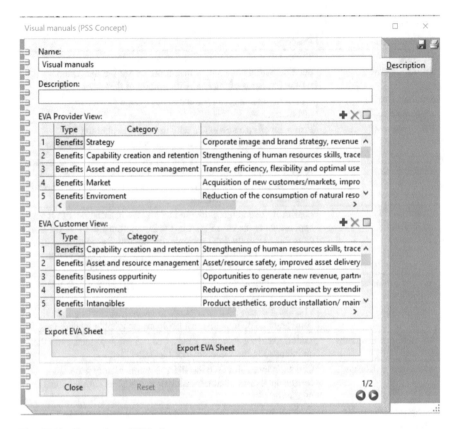

Fig. 17.10 Generation of EVA sheet

further interviews have been carried out with the same people involved in the previous phase.

The analysis of all the scores provided by the company led to the final selection of the PSS solution concepts to be developed and added to the PSS portfolio of the target company. The most valuable PSS is the delivery of *visual manuals* (preferably through an app).

It is important to emphasize that, thanks to the SEEM Modeling Toolkit, all the analyses carried out starting with the definition of the persona, the generation of the different solutions, and their evaluation become an important part of the company's knowledge and can be used for future projects. In fact, these models have the great advantage of becoming a methodological base supporting how the company manages the engineering process and generates a fundamental knowledge base for companies that want to servitize.

Starting from the most valuable solution, the Customer Journey Model and the BPMN model of the service delivery process have been defined. In the solution options of the SEEM Modeling toolkit, it is possible to automatically create the template of these two models, as shown in Fig. 17.11.

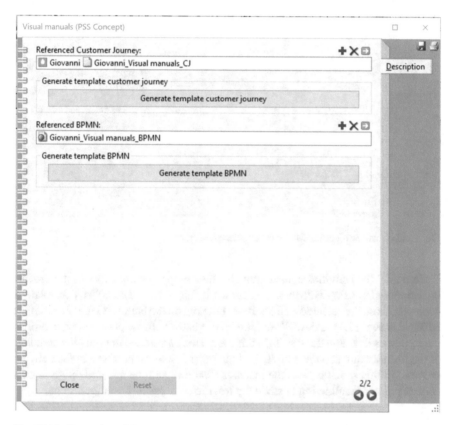

Fig. 17.11   Generation of Customer Journey Model and BPMN

Then, the Customer Journey Model (Fig. 17.12) has been built adding in the template all the activities carried out by the installer, from when he receives the call from his customer that needs an automation system to when the automation is installed. As it is possible to notice, after having received the customer request, the installer analyzes the plant where the automation must be installed, makes an offer, and, if accepted, buys the automation from a wholesaler and installs it to the customer site. During installation, he can consult the visual manual provided along with the product or in the company app, which allows him to follow step by step in an easy way installation procedure, fastening the entire process. Once the installation is concluded, he makes the needed tests for the product, releases the certificate, sends the invoice to the customer, and receives the payment.

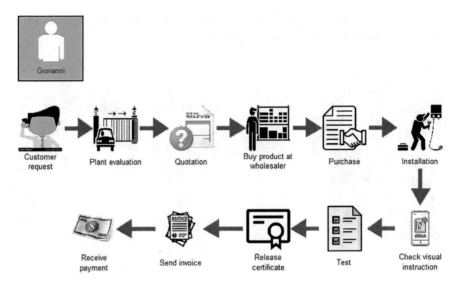

Fig. 17.12 Customer Journey Model of the selected solution

To model the activities considering also the company point of view, the process is also modeled using BPMN2.0, as shown in Fig. 17.13. The BPMN template is generated from the selected PSS solution: clicking on the button "Generate template BPMN" in Fig. 17.11, a new BPMN model is created with the pool corresponding to the resources linked in the PSCT. In this model then are added not only the activities of the installer but also the activities of the other resources involved in the delivery process (in this specific case, the installer customer and the app), highlighting the contact points and allowing to statically test different process configurations.

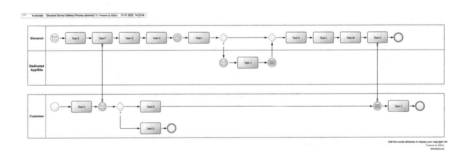

Fig. 17.13 BPMN of the service delivery process

Once the statistical process configuration has been defined, a quantitative evaluation of the process could be carried out leveraging on the time and cost assessment available in the SEEM Modeling toolkit, as shown in Fig. 17.14. This assessment will be possible to estimate, considering several scenarios, the lead time of the process, the waiting time, the resource utilization, the cost associated with the process, and so on. This will be helpful in making further decisions related to the process and supporting the decision-maker in defining its optimal configuration.

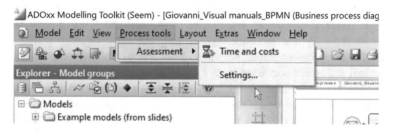

Fig. 17.14 Process assessment

17.5 Conclusion

Nowadays, companies are struggling to move from a product-oriented to a more PSS-oriented business model. The academic and scientific literature reveals a lack of suitable computer-based tools to support early PSS design activities, integrate product and service concepts since the beginning, and evaluate PSS concepts based on customer needs and company profitability. To fill this gap, the SEEM Modeling Toolkit has been proposed to implement the methods suggested in the SEEM methodology [5] and, then, to support the PSS designer in the different phases of designing and engineering PSS.

This chapter shows an application of the first two phases of the methodology and the implementation of the SEEM Modeling Toolkit in a case study focused on an Italian producer of automation systems for residential use. Thus, starting from the customer analysis, the case study has led to the definition of a set of PSS solutions to the selection of the PSS concept to be added in the company portfolio and to the design of the solution delivery process, highlighting both the customer (in the Customer Journey Model) and resource interactions (in the BPMN) point of views.

From the case study point of view, the interviews and the methodology implementation have been highlighted as a cultural change inside the company that appears to be fundamental to successfully introduce PSS offering. Indeed, the willingness of the middle management to offer services that could change the habits of customers and could allow establishing a different relationship with them is still missing. Furthermore, customers are perceived as not very prone to services but still too focused on acquisition cost and selling price. In general, there is a lack of a long-term vision in which the relationship with customers can change and offer services effectively capable of anticipating their needs. Despite the need for a business and cultural change of the company and of the industry, the implementation of this methodology has been a first valuable attempt to change the mindset of managers since it has allowed them to analyze their products from a different point of view and to design new solutions starting from customer needs rather than from a technology and product innovation point of view.

From a technical point of view, even if the SEEM Modeling Toolkit is still at the prototype phase, it has demonstrated ease of use and suitability to implementing phases foreseen by the methodology. During the design phase of the SEEM metamodel, the following challenges have been identified from a conceptual point of view and can be considered as input for further research work: The first is related to model/view synchronization, where mechanisms in the metamodel are required for an intelligent synchronization of artefacts. This is specifically interesting for personas and potential changes during the decomposition and refinement phases. The second concerns time/variants. Variants might evolve during the design, and this requires capabilities to synchronize and compare model artefacts.

In addition, the toolkit only covers a part of the methods suggested by the SEEM methodology. Further developments consist in the integration into the tool of the two steps of the EVA method. This can be done directly in the tool allowing to import the Excel sheets with the scores assigned to the different criteria, create the Excel files for the second steps, and visualize the results of the two steps of assessment in a graphical manner. Furthermore, the last phases of the SEEM should also be tested with a case study, in particular, the integration of the time and cost assessment to quantitatively evaluate the performance of the process considering different scenarios.

Tool Download: https://www.omilab.org/seem

References

1. Vandermerwe, S., Rada, J.: Servitization of business: Adding value by adding services. Eur. Manag. J. **6**(4), 314–324 (1988)
2. Mont, O.K.: Clarifying the concept of product–service system. J. Clean. Prod. **10**(3), 237–245 (2002)
3. Pirola, F., Boucher, X., Wiesner, S., Pezzotta, G.: Digital technologies in product-service systems: A literature review and a research agenda. Comput. Ind. **123**, 103301 (2020)
4. Kowalkowski, C.: Service innovation in industrial contexts. In: Toivonen, M. (ed.) Service Innovation: Novel Ways of Creating Value in Actor Systems, pp. 235–249. Springer Japan, Tokyo (2016)
5. Pezzotta, G., Pirola, F., Rondini, A., Pinto, R., Ouertani, M.-Z.: Towards a methodology to engineer industrial product-service system – Evidence from power and automation industry. CIRP J. Manuf. Sci. Technol. **15**, 19–32 (2016)
6. Pirola, F., Pezzotta, G., Andreini, D., Galmozzi, C., Savoia, A., Pinto, R.: Understanding customer needs to engineer product-service systems. IFIP Adv. Inf. Commun. Technol. **439**(Part 2), 683–690 (2014)
7. Rondini, A., Giuditta, P., Fabiana, P., Monica, R., Paulo, P.: How to design and evaluate early PSS concepts: The product service concept tree. Procedia CIRP. **50**, 366–371 (2016)
8. Rondini, A., Bertoni, M., Pezzotta, G.: At the origins of product service systems: Supporting the concept assessment with the engineering value assessment method. CIRP J. Manuf. Sci.

Technol. **29**, 157–175 (2020)

 9. Rondini, A., Marco, B., Giuditta, P.: At the origins of product service systems: Supporting the concept assessment with the engineering value assessment method. CIRP J. Manuf. Sci. Technol. **29**, 157–175 (2018) pp. 1–19

10. Bitner, M.J., Ostrom, A.L., Morgan, F.N.: Service blueprinting: A practical technique for service innovation. Available at: https://doi.org/10.2307/41166446. (2008)

11. Lynn Shostack, G.: How to design a service. Eur. J. Mark., MCB UP Ltd. **16**(1), 49–63 (1982)

12. Karagiannis, D., Kühn, H.: Metamodelling Platforms. EC-Web. Vol. 2455. 2002

Part VI
Knowledge Engineering

Chapter 18
Model-Based Guide Toward Digitization in Digital Business Ecosystems

Anna Sumereder and Tor Dokken

Abstract Digitization is popular in today's business ecosystems. However, digitization is not straightforward and introduces challenges such as sensor issues, edge computing, network dependencies, and security. Therefore, the idea is to propose a modelling method enabling to guide key aspects for the digitization process. For this reason, the proposed modelling method prototype concentrates on (a) the collection of requirements, (b) the analysis of the contextual environment, as well as (c) the monitoring by guiding the selection of an appropriate digitization device. The modelling method is extended by a physical OMiLAB Innovation Corner experiment that eases, on one hand, understanding the domain problem and, on the other hand, facilitates the selection of an appropriate digitization unit by taking into account potential physical issues as well as the requirements related to the business perspective.

Keywords Digitization · OMiLAB Innovation Corner · Physical experiment

18.1 Introduction

Digitization is popular in today's business ecosystems. However, digitization and in particular devices at the edge introduce challenges such as network stability, connectivity, and security. To minimize problems like hardware failures and to identify essential dependencies, guidance seems to be required throughout the digitization process. Benedict [1] characterizes digital (business) ecosystems as a platform-independent and sociotechnical system that focuses on coevolution, coopetition, openness, recombination, and self-organization. A differentiation between technical

A. Sumereder (✉)
RG Knowledge Engineering, University of Vienna, Vienna, Austria
e-mail: Anna.Sumereder@boc-eu.com

T. Dokken
SINTEF Digital, Oslo, Norway
e-mail: Tor.Dokken@sintef.no

© The Author(s), under exclusive license to Springer Nature Switzerland AG 2022
D. Karagiannis et al. (eds.), *Domain-Specific Conceptual Modeling*,
https://doi.org/10.1007/978-3-030-93547-4_18

411

and social relationships can be conducted, where the former is highly agile and dynamic—consisting of technology components such as digital devices or hardware parts. A basic overview of the relationships in a digital ecosystem is provided in Fig. 18.1. Here the fundamental parts of such an ecosystem are addressed like digital/smart objects and sensors. Gosh et al. [2] consider the combination of artificial intelligence (AI) and the Internet of Things (IoT) as a breakthrough that enables an easy human life, also in a business environment.

Digitization in general and the creation of a digital twin are mega trends not only in a research context but also in today's business world. For instance, small- and medium-sized enterprises in manufacturing are looking for guidance when digitizing their processes [4]. By focusing on a specific production process setting, which serves as a sample for introducing and explaining our idea, three major digitization challenges were identified in [5]. These are expected also to be relevant for other application cases. The three challenges are (1) the digitization of the production process, (2) the digitization of the raw material, and (3) the digitization of the product itself. The mentioned characteristics and challenges imply that digital ecosystems are not trivial to understand. For this reason, a sort of complexity reduction and simplification can be introduced to support transparency when tackling a specific domain problem. Particularly, the introduction of abstraction facilitates the identification of patterns so that the digitization process in similar domains is supported by concepts such as reusability, simplification, and modularity.

Therefore, the idea (see Sect. 18.2) is to propose a modelling method to guide key aspects related to the digitization process. By supporting documentation and

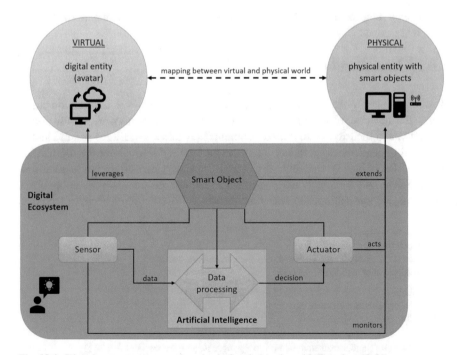

Fig. 18.1 Digital ecosystem connecting physical and virtual world (Based on [2, 3])

consulting features, understanding of the potentially complex domain problem can be highly facilitated. For this reason, the proposed modelling method prototype concentrates on the (a) collection of requirements, (b) analysis of the contextual environment, as well as (c) monitoring by guiding the selection of an appropriate digitization device. The focus areas are supported by the OMiLAB Innovation Corner and its layer-based architecture [6] (see Fig. 18.2)—consisting of three main layers—throughout all stages of digitization and digital transformation. The OMiLAB Innovation Corner facilitates digital innovation by providing a digital innovation and laboratory environment that supports design, engineering, and training activities related to digital transformation.

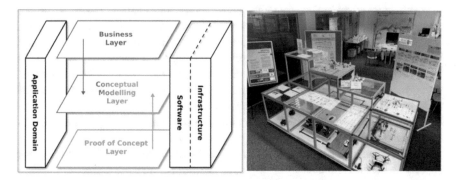

Fig. 18.2 Introduction of the three abstraction layers (left) and the realization of an industrial OMiLAB Innovation Corner at BOC in Vienna (right) [6]

The proposed model-based approach in combination with an OMiLAB Innovation Corner experiment should facilitate the requirement engineering from a business perspective (business layer). It should as well tackle questions such as if a new business model is required or if the existing business model can be used to tackle the requirements of the particular system under study. Furthermore, the organizational structure (conceptual model layer) is considered by focusing on relationships as well as dependencies. This can on the one hand leverage the customer relationship by offering additional services, while on the other hand, a need for adapting the business model might be identified based on increased information, data, and service orientation. The different abstraction layers in the OMiLAB Innovation Corner facilitate holistic considerations from multidisciplinary stakeholders. Additionally, digital devices are introduced and can be tested in the provided experimentation infrastructure (proof-of-concept layer) of the OMiLAB Innovation Corner.

To take into account different perspectives and shed light on the complexity of the digitization problem in digital business ecosystems, a combination of a bottom-up and a top-down approach was chosen. The approach is detailed in Sect. 18.3 and provides further insights on the description and foundation of the method. Furthermore, the method conceptualization including the meta-models is described. This sets the basis for the proof-of-concept experiment (see Sect. 18.4) that consists of the modelling method and a supporting physical model. Finally, an outlook is provided in a short conclusion in Sect. 18.5.

18.2 Method Description

The World Economic Forum report [7] states that the industry is transformed by technologies such as AI, autonomous vehicles, big data analytics and cloud, custom manufacturing and 3D printing, IoT and connected devices, robots and drones, and social media and platforms. These technologies have in common that they can drive new efficiencies, advanced customer experiences, and adapted business models. Agile and digital-savvy leadership, forward-looking skills, ecosystem thinking, data access and management, and technology infrastructure readiness are considered as key enabler for maximizing the return on digital investments. To establish competitive advantage, a combination of products and services can create a unique experience. Aspects such as personalization and access-based ownership models must be considered as well. Therefore, the disruption of existing businesses and the adaption of business models are required to survive the battleground of digital transformation and digitization within digital ecosystems.

Five operating/business models can be identified in the era of digital enterprises [7]. These business models are:

- Customer-centric—The major goal is to make customers' lives easier, and therefore, front office processes are focused.
- Extra frugal—This model concentrates on standardizing the organizational structure and creates a culture where fewer is better.
- Data-powered—The major focus is set on capabilities in the context of intelligence related to analytics and software.
- Skynet—The main objective for production is to increase productivity and flexibility by using machines.
- Open and liquid—Ecosystems are created, and a focus is set on the concept of sharing and collaboration.

The focus areas of those business models differ quite a lot, for instance, some are concentrating on a standardized organization for optimization and automations, while others tend to decentralize to empower people and enable collaboration and a sharing ecosystem. In general, digital transformation is expected to unlock value of more than $100 trillion not only for businesses but also for society [7].

To handle the complexity introduced by new business models and digital transformation, the OMiLAB Innovation Corner [6] has the potential to be a helpful consulting environment. It is an environment that elaborates on digitization in the light of new business models that follow a layer-based approach that ranges from business to conceptual and physical considerations. For this reason, we consider the proposed modelling method and especially the proof-of-concept experiment as a good starting point for further research and innovation relevant for digitization in industry.

To manage the complexity of the mentioned aspects, a hybrid approach was followed when designing the modelling method. The chosen combination of a bottom-up approach and a top-down approach has been tested out of a set of challenges. These range from a smart energy management ecosystem case, over standards and frameworks, to a pilot study within the context of the Horizon 2020 EU project "Change2Twin".

The foundation for this modelling method was laid by [3], where a bottom-up approach was applied to tackle the model-based application of artificial intelligence technologies within digital ecosystems. The growing demand for battery packs creates a need for improving their lifetime by battery management services. Therefore, a smart energy management ecosystem including a model-based prototype was developed. As the development of a self-ordering battery system is a quite specific use case, the goal of this modelling method is to leverage the meta-model shown in [3]. This is done by introducing more abstraction and therefore allowing a broader application domain for digitization problems.

While the mentioned bottom-up approach is based on a prototype, a top-down notion is provided by having a look at established reference frameworks such as the reference architecture model for Industry 4.0 (RAMI 4.0) [8]. This model suggests creating value based on information flows by focusing specifically on communication. This is done by introducing a layer model as well as standardization. The reference architecture model provides insights on what digitization means for companies and fosters worldwide interoperability. In particular, common standards are seen as prerequisite for digitized production including (a) communication structures such as networks and protocols, (b) guidelines for security and data protection, and (c) terminology and understanding.

RAMI 4.0, and specifically its three-dimensional reference architecture map, consists of several layers, life cycle value streams and hierarchy levels following a service-oriented architecture that serves as a foundation for a common understanding in Industry 4.0 by providing a multi-dimensional view. Therefore, the hierarchy of the factory is considered as well as the product lifecycle and the architecture layers. We assume that the presented architecture and specifically its components can serve as a starting point for the proposed modelling method. This is done to ensure that relevant considerations are captured, while at the same time, the complexity is reduced by introducing abstraction. Bridging the business and the physical world by keeping in mind various viewpoints seems to be an essential requirement for the modelling method.

Shedding light on aspects related to managing data and relationships makes the complexity of bridging physical and digital/business worlds even clearer. The role of different relationships in digital (business) ecosystems as shown in [1] creates a need for managing those by establishing a "global, digital economy with International Data Spaces (IDS), a secure, sovereign system of data exchange in which all participants can realize the full value of their data" [9]. The centerpiece of the data space idea is the connector that brings together all components and services in order to deliver value. IDS presents various white papers including criteria catalogues for the components. The IDS Association White Paper [10] focuses on the operational environment by considering, for example, aspects such as assets, business continuity, communication, security, compliance, monitoring, or access management. It provides a reference architecture consisting of business, functional, process, information, and system layer while at the same time focusing on security, certification, and governance perspectives [11]. Comparing this layer-based structure with the OMiLAB layer architecture presented in [6], a proof of concept within the OMiLAB Innovation Corner seems to be at the cutting edge.

Also, well-known members [12]—like Allianz, Audi, IBM, PWC, Rewe, SIN-TEF, TNO, Thyssenkrupp, and others—of the IDS clearly show the applicability for various industries and the importance in today's business world. In particular, as data and data exchange are cornerstones for digitization and digital (data-driven) business ecosystems, we consider the mentioned concepts as very important for the modelling method.

Based on the concepts found in reference architectures and frameworks, for example, RAMI 4.0 and IDS, the idea for a modelling method that guides digitization by transforming business environments into digital ecosystems emerged. As a result, the key concepts of [3, 8–10] were brought together to design the meta-model. This served as a foundation for the proof of concept, in Sect. 18.4, that shows the applicability of the abstract schema within an experimentation setup and established the foundation for further industrial investigations.

The introduction of abstraction and simplification fosters transparency, reusability, and understandability. To ensure that specificities of the domain are supported by expert knowledge, we propose that the modelling method is used by two actors with domain/expert knowledge. The first expert is responsible for the collection of requirements arising due to the contextual environment as well as for the description of the system under study. The second expert can provide recommendations for the selection of management units based on the gathered information. Thus, the modelling method serves as a platform that offers a playground for interoperability and interdisciplinary discussions based on information captured in models. This idea ensures that the domain experts can discuss and present their viewpoint in a simplistic way that is easy to understand by other stakeholders.

The high-level goal of the modelling method is to relate business requirements with physical world requirements. This is achieved by guiding the digitization process by instructions and through consulting capabilities. The idea is that based on a set of physical objects and/or a business process/model digitization, units can be identified. Therefore, we consider the following major steps in our prototype process. The first is the collection of data, which is realized by visual modelling, where the externalization of knowledge is conducted by humans so far. The second is monitoring of the status of candidate digitization units, which allows the following of status information. Based on the first two steps, suitable digitization units can be identified. The third step is continuous improvement and development required due to the fast development of digital devices on the market.

These steps are the foundation for the building of the meta-model. Therefore, the main concept of the meta-model and hence the centerpiece is selected to be the digitization unit. The selection of the digitization unit is highly influenced by the system under study and the environmental context. More specifically, the system under study is a physical object or a domain-specific digitization case. The abovementioned reference frameworks are currently not directly integrated in the modelling method. However, the design of the modelling method allows for the integration of a semantic lifting approach by being easily extendible in the context of introducing reference ontologies.

Summarizing, the modelling method focuses on simplification, abstraction, and transparent documentation to pave the way for improving the understandability and interdisciplinarity of different domain stakeholders. Accordingly, the complexity of digital transformation and specifically digitization problems can be reduced. The following section provides more details about the modelling method based on a description of the meta-model.

18.3   Method Conceptualization

The meta-models described in this section were created with CoChaCo [13], which is a tool that supports the creation and design of meta-models. The eponymous CoChaCo—Concept, Characteristic, and Connector—is a concept that allows the construction of a meta-model supported by Purpose and Functionality that depict the usage. The tool facilitates the meta-model creation in a framework, platform, and implementation-independent environment. The CoChaCo meta-modelling tool provides three major model types. Those are concept overview, concept pool, and procedure, which serve as a basic outline for the meta-model description section.

18.3.1   Concept Overview

A high-level meta-model was designed so that the focus is set on the characteristics of the concepts. The main concepts are displayed in Fig. 18.3, indicated by rectangles, while the major relationships are depicted by ellipses. All of the shown concepts have basic characteristics such as a name and a description attached. Furthermore, they are detailed with advanced characteristics shown in the concept pool.

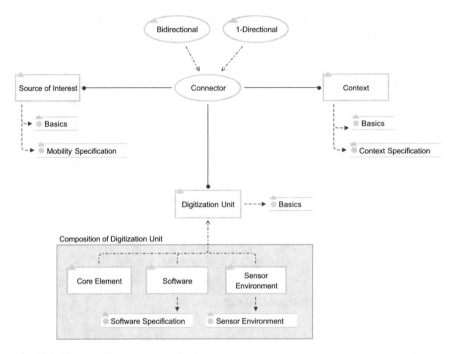

Fig. 18.3 Meta-model concept overview

As mentioned, the meta-model was designed by abstracting the meta-model shown in [3]. Therefore, the major concepts of the smart energy management system meta-model—such as an energy source, a management unit, a device, and a location/owner—are supported by introducing more abstraction. This resulted in three major concepts, which are the source of interest—also known as system under study—the context, and the digitization unit. The connector is seen as a center that connects the three major concepts. In particular, the selection of the digitization unit is highly influenced by both, the source of interest and the context.

The source of interest is characterized by having a tight relation to the business ecosystem. The major idea is to capture the varying characteristics of the system under study, which can consist of physical objects—in order to digitize the source of interest. This allows a new business model to be found or existing business models to be adapted so that they fit the complex requirements of digital business ecosystems. Remembering the smart energy/battery management sample described in [3], the source of interest could be an energy source, for instance. However, by introducing the concept of source of interest in our proposed modelling method, also, more complex problems related to (industrial) business challenges can be outlined. For example, digitizing the warehouse or raw material management can be described. In particular, the modelling method allows the transparent and easy understandable description of the digitization challenge. This is done by on the one hand allowing for a textual description as well as offering the possibility of collecting the requirements emerging based on the business case while on the other hand affecting the context and the digitization unit. In particular, the gathered business aspects might pose specific requirements on the digitization unit, for instance, the selection of particular sensors. The source of interest can have different characteristics related to mobility such as semi-mobile, mobile, and fixed. The exact source of interest addressed will have an influence when selecting the digitization unit, as some devices require a fixed power cable, while others can be operated with wireless power sources, for instance.

The context describes the external influences as well as the environment of the source of interest. Each physical object within a system under study must be seen as a component within an environment, as all objects are operated within a specific context, for instance, related to public laws or regulations. Therefore, the context can be detailed by different contextual specifications such as location, compliance, or owner. As the complexity of such environmental influences might be out of scope for this modelling language, the implementation with the open-source meta-modelling platform ADOxx [14] offers the possibility to outsource semantic lifting by means of ontologies. This is enabled by introducing a key-value pair consisting of context group and value. For example, a context can be specified by choosing a context group such as location and a specific value like Austria. Multiple context group and value pairs might be required to describe the contextual environment of the source of interest.

The digitization unit in the form of an edge device—such as an Arduino device, a Raspberry Pi, a mobile phone, or other microcomputers—is a composition of three key components. The first, the core element, describes the basic hardware. The second, the software component, describes possible operating systems or applications. In particular, close relationships and dependencies between hardware and software can be recognized, for example, most Arduinos are usually not operated with a Windows operating system. The third, the sensor environment, can be seen as an enlargement of the core hardware component that allows the introduction of further advanced functionalities, for example, enabled by software extensions. Specifically, currently available sensors range from cameras supporting image recognition, scales, or temperature sensors for monitoring to sound and visual systems allowing for detailed control. It could be recognized that the digitization unit is highly dependent on the source of interest and the context. Therefore, the clear and transparent description of the domain problem and related external influences is critical for the successful recommendation of a digitization unit.

Summarizing, this meta-model overview and the resulting modelling method should support the mapping of business requirements with physical requirements so that digitization is facilitated. The overall meta-model is geared to being flexible and generic enough so that the appropriate standard can be introduced by means of semantic lifting in order to serve various business models. Specifically, the platform [14] chosen for implementing the modelling method supports the creation of interfaces to other modelling objects by allowing the integration of standards. For instance, BPMN [15] models relevant for business process descriptions can serve as a foundation for further extension and description with attributes specifically required for digitization. On the one hand, this flexibility ensures that common standards are not changed, while on the other hand, interfaces enable the usage of BPMN concepts so that the business perspective is considered during digitization.

The OMiLAB Innovation Corner [6, 16] enables the combination of physical objects with creativity approaches so that businesses and related processes are supported with their domain-specific digital transformation challenges. The added value is the selection of a digitization unit based on the creation of a reference between the business process, the physical world, and the meta-model. This allows the tight integration of business requirements when modelling the context and the system under study. For instance, if a business requirement is that the business phone power bank is always loaded more than 10 percent, the compliance context can refine this context by describing the process of sending a low-battery warning. Such a scenario might involve some kind of warning system, either visual or sound based, which poses requirements on the digitization unit.

18.3.2   Concept Pool

The concept pool in Fig. 18.4 shows the major constructs of CoChaCo [13] in a hierarchical structure. Notice that not all potentially reasonable constructs could be captured within the concept pool, as this would have gone beyond the scope of this modelling method and unnecessarily complicate the presentation of providing a model-based digitization guide.

Most of the concepts were already outlined above; therefore, we would like to go into detail for the mobility specification only, which is detailing the source of interest by describing potential real-world samples. The mobility aspect can be specified by nomadic/semi-mobile, mobile, or fixed/stable. Selecting the nomadic characteristic can mean, for instance, that we are talking about pallets in a warehouse that are shifted from time to time. This specification might indicate that the digitization unit must be small and could be operated via a mobile battery. On the other side, when talking about fixed shelves in a warehouse, a digitization unit with a cable-based power source and a big screen providing an overview might be better.

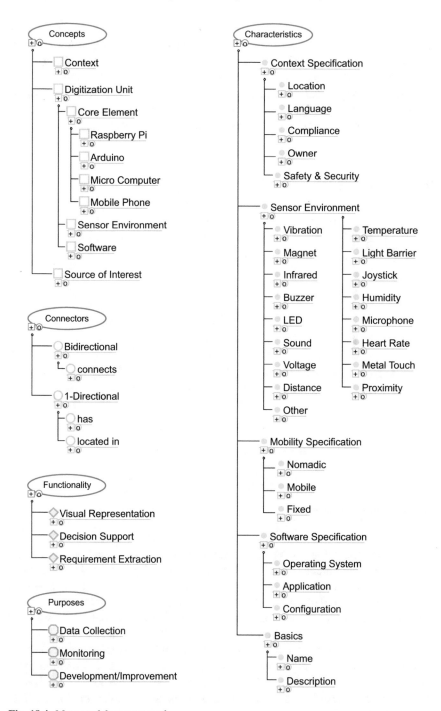

Fig. 18.4 Meta-model concept pool

As we assume that the source of interest is highly related to a domain-specific case such as the digitization of the raw material warehouse within a production company, we did not explicitly depict the requirements emerging from the business context here. Furthermore, only a sample set of characteristics is presented in the meta-model concept pool, as including all would have gone beyond the scope of the meta-model sample in Fig. 18.4. However, this kind of scope reduction should not influence the understandability of the basic idea behind the meta-model.

18.3.3 Procedure

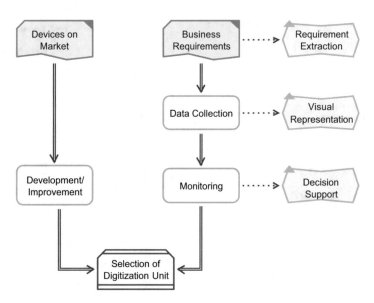

Fig. 18.5 Meta-model procedure

The procedure for the modelling method is quite generic and should mainly support the requirements mapping of business and physical world to facilitate digitization. Therefore, the procedure builds on the two key pillars shown in Fig. 18.5. These are data collection and monitoring and continuous improvement. External business requirements serve as a foundation for the data collection and provide the basis for the requirements extraction. To ease understandability, data collection is supported by visual representations and so-called notebooks, which describe modelling elements. These notebooks capture detailed information about the major concepts such as the source of interest, the context, or the digitization unit. Monitoring the aspects should ease the decision and pave the way for selecting a digitization unit. Furthermore, monitoring can indicate that the chosen digitization unit is not appropriate anymore. In this case, the devices on the market could provide external input by showing the actual status of the technology. As the development for devices is fast going, continuous improvement and development with respect to the selected digitization unit might result in exchanging the whole digitization unit or adapting components such as the software or the sensor environment, for instance.

As mentioned, we propose that two modelling actors work with the modelling method. Steps such as the data collection and the monitoring can be taken over by domain experts, while the actual selection of a digitization unit should be conducted in tight collaboration with a technical expert.

The following proof-of-concept section shows the journey from a physical object, respectively, a business process, to the selection of the digitization unit. This journey might be relatively easy when thinking about a smart energy management system that should simply reorder batteries when those are nearly empty. However, the complexity is highly increased when thinking about a production process with different materials and a set of requirements.

18.4 Proof of Concept

The proof of concept builds upon two main pillars, the modelling method and a physical experiment in the OMiLAB Innovation Corner using the Dig4Biz tool. The physical experiment serves as a playground for identifying the context and refining the source of interest, so that the findings can be used to specify the requirements for the digitization unit on the one hand and test the feasibility on the other hand. The material for the physical experiment—including documentation, videos, and a fast deployment package—is available open source online [5] and allows for accessing the experiment remote.

The major idea of the physical experiment is to provide a discussion platform that allows interdisciplinary discussions and eases the understanding of the digitization problem. The high-level domain for our physical experiment is about production processes, where a bunch of products is produced at once and afterward packaged in smaller portions. Examples would be paint production, convenience food production, or products from advanced biotech industry. As the real production of paint, food, or biotech products would go beyond the scope of a laboratory experiment, we decided to apply simplification and abstraction to develop an experiment setup that can be associated with the real production as the characteristics are similar. This results in a tea production scenario facilitating the identification of digitization challenges—three digitization challenges could be identified. Those are (1) the digitization of the production process, (2) the digitization of the raw material, and (3) the digitization of the product itself.

First, digitizing the production process can highly enhance efficiency and ensure continuous documentation while at the same time reducing manual documentation effort. To digitize the production process, the concept of timestamps was introduced that captures each production process step. The description of the source of interest, which is in this sample a shop floor, revealed that the machines are stable in fixed areas. The employees bring the material to the machines (for instance, a mixer or an oven). However, as the production facilities have currently no digital information attached, all the documentation must be handled manually, which is quite time-consuming and error prone. For this reason, the selection of a suitable digitization unit able to capture the timestamps should release the employees from this manual effort and improve the quality as well as the accuracy. To bind the information to a specific production, the order can be digitized, for example, by means of RFID technology. Therefore, we add a RFID tag to the order as the order production sheet must be controlled at each production stage anyway. Contextual considerations such as machines in a production hall with high humidity must be considered as well as legal obligations for production documentations and related standards.

Second, the digitization of the raw material seems to be critical to monitor the raw material status. A differentiation of three types of raw material [17]—ABC material—is used: (1) A material is characterized by low number and high value. (2) B material is characterized by medium amount and value. (3) C material is characterized by large amounts with low value. In the physical experiment, only B and C material was addressed so far. We focus on B material as C material is normally quite cheap and available in large amounts. For the tea production association tea bags, sugar, and milk are considered as B material. As digitizing the raw material directly could be considered as impossible, for instance, counting each crumb of sugar is simply not reasonable, the approach of digitizing the slot— where the raw material is stored—was chosen. The collection of timestamps when reducing the raw material allows continuous monitoring and facilitates production stops when charges of raw materials are considered to be problematic. Again, based on describing the scenario with the proposed modelling method, the suitable digitization unit for tackling the above-described challenge can be identified.

Third, digitizing the product itself might be important for both, customers to track their product and companies to monitor their production. The captured information can be further used for simulation and analysis such as evaluating the standard time from the raw material until the finished product leaves the company. The chosen digitization technology must allow for storing the information on the product packaging. At the same time, this information must be readable from any location and at any time. Further considerations such as easy usage are important for the customer experience.

The physical experiment architecture for tackling the digitization challenges is shown in Fig. 18.6. KPIs, data, and process models from the domain scenario serve as input to identify requirements and describe the source of interest and the context. A dashboard and simulation functionalities serve as a foundation for monitoring—supported by microservices offering database operations. On the bottom, physical devices and machines are described, extended by the digitization unit. Each layer of the experiment is supported by an expert—a method/modelling expert, a domain/business expert, and a technical expert.

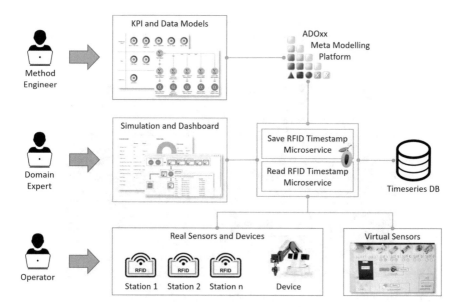

Fig. 18.6 OMiLAB Innovation Corner physical experiment architecture

The shop floor and the raw material warehouse of the experiment are shown in Fig. 18.7, where digitization units (microcontrollers with RFID readers) for capturing the timestamp information are already introduced. The physical experiment setup consists of a warehouse with silos and slots, a production area with filler and mixer, a laboratory, a final product labelling station, and an outbound warehouse.

The second pillar of the proof of concept, the modelling method, can be filled with the information resulting from the physical experiment. However, it provides not only the opportunity to describe the situation; additionally, the modelling method allows to identify requirements directly related to the business perspective. A specific feature allows using BPMN models, which can describe a real-world production process, as a foundation for extracting the tasks as requirements. This technique is also known as graph rewriting and realized by the ADOxx [14] script language AdoScript.

Figure 18.8 shows a code snippet containing the major procedure for the graph rewriting. The "dataInput" is a BPMN process file in BPMN DI format. The file is parsed, and all the tasks are extracted. The extracted tasks are directly mapped to a requirement of our proposed modelling method. The business requirement input can be triggered by the modeler. As shown in Fig. 18.9, the modeler can create a model of model type "Requirements Collection." Afterward, "Extras" and "Import Requirements" can be selected (Fig. 18.9, step 1). Choosing the path (Fig. 18.9, step 2) for the BPMN model of interest starts the creation of requirement objects based on the business tasks. The graph rewriting directly maps the BPMN tasks to the requirements (Fig. 18.9, step 3). The collection of requirements can afterward be extended by creating additional requirements not directly related to BPMN tasks or by specifying the imported requirements (Fig. 18.9, step 4) with the introduction of detailed descriptions.

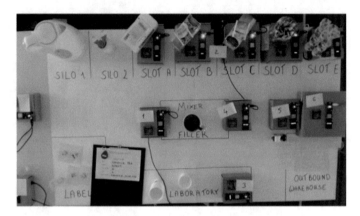

Fig. 18.7 Physical experiment setup in the OMiLAB Innovation Corner

```
29  □FOR sRow in:(dataInput) sep: "\n" {
30       SET taskNameKey:(search(sRow, "<task name=", 0))
31
32  □    IF (taskNameKey != -1) {
33            SET taskName:(token(sRow,1,"="))
34            SET taskName:(copy(taskName, 1, (LEN taskName)-2))
35            CC "Core" CREATE_OBJ modelid:(modelid) classid:(requirement) objname:(taskName)
36  □        IF (ecode != 0) {
37                CC "AdoScript" INFOBOX ("Requirement with name '" + taskName + "' already exists.")
38  ├        }
39            CC "Modeling" SET_OBJ_POS objid:(objid) x:(5cm) y:(yPos)
40            SET yPos:(yPos + 4cm)
41  ├    }
42  └}
```

Fig. 18.8 Code snippet for graph rewriting

Aside from the requirements collection models, an overview model type is also provided. This model type consists of the source of interest, one or more context elements, and the digitization unit. For the simple example shown in the middle of Fig. 18.10, we used one object of each class. Additionally, the notebooks of the objects are presented to provide further insights. In the example, the source of interest is a paint production factory. The major business process in this factory consists of four tasks—material collection, laboratory approval, filling, and outbound warehouse—which are also mapped to the requirements collection model shown in Fig. 18.9. The factory environment implies that the source of interest is fixed. The source of interest could be subdivided in smaller challenges, such as the digitization challenges presented above. For instance, an individual source of interest element for digitizing the raw material warehouse can be created. Compared to the factory, slots in a raw material warehouse must not necessarily be fixed with respect to the mobility characteristic. Therefore, wherever various characteristics seem to be relevant, a division of the major source of interest in finer grained objects is suggested.

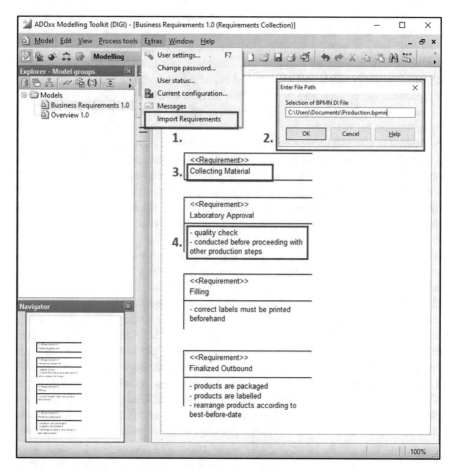

Fig. 18.9 Requirements import from business process model

With respect to the business context, domain standards can be captured for the source of interest. These standards may also have a tight interconnection with identified requirements. The basic requirements created from a BPMN process by means of graph rewriting can be connected with the source of interest. Technically, this is done by introducing the concept of model pointers, specifically "interrefs."

Those allow to refer from the attribute in the overview model directly to one or more objects in the requirements collection model. Prioritization is supported by introducing a rating of the referenced requirements. The location context in the sample is straightforward and therefore requires no further explanations. However, it is important to point out that all of the objects in the model are somehow interconnected and dependent on each other. For instance, the location context "Vienna" may create the need for specific standards and requirements posed on the source of interest by Austrian government regulations. Furthermore, specific digitization units might not be certified for use in relevant business settings. For this reason, we recommend that the identification of requirements, the description of the source of interest, and the collection of context related details are taken over by a domain expert, whereas the selection of the appropriate digitization unit is conducted in close collaboration between business and technical experts.

For the production process digitization sample, it was identified that RFID technology could be one potential solution to capture timestamp data that can be used for documentation. The original manual documentation process should be facilitated by the introduction of technological support. For this reason, the digitization unit must be capable of a RFID sensor module for our sample. Furthermore, existing databases—as mentioned currently filled with information manually—can be reused for capturing the timestamp data. This implies that the digitization unit must allow some kind of network connectivity mechanism for sending the data to the database. Assuming a stable network connection, the digitization device requires no hard disk, as all of the data should be stored in a database anyway. In addition to a simple database, also, a connection to a potentially existing ERP system might be reasonable. Due to the fixed mobility characteristic of the source of interest, different power sources ranging from mobile battery packs to a power cable are possible. To digitize the machine stations, a power cable might be more reasonable as those are fixed, and potential problems with wireless power sources must not be taken into account. Production workers might need some kind of visual confirmation that sending the data was working, as they are not familiar with capturing the production process data automatically. For our example, we assume that so far this was conducted only manually with sheet and paper. For this reason, having a small display connected to the device might be beneficial. Furthermore, the conditions in a production hall, such as dusty air, should be no problem for the digitization unit. The price performance ratio should be reasonable so that the initial investment for the digitization devices is manageable. As those are needed at several stations within the production hall and the warehouse, maintenance costs must also be considered and comparable to the benefits of digitization.

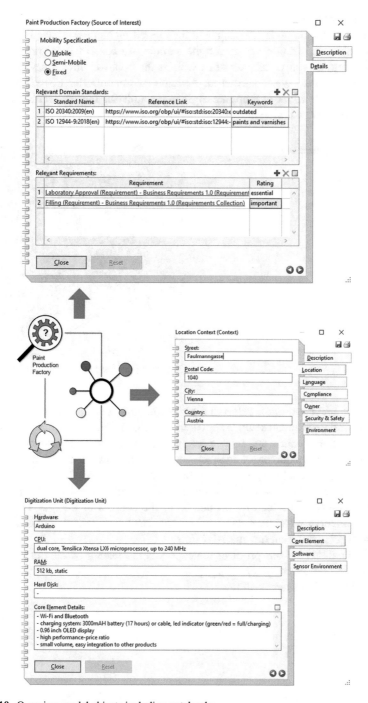

Fig. 18.10 Overview model objects including notebooks

Taking everything into account, a combination of the physical model, paving the way for a common understanding, and the modelling method allowed us to choose the suitable digitization device for the sample use case of paint production. By considering the source of interest as well as the context—involving, for instance, local regulations—we identified an Arduino microcontroller ESP32 and a NFC (RFID) module as an appropriate digitization unit for the production process as well as for the raw material.

Fig. 18.11 Digitization unit

Figure 18.11 shows the selected digitization unit. A sample overview model for the physical experiment setup is shown in Fig. 18.12. The main source of interest is the production scenario and related production processes. Those can be subdivided in more specific sources of interest—such as the raw material warehouse, the filler/mixer, the laboratory, and the outbound warehouse. All the sources of interest can be further detailed with one or more context elements posing requirements for the digitization units that are connected to the sources of interest. For instance, the raw material warehouse source of interest has five digitization units connected. Those digitize different raw material slots.

The final step of our proof of concept was the testing of the digitization unit within the physical experiment setup to identify any problems before testing the device in a real business setting.

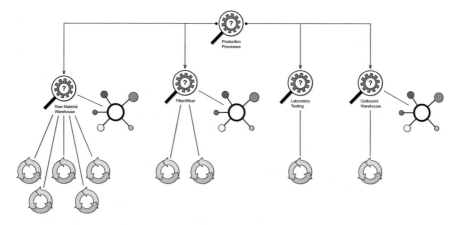

Fig. 18.12 Sample overview model for physical experiment setup

18.5   Conclusion

Digitization is popular in today's business ecosystems, in particular as digital transformation is expected to unlock incredible value for businesses as well as for society. However, digitization is not straightforward and introduces a lot of challenges. To handle the emerging complexity, the OMiLAB Innovation Corner was used as a consulting environment for testing the proposed model-based guidance approach toward more digitization in digital business ecosystems.

A hybrid approach was followed for establishing the modelling method and a modelling environment that describes and configures digitization scenarios such as the aforementioned production process. This resulted in the proposed modelling method prototype focusing on (a) the collection of requirements, (b) the analysis of the contextual environment, as well as (c) the monitoring by guiding the selection of an appropriate digitization device. The modelling method is highly supported by a physical OMiLAB Innovation Corner experiment that eases the understanding of the domain problem by serving as a discussion platform and playground for further studies. Furthermore, the experiment facilitates the selection of appropriate digitization units by taking into account potential physical issues as well as the requirements related to the business perspective.

Considerations for further research are based on the identification of patterns guiding digitization. These include but are not limited to production processes, manufacturing robotics, or mobile/driving devices in different environments. Beginning with the production process scenario, the physical experiment in combination with a model-based approach paves the way for shedding light on a specific digitization scenario from different perspectives. The physical experiment supports the description of a variety of aspects—ranging from sensors over networks to edge devices—that are potentially relevant for the description of digitization patterns.

Finally, the presented modelling method is a first prototype for guiding digitization in digital (business) ecosystems. It is planned to conduct further studies in order to improve and extend the modelling method. Currently, we are testing the applicability of the first modelling method prototype in a real-world production domain in the context of pilot studies for Change2Twin [4]. In its current version, two types of experts are needed to work with the modelling method—domain and technical experts. However, in the long run, we plan to optimize and automate the selection of the digitization unit based on the gathered information within the model to provide additional value. Although we believe that this extension will not completely supersede the technical expert, it should provide the foundation for better decision-making and continuous development to find the optimal digitization unit for any digital business ecosystem use case.

Another idea for further research is the integration of AI. This poses questions such as how the introduced concepts as well as the physical infrastructure need to change when new technologies are implemented. A good starting point for finding suitable innovation items could be the Change2Twin [4] marketplace.

Tool Download https://www.omilab.org/dig4biz

References

1. Benedict, M.: Modelling Ecosystems in Information Systems – A Typology Approach (2018)
2. Gosh, A., Chakraborty, D., Law, A.: Artificial intelligence in Internet of things. CAAI Trans. Intell. Technol. 3(4) (2018). https://doi.org/10.1049/trit.2018.1008
3. Sumereder, A.: Model-based application of artificial intelligence technologies in digital ecosystems. Masterthesis - University of Vienna (2020)
4. Change2Twin: Digital twin for every manufacturing SME! https://www.change2twin.eu/ (2021).
5. ADOxx.org: Change2Twin Development Space. https://adoxx.org/live/web/change2twin/downloads (2021)
6. Woitsch, R.: Industrial digital environments in action: The OMiLAB innovation corner. In: Grabis, J., Bork, D. (eds.) The practice of enterprise modeling. PoEM 2020. Lecture notes in business information processing, vol. 400. Springer, Cham (2020)
7. World Economic Forum: Digital Transformation Initiative. http://reports.weforum.org/digital-transformation/wp-content/blogs.dir/94/mp/files/pages/files/dti-executive-summary-20180510.pdf (2018). Accessed 4 Mar 2021
8. Plattform Industry 4.0: RAMI 4.0 – Ein Orientierungsrahmen für die Digitalisierung. Available: https://www.plattform-i40.de/PI40/Redaktion/DE/Downloads/Publikation/rami40-einfuehrung-2018.html (2018). Accessed 2 Mar 2021
9. IDS Association: International Data Spaces. Available: https://internationaldataspaces.org/ (2021). Accessed 4 Mar 2021
10. IDS Association: White paper – Criteria catalogue: Operational environments. International Data Spaces Association, Berlin, Germany. https://internationaldataspaces.org/publications/papers-studies/ (2020)
11. IDS Association: IDS-RAM. International Data Spaces Association, Berlin, Germany. Available: https://www.internationaldataspaces.org/wp-content/uploads/2019/03/IDS-Reference-Architecture-Model-3.0.pdf (2019). Accessed 4 Mar 2021

12. IDS Association: White Paper – IDSA Rule Book. International Data Spaces Association, Berlin, Germany. https://internationaldataspaces.org/publications/papers-studies/ (2020). Accessed 4 Mar 2021
13. OMiLAB NPO: MM-DSL toolkit: CoChaCo. https://www.omilab.org/activities/cochaco.html. Accessed 26 Feb 2021
14. ADOxx.org: Develop your own Modelling Toolkit with ADOxx. Available: https://www.adoxx.org/live/home (2021). Accessed 4 Mar 2021
15. OMG: BPMN 2.0. Available: https://www.omg.org/spec/BPMN/2.0/ (2010). Accessed 4 Mar 2021
16. OMiLAB Brochure: A Digital Innovation Environment. https://zenodo.org/record/3899990/files/OMiLAB%20Introduction%20Brochure_EN_FINAL.pdf?download=1. Accessed 7 June 2021
17. Springer Gabler: ABC-Analyse. Available: https://wirtschaftslexikon.gabler.de/definition/abc-analyse-28775 (2021). Accessed 6 Mar 2021

Chapter 19
Generating ROS Codes from User-Level Workflow in PRINTEPS

Takeshi Morita and Takahira Yamaguchi

Abstract To reduce the cost of developing integrated intelligent applications where multiple robots, agents, and sensors cooperate to realize multiple tasks by integrating heterogeneous intelligence, we have been developing a platform named PRINTEPS (PRactical INTElligent aPplicationS). Since PRINTEPS provides a user-friendly workflow editor and a generator based on ROS (Robot Operating System) and SOA (Service-Oriented Architecture), users who do not know robots and AI techniques will be able to execute ROS codes generated from user-level workflows. We propose the generator based on a ROS-based workflow schema. We describe how we model ROS elements such as services, publishers, and subscribers with the proposed schema and generate ROS codes from the workflows. We also evaluate the proposed schema and generator by applying it to practical applications.

Keywords Code generator · User-centric AI · Unified AI · ROS · Workflow

19.1 Introduction

While AI and service robot applications are very popular in many domains, they should be more interactive and harmonious with end users (domain experts). Although there are several interactive AI and service robot applications, many of these applications focus on a single task by a single robot or agent. It is still difficult to develop integrated intelligent applications where multiple robots, agents, and sensors cooperate to realize multiple tasks by integrating heterogeneous intelligence such as knowledge-based reasoning, image sensing, spoken dialogue, and motion

T. Morita (✉)
College of Science and Engineering, Aoyama Gakuin University, Sagamihara-shi, Kanagawa, Japan
e-mail: morita@it.aoyama.ac.jp

T. Yamaguchi
Faculty of Science and Technology, Keio University, Yokohama-shi, Kanagawa, Japan
e-mail: yamaguti@ae.keio.ac.jp

management. Additionally, it is difficult for domain experts who do not know robots and AI techniques to implement such applications. To develop such harmonious and integrated AI applications, we need agile AI platforms for not only AI system engineers but end users who are not familiar with programming.

The agile AI platforms should have the following two facilities: One facility is to integrate elemental intelligent systems, such as knowledge-based reasoning, speech dialog processing, image sensing, and intelligent planning for manipulation and motion. The other facility is automatic transformation from knowledge represented in natural language to programming codes, such as Python codes that can run over ROS (Robot Operating System) [8].

To solve these issues, we have been developing an integrated intelligent application development platform named PRINTEPS (PRactical INTElligent aPplicationS) [10]. Since PRINTEPS provides a user-friendly workflow editor and a generator based on ROS and SOA (Service-Oriented Architecture) [4], users who do not know robots and AI techniques will be able to execute ROS codes generated from user-level workflows.

We propose the generator based on a ROS-based workflow schema. We will describe how we model ROS elements such as services, publishers, and subscribers with the proposed schema and generate ROS codes from the workflows. We also evaluate the proposed schema and generator by applying it to a practical robot cafe [6, 7] and teaching assistant robot [7] applications.

19.2   Method Description

The primary motivation behind the creation of PRINTEPS was the lack of sufficient platforms and methodologies to support developing integrated intelligent applications for end users. To achieve that, we have designed the architecture for the integrated intelligent applications. Also, we have developed a user-friendly workflow editor and a generator based on ROS and SOA. This section presents the architecture, workflow editor, and generator of PRINTEPS.

19.2.1   The Architecture of PRINTEPS

Figure 19.1 shows the architecture of PRINTEPS. The modules in PRINTEPS are fully compliant with the ROS publisher, subscriber, service client, and message. PRINTEPS mainly consists of the multi knowledge-based editor, the information state, and the spoken dialogue system.

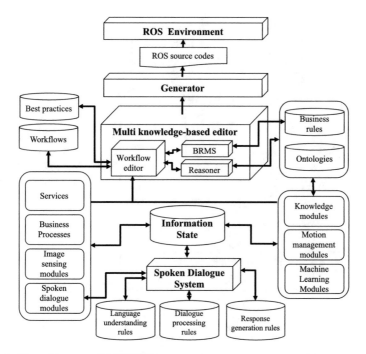

Fig. 19.1 The architecture of PRINTEPS

The multi knowledge-based editor is provided for end users to develop integrated intelligent applications easily by combining software modules from PRINTEPS. It consists of a workflow editor, a Business Rule Management System (BRMS) [1], and a reasoner. It refers to best practices, workflows, business rules, and ontologies. The elements of workflows are services, business processes, knowledge modules, image sensing modules, spoken dialogue modules, motion management modules, and machine learning modules.

Information State (IS) in PRINTEPS is a database for sharing data among the multi knowledge-based editor, the spoken dialogue system, and the modules. We use mongodb_store,[1] which is a MongoDB-based storage and analysis for data from a ROS system, as IS. In PRINTEPS, each module stores data to IS and refers data from IS. The data format in PRINTEPS is the format of messages in ROS. In addition, knowledge logs, dialogue logs, facial expression/gazing/posture/motion logs, and environment logs obtained by humans and machines' multimodal interaction are stored in IS. They become input for batch and online machine learning. They are used for creating machine learning modules.

The spoken dialogue system consists of five modules (speech recognition, language understanding, dialogue management, response generation, speech synthesis). It refers to the language understanding, the dialogue processing, and the response generation rules.

---

[1] http://wiki.ros.org/mongodb_store

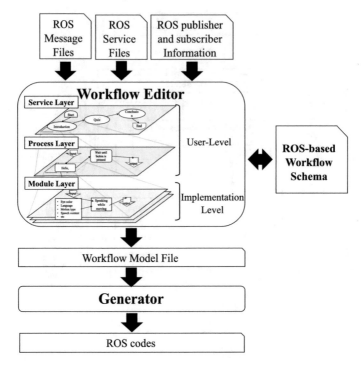

Fig. 19.2 Overview of the workflow editor and generator

19.2.2 Workflow Editor

We have developed a workflow editor based on the ROS and the SOA. Figure 19.2 shows the overview of the workflow editor and the generator. The workflow editor has service, process, and module layers. End users can create user-level workflows in the service and process layers. In contrast, developers can create workflows with the implementation level in the module layers.

There are two types of connectors in the workflow editor. One is processing flow and the other is data flow. Basically, one component is connected to the other component by only one processing flow connector. If there are two or more inputs in a component, one of them is connected to the output of a component by a processing flow connector, and the others are connected to outputs of components by data flow connectors.

The workflow editor also has three types of components: services, processes, and modules. The service is a function with the roughest grain size and is composed only of processes defined as business processes. The process plays a function-like role in which it compiles multiple processes and modules. The module is a primitive function, and it corresponds to basic modules provided by the workflow editor (e.g., variable, constant, loop, branch, etc.), the ROS publisher, subscriber, service client, or message. The Message modules are used for type conversion when the values of specific fields in a composite data type are connected to the entries of other modules.

Users can register ROS message files, service files, and publisher or subscriber information as modules in the workflow editor. Workflows in the service layers only consist of the services. Workflows in the process layers consist of the processes and the basic modules. Workflows in the module layers consist of processes and the modules.

When users connect one of the outputs of a component to another of the inputs of a component, the workflow editor automatically checks the types of the input and the output based on ROS message type. If they are not matched, they cannot be connected.

Based on the ROS-based workflow schema, the workflow editor exports a workflow model file named "workflow.json" encoded as JavaScript Object Notation (JSON) format.

19.2.3 Generator

The generator generates a source file in Python from the workflow.json file. The source file can be executed on the ROS environment.

Algorithm 1 shows an overview of generating ROS codes in Python from workflow.json. First, the generator analyzes components and connectors information in the workflow (Line 1 in Algorithm 1). Then, the generator gets the start component in the workflow and generates the ROS codes corresponding to the component (Lines 2 and 3 in Algorithm 1). After that, by referring to components and connectors information, the generator will continue to get the next component and generate ROS codes corresponding to each component until the next component cannot be obtained (Lines 4 to 24 in Algorithm 1).

In the next section, we describe the details of the ROS-based workflow schema.

19.3 Method Conceptualization

This section presents the metamodel in PRINTEPS that includes the constructs about projects, modules, and workflows and their graphical representations. Since the workflow editor in PRINTEPS has been developed as a web application, we selected JSON as the description format for the metamodel. To define the schema of JSON, we employ JSON Schema, which is a schema language that enables JSON validation. Also, we have implemented a prototype workflow editor in PRINTEPS based on ADOxx.

Algorithm 1 Overview of generating ROS codes from workflow.json

---
Input: workflow.json
Output: ROS codes in Python
 1: $AnalyzeWorkflows(workflow.json)$
 2: Let $cmpt = GetStartBasicModule()$
 3: $GenerateBasicModuleSourceCodes(cmpt)$
 4: **while** $hasNextComponent(cmpt)$ **do**
 5:    $cmpt = GetNextComponent(cmpt)$
 6:    **if** $isService(cmpt)$ **then**
 7:       $GenerateServiceSourceCodes(cmpt)$
 8:    **else if** $isProcess(cmpt)$ **then**
 9:       $GenerateProcessSourceCodes(cmpt)$
10:    **else if** $isBasicModule(cmpt)$ **then**
11:       $GenerateBasicModuleSourceCodes(cmpt)$
12:    **else if** $isROSServiceModule(cmpt)$ **then**
13:       $GenerateROSServiceSourceCodes(cmpt)$
14:    **else if** $isROSPublisherModule(cmpt)$ **then**
15:       $GenerateROSPublisherSourceCodes(cmpt)$
16:    **else if** $isROSSubscriberModule(cmpt)$ **then**
17:       $GenerateROSSubscriberSourceCodes(cmpt)$
18:    **else if** $isROSMessageModule(cmpt)$ **then**
19:       $GenerateROSMessageSourceCodes(cmpt)$
20:    **end if**
21: **end while**

19.3.1 Metamodel in PRINTEPS

We have implemented a prototype workflow editor in PRINTEPS based on ADOxx [2].[2]

The model types of the workflow editor in PRINTEPS are PRINTEPS Project, PRINTEPS Module, and PRINTEPS Workflow.

The PRINTEPS Project model type defines metadata about workflows. This model type contains ProjectInfo class that has name, description, created, and creator attributes.

The PRINTEPS Module model type defines components referred to by the workflow elements. This model type contains PRINTEPSService, PRINTEPSProcess, ROSService, ROSPublisher, ROSSubscriber, and ROSMessage classes.

The PRINTEPS Workflow model type defines compositions of instances of services and processes including instances of the modules. The classes and relation classes in this model are shown in Fig. 19.3.

The fundamental components and their graphical representations in the workflow editor are shown in Table 19.1.

---

[2] https://austria.omilab.org/psm/content/printeps/info

- Classes
    - PRINTEPSServiceElement
    - PRINTEPSProcessElement
    - ROSServiceElement
    - ROSSubscriberElement
    - ROSPublisherElement
    - ROSMessageElement
    - Constant
        - NumberConstant
        - StringConstant
        - BooleanConstant
    - Variable
        - NumberVariable
        - NumberVariableOutOnly
        - StringVariable
        - StringVariableOutOnly
        - BooleanVariable
        - BooleanVariableOutOnly

- Classes
    - SleepElement
    - IfElement
    - LoopElement
    - OneOperationElement
    - ForkElement
    - MergeElement
    - ThreadCreationElement
    - CheckElement
    - SkipElement
    - Quiz3Element
    - StartElement
    - EndElement
    - InputElement
    - OutputElement
- Relation classes
    - FlowConnector
    - DataConnector

Fig. 19.3 The classes and relation classes in the PRINTEPS Workflow model type

19.3.2 Overview of ROS-Based Workflow Schema

The workflow editor in PRINTEPS exports workflows as a workflow.json file that is encoded as JSON based on the ROS-based workflow schema. Although currently we only have developed the generator that can generate ROS source file in Python, generators can be developed to generate source codes in various programming languages and environments, such as ROS2 [5] in the future.

The workflow schema consists of info, components, and workflows. We define the workflow schema with JSON Schema [9], which is a schema language that enables JSON validation.

Listing 19.1 shows the overview of the workflow schema. Line 5 in Listing 19.1 shows the **info** part as shown in Listing 19.2, Line 6 in Listing 19.1 shows **components** part as shown in Listing 19.3, and Line 7 in Listing 19.1 shows **workflows** part of the workflow schema as shown in Listing 19.5, respectively. In the following sections, we describe the essential points of the workflow schema.

19.3.3 Info Part of the Workflow Schema

The **info** part, as shown in Listing 19.2, contains metadata about a project of the workflow editor. A project in the workflow editor contains several workflows. The properties in the info part are **name, description, created,** and **creator**. These properties are referenced by the user when selecting a project to edit in the workflow editor.

Table 19.1 The fundamental components and their graphical representations in the workflow editor

Category	Class	Graphical representation
Connector	FlowConnector	
	DataConnector	
Components	PRINTEPSServiceElement	PRINTEPS Service
	PRINTEPSProcessElement	PRINTEPS Process
	ROSPublisherElement	ROS Publisher
	ROSSubscriberElement	ROS Subscriber
	ROSServiceElement	ROS Service
	ROSMessageElement	ROS Message
Basic control statement	IfElement	If
Data-processing operations	NumberVariable	Number Variable
	StringVariable	String Variable
Others	StartElement	Start
	EndElement	End
	InputElement	Input
	OutputElement	Output

Listing 19.1 Overview of the workflow schema

```
1 {
2   "$schema": "http://json−schema.org/draft−07/schema#",
3   "type": "object",
4   "properties": {
5     "$ref": "info.json#/info",
6     "$ref": "components.json#/components",
7     "$ref": "workflows.json#/workflows"
8   }
9 }
```

Listing 19.2 Info part of the workflow schema (info.json)

```
1 {
2   "info": { "type": "object",
3     "properties": {
4       "name": {"type": "string"}, "description": {"type": "string"},
5       "created": { "type": "string" }, "creator": { "type": "string" }
6     } }
7 }
```

The **name** property stores the project name, which is displayed on the top screen of the workflow editor. The **description** property stores the description of the project. The **created** property stores the date and time when the project was created. The **creator** property stores the name of the creator who created the project.

19.3.4 Components Part of the Workflow Schema

Listing 19.3 shows the **components** part of the workflow schema. The **components** part mainly defines **id, info, shape, inputs, outputs, ros_srv**, and **ros_topic** properties of each component. These definitions are referred to by instances of components in **workflows** part of the workflow schema described in the next section.

Each component has a **shape** property which defines the type of components such as service, process, ROS service, ROS subscriber, and ROS publisher. Since each component has one or more inputs and outputs, it also has inputs and outputs properties. Each input and output mainly has **name, type**, and **kind** properties as shown in Listing 19.4. The **type** property represents the data type of input or output which is defined by .srv or .msg file in ROS. The **kind** property represents the kind of connector. There are two types of connectors in the workflow editor. One is the processing flow connector, and the other is data flow connector. Only one instance of a component is allowed to connect to the other instance of a component by only one processing flow connector. If there are two or more inputs in an instance of a component, one of them is connected to the output of an instance of a component by a processing flow connector, and the others are connected to outputs of instances of components by data flow connectors. In this case, since different inputs can be connected with processing or data flow connector, the kind of each input is **dynamic_flow** that represents the processing or data flow connector. Since some of the components have ROS-specific properties such as ROS service name and ROS topic name, we prepared optional properties (**ros_srv** and **ros_topic**).

The **type** and **kind** properties in inputs and outputs are used in the workflow editor to determine the connectivity between each instance of a component.

Listing 19.3 **Components** part of the workflow schema (components.json)

```
1 {
2  "components": { "type": "object",
3   "patternProperties": {
4    "^.*$": { "type": "object",
5     "properties": {
6      "id": { "type": "string" },
7      "info": {"type":"object",
8       "properties":{"name":{"type":"string"}}},
9      "shape": { "type": "string" },
10     "inputs": {"type":"array","$ref":"io_items.json#/items"},
11     "outputs": {"type":"array","$ref":"io_items.json#/items"},
12     "ros_srv": { "type": "object",
13      "properties": {
14       "service_name": { "type": "string" },
15       "service_package": { "type": "string" },
16       "service_type": { "type": "string" }
17      }
18     },
19     "ros_topic": { "type": "object",
20      "properties": {
21          "topic_name": { "type": "string" },
22          "msg_package": { "type": "string" }
23      }
24    } } } } }
25 }
```

Listing 19.4 IO items in the **components** part of workflow schema (io_items.json)

```
1 {
2  "items": { "type": "object",
3   "properties": {
4    "name": { "type": "string" },
5    "type": { "type": "string" }, "kind": { "type": "string" }
6   }
7  }
8 }
```

19.3.5 Workflows Part of the Workflow Schema

Listing 19.5 shows the **workflows** part of the workflow schema. The **workflows** part defines compositions of instances of services and processes. Each service consists of instances of processes. Each process consists of instances of processes and modules. Each component has inputs and outputs, and they are connected with processing or data flow connectors. In this schema, a workflow represents an instance of service or process which consists of instances of components and connectors. Therefore,

Listing 19.5 **Workflows** part of the workflow schema (workflows.json)

```
 1 {
 2   "workflows": { "type": "array",
 3     "items": { "type": "object",
 4       "properties": {
 5         "id": { "type": "string" },
 6         "info": { "type": "object",
 7           "properties": {
 8             "name": { "type": "string" }, "kind": { "type": "string" }
 9           },
10         "components": { "type": "object",
11           "patternProperties": {
12             "^.*$": { "type": "object",
13               "properties": {
14                 "id": { "type": "string" },
15                 "kind": { "type": "string" },
16                 "name": { "type": "string" },
17                 "position": { "type": "string",
18                   "properties": {
19                     "x": { "type": "number" }, "y": { "type": "number" }
20                   }
21                 },
22                 "data": { "type": "object",
23                   "properties": { "value": {
24                     "anyOf": [ {"type":"string"},{"type":"number"} ]
25                   }
26                 } } } }
27             },
28         "connectors": { "type": "array",
29           "items": { "type": "object",
30             "properties": {
31               "source": {"type":"string"}, "target": {"type":"string"},
32               "kind": { "type": "string" }
33             }
34           } } } } } } }
35 }
```

each workflow has properties for metadata (**id**, **name**, **kind**, etc.), **components**, and **connectors**.

The **components** property has a set of instances of components. Each instance of component mainly has **id**, **kind**, **name**, **position**, and **data** properties. The **kind** property represents the type of an instance of component. The type refers to the corresponding **id** as shown in Listing 19.3 that is defined in the **components** part of the workflow schema. The **position** properties represent the coordinates of an instance of component in the workflow editor. The **data** property represents the value of basic modules such as constant number and string basic modules.

The **connectors** property has a set of connectors. Each connector mainly has **source**, **target**, and **kind** properties. The **source** and **target** properties represent a source and a target port of instance of component, respectively. The source or target port is one of the inputs or outputs of the instance of a component. The value of source or target property is an array of strings. The array includes the ID of the instance of the component and the IO (input or output) ID of the instance of the component. The IO ID is automatically generated by the workflow editor. The **kind** property represents a kind of connectors described in Sect. 19.3.4.

19.3.6 Example Workflows for TurtleSim

This section describes example workflows for TurtleSim created by the prototype workflow editor in PRINTEPS. TurtleSim is a simple simulator made for teaching ROS concepts.[3]

To facilitate understanding of ROS-based workflow models, we created minimum workflows including a service, a process, a ROS service client module, and constant number basic modules. The ROS service client module is *TeleportAbsolute* that teleports a turtle to specified coordinates with an angle of the turtle. The inputs of *TeleportAbsolute* are x, y, and theta. The output of *TeleportAbsolute* is nothing, but only the movement of the turtle to the specified position with an angle in the simulator.

Here, we created workflows to move a turtle to the coordinates (10, 10) with angle 0. The blue edges represent processing flow, and the green edges represent data flow connectors in Figs. 19.4 and 19.5, respectively. The left side of Fig. 19.4 shows *TurtleSim* service in the service layer. The right side of Fig. 19.4 shows *Move to (10, 10)* process in the process layer. The left side of Fig. 19.5 shows the *TeleportAbsolute* ROS service client module and the constant number basic modules as inputs of the *TeleportAbsolute* module in the module layer. *TurtleSim* service is defined in the root service. The *Move to (10, 10)* process is defined in the *TurtleSim* service. The *TurtleSim* module is defined in the *Move to (10, 10)* process. The right side of Fig. 19.5 shows the screenshot of the TurtleSim after the turtle has moved to the coordinates (10, 10).

Listing 19.6 shows an example of JSON codes of the components part about *TeleportAbsolute* module based on the workflow schema as shown in Listing 19.3. Listing 19.8 shows an example of JSON codes of **workflows** part about *Move to (10, 10)* process based on the workflow schema as shown in Listing 19.5.

Note that some of the IDs such as **PRINTEPSService1** and **PRINTEPSProcess1** in the listings are simplified for understanding. In practice, random strings are generated so that IDs do not overlap. In addition, **ros_srv**, **service_name**, **service_package**, and **service_type** properties are added as ROS-specific properties in Listing 19.6. These properties are necessary to generate ROS codes by generator.

---

[3] http://wiki.ros.org/turtlesim

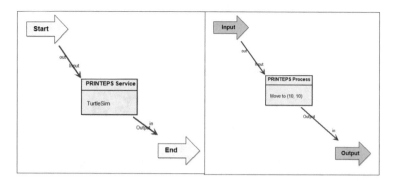

Fig. 19.4 *TurtleSim* service in the service layer (left side) and *Move to (10, 10)* process in the process layer (right side)

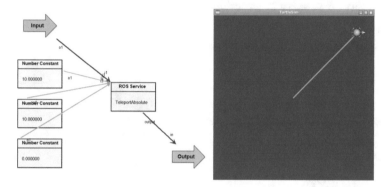

Fig. 19.5 *TeleportAbsolute* module in the module layer (left side) and the screenshot of the TurtleSim (right side)

Listing 19.7 shows a part of the generated ROS codes about *Move to (10, 10)* process. The generator generates services and processes as classes in Python. Line 11 in Listing 19.7, **/turtle1/teleport_absolute** ROS service call codes are generated based on Listing 19.8. Line 6 in Listing 19.7, constant number basic modules are generated as class attributes of the PRINTEPSProcess1 class. Methods corresponding to inputs and outputs in the processing flow are generated in the service or process class (Line 10 in Listing 19.7).

19.4 Proof of Concept

To evaluate the concept of PRINTEPS, we have developed the workflow editor in PRINTEPS and also developed several practical applications where many robots and sensors work together to perform multiple tasks using the workflow editor. In this section, we evaluate the proposed schema and generator from the workflows of robot cafe [7] and teaching assistant robot [6]. Please refer to these papers for details of each application.

Listing 19.6 Example of JSON codes of the **components** part about *TeleportAbsolute* module

```
1 "components": {
2   "rosservice./turtle1/teleport_absolute": {
3     "id": "rosservice./turtle1/teleport_absolute",
4     "inputs": [
5       {"type":"float32","kind":"dynamic_flow","name":"x"},
6       {"type":"float32","kind":"dynamic_flow","name":"y"},
7       {"type":"float32","kind":"dynamic_flow","name":"theta"}
8     ],
9     "outputs": [
10      {"type":"None","kind":"dynamic_flow","name":"output"}
11    ],
12    "shape": "rosservice",
13    "ros_srv": {
14      "service_name": "/turtle1/teleport_absolute",
15      "service_package": "turtlesim",
16      "service_type": "TeleportAbsolute"
17    },
18    "info": { "name": "TeleportAbsolute", ... }
19  }
20 }
```

Listing 19.7 Part of the generated ROS codes about *Move to (10, 10)* process

```
1 import turtlesim.srv
2 import rospy
3
4 class PRINTEPSProcess1:
5   display_name='Move_to_(10,_10)'
6   const1=10; const2=10; const3=0
7
8   def __init__(self):
9 # ...
10  def execute_i1(self,inputs):
11    r0007=(rospy.ServiceProxy('/turtle1/teleport_absolute',
         turtlesim.srv.TeleportAbsolute))(self.const1,self.const2,self.const3)
12 # ...
```

19.4.1 Practical Applications of PRINTEPS

The overview of the robot cafe application is described as follows.

The robot cafe was developed and opened during a university festival on Oct. 7 and 8, 2017. Figure 19.6 shows the setup environment of the robot cafe. It shows the layout of the robot cafe in which the entrance, the service counter, two tables to seat four people each, two tables to seat two people each, plastic bottle dispensers, a cup dispenser, a plastic bottle shelf, a trash can, a cart, arm-type robot Jaco2, concierge robot Pepper, and serving robot HSR are depicted.

Listing 19.8 Example JSON codes of the **workflows** part about *Move to (10, 10) process*

```
 1 "workflows": [
 2  ...
 3  {
 4    "id": "PRINTEPSService1",
 5    "info": { "kind": "service", "name": "TurtleSim", ... },
 6    "components": {...}, "connectors": [...]
 7  },
 8  {
 9    "id": "PRINTEPSProcess1",
10    "info": { "kind": "process", "name": "Move to (10, 10)", ... },
11    "components": {
12      "I": {
13        "id": "I", "kind": "input", "name": "Input",
14        "position": { "x": 341, "y": 93 },
15      },
16      "O": {
17        "id": "O", "kind": "output", "name": "Output",
18        "position": { "x": 717, "y": 537 },
19      },
20      "ROSServiceModule1": {
21        "id": "ROSServiceModule1",
22        "kind": "rosservice./turtle1/teleport_absolute",
23        "name": "TeleportAbsolute",
24        "position": { "x": 461, "y": 369 },
25      },
26      "NumberModule1": {
27        "id": "NumberModule1",
28        "kind": "const.double",
29        "name": "Number",
30        "position": { "x": 49, "y": 225 },
31        "data": { "value": "10" }
32      },
33      "NumberModule2": {...},
34      "NumberModule3": {...}
35    },
36    "connectors": [
37      { "source": [ "ROSServiceModule1", "o1" ],
38        "target": [ "O", "i1" ],
39        "kind": "processing_flow", },
40      { "source": [ "I", "o1" ],
41        "target": [ "ROSServiceModule1", "i1" ],
42        "kind": "processing_flow", },
43      { "source": [ "NumberModule1", "o1" ],
44        "target": [ "ROSServiceModule1", "i1" ],
45        "kind": "data_flow", }, ...
46    ],
47  }
48 ]
```

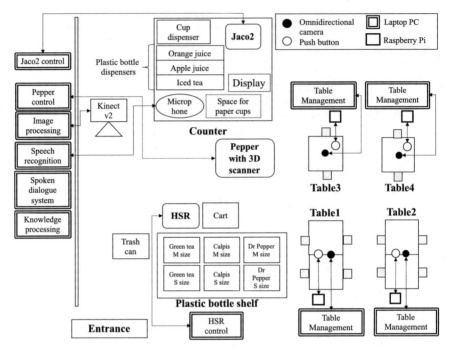

Fig. 19.6 Setup environment of the robot cafe

Figure 19.7 shows an overview of the robot cafe. The workflows in the robot cafe consist of customer detection, greeting, order taking, serving drinks at the counter, guiding customer to a table, serving drinks at the table, and cleaning up empty plastic bottles or cups.

Fig. 19.7 An overview of the robot cafe

Fig. 19.8 The counter of the robot cafe with Pepper and Jaco2

Figure 19.8 shows the counter of the robot cafe with concierge robot Pepper and arm-type robot Jaco2. Kinect v2 was positioned in front of the entrance mainly for detecting and counting incoming guests. A microphone was placed on the counter for taking orders using speech recognition. First, when customers entered the robot cafe, Kinect v2 detected the entrance to the robot cafe, and Pepper greeted the customers. Then, Pepper asked the customers whether to choose either counter service or table service. If the customers had chosen the counter service, the customers could order orange juice, apple juice, iced tea, or mixed juice. If the customers had chosen the table service, the customers could order Dr. Pepper, Calpis, or green tea.

Three plastic bottle dispensers and a cup dispenser were placed on the counter to serve orange juice, apple juice, iced tea, and mixed juice. Jaco2 took out a paper cup from the cup dispenser according to the order, placed it below the corresponding plastic bottle dispenser, and pulled the lever for a duration corresponding to the size of the order to serve the drink to the guests. If mixed juice was ordered, equal quantities of both orange juice and apple juice were poured into the cup.

After taking the orders, Pepper guided customers to a table available. Pepper had a 3D scanner to detect its own position during movement. In addition, Pepper could move while avoiding obstacles. Each table had an omnidirectional camera to detect people using the table to check if the table was unoccupied.

Figure 19.9 shows the plastic bottle shelf and the trash can of the robot cafe with serving robot HSR, respectively. HSR took plastic bottle(s) from the plastic bottle shelf according to the orders and used the cart to carry the bottles when more than one bottle was ordered. Otherwise, it directly brought the bottle(s) to the table. HSR also had a 3D scanner to detect its own position during movement. S-size and M-size plastic bottles of Dr. Pepper, Calpis, and green tea were placed on the bottle shelf as shown in Fig. 19.9.

Tables were also equipped with push buttons to call HSR so that the robot would come to the table and collect empty plastic bottles. Guests were supposed to hand the empty bottles to HSR.

Fig. 19.9 HSR with the
plastic bottle shelf and the
trash can at the robot cafe

19.4.2   Evaluation

Table 19.2 shows the statistical analysis results of each workflow, the lines of code
generated from each workflow, and each generation time. Table 19.3 shows the
details of module types for ROS in the workflows.

From Tables 19.2 and 19.3, the proposed schema can represent various modules
including ROS services, publishers, subscribers, and messages. We also confirmed
that the generation times from the workflows to the ROS codes are practical response
time (within 1 second).

As a result, we confirmed that real-world applications of the proposed schema
and the performance of the generator were enough for the development of integrated
intelligent applications.

Table 19.2 Evaluation
results

	Robot cafe	TA robot
# service types	6	9
# process types	20	46
# module types	145	143
# service instances	6	9
# process instances	41	239
# module instances	169	263
# connectors	170	476
Lines of code	1,147	3,168
Generation time (secs)	0.13	0.17

Table 19.3 The details of module types for ROS in the each workflow

	Robot cafe	TA robot
# ROS services	80	113
# ROS publishers	6	0
# ROS subscribers	11	2
# ROS messages	24	15

19.4.3   Discussion

Currently, the decomposition from the service to the process layer and the process to module layer is manually defined by developers. In other words, we have not been able to dynamically change the execution of services and processes according to the environment and available robots. Also, the decomposition of services and processes depends on the processes and modules prepared by the developers.

Services and processes are defined from both top-down and bottom-up perspectives. First, the user defines the services required for the target application in the service layer and then implements the services by combining existing processes. However, there are cases where the service cannot be realized by the combination of existing processes. Therefore, we have to develop the necessary modules and processes from the bottom up. By doing these iterations, services and processes are defined.

In the future, we would like to extend the workflow editor in PRINTEPS for dynamic decomposition from the service to the process layer.

19.5   Conclusion

To reduce the cost to develop integrated intelligent applications where multiple robots, agents, and sensors cooperate to realize multiple tasks by integrating heterogeneous intelligence, we have developed a platform named PRINTEPS based on ROS and SOA. PRINTEPS will provide a user-friendly workflow editor for end users.

We proposed a generator based on a ROS-based workflow schema. We have described how we model ROS elements such as services, publishers, and subscribers with the proposed schema and generate ROS codes from the user-level workflows. We have also evaluated the proposed schema and generator by applying it to practical robot cafe and TA robot applications. Through the evaluation, we confirmed the performance and utility of the proposed schema and the generator.

As mentioned in Sect. 19.4.3, the decomposition from the service layer to the process layer is currently done manually by the developer. Therefore, we have not been able to dynamically change the execution of services and processes according to the environment and available robots. In our future work, we would like to extend the workflow editor in PRINTEPS using action ontologies which define atomic and compound actions for robots and sensors. In our previous work [3], we have proposed an intelligent humanoid robot with Japanese Wikipedia Ontology and Robot Action Ontology. In this paper, aligning Robot Action Ontology with Japanese Wikipedia Ontology enables NAO, which is a humanoid robot, to perform related actions to dialogue topics. We extend this Robot Action Ontology to define the relationship between abstract actions and their corresponding concrete actions in the action ontology. The abstract actions are mapped to processes in PRINTEPS, and the concrete actions can be automatically selected and executed according to the environment and available robots.

Furthermore, we plan to develop modules for various types of robots and sensors, implement practical applications, and verify the usefulness of this platform.

Acknowledgments This study was supported by the project of "A Framework PRINTEPS to Develop Practical Artificial Intelligence," (JPMJCR14E3) the Core Research for Evolutional Science and Technology (CREST) of the Japan Science and Technology Agency (JST).

We thank Prof. Dr. Dimitris Karagiannis, Dr. Michael Walch, and Mr. Patrik Burzynski for the discussion and implementation advice of the prototype workflow editor in PRINTEPS based on ADOxx.

Tool Download   https://www.omilab.org/printeps

References

1. Boyer, J., Mili, H.: Agile Business Rule Development: Process, Architecture, and JRules Examples. Springer, Berlin (2011). https://doi.org/10.1007/978-3-642-19041-4
2. Fill, H.G., Karagiannis, D.: On the conceptualisation of modelling methods using the adoxx meta modelling platform. Enterprise Modelling and Information Systems Architectures (EMISAJ). Int. J. Concept. Model. **8**(1), 4–25 (2013)
3. Kobayashi, S., Tamagawa, S., Morita, T., Yamaguchi, T.: Intelligent humanoid robot with Japanese wikipedia ontology and robot action ontology. In: Proceedings of the 6th International Conference on Human-Robot Interaction, pp. 417–424. Association for Computing Machinery, New York (2011). https://doi.org/10.1145/1957656.1957811
4. Krafzig, D., Banke, K., Slama, D.: Enterprise SOA: Service-Oriented Architecture Best Practices (The Coad Series). Prentice Hall PTR, Upper Saddle River (2004)
5. Maruyama, Y., Kato, S., Azumi, T.: Exploring the performance of ros2. In: Proceedings of the 13th International Conference on Embedded Software, EMSOFT '16, pp. 5:1–5:10. ACM, New York (2016). http://doi.acm.org/10.1145/2968478.2968502
6. Morita, T., Kashiwagi, N., Yorozu, A., Suzuki, H., Yamaguchi, T.: Implementing multi-robot cafe by printeps with service quality dimensions. Proc. Comput. Sci. **126**, 1954–1963 (2018). https://doi.org/10.1016/j.procs.2018.08.035. http://www.sciencedirect.com/science/article/pii/S1877050918313139. Knowledge-Based and Intelligent Information & Engineering Systems: Proceedings of the 22nd International Conference, KES-2018, Belgrade, Serbia
7. Morita, T., Nakamura, K., Komatsushiro, H., Yamaguchi, T.: Printeps: an integrated intelligent application development platform based on stream reasoning and ROS. Rev. Socionetw. Strategies **12**(1), 71–96 (2018). https://doi.org/10.1007/s12626-018-0020-y
8. Quigley, M., Conley, K., Gerkey, B.P., Faust, J., Foote, T., Leibs, J., Wheeler, R., Ng, A.Y.: ROS: an open-source robot operating system. In: ICRA Workshop on Open Source Software (2009)

9. Wright, A., Andrews, H.: JSON schema: a media type for describing JSON documents. Internet-Draft draft-handrews-json-schema-01, Internet Engineering Task Force (2018). https://datatracker.ietf.org/doc/html/draft-handrews-json-schema-01. Work in Progress
10. Yamaguchi, T.: A platform printeps to develop practical intelligent applications. In: Adjunct Proceedings of the 2015 ACM International Joint Conference on Pervasive and Ubiquitous Computing and Proceedings of the 2015 ACM International Symposium on Wearable Computers, UbiComp/ISWC'15 Adjunct, pp. 919–920. ACM, New York (2015). https://doi.org/10.1145/2800835.2815383

Chapter 20
ECAVI: An Assistant for Reasoning About Actions and Change with the Event Calculus

Nena Basina, Theodore Patkos, and Dimitris Plexousakis

Abstract Reasoning about actions, change, and causality constitutes an important field of research in artificial intelligence. Several formal action languages have been proposed, addressing the need to qualify change and facilitate (commonsense) reasoning in dynamic settings. The Event Calculus (EC), in particular, permits the representation of causal and narrative information. Although action languages are well established as a means to model dynamic domains, their adoption by knowledge engineers is often hindered by modelling errors and steep learning curves. It has been argued that visual modelling tools could assist knowledge engineers in their modelling tasks and improve the quality of the resulting models by obtaining a better understanding of the semantics. We present ECAVI (Event Calculus Analysis and VIsualisation), a domain-independent visual modelling tool for designing dynamic domains in the Event Calculus. ECAVI is mainly addressed to inexperienced modellers, aiming to acquaint them with the features of the Event Calculus and to guide them during the process of designing their dynamic problem settings.

Keywords Visual modelling · Event Calculus · Answer Set Programming · Model-driven engineering

20.1 Introduction

Reasoning about actions, change, and causality has been an important challenge from the early days of artificial intelligence (AI). Action languages are well-established logical theories for reasoning about the dynamics of changing worlds, aiming at "formally characterising the relationship between the knowledge, perception and the action of autonomous agents" [26]. One of the most prominent, widely

N. Basina · T. Patkos · D. Plexousakis (✉)
Institute of Computer Science, FORTH, Heraklion, Greece
e-mail: basina@ics.forth.gr; patkos@ics.forth.gr; dp@ics.forth.gr

applied action languages is the Event Calculus (EC) [13, 18], which incorporates useful features for representing causal and narrative information and has been applied in domains as diverse as high-level robot cognition, complex event detection [27], and others. EC implementations can be encoded in different languages, such as Answer Set Programming (ASP), a form of knowledge representation and reasoning paradigm oriented toward solving complex combinatorial search problems. ASP programs define a set of logical rules, whose models, called answer sets, correspond to solutions to a reasoning task, such as progression or planning. However, both ASP and the EC can be quite difficult to axiomatize by the non-expert, and novice practitioners find it hard to properly model a domain of interest.

Visualizations generally help knowledge engineers understand better the ramifications of their modelling decisions [19]. Fill and Karagiannis [6] investigated the role of visualization in the conceptualization of modelling methods and commented on the fact that "*the absence of a graphical representation during modelling will inevitably force the engineer to develop an adequate visualization for the elements of the syntax of the modelling language, by taking into account the corresponding semantics.*" This realization is also enforced by many popular efforts in visualization, such as the introduction of UML [7] in the context of software engineering or Protégé [21] as a visual tool for ontology editing.

To the best of our knowledge, there does not exist any tool that focuses on the visualization of Event Calculus axiomatizations. Visic et al. [28] introduced the only relevant point of reference for our case, a domain-specific language (DSL) that considers the "modelling method engineering" as the application domain and allows the method engineer to focus on the conceptual building blocks of a modelling method rather than on a metamodelling platform's technical specificity.

In the context of Event Calculus, we argue that a visual representation of the various axiom types may help knowledge engineers understand the semantics of the different axiom types, thereby simplifying the learning process for inexperienced modellers and reducing the number of modelling mistakes. We propose ECAVI (Event Calculus Analysis and VIsualisation), a domain-independent modelling tool which offers a visual language for designing dynamic domains in the Event Calculus, based on the syntax and semantics of the Answer Set Programming formal language, while assisting the user in the process of knowledge engineering, through the ADOxx Metamodelling Platform and with the help of a state-of-the-art reasoner, Clingo.

The ECAVI modelling tool relies on the following contributions:

- It offers a visual language for designing causal dynamic domains, supporting phenomena such as context-dependent event occurrences, context-dependent effects of events, and concurrency. Next versions will further extend the language with more features, such as non-determinism, indirect effects of events, and others.
- The tight coupling of the visual domain representation with two powerful logical formalisms, namely, the Event Calculus and Answer Set Programming (ASP),

which enable the knowledge engineer to perform complex reasoning tasks, such as progression, observation explanation, etc.

- It assists the user in the process of knowledge engineering, reducing the possibility for syntactical errors. More importantly, our current work concerns also the raising of warnings and exceptions whenever logical fallacies are detected, which may lead to contradicting or counter-intuitive behavior, e.g., when the same property may become true and false at the same time.
- Adoption of a pedagogical approach in the process of designing causal domains, aiming to help non-experts, such as students, to learn the basics of how a conceptual model can be translated and executed through the logic programming paradigm.

Even though ECAVI is still a work in progress, with several features that have been planned but not implemented yet, we argue that the tool will be useful to a diverse audience of knowledge modellers as a teaching assistant for the fundamental concepts of reasoning about actions and change and also as a way to visualize full ASP programs.

In order to display a comprehensive overview, we organize the rest of the chapter as follows: Sect. 20.2 explains the context of the method development—i.e., the project background, an overview of related works so far, and an analysis of the requirements that the project needs to meet. Section 20.3 presents design decisions and specification of the notation, syntax, and semantic requirements. Section 20.4 highlights the proof of concept with a use case and a heuristic evaluation. The paper ends in Sect. 20.5 with concluding remarks and future work mentions.

20.2 Method Description

ECAVI comprises three main parts that define our tool and are essential to our methodology and implementation: Event Calculus, Answer Set Programming, and the ADOxx Metamodelling Platform.

20.2.1 Event Calculus and Answer Set Programming (ASP)

Commonsense reasoning is essential to intelligent behavior and thought. It allows us to fill in the blanks, to reconstruct missing portions of a scenario, to figure out what happened, and to predict what might happen next. Reasoning about the world requires a large amount of knowledge about the world and the ability to use that knowledge. Commonsense reasoning can be used to make computers more human-aware, easier to use, and more flexible. Although it comes to us naturally and appears to be simple, it is actually a complex process [20].

The Event Calculus is a narrative-based many-sorted first-order language for reasoning about action and change, which explicitly represents temporal knowledge, enabling reasoning about the effects of a narrative of events along a timeline. It also relies on a non-monotonic treatment of events, in the sense that by default there are no unexpected effects or event occurrences.

Several fundamental entities must be represented: objects in the world and agents such as people and animals, properties in the world that change over time which we call fluents and such is the location of an object, events or actions that occur in the world such as the action of a person moving an object, and at last we need to represent time.

Formally, a sort $\mathcal{E}$ of *events* indicates changes in the environment, a sort $\mathcal{F}$ of *fluents* denotes time-varying properties, and a sort $\mathcal{T}$ of *timepoints* is used to implement a linear time structure. The calculus applies the *principle of inertia* for fluents, in order to solve the frame problem, which captures the property that things tend to persist over time unless affected by some event.

A set of predicates is defined to express which fluents hold when ($holdsAt \subseteq \mathcal{F} \times \mathcal{T}$), which events happen ($happens \subseteq \mathcal{E} \times \mathcal{T}$), which their effects are ($initiates$, $terminates, releases \subseteq \mathcal{E} \times \mathcal{F} \times \mathcal{T}$), and whether a fluent is subject to the law of inertia or released from it ($releasedAt \subseteq \mathcal{F} \times \mathcal{T}$).[1] An event may occur or happen at a timepoint, and a fluent has truth value at a timepoint or over a timepoint interval (true or false). The occurrence of an event may affect the state of a fluent. We have commonsense knowledge about the effects of events on fluents, specifically about events that initiate fluents and events that terminate fluents.

The commonsense notions of persistence and causality are captured in a set of *domain-independent* axioms, referred to as $\mathcal{DEC}$ [20], that express the influence of events on fluents and the enforcement of inertia for the $holdsAt$ and $releasedAt$ predicates. In brief, $\mathcal{DEC}$ states that a fluent that is not released from inertia has a particular truth value at a particular time if at the previous timepoint, either it was given a cause to take that value or it already had that value. For example, $initiates(e, f, t)$ means that if action e happens at timepoint t, it gives cause for fluent f to be true at timepoint $t + 1$.

In addition to domain-independent axioms, a particular domain axiomatization requires also axioms that describe the commonsense domain of interest, observations of world properties at various times, and a narrative of known world events. The role of the ECAVI tool is to assist knowledge engineers in designing Event Calculus domain axiomatizations, without requiring them to master the complexities of logic programming.

Satisfiability and logic programming-based implementations of Event Calculus dialects have been proposed over the years. Recently, progress in generalizing the definition of stable model semantics [5] used in ASP has opened the way for the

---

[1] In the sequel, variables, starting with a upper-case letter, are implicitly universally quantified, unless otherwise stated. Predicates and constants start with a lower-case letter.

reformulation of Event Calculus axiomatizations into logic programs that can be executed with ASP solvers [14].

Answer Set Programming (ASP) is a form of knowledge representation and reasoning paradigm oriented toward solving complex combinatorial search problems. A domain is represented as a set of logical rules, whose models, called answer sets, correspond to solutions to a reasoning task, such as progression or planning. ASP enables default reasoning, which is required in commonsense reasoning. The syntax of answer set programs derives from the Prolog language, and the semantics is defined by the stable model semantics introduced by Gelfond and Lifschitz [9, 16], where a conclusion is inferred only if there is explicit evidence to support it.

An answer set program consists of a set of rules of the form:

$$\alpha : -\beta.$$

which represents that α, the head of the rule, is true if β, the body of the rule, is true. Here is an answer set program:

```
p.
r :- p, not q.
```

The first rule p. is called a *fact*. It has an empty body and is written without the : - (if) connective. The symbol , indicates conjunction ($\wedge$). The token not refers to negation as failure and is different from classical negation ($\neg$). The expression not q represents that q is not found to be true.

We can perform automated reasoning on this program by placing it in a file example.lp and running the answer set grounder and solver clingo on the file. The Clingo reasoner is a combination of the answer set grounder gringo and the answer set solver clasp, offering more control over the grounding and solving processes. ECAVI implements a translation of Event Calculus theories into ASP rules, which are then executed by clingo.[2]

20.2.2   Related Work

As the main components of ECAVI are the Event Calculus and the ADOxx platform, and the tool is targeted toward the integration of those two components in order to implement a visualization tool, we studied in more detail other works related to ours. Other visualization tools have been made for many purposes, and they have pointed out the advantages of visualization. In addition, extensive work with Answer Set Programming has pointed out the capabilities of the language.

---

[2] https://potassco.org/, last visit 03.28.2021

There exists a variety of modelling toolkits implemented with the ADOxx Metamodelling Platform. Most of those modelling method projects are available on the OMiLAB website and have been extensively documented in this book and the previous edition [10]. A notable related work has been made by Choe and Lee [2] introducing a newly proposed process algebra (δ-calculus) that deals with changes and movements in time and space. They consider δ-calculus as one of the most suitable methods to model IoT and develop a tool for visualizing and testing the feasibility of their method, using the ADOxx Metamodelling Platform. Although focusing on a different domain, their approach presents similarities to ours: their tool consists of a modeler and a verifier for testing the corresponding models, relying also on the AdoScript language to program the detailed logics of the underlying procedures. They further incorporate a simulator to produce diagrams of the execution paths.

Visualization techniques are used as part of model-driven engineering (MDE) to visualize the code, the problem domain, and the models used to describe the domain. Morgan et al. [19] introduced a *platform-independent* and extensible modelling language, VizDSL, which allows non-IT experts to describe, model, and create interactive visualizations, quickly and easily. VizDSL is based on the Interaction Flow Modeling Language (IFML) for creating highly interactive visualization. It can be used to model, share, and implement interactive visualization based on model-driven engineering principles.

Dogmus et al. [3] presented an interactive educational tool for artificial intelligence (AI) planning for robotics. ReACT! enables students to describe robots' actions and change in dynamic domains via interactive user interface without first having to know about the syntactic and semantic details of the underlying formalism. They also can solve hybrid planning problems using state-of-the-art reasoners for hands-on applications of cognitive robotics without having to know about their input/output language or usage. The teaching of AI planning in robotics class for students from various departments and with different backgrounds can be a very challenging and time-consuming work. The job of the tool is to guide the students toward the representation of dynamic domains generically and the solving of planning problems using various planners/reasoners, without having to know the particular specifics.

SeaLion is an Integrated Development Environment (IDE) for Answer Set Programming (ASP) [22]. It is developed as part of an ongoing research project on methods and methodologies for developing answer set programs. It is designed as an Eclipse plugin, providing useful and intuitive features for ASP, and targets both experts and software developers new to ASP, but with familiarity with support tools as used in procedural and object-oriented programming. The goal is to fully support the languages of the state-of-the-art solvers Clasp and DLV, as opposed with other IDEs that support only a single solver. The IDE is in an alpha version that already implements important core functionality. The editor provides syntax highlighting, syntax checks, error reporting, error highlighting, and automatic generation of a program outline. There is functionality to manage external tools such as answer set solvers and to define arbitrary pipes between them, as needed when using separate grounders and solvers. The visualization functionality of SeaLion is itself represented in an Eclipse plugin, called Kara [12].

For the implementation of ECAVI, we studied the techniques used by the mentioned tools. The ECAVI tool distinguishes from those by offering the contributions described in Sect. 20.1.

20.2.3   Requirement Analysis

The process, as well as the outcome, of knowledge engineering can benefit by following certain guidelines and good practices, especially in complex cases, such as the domains that action languages are focusing on, which are dynamic and incorporate perplex causal relations. The ECAVI tool intends to facilitate this process, by offering a smooth introduction to the underlying formalisms for the non-expert user.

According to Mueller [20], any method for automated commonsense reasoning must incorporate five main key aspects. We incorporate these aspects in ECAVI with the use of the Event Calculus syntax and semantics and by separating the design into four sub-models (Fig. 20.2).

Our aim is for this tool to be used as an assistant for teaching the fundamental concepts of reasoning about actions and change. For this purpose, at this point of the tool's development, we focus on a target group of novice knowledge engineers and students with little or no knowledge of the Event Calculus formalism. Siau and Loo [24] have highlighted the challenges faced by students who learn modelling of any type, including not only inexperienced students but also experienced students whose prior knowledge differs and interferes with the learning process.

We must first distinguish each group of users we focus on. We separate them into four sub-groups:

1. Users with some knowledge and a little experience in logical programming (e.g., Prolog) but no previous knowledge in Event Calculus.
2. Users with no knowledge in logical programming but with programming background (e.g., knowledge of C, C++, Java, etc.)
3. Users with no programming knowledge whatsoever but with some experience in modelling (e.g., people who have worked with other modelling tools implemented on ADOxx such as the Business Process Management tool, ADONIS).
4. Users with no programming knowledge neither any modelling experience.

Then we identify our tool's requirements according to the needs of those users.

On Table 20.1, we pinpoint the needs for our target group of users. Notice that, in some cases, a certain target group does not necessarily have a certain need. For example, a user that has previous experience with other modelling tools made on the ADOxx platform (e.g., ADONIS) may not need tooltips that show how to make the first model.

Table 20.1 Requirements specified for each distinct group of users in our target group

	User Group 1	User Group 2	User Group 3	User Group 4
Walk-through wizard/tooltips to help make the first steps into the tool making the first model	X	X		X
Tooltips that explain what each object of the design represents	X	X	X	X
Help to become acquainted with specific features of the language (e.g., delayed effect axioms)		X	X	X
Assistance in the process of building an axiom, avoiding syntactical errors	X	X	X	X
Build ASP programs without needing to know how the answer set solver works			X	X

We also want to help the users that already know how Event Calculus works (e.g., knowledge engineers) visualize their programs. Those users, however, will need the support of further features from our tool such as non-determinism, indirect effects of events, and others. The need for our tool to support those users as well is considered part of our future work.

In addition, for the knowledge engineer that wants to interoperate with different teams in the same project, quickly communicating the high-level behavior of a component without delving into the code details (by exchanging visual representation of the model) can be a key aspect in promoting productivity.

20.3 Method Conceptualization

Following the proposed framework by Karagiannis and Kühn [11], we realize the modelling language for our tool. We define the conceptual aspects of the implementation of our modelling language (namely, the Event Calculus in our case), and then we move to the realization of the Event Calculus metamodel with ADOxx.

A model represents a partial and simplified view of a system, so, the creation of multiple models is usually necessary to better represent and understand the system under study. Models make the project planning more effective and efficient while providing a better view of the system. The concepts of system, model, metamodel, and their relations are the essential concepts of model-driven engineering (MDE) [25]. MDE focuses on the models, rather than the code, using them as primary engineering artifacts [1]. ECAVI takes a model-based approach, where the code is generated directly from the models, in order to meet integration and interoperability requirements in the context of MDE.

20.3.1   *Implementation of the Modelling Language*

In ECAVI, we rely on the ASP syntax and semantics, which implement Event Calculus theories. As for the visual notation deployed to model the key aspects of the formal languages, we developed a set of visual cues shown in Fig. 20.1.

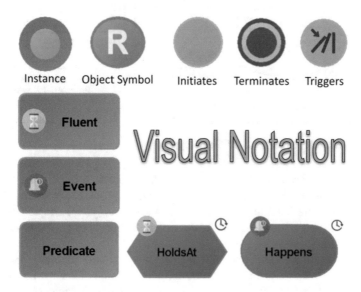

Fig. 20.1   Graphical notation of ECAVI

20.3.1.1   Modelling Procedure

To accommodate the modelling process, we follow a common practice in knowledge engineering for dynamic domains, which breaks down the modelling tasks into four sub-models:

- The *Domain Object* model, which specifies all *Object Symbols* (or Roles) and the *Instances* (or Constants) that populate our domain.
- The *Fluent and Event* model, which specifies all dynamic aspects of our domain, in the form of *fluents*, *events* , and other user-defined *predicates*. Together with the Domain Object model, this part defines the *signature* (or *alphabet*) of our domain axiomatization.

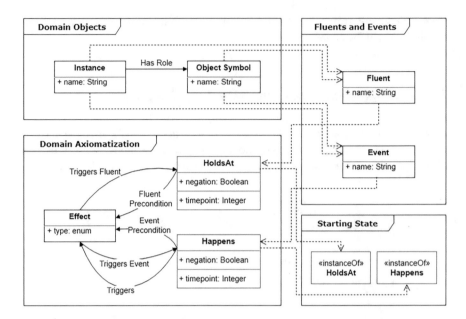

Fig. 20.2 Class diagram for the ECAVI model types

- The *Domain Axiomatization* model, which axiomatizes the dynamics of our domain. This is the main part of the modelling process, supporting the user in defining effect axioms (*Initiates, Terminates, Triggers*), coupled with pre-conditions and effects defined in the previous models, e.g., fluent and event expressions.
- Finally, the *Starting State* model, which defines the initial state of a domain and the narrative of events that happen at various timepoints. This is used as input to the **Clingo** solver, to find answer sets satisfying the domain dynamics.

Figure 20.2 provides a diagram of the model types and their semantic inter-connections, achieved via the InterRef functionality. With the help of Event Calculus, we can represent commonsense knowledge and scenarios and use the knowledge to reason about the scenarios (Erik Mueller [20]).

20.3.2   Translation into ASP

The axiom shown in Fig. 20.3 when translated into ASP composes the following:
```
happens (turnRed(tl_cars),T+1)  :-
     not holdsAt(isRed(tl_cars),T),
     holdsAt(waitingP(PERSON2),T),
     happens(newPedestrian(PERSON1),T),
     PERSON1!=PERSON2.
```

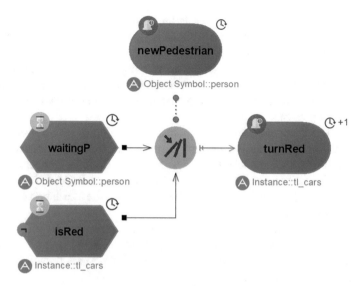

Fig. 20.3 Triggering axiom with two fluent preconditions

Meaning:

At a certain timepoint T, if a new pedestrian (PERSON1) arrives at the traffic light (tl_cars) for the purpose of crossing to the other side of the road, and the light is not red and there is already another pedestrian waiting (PERSON2), then the traffic light will turn red at the next timepoint T+1.

The effects of events may have preconditions that define if the event will have its intended effect (qualification):

- A **fluent precondition** is a requirement that must be satisfied for an event to have an effect. We express the fluent preconditions in the form of HoldsAt.
- An **action precondition** is a requirement that must be satisfied for the occurrence of an event. We express the fluent preconditions in the form of Happens.

For simplicity, we assume that there is only one traffic light in this case with two states: When the light is green, the cars can move through and the pedestrians have to wait, and when the light is red, the cars will have to stop and the pedestrians can cross the road.

In ASP, it is a common practice for predicates and constants to start with a lower-case letter and for variables to start with an upper-case letter. In our example, *tl_cars* is a constant that has already been defined with the role of a traffic light. *PERSON1* and *PERSON2* are variables of the type person that will each be mapped to an already defined constant of a person when the resulting answer sets are produced by the reasoner. Moreover, *T* is a variable that represents a timepoint which can equal to an integer. In this example, there are two fluents, *isRed* and *waitingP*, and two events: *turnRed* and *newPedestrian*.

In order to achieve the correct translation of the models, we export them into XML format (a feature supported by ADOxx), and then an intermediate Java program performs the required analysis on the XML exported file where for each complex object it finds all the relations of this object (incoming and outgoing), translates them according to the ASP syntax, and writes the corresponding ASP rules and axioms into the file that compiles the final ASP program that the Clingo reasoner is going to run.

The InterRef functionality enables us to make mappings between objects that belong in different models. For example, each instance of the HoldsAt class (in Domain Axiomatization model) is linked with a fluent from the Fluents and Events Model. These kinds of links are essential for the translation into ASP. If any essential InterRef is missing, then our program cannot move on to the translation of the XML extract into ASP code.

For better visualization, the preconditions are shown before the effect, and the triggering event is shown above the effect and the triggered event/fluent on the effect's right side. This order and the connectors (arrows) are drawn this way to better represent the flow of time.

20.3.3 Meta-reasoning and Integrity Checks

The basic idea of ASP is to find solutions to a problem, in the form of answer sets (usually stable models) of a logic program, which consists of rules and constraints that define properties of the solutions. The problem is solved by computing stable models using answer set solvers like $clasp$ [8]. Simple reasoning over answer sets is frequently supported by ASP systems, but more specialized reasoning tasks require more processing and are not easily done. In the previous years, there have been some works focused on the job of meta-reasoning on answer sets [4, 23].

The adoption of the logic programming paradigm offers certain leverage to the knowledge engineer, such as the ability to prove properties or to easily find optimal solutions, yet the process of detecting and ironing out logical errors is often cumbersome. This is due to the declarative nature of program execution, which does not follow a procedural execution, but instead relies on logical dependencies among rules in the encoding.

We aim to implement some extensive meta-reasoning into our tool that will help the more experienced users run and visualize their programs better, but at this point of ECAVI's development, we focus on implementing simple meta-reasoning tasks and integrity constraints that are designed for the purpose of helping the user create full and syntactically correct programs.

AdoScript, the macro language of ADOxx, is designed for the purpose of providing the metamodeller with significant extension possibilities with low programming effort. We make use of AdoScript for implementing a number of features that make the user's work with building axioms easier and also enable us to support a number of integrity checks.

In ECAVI, we implement simple but fundamental checks for syntactical errors with the help of AdoScript at design time before the run of the Clingo reasoner. In more detail:

- **An instance must always have at least one role** (object symbol). For this purpose, the Java programs check the Domain Object Model for whether an Instance isn't mapped to any Object Symbol.
- **Whatever the type of an Effect (Initiates, Terminates, or Triggers), there must always be an event that triggers this effect.** For this purpose, we developed a script in AdoScript that automatically generates the triggering event for an Effect.
- **An effect, with the type of Initiates or Terminates, requires a fluent to be triggered.** So it must always have an outgoing relation to a fluent. **And if an effect is of type Triggers, it must always have an outgoing relation to an event to be triggered.** Similar with the triggering event, a script is developed for the auto-generation of the corresponding objects.
- **In order for an ASP program to run on the Clingo reasoner, the starting state of the world of the designed domain has to be defined.** At the start of the script that implements all the main functionality of the ADOxx External Coupling with Java and Clingo, we check whether the script was called from a Starting State Model. This model has to be designed before we can move on to the translation into ASP.

Preconditions are not necessary for an effect. However, effects often have one or more preconditions. The user can generate a new precondition for an effect using a new menu option of the effect class. With this process, we point the user to the right way of modelling an axiom, minimizing as well this type of syntactical errors.

After the user clicks the "Run" option and chooses which models define his/her program, those models are then exported into XML, and the Java intermediate program checks if there is an object with a missing relation before doing any other activity (e.g., an Instance has no Role, a HoldsAt precondition has no InterRef to a fluent, etc.). If any missing relation is found, then an error is raised pointing the user to the object that is undefined, highlighting it as well.

An error logging window has been added into the platform, in order to help the user inspect the errors that may arise and find the objects responsible for them.

20.4   Proof of Concept

20.4.1   Architecture

ECAVI is developed with the use of the ADOxx Metamodelling Platform. We try to develop a modelling language that is tailored to the Event Calculus way of representing causal relations, making use of the ADOxx External Coupling

Fig. 20.4 The architecture of the ECAVI modelling toolkit

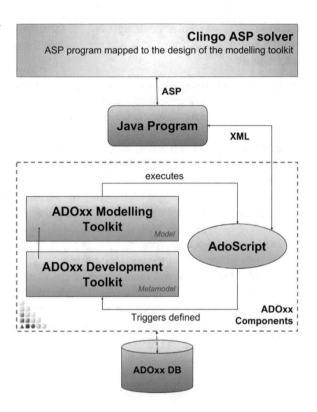

functionality with the AdoScript macro language. A high-level overview of the tool's architecture is shown in Fig. 20.4.

The ADOxx Metamodelling Platform comprises the *Development Toolkit* and the *Modelling Toolkit*. The whole realization of the ECAVI metamodel happens on the Development Toolkit, which we use in order to build the modelling language of our tool, by defining our modelling constructs (classes, model types, and attributes) stepping on some ADOxx predefined abstract classes, and to define our modelling procedure by separating the process of building a full ASP program into four sub-models. We design the graphical representation for each class and relation class by defining the class attribute GraphRep and with the help of the GraphRep online repository. Furthermore, we use the Development Toolkit to realize the external coupling that provides the tool with additional functionality, with the help of the AdoScript macro language.

The AdoScript MessagePorts and Commands enable us to define new menu entries, realize specific model checking, and provide additional add-on programming. AdoScript is the actual link between ADOxx and Clingo following these steps:

1. Export the designed models in XML.
2. Provide the XML files as input to the Java program that implements the translation of the designs into ASP programs.

3. Run the translated ASP program on the Clingo reasoner and save the resulting answer sets into a file.
4. Provide the Clingo results as input to the Java program that parses them into XML format which is needed for the results to be displayed back into the model.

In the Modelling Toolkit, the end user makes use of the modelling language that was realized in the Development Toolkit. The user will follow the modelling procedure steps in order to design a new domain of application that will be translated into an ASP program and given into the Clingo reasoner to produce the resulting answer sets. During the user's work in the Modelling Toolkit, the various functionalities implemented in AdoScript and defined in the Development Toolkit will be triggered either consciously by the user (e.g., when a user chooses to add a precondition to an Effect from its context menu) or automatically when another event happens and causes the functionality to be triggered (e.g., when an Effect is created and its type is chosen, a couple of object instances are automatically created and linked with it).

The Java intermediate program is made for the purpose of translating the designed models into an ASP program and vice versa (Sect. 20.3.2). On the way to making the translation from XML to ASP and vice versa easier and more efficient, we implemented Java classes that imprint the full structure of each type of "object" in ASP. In more detail, each model designed in ADOxx is exported as an XML file. The Java program parses each one of the XML files and with a certain order that follows the common practice of writing ASP programs (first constants, then events and fluents, then the axioms, and at the end the starting state), translates them into ASP, and writes them into the file that the Clingo reasoner runs and produces the desired answer sets. It then parses the results and produces the XML file that is read by AdoScript and displayed back into the model.

20.4.2 An Example of Application: Use Case

In this section, an example of application (i.e., a *use case*) is described. Even though we made the use case intentionally trivial, it can be generalized to account for more complex domains with larger knowledge bases.

As part of a general-purpose smart city project, an engineer wishes to model the behavior of a particular type of traffic lights that change from red to green and back according to some rules. The desirable behavior is for the light to stay green for cars as long as a predefined number of pedestrians show up and wait to cross the road. The idea is to model the dynamics of the traffic light domain with a given ruleset, so that it can be integrated in the overall smart city system and be stress-tested through simulation to fine-tune its parameters.

Figures 20.5, 20.6, and 20.7 show the realization of the traffic lights use case. Fluents and events need object symbols and/or instances as arguments. We use the InterRef relation class in order to set the arguments of an object and set the necessary interlinks of our models. The domain objects have to be created first in order to be

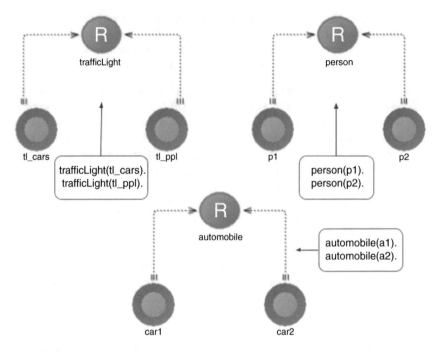

Fig. 20.5 Domain Object Model of the traffic lights example

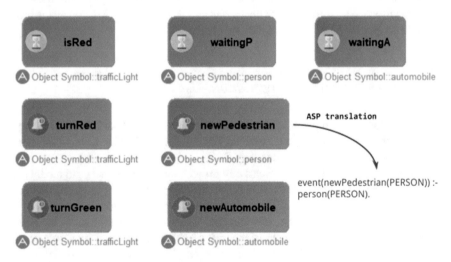

Fig. 20.6 Fluents and Events Model of the traffic lights example

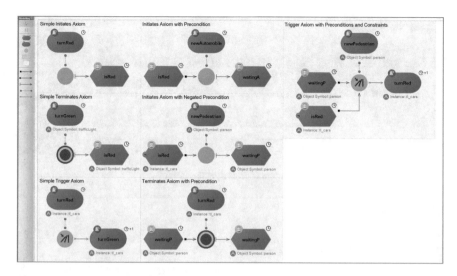

Fig. 20.7 Screenshot of the Domain Axiomatization model of the traffic lights example

used as arguments, same with the fluents and events that need to be used in the Domain Axiomatization model.

The graphic representation of the axioms aims to visualize a certain flow of actions. In particular, the effects have incoming arrows from the fluents and the events that are considered as preconditions to them. The connector between the events that are the triggering point for an effect to take place (if all the preconditions are met) and the corresponding effect is drawn with a bullet on each edge, and the fluent or event that is the result of the effect has an arrow pointing to it.

In order to define more complex axioms, adding some constraints, we make use of the Notebook, adding a chapter to the Happens objects. The user can define one or more constraints, as shown in Fig. 20.8, for the axiom described in Sect. 20.3.2. In this example of a trigger axiom, the constraint we have added is for the two instances of type person to be different, PERSON1 != PERSON2. Those arguments are part of the triggering event and one of the fluent preconditions (newPedestrian & waitingP) so we define the InterRefs to those two objects. Then we choose the role these arguments have, person in our case, and then choose the operator from the drop-down list. A description of each class type has been added to its Notebook, in order to help the user learn the semantics and syntax of the models (Fig. 20.9).

The user is free to implement the models in any order he desires, but in order to make the desired mappings (InterRefs) to other models, a certain order of implementation has to be applied.

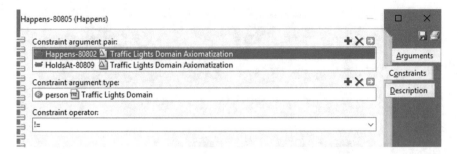

Fig. 20.8 Example of defining constraints for a triggered event

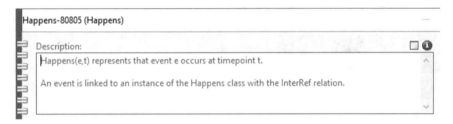

Fig. 20.9 Example of a description of an object class

20.4.3   Tutorial and Evaluation

To facilitate the use of the tool, a tutorial has been implemented, using traffic lights as a sample use case, as part of the general-purpose smart city scenario described in Sect. 20.4.2. The tutorial is in the form of a walk-through wizard, which guides the user step by step through the process of defining the domain of interest. The user can choose to start the tutorial either when the modelling toolkit has started and he is asked about it or later via a menu option. When the tutorial is active, a description of each model type is displayed when created, and tooltips appear to help the user follow the steps.

A heuristic evaluation was performed first, as a preliminary evaluation, so that the most "obvious" usability problems would be addressed, before moving on to user testing with a bigger sample of users. Heuristic evaluation is a usability inspection technique where a small number of usability experts evaluate the interface of a product. We conducted one with a group of four experts, each one with a different level of knowledge of the domain (Table 20.2). The experts had to follow the tutorial of ECAVI, and the goals we wanted to answer from this process are:

- Can the tutorial be successfully completed?
- Is it easy for the user to follow the steps?
- At the end of the tutorial, did the user feel a better understanding of modelling with Event Calculus techniques?

Table 20.2 Knowledge of the domain for each evaluator and meeting of end goal

	Evaluator 1	Evaluator 2	Evaluator 3	Evaluator 4
Experience with other ADOxx-based tools (e.g., ADONIS)	Yes	None	Yes	None
Knowledge of event calculus	Limited	None	Yes	Limited
Tutorial successfully completed	Yes	Yes	Yes	Yes
Steps easy to follow	Yes	Yes	Yes	Yes

The evaluation process was to let the users take their time following the tutorial steps, while an observer was taking notes. The observer was also available for answering any questions by the users, and for that reason, it was a person with knowledge of the application and its interface.

As general remarks from the users in this pilot evaluation, the tutorial steps are very well described and guide the user to the end goal. Each individual was able to complete the tutorial successfully, even those that had very limited knowledge of the domain.

As a result from the preliminary evaluation, some weak features have been identified, and minor revisions have been made to fix the issues we found. Small changes have been made to the text for better clarification; several minor visual bugs and several bugs regarding the progress of the steps of the tutorial have been fixed. Some useful suggestions for improving the usability of the tool have also been made.

20.5 Conclusion and Future Work

We presented a first prototype of the ECAVI tool. The features presented have already proven their usefulness in some preliminary tests, but cannot be considered complete, and do not fully realize our vision toward a metamodelling platform for modelling dynamic domains.

Despite the encouraging feedback from the preliminary evaluation, we still need to perform a more extensive normative evaluation of the current features of ECAVI that will quantify the gains in terms of modelling time and task completion time that users of different levels have while using the tool (as opposed to the standard baseline of using a plain text editor). Specifically, we will further evaluate the tool's usability in terms of *satisfaction*, *efficiency*, and *effectiveness* by means of user studies both from the perspective of the variety of students with different backgrounds and the perspective of the teacher. With a bigger testing sample, we expect to find the need for more minor revisions of the current features.

Upcoming versions will consider more features of the Event Calculus such as non-determinism, indirect effects of events, and others, which may be useful for modelling large domains with complex rules. Furthermore, we plan to extend our focus to other types of users, with different levels of modelling experience. As more experienced users have different needs, new features will have to be supported, such as more complex meta-reasoning tools and tools analyzing the resulting models to identify potential errors or poor modelling choices. Such features may be useful to experienced users who typically model large domains with hundreds of rules. With the integration of more capabilities in our tool, full programs that have already been implemented in ASP can be imported and visualized with the help of ECAVI.

We also plan of making use of the ADOxx web service interface which will help decrease the time needed in order to communicate with the reasoner, compared to the manual XML export/import of the models. The use of SOAP and RESTful web services for triggering the AdoScript commands remotely can help improve streamlining.

In the long run, we envision ECAVI to take the form of a fully visual integrated development environment for modelling dynamic domains, complemented with a debugger, step-by-step execution, and other features typically found in IDEs, while supporting alternative action languages, such as the Situation Calculus [15, 17, 29] or similar action formalisms.

Tool Download and Tutorial Description https://www.omilab.org/ecavi

References

1. Brambilla, M., Cabot, J., Wimmer, M.: Model-Driven Software Engineering in Practice: Second Edition, 2nd edn. Morgan & Claypool Publishers (2017)
2. Choe, Y., Lee, M.: Algebraic method to model secure IoT. In: Domain-Specific Conceptual Modeling, pp. 335–355 (2016). https://doi.org/10.1007/978-3-319-39417-6_15
3. Dogmus, Z., Erdem, E., Patoglu, V.: ReAct!: An interactive educational tool for AI planning for robotics. IEEE Trans. Educ. **58**, 15–24 (2015). https://doi.org/10.1109/te.2014.2318678. https://app.dimensions.ai/details/publication/pub.1061587896
4. Faber, W., Woltran, S.: Manifold answer-set programs for meta-reasoning. In: Logic Programming and Nonmonotonic Reasoning, LPNMR 2009 (2008). https://doi.org/10.1007/978-3-642-04238-6_12
5. Ferraris, P., Lee, J., Lifschitz, V.: Stable models and circumscription. Artificial Intelligence **175**(1), 236–263 (2011)
6. Fill, H.-G., Karagiannis, D.: On the conceptualisation of modelling methods using the ADOxx meta modelling platform. Enterp. Modell. Inf. Syst. Archit. **8**, 4–25 (2013)
7. Fowler, M.: UML Distilled: A Brief Guide to the Standard Object Modeling Language, 3rd edn. Addison-Wesley Longman Publishing (2003)
8. Gebser, M., Kaufmann, B., Neumann, A., Schaub, T.: Clasp: A conflict-driven answer set solver. In: Logic Programming and Nonmonotonic Reasoning, LPNMR 2007 (2007). https://doi.org/10.1007/978-3-540-72200-7_23
9. Gelfond, M., Lifschitz, V.: The Stable Model Semantics For Logic Programming, pp. 1070–1080. MIT Press (1988)
10. Karagiannis, D., Mayr, H.C., Mylopoulos, J.: Domain-Specific Conceptual Modeling: Concepts, Methods and Tools, 1st edn. Springer Publishing Company (2016)
11. Karagiannis, D., Kühn, H.: Metamodelling platforms. In: Proceedings of the Third International Conference on E-Commerce and Web Technologies, EC-WEB '02, 182 (2002). https://doi.org/10.5555/646162.680499

12. Kloimüllner, C., Oetsch, J., Pührer, J., Tompits, H.: Kara: A system for visualising and visual editing of interpretations for answer-set programs. In: Applications of Declarative Programming and Knowledge Management, INAP 2011, WLP 2011 (2011). https://doi.org/10.1007/978-3-642-41524-1_20

13. Kowalski, R., Sergot, M.: A logic-based calculus of events. New Gener. Comput. **4**, 67–95 (1986). https://doi.org/10.1007/BF03037383

14. Lee, J., Palla, R.: Reformulating the situation calculus and the event calculus in the general theory of stable models and in answer set programming. J. Artif. Intell. Res. **43** (2012). https://doi.org/10.5555/2387915.2387930

15. Levesque, H., Pirri, F., Reiter, R.: Foundations for the situation calculus. Electron. Trans. Artif. Intell. **2**, 159–178 (1998). https://ep.liu.se/ej/etai/1998/005/

16. Lifschitz, V.: What is answer set programming? In: Proceedings of the 23rd National Conference on Artificial Intelligence - Volume 3, pp. 1594–1597 (2008). https://doi.org/10.5555/1620270.1620340

17. McCarthy, J.: Stanford Artificial Intelligence Laboratory (1963). Situations, Actions, and Causal Laws. Memo (Stanford Artificial Intelligence Project). Comtex Scientific https://books.google.gr/books?id=iF8iGwAACAAJ

18. Miller, R., Shanahan, M.: Some alternative formulations of the event calculus. Comput. Logic Logic Programm. Beyond, 452–490 (2002). https://doi.org/10.1007/3-540-45632-5_17

19. Morgan, R., Grossmann, G., Schrefl, M., Stumptner, M., Payne, T.: VizDSL: Towards a graphical visualisation language for enterprise systems interoperability. In: Advanced Information Systems Engineering, CAiSE 2018 (2017). https://doi.org/10.1007/978-3-319-91563-0_27

20. Mueller, E.: Commonsense Reasoning, 1st edn. Morgan Kaufmann (2006)

21. Musen, M.A., Protégé, T.: The Protégé Project: A look back and a look forward. In: AI Matters. Association of Computing Machinery Specific Interest Group in Artificial Intelligence, vol. 1(4) (2015). https://doi.org/10.1145/2757001.2757003

22. Oetsch, J., Pührer, J., Tompits, H.: The SeaLion has landed: An IDE for answer-set programming–preliminary report. In: Applications of Declarative Programming and Knowledge Management, INAP 2011, WLP 2011, pp. 305–324 (2013). https://doi.org/10.1007/978-3-642-41524-1_19

23. Ribeiro, T., Inoue, K., Bourgne, G.: Combining answer set programs for adaptive and reactive reasoning. Theory Pract. Logic Programm. **13** (2013). https://hal.archives-ouvertes.fr/hal-01562133

24. Siau, K., Loo, P.-P.: Identifying difficulties in learning UML. IS Management **23**, 43–51 (2006). https://doi.org/10.1201/1078.10580530/46108.23.3.20060601/93706.5

25. Silva, A.R.da.: Model-driven engineering: A survey supported by the unified conceptual model. Comput. Lang. Syst. Struct. **43**, 139–155 (2015)

26. Van Harmelen, F., Lifschitz, V., Porter, B.: Handbook of Knowledge Representation. Elsevier Science (2007)

27. Van Lambalgen, M., Hamm, F.: The Proper Treatment of Events (2006)

28. Visic, N., Fill, H.-G., Buchmann, R.A., Karagiannis, D.: A domain-specific language for modeling method definition: From requirements to grammar. In: 2015 IEEE 9th International Conference on Research Challenges in Information Science (RCIS), pp. 286–297 (2015). https://doi.org/10.1109/RCIS.2015.7128889

29. Yamasaki, S., Sasakura, M.: A calculus effectively performing event formation with visualization. In: High-Performance Computing, ISHPC 2005, ALPS 2006, pp. 287–294 (2008). https://doi.org/10.1007/978-3-540-77704-5_27

Part VII
Technology Enhanced Education

Chapter 21
Tree Diagrams and Unit Squares 4.0: Digitizing Stochastic Classes with the Didactic Modeling Tool PROVIS

Victoria Döller and Stefan Götz

Abstract PROVIS—*Probability Visualized*—is a tool for constructing tree diagrams and unit squares. Tree diagrams are often used in mathematics education to structure multi-stage random experiments. Unit squares illustrate dependencies between two-dimensional characteristics and their values. The intention of this project is to foster the use of digital tree diagrams and unit squares in the classroom. PROVIS exempts the students from operating and gives them opportunity to model, interpret, and analyse complex statistical situations. For the development of PROVIS, seven requirements based on didactic considerations are proposed, which a statistical education software should fulfil. The metamodel of the method underlying PROVIS is presented. Also the related functionalities are outlined. The realization of the metamodel and the implementation of the involved concepts appear to be complex in construction as well as in interdependence. Nevertheless, it was the intention of the developers to realize a software, which is quite easy to handle. For this reason, a convenient interface is offered. The features of PROVIS are demonstrated by discussing a case study in a recent context. PROVIS is implemented on the metamodeling platform ADOxx. It is available for free on the OMiLAB-Austria homepage.

Keywords Tree diagram · Unit square · Stochastics · PROVIS · Metamodeling · ADOxx

V. Döller (✉)
Research Group Knowledge Engineering, University of Vienna, Vienna, Austria
e-mail: victoria.doeller@univie.ac.at

S. Götz
Faculty of Mathematics, University of Vienna, Vienna, Austria
e-mail: stefan.goetz@univie.ac.at

© The Author(s), under exclusive license to Springer Nature Switzerland AG 2022   481
D. Karagiannis et al. (eds.), *Domain-Specific Conceptual Modeling*,
https://doi.org/10.1007/978-3-030-93547-4_21

21.1   Introduction

Visualization is a permanent requirement in mathematical education especially for applied and realistic aspects. In this sense, we view stochastics as an applied topic of mathematics (education) [8]. Stochastic situations (random experiments) and statistical data can often be illustrated by tree diagrams and unit squares, respectively. The creation of these graphical methods by hand is time-consuming and monotonous. Thus, a typical indication for using technological support is present.

To the best of our knowledge, there are no established technological tools for constructing tree diagrams and unit squares in mathematics education. The first author has already developed such a tool, called PROVIS (*Probability Visualized*), which is presented in our contribution as well as in [6, 7]. Furthermore, seven requirements are postulated concerning didactic aspects, which a stochastic software should fulfil. By a case study, we prove that PROVIS conforms to these requirements.

Related to the Fourth Industrial Revolution ("Industry 4.0"), we complement our approach with the extension 4.0 to emphasize our intention to contribute an option to a digital classroom 4.0. PROVIS is realized on the metamodeling platform ADOxx. It is available for free on the OMiLAB-Austria homepage.[1]

21.2   Method Description

In Austria, stochastics education does not play an important role in the curriculum in contrast to many other countries. At secondary level 1 (age 10–14), only elementary statistics is taught [10]. The concept of probability is reserved for secondary level 2 (age 15–18) [1]. (Note that in Austria, there is no graduation for a lower secondary education.) To bridge this gap between elementary statistics and calculus of probability, we suggest two concepts: tree diagrams and unit squares.

While the former is established in stochastics education (also in Austria), the latter is almost unknown in Austrian mathematics classes. This is unfortunate because both concepts entail the potential to connect frequencies with probabilities. This is the reason for our conviction to provide a digital tool to bridge the gap mentioned above.

At secondary level 1, Austrian students are confronted with frequencies, diagrams, mean values, and scattering parameters in statistics education. In addition, they learn about probabilities, probability distributions, expected values, variances, and so on 2 years later.

In this paper, we want to introduce a digital tool to create tree diagrams and unit squares. With this automatization, we intend to make the use of these visualizations in class easier for the teachers. The simple usability of the program is an enabler for a more widespread distribution of those concepts.

---

[1] austria.omilab.org/psm/content/provis/info.

21.2.1 Involved Stochastic Concepts for Visualization

Tree diagrams are a lucid way of structuring multi-level random experiments. The concept can also be used to model stochastic situations including frequencies or probabilities. The visualization of such situations can help the students to understand complex processes, connections, and dependencies.[2] Figure 21.1[3] shows the smoking behaviour of the Austrian population older than 16 years in 2019.[4] The indicated values are absolute frequencies in thousands. The last line in Fig. 21.1 shows the total numbers of male smokers (1,091,000), male non-smokers (2,533,000), female smokers (853,000), and female non-smokers (2,941,000). Figure 21.2 describes the well-known Monty Hall dilemma [2]. The first item in the last line means that the probability is zero for the event that the host opens door No.1 and the car is also behind this door, if the candidate chooses door No.1 at the beginning of the game. For an extended introduction to tree diagrams, see [5, Chap. 5].

Fig. 21.1 Adults' smoking behaviour in Austria depending on gender 1

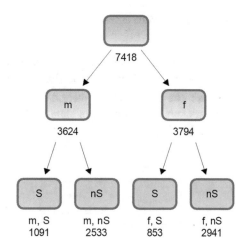

An example of a unit square is given in Fig. 21.3, left, depicting adult smokers in Austria in 2019. The entry 1091 in the top left rectangle, for example, is the number of male smokers (older than 16) in thousands. The square is divided into four rectangles. Their surface areas correspond to the relative proportions of the four subgroups mentioned above. The width of the top left rectangle is related to the proportion of men relative to the whole Austrian population older than 16: $\frac{3624}{7418} \approx 48.9\%$. This can be directly inferred from Fig. 21.1. The height of the top

---

[2] Tree diagrams arising from absolute frequencies have a similar structure as decision trees [14, Sect. 19.3].

[3] All figures are made by using ProVis.

[4] https://www.statistik.at/web_de/statistiken/menschen_und_gesellschaft/gesundheit/ gesundheits\discretionary-determinanten/rauchen/index.html.

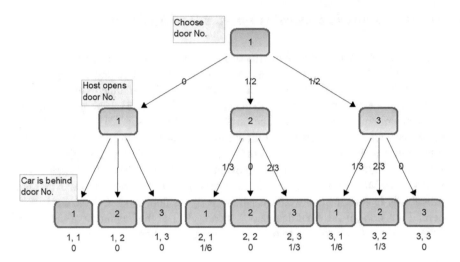

Fig. 21.2 A schematic representation of the Monty Hall dilemma

left rectangle corresponds to the relative proportion of male smokers to all men: $\frac{1091}{1091+2533} \approx 0.30$. This is a conditional frequency.

Note: The product of height and width gives the relative proportion $\frac{1091}{7418}$ for the male smokers to the whole population. For an extended introduction to unit squares, see [4], [9, Chap. 3.1].

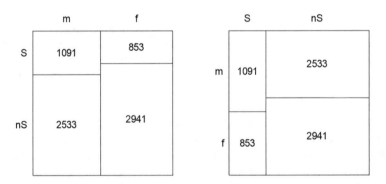

Fig. 21.3 Adults' smoking behaviour in Austria depending on gender 2

The calculations above show the complexity of unit squares, which make their manual construction very time-consuming. This drawback is overcome by a suitable digital tool.

By comparison, tree diagrams seem to be a bit more intuitive than unit squares. This may be caused by the fact that unit squares are not self-descriptive, because the involved frequencies are represented by quite different geometric elements: areas and line segments. A consequence could be the unequal popularity of these two concepts mentioned at the beginning of Sect. 21.2.

For the digital realization of the two visualization methods introduced above, we postulate seven requirements based on didactic considerations, which are very important for a successful implementation, following [6].

21.2.2 Requirements for a Digital Tool in Stochastics Education

Our main intention is to support students in handling (complex) stochastic situations on their own [15, p. 1]. This purpose requires a high flexibility of the stochastic tool to adapt to any conditions of a given stochastic situation.

Requirement 1: Realize Different Types of Tree Diagrams
A digital tool to support modeling with tree diagrams should allow the creation of both probability trees and (absolute and relative) frequency trees [3], as well as complete and incomplete, and reduced trees.

Figure 21.2 shows an incomplete tree diagram: for completeness, the two branches of the candidate choosing door number 2 or 3 would have to be added. An example of a reduced tree can be seen in Fig. 21.4. We roll a dice four times, and we observe the drawn number of eyes. Here the elementary events of all possible results except for a six are collected in one event ("rolling no six"). The universal set of events T has only two elements: 6 and n6 (non six) in Fig. 21.4.

Requirement 2: Automate Calculation Work
A technical support for tree diagrams should offer an automatic calculation of frequencies and probabilities, respectively. Depending on the known quantities, probabilities are calculated by multiplying and adding following the rules of conditional probability ("Pfadregeln" in German). Moreover, the probabilities or frequencies along the paths are computed by the program.

In Fig. 21.4, we can see the probabilities, which can be calculated automatically at the ends of the branches.

Requirement 3: Support the Construction of Tree Diagrams According to the Spiral Curriculum [11]
Students should be given a low-threshold introduction to the ideas of tree diagrams. The mental process of constructing a tree should be run through step by step and event by event, and the tree should optionally deal with probabilities or frequencies. In addition, useful functions should be offered for an advanced learning stage in order to be able to manipulate tree diagrams quickly and efficiently. For example, the program should provide the feature of generating tree diagrams from few details of their partial events (a multi-level random experiment consists of several single-level partial events) or the option of checking manually calculated probabilities for correctness.

In Fig. 21.4, we see a four-level process, and each stage stands for a partial event. All stages have the same universal set of events *T*. At stage 1, we have 2 possible outcomes; at stage 2, there are 4; at stage 3, there are 8; and at stage 4, there are 16.

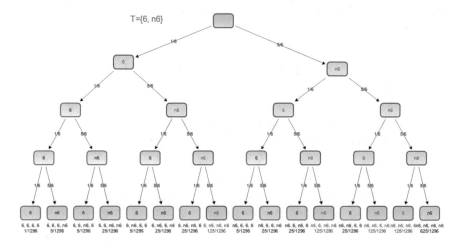

Fig. 21.4 A reduced tree diagram

Requirement 4: Create Unit Squares Automatically
A digital tool for teaching stochastics should be able to create quickly and easily unit squares directly from the information of a 2 × 2 contingency table.[5] In addition, the derivation of the transposed unit square shall be supported by a digital tool; see Fig. 21.3, right.

To get the unit square in Fig. 21.3, left, the universal set is primarily separated in men and women. In contrast to this, in Fig. 21.3, right, the primary classification criterion is the smoking behaviour. In both squares, the leading separation is marked by the continuous vertical line. Note that there are mathematical dependencies between these two representations (see Sect. 21.3).

Requirement 5: Connect Tree Diagram and Unit Square
A digital tool should connect the two visualization methods unit square and tree diagram and should offer the possibility to derive the corresponding tree diagram from a unit square. If a tree diagram fulfils the necessary requirements, the reverse way shall also be supported (compare Fig. 21.3, left, with Fig. 21.1).

---

[5] The two-by-two or fourfold contingency table represents two characteristics of a set of counts or frequencies. The rows represent two values of one characteristic (e.g. male/female), and the columns represent two values of another characteristic (e.g. smoker/non-smoker).

Requirement 6: Dynamize Graphical Representations and Support Visualizations
A digital tool for creating tree diagrams and unit squares should support a clear, situation-appropriate representation. This includes options for editing trees, integrating changes such as new branches in a uniform manner, and switching between horizontal and vertical arrangements (e.g. rotating Fig. 21.2 by 90°; a result can be seen in Fig. 21.12 in Sect. 21.4.1). Further helpful functions are, for example, the visual differentiation of special nodes in tree diagrams or the highlighting of the measure of association and other distances and areas in unit squares. Likewise, scaling the side length of a unit square and the uniform alignment of trees should be possible.

The measure of association describes the dependency of two nominal scaled characteristics [9, Chap. 3.1]. A detailed explanation can be found in the next section.

Requirement 7: Stimulate Experimentation
A digital tool that supports the visualization methods tree diagram and unit square should stimulate students to ask "what if . . . " questions by making these methods efficient to use. For example, the numbers in a unit square can be varied, and the change in areas can be observed instantly. Similarly, the tree structure changes immediately, when the event space of a sub-process is adjusted or the order of sub-processes is changed. In addition, new perspectives should be opened, such as the possibility of deriving one form of representation from the other (Requirement 5 targets the technical feature for this reason).

In summary, these features should relieve students from calculating and drawing in order to strengthen their abilities to analyse and to interpret complex stochastic situations.

21.3 Method Conceptualization

Figure 21.5 shows the metamodel of PROVIS. The process of developing a modeling method is a creative act in a variety of domains, and it has quite different requirements than software modeling with UML class diagrams, which are frequently used for representing metamodels. Therefore, we use the method *CoChaCo* for the graphical representation of the metamodel [12], which is semantically specialized on this process of engineering modeling methods.

Remark: The method PROVIS contains only three conceptions, Unit Square, Event, and Partial Event, and one relation, Transition, but each conception incorporates a complex structure.

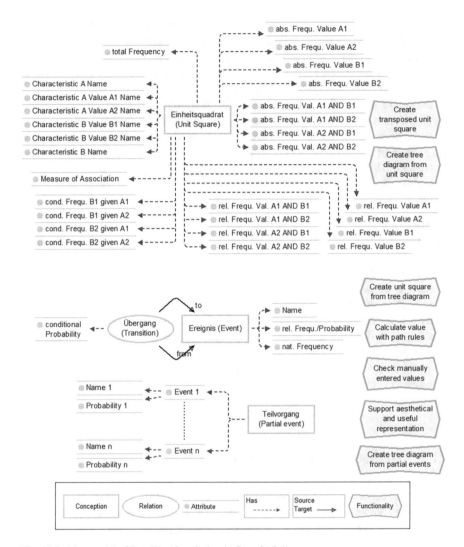

Fig. 21.5 Metamodel of PROVIS (description in Sect. 21.3.1)

21.3.1 Syntax of PROVIS

21.3.1.1 Unit Squares

If we start with the concept Unit Square, we will have to define two characteristics, for instance, smoking behaviour and gender in Fig. 21.3. Each of the characteristics has two values. In our case, these are smokers and non-smokers, as well as male and female. In total, there are four possible combinations of the values; see Sect. 21.2.1. For each combination, we gather the absolute frequency of the incidents. From these frequencies, we derive the absolute frequency of the values (the total number of smokers, for instance). Summing up these values, we get the total frequency of the universal set.

To get insight into the dependency of the two characteristics, we change from absolute frequencies to relative frequencies f by division by the cardinality of the universal set. This transfer opens the possibility to use methods coming from probability theory. Along the lines of absolute frequencies, we can calculate the relative frequency of each value with respect to the universal set.

The relative frequency $B1$ given $A1$ is defined by

$$f(B1|A1) = \frac{f(A1 \cap B1)}{f(A1)},$$

where $f(A1)$ is not equal to zero. This means we refer to a new universal set, namely, $A1$.[6]

Fig. 21.6 Schema of a unit square

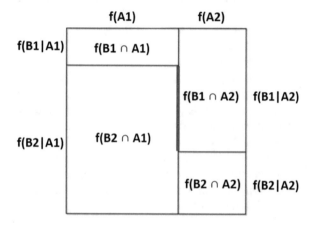

A schema for the construction of a unit square can be seen in Fig. 21.6. We divide the square vertically according to the relative proportions of the leading characteristic values $f(A1)$ and $f(A2)$ (in our example, we have to choose between smoking behaviour and gender). In order to divide the left area, we use the conditional relative frequencies of $B1$ and $B2$ given the leading characteristic value $A1$, which gives us the height of the top left rectangle $f(B1|A1)$ and the one of the bottom left rectangle $f(B2|A1)$. Analogously, we treat the right half of the square with respect to $A2$.

---

[6] Remark: The famous Bayesian theorem deals with conditional frequencies and probabilities, respectively [13, Chap. 1.6].

The difference between the frequencies $f(B1|A1)$ and $f(B1|A2)$ measures the dependency of the two characteristics. This measure—the so-called measure of association—can be identified easily in the unit square by observing the different heights of the part rectangles in the upper part of the square (thick red line segment in Fig. 21.6). A small value[7] of the measure of association is an indicator for the independence of the two characteristics.

It seems to be clear that the measure of association $\mathcal{A}$ in the transposed unit square $\bar{U}$ (see Sect. 21.2.2) is different to the equivalent in the original square U in general, but there is a strong connection [6, p. 21]:

$$\mathcal{A}_U \cdot f(A_1) \cdot f(A_2) = \mathcal{A}_{\bar{U}} \cdot f(B_1) \cdot f(B_2).$$

21.3.1.2 Tree Diagrams

In the following, we describe tree diagrams with probabilities. An outcome is a result of a random experiment. The set of all possible outcomes is called sample space. An event is a subset of the sample space. A tree is constituted by events or outcomes and transitions between them. The transitions comprise (conditional) probabilities. In Fig. 21.4, we focus on the outcome *six* and the event *non six* (this is the subset $\{1, 2, 3, 4, 5\}$ of the sample space $\{1, 2, 3, 4, 5, 6\}$). There are two transition probabilities, $1/6$ for rolling a six and $5/6$ for the event *non six*.

Alternatively, it is possible to deal with absolute frequencies instead of events and outcomes, respectively (see Fig. 21.1), and with relative frequencies instead of (conditional) probabilities.

A tree diagram has two functionalities. First, it provides a systematic overview of a (complex) stochastic situation (Fig. 21.4). Second, we can calculate the probabilities of composed events of random experiments using so-called path rules. By Fig. 21.7, we obtain

$$P(A \cap B) = P(B|A) \cdot P(A)$$

for the uppermost branch, for instance. Note that the definition of the conditional probability of B given A is

$$P(B|A) = \frac{P(A \cap B)}{P(A)}$$

for $P(A) > 0$. This rule can be generalized to finitely many events by

$$P(A_1 \cap \ldots \cap A_n) = P(A_1) \cdot P(A_2|A_1) \cdot \ldots \cdot P(A_n|A_1 \cap \ldots \cap A_{n-1})$$

for $P(A_1 \cap \ldots \cap A_{n-1}) > 0$.

---

[7] Note that the measure of association always ranges between $+1$ and -1.

Fig. 21.7 Schema of a tree diagram

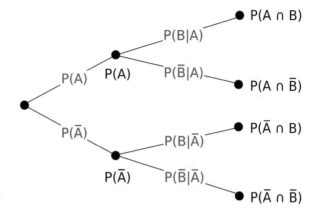

So each probability at the end of a branch is the product of the transition probabilities along the branch. This is the first path rule (multiplication rule). We can see these AND-probabilities in Fig. 21.4 at the end of each branch:

$$\frac{5}{6} \cdot \frac{5}{6} \cdot \frac{5}{6} \cdot \frac{5}{6} = \frac{625}{1296}$$

is the related calculation to the uppermost branch for not rolling any sixes in four consecutive rolls.

If we are interested in the event of rolling exactly two sixes, then we shall sum up the probabilities of the respective events at the ends of the branches:

$$\frac{25}{1296} + \frac{25}{1296} + \frac{25}{1296} + \frac{25}{1296} + \frac{25}{1296} + \frac{25}{1296} = \frac{150}{1296}$$

for the six possibilities $(6, 6, n6, n6)$, $(6, n6, 6, n6)$, $(6, n6, n6, 6)$, $(n6, n6, 6, 6)$, $(n6, 6, n6, 6)$, and $(n6, 6, 6, n6)$. This is the second path rule (addition rule). It is a consequence of the third axiom by Kolmogorov [13, p. 8].

The concept of a partial event (compare to Requirement 3 in Sect. 21.2.2) is a way to describe single-stage events, which can be used to build up multi-stage random experiments like in Fig. 21.4. It allows to preserve information about the involved outcomes and their probabilities in order to use this information in more complex experiments. In Fig. 21.4, for example, we repeat four times the same partial event—rolling a six or no six. This is due to the mutual independence of the throws.

21.3.2 Functionality

Figure 21.5 includes seven functionalities:

1. Create the transposed unit square from a given square.
2. Create the corresponding tree diagram from a given unit square.

3. Create a unit square from a tree diagram.
4. Calculate probabilities or frequencies due to the path rules (Sect. 21.3.1.2).
5. Provide checking mechanisms on manually entered probabilities.
6. Aesthetic and useful possibilities of representations: Align tree diagrams horizontally or vertically and highlight line segments and their lengths (e.g. the
   measure of association) in unit squares.
7. Create a tree diagram from a row of partial events.

In the following, we explain each functionality in more detail.

In Fig. 21.8, we present a schematic unit square and its transposition (Sect. 21.2.2 and Fig. 21.3). Note that the squares explicate different conditional relative frequen-cies. For this reason, the user has to decide on which characteristic he or she will focus on primarily. Having constructed the unit square in PROVIS according to this decision, the transposed should also be made by this tool.

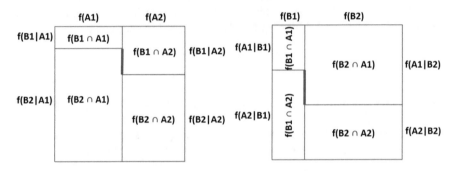

Fig. 21.8 Schema of a unit square and its transposition

The second and third functionalities are illustrated by Figs. 21.7 and 21.8, left.[8] (A unit square corresponds to a binary tree with two stages.) In this case, we identify relative frequencies ($f(A_1)$) with probabilities ($P(A)$). A tree diagram represents the procedural structure of the discussed random (multi-level) experiment. The root of the diagram marks the beginning of the process; the leaves indicate the end. In a unit square, we see at a glance the proportions and dependencies of the involved probabilities and frequencies, respectively.

The PROVIS method should also provide checking mechanisms (Functionality 5) for the results of the path rules (compare Functionality 4). This can be observed in the last entries of Fig. 21.2, which are calculated automatically. Due to the second path rule, the sum of the last entries is one. If a student replaces one entry with a manually calculated result, an error will be marked by the program (Fig. 21.12, right, in Sect. 21.4.1). Furthermore, compliance with the normalization of the (transition) probabilities can be checked (compare also to the subtrees in Fig. 21.2). In frequency trees, the sum of frequencies at a certain stage of the related (sub)tree must be equal

---

[8] Note that we have to identify $A1$ with A and $A2$ with $\bar{A}$ and also for the characteristic B.

to the frequency at the stage above in the same (sub)tree. In Fig. 21.1, the mentioned relations can be evaluated.

The sixth functionality is illustrated by Figs. 21.4 and 21.9. The highlighted (red) part of the tree diagram in Fig. 21.4 means the event of rolling exactly one six when rolling the dice four times. It is difficult to overlook this new situation. If we delete all branches except for the focused ones, we have to rearrange the obtained incomplete tree for aesthetic reasons. This shall be done automatically. A possible result is shown in Fig. 21.9.

Fig. 21.9 A rearranged incomplete tree diagram

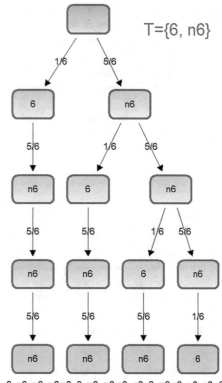

6, n6, n6, n6 n6, 6, n6, n6 n6, n6, 6, n6 n6, n6, n6, 6

The last functionality requires the automatic generation of a tree diagram, when the constituting partial events of each stage are given; see also Sect. 21.3.1.2. If these partial events are independent from each other, the transition probabilities can be deduced, too; see, for example, Fig. 21.4.

21.4   Proof of Concept

In this section, we want to demonstrate and explain how to apply the capabilities, and functionalities, of our developed modeling tool.

21.4.1   Tool Implementation

To realize a tool satisfying the requirements proposed in Sect. 21.2.2, the software PROVIS—*Probability Visualized*—was implemented on the metamodeling platform ADOxx.[9] The tool can be downloaded from the OMiLAB project homepage.[10]

The creation of models is very simple due to the small amount of available concepts. The power of these concepts lies in their visual expressiveness and the numerous computational dependencies. The effort of construction and computation is undertaken by the tool, and thereby PROVIS frees the user from the monotonous operational work. This allows students in school to focus on the interpretation and analysis of the stochastic situation.

The tool interfaces are realized in German, as it is intended to be used by students in Austrian schools. The intention is to make both visualization methods—tree diagrams and unit squares—available next to each other, so that the strengths of both can be used simultaneously. Therefore, we decided to realize only one model type containing both.

To trigger the algorithms mentioned in Sect. 21.3.2 or display the automatically calculated values in the model, the user interacts with the concepts via the notebook; see Fig. 21.10.

Fig. 21.10 The notebook of a unit square on the left and of a tree diagram on the right

The notebook is structured in tabs for (a) the input of names and numbers (frequencies or probabilities) of events, characteristics, and values, (b) the graphical representation, and (c) the functionality. The input tabs can be seen in Fig. 21.10. The tab for graphical adjustment ("Grafische Darstellung") of a unit square is shown in Fig. 21.11, right. (We know the data in Fig. 21.11, left, from Fig. 21.3.)

---

[9] adoxx.org.

[10] austria.omilab.org/psm/content/provis.

There we can change the absolute size of the square, the number of rounded decimals (radio button "5" is chosen in Fig. 21.11, right), and the optional display of measure of association ("Assoziationsmass anzeigen" is ticked), row and column sums ("Summen anzeigen" is ticked), as well as concrete conditional frequencies at the corresponding line segments ("Bedingte Haeufigkeit B1 unter A1" is chosen in a drop-down menu). This configuration results in the (green) highlighting of the measure of association 0.07622 (rounded to five decimals) and the (blue) marking of the line segment corresponding to the conditional frequency $h(S|m) = 0.30105$ in Fig. 21.11 on the left.[11] (From the small value of the measure of association, we infer that the smoking behaviour of Austrian adults in 2019 is almost independent from the gender.)

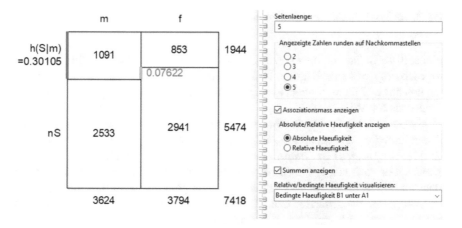

Fig. 21.11   A unit square and its graphical configuration in the notebook

The tab for triggering the functionality ("Funktionalitaet") on a unit square offers algorithms to create the transposed square, e.g. Fig. 21.3, as well as the corresponding tree diagram. Figure 21.1 can be derived from Fig. 21.3 using this functionality.

In a tree diagram, we offer mechanisms to structure the tree vertically, for example, Fig. 21.4, or horizontally, for example, Fig. 21.12, besides the choice of the number of rounded decimals.

For tree diagrams, the following algorithms are available: it is possible to apply the path rules (see Sect. 21.3.1.2), to create the corresponding unit square (see Sect. 21.3.2), or to check the tree for incorrect states. The right tree diagram in Fig. 21.12 includes one wrong result: The event shown on the bottom right is evaluated with a wrong probability as we can see by comparison with Fig. 21.12, left. The tool highlights the whole column (in red) because the sum of the

---

[11] Note that the German abbreviation h ("Häufigkeit") in PROVIS means the relative frequency f.

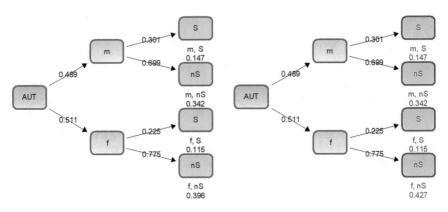

Fig. 21.12 Two horizontally aligned tree diagrams

probabilities in this column exceeds one. This function of evaluation is implemented for each stage of a tree diagram. Note that these mechanisms are accessible only in the notebook of the root node, as they concern the whole tree consisting of several events and transitions.

Moreover, partial events can be used to automatically create a tree diagram. This is configured via the menu tab *Baumdiagramme/Erstelle Baum aus (unabhaengigen) Teilvorgaengen (Tree diagrams/Create tree diagram from (independent) partial events)*. For each stage, the corresponding partial event has to be chosen. If the stages are independent of each other, it is even possible to transfer the transition probabilities to the generated tree. The partial event shown in Fig. 21.13 is the basis for the automatically generated tree diagram in Fig. 21.4.

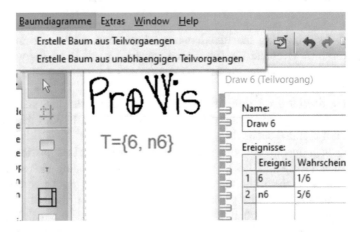

Fig. 21.13 A partial event to be used for the automatic generation of a tree diagram

21.4.2 Case Study

For our case study, we focus on a statistical analysis of diagnostic procedures for detecting COVID-19. For the implementation in PROVIS, we need specific parameters like the sensitivity and specificity of antigen tests. Furthermore, the prevalence of a certain population is required. We take the recommendations of the WHO for a minimal performance of rapid antigen tests: 80% sensitivity and 97% specificity.[12]

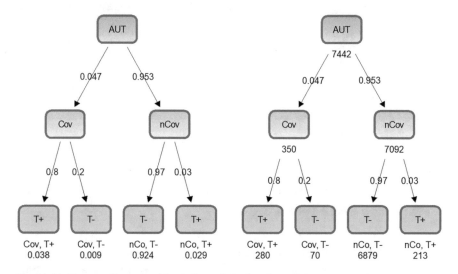

Fig. 21.14 Two tree diagrams with relative and absolute frequencies

In Fig. 21.14, there are two tree diagrams with relative and absolute frequencies (numbers in thousands). They are based on a prevalence of 4.7%. This value is the prevalence of COVID-19 among the Austrian population older than 16 years in November 2020, as found in a study conducted by Statistics Austria.[13] Note that the sensitivity and specificity are interpreted as the conditional transition probability given the infection status.

At the end of the very left branch in Fig. 21.14, left, we see the probability of being infected and getting a positive test result, which is 3.8% (= $0.047 \cdot 0.8$ due to the first path rule; see Sect. 21.3.1.2). In the right tree of Fig. 21.14, the corresponding branch shows the absolute frequency "280" (= $7{,}442 \cdot 0.047 \cdot 0.8$), which means 280,000 (rounded). This is the number of Austrian people older than

---

[12] apps.who.int/iris/rest/bitstreams/1323285/retrieve.

[13] www.statistik.at/web_de/statistiken/menschen_und_gesellschaft/gesundheit/covid19/index.html.

16 years in November 2020 being infected and getting a positive test result, if they were tested (antigen test).

This complex stochastic situation is structured by two tree diagrams created in PROVIS. After the input of the sensitivity, the specificity, and the prevalence, PROVIS automatically calculates the other values in Fig. 21.14. For didactic reasons, it is important to visualize the proportions of the crucial statistical quantities. This can be managed by constructing unit squares; see Sect. 21.3.1.1.

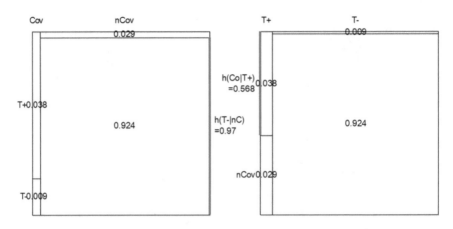

Fig. 21.15 A unit square and its transposed one

In Fig. 21.15, we can see the unit squares, which were automatically derived by PROVIS from the tree diagram in Fig. 21.14, left. Now the probabilities at the ends of the branches in the tree diagram are illustrated by rectangular areas in the unit squares. Note that the four rectangles in the left and in the right unit squares have corresponding surface areas but they are not congruent to each other.

We have highlighted two important relative conditional frequencies (in blue): in the left unit square, we can see $h(T - |nC) = 0.97$ as the minimal specificity of the test, which the WHO recommends for antigen tests. For the patient, it is more relevant to know the probability of being infected given a positive test result. This probability in question is marked in the right unit square: $h(Co|T+) = 0.568$. Due to the low prevalence, this probability is considerably smaller than the sensitivity. The mathematical background is given by the Bayesian theorem [13, Chap. 1.6].

The measure of association is quite different in these two unit squares (requirement 6 in Sect. 21.2.2). In the left one, it is 0.77 and in the right one 0.558 (these values are calculated by PROVIS); compare Sect. 21.3.1.1. But in both cases, the measure of association is far away from zero. Otherwise, a value close to zero would mean that the characteristics infection status and test result are independent from each other. Of course, this would not be desirable.

PROVIS supports a fast and easy variation of the underlying values (prevalence, sensitivity, specificity). For instance, the prevalence of a certain age period cohort is considerably higher than the general one: 10.1% for the group of people aged 16–24 in Austria (in November 2020).[14] Of course, we would get diagrams different to Figs. 21.14 and 21.15, respectively. Figure 21.16 shows the transposed unit square and the tree diagram, which is derived from it. Note that the new prevalence is not visible in Fig. 21.16 but the interesting relative conditional frequency $h(Co|T+) = 0.75$ is provided there. It is quite different to the corresponding relative conditional frequency in the total population of Austria (0.568). Interestingly, the change in the prevalence is 5.4% points, but the change in the conditional frequency of being infected given a positive test result is 18.2% points!

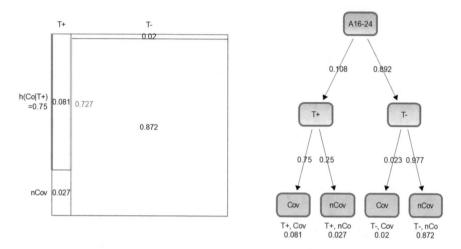

Fig. 21.16 (Transposed) unit square and tree diagram based on a different prevalence

The measure of association is also different to the analogon determined in the total population: 0.727 (Fig. 21.16, left) versus 0.558. Last but not least of course, the AND-frequencies have changed, too. For instance, the proportion of negatively AND not infected persons is lower (0.872 in Fig. 21.16, right) than the equivalent proportion in the population as a whole (0.924 in Fig. 21.15, left).

21.5 Conclusion and Outlook

PROVIS is a tool for constructing tree diagrams and unit squares, which are used for statistical representations of random experiments and two binary characteristics, respectively. For a good performance, certain requirements are needed

---

[14] www.statistik.at/web_de/statistiken/menschen_und_gesellschaft/gesundheit/covid19/index.html.

(Sect. 21.2.2), which PROVIS fulfils to a great extent. This is proved in this contribution by discussing a case study (Sect. 21.4.2).

Because of the nature of multi-stage random experiments, tree diagrams are the appropriate and therefore established way of visualizing them ([5, Sect. 5.3], for instance). Nevertheless, there is no convenient tool support for creating them automatically. For the same reason, unit squares are not popular among math teachers (in Austria). Their construction is time-consuming and operation-intensive. We close this gap with the presented tool PROVIS implemented on the ADOxx platform.

A digital classroom needs sophisticated technological tools for supporting education in a didactically adequate way. To explicate this agenda, we have postulated seven requirements in Sect. 21.2.2 for an orientation. As a consequence, this also means that the students are exempt from operating and they can focus on the interpretations of statistical results and consequences. This is what is needed in every day life. In consequence, digitization in the classroom 4.0 means a shift from operating to proving, modeling, interpreting, experimenting, and so on. These skills are reserved for human beings (maybe except for artificial intelligence).

This is a tedious process because school systems are not very flexible regarding changes of paradigms. Therefore, it is necessary to support the teachers who are the main drivers of this development. PROVIS is a first attempt concerning the statistical visualizations mentioned above.

Although the basic idea was to create a tool for stochastic education, from a conceptual modeling point of view (e.g. enterprise modeling or data modeling), there are intersections with data science, in particular clustering. For instance, we can identify some application scenarios outside of teaching statistics: An example is the use of probabilistic reasoning in artificial intelligence [14, Chap. 13].

For a deeper implementation in mathematics education, PROVIS must provide more features like checking mechanisms and exam construction tools. For instance, students have to complete a tree diagram, and PROVIS checks the entries and gives feedback or hints to the users (e.g. a reaction on a given error).

We have to distinguish between an instruction and exercise phase on the one hand and the testing phase on the other hand in mathematics education. For the last one, it can be necessary to restrict the available features of PROVIS depending on what the teacher wants. So another mode of PROVIS is needed for testing situations.

For presenting important mathematical interdependencies in probability theory, the possibility to highlight certain line segments or certain probability values should be extended; see, for example, Fig. 21.16.

Of course, to evaluate our computer-aided tool, it would be necessary to conduct empirical investigations in an educational setting. In detail, we have to find out if the use of our tool has a positive impact on the understanding of conditional probabilities and conditional frequencies, respectively. To be more precise, the tool should foster the students' capabilities of handling two-dimensional characteristics and of interpreting their representations and dependencies. This could be done by case studies. If the results are positive, PROVIS will be a contribution to support the instruction of both complex approaches in stochastic education.

Summarizing, PROVIS is a contribution to a future mathematical education, which will focus on essential aspects of stochastic thinking and exempt students from monotonic calculations of routines.

Tool Download https://www.omilab.org/provis

References

1. Aue, V., Bleier, G., Lechner, J., Malle, G.: Handreichung zum Lehrplan Mathematik 2016 Oberstufe AHS (Secondary level two). Bundesministerium für Bildung Lehrplangruppe Mathematik AHS Oberstufe, Vienna (2016)
2. Bennett, K.: Teaching the monty hall dilemma to explore decision-making, probability, and regret in behavioralscience classrooms. Int. J. Scholarship Teach. Learn. **12**(2), Article 13 (2018). https://doi.org/10.20429/ijsotl.2018.120213
3. Binder, K., Krauss, S., Bruckmaier, G.: Effects of visualizing statistical information—an empirical study on tree diagrams and 2—2 tables. Front. Psychol. **6**, Article 1186 (2015). https://doi.org/10.3389/fpsyg.2015.01186
4. Böcherer-Linder, K., Eichler, A., Vogel, M.: Visualising conditional probabilities—Three perspectives on unit squares and tree diagrams. In: Batanero, C., Chernoff, E. (eds.) Teaching and Learning Stochastics, pp. 73-88. ICME-13 Monographs. Springer, Cham. (2018). https://doi.org/10.1007/978-3-319-72871-1_5
5. Brase, C.H., Brase, C.P.: Understanding Basic Statistics, 8th edn. Cengage, Boston (2019)
6. Döller, V.: ProVis—Probability Visualized: Technologische Unterstützung für den Einsatz von Einheitsquadraten und Baumdiagrammen im Stochastikunterricht. University of Vienna: Diploma Thesis (2020). http://othes.univie.ac.at/61461/
7. Döller, V.: ProVis—probability visualized: a modeling tool for teaching stochastics. In: Companion Proceedings of Modellierung 2020 Short, Workshop and Tools & Demo Papers. CEUR Workshop Proceedings, vol. 2542, pp. 222–226. CEUR-WS.org (2020)
8. Döller, V., Götz, S.: Baumdiagramme und Einheitsquadrate 4.0. Stochastik in der Schule **41**(3), 9–19 (2021)
9. Eichler, A., Vogel, M.: Leitidee Daten und Zufall: Von konkreten Beispielen zur Didaktik der Stochastik, 2nd edn. Springer Fachmedien, Wiesbaden (2013)
10. Gesamte Rechtsvorschrift für Lehrpläne—allgemeinbildende höhere Schulen, Fassung vom 16.02.2021, pp. 79-85 (Secondary level one). Bundesministerium Bildung, Wissenschaft und Forschung, Vienna (2021)
11. Johnston, H.: The Spiral Curriculum. Research into Practice. Education Partnerships, (2012) https://eric.ed.gov/?id=ED538282
12. Karagiannis, D., Burzynski, P., Utz, W., Buchmann, R.A.: A metamodeling approach to support the engineering of modeling method requirements. In: 27th IEEE International Requirements Engineering Conference, pp. 199–210 (2019)
13. Olofsson, P., Andersson, M.: Probability, Statistics, and Stochastic Processes, 2nd edn. Wiley, New York (2012)
14. Russel, S., Norvig, P.: Artificial Intelligence: A Modern Approach, 4th edn. Pearson Education, Harlow (2021)
15. Winter, H.: Entdeckendes Lernen im Mathematikunterricht. Einblicke in die Ideengeschichte und ihre Bedeutung für die Pädagogik, 3rd edn. Springer Spektrum, Wiesbaden (2016)

Chapter 22
Improving Student Mobility Through Automated Mapping of Similar Courses

Martina Tomičić Furjan, Bogdan Okreša Djuric, and Tomislav Peharda

Abstract Internationalization is a global trend of society development. In order to get on board with this trend, universities are making great efforts to create possibilities for students to participate in mobility and exchange programs and learn from others. Students' decision to take this great step get out of their comfort zone and manage their stay in an unknown environment depends on many influencing factors, the most important one being a smooth recognition process of the study period and credits earned abroad. SCoRe4Mobility is a tool supposed to help students and responsible people at the home university to find similar courses at other universities and make the selection of the most compatible destination for mobility easier.

Keywords Mobility · Course comparison · Natural language processing · Latent semantic analysis

22.1   Introduction

Global migration of people, goods, and services is defining the way in which today's world is growing and developing in terms of cultural and personal diversification, multi-nationalization, and internationalization.

"Internationalization" can, among others, refer to physical mobility of students and academic staff across countries [1].

International mobility of students represents a great part of the efforts universities undergo in order to increase their visibility, prestige, and reputation within the worldwide academic community. The advantages are manifold, firstly for students and then for sending and receiving universities, but also for the whole community and society. Students that go through the experience of managing their stay and

M. Tomičić Furjan (✉) · B. Okreša Djuric · T. Peharda
Faculty of Organization and Informatics, University of Zagreb, Zagreb, Croatia
e-mail: mtomicic@foi.unizg.hr; dokresa@foi.unizg.hr; tpeharda@foi.unizg.hr

study in an unknown environment are becoming better prepared for their future work life.

International mobility is supposed to ensure experience and knowledge exchange between students coming from different countries and environments, whereby the credits earned have to be recognized and built in the student's original study programs, "without compromising academic progress or generating increased costs associated with an additional year of study" [2].

Advantages of undertaking short-term mobilities, ranging from 1 week to 1 year, have been explored in [3], and they can be cultural (such as cultural awareness and intelligence, global mind openness, empathy development, or language and communication skills advancement), personal (such as better academic performance, better understanding of others, and personal confidence), and employment related (e.g., better employability, greater career choices, international contacts leading to international careers and better overall success). The experience of migration and international mobility can also lead to a higher level of multicultural self-efficacy, increased intercultural competence, as well as a lower level of intergroup anxiety [4].

The decision on taking the opportunities that are available for student international mobility depends on many factors, including opinion of the direct environment (like family and friends), personal mobility aspirations and personal skills (like communication and language skills), demographic characteristics (such as gender, age, and field of study), and availability of information on possibilities [5].

Thereby, students also face many barriers, as systemized by [6], that can be grouped into human (such as cultural differences and motivation), organizational (management of the student mobility through bureaucracy and procedures), strategic (as of strategy of the home university to increase and speed up the recognition process), and financial. Costs of life are the main cause of uncertainty for potential applicants, followed by the lack of knowledge about opportunities and possibilities and students just not knowing whom to contact [7].

The Bologna Declaration [8] has created the European Higher Education Area, whereby one of its six main goals was to increase mobility of students, teachers, and researchers and to ensure that the qualifications and credits gained at the mobility will be recognized at the home university.

The Erasmus program, which was established in 1987, is currently active in all EU member states and some close regions. During more than 30 years over, 4 million students, trainees, and members of the faculty have participated in its exchange program. To achieve all the set objectives, the budget for Erasmus program was greatly increased in the EU budgetary cycle of 2014–2020, and the budget for the next program will be increased even more, in order to triple the number of existing mobilities achieved [9].

Every university defines their way of how to motivate and get students to use those opportunities and possibilities that the mobility programs offer. Usually, a great help and motivator are a smooth and clear credits recognition process, whereby the goal is either that the students choose courses mostly different from the ones they can enroll at their own university, and ensure thereby learning of something new and different, or that students are supposed to choose courses similar to the ones that are obligatory to pass at their home university, so they still achieve all the learning outcomes their original program is offering. In this chapter, there is a focus on the latter, trying to develop a tool which will help in finding the most similar courses at targeted universities. In order to develop such a tool, natural language processing methods have been explored, and the best was chosen.

22.2 Method Description

Natural language processing (NLP) methods are supposed to help computer programs understand human spoken languages and enable analysis on the recognized text strings according to the purpose they are used for. In general, there are five steps of NLP: Morphological and Lexical Analysis (analysis of the structure of words and expressions within the vocabulary), Syntactic Analysis (investigation of the words relation within the sentences they occur in), Semantic Analysis (exploration of the meaning of words and sentences in relation to the context they are related to), Discourse Integration (analysis and integration of words and sentences in relation to others they precede or follow), and Pragmatic Analysis (investigation on the interpretation of the analyzed word or sentences as to what they really mean) [10].

The algorithms within NLP are supposed to compare text strings and give suggestions for their interpretation in various fields of applications, in order to decrease human work and give an efficient output that can be used further [11].

In investigating course similarities, the work is usually done by a responsible person within the university, by manual comparison of different course descriptions, goals, and learning outcomes. When taking into account the great number of obligatory courses within different study programs, distributed through years of study, semesters, and study modules, usually the selection of appropriate courses for each student wishing to study abroad leads to creation of a study abroad semester or year, which is a setup individualized for each student.

22.2.1 NLP Algorithms

Several NLP algorithms were considered to be used for the purposes of the tool described within this chapter. The initial set of considered algorithms was motivated by the goal of the tool, i.e., selecting a course from a list of courses that is the most similar ones to the reference course, and similar conducted and published projects. The specific features used to evaluate and compare the selected algorithms, and thus choose the right one, include, but are not limited to, the following: the speed of processing and performance regarding the current scale of the model and its functionalities, the complexity of implementation, the use of computational resources, and the provided semantic similarity score, compared to the similarity score provided by the employed expert. The following NLP algorithms were considered initially: (i) term frequency-inverse document frequency (TF-IDF) [12, 13], (ii) document similarity algorithm used by spaCy [14, 15] (an NLP framework for Python), (iii) latent semantic analysis (LSA) [16, 17], and (iv) bidirectional encoder representations from transformers (BERT) [18]. A short analysis of each of the initially considered NLP algorithms is given before the particular algorithm utilized by the tool (LSA) is described in some more detail.

Before describing the algorithms themselves, it should be noted here that the concept of a document, used frequently in the context of NLP algorithms, can be applied to essentially any string of characters. Anything from a book to a single sentence, or even a single word, can be classified as a document. In the context of the tool described within this chapter, a document represents a concatenated set of features that describe a course: its name, its description, and its goals, among others.

When document similarity is considered, one of the basic algorithms that can be used to determine whether a given document is in any way similar to the reference document is the one that relies on the occurrence of terms in a document. Term frequency [12] denotes the weighting scheme wherein a weight is assigned to each term of a document based on the number of occurrences of the term in the document. A problem arises here when too many words occur in all of the compared documents, yet they bear no real meaning, e.g., English words "in," "the," and similar, usually referred to as stop words. In order to counter this, term frequency is used alongside document frequency [12, 13], i.e., the number of documents in a given collection of documents that contain the given term. Their combination provides a good indication of which documents are relevant considering the reference document. This effect is trifold [19]: Frequently occurring words are given higher scores (term frequency), words that appear in a large number of documents are given a low score (inverse document frequency), and short and concise documents that mention all the reference words are recognized as higher quality than long documents that mention all the reference words.

In order to utilize the power of mathematics and methods of mathematical modelling, analysis, and transformations, documents and their respective terms, along with their applicable values, are often transformed into mathematical vectors. Word vector is the key concept in this context. A word vector [20] represents a single word with a set of factors or dimensions in a semantic space. In other words, a word vector is a multidimensional meaning representation of a word. These word vectors are then combined, and their computed vector addition is a representation of new passages and documents. The level of similarity of two words, as described in [20], is measured as "the cosine (or dot product or Euclidean distance, depending on the application) between the vectors, and the similarity of two passages (of any length) as the same measure on the sum or average of all its contained words." One of the most popular techniques for generating a set of word vectors based on the provided corpus of text is word2vec [21], which uses a shallow neural network to learn word embeddings.

The second considered NLP algorithm [15], featured in spaCy, determines the semantic similarity of two documents using the measures based on the applicable word vectors, and comparing them.

A different approach to the mechanism of determining word vectors (called hereinafter term vectors) is utilized by the NLP algorithm of latent semantic analysis (LSA) [17], sometimes referred to as latent semantic index (LSI) as well. LSA "models a passage as a simple linear equation, and a large corpus of text as a large set of simultaneous equations" [20]. Instead of simply taking into account the co-occurrence of the words or terms in common passages, sentences, and documents, LSA builds a meaning of a word that is updated every time the word is met in the corpus and the features of document parts where it does not occur. The process is based on singular value decomposition (SVD) [22], which decomposes a collection of documents into a vector space of type and document vectors. The resulting similarity is taking into account semantic values of the observed terms.

The most recent of the considered NLP algorithms is bidirectional encoder representations from transformers (BERT) [18]. BERT was, at the time of its publishing, considered [23] as a significant improvement in understanding natural language queries, and the biggest leap forward in the 5 years prior to its publishing. Therefore, BERT, using transformer architecture to learn embeddings for words, excels as an algorithm in the domain of question answering, yet it can be applied to comparing documents, i.e., determining document similarity. Question answering is one of the domains NLP can be applied to [19], with the others including, but not limited to, text classification, information retrieval, and information extraction.

The considered NLP algorithms were tested on a limited corpus of description of 10 courses wherein each course document consisted of values of the following attributes: course name, course description, and course goals. The documents of the corpus were compared against the input (reference) document, which consisted of values of the same attributes, and the most similar document was observed. Prior to analyzing the test results, the same dataset used as the corpus was given to an expert to provide their opinion on similarity of the documents of the corpus, i.e., the collected course descriptions, which comprise courses of an external institution, to the input document that represents a course of our home institution.

The conducted test was minimal and served the purpose of further establishing, testing, and proving that the algorithm that should be chosen for the tool presented in this chapter is LSA. This initial choice was made based on the available publications regarding a similar type of a system, mainly [24–26], and was made certain after the conducted test, when performance, similarity score, implementation, and runtime environments were analyzed. LSA was selected for a number of reasons, the most prominent of which are as follows: because it is fast enough for the currently envisioned scale of the tool described in this chapter, because implementation is not complex and demanding resource-wise, and because the similarity scores provided during the testing described above were most aligned with the scores provided by the employed expert.

22.2.2 Latent Semantic Analysis

LSA is not only a method of NLP, as described earlier, but is considered a theory of meaning as well [16, 20, 27], since "meaning is constructed through experience with language" [27]. Thus, it gains a more interdisciplinary context, which is appropriate for the domain of this chapter's topic. Mathematically, the foundations of LSA can be found in the Vector Space Model (VSM) [28] that converts documents to vectors of as many dimensions as there are terms in their dictionary.

Formally, matrix X as $t \times d$ is a VSM of a corpus d in a space of dictionary terms t. Term dimensionality of VSM is subjected to reduction techniques of term filtering and term conflation (stemming or lemmatization); frequency transformations, such as TF-IDF described earlier; and normalization. Such an approach allows for calculations of term-based and document-based similarities.

The approach introduced by LSA [16] ensures that the terms that are similar in meaning, i.e., semantically related, bear some weight in the calculations on similarity of documents, based on the patterns of how individual terms are used in the corpus. Therefore, it provides a different treatment for the matrix X. The first step becomes application of matrix operation of SVD which decomposes the td matrix into three components: term eigenvectors U, document eigenvectors V, and singular values Σ. Therefore, $X = U\Sigma T^T$. This term frequency matrix is then truncated to $X_k = U_k \Sigma_k V_k^T$, where k is the most important dimensions (or highest singular values), which are "the square roots of common eigenvalues in the simultaneous principal component analysis of terms as variables (with documents as observations) and documents as variables (with terms as observations)" [27]. It is interesting to note here that matrix X_k is a result [27, 29] of the original term frequencies being transformed using a hidden topic structure upon which projected terms and documents are. Further detailed mathematical features of LSA are suggested to be found in [22, 27].

22.3 Method Conceptualization

In the following subsections, the development of the method for comparison of courses, authors of this chapter named it SCoRe4Mobility, is described. The logic of the method is shown first, followed by the conceptual metamodel as an entry to the tool developed to support the method.

22.3.1 Method of SCoRe4Mobility

To begin with, a set of course descriptions was established, comprising course descriptions from various study programs of universities and their constituents with which the Faculty of Organization and Informatics has a valid and active Erasmus+ agreement. The courses are described using the following set of attributes: host university, semester when the course is performed, ID of the course for indexing and communication purposes, the name of the course, number of credits awarded for the course, goals of the course, its description, and the expected learning outcomes. Considering the diversity of the used sources (publicly available course descriptions), some of the attributes (especially learning outcomes) are omitted in some entries.

A selected subset of these attributes is used in the similarity-determining process, while the rest of them are used for the final result representation and filtering courses. The prepared LSA model, which is built on the whole corpus consisting of all the courses, is run using a subset of the whole corpus, consisting of only the courses that the user is interested in. This approach is useful for limiting the resources necessary to run the model and the used similarity algorithm. The query document, which is built based on the user's input, and represents the description of the course that the user wants to find similar courses to, is described by the same subset of attributes that are used for the other courses: course goals, course description, and its learning outcomes.

LSA is usually, in the context of determining document similarity, performed in pairwise comparison. Such an approach is applied in SCoRe4Mobility as well, but the query document set comprises only a single element. The number of elements of the set the query document is compared to depends on the set filters. The filtered set of documents is first preprocessed insomuch that the document is split into words, and then usual English stop words are discarded, along with the words that can be found in a single document only once. A corpus is built based on the subset of documents processed in such a manner. The method to determine similarity utilized by SCoRe4Mobility is implemented using Python library Gensim [29].

Once the similarity is calculated between all the pairs of the query document and the corpus, the top similarity result is presented to the user in the format they choose within the model. Depending on the result, the user then can create a list of courses, which will be enrolled at the targeted university.

The simplified process model, describing the logic of the method implementation, is shown in Fig. 22.1. The swimlanes represent the user and the developed tool. Future work on the tool improvement could automate some of the listed activities, i.e., *Create content of obligatory courses* (which could be fetched from a database) and *Create list of courses at target University to enrol* (which could be automatically be enrolled at the target University), but for that improvement, digitalization of course catalogues (in a machine retrievable format) and of the enrolment process should be established.

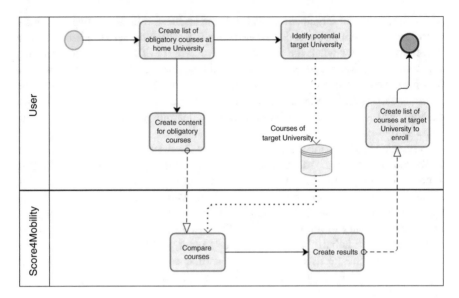

Fig. 22.1 Simplified process model

The described process is, for the purposes of this chapter, implemented as a single service providing a single (user-wise) process, as described in the rest of this chapter. Such an approach is one of the segments where the authors observe room for improvement. Most importantly, the single service could be broken down into coordinated microservices. Utilizing such a microservice architecture, coupled with the paradigm of a distributed system, e.g., a multiagent system, would provide welcome additions to the robustness, scalability, and load management of the implemented system. An identified applicable approach is outlined, in general concepts, in a currently ongoing project Orchestration of Hybrid Artificial Intelligence Methods for Computer Games described briefly in [30].

22.3.2 The Metamodel

The foundations of the metamodel of SCoRe4Mobility can be found in the fundamental elements of a class (or entity) and relationship model [31, 32]. Therein a class represents a type of an entity, where an entity represents an element that can be abstracted using any standalone concept. A relationship is a concept that connects at least two entities (not necessarily distinct), thus having at least one source, and at least one target element.

The elements of the metamodel for SCoRe4Mobility, shown in Fig. 22.2, are derived from the elements of this, in this instance, meta^{2}model. The central element of the metamodel for SCoRe4Mobility is a *Similar course recommender algorithm.* This class describes all the NLP algorithms that are at the user's disposal, which can be used for performing the task of determining the similarity score of given inputs, and which is provided by a related *Service* element.

A *Service* is an external service available online that provides one or more NLP algorithms that are replaceable and can be implemented by the provider of the service. The intention of abstracting and modelling the approach in this way is to provide the modular and generalized implementation that can utilize various provided NLP algorithms, thus rendering the currently suggested tool somewhat future-proof. Such a service can be self-hosted.

It was mentioned that an NLP algorithm is provided with a set of inputs. The *Input* element describes all the types of entities that provide input for an NLP algorithm entity. An input can be a string of characters, an otherwise specified value, or it can be a *Set of courses*, or a *Reference course*, which is a key user input in SCoRe4Mobility. The set of courses is provided as a source of stored course descriptions, a set of documents against which the reference course will be compared against, and among which the most similar course will be selected and suggested to the user.

Various *Filter* instances can be applied to a specified data source, thereby constraining the data source and creating a subset of data that is to be used in the similarity-determining process.

The latter special type of input is the *Reference course* which constitutes a collection comprising a description of the reference course and its goals—the two *Reference course attribute* instances. Both of these values are input by the user, and together they form the content that is used to find the most similar course in the provided data source (or its subset, based on the applied filters).

Once the NLP algorithm is run, and the similarity process is conducted, the output is provided to the user. Not specified in the metamodel for the sake of retaining its general applicability, the output of SCoRe4Mobility model's similarity-determining process is established based on the user's chosen output format, e.g., JSON, CSV, etc.

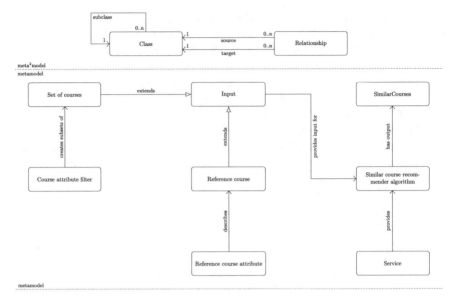

Fig. 22.2 The meta^2 model and metamodel for SCoRe4Mobility

22.4 Proof of Concept

The tool developed to support the method of comparing and identifying similar courses was developed using the ADOxx platform [33]. It can be freely downloaded and used. The AdoXX model is presented in this section first, followed by the service implementation description.

22.4.1 ADOxx Model

The tool implemented in ADOxx comprises elements that are to be considered as specialized types, when compared to the classes defined in the SCoRe4Mobility metamodel. Each of the elements can be instantiated within the modelling canvas, as shown in Fig. 22.3, although some of them should not be instantiated more than once, at the current stage of development of the SCoRe4Mobility tool. The elements that can be used within ADOxx represent various stages of the process, from sourcing the necessary data from a set of courses, filtering them based on the values of specific course attributes, and providing the attribute values of a reference course to the algorithm that should be used to compute and recommend the most similar courses, and its output.

The ADOxx model represents a user-oriented part of the two parts that the whole tool consists of. The ADOxx model can be considered as a user interface of the service that is located in the backend. The input provided by the user is forwarded

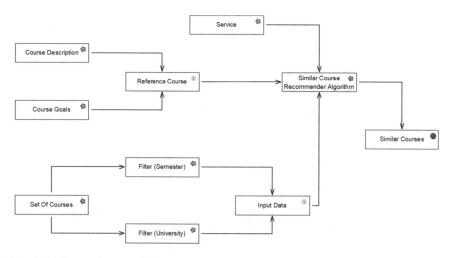

Fig. 22.3 The ADOxx tool SCoRe4Mobility

to the service specified in the *Service* element, where the necessary computing is performed.

The elements that expect an input from the user are designated as such using the small cogwheel icon in the upper-right part of their visual representation. The kind of expected user input, and what it is, can be determined in the notebook view of the specific element. The elements that provide some information to the user, e.g., aggregated information of the connected input elements, have a small *i* icon in their upper right. Finally, the output element, *Similar Courses*, has a red icon, while no response is present, which turns green when a response has been generated by the given service, i.e., when some courses are deemed as similar, and the user can view them.

The input of *Course Description* and *Course Goals* define values of attributes *description* and *goals*, respectively, of the reference course. The input of *Data Source* provides the address of the set of course descriptions that the reference course should be compared against, and wherefrom the recommended similar courses are to be sourced. Input of *Filter* elements is used (if specified, as *Filter* elements are optional) to filter the courses of the used source of courses, e.g., based on their home universities or the semester when they are taught. Such a filtered (or unfiltered, if no *Filter* elements are used) dataset is prepared for processing in the *Input Data* element. The algorithm that is used to recommend similar courses is specified in its element of the model. The specified algorithm is provided by the source the address of which is the value of user input of the *Service* element. Finally, *Similar Courses* provides the output of the whole process, i.e., top three courses from the *Input Data* that are the most similar to the reference course, as shown in Fig. 22.4 formatted as JSON content.

A dropdown menu that provides a trigger to execute the model is located in the ADOxx Modeling Toolkit toolbar under the SCoRe4Mobility item (Fig. 22.5).

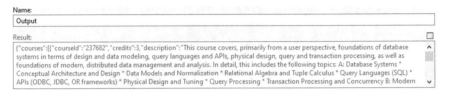

Fig. 22.4 Response content example

The expanded dropdown menu contains *Find similar courses* which, when clicked, executes AdoScript code.

Fig. 22.5 SCoRe4Mobility dropdown in toolbar

Once the input is set, and the model is run, in the current version of the SCoRe4Mobility tool, the filters, and the reference course attributes, are sent to the service that provides the NLP algorithm necessary for determining and retrieving similar courses. The service is open to the public through an application programming interface (API) and is described in detail in the following section.

22.4.2 Service Implementation

The role of the API is to abstract away the logic behind derivation of the courses' similarity as well as to provide a simple communication interface to the user (in our case, ADOxx model) and the business logic. That being said, the request that arrives to API must accommodate a predefined format. The response contains three courses that are the most similar to the reference course, and their respective similarity scores, from the set of input data consisting of a possibly filtered initial set of course descriptions.

The main technology used for the development of the API is Python, more concretely, the Flask web framework [34]. Flask deals with setting up the API in terms of launching an HTTP server and processing incoming requests to previously created endpoints. Flask is described as a microframework due to the fact that it does not provide built-in functionalities to validate the input data, connect to a database, or any other form of integration with third-party libraries or application layers.

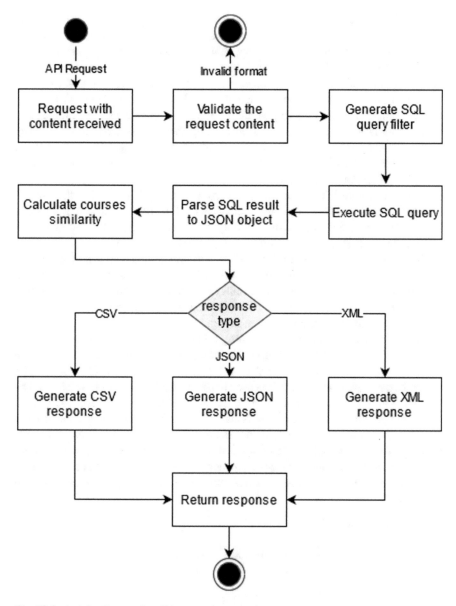

Fig. 22.6 Activity diagram describing steps in generating output

From a technical perspective, the API provides the following functionalities: processes incoming requests, validates the request content data, communicates with the database storage, derives similarity percentage, and generates different types of output response, as visualized in Fig. 22.6.

All of the listed functionalities are incorporated in a single service, although that does not necessarily need to be the case. Microservice architecture [35] describes an approach to architectural modeling that introduces lightweight services and decoupling of the independent functionalities by separating them into multiple services (APIs), as some of the key elements. In this particular case, none of the functionalities are tightly bound; hence, they could live independently. A proposal for such implementation could potentially be in having database communication, courses similarity calculation, and a user-facing interface as separate APIs. Even though the user would only communicate with the user-facing API, while the end user uses the ADOxx tool, behind the scenes, all the APIs would be mutually related and included in shaping the result for a user.

Supporting libraries and technologies used in the API to deliver the desired service are: Cerberus for the request content data validation, SQLite as a lightweight internal storage, LSA algorithm including associated libraries for the similarity calculation and pandas, json & json2xml to generate a response.

The API exposes two endpoints which are/score/compute and/score/fetchdata. The first one's request body requires a description of the course that shall be tested against the stored courses, an optional filter to specify what are the constraints for the stored courses, and a required output format type. The second endpoint is for retrieving data from the database, with no processing.

The endpoints are accessed by sending a POST, GET, or a JSON request. The request body for the/compute endpoint must be in JSON, and it consists of three attributes: *input, filter,* and *outputFormat. input* attribute is a JSON object with attributes *description* and *goals*. It is used to describe the course which shall then be compared to the bucket of courses from the storage and provide a similarity. *filter* is an optional attribute that is a JSON object with *uni* and *semester* as attributes. *uni* attribute is a list of university names to be used as an inclusion constraint when preparing the set of courses. In a similar fashion, *semester* is a list that accepts either *summer* or *winter* as values. *outputFormat* accepts a string value that is either JSON, XML, or CSV that will be used to shape the output. An example request is shown in Fig. 22.7.

Fig. 22.7 Request content example

```
{
"input": {
"description": "description of the reference course",
"goals": "learn how to learn"
},
"output": {
"format": "json"
},
"filter": {
"semester": ["winter"]
}
}
```

Once the request content is validated, the filter attribute is consumed to generate an SQL query to fetch courses from the SQLite storage, which meet the constraints on uni and semester attributes. Data retrieved from the storage is parsed and formatted as a JSON. Since JSON is a format that provides easy access and manipulation, it is used in the API to transfer data.

Calculate courses similarity activity takes as input course description from the input attribute of the request and filtered courses. The computing utilizes the LSA algorithm. The output of this activity is similarity represented in percentages that indicates how much an individual stored course relates to the input reference course. Such a function can be formally described as *similarity(X, N)* $\rightarrow$ *Y*, where *X* is the reference course, *N* is an individual course from the potentially filtered set of the stored courses, and Y is the result of the similarity function, i.e., percentage of similarity.

At that point, the response content is ready, and it is no longer involved in any kind of process that would change the semantics around it, except for the format it is served in to the user. Depending on the defined response type, the endpoint result may be provided in JSON, XML, or CSV format. For each of these formats, a handler function is put in place to apply the transformation. Eventually, a response is returned to the user which also indicates the ending point of the process. Example response, formatted as a JSON string, is shown in Fig. 22.8. The currently implemented ADOxx model provides the user with the ability to choose how the output is formatted, based on a defined set of formats: JSON, XML, or CSV. These output formats are selected as they provide data in a computer-readable format. Such data can be further processed, easily imported to a spreadsheet or various analysis software. Subject to the future development is implementing a more structured and human-readable data format.

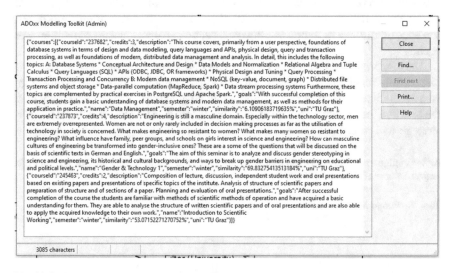

Fig. 22.8 Response content example in AdoXX

22.5   Conclusion

SCoRe4Mobility is a tool created to support internationalization efforts of universities by increasing student mobility. The main goal that the tool is helping to achieve is to enable an automated comparison and mapping of similar courses within different university study programs and to find the best matching courses, i.e., their description and goals similarity. The result is one or several similar courses at different universities, which are then recommended to be chosen for enrollment. Proper selection of courses that are recognized by the home university makes students' decisions about whether and where to travel clearer and easier.

Some efforts have previously been made on this matter through a variety of approaches and methodologies used. In this chapter, we have chosen and presented how the natural language processing logic through latent semantic analysis algorithm implementation can be used in performing the matching process.

The identified classes, as well as related filters like mobility semester and desired university, are the foundation for the tool's building blocks, whereby existing code and graphics within the OMiLAB have been analyzed and, if applicable, integrated into the developed tool.

Further upgrade of the tool, as the next step within this process of methodology creation, is planned through analysis of its practical utility. There are many identified directions of improvement and further development of the tool, and its underlying backend service. These improvements include, but are not limited to, decomposing the implemented backend service on multiple microservices that would be more specialized, thus utilizing the idea and the concept of distributed systems and the microservice architecture; real-time filtering of the available courses, so that the user can observe the effect of introduced filters in real time; and combining the tool, or the connected service backend, with other services that would utilize different methods of artificial or hybrid intelligence, such as chatbots, voice recognition, and agents.

The tool presented in this chapter is in a proof-of-concept stage, yet it already features a fully functioning service in the sense that its main purpose—recommending courses similar to the reference course—can be achieved. Further development of the tool and the service is expected, especially considering that the ultimate goal is strategic and student-oriented.

Acknowledgments This work has been supported in part by Croatian Science Foundation under project number IP-2019-04-5824.

Tool Download https://www.omilab.org/score4mobility

References

1. Teichler, U.: Internationalisation trends in higher education and the changing role of international student mobility. J. Int. Mobil. **5**, 177 (2017). https://doi.org/10.3917/jim.005.0179
2. Courtois, A.: 'It doesn't really matter which university you attend or which subject you study while abroad.' The massification of student mobility programmes and its implications for equality in higher education. Eur. J. High. Educ. **8**, 99–114 (2018). https://doi.org/10.1080/21568235.2017.1373027
3. Roy, A., Newman, A., Ellenberger, T., Pyman, A.: Outcomes of international student mobility programs: a systematic review and agenda for future research. Stud. High. Educ. **44**, 1630–1644 (2019). https://doi.org/10.1080/03075079.2018.1458222
4. Zimmermann, J., Greischel, H., Jonkmann, K.: The development of multicultural effectiveness in international student mobility. High. Educ. (2020). https://doi.org/10.1007/s10734-020-00509-2
5. Bartha, Z., Gubik, A.S.: Institutional determinants of higher education students' international mobility within the Erasmus Programme countries. Theory Methodol. Pract. **14**, 3–13 (2018). https://doi.org/10.18096/TMP.2018.02.01
6. Pagani, R.N., Ramond, B., Da Silva, V.L., Zammar, G., Kovaleski, J.L.: Key factors in university-to-university knowledge and technology transfer on international student mobility. Knowl. Manag. Res. Pract. **18**, 405–423 (2020). https://doi.org/10.1080/14778238.2019.1678415
7. Bartha, Z., Gubik, A.S., Rethi, G.: Management of innovations in Hungarian HEIs: enhancing the Erasmus mobility Programme. Mark. Manag. Innov. **84–95** (2019). https://doi.org/10.21272/mmi.2019.1-07
8. European Ministers in charge of Higher Education. The Bologna Declaration of 19 June 1999: Joint Declaration of the European Ministers of Education (1999).
9. Council of the EU. Erasmus + 2021 2027: Council Reaches a Provisional Agreement with the European Parliament. In: Council of the European Union. https://www.consilium.europa.eu/en/press/press-releases/2020/12/11/erasmus-2021-2027-council-reaches-a-provisional-agreement-with-the-european-parliament/ (2020). Accessed 22 Mar 2021
10. Chopra, A., Prashar, A., Sain, C.: Natural language processing. Int. J. Technol. Enhanc. Emerg. Eng. Res. **1**, 131–134 (2013)
11. Jain, A., Kulkarni, G., Shah, V.: Natural language processing. Int. J. Comput. Sci. Eng. **6**, 161–167 (2018). https://doi.org/10.26438/ijcse/v6i1.161167
12. Manning, C.D., Raghavan, P., Schutze, H.: Introduction to Information Retrieval. Cambridge University Press, Cambridge, UK (2008)
13. Luhn, H.P.: A statistical approach to mechanized encoding and searching of literary information. IBM J. Res. Dev. **1**, 309–317 (1957). https://doi.org/10.1147/rd.14.0309
14. spaCy. ExplosionAI GmbH (2021)
15. ExplosionAI GmbH. Linguistic Features: Word Vectors and Semantic Similarity. In: SpaCy Usage Doc. https://spacy.io/usage/linguistic-features#vectors-similarity (2021). Accessed 17 Mar 2021
16. Landauer, T.K., Foltz, P.W., Laham, D.: An introduction to latent semantic analysis. Discourse Process. **25**, 259–284 (1998). https://doi.org/10.1080/01638539809545028
17. Deerwester, S., Dumais, S.T., Furnas, G.W., Landauer, T.K., Harshman, R.: Indexing by latent semantic analysis. J. Am. Soc. Inf. Sci. **41**, 391–407 (1990)
18. Devlin, J., Chang, M.-W., Lee, K., Toutanova, K.: BERT: pre-training of deep bidirectional transformers for language understanding. ArXiv181004805 Cs (2019)
19. Russell, S., Norvig, P.: Artificial Intelligence: A Modern Approach, 3rd edn. Prentice Hall, Hoboken, NJ (2010)
20. Landauer, T.K.: LSA as a theory of meaning. In: Landauer, T.K., McNamara, D.S., Dennis, S., Kintsch, W. (eds.) Handbook of latent semantic analysis, pp. 3–34. Routledge, New York (2011)

21. Mikolov, T., Sutskever, I., Chen, K., Corrado, G., Dean, J.: Distributed representations of words and phrases and their compositionality. ArXiv13104546 Cs Stat (2013)
22. Martin, D.I., Berry, M.W.: Mathematical foundations behind latent semantic analysis. In: Landauer, T.K., McNamara, D.S., Dennis, S., Kintsch, W. (eds.) Handbook of latent semantic analysis, pp. 35–56. Routledge, New York (2011)
23. Nayak, P.: Understanding searches better than ever before. In: Google. https://blog.google/products/search/search-language-understanding-bert/ (2019). Accessed 24 Feb 2021
24. Guberović, E., Turčinović, F., Relja, Z., Bosnić, I.: In search of a syllabus: comparing computer science courses. In: 2018 41st International Convention on Information and Communication Technology, Electronics and Microelectronics (MIPRO), pp. 0588–0592. IEEE, Opatija (2018)
25. Fu, Q., Zhuang, Y., Gu, J., Zhu, Y., Guo, X.: Agreeing to disagree: Choosing among eight topic-modeling methods. Big Data Res. **23**, 100173 (2021). https://doi.org/10.1016/j.bdr.2020.100173
26. Miller, T.: Essay assessment with latent semantic analysis. J. Educ. Comput. Res. **29**, 495–512 (2003). https://doi.org/10.2190/W5AR-DYPW-40KX-FL99
27. Evangelopoulos, N.E.: Latent semantic analysis. Wiley Interdiscip. Rev. Cogn. Sci. **4**, 683–692 (2013). https://doi.org/10.1002/wcs.1254
28. Salton, G., Wong, A., Yang, C.S.: A vector space model for automatic indexing. Commun. ACM. **18**, 613–620 (1975). https://doi.org/10.1145/361219.361220
29. Řehůřek, R., Sojka, P.: Software framework for topic modelling with large corpora. In: Proceedings of the LREC 2010 workshop on new challenges for NLP frameworks, pp. 45–50. University of Malta, Valletta, MT (2010)
30. Schatten, M., Tomičić, I., Okreša Đurić, B.: Orchestration platforms for hybrid artificial intelligence in computer games – a conceptual model. In: Strahonja, V., Steingartner, W., Kirinić, V. (eds.) Central European conference on information and intelligent systems, pp. 3–8. Varaždin, Faculty of Organization and Informatics, University of Zagreb (2020)
31. Karagiannis, D., Buchmann, R.A., Burzynski, P., Reimer, U., Walch, M.: Fundamental conceptual modeling languages in OMiLAB. In: Karagiannis, D., Mayr, H.C., Mylopoulos, J. (eds.) Domain-Specific Conceptual Modeling, 1st edn, pp. 3–30. Springer, Cham (2016)
32. Karagiannis, D., Kühn, H.: Metamodelling platforms. In: Bauknecht, K., Tjoa, A.M., Quirchmayr, G. (eds.) E-commerce and web technologies, pp. 182–182. Springer, Aix-en-Provence (2002)
33. BOC Gmbh. ADOxx. BOC Gmbh, Vienna, AT. (2016)
34. Grinberg, M.: Flask web development: developing web applications with python, 2nd edn. O'Reilly Media, Sebastopol, CA (2018)
35. Lewis J, Fowler M.: Microservices. In: martinfowler.com. https://martinfowler.com/articles/microservices.html. Accessed 27 Mar 2021

Part VIII
Digital Humanities

Chapter 23
Aggregation and Curation of Historical Archive Information

Panos Constantopoulos, Vicky Dritsou, Maria Ilvanidou, and Alexandra Chroni

Abstract Integrating archival information from different cultural heritage institutions to support historical research has been a commonly pursued goal among humanities digital research infrastructures. Due to the lack of standards in performing such processes, there is a need to provide guidance to interested parties and share knowledge deriving from successful practices. In this chapter, we introduce the Historical Information Curation (HIC) model that aims to address this need. Based on our experience with aggregating and curating archival collections, we have developed a two-faceted model for such processes, capable of supporting both the structural representation of the required workflows and the analysis of their dynamics.

Keywords Digital curation · Aggregation · Process modeling · Ontologies · Digital humanities · Archive metadata

P. Constantopoulos (✉) · V. Dritsou
Department of Informatics, Athens University of Economics and Business, Athens, Greece

Digital Curation Unit, Information Management Systems Institute, Athena Research Centre, Athens, Greece
e-mail: panosc@aueb.gr; vdritsou@aueb.gr

M. Ilvanidou
Digital Curation Unit, Information Management Systems Institute, Athena Research Centre, Athens, Greece
e-mail: m.ilvanidou@dcu.gr

A. Chroni
Department of Informatics, Athens University of Economics and Business, Athens, Greece
e-mail: achroni@aueb.gr

23.1   Archival Integration for Historical Research in Digital Humanities Infrastructures

During the last decade or so, there has been a significant effort from several digital humanities research infrastructures to aggregate content from various cultural heritage institutions, thus enabling historical research, while establishing more standardized processes in doing so. Their focus is to integrate access to archives, connect resources, and, in many cases, support research processes. Some of them are domain- and/or theme-specific, while others are broader in scope.

Europeana,[1] the European Union's Digital Service Infrastructure for cultural heritage launched in 2008, falls in the latter category. It aggregates content from thousands of cultural heritage institutions (museums, libraries, archives) throughout Europe, acting as a single point of access to millions of digitized records of cultural objects. Within the Europeana ecosystem, there are specific collections and projects on topics related to history, such as "Europeana 1914–1918,"[2] "Historiana,"[3] etc. Similarly, an explicit interest in gaining insights into researchers' needs can be traced back to initiatives such as the Europeana Cloud[4] project and the Europeana Research Community[5] [1]. In addition, the Europeana Data Model, which was community-developed in order to harvest, manage, and publish cultural heritage metadata, is now used by several other cultural aggregators.

The European Holocaust Research Infrastructure (EHRI),[6] launched in 2010, aims to advance Holocaust studies by transforming archival research on the Holocaust and connecting sources, institutions, and people across Europe and beyond. EHRI has come up with the concept of research-driven archival integration, choosing to "focus on the content as a researcher would need it" [2] and using graph databases to implement the EHRI integrated information resource.

From 2012 to 2016, the Collaborative European Digital Archive Infrastructure (CENDARI)[7] created a virtual research environment (VRE) to integrate digital archives and tools for advanced historical research, focusing on two case studies: medieval culture and World War I. It has been built to support the historian research workflow, and it does so through a data integration platform, supporting semantic enrichment, and a note-taking environment with faceted search, sharing, and collaboration capabilities [3].

---

[1] https://www.europeana.eu/ (Accessed 30.03.2021).

[2] http://www.europeana1914-1918.eu/ (Accessed 30.03.2021).

[3] https://historiana.eu/ (Accessed 30.03.2021).

[4] https://pro.europeana.eu/project/europeana-cloud (Accessed 30.03.2021).

[5] https://pro.europeana.eu/page/europeana-research (Accessed 30.03.2021).

[6] https://www.ehri-project.eu/ (Accessed 30.03.2021).

[7] http://www.cendari.eu/ (Accessed 30.03.2021).

Equally oriented toward supporting research processes—although focusing on archaeology rather than history—is the ARIADNE and ARIADNEplus[8] infrastructure. It was launched in 2012 and has already integrated in its repository existing archaeological data infrastructures in Europe. It currently seeks to develop a Linked Open Data approach and create a VRE that will provide tools and services for data analysis and synthesis, enabling researchers to reuse data accessible through its catalogue and carry out collaborative research.

Drawing on the experience of these pan-European platforms, but also taking into consideration the smaller-scale, local characteristics and different needs of a national infrastructure, APOLLONIS, the Greek Infrastructure for Digital Arts, Humanities, and Language Research and Innovation,[9] has taken a similar, yet slightly different, approach in its Greek 1940s case study. Launched as a federated infrastructure in 2018, APOLLONIS brings together two ESFRI-related national networks in the Social Sciences and Humanities area with a long presence in Greece, CLARIN:EL[10] and DARIAH-GR,[11] creating bridges where commonalities are observed. In the Greek 1940s case study, what we had in mind was not only the needs of historians and digital humanists but also those of research infrastructures and what we consider to be a part of their mandate, i.e., providing guidance and sharing knowledge deriving from successful practices. Thus, we decided to aggregate, index, and enrich archival metadata for historical research and at the same time take it a step further, documenting the digital curation processes and workflows we followed and the tools and methods we used in order to do so.

Humanities research can be differentiated from research in the natural sciences "by its interest in the particular: a concrete work or corpus, a historical event or period, a culture, an artefact, or an artist" [1]. As noted by Dallas [4], it is often hermeneutic rather than experimental, and idiographic—aiming to provide understanding of a particular phenomenon—rather than nomothetic—aiming to produce generally applicable laws or generalizations. A wealth of historical information lies in material objects (documents, photographs, maps, audiovisual collections, etc.) held in archives and other cultural heritage institutions, with millions of records searchable and accessible through their analogue catalogues. The "digital turn" in historical scholarship and archival research holds the promise of breaking down the barriers to physical access, through digitization and open access to archival records. Archives, though, are in general much less advanced than libraries and

---

[8] https://ariadne-infrastructure.eu/ (Accessed 30.03.2021).

[9] https://apollonis-infrastructure.gr/ (Accessed 30.03.2021).

[10] https://www.clarin.gr/en (Accessed 30.03.2021).

[11] http://www.dyas-net.gr/?lang=en (Accessed 30.03.2021).

museums in sharing their content online, and provision of digital access can be quite uneven, due to lack of resources and familiarity with digital processes [5]. For all these reasons and due to the lack of standards in performing such processes, digital projects and institutions often resort to ad hoc practices—that are not reproducible or sustainable—when aggregating archival content. Moving beyond ad hoc practices and establishing a methodology for aggregating and curating archival metadata to enable historical research is the main challenge addressed by our work. By introducing the Historical Information Curation (HIC) model, we aim to address this need and provide guidance to interested parties, i.e., institutions and individuals, proposing standardized, reusable processes as the field matures beyond organizational silos into digital humanities research infrastructures.

23.2   Curating Information in the APOLLONIS Infrastructure

The development of the Greek 1940s use case within APOLLONIS addressed the challenge of aggregating and curating different historical archives and, more precisely, six related digitized archival collections coming from different data providers. It comprises a set of tasks, each one aiming at a different goal. These tasks derive from the Extended Digital Curation Lifecycle Model [6] and are presented in Fig. 23.1. Our aim was twofold: the assembly, aggregation, and curation of material from the distinct archives on one hand, thus enabling their joint indexing, while on the other hand, we have focused on the identification of the aggregation and digital curation workflows for the reusability of the processes. Toward the latter aim and in an attempt to provide a curation methodology for interested parties, we have developed a BPMN model, presented in Fig. 23.2, which captures the causal precedence relations and the decisions of the whole process. The workflow model contains 15 tasks, which can be grouped into 2 categories, based on the challenges they address: data heterogeneity and knowledge enhancement and representation. Though our work is described in what follows as a sequence of tasks, one should bear in mind that the actual workflow has not always been strictly sequential: Most tasks were indeed performed sequentially, but there existed cases with simultaneous processing or cases with completed tasks that had to be revisited after the production of a later outcome.

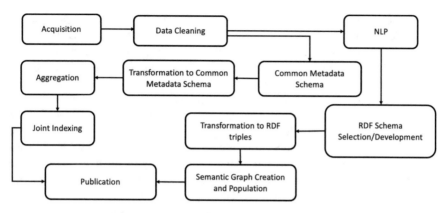

Fig. 23.1 Information aggregation and curation processes

23.2.1   Data Heterogeneity

Starting from the acquisition of the data (illustrated on the right of Fig. 23.2), we have acquired six independent digitized archival collections containing 92,000 records in total, which produced a complete dataset of approximately 4.6 million metadata values. These individual collections were obtained in different file formats and following different data structures. Therefore, our first task was to overcome their syntactic heterogeneity. Through multiple transformations (with the use of existing software and/or programmatically), we have homogenized a variety of file formats, and we have then organized the initial complete dataset in comma-separated values (csv) format. We have chosen this format due to its user-friendliness, so that even non-experienced users can easily work with it. The outcome of this process was the production of six csv files, one for each acquired collection.

The next goal was the cleaning of the metadata values, in an attempt to face the challenges arising from the lack of standardization. Typographic and spelling issues, erroneous mixing of Latin and Greek alphabets, abbreviations and acronyms, and uppercase and lowercase writing styles were dealt in this task of cleaning using the open-source software OpenRefine.[12] Data cleaning was performed semi-automatically and individually for each acquired collection. Moreover, by using the same software, we have performed segmentation of complex data that included repeating values in single data fields.

---

[12] https://openrefine.org/ (Accessed 03.04.2021).

We then focused on overcoming the structural and semantic heterogeneity of the data. Each acquired collection followed a different metadata schema; therefore, the subject data were organized using different structures and different semantics and with varying complexity. Since our goal is to unify the individual data sets and provide uniform access using joint indices, it is crucial that these are structurally homogenized and that semantic ambiguities are eliminated. The solution we have provided to face heterogeneity and achieve data disambiguation was the application of one common metadata schema. For this purpose, we have selected the Europeana Data Model (EDM),[13] a model for cultural heritage metadata developed in the context of the Europeana initiative. After careful study of all fields within each individual metadata schema and their actual values, we have manually mapped each field to a corresponding one of the adopted schema. Cases where the fields in hand revealed more specific descriptions (and/or definitions) than those of EDM were treated by adding extensions to the latter. Finally, all data have been programmatically expressed in terms of the extended EDM schema (encoded in XML format).

The unification of the individual collections has been completed by ingesting the outcome of the transformation process into our previously developed MORe aggregator [7]. After validating the unified collection using the MORe micro-services, we proceeded to the development of the joint indices. According to our predefined criteria and with the use of the open-source search engine Elasticsearch,[14] we have developed five indices for information regarding Actors (Persons and Groups), Places, Time, Events, and Topics. Finally, we have implemented a user-friendly interface, where the unified collection is published and interested users can interact by exploiting the joint indices.

---

[13] https://pro.europeana.eu/page/edm-documentation (Accessed 30.03.2021).

[14] https://www.elastic.co/elasticsearch/ (Accessed 30.03.2021).

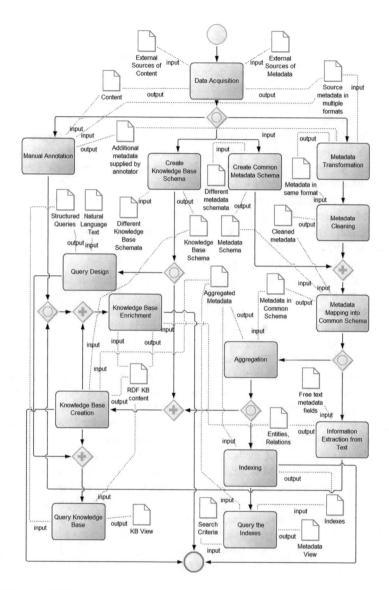

Fig. 23.2 The BPMN model representing the aggregation and curation workflow

23.2.2   *Knowledge Enhancement and Representation*

The second group of tasks undertaken addresses the challenge of both enriching the existing information (bottom right of Fig. 23.2) and representing knowledge using an efficient structure (left part of Fig. 23.2).

While executing the curation steps presented in Sect. 23.2.1 and, more precisely, after having completed data cleaning, a detailed investigation of the data values has revealed complex fields containing information—or referring to information—that had not been annotated. Such values included valuable information resources with respect to our selected criteria. In an attempt to enhance the primary data in hand and exploit methods to enrich our unified collection, we decided to follow an additional curation path, executed in parallel with the sequence of steps described above. In order to exploit this additional information, we have applied Natural Language Processing (NLP) methods to a subset of collections containing such rich values. Using the Apache UIMA Ruta[15] rule language, we have expressed and applied the necessary rules to extract (previously not annotated) information. This process resulted in the successful identification of 15723 Actors, 9949 Document types, 4545 Dates, 3851 Topics, and 2125 Places. The extracted values have been annotated and are considered as secondary data, complementing the primary data to produce an enriched dataset.

We have chosen to organize the enriched information (primary and secondary data together) in a separate structure, so as to distinguish it from the original information coming from the providers and to support its separate evolution. Since one of our main objectives throughout this work was to interrelate resources coming from different digital collections that would otherwise remain unrelated and exploit their semantic associations, we decided to organize this information using a knowledge graph. The knowledge graph would also enable highly complex queries, not feasible using just the five-criteria joint index. The first step toward this goal is the adoption of a common schema—an ontology—for conceptualizing and representing domain knowledge. Since compliance with standards is essential for RIs, after studying the available standards, we have adopted the CIDOC Conceptual Reference Model (CIDOC CRM 2014), which provides a common ground for knowledge integration and exchange of cultural heritage data. We have further extended the CIDOC CRM schema by 13 entities and 12 relationships, in order to capture all the required information regarding the domain of historical archives. The extended schema has been expressed using RDF. We then programmatically transformed the enriched data into RDF triples, according to the adopted schema. Finally, an RDF knowledge graph has been created using the open-source graph database system Blazegraph,[16] which was populated by the generated RDF triples, and made publicly available for direct access by interested parties.

---

[15] https://uima.apache.org/ruta.html (Accessed 30.03.2021).

[16] https://blazegraph.com/ (Accessed 30.03.2021).

23.3 An Ontological Framework for Contextual Curation Modeling

The BPMN model enables the representation of causal precedence relations along with the decisions, thus introducing interested parties to the workflow they should undertake to perform information aggregation and curation while also supporting performance analysis. However, we consider it crucial to also develop a formal semantic representation of these processes, which enables their better understanding in each context. Monitoring, communication about, and training on the respective workflows are also greatly facilitated. Based on Scholarly Ontology (SO), an ontology of scholarly work, we develop a structural model for the aggregation and curation of the metadata of historical archival records, which models the processes in detail and complements the BPMN flow model. We first give a brief introduction to the ontology.

The Scholarly Ontology (SO) [8] is a discipline-neutral ontological model for representing scholarly and scientific work as a kind of business process. It has evolved as a generalization of the NeDiMAH Methods Ontology (NeMO) [9, 10], targeted at the humanities and developed within the ESF Network for Digital Methods in the Arts and Humanities, following yet earlier work on a Scholarly Research Activity Model [11, 12] carried out in the context of the initial phases of the European Digital Research Infrastructure for the Arts and Humanities (DARIAH-EU) and the European Holocaust Research Infrastructure (EHRI). In line with Cultural-Historical Activity Theory [13], SO introduces a concept of activity as an intentional act, hierarchically composed of smaller acts aimed at meeting hierarchically structured goals. The notions of goal and agency are also central in requirements analysis and business process re-engineering [14]. Furthermore, in business process modeling, the distinct notions of process and procedure play an important role in modeling what actions are performed by actors and how [15, 16], enabling to capture both alternative activity specifications and discrepancies of implementation. In the domain of cultural documentation, on the other hand, the ISO 21127 standard ontology CIDOC CRM (CIDOC CRM 2014) introduces a concept of activity representing intentional acts about which we may record by whom, why, how, when, and where they were performed, as well as the structure they may possess.

The SO conforms by design with CIDOC CRM and is built around the central notion of *activity*. All the concepts defined in the ontology can be grouped into four perspectives corresponding to points of view in the analysis of working practices: the *activity perspective*, concerning the description of activities as they actually take place; the *agency perspective*, concerning actors and goals; the *procedure perspective*, concerning the methods and organization of work; and the *resource perspective*, concerning the material and immaterial objects consumed, used, or produced in the course of activities. The development of SO has followed an iterative process to ensure empirical grounding and validation, as well as usability in annotation tasks. The hierarchy of SO classes is presented in Fig. 23.3.

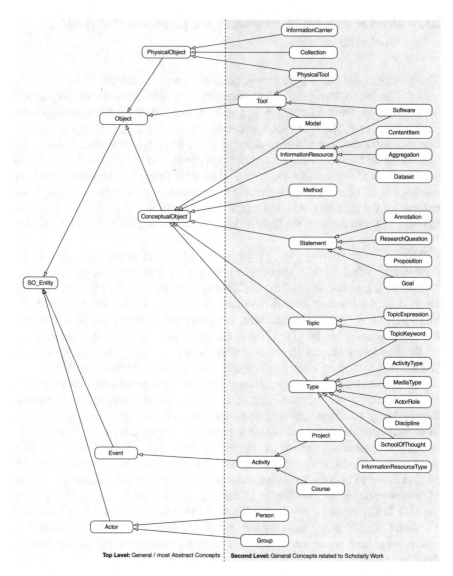

Fig. 23.3 Class hierarchy of the Scholarly Ontology [8]

There is a top abstract class, *SO_Entity*, from which all classes in SO inherit the basic properties *identifier*, *type*, and *description*. *Identifier* supports identification by name or preferred identifiers; *type* supports flexible characterization in parallel with a distinction of ontological classes; and *description* allows free text description.

The *Activity* class represents intentional acts carried out by actors, e.g., a survey, an evaluation, an excavation, a chemical experiment, etc. An activity can be composed of sub-activities, represented by a *partOf* relation. It can also be causally linked with other activities which are preconditions to the activity taking place; such causal links are represented by a *follows* relation. An activity is a real process carried out by an *actor* in a specific time and place using specific *methods*, *tools*, and *information resources*, producing specific results and addressing specific *goals*. It is classified under an *activity type*. The class *Method* represents specifications, recipes, or procedures for carrying out activities of given *activity types* in order to address given goals. A method prescribes the use of specific *tools*, *information resource types*, and *media types* depending on the activity type. It can also have a structured representation showing its composition from *steps*, via *partOf* relations, and causal links between steps, via *follows* relations. The *Actor* class, with subclasses *Person* and *Group*, represents entities capable of performing intentional acts they can be accounted for or referenced for, actively or passively participating in activities, in one or more roles. The *InformationResource* class refers to conceptual objects that can be used in or produced by or document activities. Other subclasses of *ConceptualObject* are *Type*, *Topic*, *Model*, *Method*, and *Assertion*.

Representing the structure of information aggregation and curation in terms of SO involves only a subset of the ontology and is, in fact, a good example of reuse in a different context. We might have used some other ontological framework instead; however, the conformance of SO with CIDOC CRM ensures ease of possible future integration with other CRM-compliant cultural documentation information bases, in addition to offering a well-developed framework for representing processes and procedures.

We have already explained the difference between activity, activity type, and method: a method specifies the way of performing an activity type, while an activity is an actual instance of some activity type; the method may or may not be faithfully enacted in the course of the activity. The class *ActivityType* is therefore a metaclass that is a power type of the *Activity* class: the instances of *ActivityType* are disjoint subclasses of *Activity* that also form a covering of it. Structural information concerning activity types can be attributed to them. These will then be instantiated by specific activities each time actual aggregation or curation operations take place.

The model we define for *ActivityType* parallels that of *Activity*, but one instantiation level higher, except for elements, such as time, place, and assertion, which are not type-specific. Each activity type is related with the relevant application context, goal(s), input and output information resource types, and methods. Differences may occur between activity instances regarding context, goals, or resources, which may in turn entail the use of different methods, even though the activity type may be the same. Activity types are also characterized by properties of composition and causality. Aggregation and curation processes can be seen as instances of composite activity types comprising other activity types linked by causal relations. Such relations prescribe the process structure at the level of activity types, while process instances might, in general, display structural deviations. In the simplest case, a process is linear. In the general case, it is a directed acyclic graph.

Methods carry all the information specifying how activity types are to be performed, and that specification is also directly related to the context, the goals pursued, and the available resources. Although both activity types and methods can have structural descriptions, the level of granularity of those descriptions differs. At the level of large-scale composite activity types, such as aggregation or curation processes, the structure and the causality links are essential and need to be explicitly modeled. This is not the case at the smaller scale of unary activity types that can be assigned a textual definition leaving implementation details to be specified by the related method. On the other hand, if a method has high complexity, it is worth having a structured description regardless of the activity type being considered unary or composite.

Figure 23.4 shows the ontological model derived from SO to serve as a modeling framework for the representation of aggregation and curation processes. For illustration purposes, the figure also shows an activity type, AT1, and an activity, a1, instance of AT1. The implementation and evaluation of this modeling framework are discussed in Sect. 23.4.

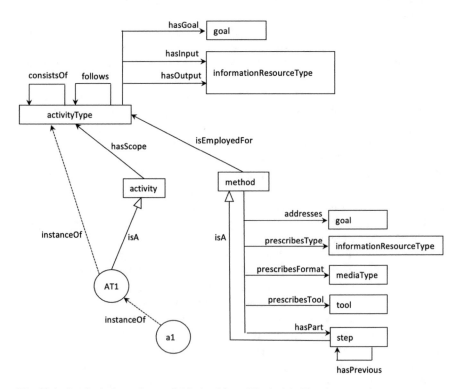

Fig. 23.4 Ontological curation model derived from SO. ActivityType is a metaclass

23.4 Modeling and Analyzing Aggregation and Curation Processes

The modeling framework for the representation of aggregation and curation processes serves as a pattern that users can follow, in order to identify the required processes and guide their activities. As of proof of concept, we have implemented this framework using the ADOxx Metamodelling Platform and applied it to the "Greek 1940s" use case of APOLLONIS. The implementation comprises the development of two complementary models:

1. A BPMN model representing the workflows, i.e., causal precedence relations along with decisions
2. A UML model derived from SO supporting a rich description of aggregation and curation processes

Starting with the analysis of the workflow, we have first implemented the BPMN model using the Bee-Up tool (see Fig. 23.2). By instantiating the ADOxx BPMN metamodel, we have implemented a model at class level that captures the curation workflow. No instance level models have been implemented under this model, since these represent the actual enactments of the workflow, which are out of scope of our work. The model represents the workflow by combining the established causal relations with the relevant decisions. Its aim is to support the understanding, analysis, and validation of the workflows. It can serve as the basis for both static and performance analysis of the aggregation and curation processes. As a matter of fact, a previous partial study focusing on the function of the MoRE aggregator using BPMN and Petri net models has shown the process to be sound, as well as efficient when dealing with large yet temporally dispersed payloads, which is the case with the ingestion of scholarly and cultural content [17].

We have next turned to implementing the ontological curation model described in Sect. 23.3, using the UML metamodel of ADOxx. For ease of implementation, a simplification was made so as to contain the entire application model in one instantiation level, rather than two. Specifically, the metaclass *activityType* is replaced by a class. The exact semantics of the power type are thus compromised; however, this is practically harmless, as they are not really used in our case. This simplification is depicted in Fig. 23.5, where *activityType* is placed at the class level, like the other application domain classes in the model. For illustration purposes, three instances, *AT1*, *a1*, and *m1*, are also shown in Fig. 23.5. The class *activity* is also depicted for reference: the curation process is expressed in terms of activity types, goals, methods, steps, information resource types, media types, and tools; activities capture the actual enactments of the curation process. Under the schema of Fig. 23.5, any specific curation process is represented at the instance level, comprising instances of the classes *activityType, method, step, goal, informationResourceType, mediaType,* and *tool*. Our curation process model includes a core model capturing the overall workflow and 15 submodels, one for each activity type included in the process.

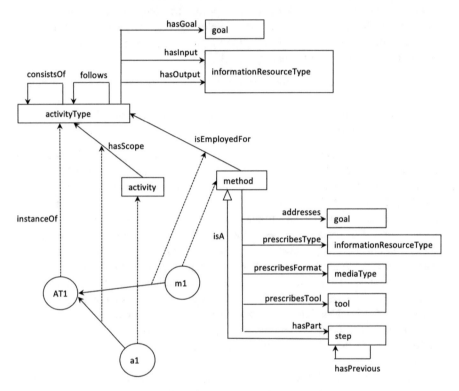

Fig. 23.5 Simplified curation model. ActivityType is rendered as a simple class

The core part of the implemented model for the historical archive information aggregation and curation processes is depicted in Fig. 23.6, showing the overall directed graph structure generated by the causality relations between the activity types involved. Two examples of the 15 implemented activity type models are given in Figs. 23.7 and 23.8, while Fig. 23.9 shows an example of a complex procedure (a method) for performing information extraction from text (an activity type).

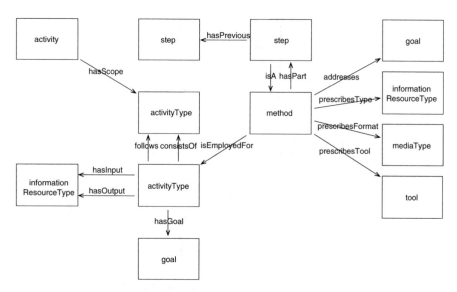

Fig. 23.6 The core of the metadata curation model implemented in ADOxx

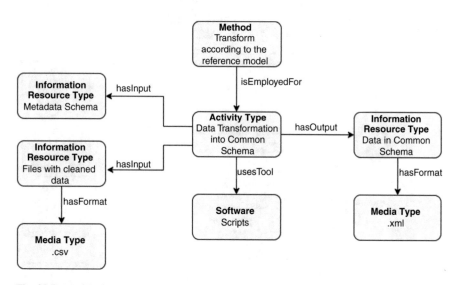

Fig. 23.7 Model of an activity type: data transformation into common schema

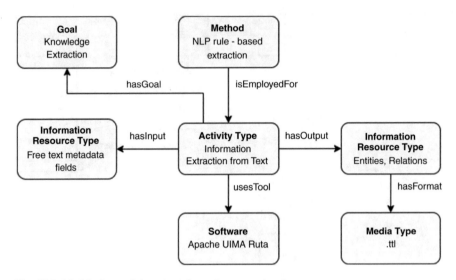

Fig. 23.8 Model of an activity type: information extraction from text

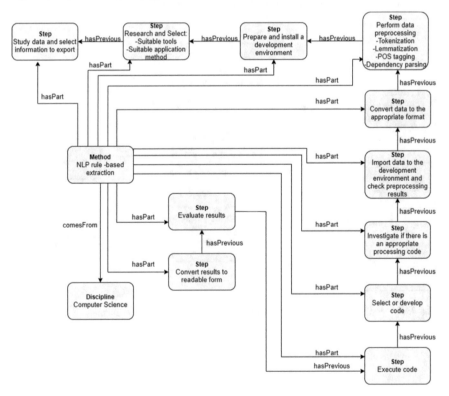

Fig. 23.9 Complex procedure (method) for performing information extraction from text (activity type)

The complete representation of the aggregation and curation processes of historical archive information is the *Historical Information Curation (HIC) Model*, a two-faceted model: The first facet instantiates the BPMN curation workflow model and supports, as explained, the analysis of the dynamics of the processes. The second facet instantiates the SO-based curation model, comprises 16 submodels (core +15) as explained above, and offers a rich structured documentation of the aggregation and curation processes, capable of supporting all sorts of complex queries. They jointly capture the knowledge about these processes and support reasoning about, training on performing, as well as controlling them, the processes being highly interactive, only partially susceptible to automation.

23.5 Conclusion

Aggregating and curating historical information is a complex process, consisting of a set of tasks, some enacted sequentially while others in parallel. In this chapter, we have described the HIC model which aims at facilitating and guiding researchers and infrastructures in organizing and performing this process. Its two-faceted approach supports both the representation of the curation workflow and the structural representation of information. The BPMN model emphasizes causal relations and decisions thus capturing the workflows and supporting the verification of the whole process. The SO-based structural model provides a framework for the detailed implementation of the process.

Our models have been tested using a real case scenario, the "Greek 1940s" case study of the APOLLONIS infrastructure. Throughout this study, we have applied the models and validated the correctness of both the workflow and the structural representation. Moreover, the BPMN model has been verified to be bounded and deadlock-free. Work is under way on optimizing process performance in view of larger-scale applications.

The approach presented here can enjoy wider applicability and serve as a reproducible established methodology for researchers. Aggregation and curation processes in different domains may display differences from the HIC model; still, the BPMN workflow model with possible adaptations would serve in capturing causal relations and decisions. Moreover, the SO-based curation model is quite generic; processes of different domains would lead to corresponding domain-specific models derived by instantiation of the presented generic model.

Acknowledgments We acknowledge support of this work by the project "APOLLONIS: Greek Infrastructure for Digital Arts, Humanities and Language Research and Innovation" (MIS 5002738), which is implemented under the Action "Reinforcement of the Research and Innovation Infrastructure" funded by the Operational Programme "Competitiveness, Entrepreneurship and Innovation" (NSRF 2014-2020) and co-financed by Greece and the European Union (European Regional Development Fund).

Tool Download https://www.omilab.org/hicmodel

References

1. Benardou, A., Champion, E., Dallas, C., Hughes, L.: Introduction: a critique of digital practices and research infrastructures. In: Benardou, A., Champion, E., Dallas, C., Hughes, L. (eds.) Cultural Heritage Infrastructures in Digital Humanities Digital Research in the Arts and Humanities, pp. 1–14. Routledge, Abingdon (2018)
2. Blanke, T., Kristel, C.: Integrating Holocaust research. Int. J. Humanit. Arts Comput. **7**(1–2), 41–57 (2013)
3. Boukhelifa, N., Bryant, M., Bulatović, N., Fekete, J.-D., Knežević, M., et al.: The CENDARI infrastructure. J. Comput. Cult. Herit. **11**(2), 1–20 (2018)
4. Dallas, C.: Humanistic research, information resources and electronic communication. In: Meadows, J., Boecker, H. (eds.) Electronic Communication and Research in Europe, pp. 209–239. European Commission, Luxembourg (1999)
5. Beneš, J., Bulatovic, N., Edmond, J., Knežević, M., Lehmann, J., et al.: The CENDARI white book of archives: data exchange recommendations for cultural heritage institutions and infrastructure projects. [Research Report] Trinity College Dublin (2016)
6. Constantopoulos, P., Dallas, C., Androutsopoulos, I., Angelis, S., Deligiannakis, A., Gavrilis, D., Kotidis, Y., Papatheodorou, C.: DCC&U: an extended digital curation lifecycle model. Int. J. Digit. Curation. **4** (2009). https://doi.org/10.2218/ijdc.v4i1.76
7. Gavrilis, D., Nomikos, V., Kravvaritis, K., Angelis, S., Papatheodorou, C., Constantopoulos, P.: MORe: a micro-service oriented aggregator. In: Metadata and Semantics Research 2016, pp. 15–26. CABI, Göttingen, Germany (2016)
8. Pertsas, V., Constantopoulos, P.: Scholarly ontology: Modelling scholarly practices. Int. J. Digit. Libr. **18**(3), 173–190 (2017)
9. Constantopoulos, P., Hughes, L., Dallas, C., Pertsas, V., Papachristopoulos, L., Christodoulou, T.: Contextualized integration of digital humanities research: using the NeMO ontology of digital humanities methods. In: Digital Humanities 2016: Conference Abstracts, pp. 161–163. Jagiellonian University & Pedagogical University, Kraków (2016)
10. Hughes, L., Constantopoulos, P., Dallas, C.: Digital methods in the humanities: understanding and describing their use across the disciplines. In: Schreibman, S., Siemens, R., Unsworth, J. (eds.) A New Companion to Digital Humanities. Wiley-Blackwell, Oxford (2016)
11. Benardou, A., Constantopoulos, P., Dallas, C., Gavrilis, D.: Understanding the information requirements of arts and humanities scholarship: implications for digital curation. Int. J. Digit. Curation. **5**(1), 18–33 (2010)
12. Benardou, A., Constantopoulos, P., Dallas, C.: An approach to analyzing working practices of research communities in the humanities. Int. J. Humanit. Arts Comput. **7**, 105–127 (2013)
13. Kaptelinin, V.: Acting with Technology: Activity Theory and Interaction Design. MIT Press, Cambridge (2006)
14. Yu, E., Giorgini, P., Maiden, N., Mylopoulos, J., Fickas, S.: Modelling strategic relationships for process reengineering. In: Yu, E., Giorgini, P., Maiden, N., Mylopoulos, J. (eds.) Social Modelling for Requirements Engineering. MIT Press, Cambridge (2010)
15. Dietz, J.L.G.: Enterprise Ontology: Theory and Methodology. Springer, New York (2006)
16. Weske, M.: Business Process Management. Springer, New York (2012)
17. Kotzantonoglou, L.: Modeling and analysis of a business process. MSc Thesis (in Greek). MSc Programme in Information Systems, Athens University of Economics and Business (2017)

Part IX
Modelling Method Conceptualization

Chapter 24
Conceptualization of Modelling Methods in the Context of Categorical Mechanisms

Daniel-Cristian Crăciunean and Daniel Volovici

Abstract This chapter focuses on identifying a process of methodological conceptualization of a modelling method, in the context of categorical mechanisms, starting with the conceptualization phase of the domain and ending with its implementation and validation. Our approach is motivated by the finding that, at least in some phases, the process of conceptualization and implementation of the modelling method is not supported by sufficiently strong semantic foundations in relation to its importance. In this idea, we will pay special attention to the phase of mathematical formalization of the concept of modelling method by identifying or defining categorical mechanisms with implicit semantics appropriate to this concept. We will also identify a way to specify a modelling tool, independent of the metamodelling platform. Our approach is supported by conceptualizing and implementing a modelling method.

Keywords Model · Metamodel · Modelling method · Domain-specific modelling language · Categorical sketch · Semantics · Syntax · Graph transformation · Behavioural rule

24.1 Introduction

We believe that modelling is the main factor supporting man/woman in his/her effort to master the complexity and heterogeneity of the systems involved in all areas vital to the progress of humanity. Modelling manufacturing systems, which are among the most complex and heterogeneous systems in the context of today's competitive conditions, is a major challenge for Model-Driven Development (MDD).

Increasing the competitiveness of the factory of the future means making manufacturing processes more flexible through advanced technologies based on agile,

D.-C. Crăciunean (✉) · D. Volovici
Faculty of Engineering, Lucian Blaga University of Sibiu, Sibiu, Romania
e-mail: daniel.craciunean@ulbsibiu.ro; daniel.volovici@ulbsibiu.ro

© The Author(s), under exclusive license to Springer Nature Switzerland AG 2022
D. Karagiannis et al. (eds.), *Domain-Specific Conceptual Modeling*,
https://doi.org/10.1007/978-3-030-93547-4_24

collaborative, mobile, intelligent and adaptive systems. The factory of the future is based on an iterative design model, which can be optimized by virtually simulating a spiral life cycle model similar to that used in software engineering. The agility of manufacturing systems has been addressed over time in various approaches such as Intelligent Manufacturing Systems, Reconfigurable Manufacturing Systems, Holonic Manufacturing Systems, and Industrial Agents. All of these approaches converge on the concept of Cyber-Physical Production Systems (CPPS), which inherits and integrates these older approaches [1]. In this context, modelling and simulation become essential factors in the design of flexible manufacturing cells because they offer facilities for test, analysis and optimization of manufacturing processes, with minimal costs, before they are physically built.

The modelling activity aims to build a model that facilitates the verification, validation, simulation and analysis of the real system in order to optimize it [2]. An essential step in the process of building an executable model is to specify it in a language endowed with a precise and unambiguous syntax and semantics. Diagrammatic modelling languages are generally preferred for model specification, as they possess important intuitive features and are therefore easier to learn and understand by all parties involved in the modelling process [3].

The MDD objective of moving the software development effort to modelling requires the specification of formal models, and this assumes that the modelling language is formal and therefore allows the exact and unambiguous specification of the models. Such a tool results in an increase in efficiency similar to the efficiency increase resulting from the transition from assembly languages to high-level programming languages. Therefore, it is obvious the importance of building modelling tools endowed with Domain-Specific Modelling Language (DSML), but this stage of the modelling process involves additional costs that must be minimized.

In this idea, we aim to identify and define the theoretical and practical mechanisms that ensure the optimal methodological construction of modelling tools. The theoretical model of a modelling tool, in our approach, is the concept of modelling method introduced by Karagiannis and Kühn [4]. Our proposal will be supported by conceptualizing and implementing a modelling method we called Modelling Method for a Digital Manufacturing Planner (MM-DiMaP), in a modelling tool we called Digital Manufacturing Planning Tool (DiMaP).

While classical mathematics offers a wide range of formal mechanisms, suitable for specifying atomic concepts, it does not provide satisfactory mechanisms for specifying and reasoning on the inter-structural interactions and operations of these concepts that are essential in specifying metamodels. These mechanisms, specific to modelling, are the very essence of category theory. Even the notion of category is defined as a collection of objects and a set of arrows that respect two important axioms in modelling, namely the associativity of the composition of the arrows and the existence of the identity arrow for all objects in the category.

In Sect. 24.2, we describe the purpose and objectives of this chapter, the conceptualization of the domain and the life cycle of the MM-DiMaP modelling method in the context of Agile Modelling Method Engineering (AMME) [5]. In Sect. 24.3, we present the conceptualization of the MM-DiMaP modelling method in the context of categorical mechanisms. In Sect. 24.4, we present the DiMaP modelling tool resulting from the implementation of the MM-DiMaP method using as an intermediate language the MM-DSL language. Section 24.5 concludes the chapter with some observations and conclusions.

24.2   Method Description

Modelling is a method of knowing reality that involves replacing real or virtual systems with models that mimic their behaviour, from a certain point of view, in order to facilitate the process of reasoning and reflection on them [6]. Imitation of the behaviour of real systems by models often involves imitating interactions with other real systems or with other models in a similar way to the real system.

If we intend to specify a model for manufacturing cells in a profile company, we must also consider the interaction of the models with the physical components specific to a manufacturing cell such as robots, manipulators, workstations, etc., or software components such as the control components. The resulting model is therefore a model of a Cyber-Physical Production System (CPPS), that is, a very complex model that contains a heterogeneous mixture of physical components and software that interact with each other.

24.2.1   Goals and Motivation

For a model to be able to run and interact with real systems and other models, it must be specified in a language that can be executed by a physical or virtual machine, that is, to be an executable model. The process of moving from real-world systems to executable models is a complex process that involves specifying at least two more intermediate models, namely the conceptual model and the formal model.

The specification of the formal model implies the use of a language defined by precise syntactic and semantic rules and that offers facilities of reasoning on the model. The formal model can be specified using two different types of formal languages depending on the purpose we are pursuing, namely a mathematical language in order to share the results of research with the scientific community or a formal modelling language in order to be automatically transformed into an executable model. For the first purpose, in this chapter we used the language offered by the category theory. This language provides appropriate mechanisms for specifying models and reasoning about them.

To specify the formal model in order to automatically generate the executable model we need a formal modelling language, that is, a language with precise syntactic and semantic rules and without ambiguity. The activity of specifying such a model requires an expertise from the modeller that can be obtained only after an important training and experience. This shortcoming can be avoided by using a modelling language with a syntax and semantics appropriate to the modeller's domain of expertise, that is, a domain-specific modelling language.

On the other hand, the conceptual model is constructed in order to be converted into a formal model, specified into a formal modelling language. The efficiency of this conversion operation is directly dependent on the compatibility between the conceptual model and the modelling instrumentation used. The optimization of this operation can be done by ensuring a morphism between the conceptual model and the formal model, a morphism that leads to the reduction of the number of iterations in the design cycle and the reduction of the complexity of the formal model.

The conflict between the need to understand the conceptual model by all participants in the modelling process and the need to ensure compatibility between the conceptual model and the formal model has only one practical solution, namely the use of a modelling tool appropriate to the specific modelling domain to facilitate the conversion from the conceptual model to the formal model.

These requirements related to the complexity and heterogeneity of real-world systems explain why it is impossible to develop a modelling tool suitable for all modelling domains and therefore lead us to the idea that the development of domain-specific modelling tools is a central phase of the modelling process.

For a modelling language to allow the precise specification of a model with minimal effort, it must be as close as possible to the language of the end user and not to the language of the machine on which it is to be executed and therefore has a limited scope [7].

Following a systematic study of research that addresses the mechanisms and technologies of metamodelling, we found that the main focus is on the study or expansion of existing languages and the construction of new languages to cover the widest possible areas of use. Concerns about the mechanisms and tools to enable the rapid and efficient specification of modelling tools to facilitate the precise, systematic and incremental specification of complex systems in a narrow domain are insufficient in relation to their importance.

Another important shortcoming, which we found, is related to the lack of portability from one metamodelling platform to another. The solution we propose to this problem is a metamodelling language independent of the metamodelling platform. Platform independence is achieved by building translators for multiple platforms.

Although formal specification in mathematical language is very important for sharing research results but especially for its use as a source of mechanisms that facilitate reasoning on modelled systems, in the case of modelling tools this activity is based on surprisingly weak semantic foundations. Although the language offered by category theory has adequate syntax and implicit semantics for model representation and is the most expressive mathematical language [8–10], it is far too rarely used.

Therefore, the motivation and objectives of our approach derive from the imperative need to develop modelling tools specific to the domain in contrast to the timid concerns in this domain, the lack of portability between metamodelling platforms and last but not least the retention with which categorical mechanisms are used in contrast to the expressiveness appropriate to the modelling domain.

In this idea, we aim to identify or define the theoretical and practical mechanisms that ensure the optimal methodological construction of modelling tools. Our proposal will be supported by conceptualizing and implementing a modelling method we called Modelling Method for a Digital Manufacturing Planner (MM-DiMaP), in a modelling tool we called Digital Manufacturing Planning Tool (DiMaP).

Our research approach is based on the concept of modelling method on the methodical dimension, on the categorical mechanisms, on the dimension of mathematical formalization and on the environment offered by the Open Model Initiative Laboratory (OMiLAB) [11] on the methodological and technological dimension.

Our approach is based on the concept of modelling method introduced by Karagiannis and Kühn [4], which integrates three essential components of a modelling tool, namely the modelling language, algorithms and mechanisms and the modelling procedure.

24.2.2 Domain Conceptualization

An important phase that precedes the conceptualization process of the modelling method is the conceptualization process of the specific modelling domain. By conceptualizing the domain, we will understand the process of acquiring knowledge in the domain of modelling in order to identify the atomic concepts in this domain and the interactions between them. These concepts will represent entities or classes of entities in the modelling domain and will be the basis for defining the components of the modelling method. A concept is characterized by the state in which it is and the context in which it is at a given time, and therefore, they can cause a change of state of the concept. This transition from one state to another defines the behaviour of a concept.

In modelling, the state of an atomic concept is given by the values of some attributes, and the state of a concept composed by aggregating several atomic concepts is given by the states of the components and their aggregation structure.

Multi-level modelling is based on generic concepts, which are specified by potential properties, potential contexts and potential transformations. The genericity of the concepts is obtained by endowing them only with a minimum set of properties common to a class of entities and with facilities to extend the number of properties to represent concrete entities in this class. A generic concept facilitates two fundamental processes in multi-level modelling, namely a process of refining from abstract to concrete on two or more levels as well as a process of abstraction from concrete to generic. The abstraction process is accomplished by mapping several concepts from a lower level of abstraction to the same concept from a higher level of abstraction. The processes of refining and abstracting generic concepts are important in multi-level modelling because they define a classification relationship of concepts.

24.2.3 AMME Life Cycle

The design and development of a modelling tool for manufacturing planning is an iterative process characterized by a continuous interaction of the designer with the environment containing the entities in the domain, such as companies, real manufacturing systems, with specialists in manufacturing cell design, with end users, as well as with the knowledge base in the domain, that is, existing methodologies, tools, models and methods.

The sequencing of the build phases of the modelling tool is in line with the Agile Modelling Method Engineering (AMME) methodology proposed in [5]. AMME has been defined as a reaction to traditional rigid practices that dominate the conceptualization and implementation of modelling methods, similar to the reaction of Agile Manifesto [12] to traditional rigid models in software application development.

In the AMME life cycle, each phase is also an evaluation phase of the previous phase that can determine the redoing or completion of the previous phase. Also, the resumption of the cycle can be done from any phase if the propagation of new requirements requires it. Thus, the semantics of the model is integrated into the model and evolves iteratively as the participants in the modelling process gradually understand the modelling domain [5, 13].

In the continuation of this section, we present briefly the activities specific to each phase defined by the Open Model Initiative Laboratory (OMiLAB) of the AMME Framework.

Create In this phase, we followed the acquisition of knowledge in the domain of real manufacturing systems that must be modelled by observing the manufacturing cells and interaction with specialists in the domain and we identified the concepts that will represent them in models in relation to modelling requirements. Mostly in the case of the MM-DiMaP modelling method, the actual system observed is represented by a company that produces medical laser, mainly by assembling components. The specialists and end users of this company needed a specific modelling tool to support them in the design and reconfiguration of manufacturing cells. They wanted the modelling tool to provide them with facilities for specifying, simulating and optimizing manufacturing cells. Also, an important requirement was that the behavioural dimension has to be included, in its entirety, at the metamodel level, that is, to be transparent to the end user of the modelling tool.

The activities in this phase refer especially to the process of conceptualizing the domain, described in Sect. 24.2.2. Following this phase, we identified the atomic concepts of manufacturing cells and the rules for aggregating these concepts into manufacturing cell models as well as a way to specify the models specific to this community. The generic atomic concepts identified in this phase are workstations, transport machines, buffers and ports that are connected to each other according to the interactions between them to form manufacturing cells.

Design In this phase, we defined the components of the MM-DiMaP modelling method at the metamodel level. Thus, the atomic concepts identified in the creation phase become lexical atoms of the modelling language and the rules for connecting these concepts in manufacturing cells become syntactic rules in the grammar of the modelling language. Also, the specific functionalities of the atomic concepts and of the syntactic constructions specified on the basis of the connection rules will constitute the semantics of the modelling language.

Formalize In this phase, detailed in Sect. 24.3, we specified the components of the MM-DiMaP modelling method in the language provided by the category theory in order to highlight the generic mechanisms offered by this language and to share research results with the scientific community.

If in the case of textual languages, the standard metamodel is context-free grammar that offers efficient algorithms for lexical and syntactic analysis, in the case of diagrammatic languages similar mechanisms are far from providing support for implementation. The complexity of these languages derives from the fact that a model is no longer a sequence of lexical atoms, as in the case of textual languages, but as a graph structure with multiple connections between lexical atoms. We believe that categorical mechanisms provide adequate support for specifying and implementing this type of language.

Develop In the first iteration of this phase, we specified in the Modelling Method Domain-Specific Language (MM-DSL) an initial prototype of the DiMaP modelling tool. In the following iterations, this prototype was enriched with new facilities in relation to the propagation of the new requirements appeared in the following iterations.

Deploy/Validate In this phase, we specified with the DiMaP tool a series of theoretical models in the domain of modelling. Different types of errors, deficiencies or new requirements found in this phase caused new iterations in which we fixed these deficiencies in all phases in which these changes spread. Following these successive iterations of DiMaP modelling instruments, it has reached the form presented in Sect. 24.4 and can be seen on the OMiLAB website.

24.3   Method Conceptualization

The MM-DiMaP modelling method is an instance of the concept of modelling method [14, 15] which abstracts the notion of modelling tool, by integrating their essential components at abstract level. For the MM-DiMaP method to exist in reality, it will have to be specified in a formal language, otherwise it exists only in the mind of the modeller. The specification of the MM-DiMaP method implies the adequate specification of the essential components of the modelling method concept, in the context of the facilities offered by the modelling tool implementation platform. We will call this process of specification the process of conceptualizing the modelling method [2].

In general, all metamodelling platforms offer at least two important meta-elements from which model-level elements are constructed, namely object types from which objects are obtained by instantiation and connector type from which connectors are obtained by instantiation [16]. Although the syntax and semantics of these meta-elements are different from one platform to another, they can be refined at the model level by attributes.

The components that interact in a model represent concepts in the specific field of modelling and therefore are encapsulated algebraic structures, and the metamodelling effort consists primarily in specifying the relationships between these structures considered holistic entities. But the mechanisms for specifying structures and the interactions between them are the very essence of category theory. Thus, the category theory offers us this type of thinking on arrows [17, 18] specific to the modelling process, and therefore, we will use the categorical mechanisms to conceptualize the modelling method.

24.3.1 Categorical Specification of DiMaP-DSML

As we saw in Sect. 24.2, a diagrammatic model integrates two dimensions: a static dimension and a behavioural dimension. Therefore, the metamodel of our language that we have called Digital Manufacturing Planning DSML (DiMaP-DSML) must include syntax and semantics specifications for each of these two dimensions. The resulting DiMaP-DSML language will have to allow the specification of all models in the domain, based on static syntax and semantics, and these models to ensure a behaviour similar to that of the manufacturing cell that it models, from certain points of view, based on the behavioural dimension specified and implemented at the metamodel level.

24.3.2 The Static Dimension of DiMaP-DSML

The formalization of the DiMaP-DSML language is preceded by the conceptualization of the specific domain, which involves identifying the atomic concepts in the domain, identifying the rules for aggregating atomic concepts in syntactic constructions and then identifying the semantic domain and the mechanisms for mapping syntactic constructions to the semantic domain.

The generic atomic concepts identified in the specific domain of modelling and which will become types of lexical atoms in the DiMaP-DSML language are: concepts of type workstation that we denote with x_{ws}, concepts of type transport machine that we denote with x_{ts}, concepts of type buffer that we denote with x_{bf} and concepts of type port that we denote with x_{mp}. The concepts of type x_{ts} will be partitioned into the subtypes: autonomous guided vehicle (AGV) that we denote with x_{avg}, conveyor that we denote with x_{cbp} and manipulator that we denote with x_{man}.

From a syntactic point of view, a specified model with atomic components of these types, as nodes, and with the corresponding connections between them, as arcs, is a graph $\mathcal{G}$, which respects the constraints identified in the conceptualization phase of the domain. These constraints are: (1) the graph $\mathcal{G}$ is connected; (2) there is at most one arc between any two nodes; (3) the sets of components of types x_{ws}, x_{ts}, x_{bf} and x_{mp} form a partition on the set x of all atomic components of the model; (4) the sets of components of types x_{avg}, x_{cbp} and x_{man} form a partition on the set x_{ts} of all atomic components of type transport machine.

24.3.2.1 Syntax of the Static Dimension of DiMaP-DSML

To specify the syntactic constructions of the language, related to the static dimension of the models, at the metamodel level we use the categorical sketch, which offers a formal declarative language endowed with an implicit semantics. A categorical sketch is a tuple $\mathcal{S} = (\mathcal{G}, \mathcal{C}(\mathcal{S}))$, where $\mathcal{G} = (x, \gamma, \sigma, \theta)$ is a graph specified by the set of nodes x, the set of arcs γ with source $\sigma(\gamma)$ and the target $\theta(\gamma)$, and $\mathcal{C}(\mathcal{S})$ is a set of constraints defined on the graph components.

The graph of the sketch that specifies the syntax of the DiMaP-DSML language is the one in Fig. 24.1. The nodes of the graph represent the lexical atoms of the language, and the admissible connections between them and the arcs of the graph represent the operators of the sketch. The constraints $(\mathcal{S})$ are introduced by a diagram predicate signature [19, 20], which is defined as a tuple $\Theta = (\Pi, ar)$ consisting of a set of predicates Π and an application $ar: \Pi \to Graph_0$ which maps the predicates $P \in \Pi$ to objects in the Graph category. The objects $ar(P)$ are called shape graph arity. These shape graph arities are then mapped accordingly to the graph of the sketch by diagram functors. The static models of the sketch $\mathcal{S}$ are the images of the graph $\mathcal{G}$ of the sketch in the category of sets and functions, which we denote by Set, by functors that respect the constraints $(\mathcal{S})$.

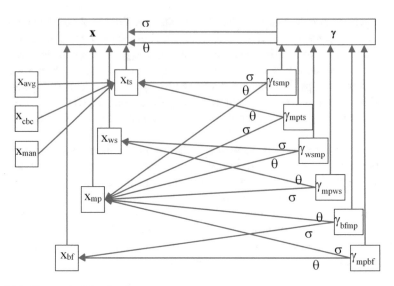

Fig. 24.1 The graph of the sketch

Therefore, we will have to define the diagram predicate signature $\Theta = (\Pi, \text{ar})$ corresponding to the four syntactic constraints imposed on the DiMaP-DSML language. The definition of these constraints is made so that they are respected by the graph structures of all the sketch models.

For example, in order to impose the condition that any model graph is connected we use the fact that the set of connected components of a graph is isomorphic with the pushout of σ with θ in the Set category. But a graph is connected if it has a single connected component and therefore this constraint can be put by a predicate of the form $P_1(n_1, n_2, n_3, a_{31}, a_{32}) = |\text{CoLim}(D_1)| = 1$, where: $\text{CoLim}(D_1)$ is the colimit of diagram D_1:Span$(1,2,3,r_{31},r_{32}) \rightarrow$ Span$(x,x,\gamma,\sigma,\theta)$ where $D_1(1) = x$, $D_1(2) = x$, $D_1(3) = \gamma$, $D_1(r_{31}) = \sigma$, $D_1(a_{32}) = \theta$; $\text{ar}(P_1(n_1, n_2, n_3, a_{31}, a_{32})) =$ Span$(1,2,3,r_{31},r_{32})$ defined as: $\text{ar}(n_1) = 1$, $\text{ar}(n_2) = 2$, $\text{ar}(n_3) = 3$, $\text{ar}(a_{31}) = r_{31}$, $\text{ar}(a_{32}) = r_{32}$, and Span$(x,y,z,r_{zx},r_{zy}) = (x \xleftarrow{r_{zx}} z \xrightarrow{r_{zy}} y)$.

In a similar way the predicates P_2, P_3, P_4 will be defined, which will be mapped to the components of the sketch by corresponding diagrams that we denote by D_2, D_3 and D_4. It follows that $\mathcal{S}(\Pi) = \{\mathcal{S}(P_1), \mathcal{S}(P_2), \mathcal{S}(P_3), \mathcal{S}(P_4)\}$ where: $\mathcal{S}(P_1) = \{(P_1, D_1:\text{ar}(P_1) \rightarrow \mathcal{G})\}$, $\mathcal{S}(P_2) = \{(P_2, D_1:\text{ar}(P_2) \rightarrow \mathcal{G})\}$, $\mathcal{S}(P_3) = \{(P_3, D_2:\text{ar}(P_3) \rightarrow \mathcal{G})\}$, $\mathcal{S}(P_4) = \{(P_4, D_3:\text{ar}(P_4) \rightarrow \mathcal{G})\}\}$.

These constraints imposed at the metamodel level by diagram predicate signature will be mapped in concrete static models, from the Set category, by the model functors.

24.3.2.2   Semantics of the Static Dimension of DiMaP-DSML

In order to define the semantics of the static dimension at metamodel level, the nodes of the categorical sketch that represent atomic concepts in the modelling domain will be endowed with attributes. In this context, the semantics of a static model is defined by mapping the attributes associated with the sketch nodes to data domains and the graphical structures of the static model to graphical structures with well-defined semantics. In the case of the DiMaP-DSML language, the atomic components represented by the nodes of the sketch graph are endowed with the attributes presented in Sect. 24.4.2.3.

A static model endowed with syntax and semantics represents in our approach a state of the behavioural model.

24.3.3   The Behavioural Dimension of DiMaP-DSML

The behavioural dimension of a model is generally transparent to the end user of the modelling tool and has the role of ensuring a behaviour of the specified model, through the syntax of the static dimension by the end user, similar to the behaviour of the modelled system.

Therefore, the syntax and semantics of the behavioural dimension must be specified generically so that they can be implemented at the metamodel level. To achieve this goal, we introduced the concept of behavioural rule. We defined a behavioural rule as an aggregation between a graph transformation and a behavioural action. Thus, the static models of the categorical sketch become states of the behavioural model, and the behavioural rules become transitions of the behavioural model.

24.3.3.1   Syntax of the Behavioural Dimension of DiMaP-DSML

The behaviour of DiMaP models is not based on structural transformations but only on changes in attributes, and therefore, the role of graph transformations, in this case, is reduced to locating the area of definition of behavioural actions.

The syntax of a graph transformation p is defined as a pair of graphs $p = (L, R)$, and the semantics of this graph transformation is defined by a mechanism that specifies how to replace the subgraph L with the subgraph R in the graph structure of a static model. In the context of categorical mechanisms, there are two ways to approach graph transformations, namely: as a single-pushout (SPO) or as a double-pushout (DPO) [21–26]. In the SPO variant, a graph transformation is denoted as $p = (L \rightarrow R)$, where $p{:}L \rightarrow R$ is a partial graph monomorphism. In the DPO variant, a graph transformation is denoted as $p = (L \leftarrow K \rightarrow R)$ and contains three graphs: a left graph L, a right graph R and a graph K common to R and L. Applications $p_L{:}K \rightarrow L$ and $p_R{:}K \rightarrow R$ are total inclusion monomorphisms.

Because the SPO version does not include deletion in the model, but only the addition, we chose the DPO version that also allows deletion. A behavioural action, which we denote with Act, is a mathematical function defined on the value range of the attributes of a sub-model of a static model, with values in the value range of the attributes of a sub-model of another static model. An action is executed after the execution of the associated graph transformation. In order for a behavioural rule to be applied, its action graph structure must meet a precondition that we denote with C_L and a postcondition that we denote with C_R.

We will define the behaviour of a model by a behavioural signature which is a set of signatures of a behavioural rule, and which we denote by Σ. A signature of a behavioural rule is a tuple $\sigma = (p, C_L, \text{Act}, C_R, \alpha)$, where $p = L \xleftarrow{l} K \xrightarrow{r} R$ is a graph transformation, Act is the graph signature of the action, C_L is the graph signature of a precondition predicate, C_R is the graph signature of a postcondition predicate and $\alpha: \{C_L, \text{Act}, C_R\} \to p$ is an application that maps the parameters of the action Act and the predicates C_L, C_R to the nodes of the graphs L and R, and which we call the graph arity of the behavioural rule.

In the case of the DiMaP-DSML language, we have a single signature of a behavioural rule $\sigma = (p, C_L, \text{Act}, C_R, \alpha)$, where p is the graph transformation $p = L \xleftarrow{l} K \xrightarrow{r} R$ from Fig. 24.2, L and R are shape graph and $\alpha: \{C_L(x_1, x_2, x_3, x_4, x_5, x_6, x_7, x_8, x_9),$ $\text{Act}(x_1, x_2, x_3, x_4, x_5, x_6, x_7, x_8, x_9)$ and $C_R(x_1, x_2, x_3, x_4, x_5, x_6, x_7, x_8, x_9)\} \to p$ are defined as follows: $\alpha(x_i) = n_i$, for all $i = 1, 9$. Therefore, the behavioural signature of the DiMaP-DSML language is $\Sigma = \{\sigma\}$.

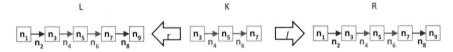

Fig. 24.2 Graph transformation p

The behavioural signature $\Sigma = \{\sigma\}$ of the DiMaP-DSML language is mapped to the nodes of the graph of the categorical sketch $\mathcal{S} = (\mathcal{G}, \mathcal{S}(\Pi))$ from Fig. 24.1, through two functor diagrams D_w and D_t, and thus the components of the shape graphs L and R from the signature of a behavioural rule, receive appropriate attributes, which will be used to specify the action Act and the C_L and C_R conditions.

The functor D_w maps the components of the shape graphs L and R of the graph transformation p to the objects of the sketch corresponding to the area of action of a component of workstation type and is defined as follows: $D_w(n_1) = x_{bf}$; $D_w(n_2) = \gamma_{bfmp}$; $D_w(n_3) = x_{mp}$; $D_w(n_4) = \gamma_{mpws}$; $D_w(n_5) = x_{ws}$; $D_w(n_6) = \gamma_{wsmp}$; $D_w(n_7) = x_{mp}$; $D_w(n_8) = \gamma_{mpbf}$; $D_w(n_9) = x_{bf}$.

The functor D_t maps the components of the shape graphs L and R of the graph transformation p to the objects of the sketch corresponding to the area of action of a component of the transport machine type and is defined as follows: $D_t(n_1) = x_{bf}$;

$D_t(n_2) = \gamma_{bfmp}$; $D_t(n_3) = x_{mp}$; $D_t(n_4) = \gamma_{mpws}$; $D_t(n_5) = x_{ts}$; $D_t(n_6) = \gamma_{wsmp}$; $D_t(n_7) = x_{mp}$; $D_t(n_8) = \gamma_{mpbf}$; $D_t(n_9) = x_{bf}$.

Thus, the behavioural signature $\Sigma = \{\sigma\}$ generates a behavioural model at the level of the categorical sketch $\mathcal{S}$, which we denote by $\mathcal{S}(\Sigma)$ and which contains two behavioural rules at the level of the categorical sketch $\mathcal{S}(\Sigma) = \{D_w(\sigma), D_t(\sigma)\}$, where $D_w(\sigma) = (D_w(p), D_w(\alpha(C_L)), D_w(\alpha(\text{Act})), D_w(\alpha(C_R),))$ and $D_t(\sigma) = (D_t(\alpha(p)), D_t(\alpha(C_L)), D_t(\alpha(\text{Act})), D_t(\alpha(C_R)))$.

24.3.3.2 Semantics of the Behavioural Dimension of DiMaP-DSML

The semantics of the behavioural dimension of a model must specify a process characterized by states and transitions, which is similar to the dynamic behaviour of the modelled system. In our approach each state of the model is an instance of the categorical sketch $\mathcal{S} = (\mathcal{G}, (\mathcal{S}))$, that is, the image of this sketch through a functor $\mathcal{J}:\mathcal{S}\rightarrow$ Set in the Set category. The graph $\mathcal{G}$ of the sketch $\mathcal{S}$ is a typed graph, with nodes endowed with attributes that are mapped to data domains and which through the functor $\mathcal{J}$ receive values from the specified data domain. Behavioural rules are algorithms that transform one instance of the sketch $\mathcal{S}$ into another instance of this sketch. The successive execution of the behavioural rules simulates the dynamic evolution of the real modelled system [27, 28].

As we saw, in the previous section, the behavioural model $\mathcal{S}(\Sigma)$, of the DiMaP-DSML language is represented by two behavioural rules at the level of the sketch $\mathcal{S}$, obtained by mapping the behavioural signature Σ to the nodes of the graph of this sketch, that is, $\mathcal{S}(\Sigma) = \{\tau_w, \tau_t\}$ where $\tau_w = (D_w(p), D_w(\alpha(C_L)), D_w(\alpha(\text{Act})), D_w(\alpha(C_R),))$ and $\tau_t = (D_t(\alpha(p)), D_t(\alpha(C_L)), D_t(\alpha(\text{Act})), D_t(\alpha(C_R)))$. By mapping the shape graphs components L and R from the definition of the graph transformation p to the sketch graph $\mathcal{S}$, they become typed shape graphs, endowed with the attributes and data domains corresponding to the components of this graph. Therefore, the preconditions and postconditions of the behavioural rules τ_w and τ_t become logical predicates defined on the attributes of the components L and R, and the actions of the behavioural rules τ_w and τ_t become mathematical functions defined on these attributes and can be mapped to mathematical expressions. In our approach, the graph transformations corresponding to the behavioural rules are mapped to the DPO model. In the case of the DiMaP-DSML language, the DPO transformation is an identity transformation, because the DiMaP models do not undergo structural behavioural transformations.

Applying a behavioural rule begins with finding a match μ of shape graph L in the current instance $\mathcal{J}^1$ of the sketch $\mathcal{S}$. If the rule has been successfully applied, then the result obtained must be a new instance $\mathcal{J}^2$, of the sketch $\mathcal{S}$. In general, if there is a behavioural rule τ, which transforms an instance $\mathcal{J}^1$ of the sketch $\mathcal{S}$ into an instance $\mathcal{J}^2$ of this sketch, then the tuple $(\mathcal{J}^1, \tau, \mathcal{J}^2)$ is a transition in the behavioural model of the DiMaP-DSML language. If there are several matches of a behavioural rule in an instance of the sketch and these matches are independent, then the rule can be applied simultaneously for all matches. Also, if there are independent matches in a draft instance for multiple behavioural rules, they can be applied simultaneously.

On the other hand, any two sequential graph transformations can be composed and form a new transformation that cumulates the effect of both transformations [23]. It is obvious that behavioural actions, which are mathematical functions, can also be composed and therefore two successive behavioural rules can be composed. It follows that the set of instances of a categorical sketch together with the behavioural rules form a category that we call category of instances and behavioural rules (CIBR).

24.4 Proof of Concept

The conceptualization and implementation of the MM-DiMaP modelling method were done in the context provided by the Open Model Initiative Laboratory (OMi-LAB). OMiLAB is an open ecosystem that incorporates principles, methodologies, tools, services and practices for research in the field of modelling methods and agile development of modelling tools [11, 14]. To implement the DiMaP modelling tool, we used the MM-DSL metamodelling language.

The MM-DSL language is a textual metamodelling language that is an integral part of the OMiLAB ecosystem, and which was designed and specified at the University of Vienna in order to allow platform independence of the process of conceptualization and implementation of modelling methods.

The conceptualization and implementation of a modelling method are dependent on the facilities offered by the metamodelling platform used [2]. This platform must provide in the first phase the facility for specifying the syntax and semantics of the modelling language as well as the generic algorithms and mechanisms, and in the phase of specifying the models in the specific modelling domain, it must offer mechanisms for model manipulation and analysis. The MM-DSL language allows the change of the metamodelling platform with minimal costs, during the modelling process, in case it is found that the facilities offered by the initial platform prove to be unsatisfactory.

The platform dependence of the modelling tools development process and the lack of portability between the metamodelling platforms are the main reasons that led to the design and implementation of the MM-DSL language. The platform independence of the MM-DSL language is conditioned by the construction of translators specific to the metamodelling platforms in question. We used in the process of implementing the MM-DiMaP modelling method a translator specific to the ADOxx metamodelling platform, which is also the first translator developed for this language.

The MM-DSL language was designed to facilitate the implementation of modelling methods through appropriate descriptive instructions for specifying concepts in the domain of modelling and through calculation and control instructions of the flow that allow the specification of algorithms and mechanisms [29]. The set of declarative instructions includes statements that allow specifying the name of a modelling method and external code; statements that allow specifying typical structures of a modelling method such as classes, relationships, attributes and model types; and statements that allow defining graphical notations associated with classes and relationships. The set of calculation and control instructions contains the instructions specific to the programming languages for specifying the algorithms.

24.4.1 Digital Manufacturing Planning Tool (DiMaP)

The DiMaP modelling tool implements the MM-DiMaP modelling method instance specified, in the context of categorical mechanisms, in Sect. 24.3. To implement the DiMaP tool, we used the MM-DSL metamodelling language and the specific translator to the ADOxx metamodelling platform. DiMaP is a modelling tool built to facilitate the design and digital optimization of manufacturing processes. Modelling and simulation are essential for the optimal design of flexible manufacturing lines because they offer the possibility to create, test, compare and optimize manufacturing processes, with minimal costs. The models thus become primary artefacts from which the software components necessary for the coordination and supervision of the physical manufacturing processes can be generated.

This tool offers facilities for integrating the logical and functional dependencies of the activities of a manufacturing process into models and for simulating these models in order to optimize the manufacturing process. In our approach, a model is characterized by two dimensions: the static dimension and the behavioural dimension. The behavioural dimension is fully integrated into the algorithms and mechanisms component of this tool. From the end user's point of view, the most important component of the DiMaP tool is the DiMaP-DSML modelling language, which we will present below.

24.4.2 The DiMaP-DSML Language

The DiMaP-DSML diagrammatic modelling language provides notations for specifying the static dimension syntax and features, based on attribute values and model structuring, for specifying the static dimension semantics of a model. Thus, this language provides the appropriate mechanisms for specifying a model in the specific domain of modelling in a clear, simple form that integrates all the information necessary to simulate and optimize manufacturing processes.

A model specified in the DiMaP-DSML language is a graph that has as nodes concepts in the modelling domain, as arcs the flow connections between these components and that respects the constraints placed in the metamodel on these components.

There is a logical barrier between how language syntax and semantics were specified at the metamodel level and how the end user understands and uses language syntax and semantics. In the continuation of this section, we present the notations, syntax and semantics of the DiMaP-DSML language from the perspective of the end user.

24.4.2.1 Notations

Defining the notation associated with a diagrammatic modelling language involves associating suggestive notations to the lexical atoms of the language, which represent atomic concepts in the specific domain of modelling. The notation used to specify the atomic components of a language is important because it provides an intuitive character for specifying and interpreting models. From the point of view of the end user, the notation is endowed with the semantics of the concepts in the modelling domain they represent.

In the case of the DiMaP-DSML language, the lexical atoms are buffers, workstations, conveyers, autonomous guided vehicles, manipulator and ports, which represent the atomic concepts in the specific modelling domain and which will be aggregated in a manufacturing flow through flow relations.

Buffers are static components of the manufacturing flow that temporarily store certain materials and semi-finished products involved in the manufacturing process. These are represented in a model by the notation shown in Fig. 24.3.

Workstations are active components in the manufacturing process that turn a set of input materials or semi-finished products into a set of output semi-finished products. These are represented in a model by the symbolic notation shown in Fig. 24.4.

Transport machines are also active components in the manufacturing flow that have the role of moving materials and semi-finished products from a source buffer to a destination buffer. This type of lexical atoms of the language is of three subtypes, namely the Conveyor subtype for which we use the notation from Fig. 24.5a, the autonomous guided vehicles (AGV) subtype for which we use the notation from Fig. 24.5b and the Manipulator subtype for which we use the notation from Fig. 24.5c.

Ports are specific intermediate components connecting in the manufacturing flow through which any two components of the other types are connected to each other. These are represented in a model by the symbolic notation shown in Fig. 24.6. The connection of these ports to other atomic components will be done by arrows (Fig. 24.7), which represent the flow of materials and semi-finished products in the manufacturing process.

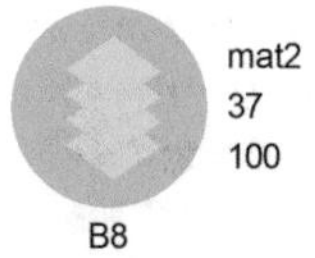

Fig. 24.3 Buffer

Fig. 24.4 Workstation

 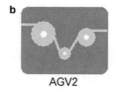

Fig. 24.5 Conveyor (**a**), AGV (**b**), Manipulator (**c**)

Fig. 24.6 Port

Fig. 24.7 Flow connector

24.4.2.2 Specifying the Model Syntax in the DiMaP-DSML Language

The end user views the DiMaP-DSML language syntax as a way to specify the semantics of manufacturing models. The specification of the syntax of a manufacturing cell consists in the aggregation of a set of atomic components, represented by the symbols defined in Sect. 24.4.2.1, according to the workflow corresponding to the manufacturing process.

For example, the manufacturing cell, specified in terms of the DiMaP-DSML language, from Fig. 24.8, is, from a syntactic point of view, a graph that has the nodes and arcs represented by the notations associated with the atomic components in Sect. 24.4.2.1. The graph structure of the model reflects the physical structure of the manufacturing cell and the associated workflow and therefore specifies its semantics. Thus, the specified model connects through the ports: two transport machines, one of type conveyor (Conveyor 1) and one of type manipulator (Manipulator 1); a workstation (Workstation 1); and six buffers.

To specify a functional aggregation of atomic components, the end user of the DiMaP modelling tool will need to consider the functionality of the actual atomic components represented in the model by the associated symbols, as well as their aggregation rules in the models.

Therefore, a model of a manufacturing cell is, from a syntactic point of view, a directional graph that has the set of nodes represented by a set of buffers, workstations, conveyors, autonomous guided vehicles, manipulators and ports, and the arcs between them represent the flow of materials and semi-finished products in the manufacturing process. The lexical atoms of the language that represent these atomic concepts in the modelling domain are represented in the toolbox of the DiMaP tool (Fig. 24.8), through the associated notations, to be used by the modeller in the syntactic specification activity of the models.

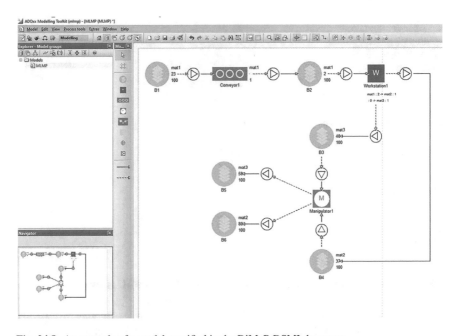

Fig. 24.8 An example of a model specified in the DiMaP-DSML language

Therefore, for a graph with nodes of the types workstations, conveyors, AGV, manipulators, buffers and ports to represent a correct model from a syntactic point of view, it must respect the conditions imposed by the categorical sketch defined in Sect. 24.3.2.1, that is, it must be connected, there should be at most one arc between any two nodes, the subtypes should partition the types accordingly, etc.

24.4.2.3   Specifying Model Semantics in DiMaP-DSML Language

The lexical atoms of the DiMaP-DSML language semantically represent atomic components of a flexible manufacturing system that are autonomous, distributed, cooperative and intelligent, and that can be assembled into a manufacturing cell that performs the functions specific to a manufacturing process. The semantics of a model thus specified is given by the graph structure of the model, that is, the type of components, their number and their functional assembly mode as well as the semantics of each component represented by the values of some attributes associated with atomic components.

In the example from Fig. 24.8, we have a model with a graph structure that represents a conveyor that moves materials from the source buffer B1 to the destination buffer B2, a manipulator that alternately moves materials from the source buffers B3 or B4 to the destination buffers B5 or B6 and a workstation that feeds on material entities from buffer B2; processes these materials through specific operations; and stores the resulting new material entities in one of the buffers B3 or B4, depending on the type of entity results.

The state of the model at a given time is represented by the graph structure of the model and the values of some attributes associated with the atomic components at that time. The attributes associated with the atomic components of a model are the parameters that, on the one hand, contribute to the specification of the states of a model and, on the other hand, customize the actions of behavioural rules.

All atomic components of a model are endowed with attributes that are mapped to data domains at the metamodel level and can be customized by the modeller when specifying a model by assigning appropriate values to the manufacturing cell it represents.

Workstation components are endowed with the following attributes and corresponding data fields: Name: string, (MaterialTypeIn: string, MaterialAmountIn: integer, MaterialTypeOut: string, MaterialAmountOut: integer, Duration: time): record, OperationCode: longstring. The mechanism for initializing and customizing the values of these attributes can be seen in Fig. 24.9. These attributes customize the application of behavioural rules and remain constant in the execution process of the model. The OperationCode attribute contains ADOScript code that specifies the location of a physical device that performs the operations defined by the workstation component, through the URL, and the operations that it must perform.

Atomic components of the transport machine type can be customized by appropriate attributes: Name: string, (MaterialType: string, CapacityUnit: integer, Capacity: integer, TransportTime: time, OperationCode: longstring): record.

The personalization of the components of this type is done, as in the case of the previous components, by values from the data domain associated with these attributes. These attributes customize the application of appropriate behavioural rules and remain evident in the execution process of the model. As with workstation components, the OperationCode attribute contains ADOScript code that specifies the location of a physical device that performs the operations defined by the component, through the URL, and the operations that it must perform.

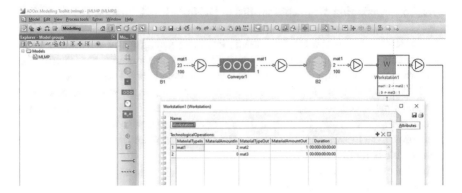

Fig. 24.9 Workstation customization

Buffer components are endowed with the following attributes mapped to the specified data domains: Name: string, MaterialType: string, Capacity: integer, OccupiedCapacity: integer. In the model execution process, the values of the Name, MaterialType and Capacity attributes remain constant and the value of the OccupiedCapacity attribute will be recalculated at each step by applying behavioural rules.

Port-type components are also endowed with specific attributes that can be customized similar to those of the components described above: Name: string, MaterialKind: string, PortName: string, PortDirectionType: enum {Incoming, Outgoing}, Direction: enum {Right, Left, Up, Down}.

The behaviour of a model specified in the DiMaP-DSML language is defined by the behavioural dimension of the model that was implemented at the metamodel level by the behavioural rules defined in Sect. 24.3.3. The matches of these behavioural rules in a model have as matching pivot components the active atomic components of the model, that is, components such as workstation and transport machines.

Each workstation component is fed from one or more input buffers with material entities, according to the types and quantities specified in the customization phase, and stores the resulting material entities in one or more output buffers, according to types and quantities specified by custom attribute values. The transport machine components have limited transport capacities and can only transport the types of material entities specified in the customization phase. Both workstation and transport machine components work asynchronously if they find in source buffers the types of materials specified in the configuration, in the specified quantities and there is space available for storage in the output buffers. The operations performed by these active components have an execution duration and begin to be executed immediately when these conditions are met and enter the standstill when these conditions are no longer met. Behavioural rules that fit the model are executed simultaneously if they are independent.

24.5   Conclusion

In this chapter, we propose some theoretical and practical mechanisms that, in our opinion, are of major importance for the process of methodological construction of domain-specific modelling tools. The motivation and objectives of our approach derive from the imperative need to develop domain-specific modelling tools in contrast to the timid concerns in this domain.

The mathematical formalization in Sect. 24.3 highlights the very good compatibility between the categorical mechanisms and the concepts involved in metamodelling, in general, and especially in the metamodelling of manufacturing processes. Category theory provides adequate mechanisms for specifying inter-structural relations, for composing structures and for reasoning on these constructions. The categorical sketch becomes a natural metamodel that attributes to a diagrammatic language the quality of formal language. The implicit semantics of the categorical sketch components make it possible to verify the syntactic correctness of a model by generic algorithms specified at the metamodel level. Also, the concept of behavioural rule that we have defined as an association between a graph transformation and a behavioural action naturally serves as a formal metamodel for behavioural semantics.

Our approach by category of instances and behavioural rules (CIBR), defined in Sect. 24.3.3.2, also offers a solution for the faithful modelling of the simulation and execution space of a model. CIBR category paths define the possible evolutions of a model during simulation or execution by states, represented by static models, and transitions, represented by behavioural rules.

In the process of specifying the metamodel, we found a very good compatibility of the categorical mechanisms with the syntax and semantics of the MM-DSL language. The MM-DSL language also allows the platform-independent specification of the modelling method components.

The feasibility and efficiency of our methodological approach are demonstrated by treating the MM-DiMaP modelling method from the conceptualization phase in the context of categorical mechanisms, to the specification phase in the MM-DSL language and to the translation and testing phase on the ADOxx metamodelling platform. The result of this process is the DiMaP modelling tool, endowed with the DiMaP-DSML diagrammatic modelling language.

Although the DiMaP modelling tool is only a prototype, with a small set of features, it highlights the advantages of a domain-specific modelling tool through intuitiveness, simplicity and compatibility with the modelling domain. Therefore, although the DiMaP-DSML language is a formal language, it is simple and intuitive enough to be accessible to all parties involved in the design of manufacturing cells due to its visual character and its compatibility with the specific modelling domain.

Tool Download   https://www.omilab.org/dimap

References

1. Cardin, O.: Classification of cyber-physical production systems applications: proposition of an analysis framework. Comput Ind. **104**, 11–21 (2019)
2. Fill, H., Karagiannis, D.: On the conceptualization of modelling methods using the ADOxx meta modelling platform. Enterp. Modell. Inf. Syst. Arch. **8**(1), 4–25 (2013)
3. Wolter, U., Diskin, Z.: The next hundred diagrammatic specification techniques, a gentle introduction to generalized sketches. https://www.researchgate.net/publication/253963677 (2015)
4. Karagiannis, D., Kühn, H.: Metamodelling platforms. Invited paper. In: Bauknecht, K., Tjoa, A.M., Quirchmayer, G. (eds.) Proceedings of the Third International Conference EC-Web 2002 - Dexa 2002, Aix-en-Provence, France, September 2–6, 2002, LNCS 2455. Springer, Berlin, Heidelberg (2002)
5. Karagiannis, D.: Agile modeling method engineering. In: Proceedings of the 19th Panhellenic Conference on Informatics, pp. 5–10. ACM, Athens, Greece (2015)
6. Zeigler, B.P., Muzy, A., Kofman, E.: Theory of Modeling and Simulation Discrete Event and Iterative System Computational Foundations. Academic Press, New York (2019)
7. Fowler, M., Parsons, R.: Domain Specific Languages, 1st edn. Addison-Wesley Longman, Amsterdam (2010)
8. Barr, M., Wells, C.: Category Theory For Computing Science - Reprints in Theory and Applications of Categories, No. 22 (2012)
9. Diskin, Z., Maibaum, T.: Category theory and model-driven engineering: from formal semantics to design patterns and beyond. ACCAT. **93**, 1–21 (2012)
10. Milner, R.: The space and motion of communicating agents. Cambridge University Press, Cambridge (2009)
11. Bork, D., Buchman, R.A., Karagiannis, D., Lee, M., Miron, E.T.: An open platform for modeling method conceptualization: the OMiLAB digital ecosystem, Communications of the Association for Information Systems. http://eprints.cs.univie.ac.at/5462/1/CAIS-OMiLAB-final-withFront.pdf (2019)
12. Manifesto for Agile Software Development website, https://agilemanifesto.org/. Accessed 15 March 2021
13. Efendioglu, N., Woitsch, R., Utz, W., Falcioni, D.: A product-service system proposal for agile modelling method engineering on demand: ADOxx.org. In: Rossmann, A., Zimmermann, A. (eds.) Digital Enterprise Computing 2017, Lecture Notes in Informatics (LNI). Gesellschaft für Informatik, Bonn (2017)
14. Karagiannis, D., Mayr, H.C., Mylopoulos, J.: Domain-Specific Conceptual Modeling Concepts, Methods and Tools. Springer, Cham (2016)
15. Karagiannis, D., Višić N.: Next generation of modelling platforms, perspectives in business informatics research. In: 10th International Conference, BIR 2011 Riga, Latvia, October 6–8, 2011 Proceedings (2011)
16. Bork, D., Karagiannis, D., Pittl, B.: A survey of modeling language specification techniques. Inf. Syst. **87**, 101425 (2020)
17. Crăciunean, D.C., Karagiannis, D.: Categorical modeling method of intelligent WorkFlow. In: Groza, A., Prasath, R. (eds.) Mining Intelligence and Knowledge Exploration. MIKE Lecture Notes in Computer Science, vol. 11308. Springer, Cham (2018)
18. Crăciunean, D.C.: Categorical grammars for processes modeling. Int. J. Adv. Comput. Sci. Appl. **10**(1) (2019). https://doi.org/10.14569/IJACSA.2019.0100105
19. Diskin, Z., Wolter, U.: A diagrammatic logic for object-oriented visual modeling. Electron. Notes Theor. Comput. Sci. **203**(6), 19–41 (2008)
20. Wolter, U., Diskin, Z.: The next hundred diagrammatic specification techniques – an introduction to generalized sketches. Technical Report No 358, Department of Informatics, University of Bergen (2007)

21. Campbell, G., Courtehoute, B., Plump, D.: Linear-time graph algorithms in GP2, Department of Computer Science, University of York, UK, Submitted for publication [Online]. https://cdn.gjcampbell.co.uk/2019/Linear-Time-GP2-Preprint.pdf (2019)
22. Campbell, G.: Algebraic graph transformation: a crash course, Department of Computer Science, University of York, UK, Technical Report [Online]. https://cdn.gjcampbell.co.uk/2018/Graph-Transformation.pdf (2018)
23. Ehrig, H., Ermel, C., Golas, U., Hermann, F.: Graph and model transformation general framework and applications. Springer, Berlin (2015)
24. Plump, D.: Checking graph-transformation systems for confluence. ECEASST. **26** (2010). https://doi.org/10.14279/tuj.eceasst.26.367
25. Plump, D.: Computing by Graph Transformation: 2018/19. Department of Computer Science, University of York, York (2019)
26. Rozsnberg, G.: Handbook of Graph Grammars and Computing by Graph Transformation. World Scientific Publishing, Singapore (1997)
27. van der Aalst, W.M.P.: Process Mining Discovery, Conformance and Enhancement of Business Processes. Springer, Berlin (2011)
28. van der Aalst, W.M.P., van Hee, K.M.: Workflow Management: Models, Methods, and Systems. MIT Press, Cambridge, MA (2004)
29. Višić, N.: Language-oriented modeling method engineering, Doctoral Thesis, University of Vienna, Scientific Advisor: o. Univ.-Prof. Prof.h.c. Dr. Dimitris Karagiannis (2016)

Chapter 25
Conceptualizing Design Thinking Artefacts: The Scene2Model Storyboard Approach

Christian Muck and Silke Palkovits-Rauter

Abstract The need for innovative products and business models has increased in recent years, as they are seen as an important selling point in today's economy. As a consequence, various approaches and tools were introduced to tackle such design problems. Even though these approaches have their advantages, we found a lack in approaches that consider the synergies from using tangible methods (like organising sticky notes on a whiteboard) and computer-aided tools to capture and share the knowledge beyond pictures and lengthy texts. Therefore, we propose an approach to link these two worlds (tangible and digital) and a corresponding proof-of-concept prototype in the form of the Scene2Model tool, which offers an automated transformation from tangible objects to digital models.

Keywords Conceptual modelling · Diagrammatic modelling · Design thinking · Storyboards

25.1 Introduction

Being innovative and meeting the users' needs are becoming more and more important in today's economy. But designing such solutions is a complex undertaking. In [4] the authors call such problems "*wicked problems*", which means that they have a weakly defined problem space, with multiple stakeholders having different requirements and goals towards the complex system which should be designed. Often such problems need unique solutions in a given environment, which makes it difficult to propose a general approach to solve them.

C. Muck (✉)
Research Group Knowledge Engineering, University of Vienna, Vienna, Austria
e-mail: christian.muck@univie.ac.at

S. Palkovits-Rauter
University of Applied Sciences Burgenland, Eisenstadt, Austria
e-mail: silke.palkovits-rauter@fh-burgenland.at

© The Author(s), under exclusive license to Springer Nature Switzerland AG 2022   567
D. Karagiannis et al. (eds.), *Domain-Specific Conceptual Modeling*,
https://doi.org/10.1007/978-3-030-93547-4_25

One approach to tackle these problems is *design thinking*, which usually concentrates on a strong user focus and creativity. Within the overall process of design thinking (examples for design thinking processes can be found in [18, 24]), different methods can be used to gain insight or design different parts of the novel idea, which should be created. In [24] such methods are introduced, which are often applied in workshops and aided by tangible resources like sticky notes, flipcharts, printed templates, paper figures and so on, which are used to create an artefact to visualize the created idea or design. The interaction with and through these tangible means should foster the interaction and creativity in such workshops. This leads to thorough knowledge by the participants, the created artefacts or pictures of them and maybe a separate created textual explanation. The latter two can then be used to share the created knowledge with other stakeholders.

With the approach and prototype introduced in this chapter, we want to propose a way to support the exchange of knowledge with stakeholders, who cannot participate in the workshops, without losing the physical interaction of workshop participants. For supporting the knowledge exchange, we use conceptual modelling, as it is an established approach to capture, represent and exchange knowledge in various domains, like software engineering or business process management. Conceptual modelling itself uses abstraction to capture and represent knowledge in a comprehensible way, in the context of a specific purpose (cf. [13]). Such models are especially useful to communicate knowledge if computer-aided tools are used. The digital representation can then be saved, adapted over time and shared with other stakeholders. An additional benefit of using digital models in the introduced context is that they can be enriched with additional information, which leads to a more sophisticated representation.

The goal of Scene2Model (cf. [15]) is not to replace the tangible technique (like the paper figures of SAP Scenes[TM] [21]) within a workshop through the modelling tool or to offer another way to manually create digital artefacts additionally to the tangible ones. The aim is to connect the tangible method with the digital modelling tool, by allowing an automated transformation from the tangible artefacts into digital models. The created models can then be enhanced and used like other models. So, not only the modelling tool with the used design thinking method is needed but also an environment where the tangible objects can be recognized and enriched by a machine to allow the automated creation of the digital models. To show and evaluate this approach, the Scene2Model prototype was created, for which one design thinking method was chosen, and the needed environment was designed and implemented.

In the remainder of this chapter, first the background to related topics is given, and then the method will be introduced and conceptualized. Afterwards we will introduce the prototype with the aid of a use case. Last but not least, thoughts on future work will be given.

25.2   Method Description

In this chapter, we introduce an approach, aiming at supporting the automated transformation from tangible representations to digital models and a proof-of-concept prototype for one chosen tangible technique. With tangible we mean to represent knowledge by arranging physical objects like paper figures or sticky notes, as it is done in many design thinking methods within workshop settings. We follow the thesis that this way of working, using the physical objects in a closed setting (e.g. workshops), is useful and therefore often proposed. For example, the book [24] or websites like digitrans.me,[1] designthinking-methods.com,[1] http://www.designkit.org/,[1] . . . contain multiple methods, aimed to be used in workshops.

Before we chose a design thinking technique for the prototype, we researched tangible techniques and divided them rough into two categories: picture based and text based. With tangible we mean that the method uses artefacts that participants of workshops can physically touch and rearrange, like sticky notes with text or paper figures. In a broader interpretation of these categories, one could also add sketches and texts written on a whiteboard. But such techniques were not considered for the prototype, just as pictures and texts that are created purely digital (like the ones introduced in Sect. 25.2.2.1). This is based on our goal to support the tangible and digital knowledge representation in creative settings.

The first category uses graphical representations, like storyboards which usually can be interpreted and understood by humans. Therefore, semantic-rich pictures are used to showcase the interaction of a user with a system, product, service or something similar. The second category uses natural language texts to describe certain aspects of the system under study. In the context of design thinking, these are usually short notes or word groups written on sticky notes and arranged on a white board or a printed template. One well-known example would be the *Business Model Canvas (BMC)* (cf. [17]). An example for a picture-based approach would be SAP Scenes[TM] (cf. Sect. 25.2.1.1 for more information). Here graphical paper figures are used to create visual storyboards of the users' story. This technique is also used for the Scene2Model prototype, which is the focus of this chapter. The prototype allows to transform the paper figures into a digital model, and this graphical representation can then be enriched with additional information, to better capture the essence of the portrayed user story.

In the rest of this section, we want to introduce related work, which we used within the motivation, conceptualization and implementation of the Scene2Model tool. To prevent confusion, for the rest of the chapter, we will call tangible methods with paper figures or sticky notes techniques and the term methods will refer to conceptual modelling methods, as defined by Karagiannis and Kühn [10].

---

[1] Last visited: 2021-03-08.

25.2.1 Design Thinking

Design thinking has been developed by researchers at the Stanford University and the design agency IDEO with the aim to be able to focus on user-centred aspects rather than technical ones during the development of new products [8]. In [24] it is further stated that design thinking can be used as an innovation method, which is based upon an iterative and user-oriented process for solving complex problems. Razzouk and Shute [19] further argue that design thinking is an important skill for staying competitive in today's economy.

In this context, [3, 24] argue that among other things it is important to make low fidelity prototypes fast, often to make the innovative idea itself more concrete and to improve discussion and feedback collection with further stakeholders.

In [9] the authors claim that the physical environment (e.g. for workshops), in which design thinking is applied, is important for the design thinking process itself. It usually has enough space, a changeable layout (flexible furniture) and materials and resources to visualize new ideas. Further, [1] argues that the work environment has an important contribution to finding creative solutions. Design thinking can then further improve the finding of solutions by providing guidelines in the way of working, inside and outside of workshops.

One famous design thinking process is introduced by the Stanford d.school (cf. [7]) which contains a five-phased cycle which is iterative applied to a given problem. The five phases are called *Empathize, Define, Ideate, Prototype* and *Test*. The first phase focuses on exploration of the problem and its context. The second phase shares and interprets the relevant findings. The third phase then creates various ideas, which are prototyped in the fourth phase. In the fifth phase, these prototypes are then tested.

The goal of the approach introduced in this chapter is to support methods like design thinking by allowing to use the tangible techniques in physical workshops and support the automated creation of a digital representation, which can then be shared between the different phases and exchanged between various stakeholders. For the Scene2Model prototype, one design thinking technique was chosen, which is described in the next subsection.

25.2.1.1 Storyboarding with SAP Scenes[TM]

For the implementation of the Scene2Model tool and a first evaluation of the combination of tangible and digital support for design thinking techniques, the SAP Scenes[TM] (cf. [21]) approach was chosen. The reason was that the technique itself is intuitive to understand, and it uses individual concepts, which can be easily interpreted by humans. So, for applying the Scene2Model tool, not much energy has to be spent for explaining the design thinking technique.

In the design of new products/services, storyboards can be used to create an understandable and shareable visualization. Van der Lelie [25] argues that this kind of visualization helps the designer of the product to better understand the users and their needs. In addition, the designer can explore the context and flow of time, within the visualized story. Last but not least, created storyboards can be shared with other stakeholders to collect further insights from them. Another benefit from using storyboards is that they are easily comprehensible by humans [25].

According to [21], SAP Scenes^{TM} are based on the idea of storyboards to explore, analyse and capture a user's story in a visual way within a workshop. The difference to other storyboard approaches is that sets of predefined paper figures with which the storyboards are created are provided. Their thesis is that many participants are hindered to participate, because they do not want to draw themselves. So, by offering a predefined set of figures, the approach should include more participants. Cutting out the paper figures and arranging them on a table should make the storyboards more tangible and foster participation in the workshop setting [21].

25.2.2 Challenges of Digital Tool Support for Design Thinking Techniques

Many design thinking techniques are used in workshops with a limited number of participants and use tangible objects to represent and structure information about ideated products, services, business models and so on.

Even though there are different computer-aided tools to create similar representations of the information as the created tangible artefacts (cf. Sect. 25.2.2.1 for a short overview on possible tools), in design thinking still face-to-face workshops with tangible techniques are used to foster participation and creativity. Such approaches are location and time dependent, and the number of possible participants is restricted. This supports a thorough understanding for the participants, but for other involved stakeholders, the information is often limited to textual summaries, pictures of the created (tangible) artefacts or other means of manually summarized knowledge transfer.

Digital tools which can be used for creating design thinking technique artefacts are useful in offering an adaptable and shareable representation of the captured information. Some of them also offer capabilities to work distributed on a shared artefact in a synchronous manner, but according to [5], directly using such tools can hinder a design thinking workshop and its result.

With the proposed Scene2Model tool, we aim to support the linkage of both sides (tangible and computer-aided design thinking techniques) while minimizing the manual steps and reducing the media break. We achieve this by supporting a tangible design thinking technique with a corresponding modelling tool and offer an environment, where the used tangible objects can be recognized via a camera and mapped to modelling objects in a tool. In this way the tangible representation can be automatically transformed into a digital model, which can later be adapted, shared and evolved.

25.2.2.1 State of the Art in Design Thinking Tooling

Literature is limited when searching for IT tools supporting the creative process in the design thinking approach. There exist online collaboration whiteboard tools or realtimeboards [20] such as Wiki-Wall, Glogster, Padlet, Linoit, Twiddla, Trello, Miro, Rizzoma or Mural [2], providing methods for all stages of design thinking, such as ideation and brainstorming, mind mapping, brain writing, planning boards or SWOT analyses. These modern cloud services are researched in concern of their capabilities in educational settings [22] or in agile sprint planning sessions [6].

There is still a demand for a digital tool, which focuses on the benefits of applying the tangible design thinking techniques in combination with the digital enrichment, like it was done with the Scene2Model prototype.

25.2.3   Modelling as Shareable Knowledge Representation

According to [13], models are widely used for analysing, representing and communicating specific aspects of real-world systems or objects. It thereby does not matter if the original (a.k.a., the real-world system) is already existing or the model is used to design a future original. One key aspect of models is abstraction, which means the model does not contain all the details of the original, but selected characteristics which are important. The importance of the characteristics is specified by the purpose of the model creation.

For the Scene2Model approach, we found modelling as a beneficial way to conceptualize the design thinking technique and what should be captured of the created user story. It allowed to reuse the graphical rich expression of the SAP Scenes™ paper figures and equip them with attributes to define further information about the represented concepts. Adding this additional information would not be possible by using drawing tools like Microsoft PowerPoint or Paint.

An often used approach to define modelling method is metamodelling (e.g. cf. [10, 13, 23]). Using this approach to describe the Scene2Model modelling method further supported the implemented environment, because the created metamodel was used to transform and enrich the used paper figures into the digital model. In this way, the metamodel served as the common conceptual representation between the different components of the Scene2Model prototype (for more information, see Section 25.3)

25.3   Method Conceptualization

To reach the goal of offering the benefits of using tangible objects and a computer-aided modelling tool, we identified the need for four components: tangible objects and a way to digitize them (e.g. camera), the modelling tool, the recognition of the paper figures and the mapping between the tangible objects and their digitized representations. These four components are represented in Fig. 25.1. Even though the figure focuses on the Scene2Model approach, a similar setting could be used for text-based approaches, like the ones mentioned in Sect. 25.2.

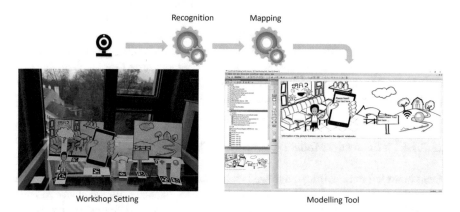

Recognition   Mapping

Workshop Setting   Modelling Tool

Fig. 25.1 General approach of the Scene2Model tool (based on figure 1 from [14]) (the figure contains graphics from SAP Scenes™ [21])

On the left side of Fig. 25.1, we see an example of the tangible environment, which could be applied in a workshop environment. In this case it is a scene created with figures from SAP Scenes™. Then we need some device for creating a digital representation of the physical environment, which is shown in Fig. 25.1 through the camera (icon above the paper figures). On the right side of the figure, we see the modelling tool, which shows the same figures as the physical environment. But the figures in the modelling tool can be enriched with additional information by filling in their attributes. Of course, the modelling tool can be used on its own. But to gain the benefit of the automated transformation, other important components are needed.

In Fig. 25.1 these important parts are named *Recognition* and *Mapping*, which symbolize the comprehension of the digital input and mapping it to the used modelling method. This of course depends on the specific applied context. For example, identifying handwritten text will need another approach and then identifying paper figures and their position. The recognition and mapping must also be adjusted to the physical environment, considering which information is available and can be used for the processing. For example, for the Scene2Model prototype, we added markers to the paper figures to reduce the preparation time and to have a stable and fast recognition.

The remainder of this section focuses on the chosen storyboard technique and the implementation in the context of the Scene2Model prototype.

25.3.1   The Scene2Model Modelling Method

According to [10] a modelling method is composed of three parts: *modelling language, modelling procedure* and *mechanisms & algorithms*. The modelling language describes the syntax, notation and semantics of the models that can be created. Syntax contains the available concepts and rules how they are connected. Semantic describes the meaning of the concepts, and last but not least, the notation defines how the concepts are visualized. The modelling procedure contains guidelines on how to create models, which can be supported by mechanisms and algorithms. Mechanisms and algorithms contain automated ways of processing or creating models and support the user or extract implicit knowledge from the models.

25.3.1.1   The Scene2Model Diagrammatic Modelling Language

Even though the modelling language is important for the Scene2Model approach, it is not the main focus, because it is mainly used to visualize graphical storyboards and set attributes. It contains classes to group the representation of the paper figures and a concept to contain a whole scene. Additional to the concept for describing storyboards, a class for creating textual notes and a concept to link business processes were added. The capability to link business processes (with *Process*) was added to Scene2Model to gain a first insight on how other modelling methods can be used to add specialized knowledge to scenes. Business processes were chosen because they are a widely recognized approach (e.g. *Business Process Model and Notation (=BPMN)*). But using such processes is not a core capability of Scene2Model. An excerpt of the metamodel can be seen in Fig. 25.2 which was visualized with the *CoChaCo* tool (cf. [11]).

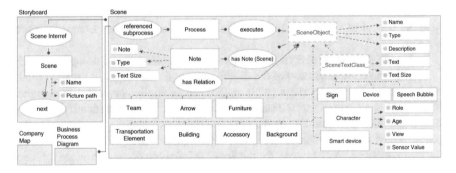

Fig. 25.2 Metamodel of the Scene2Model approach

The purple rectangles represent the used modeltypes. The *Storyboard* and *Scene* modeltypes are the core model types of the Scene2Model approach. They represent the created storyboards and the different scenes, which show key moments in the told story of the user or the system. The *Scene* modeltype contains the different figures to create the visual user stories. *Storyboard* is then used to combine different scenes, order them in a chronological manner and give an overview over the complete user story. The *Company Map* and *Business Process Diagram* are used to visualize the added business process models.

For the *Scene* modeltype, an important class is the abstract class *_SceneObject_*. It is the superclass of all classes which are used to represent figures, defines their available standard attributes and severs as endpoint for the relations. The attributes are:

- *Name*: gives an identifier to the object and must be unique within a model.
- *Type*: specifies a type of the class and the notation in form of a graphic.
- *Description*: holds a textual description of the object.

The abstract class *_SceneTextClass_* is the superclass of those classes, which are able to add text to their graphical representation. For example, in Fig. 25.3h you can see text in a thought bubble. The *_SceneTextClass_* is used to cluster these classes and provide the ability to attach the needed information, like the text that should be represented. Thereby, the *Text* attribute captures the string which should be shown and *Text Size* defines the size of the shown text. Of course, every subclass of *_SceneTextClass_* is also a subclass of *_SceneObject_*.

The classes which specialize *_SceneObject_* or *_SceneTextClass_* (*Team, Arrow, Furniture, Transportation Element, Building, Accessory, Background, Speech Bubble, Device, Sign, Character* and *Smart device*) are used to group figures together, which belong semantically together. The *Type* attribute from the superclass is used to specify the concrete representation of the created modelling object. For example, the class *Character* has the types businesswoman (see Fig. 25.3a) and businessman (see Fig. 25.3c), which have their certain figures mapped to them. The subclasses *Character* and *Smart device* (see Fig. 25.3f) possess additional attributes to further describe the represented objects. For example, the class *Characters* uses the attribute *View* to switch between front and back view (see Fig. 25.3a, b). *Smart device* has the attribute *Sensor Value* which influences the colour coding of the visualization.

The classes specified as specializations of *_SceneObject_* (see Fig. 25.2) should not be seen as fixed, but as a starting set of possible classes and corresponding figure representations. Of course, no predefined set of figures can be used to represent all possible use cases. Therefore, by facilitating the underlying metamodelling platform (ADOxx, which is explained in more detail in Sect. 25.3.2), the available classes and figures for the Scene2Model tool can be adapted. But to do so, more sophisticated knowledge about the Scene2Model tool and ADOxx is needed. For example, the class *Smart device* is not predefined in SAP Scenes™, but was needed for a teaching case and was therefore added to the tool.

Apart from the specializations of *_SceneObject_*, also the classes *Note* and *Process* are available in the *Scene* modeltype. Examples of their visualization can be seen in Fig. 25.3d, e. Further, within an instance of the *Process* class, a link can be set to a model of the *Business Process Diagram* modeltype. With this link the user can directly navigate from a scene to a linked business process diagram.

To support the adding of textual notes to the created scenes, the *Note* class was created. It can display text directly in each visualization and its size can be dynamically adjusted to the needs. The attribute *Note* contains the string which will be shown. But not only the specially entered string can be shown, but also the content of the *Description* attribute of a connected object can be visualized. Therefore, a specialization of *_SceneObject_* must be related to the *Note* instance via the *has Note (Scene)* relation. The *Type* attribute can then be used to switch a *Note* object from showing the string of the *Note* attribute to showing the string of the *Description* attribute of a related object. The attribute *Text Size* can be used to influence the size of the shown text.

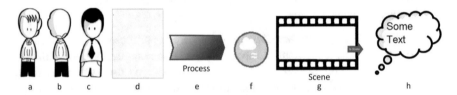

Fig. 25.3 Notation example for model objects (the figure contains graphics from SAP Scenes[TM][21]): (**a**) businesswoman front, (**b**) businesswoman back, (**c**) businessman, (**d**) note, (**e**) process, (**f**) smart device, (**g**) scene, (**h**) thought bubble with text

The goal of the modeltype *Storyboard* is to give an overview of the whole story, created with the separated scenes. It therefore uses the *Scene* class (see Fig. 25.3g) to represent one specific scene. *Scene* objects can be connected to each other with the *next* relation, and thus they can be ordered within a use case. For example, this could be the chronological order, in which the scenes play through during the story. A scene also possesses a name which should encompass the essence of the scene. An object of the *Scene* class can directly be linked to an instance of the *Scene* modeltype. Therefore, the attribute *Scene Interref* can be used. Using this link the user can directly navigate from the storyboard to the linked model by clicking on the blue arrow or the shown name. Further, a static picture of the scene can be shown in the graphical representation of the *Scene* class object. Or rather any picture can be shown in the visualization, as long as the system path to the picture is entered into *Picture path* attribute. During the automated creation of a *Storyboard* model from separate scene, this picture can also be set automatically (see Sect. 25.3.1.3 for more details). Examples of a *Scene* and *Storyboard* model can be found in Sect. 25.4.2.1.

The *Business Process Diagram* modeltype can be used to describe business processes in the *BPMN* notation. The *Company Map* modeltype can be used to give an overview over the created processes within the scenes. This modeltype is used in the automated creation of the process overview, which is explained in Sect. 25.3.1.3. For these two modeltypes, no classes are given because this would go beyond the scope of this chapter. But they both are based on the *BPMN@ADOxx* library, which is available at www.adoxx.org.

25.3.1.2   Modelling Procedure: Creating Models with Scene2Model

As defined in [10], the modelling procedure guides a user in creating high-quality models. On one side, this can be guidelines in form of steps and rules, which support the user. On the other hand, this can mean implemented functionality, which checks if certain constraints are violated or helps to generate (parts of) models automatically.

For the Scene2Model approach, the modelling procedure is an important part, because the main idea is that users are not creating their models through the graphical user interface (GUI) but through paper figures placed on a table. Of course, the interaction through the GUI is still possible and needed to refine the models. But the idea is that the initial state of a *Scene* model, containing the available figures and their arrangement, is done through paper figures. This of course is supported by *mechanisms & algorithms*, which are explained in Sect. 25.3.1.3.

The creation of *Storyboard* models is also supported through automated means. After all the individual scenes are created within the tool, the overview in form of a storyboard can be generated out of the different models. More information on this mechanism itself can be found in Sect. 25.3.1.3.

The general approach of creating models with the Scene2Model prototype is therefore to use the tangible paper figures, which are imported through an automated transformation. Of course, these models should then be enriched, shared with other stakeholders and adapted if the design of the novel idea progresses.

25.3.1.3   Supporting the User Through Mechanisms and Algorithms

This section focuses on the main functionalities which are proposed for the Scene2Model approach and were implemented within the prototype. According to [10], *Mechanisms & Algorithms* are based upon the modelling language and process or evaluate the created models. They can be generic, hybrid or specific.

As the prototype was implemented with ADOxx (see Sect. 25.3.2 for a short introduction), provided generic mechanisms are used in the Scene2Model modelling tool, which adds value for the users. For example, models can be saved in files, exported as pictures, analysed with queries and so on. For this chapter, we will not go into detail about the generic mechanisms but focus on the ones specifically created for Scene2Model.

For the introduced Scene2Model approach, the most important mechanism is the automated creation of digital models from scenes created with paper figures. In Fig. 25.1 the basic idea of the transformation mechanism can be seen.

First of all, the modelling tool (shown on the right side of Fig. 25.1) has the main task to create and manage the models and their export. This also includes to get information from the tangible paper figure environment and create models out of it. We decoupled the recognition and the mapping from the modelling tool to support the connecting of multiple modelling tools with one environment within a workshop. For example, each participant could bring its own device with the Scene2Model tool to the workshop and import the paper figures. Therefore, the modelling tool must be able to communicate with the external service and get the information it needs to create the *Scene* models.

In Fig. 25.1 the components *Recognition* and *Mapping* are located between the paper figures and the modelling tool. *Recognition* symbolizes the identification of the used paper figures and their position. The input to this component is a picture or a frame of a video. The output which is used as input of the *Mapping* component is for each recognized figure an identifier and the position of the paper figure. The identifier is needed to add additional information in the *Mapping* component, and the position is needed to correctly place the figures within the digital model. Thereby, it is not important to get some kind of absolute position, but rather the relative positioning between the paper figures is needed to recreate the general look of the scene. Of course, if not only paper figures should be recognized but also text, the capabilities of the *Recognition* component must be enhanced accordingly.

In the *Mapping* component, the information gathered from *Recognition* will be taken as input and enhanced with additional information. This can be the available characteristics associated with the concept behind the paper figure, a set of filled-out characteristics or both. On one hand it needs a way to assign the characteristics to the concept of the paper figure and on the other hand to describe the characteristics and their values. This information must then be provided in a format that the modelling tool can process.

The other two introduced specific mechanisms follow a similar goal. One is to create *Storyboard* models out of a set of scenes, and the other one is to generate *Company Maps* out of them. The goal is to get an overview of different aspects of the created scenes and to save the user cumbersome work through an automated process. To do this first the scenes which belong together must be identified, and also an order between them must be established. Because storyboards usually contain the notion of a flow of time in the visualized story (cf. [25]), this flow can also be used to order the storyboard and the company map, if it can be communicated to the tool. The automatically created *Company Maps* give an overview of the business processes linked in the different *Scene* models.

25.3.2   Scope and Objectives of the Prototype

The previously defined Scene2Model method was implemented in a proof-of-concept prototype to gain first insights on how the combination of tangible design thinking techniques and tool-aided conceptual modelling can be combined and supported. To increase the added value of the approach, the transformation should be automated as much as possible. With this we mean that the user should be supported during the creation of the digital models and have the ability to enrich and adapt them.

Therefore, one specific technique was chosen, in our case SAP Scenes[TM] (cf. [21]), and the tool and the environment were designed and implemented for this technique. It was chosen because it is intuitive to use, so the prototype is not as dependent on potential users to understand and rightfully apply the chosen design thinking technique.

ADOxx was chosen as metamodelling platform (www.adoxx.org) because it supports the implementation of an automatic processing or creation of models and offers generic functionality out-of-the-box which is beneficial to the Scene2Model prototype. Examples are the automatic possibility to search through models, export pictures, share models between tool instances, allow the creation of an installable tool and so on.

For Scene2Model the goal was to create an environment where the SAP Scenes^{TM} paper figures can be used, automatically identified and transformed into a digital model. Additionally, the identified paper figures should be enhanced with information to further minimize the workload for the user. To achieve that goal, we created the environment described in Sect. 25.4.1.

The first version of the ADOxx-based Scene2Model tool was created in the context of the EU-funded *DIGITRANS* project (http://www.interreg-danube.eu/approved-projects/digitrans), and the actual version 1.5.2 can be found at https://austria.omilab.org/psm/content/scene2model/info.

25.4 Proof of Concept

This section will focus on how the Scene2Model prototype was applied to a fictitious scenario to discuss the proposed way of working. The general aspects of the design for this proof-of-concept tool can be found in Sect. 25.3. Before we start with the scenario, the environment for using the Scene2Model prototype will be described.

25.4.1 The Proof-of-Concept Environment

As shown in Fig. 25.1, the proposed environment for the Scene2Model prototype consists of four components: paper figures, recognition, mapping and the modelling tool. For the typical environment, this four components are separated into two main parts. First the setup in the workshop place consisting of the paper figures and the recognition. The second part contains the devices of the participants which are running the modelling tool and the mapping component.

For the Scene2Model tool, the identification and the calculation of the position are done via tags. These tags are attached directly to the paper figures and on the surface, where the paper figures are placed. The tags on the surface are used to calculate the position of the paper figures, and the tags on the paper figures are used for the identification. The tags, the position calculation and the tag recognition are using *ArUco* (cf. https://www.uco.es/investiga/grupos/ava/node/26). Each tag represents an integer value. The camera is connected to the recognition component, which offers the *id*, *x* and *y* coordinates via a websocket. Additionally, the component offers a web interface, which can be accessed via a browser and shows a live stream of the video from the camera overlayed with the identified tags and their IDs. This web interface is helpful, because the recognition of the tags depends on the position of the paper figures, the camera and light conditions. Through the video stream, the participants can check what is recognized and where a problem may have occurred. For example, maybe a paper figure partially covers the tag for the camera.

The websocket is received by the mapping component which takes the *id* and the coordinates and enhances them with the information needed to create the objects in the modelling tool. The mapping component can be started and stopped directly via the modelling tool, and the information for the enrichment is saved in an ontology and is processed by using Apache Jena (cf. https://jena.apache.org/). The file with the ontology is saved in the installation folder of the modelling tool and can there be manually adapted. Tailoring the locally saved ontology, if needed, is the reason why the mapping component is located at the same device as the modelling tool. The ontology itself contains the standard values for the attributes of the modelling objects, which are set during the creation. The mapping component then offers a *REST (Representational State Transfer)* interface which can be called directly from the modelling tool via an HTTP call. Multiple mapping components can connect to the recognition component, so that if multiple participants of the workshop bring their device, they could connect to a central installation of the recognition component.

The modelling tool also allows to configure a locally started mapping component and the connection to it. Also, it can be decided if the mapping component starts automatically with the modelling tool or if this must be done manually.

A picture of the paper figures can be seen on the left side of Fig. 25.1. In this figure, also the tags for identifying the figures can be seen. The camera must be able to see the tags of the figures to be able to recognize them and calculate their positions.

25.4.2   Use Case Introduction

This section will introduce the general use case, from which a portion will later be used to describe how the prototype can be applied. This use case was chosen to discuss different aspects of the Scene2Model approach. Therefore, an innovative idea which uses technologies to help some users to reach a goal was chosen. Thereby, different stakeholders with various backgrounds should be included. For our fictitious use case, we assume that a start-up wants to support urban citizens by growing their own crops nearby the city. Urban citizens are often responsible consumers with a bias to regional and biologically grown food. Unfortunately, this group of people cannot afford land to grow fruits and vegetables. Land became expensive, and even in rural areas square meters cost a fortune to only grow food.

Another important factor is the necessity of time and expert knowledge that is needed to be a successful farmer.

The solution for this problem is a mixture of both, providing arable crop paired with expert knowledge and supported by technology. An urban citizen rents farmland in the closer rural surroundings, so that it is reachable within 1 or 1.5 hours of driving. The owner of the farmland is a farmer who would otherwise cultivate the land by himself/herself. The townsman/townswoman decides what crops he or she would like to grow supported by the farmer's expertise. Both parties communicate with the help of an application that provides numerous data sets for the urban citizen such as weather data, humidity of the air and the land, real-time videos of the crop or the timing when the harvest can begin.

But the technology should not only show data from the field but support the different kind of users (urban citizens and farmers) to reach their goals. Further, it should have the ability to include expert knowledge (from farmers) and make suggestions to the urban citizens.

In this use case, the start-up offers the software and platform containing the interface for the urban citizen and the farmer. For this business model, the start-up must have an exact idea on how the different tasks of the platform work, who is involved and what is needed. Further, the idea has to be explained to farmers, who offer the core aspect of the idea which is not provided by the start-up itself. Additionally, the fields must be enhanced with different sensors and cameras, so that the urban citizen has a more sophisticated online access to his rented field. This knowledge about installing and maintaining the hardware can neither be provided by the start-up nor the farmers. This leads to the inclusion of local electricians.

In this environment Scene2Model could be used to design the novel idea internally and also include the farmers and electricians, because they do not need to know or learn a new modelling method but use figures to build a joined story. This helps that every stakeholder better understands their role and what needs to be done and provided. Further, the digital models can help to document the ideas and support the implementation of the design, especially for the start-up.

25.4.2.1 Visualizing the Use Case

This section focuses on giving an introduction on how the Scene2Model tool can be used. Therefore, we will show how a part of the use case can be visualized and discuss how the tool can support the start-up in designing their novel idea. We do not visualize and create storyboards for every part of the use case, because this would go beyond the scope of this chapter and would not lead to additional value, but the idea behind the Scene2Model prototype will still be noticeable.

A graphical representation of the automatically created storyboard can be seen in Fig. 25.5. Each rectangle thereby contains one scene, which is described in a separated but linked model. An example for the scene with paper figures can be seen on the left side of Fig. 25.1. Such a scene can be created within a workshop. Later it is digitized and enriched and becomes to a scene like shown in Fig. 25.4.

The chosen part for discussing the realization of the use case is harvesting and storing the crops of a user, who is called Patrick. First, he receives a message, from the central-processing unit of the start-up, recommending that the crops should be harvested next week. See Fig. 25.4 for an example representation. After the message he quickly looks at his rented field via his smartphone. He wants to check the data and video of the field, additionally to the available harvesting times. Through visualizing this part of the process, the start-up gets a better feeling on what the central-processing unit and the user interface must be capable of and what tasks a user really wants to accomplish at certain point in time during the usage.

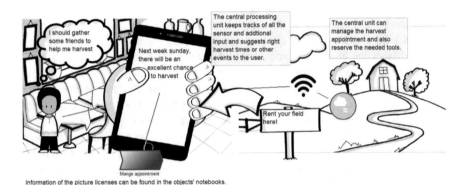

Information of the picture licenses can be found in the objects' notebooks.

Fig. 25.4 Enhanced example scene for the notification of the user (the figure contains graphics from SAP Scenes[TM][21])

But the start-up stakeholders have no idea how they can determine the proposed harvesting time. The farmer states that this depends on the weather, the rainfall in this year, the size of the crop and so on. With this information the electrician can then start to search for fitting sensors, like temperature sensors and outdoor video cameras. Discussing this process with the farmers leads to insights on what the farmer must be able to see and which information she/he has to be able to enter. The farmer mentions that she/he can also offer different tools for the harvest and the knowledge on which tool is needed for which kind of crop. This springs the idea in the start-up that they include a reservation and recommendation system for the harvesting tools.

After the user gets the notification, he can gather some friends and make an appointment for the harvest. The farmer has access to all the appointments and can check them with her/his experience. If needed, suggestions for appointment modifications can be given. At the date of the appointment, the user and his friends arrive at the farm guided by his smartphone and harvest the crops. Of course, there are more crops which can be eaten before they get rotten. Therefore, the farmer offers an optimized storage place, where the crops can be kept for a longer period of time. Registered in the platform, the user can check his stock via the Internet and get a new portion, if needed.

This story can be discussed with the farmers and electricians in a workshop using the paper figures, which lead to a visual story. Of course, the number of participants in a workshop is limited, and the digitized story can then be sent to other stakeholders. Further, in the digital form, additional information can be added to the modelled objects, which is saved within a figure or visually shown on the drawing area. For example, some figures (like the smartphone) can show text directly in its notation. In Fig. 25.5 an overview of the automatically created storyboard can be found. The figure should give an expression, how such a storyboard can look like. In Fig. 25.4 an example of a singular digital scene, enhanced with additional information, can be seen. For example, one can see that text was written in the smartphone and the thinking bubble. Additionally, two notes with explanations and a high-level business process were added, to further give insights into the idea.

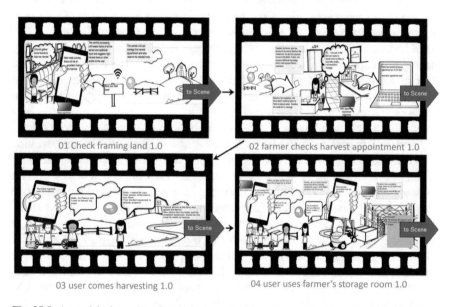

Fig. 25.5 An enriched storyboard model of a part of the use case introduced in Sect. 25.4.2 (the figure contains graphics from SAP Scenes™[21])

25.5 Future Work

Based on the insights gained in an evaluation presented in [15] and applying the Scene2Model prototype with students and at workshops, we find the general idea of providing tangible techniques with digital modelling and the automated transformation useful and worthy for further research. In this section we will provide an overview of our planned future work.

One improvement would be to allow an easier adaptation of the available figures (both paper and digital) to allow a more tailored application in various domains. Allowing this adaption by the users directly allows to use the right figures for the given project by not offering too many figures at once, which could overwhelm the user during the selection of the right figure. At the moment, this adjustment can be done, if the changes are implemented into the modelling tool. The sources (modelling tool and additional components) to do this are freely available over OMiLAB. But the adjustment needs more elaborated knowledge about the Scene2Model prototype and ADOxx. And because the tool should not only be used by sophisticated modellers but by everyone with a novel idea, this improvement could be helpful. One way to support an easier adaptation would be an on-the-fly adaptation of the available concepts in a modelling tool, like discussed in [12].

A useful extension for the Scene2Model prototype would be the support of text recognition of handwritten texts on the paper figures or sticky notes. This would further support the users, by allowing to automatically transform the text, which could be written on some of the paper figures (e.g. smartphones or speech bubbles). Having this capability of recognising text on tangible objects would also open the door to support many other design thinking techniques, like the ones which use sticky notes to organize important terms on a white board or templates. One way to tackle such a text recognition is introduced in [26].

Another aspect which would further support the application of the Scene2Model approach and prototype would be a more computer-understandable representation of the created storyboards and the used concepts. The models can then be internally linked to this enhanced knowledge representation and allow the system to offer a more sophisticated support. Thereby, not everything of this enhanced representation must be shown in the models, but the system is able to access the information to fulfil certain tasks. If the system better understands the created story and the context, it can offer adapted attributes for the modelling objects or fill the available attributes with meaningful values. Further, the system can propose additional information or warnings to the user. An example would be that, based on the additional available information, the system better understands what is represented in a scene and proposes already available business processes of the company, which can be used in the scene. Or that the usage of a certain concept in the scene has a perquisite, which is not yet met. For example, it could be proposed that if a user interface is represented in a scene, there should also be a user. In [16] we introduce further thoughts on such an enhanced representation, in the form of RDF ontologies.

Last but not least, the application of design thinking techniques usually does not have the goal to create an artefact (e.g. based on paper figures or sticky notes), but to design a new product or service which should later be implemented. The creation of the artefact is thereby a support for designing and clarifying the novel idea. Having a linked semantic-rich representation in this context can be used as a connection to other approaches or tools, for example, if other modelling methods are used to describe further aspects of the implementation of the new product, e.g. Entity-Relationship diagrams or UML. If they are connected to the same machine-readable representation, their linkage can be supported through automated means, and changes in one aspect can trigger an adaptation in the other. Further, automatic mappings between different methods can be supported if they are linked over an additional description. So, that for novel storyboards, existing aspects from other modelling methods can be proposed.

25.6 Conclusion

Tangible design thinking techniques are widely used in workshops to ideate and design novel products, services or whole business models. In this context we discussed an approach to support such techniques through tool-based conceptual modelling and an automatic transformation and enrichment of the used tangible objects into their digital representation in a modelling tool. Therefore, we introduced the ADOxx-based Scene2Model prototype, where the discussed approach is implemented for one chosen design thinking technique. The prototype itself was created to get an insight in the applicability of the proposed approach. Afterwards we described a conceptual use case and how the Scene2Model prototype can be applied to it. Last but not least, we discussed our thoughts on possible future developments.

We argue that the tangible aspect of design thinking techniques offers added value to the users in the workshops, but lacks ways of capturing the created knowledge for sharing it with stakeholders who could not physically attend. Furthermore, in such workshops the knowledge is captured in tangible artefacts (e.g. storyboards out of paper figures or sticky notes on a template), which cannot easily be enhanced or adapted after the workshop is finished. To counter these identified shortcomings, we propose to use digital conceptual modelling, as it is often used as a way to capture, process and share knowledge within a group of stakeholders. To further bring together the tangible (artefacts from design thinking techniques) and digital (conceptual models) world, we propose to apply an automated transformation of the tangible objects into their digital representation. Therefore, a recognition and semantic enrichment of the tangible objects are needed. Even though the Scene2Model prototype can create benefits for its users, these benefits can be further increased by improving upon the recognition and enrichment of the used concepts, not only for the automatic transformation but for the further processing. And with the current advances in the fields of artificial intelligence and semantic technologies, we are optimistic that this goal can be reached.

Tool Download https://www.omilab.org/s2m

References

1. Amabile, T.M., Mueller, J.S.: Studying creativity, its processes, and its antecedents: an exploration of the componential theory of creativity. In: Handbook of Organizational Creativity, vol. 3162. Elsevier, Amsterdam (2008)
2. Bodnenko, D.M., Kuchakovska, H.A., Proshkin, V.V., Lytvyn, O.: Using a virtual digital board to organize student's cooperative learning. In: Proceedings of the 3rd International Workshop on Augmented Reality in Education (AREdu 2020), Kryvyi Rih (2020)

3. Brown, T., Katz, B.: Change by design. J. Product Innov. Manag. **28**(3), 381–383 (2011). https://doi.org/10.1111/j.1540-5885.2011.00806.x
4. Buchanan, R.: Wicked problems in design thinking. Des. Issues **8**(2), 5–21 (1992)
5. Chasanidou, D., Gasparini, A.A., Lee, E.: Design thinking methods and tools for innovation. In: Marcus, A. (ed.) Design, User Experience, and Usability: Design Discourse, pp. 12–23. Springer, Cham (2015)
6. Courtney, J.: From idea to app store: a design sprint case study (2018). https://uxplanet.org/from-idea-to-appstore-a-design-sprint-case-study-a7781093de8d. Accessed 04 Mar 2021
7. d.school: bootcamp bootleg. https://static1.squarespace.com/static/57c6b79629687fde090a0fdd/t/58890239db29d6cc6c3338f7/1485374014340/METHODCARDS-v3-slim.pdf. Accessed 16 Mar 2021
8. Fleischmann, A., Oppl, S., Schmidt, W., Stary, C.: Ganzheitliche Digitalisierung von Prozessen: Perspektivenwechsel–Design Thinking–wertegeleitete Interaktion. Springer, Berlin (2018)
9. Grots, A., Pratschke, M.: Design thinking—kreativität als methode. Market. Rev. St. Gallen **26**(2), 18–23 (2009)
10. Karagiannis, D., Kühn, H.: Metamodelling platforms. In: International Conference on Electronic Commerce and Web Technologies (EC-Web), vol. 2455, p. 182 (2002)
11. Karagiannis, D., Burzynski, P., Utz, W., Buchmann, R.A.: A metamodeling approach to support the engineering of modeling method requirements. In: 2019 IEEE 27th International Requirements Engineering Conference (RE), pp. 199–210. IEEE, Piscataway (2019)
12. Laurenzi, E., Hinkelmann, K., Montecchiari, D., Goel, M.: Agile visualization in design thinking. In: New Trends in Business Information Systems and Technology, pp. 31–47. Springer, Berlin (2021)
13. Mayr, H.C., Thalheim, B.: The triptych of conceptual modeling. Softw. Syst. Model. **20**, 7–24 (2021)
14. Miron, E.T., Muck, C., Karagiannis, D., Götzinger, D.: Transforming storyboards into diagrammatic models. In: International Conference on Theory and Application of Diagrams, pp. 770–773. Springer, Berlin (2018)
15. Miron, E.T., Muck, C., Karagiannis, D.: Transforming haptic storyboards into diagrammatic models: the scene2model tool. In: Proceedings of the 52nd Hawaii International Conference on System Sciences (2019)
16. Muck, C., Miron, E.T., Karagiannis, D., Moonkun, L.: Supporting service design with storyboards and diagrammatic models: the scene2model tool. In: Joint International Conference of Service Science and Innovation (ICSSI 2018) and Serviceology (ICServ 2018) (2018). http://eprints.cs.univie.ac.at/5936/
17. Osterwalder, A., Pigneur, Y.: Business Model Generation: A Handbook for Visionaries, Game Changers, and Challengers. Wiley, Hoboken (2010)
18. Plattner, H.: An introduction to design thinking process guide (2010). https://dschool-old.stanford.edu/sandbox/groups/designresources/wiki/36873/attachments/74b3d/ModeGuideBOOTCAMP2010L.pdf. Accessed 19 Nov 2018
19. Razzouk, R., Shute, V.: What is design thinking and why is it important? Rev. Edu. Res. **82**(3), 330–348 (2012)
20. Runge, P.: Technology in IVC classes. J. Empower. Teach. Excell. **1**(1), 6 (2017)
21. SAP-AppHaus: Every great experience starts with a great story - scenes. https://experience.sap.com/designservices/resource/scenes. Accessed 09 Feb 2020
22. Semenova, N., Lebedeva, N., Polezhaeva, Z.: Modern cloud services: key trends, models and tools for interactive education. In: Proceedings of the Conference "Integrating Engineering Education and Humanities for Global Intercultural Perspectives", pp. 883–890. Springer, Berlin (2020)
23. Sprinkle, J., Rumpe, B., Vangheluwe, H., Karsai, G.: 3 Metamodelling, vol. 6100, pp. 57–76. Springer, Berlin (2010). https://doi.org/10.1007/978-3-642-16277-0_3
24. Uebernickel, F., Brenner, W., Pukall, B., Naef, T., Schindlholzer, B.: Design Thinking: Das Handbuch. Frankfurter Allgemeine Buch (2015)

25. Van der Lelie, C.: The value of storyboards in the product design process. Pers. Ubiq. Comput. **10**(2–3), 159–162 (2006)
26. Walch, M., Karagiannis, D.: Design thinking and knowledge engineering: a machine learning case. Int. J. Mach. Learn. Comput. **10**(6), 765–770 (2020). https://doi.org/10.18178/ijmlc.2020.10.6.1003

Chapter 26
An Approach to the Information System Conceptual Modeling Based on the Form Types

Ivan Luković, Milan Čeliković, Slavica Kordić, and Marko Vještica

Abstract Nowadays, we still identify a plethora of methods and techniques that can be deployed in the development of information systems (ISs). "Optimal" methods are still far from obvious. For decades we have developed a methodology approach and a framework, named IIS*Studio, for support of the IS development process. IIS*Studio can be categorized as a Model-Driven Software Development and Domain-Specific Modeling framework and relies on a specific meta-model named as IIS*Case Meta-model. It is aimed at improving the IS development process by increasing designers' efficiency and the overall quality of the systems being developed. In this chapter, we present an implementation of a selected part of the IIS*Case Meta-model in the ADOxx Modeling and Configuration Platform and demonstrate its usage in a small case study. By such an experiment, we create a new possibility of the meta-model verification and validation.

Keywords Information systems · Databases · Domain-specific modeling · Model-driven engineering

26.1 Introduction

In recent years, we have been the witnesses of a constant growth and development of various information technologies that bring new possibilities in the development and deployment of new generation Information Systems (ISs). Although such growth enriches ISs with novel capabilities as we stated in [1], the "optimal" methods and techniques to develop an IS are still far from obvious. However, there are many ways and approaches that may be deployed to improve the process of IS development.

I. Luković (✉)
Faculty of Organizational Sciences, University of Belgrade, Belgarde, Serbia
e-mail: ivan.lukovic@fon.bg.ac.rs

M. Čeliković · S. Kordić · M. Vještica
Faculty of Technical Sciences, University of Novi Sad, Novi Sad, Serbia
e-mail: milancel@uns.ac.rs; slavica@uns.ac.rs; marko.vjestica@uns.ac.rs

According to [1], the evolution of IS development process can be divided into three historical phases, following the important transitions that had happened in software engineering. Those are the phases of (i) traditional IS development; (ii) IS development based on Model-Driven Engineering (MDE) and Model-Driven Architecture (MDA) paradigms; and (iii) IS development based on the deployment of Domain-Specific Modeling Languages (DSMLs).

In the first phase of the evolution of IS development process, the traditional IS development is already based on models and model transformations. One taxonomy of IS modeling techniques is proposed in [2]. The author reviewed some of the popular IS modeling techniques, such as data flow diagramming, Entity-Relationship (ER) diagramming, state transition diagramming, Integration DEFinition for information modeling (IDEF1x), and Unified Modeling Language (UML), and categorized them according to their breadth (modeling goals and objectives) and depth (offered perspectives). In this phase, models are predominantly used for documentation purposes, while transformations are performed mostly "by hand." The IS modeling process and supported techniques are provided by traditional Computer-Aided Software Engineering (CASE) tools. In the late 1980s and early 1990s, some of the authors from the Faculty of Technical Sciences of University of Novi Sad were a part of a research team that initiated a development of a CASE tool named Integrated Information System CASE Tool or IIS*Case for short [3]. The main goal was to provide conceptual IS modeling based on the form type concept. Then, relational database (DB) schema design and generation of SQL DB implementation scripts were performed by means of a chain of transformations of the initial conceptual model.

The evolution of the IS development process in the early 2000s led to the deployment of MDE and MDA paradigms in their next phase. Some of the CASE tools in this phase evolved to the Model-Driven Software Development (MDSD) tools. Hundreds of engineering man-years had been invested in such a paradigm shift. The benefits of utilizing the MDE and MDA approaches can be seen in the improved productivity of the developer, portability of generated software, cross-platform interoperability, and the facilitation of software documenting and maintenance [4]. In this phase, the IS development process is based on the creation of Platform Independent Models (PIMs) which are in the later stage mapped to the Platform-Specific Models (PSMs) by means of a chain of model-to-model transformations. Afterward, PSM specifications are mapped to the executable program code by means of model-to-code transformations. Some examples of research results of such kind are [5–7], as well as a commercial software tool, Oracle Designer 10 g. IIS*Case has also evolved to an MDSD tool that provides IS modeling and prototype generation [8–10]. At the level of PIM specifications, IIS*Case provides conceptual modeling of database schemas and business applications. Starting from such PIM models as a source, a chain of model-to-model and model-to-code transformations is performed in IIS*Case to obtain executable program code of software applications and database scripts for a selected target platform. There are lots of authors' references describing the main idea and concepts embedded into the IIS*Case tool and the accompanying methodology approach. Some of them are [11–13].

All our experience collected from the research and development of MDSD tools for IS design led to the conclusion that the development of such tools is extremely time consuming. It comes from the fact that providing model-to-model transformations from PIM to PSM models and model-to-code transformations from PSM models to the executable program code is quite sensitive to the selected target programming and database technologies. As the 2000s bring significant or almost revolutionary shifts from "traditional" to multilayer web programming technologies, we were witnesses of many MDSD tools dying, not being able to follow such technology shifts. Unfortunately, in some segments, it has caused a retrograde shift of the IS development process to the level of manual programming of IS applications, while a generation of SQL DB scripts is still well supported by the tools. To address such an issue, recent years have led the IS development process to a level of deployment of the DSML paradigm, while the integration of MDSD and DSMLs in a single approach has been repeatedly proved worthwhile [1].

In [1], we presented many examples of Domain-Specific Languages (DSLs) being used in different software development phases and contexts relevant to the IS development. Apart from the conceptual modeling, they are used in support of many other IS development tasks in various problem domains. A commercial tool Mendix [14] is worth to mention as an emerging, integrated modeling tool based on the deployment of MDSD and DSML approaches that support almost the whole IS development process on a proprietary platform. In the context of MDSD and DSMLs integration, the deployment of model transformation languages is essential. Apart from "general purpose" model transformation languages such as ATL, Query/View/Transformation (QVT), or Kermeta, there are efforts to create even more specific languages that would be restricted to the transformations of models belonging to a particular domain. These languages are known as Domain-Specific Transformation Languages (DSTLs) [15, 16]. In support of effective DSMLs development, there are a number of meta-modeling approaches and tools. Some of them are as follows: Generic Modeling Environment (GME) [17], a toolkit for domain-specific modeling and program synthesis based on UML meta-models; MetaEdit+ [18] for the creation of meta-models using the Graphical Object-Property-Role-Relationship (GOPRR) data model; Eclipse Modeling Framework (EMF) [19] based on the meta-meta-model named Ecore; and ADOxx Modeling and Configuration Platform or ADOxx for short [20], which is used for the purpose of a research presented in this chapter. More details about the formalisms for description of the ADOxx meta-model and ADOxx models can be found in [21, 22].

In the evolution phase of coupling MDSD and DSML paradigms, our IIS*Case tool evolved into the IIS*Studio IS development framework. During the decades, we have been developing the IIS*Case Meta-model in order to provide the design of various models. It comprises a number of modeling, meta-level concepts, and formal rules that are used in the design process. In early stages of our research, we formally specified the IIS*Case Meta-model by means of predicate calculus formulas and additionally described its semantics in a form of free text [3]. We also developed and embedded into IIS*Case visual and repository-based tools (visual DSLs) that fully apply the IIS*Case Meta-model through a repository implemented as a relational database, named IIS*Case Repository. They assisted designers in creating formally valid models and their storing as repository definitions in a guided way. Its Ecore implementation, among other references, is presented in [23]. In [24], we have presented IIS*CDesLang—a textual DSML for representation of the IIS*Case Meta-model in a visual programming environment for attribute grammar specifications, named VisualLISA [25]. In [26], we experimented with GOPRR and compared Ecore and GOPRR through our IIS*Case Meta-model and its support for IS conceptual modeling. Some of our further research efforts devoted to the integration of MDSD and DSML approaches in IIS*Studio are also presented in [27–30].

The goal of this chapter is to present the implementation of a selected part of the IIS*Case Meta-model in ADOxx and demonstrate its usage in a small case study. By such an experiment, we create a new possibility of the meta-model verification and validation. We also gain a new, valuable experience about strengths and weaknesses of various meta-modeling environments. We believe that in this way we contribute to the overall progress of IS development methods based on MDSD and DSML paradigms and to its overall efficiency and quality increase.

26.2   IIS*Studio MDSD Method

One of the main motives for developing IIS*Case and then IIS*Studio is in the following. For decades, the most favorable conceptual data model is ER data model. Many research efforts are already invested in providing conceptual modeling of DB schemas by advanced forms and formal meta-specifications of ER data model and then a generation of relational DB schemas based on formal transformations defined between ER and relational data models. Some of the successful approaches deploying in a large extent of MDSD and DSML approaches are presented in [31, 32]. A typical scenario of a DB schema design process, provided by a majority of existing modeling tools, is to create an ER DB schema first and then transform it into a relational DB schema. Such a scenario has many advantages, but also there are serious disadvantages [12]. Deploying IS design methodologies based on such an approach and using UML or related modeling languages require advanced knowledge, skills, and high perception power. Failing to find an appropriate number of designers that possess these properties may lead to a risk of designing poor quality ISs [1, 33]. Besides, these methods and techniques are often incomprehensible to end-users. In practice, that may lead to problems in communication and to misunderstanding between designers and end-users. As a rule, misunderstanding results in a poorly designed DB schema or a software application, because support of all the specified user requirements is not ensured. Usually, both designers and end-users become aware of that too late, when a DB schema or a software application is already implemented.

To overcome these disadvantages, we created an alternative approach and related techniques that were mainly based on the usage of MDSD and DSML paradigms.

The main idea was to provide designers with a methodology approach and tools for conceptual IS design and model transformations providing formal methods and complex algorithms without any considerable expert knowledge. Instead of the concepts embedded into the ER data model, our approach to conceptual IS design is based mainly on a concept of a form type, which is an abstraction derived from the notion of a business document that is widely used in various business domains. Therefore, end-users are typically quite familiar with this notion.

IIS*Studio together with the proposed methodology approach [8, 11] is a set of MDSD tools for assisting in IS design and generating executable application prototypes. The IS development process based on IIS*Studio is evolutive and incremental. It supports a forward IS design by means of the IIS*Case tool, as well as reengineering of legacy systems with an additional support of our IIS*Re tool. It enables early delivery of software prototypes that can be easily upgraded or amended according to the new or changed users' requirements. IIS*Studio currently provides the following functionalities: (i) conceptual modeling of DB schemas, transaction programs, and business applications of an IS; (ii) automated design of relational database subschemas in the 3rd normal form (3NF); (iii) automated integration of subschemas into a unified database schema in 3NF; (iv) automated generation of SQL Data Definition Language (SQL/DDL) code for various Database Management Systems (DBMSs); (v) conceptual design of common User-Interface (UI) models; (vi) automated generation of executable prototypes of business applications; and (vii) automated reverse engineering of implemented relational DB schemas as SQL/DDL specifications into the IIS*Case Meta-model.

By (i), (ii), (iii), and (v) functionalities, IIS*Studio provides a logical system design at the two levels: (a) the conceptual design of DB schemas and IS applications throughout the creation of fully PIM models; and (b) the implementation design of DB schemas and IS applications throughout the creation of models that can be characterized as combined PIM/PSMs. For example, for DB schema design performed by (ii) functionality, generated relational DB schema models are still independent of any particular DBMS, and therefore, they can be characterized still as PIMs. On the other hand, they are specific to the class of Relational DBMSs (RDBMSs), and therefore, they can be characterized as PSMs. By (iv) and (vi) functionalities, IIS*Studio provides a system implementation that includes aspects of physical system design. For example, by a generation of executable SQL/DDL scripts from a relational DB schema model, IIS*Studio produces its implementation in a syntax of a specific RDBMS, with the defaulted values of physical data organization parameters. However, conceptual and implementation design of the physical data organization with a full consideration of numerous physical mechanisms and parameters specific to each RDBMS (such as memory organization, DB physical organization, table organization, table indexing and partitioning, view materialization, etc.) is a matter of our further research.

Detailed information about IIS*Studio may be found in several authors' references. In the rest of this section, we present in short a selected part of the IIS*Case Meta-model which is necessary to understand its ADOxx implementation that is created throughout the research presented in this book chapter.

At the abstraction level of PIMs, the IIS*Case tool provides conceptual modeling of DB schemas by means of the form type concept that includes specifications of various DB constraints, such as domain, not null, check, key, and unique constraints, as well as various kinds of inclusion dependencies. Such model is automatically transformed into a model of relational DB schema, which is still technology-independent specification. Then, the SQL/DDL code generator produces DDL scripts for selected DBMSs. IIS*Case also provides conceptual modeling of business applications that include specifications of (i) UI; (ii) structures of transaction programs aimed to execute over a database; and (iii) application functionality. Apart from the following "standard" Create, Retrieve, Update, and Delete (CRUD) data operations, it covers complex, application-specific functionalities, specified at the PIM level by our IIS*CFuncLang DSML [27]. A PIM model of business applications is automatically transformed into the executable program code. In this way, fully executable application prototypes are generated.

26.2.1   IIS*Case Meta-Model

The IIS*Case Meta-model contains an extensive number of meta-level concepts, their properties, relationships, and rules. Here we focus on a brief overview of the selected PIM meta-level concepts only. By this, we present the concepts: project, application system, form type, component type, application, call type, as well as fundamental concepts: domain, attribute, function, and inclusion dependency.

A work in IIS*Studio is organized through projects. Everything that exists in IIS*Case Repository is stored in the context of a project. A project is one IS specification and has a structure represented by the project tree. Each project has its (i) name, (ii) fundamental concepts or fundamentals for short, and (iii) application systems. A designer may define various types of application systems—application types for short—and introduce a classification of application systems by associating application systems to a selected application type. Application systems are organizational units, that is, subsystems of a project. By the application system concept, we provide a mechanism for decomposing large projects into trees of manageable project units. We suppose that each application system is normally sized to be designed by one designer, but more designers may also be engaged.

26.2.2   Fundamental Concepts

Fundamental concepts are formally independent of any application system. They are common for a project as a whole. They are created at the level of a project and may be used in various application systems [24].

A notion of a domain denotes a specification of allowed values of some DB attributes. We classify domains as (i) primitive and (ii) user defined. Primitive domains exist "per se," like primitive data types in various formal languages. We have a small set of primitive domains already defined, but we allow designers to create their own primitive domains, according to the project needs. User-defined domains are created by referencing primitive or previously created user-defined domains. Domains are referenced later from attribute specifications.

A user-defined domain specification includes a default value, domain type, and check condition. We distinguish the following domain types: (i) domains created by the inheritance rule and (ii) complex domains that may be created by the (a) tuple rule, (b) choice rule, or (c) set rule [24]. The inheritance rule means that a domain specification is created by inheriting a specification of a superordinated domain—a primitive one or user defined. It may be stronger, but not weaker than the superordinated domain specification. The check condition or the domain check expression is a regular expression that further constrains possible values of a domain. We have a formal syntax developed and the *Expression Editor* tool that assists in creating such expressions. We also have a parser for checking the syntax correctness. Currently, we do not support the specification of operators over a domain in IIS*Case Repository. It is a matter of our future work.

Each attribute in an IIS*Case project is identified by its name only. Therefore, we obey the Universal Relation Scheme Assumption (URSA) [12], well known in the relational data model for many years. We also specify whether an attribute is included in database schema, derived, or renamed.

Most of the project attributes are to be included in the future DB schema. However, we may have attributes that will present some calculated values in reports or screen forms, and they are not included in the DB schema. They derive their values on the basis of other attributes and their values by some function, representing a calculation. Therefore, we classify attributes in the IIS*Case Meta-model as (i) included or (ii) non-included in a DB schema. Also, we introduce another classification, by which we may have: (a) elementary or non-derived and (b) derived attributes. If an attribute is specified as non-derived, it obtains its values directly from end-users. Otherwise, values are derived by a function that may represent a calculation formula or any algorithm. Any attribute specified as non-included in a DB schema must be declared as derived one.

An elementary attribute can be additionally declared as a renamed one. By this, a concept of attribute renaming from the relational data model is provided here, too. A renamed attribute references a previously defined attribute and has to be included in a DB schema. It has its origin in the referenced attribute, but with a slightly different semantics. The attribute renaming in fundamental concepts is inspired by the renaming that is applied in mapping ER DB schemas into the relational data model. If a designer specifies that an attribute A1 is renamed from an attribute A, actually she or he introduces at the level of fundamental concepts an inclusion dependency of the form $[A1] \subseteq [A]$ as a constraint of a universal relation scheme. By means of such inclusion dependencies, IIS*Studio can generate "recursive" referential integrity constraints where the same relation scheme serves both as a referencing and referenced one. The concept is inspired by Recursive Relationship Sets and Roles from [31]. Also, a designer can define "by hand" various and more complex inclusion dependencies over domain-compatible attributes at the level of a universal relation scheme. They are considered later on in the relation DB schema generation process.

Each attribute specification also includes a reference to a user-defined domain, default value, and check condition. The check condition or the attribute check expression is a regular expression that further constrains possible values of an attribute. It is specified in a similar way as it is for domain check expressions. If the attribute check expression and the domain check expression are both defined, they will be connected by the logical AND.

Both user-defined domain and attribute specifications include a number of display properties of screen items that correspond to the attributes and their domains. Such display properties are used by the IIS*Case *Application Generator* aimed at generating executable application prototypes.

A concept of a function is used to specify any application-specific functionality that may be used in other project specifications. Functions typically include a series of various DB operations and calculations, instead of sole CRUD operations over a DB relation. Each function has its name, a list of formal parameters, and a return value type. Besides, it encompasses a formal specification of function body in our platform-independent DSL that is created by the *Function Editor* tool of IIS*Case [27].

26.2.3   Form Type and Business Application Concepts

An application system of some IIS*Case projects may comprise various kinds of IIS*Case Repository objects. For PIM specifications, only two kinds of objects are important: (a) form types and (b) business applications or applications for short.

A form type is the main modeling concept in IIS*Case. It generalizes document types, that is, screen forms or reports by means of users communicate with an IS [3]. It is a structure defined at the abstraction level of schema. By using the form type concept, a designer specifies a set of screen or report forms of transaction programs and, indirectly, specifies DB schema attributes and constraints at the conceptual level. Each particular business document is an instance of a form type. Similar ideas about our form type concepts can be found in several research works. Some of them are [34, 35]. In [34], the authors propose a model of transformations of their screen form specifications to an ER DB schema, while in [35] the authors propose a DSML named Parsimonious Data Modeling Language (PD) for conceptual DB schema design and then relatively simple transformations of PD specifications into a relational data model. In contrast, by our approach, a set of designed form types is used to infer an initial set of DB constraints, including domain constraints, check constraints, functional, non-functional, and special functional dependencies, as well as inclusion dependencies [3, 9, 11]. The initial set of constraints is used as the input to the improved synthesis algorithm, by means of IIS*Case generates a formal specification of relational DB schema [12] that includes specifications of domain constraints, not null constraints, check constraints, primary and all equivalent keys, uniqueness constraints, and inclusion dependencies of various forms, such as referential integrity constraints, inverse referential integrity constraints, and extended referential integrity constraints [9].

Business applications are structures of form types. Each application must have one form type marked as the entry form type of the application. The execution of generated application always starts from the entry form type. Form types in an application are related by form type calls. A form type call always relates two form types: a calling form type and a called form type. By a form type call, a designer specifies how values are passed between the forms during the call execution. *Business Application Designer* is a visually oriented tool for modeling business applications in IIS*Case.

Form types are classified as menus or programs. Menu form types are used to generate just menus without any data items. Program form types specify transaction programs with a UI. They have a complex structure and may be designated as (i) considered or (ii) not considered in database schema design. The first option is used for all form types aimed at DB updatings, as well as for some report forms. Only the form types that are "considered in database schema design" participate later on in generating a DB schema. The former option is used for report form types only. Those form types can be used later on for the generation of database (relational SQL) views, while report form types that are "considered in database schema design" can be used later on for the generation of database materialized views.

Each program form type is a tree structure of component types. It must have at least one component type. The following two properties of a component type are distinguished: "number of occurrences" and "operations allowed." The "number of occurrences" may be specified as (i) 0-N or (ii) 1-N. 0-N means that for each instance of the parent component type, zero or more instances of the subordinated component type are allowed. 1-N means that for each instance of the parent component type we require the existence of at least one instance of the subordinated component type. By the allowed operations, a designer may specify CRUD operations over the component type instances.

Each component type has a set of attributes included from the IIS*Case Repository. An attribute may be included in a form type at most once. Each attribute included in a component type may be declared as: (i) mandatory or optional, and (ii) modifiable, query only or display only. Also, a set of allowed operations over an attribute in a component type is specified. It is a subset of the set {Insert, Retrieve, Update, Nullify} (IRUN) operations. Each component type must have at least one key, consisting of at least one component type attribute. Each component type key provides identification of each component instance, but only in the scope of its superordinated component instance. Also, a component type may have uniqueness constraints, each of them consisting of at least one component type attribute. A uniqueness constraint provides an identification of each component instance, but only if it has a non-null value. On the contrary to keys, attributes in a uniqueness constraint may be optional. Finally, a component type may have a check constraint defined. It is a logical expression constraining values of each component type instance. Like domain check expressions, they are specified and parsed by *Expression Editor*.

Both component type and form type attribute specifications provide a vast number of display properties of generated screen forms and their various UI elements. There are also the *Layout Manager* tool that assists designers in specifying component type display properties, and the *UI*Modeler* tool that is aimed at designing templates of various common UI models. All display properties combined with a selected common UI model are used by the *Application Generator* tool.

In Sect. 26.3, we give some more detailed information about the form type and related concepts through the ADOxx presentation of IIS*Case Meta-Model, while in Sect. 26.4, we give an example of a form type being created in the scope of a selected case study.

More detailed information about IIS*Case Meta-model PIM concepts—particularly fundamental concepts and the form type concept—and their formal specifications, examples, and some case studies can be found in a number of authors' references. Some of them are [1, 3, 8, 9, 11, 13, 23, 24, 28]. Apart from already presented advantages of our MDSD approach and IIS*Studio, there are also some limitations at the level of conceptual modeling. One of them is a lack of possibility to model generalizations and specializations, as it can be done with IS-A hierarchies in the ER data model. Also, categorizations, that is, EX-OR relationship types can be modeled in an indirect way only, by means of component type check constraints. In our future work, we plan to extend our IIS*Case Meta-model with the new concepts so as to overcome these limits.

26.3   IIS*Case Meta-Model and Its ADOxx Implementation

In this section, we present an implementation of selected IIS*Case functionalities in the ADOxx platform. Our initial hypothesis that ADOxx is a suitable platform to support the goal of our research and a decision to utilize it for meta-modeling of a part of IIS*Case is highly inspired by the research presented in [32], where the authors proposed the HERM DSML to support the design of ER DB schemas and their further transformations, where the approach is also implemented in ADOxx.

In Sect. 26.3.1, we present an implementation of the IIS*Case Meta-model in ADOxx. Afterward, a concrete graphical syntax of the meta-model is presented in Sect. 26.3.2. A model-to-code transformation from IS models to SQL/DLL code implemented by using AdoScript is presented in Sect. 26.3.3.

26.3.1   ADOxx Implementation of IIS*Case Meta-Model

As an extensive meta-structure, IIS*Case Meta-model provides various concepts, some of which include implementation details. In this section, we present the ADOxx implementation of a part of the IIS*Case Meta-model that provides PIM concepts for conceptual IS design only. We name it IIS*Case PIM Meta-model. To improve readability, the ADOxx implementation of the IIS*Case PIM Meta-model is represented in a form of two class diagrams, shown in Figs. 26.1 and 26.2. Such visual representation is created by Microsoft Visio class diagrams. Hereby we cover the following main IIS*Case PIM concepts: *ISApplicationModel, Domain* and *Attribute, Application system, Form type*, and *Component type.*

   The central concept in the meta-model from Fig. 26.1 is *ISApplicationModel.* It represents a concept of an IIS*Case project. For the application model, that is, a project, the name is a mandatory property. All IIS*Case Repository objects are always created in the context of an application model. *Fundamental concept* instances are defined at the level of an *ISAppliactionModel* instance, as they are independent of any application system and can be used in more than one application system. *Application systems* are also subunits of an *ISAppliactionModel* instance. Fundamental concepts comprise zero or more: *Attributes, Domains*, and *Inclusion dependencies*. For each *ISApplicationSystem*, we can define zero or more instances of the *ApplicationSystem* concept.

   Following a classification of domains on Primitive and User defined, we introduce here two meta classes: *PrimitiveDomain* and *UserDefinedDomain. Primitive-Domain* is a subclass of the *Domain* class, while *UserDefinedDomain* is a subclass of the *PrimitiveDomain* class.

   Primitive domains must exist in modeling languages of such kind. The reason behind the existence of user-defined domain concept is to provide designers a possibility to create their own data types in order to raise the expressivity of their models. Each domain has its name, description, and a default value. At the level of a primitive domain, a designer specifies if the maximal length is a required property for the domain being specified. It specifies whether a numeric length: must be given, could be given, or should be given. For user-defined domains, a designer defines a domain type and a check condition, as a regular expression of the Boolean type.

   Each attribute is identified by its name. To each attribute, a domain must be associated. The check condition is an optional property. It is the Boolean expression that additionally constrains the value of the attribute.

   As an organizational unit of the project, each Application System belongs to an *ISApplicationModel* instance and has its name and description as mandatory properties. Besides, an application system may reference subordinated application

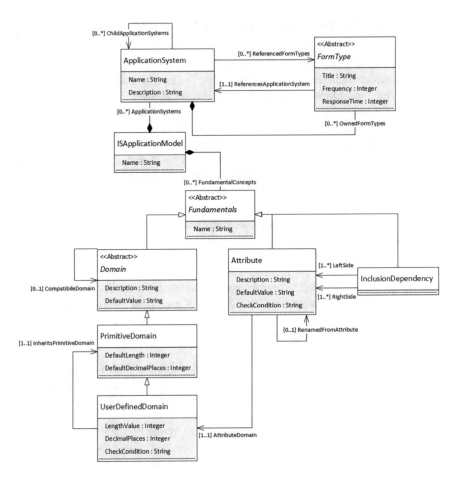

Fig. 26.1 IIS*Case PIM Meta-model diagram—Part I

systems that we call child application systems. By this, a designer may create a hierarchy of application systems in a project. The application system hierarchy is modeled by a recursive reference.

The ADOxx meta-model of the Form Type concept is presented in Fig. 26.2. It abstracts future screen forms or reports that end-users of an IS may use in a daily job. By means of the Form Type concept, designers indirectly specify, at the level of PIMs, a model of a DB schema with attributes and constraints included. At the same time, they also specify a model of IS transaction programs and applications.

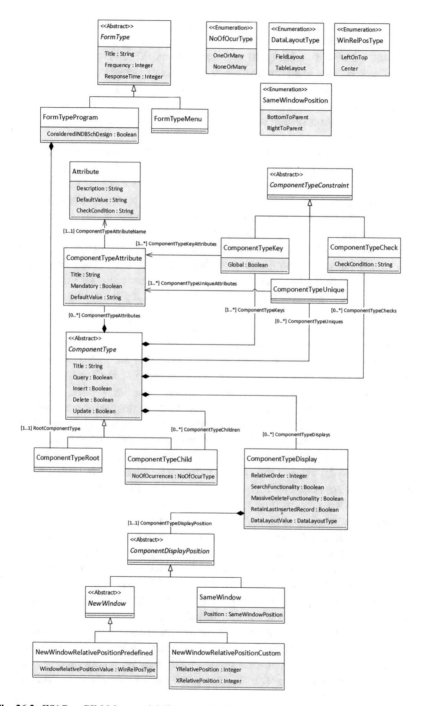

Fig. 26.2 IIS*Case PIM Meta-model diagram—Part II

Apart from creating their own form types in application systems, designers may include form types created in other application systems by referencing or copying. Therefore, we classify form types as (a) owned and (b) referenced. A form type is owned if it is created in an application system either by creating from scratch or by copying from another application system. It may be modified later on through the same application system without any restrictions. A referenced form type is created in another application system and then just included in the application system as a read-only structure.

Each form type has a name that identifies it in the scope of a project, a title, frequency of usage, response time, and usage type. The frequency is an optional property that represents the expected number of executions of a corresponding transaction program per time unit. The response time is also an optional property specifying expected response time of a program execution. By the usage type property, we classify form types as (a) menus and (b) programs.

Menu form types are used to model menus without data items. Program form types model transaction programs providing DB operations. They may represent either screen forms for data retrievals and updates, or just reports for data retrievals. As a rule, a user interface of such programs is rather complex. A program form type may be designated as "considered in the DB schema design" or "not considered in the DB schema design." Form types considered in the DB schema design are only used later as an input specification for the DB schema generation process. Form types not considered in database schema design are just used later for the generation of IS report programs, aimed at data retrievals only. Each program form type is a tree of component types. A component type has a name, title, number of occurrences, allowed operations, and a reference to the parent component type, if it is not a root component type. Name is the component type identifier. All subordinated component types of the same parent must have different names.

Each instance of the superordinated component type in a tree may have more than one related instance of the corresponding subordinated component type. The number of occurrences constrains the allowed minimal number of instances of a subordinated component type related to the same instance of a superordinated component type in the tree. It may have one of two values: 0-N or 1-N. The 0-N value means that an instance of a superordinated component type may exist while not having any related instance of the corresponding subordinated component type. The 1-N value means that each instance of a superordinated component type must have at least one related instance of the subordinated component type.

The allowed operations of a component type denote CRUD operations that can be performed over instances of the component type.

Component type display properties, defined at the level of a PIM model, are used by the program generator. The concept of a component type display is defined by properties: window layout, data layout, relative order, layout relative position, window relative position, search functionality, massive delete functionality, and retain last inserted record.

The window layout allows the values: "New window" and "Same window," specifying whether a component type is to be placed in a new window or in the same window as the parent component type. The data layout specifies the way of a component type representation in a screen form. Two values are allowed: "Field layout" or "Table layout." By the "Field layout" value, only one record at the time is displayed in a form. By the "Table layout," a set of records at the time is displayed in a screen form, in a form of a table. The relative order is a sequence number representing the order of a component type relative to other sibling component types of the same parent in a form type tree. The layout relative position represents a component type relative position to the parent component type. We may select the "Bottom to parent" value if we want to place the component type below the layout of the parent component type in a generated screen form, or the "Right to parent" value if we want to place it right to the parent one. The window relative position is to be specified only when the "New window" layout is selected. A designer may specify one of the three possible values: "Center," "Left on top," or "Custom." The "Center" value denotes that the center of a new window is positioned to match the center of the parent window. "Left on top" specifies that the top left corner of the new window will match the top left corner of the parent window. By selecting the "Custom" value, a relative position of the new window top left corner to the top left corner of the parent window is explicitly specified by giving X and Y relative positions.

The "search functionality" represents a Boolean property that enables generation of the filter for data selection. If search functionality is enabled, end-users are allowed to refine the WHERE clause of an SQL SELECT statement. If checked, the "massive delete functionality" provides a generation of a delete option next to each record in a table layout. The "retain last inserted record" property specifies if the last inserted record is to be retained on the screen for future use.

Each component type includes one or more attributes. A component type attribute is a reference to a project attribute from fundamentals. It has a title that will appear in the generated screen form. Also, it may be declared as mandatory or optional in the form. For such attributes, the IIS*Case PIM Meta-model allows a definition of IRUN operations, as well as various display properties.

Each component type has one or more keys. Each component type key comprises one or more component type attributes. It represents the unique identification of a component type instance but only in the scope of its superordinated component instance. Uniqueness constraints may be defined for each component type. Each component type uniqueness constraint comprises at least one component type attribute. If uniqueness constraint attributes have non-null values, it is possible to uniquely identify a component type instance but only in the scope of the superordinated component instance. Each component type may have check constraints to specify constraints on possible values within a single component type instance. The *ComponentTypeCheck* concept represents check constraints in the meta-model. The logical expression by which the value of each component type instance is checked is modeled by the *CheckCondition* attribute into the *ComponentTypeCheck* meta-class.

26.3.2 IIS*Case Concrete Syntax Specification in ADOxx

A specification of the concrete syntax is one of the important steps in the process of a DSML implementation. The IIS*Case Meta-model represents an abstract syntax of our DSML for IS specifications. The advantages of using DSML for modeling IS specifications instead of General Purpose Languages (GPLs) are twofold. A DSML is focused on a specific domain of application, so the set of supported concepts of such language is narrowed in relation to the set of supported GPL concepts. This feature makes a DSML much easier to learn and use. Language concepts are close to the domain of application, which affects their easiness for use. IS specifications created by a DSML do not depend on the specific platform and can be translated into platform-independent code. By choosing a new platform, it is not necessary to redefine the concepts for modeling IS specifications.

In Table 26.1, we present symbols of the concrete graphical notation of IIS*Case PIM concepts created in the ADOxx platform.

The efficiency of some concrete syntax designs highly depends on the capabilities of a meta-modeling framework. Recently, some of the authors have investigated a domain of production process modeling [36] and implemented abstract and concrete syntaxes of a production process modeling language [37, 38] by using EMF [19] and Sirius [39] frameworks. Based on our experience with these frameworks, as well as with the ADOxx framework, we have noticed some differences. ADOxx mostly relies on a tree-like structure of classes and a textual specification of classes and their attributes, while EMF mostly relies on its class diagram or a tree-like structure of classes. For unexperienced users, EMF could be seen easier to manage, but ADOxx textual syntax could probably be faster to use when learned. ADOxx presents a meta-model as a tree-like structure, and it would be a very useful feature to automatically generate a class diagram from it so that a meta-model could be more readable and easier to present.

To create graphical symbols of classes and relations, ADOxx relies on its textual syntax, while Sirius relies on different predefined symbols that can be customized, and it is also possible to include new ones. The ADOxx textual syntax could be difficult for beginners. However, there is the GraphRep Generator tool [40] that helps users draw a symbol and automatically generate its textual representation that is used in ADOxx. Still, fine tuning of graphical symbols requires a knowledge of the ADOxx textual syntax.

Using a single framework only—ADOxx, instead of the two EMF and Sirius—is very practical. A meta-model and a graphical syntax are specified in a single framework by using ADOxx. Also, we notice here less framework configuration steps when using ADOxx instead of EMF and Sirius. For example, a tool pallet can be generated faster by using ADOxx, and the object property section is easier to customize. An additional advantage of ADOxx is that the framework supports a user management system, which could be very useful for large projects such as IIS*Studio. Deployment of a newly created modeling tool is much easier to be done by using ADOxx instead of the Eclipse framework.

Table 26.1 The symbols of the concrete graphical notation of IIS*Case PIM concepts

Model / Model Name, System / System Name		ISApplicationModel ApplicationSystem
Primitive / Domain Name, UserDefined / Domain Name		PrimtiveDomain UserDefinedDomain
Attribute, ●		Attribute InclusionDependency
FormTypeMenu / Name, FormTypeProgram / Name		FormTypeMenu FormTypeProgram
CT Root Name, CT Child Name		ComponentTypeRoot ComponentTypeChild
CT Key Name, CT Unique Name, CT Check Name		ComponentTypeKey ComponentTypeUnique ComponentTypeCheck
CT Display Name, CT Attribute Name		ComponentTypeDisplay ComponentTypeAttribute
Same Window Name, New Window RPP Name, New Window RPC Name		SameWindow NewWindowRelative-PositionPredefined NewWindowRelative-PositionCustom

26.3.3 ADOxx Implementation of IIS*Case Transformations

By using code generators provided in IIS*Studio, IS designers can generate fully executable application prototypes from models. As shown in Fig. 26.3, it is possible to generate: (i) relational DB schemas; (ii) SQL/DDL scripts from a generated relational DB schema; (iii) structures of transaction programs; (iv) UI; and (v) CRUD and specific application functionalities. We chose to develop the SQL/DDL code generator within ADOxx, as it is one of the prerequisites for generators of IS applications and transaction programs. By implementing the SQL/DDL code generator, we can make a proof of concept that it is possible to implement IIS*Studio code generators by transformation specifications within the ADOxx platform.

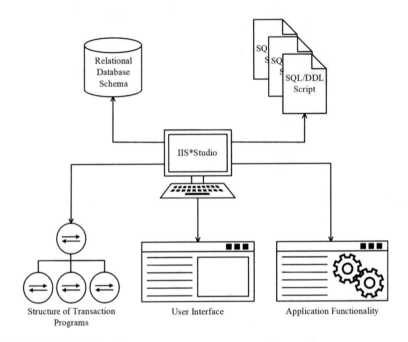

Fig. 26.3 The IIS*Studio code generators

To implement a prototype code generator within the ADOxx platform, we have used the AdoScript language [20]. To provide a generation of SQL/DDL code from a DB schema specification, we created an AdoScript file that can be called and executed from the ADOxx platform by adding action buttons in the modeling tool. To generate SQL/DDL code, end-users need to complete the following steps: (i) select a conceptual IS model as an active model; (ii) initiate the code generation by the modeling tool action button; and (iii) choose an SQL file name and a location in which it is to be saved.

An excerpt of the code generator used for the automatic generation of SQL check constraints is presented in Fig. 26.4. This code is divided into the following sections: (i) get the currently active model; (ii) choose SQL file name and location; (iii) get ComponentTypeRoot (CTR) and ComponentTypeChild (CTC) objects as they represent tables in the context of SQL; (iv) iterate through CTR/CTC objects to find all the constraints; (v) get CTR/CTC name and output relations; (vi) iterate through CTR/CTC relations as some of them are ComponentTypeChecks relations which leads to ComponentTypeCheck objects; (vii) whether the relation is ComponentTypeChecks, get its target object name, and check condition; and (viii) create a check constraint SQL statement and write it into the SQL file. Other constraints and create table statements are generated in a similar manner, but are more complex, as many other class objects are involved in the code generation.

```
#Get the active model
CC "Modeling" GET_ACT_MODEL
SET nCurrentModelId:(modelid)
  ... ... ...
#Create an SQL file
CC "AdoScript" FILE_DIALOG saveas filter1:"SQL Files" type1:"*.sql" default-ext:"sql"
SET sSQLFileLocation:(path)

#Get ComponentTypeRoot and ComponentTypeChild objects
CC "Core" GET_ALL_OBJS_OF_CLASSNAME modelid:(nCurrentModelId) classname:"ComponentTypeRoot"
SET sComponentTypeIds:(objids)
CC "Core" GET_ALL_OBJS_OF_CLASSNAME modelid:(nCurrentModelId) classname:"ComponentTypeChild"
SET sComponentTypeIds:(sComponentTypeIds + " " + objids)

#Add create table statements
  ... ... ...
#Add primary key, unique, check and foreign key constraints
FOR sCTId in:(sComponentTypeIds) sep:(" ") {
  SET nCTId:(VAL sCTId)
  CC "Core" GET_ATTR_VAL objid:(nCTId) attrname:"Name"
  SET sCTName:(val)
  CC "Core" GET_CONNECTORS objid:(nCTId) out

  #Iterate through ComponentType relations
  FOR sComponentTypeRelationId in:(objids) {
    CC "Core" GET_CLASS_ID objid:(VAL sComponentTypeRelationId)
    CC "Core" GET_CLASS_NAME classid:(classid)
      ... ... ...
    #Check if the relation is ComponentTypeChecks
    ELSIF (classname = "ComponentTypeChecks") {
      CC "Core" GET_CONNECTOR_ENDPOINTS objid:(VAL sComponentTypeRelationId)
      SET nCheckId:(toobjid)
      CC "Core" GET_ATTR_VAL objid:(nCheckId) attrname:"Name"
      SET sCheckName:(val)
      CC "Core" GET_ATTR_VAL objid:(nCheckId) attrname:"CheckCondition"
      SET sCheckCondition:(val)

      #Create alter table statement and write it into the file
      SET sTextValue:("ALTER TABLE " + sCTName + " ADD CONSTRAINT " + sCheckName + " CHECK(" + sCheckCondition + ");\n")
      CC "AdoScript" FWRITE file:(sSQLFileLocation) text:(sTextValue) append:1
    }
  }
  ... ... ...
}
```

Fig. 26.4 AdoScript code for automatic generation of SQL check constraints

From our previous experience with EMF and the Xtend language [41] in the implementation of different code generators, we notice some differences in comparison to ADOxx and AdoScript. By using ADOxx, it is easier to add new features and action buttons into the modeling tool than it is with EMF. As for the AdoScript language, it seems that greater amount of code lines is needed to implement the same functionalities compared to Xtend. However, due to a lack of our previous experience with AdoScript, we allow that we missed some code optimization or shortcuts. Nevertheless, the AdoScript language is easy to learn and understand, and can be used to successfully implement all the code generators embedded in IIS*Studio.

26.4   A Case Study as a Proof of Concept

In this section, we illustrate a usage of our IIS*Case PIM Meta-model and its
ADOxx implementation in a small case study of a specification of the Student
Service IS model. In Fig. 26.5, we present an excerpt of the formal specification
of *Student Service IS*, created by means of IIS*Case PIM concepts. In the following
text, we explain the model from Fig. 26.5 in more detail.

The modeled IS consists of the *Student Service* application system which is
created as a child application system of the *Faculty Organization* application system.

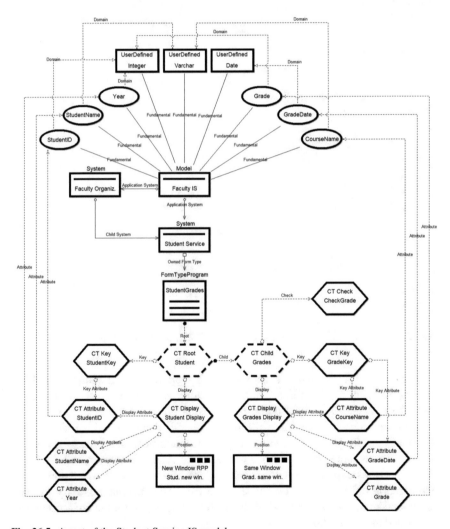

Fig. 26.5 A part of the Student Service IS model

In Fig. 26.5 at the level of the *FacultyIS* application model, we created a set of attributes, including: *StudentID*, *StudentName*, *Year*, *CourseName*, *GradeDate*, and *Grade*. The set of attributes is specified in the Fundamentals category. The attributes from Fundamentals are later used in the specification of other IS components. The set of domains is also specified in Fundamentals, representing *Integer*, *Varchar*, and *Date* domains. Each attribute references one of these domains.

A usage of the FormType concept is illustrated by creation of the *StudentGrades* form type. It comprises two component types: *Students* and *Grades*. The *Student-Grades* form type is presented in Fig. 26.5 as the Owned Form Type at the level of the *StudentService* application system. It refers to the information about students and their grades. In Fig. 26.6, we present a visual representation of the *StudentGrades* form type, for which we expect to be more readable to the end-users. While the *Student* component type represents instances of students, the *Grades* component type represents instances of grades for each student. The *Student* component type is the parent to the *Grades* component type. For each of the component type attributes, we specify its *Name* and *Title*. Thus, *Student* is specified with attributes *StudentId*, *StudentName*, and *Year*. After the component type attribute specifications, a list of component type constraints is given. We specify key, uniqueness, and check constraints. For the *Student* component type, a key constraint is specified only. In Fig. 26.5, it is the *StudentKey* instance of the ComponentTypeKey concept. It is composed of the *StudentId* attribute only, via the *StudentId* component type attribute. In Fig. 26.6, component type keys are underlined. By this, *StudentId* is underlined as a key attribute of the *Student* component type.

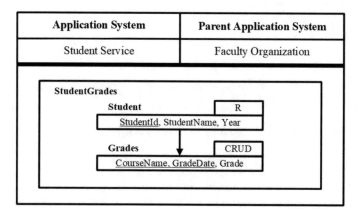

Fig. 26.6 The StudentGrades form type

In a similar way, we specify the *Grades* component type with attributes: *CourseName*, *GradeDate*, and *Grade*, and the constraints: *GradeKey* and *Check-Grade*. *GradeKey* represents a key constraint that is composed of the following component type attributes: *StudentId*, *CourseName*, and *GradeDate*. *CourseName* and *GradeDate* are the attributes from the *Grades* component type, while *StudentID* is just inherited as a consequence of the rule that for each subordinated component type, its key is composed as a union of the keys of all component types that belong to the path in a tree from the root component type to the component type being observed. *CheckGrade* represents a check constraint to check whether a final student's grade is between values 5 and 10.

In Fig. 26.7, we present the generated SQL/DDL script obtained from the excerpt of the conceptual Student Service IS model given in Fig. 26.5. Based on the *StudentGrades* form type and its *Student* and *Grades* component types, related attributes, and domains, CREATE TABLE statements are generated from the model. Whenever some of the component type attributes are mandatory, a NOT NULL constraint is generated next to the attribute domain, that s, a table column type. From the *Student* component type key, a PRIMARY KEY constraint of the *Student* table is generated. From the *Grades* component type key, a PRIMARY KEY constraint of the *Grades* table is generated. The *Grades* primary key consists of the three attributes: *StudentId*, *CourseName*, and *GradeDate*. Also, from the *CheckGrade* constraint, a CHECK constraint of students' grades is generated. As the *Grades* component type is a child of the *Student* component type, a FOREIGN KEY constraint is generated, referencing *Student* from *Grades*.

```
CREATE TABLE Student (
    StudentID Integer NOT NULL,
    StudentName Varchar(30) NOT NULL,
    Year Integer NOT NULL
);

CREATE TABLE Grades (
    CourseName Varchar(30) NOT NULL,
    GradeDate Date NOT NULL,
    Grade Integer DEFAULT 5 NOT NULL,
    StudentID Integer
);

ALTER TABLE Student ADD CONSTRAINT StudentKey PRIMARY KEY(StudentID);

ALTER TABLE Grades ADD CONSTRAINT GradeKey PRIMARY KEY(CourseName, GradeDate, StudentID);
ALTER TABLE Grades ADD CONSTRAINT CheckGrade CHECK(Grade >= 5 AND Grade <= 10);
ALTER TABLE Grades ADD CONSTRAINT Grades_Student_FK FOREIGN KEY(StudentID) REFERENCES Student(StudentID);
```

Fig. 26.7 Generated SQL/DDL code from the IS model excerpt

It is important to say that in our approach, a generation of SQL/DDL scripts is not performed by a direct transformation of the conceptual model being created, as it is assumed in this section just for the sake of simplicity. In practice, it is a two-phase transformation composed of rather complex algorithms that cannot be easily presented in a limited space. In the first phase, a conceptual model being created is transformed into the relational DB schema as a model that is independent of any target relational DBMS. Then, in the second phase, a relational DB schema is transformed into SQL/DDL scripts specific for the selected DBMS.

Due to space limits, in this section we presented just a very small segment of our Student Service IS model, with the aim to illustrate the design of a form type in the IIS*Case PIM Meta-model, and how it can be utilized for SQL code generation. A more extensive illustration of the Student Service IS model would contain at least 10 form types and more than 50 attributes. In practice, IS PIM specifications of integrated ISs of some companies consist of several hundreds or even thousands of form types, and several thousands of attributes, organized in several application systems, where the number of application systems probably may exceed 20. To provide a development of such large ISs, our IIS*Case Repository has been implemented in a relational DBMS, while IIS*Studio is to provide a multiuser and concurrent work of several IS designers.

26.5   Conclusion

In this chapter, we presented an ADOxx implementation of an IS modeling toolset named IIS*Studio, with its main tool IIS*Case. A selected rather small part of the IIS*Case Meta-model for conceptual IS modeling is implemented within the ADOxx platform. We developed a new concrete graphical syntax for IIS*Case PIM Meta-model and selected the SQL/DDL code generator to be implemented by the AdoScript language. The generator is implemented in the ADOxx platform. The usage of ADOxx to implement such a complex meta-model as the IIS*Case Meta-model has provided us with new insights into meta-modeling, tooling support, and code generation.

One of the lessons learned from our experimental work in this research is that the ADOxx framework successfully addresses some of the issues present in other meta-modeling frameworks, such as a complexity of procedure to integrate abstract and concrete syntaxes, a lack of user management system, deployment issues, and a complexity of procedure to add new features, action buttons, or customize an object property section or the tool palette. Usually, there is a lot of framework configuration steps needed to integrate abstract and concrete syntaxes. ADOxx requires only a few of these steps, which make the integration of abstract and concrete syntaxes very user-friendly. When working on a very large project with multiple users participating, a user management system can be very useful but is often omitted in other frameworks. However, ADOxx makes user management easy and practical. Also, we experienced different issues when deploying the tool with other frameworks, but with ADOxx such issues were resolved without much effort. Additionally, implementing new features in a tool or adding action buttons and menus can be done easily by using the ADOxx platform, as well as the customization of objects property sections and the tool palette.

The only feature that we did not encounter using ADOxx is a diagram-like representation of meta-models. It would be useful to create meta-models as diagrams or to automatically generate meta-model diagrams from their tree-like structure representations, in order to see them as whole and provide discussion with potential tool users. ADOxx mostly relies on a textual syntax when developing abstract and concrete syntaxes, which may be a bit difficult for beginners. However, we believe such an approach is very useful for experienced users, as they can probably use textual syntax faster than clicking on multiple buttons within user interfaces.

Our overall experience with ADOxx leads us to a conclusion that it can be efficiently used in different problem domains, in various scenarios. As for the IS modeling domain, our opinion is that the ADOxx platform can be effectively used to fully implement IIS*Studio as a toolset for modeling ISs and to generate fully executable application prototypes. Some of our future work can lead in this direction, and one of the next steps would be experimentation on a more extensive case study, necessary for collecting deeper experiences required for a future full implementation of IIS*Studio in ADOxx.

Tool Download   https://www.omilab.org/iisc

References

1. Luković, I., Ivančević, V., Čeliković, M., Aleksić, S.: DSLs in action with model based approaches to information system development. In: Mernik, M. (ed.) Formal and Practical Aspects of Domain-Specific Languages: Recent Developments, pp. 502–532. IGI Global, New York (2013). https://doi.org/10.4018/978-1-4666-2092-6
2. Giaglis, G.M.: A taxonomy of business process modeling and information systems modeling techniques. Int. J. Flex. Manuf. Syst. **13**, 209–228 (2001)
3. Mogin, P., Luković, I., Karadžić, Ž.: Relational database schema design and application generating using IIS*CASE tool. In: Proceedings of International Conference on Technical Informatics, pp. 49–58. "Politehnica" University of Timisoara, Timisoara, Romania (1994)
4. Kleppe, A., Warmer, J., Bast, W.: MDA Explained: The Model Driven Architecture - Practice and Promise. Addison-Wesley, New York (2003)
5. Vara, J.M., Vela, B., Bollati, V., Marcos, E.: Supporting model-driven development of object-relational database schemas: a case study. In: Paige, R. (ed.) Proceedings of the International Conference on Model Transformation, pp. 181–196. Springer, Berlin (2009)
6. Gudas, S., Lopata, A.: Meta-model based development of use case model for business function. Inf. Technol. Control. **36**, 302–309 (2007)
7. Pastor, O., Gómez, J., Insfrán, E., Pelechano, V.: The OO-method approach for information systems modeling: from object-oriented conceptual modeling to automated programming. Inf. Syst. **26**, 507–534 (2001)
8. Luković, I., Ristić, S., Mogin, P., Pavićević, J.: Database schema integration process – a methodology and aspects of its applying. Novi Sad J. Math. **36**, 115–150 (2006)
9. Pavićević, J., Luković, I., Mogin, P., Govedarica, M.: Information system design and prototyping using form types. In: Proceedings of INSTICC I International Conference on Software and Data Technologies (ICSOFT), pp. 157–160. Institute for Systems and Technologies of Information, Control and Communication (INSTICC) and School of Business of the Polytechnic Institute of Setubal, Setubal, Portugal (2006)
10. Luković, I., Ristić, S., Aleksić, S., Popović, A.: An application of the MDSE principles in IIS*case. In: Model Driven Software Engineering - Transformations and Tools, pp. 85–95. Logos Verlag Berlin GmbH, Berlin, Germany (2009)
11. Luković, I., Mogin, P., Pavićević, J., Ristić, S.: An approach to developing complex database schemas using form types. Softw. Pract. Exp. **37**, 1621–1656 (2007). https://doi.org/10.1002/spe.820

12. Luković, I.: From the synthesis algorithm to the model driven transformations in database design. In: Proceedings of the 10th International Scientific Conference on Informatics (Informatics 2009), pp. 9–18. Slovak Society for Applied Cybernetics and Informatics and Technical University of Košice - Faculty of Electrical Engineering and Informatics, Herlany, Slovakia (2009)

13. Ristić, S., Kordić, S., Čeliković, M., Dimitrieski, V., Luković, I.: A model-driven approach to data structure conceptualization. In: Proceedings of the Federated Conference on Computer Science and Information Systems (FedCSIS), pp. 977–984. IEEE Computer Society Press and Polish Information Processing Society, Lodz, Poland (2015). https://doi.org/10.15439/2015F224

14. Mendix: Mendix low-code application development platform. https://www.mendix.com/. Accessed 20 Mar 2021

15. Irazábal, J., Pons, C., Neil, C.: Model transformation as a mechanism for the implementation of domain specific transformation languages. SADIO Electron. J. Inform. Oper. Res. **9**, 49–66 (2010)

16. Reiter, T., Kapsammer, E., Retschitzegger, W., Schwinger, W., Stumptner, M.: A generator framework for domain-specific model transformation languages. In: Proceedings of the Eighth International Conference on Enterprise Information Systems Databases and Information Systems Integration, pp. 27–35. ICEIS Press, Paphos, Cyprus (2006)

17. GME: Generic Modeling Environment. https://www.isis.vanderbilt.edu/Projects/gme/. Accessed 20 Mar 2021

18. MetaCase: MetaEdit+. https://www.metacase.com/. Accessed 20 Mar 2021

19. EMF: Eclipse Modeling Framework. https://www.eclipse.org/modeling/emf/. Accessed 20 Mar 2021

20. ADOxx: ADOxx Modeling and Configuration Platform. https://www.adoxx.org/live/home. Accessed 20 Mar 2021

21. Fill, H.-G., Redmond, T., Karagiannis, D.: FDMM: A formalism for describing ADOxx meta models and models. In: Proceedings of the 14th International Conference on Enterprise Information Systems, pp. 133–144. SciTePress - Science and Technology Publications, Wroclaw, Poland (2012). https://doi.org/10.5220/0003971201330144

22. Fill, H.-G., Karagiannis, D.: On the conceptualisation of modelling methods using the ADOxx meta modelling platform. Enterp. Model. Inf. Syst. Archit. **8**, 4–25 (2013). https://doi.org/10.1007/BF03345926

23. Čeliković, M., Luković, I., Aleksić, S., Ivančević, V.: A MOF based meta-model and a concrete DSL syntax of IIS*Case PIM concepts. Comput. Sci. Inf. Syst. **9**, 1075–1103 (2012). https://doi.org/10.2298/CSIS120203034C

24. Luković, I., Varanda Pereira, M.J., Oliveira, N., Cruz, D., Henriques, P.R.: A DSL for PIM specifications: design and attribute grammar based implementation. Comput. Sci. Inf. Syst. **8**, 379–403 (2011). https://doi.org/10.2298/CSIS101229018L

25. Oliveira, N., Varanda Pereira, M.J., Henriques, P.R., Cruz, D., Cramer, B.: VisualLISA: a visual environment to develop attribute grammars. Comput. Sci. Inf. Syst. **7**, 265–289 (2010)

26. Dimitrieski, V., Čeliković, M., Ivančević, V., Luković, I.: A comparison of Ecore and GOPPRR through an information system meta modeling approach. In: Proceedings of the 8th European Conference on Modelling Foundations and Applications (ECMFA 2012), pp. 217–228. Technical University of Denmark, Kongens Lyngby, Denmark (2012)

27. Popović, A., Luković, I., Dimitrieski, V., Đukić, V.: A DSL for modeling application-specific functionalities of business applications. Comput. Lang. Syst. Struct. **43**, 69–95 (2015). https://doi.org/10.1016/j.cl.2015.03.003

28. Obrenović, N., Luković, I., Ristić, S.: Consolidation of database check constraint. Softw. Syst. Model. **18**, 2111–2135 (2019). https://doi.org/10.1007/s10270-017-0637-2

29. Aleksić, S., Ristić, S., Luković, I., Čeliković, M.: A design specification and a server implementation of the inverse referential integrity constraints. Comput. Sci. Inf. Syst. **10**, 283–320 (2013). https://doi.org/10.2298/CSIS111102003A

30. Ristić, S., Aleksić, S., Čeliković, M., Luković, I.: Generic and standard database constraint meta-models. Comput. Sci. Inf. Syst. **11**, 679–696 (2014). https://doi.org/10.2298/CSIS140216037R
31. Embley, D.W., Mok, W.Y.: Mapping conceptual models to database schemas. In: Embley, D.W., Thalheim, B. (eds.) Handbook of Conceptual Modeling: Theory, Practice, and Research Challenges, pp. 123–163. Springer, Berlin, Heidelberg (2011). https://doi.org/10.1007/978-3-642-15865-0_5
32. Kramer, F., Thalheim, B.: Holistic conceptual and logical database structure modeling with ADOxx. In: Karagiannis, D., Mayr, H.C., Mylopoulos, J. (eds.) Domain-Specific Conceptual Modeling: Concepts, Methods and Tools, pp. 269–290. Springer, Cham (2016). https://doi.org/10.1007/978-3-319-39417-6_12
33. Kosar, T., Oliveira, N., Mernik, M., Varanda Pereira, M.J., Črepinšek, M., da Cruz, D., Henriques, P.R.: Comparing general-purpose and domain-specific languages: an empirical study. Comput. Sci. Inf. Syst. **7**, 247–264 (2010). https://doi.org/10.2298/CSIS1002247K
34. Choobineh, J., Mannino, M.V., Nunamaker, J.F., Konsynski, B.R.: An expert database design system based on analysis of forms. IEEE Trans. Softw. Eng. **14**, 242–253 (1988)
35. Draheim, D., Weber, G.: Form-oriented analysis: a new methodology to model form-based applications. Springer, Berlin, Heidelberg (2005). https://doi.org/10.1007/b138252
36. Vještica, M., Dimitrieski, V., Pisarić, M., Kordić, S., Ristić, S., Luković, I.: Towards a formal specification of production processes suitable for automatic execution. Open Comput. Sci. **11**, 161–179 (2021). https://doi.org/10.1515/comp-2020-0200
37. Vještica, M., Dimitrieski, V., Pisarić, M., Kordić, S., Ristić, S., Luković, I.: The syntax of a multi-level production process modeling language. In: Proceedings of the 2020 Federated Conference on Computer Science and Information Systems (FedCSIS 2020), pp. 751–760. Polish Information Processing Society, Sofia, Bulgaria (2020). https://doi.org/10.15439/2020F176
38. Vještica, M., Dimitrieski, V., Pisarić, M., Kordić, S., Ristić, S., Luković, I.: An application of a DSML in industry 4.0 production processes. In: IFIP Advances in Information and Communication Technology (AICT), pp. 441–448. Springer Nature, Novi Sad, Serbia (2020). https://doi.org/10.1007/978-3-030-57993-7_50
39. Vujović, V., Maksimović, M., Perišić, B.: Sirius: a rapid development of DSM graphical editor. In: Proceedings of IEEE 18th International Conference on Intelligent Engineering Systems (INES 2014), pp. 233–238. IEEE, Tihany, Hungary (2014). https://doi.org/10.1109/INES.2014.6909375
40. OMiLAB: GraphRep Generator. http://vienna-omilab.dke.univie.ac.at/GraphRepGenerator/editor/svg-editor.html. Accessed 20 Mar 2021
41. Xtend: Xtend. https://www.eclipse.org/xtend/. Accessed 20 Mar 2021

Part X
Conceptual Modelling Language Extension

Chapter 27
BPMN4MoPla: Mobility Planning Based on Business Decision-Making

Emanuele Laurenzi, Oliver Ruggli, and Alta van der Merwe

Abstract This chapter presents a domain-specific modelling language, BPMN4MoPla, which extends the standard BPMN for the purpose of supporting business decision-making in mobility planning. Specifically, requirements for robotic car movements were derived and used for the modelling language extension. To achieve greater support of decision-making in mobility planning, the new modelling method was implemented as a cyber-physical system. Validation of the method was carried out in two complementary ways: (1) with respect to the extended language by modelling a mobility plan use case with BPMN4MoPla and (2) with respect to the expected execution behaviour by transforming and then executing the BPMN4MoPla model in two different modelling environments widely used in research and industry, respectively.

Keywords BPMN extension · Mobility planning · Transportation movements · Cyber-physical system · Model design and execution

27.1 Introduction

The movement of people and goods provides access to jobs, education, healthcare and trade, which ultimately results in economic growth [1]. The global population is estimated to grow to 10 billion by 2050, causing urban trips to have a threefold increase [2]. As a consequence, mobility systems in megacities are intended to be overstretched while rural areas will fall further behind. Growing motorization causes congestion, emissions (the transport sector is estimated to contribute 30%–50% of all emissions by 2050 [3]) and noise, takes up land, and affects road safety,

E. Laurenzi (✉) · O. Ruggli
FHNW University of Applied Sciences and Arts Northwestern, Olten, Switzerland
e-mail: emanuele.laurenzi@fhnw.ch; oliver.ruggli@students.fhnw.ch

A. van der Merwe
Department of Informatics, University of Pretoria, Pretoria, South Africa
e-mail: alta.vdm@up.ac.za

© The Author(s), under exclusive license to Springer Nature Switzerland AG 2022
D. Karagiannis et al. (eds.), *Domain-Specific Conceptual Modeling*,
https://doi.org/10.1007/978-3-030-93547-4_27

resulting in environmental, economic and social costs. For example, only in the European Union the total cost for congestion, air quality, accidents, noise and CO_2 emissions in urban areas reaches 230 billion euros [4]. This class of problems has led to initiatives that strive to create the "mobility of the future", offering efficient infrastructures capable of ensuring safety, cleanliness and inclusiveness [1].

Among others, mobility planning is a practice that contributes to creating conditions for such mobility of the future (in the EU it is also known as *integrating planning* [5]). If mobility is the ability to move about and make transport choices, mobility planning is the practice that supports urban mobility managers in the creation of transport choices towards a more sustainable urban mobility [6].

Models are a valuable means for mobility planning [7] in that they allow abstraction from a certain complexity and focus on relevant aspects of a "system under study" for a specific purpose [8]. Hence, models serve as a basis for discussions, analysis, improvements, and the support of decision-making.

While business-like activities and decisions can be specified in a BPMN model, the standard is not expressive enough to cover mobility planning aspects such as transportation types, routes, and movements. An example of this is a mobility plan that specifies a route for citizens to travel from home to the airport, consisting of a particular combination of public transportation means (a public bicycle, a tram and a train), based on travelling conditions such as the size of luggage. Such inability to represent specific aspects of mobility planning hinders the benefits of models.

In this chapter, we focus on this problem by proposing a modelling method that extends the modelling standard BPMN to cover mobility planning aspects: BPMN4MoPla. To achieve a higher support of the decision-making, the language extension is engineered to create a cyber-physical system (CPS). CPSs have the benefit of promoting mutual feedback loops between the cyber spaces and physical spaces, leading to quick and incremental improvements [3]. To create the conditions for a mutual feedback loop between the cyber and the physical space, executable BPMN4MoPla models are created and validated in two different modelling environments.

This chapter is structured as follows. Section 27.2 outlines the theoretical background and related work in language extensions for CPSs. Section 27.3 describes the methodology that was followed to create the new modelling method. The conceptualization of the artefact is discussed in Sect. 27.4 while its implementation in BPMN4MoPla and the proof of concept are presented in Sect. 27.5. Finally, Sect. 27.6 concludes by summarizing the chapter as well as mentioning some future developments.

27.2 Background

This section elaborates on the relevant theoretical background of this chapter. Firstly, the basis for the definition of Domain-Specific Modelling Languages (DSMLs) is presented along with the techniques for their creation, and the DSML user. Then, the concept of the cyber-physical system (CPS) is explained, and related work is presented with a particular focus on DSMLs (or extended languages) that implement CPSs within the mobility application domain.

27.2.1 DSML and Modelling Language Extension

As suggested by Laurenzi [9], a DSML can be defined as a graphical language that offers expressive power focused on a particular problem domain, through cognitive adequate notations and abstractions for humans. With their higher level of specificity, DSMLs enable domain experts to handle the designing and editing of models in a meaningful and less error-prone way, thus supporting the production of high-quality models [10]. Additionally, the domain experts deal directly with language constructs they are familiar with, which makes the language easy to learn and improves its applicability [11]. Given the adequate graphical notations targeting the domain experts, models that are built through DMSLs have the benefit of fostering productivity in design time, where an application domain can be better understood and issues can rapidly be identified [12].

While a DSML can be created from scratch by designing a new meta-model that addresses all the domain requirements, a more convenient way is to extend existing modelling standards [13]. Modelling standards come with sets of proven and well-known concepts with clear syntax and a widely accepted semantics. In contrast to the DSML built from scratch, this approach avoids the creation of yet another modelling language, which possibly has redundant overlaps with basal concepts from standard enterprise modelling languages [14]. Especially Atkinson et al. [15] consider the extensibility of modelling languages extremely relevant in the enterprise modelling domain, especially to the vast number of stakeholders in relation to their perspectives on the enterprise.

In this chapter, we adopt the modelling standard extension approach in order to leave the full expressivity of the selected language available to design various future use cases for mobility planning.

One of the most adopted techniques for enterprise modelling language extension is the *meta-models customization* [16], which refers to the ad hoc customization of meta-models (see, e.g., [17]). In contrast to the other prominent extension technique, namely UML *profile*, the meta-model customization often leads to well-structured, constraint-free and thus high-quality extension definitions [13].

In this chapter, the *urban mobility manager* is regarded as a domain expert and DSML user. As such, the domain expert is any person who is skilled in the mobility planning domain. The mobility manager can cooperate with a modelling expert to create models pertaining to the underlying domain [18]. In the case of business-like modelling languages (e.g. BPMN, DMN or DSMLs) this role has the ability to intervene in the design of models or even in creating them without assistance from the modelling expert.

27.2.2 Cyber-Physical Systems

Cyber-physical systems (CPS) are driving innovation across diverse application domains including mobility (or transportation) [3].

In [19], a cyber-physical system is defined as follows:

> Cyber-Physical Systems are systems with embedded software (as part of devices, buildings, means of transport, transport routes, production systems, medical processes, logistic processes, coordination processes and management processes), which:
> - directly record physical data using sensors and affect physical processes using actuators;
> - evaluate and save recorded data, and actively or reactively interact both with the physical and digital world;
> - are connected with one another and in global networks via digital communication facilities (wireless and/or wired, local and/or global);
> - use globally available data and services;
> - have a series of dedicated, multi-modal human-machine interfaces.

More concisely, CPSs are engineered systems that integrate the physical space with the cyber (or virtual) space and offer close interaction between the components of the two spaces [20]. The cyber space is characterized by a set of applications, services, data and decisions that control, collaborate and communicate with physical resources to reach a common goal [21]. The physical space, on the other hand, consists of physical resources (e.g. entities, objects, infrastructure or material) that monitor or actuate to change physical entities or the state of real-world objects [21].

Specifically, physical resources can be categorized as either static (e.g. medical devices, sensor networks) or mobile (e.g. robots) [22]. Physical mobile resources can be further characterized by constrained movements, i.e., based on a particular context, time and resource characteristics [23]. Such constraints contribute to the process and decision logic of the related cyber space, which embeds the ability to invoke software services to operate the movements of the physical resource, e.g., a robotic car.

Compared to traditional systems, CPSs allow the achievement of higher efficiency and reliability by enabling increased feedback-based interactions between the cyber system and the physical system [3].

The left side of Fig. 27.1 illustrates the two different but integrated spaces, i.e., on top the cyber space and on the bottom the physical space. Figure 27.1 also shows the relation of the term CPS to the closely related paradigms Digital Twins (DT) and Internet of Things (IoT). On the one hand, DT relates to a virtual representation that serves as the real-time digital counterpart of a physical resource [25]. On the other hand, IoT is described as a network of physical objects that are equipped with sensors and other technologies to connect and exchange data over the Internet [26].

In this sense, both DT and IoT represent the prerequisites for the development of CPSs.

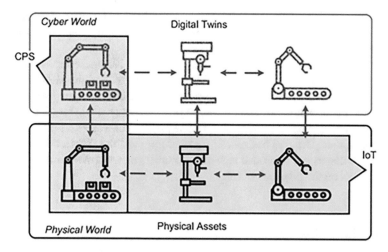

Fig. 27.1 Cyber-physical systems, Digital Twins and IoT and their relations [24]

27.2.3 Modelling Language Extension with Physical Components

Several authors have extended the standard BPMN with physical components [27]. Such language extensions mainly refer to the Internet of Things (IoT) paradigm in which the physical part of the processes shows how components are connected through the web. When addressing a CPS scenario, this is not sufficient because the representation of cyber parts and their relations is also important. In contrast to IoT, CPS applications provide the interaction not only from the cyber to the physical components but also the other way around.

The authors in [3] presented various CPSs in the transportation sector, i.e., aviation transportation CPS, rail transportation CPS, road transportation CPS and Marin transportation CPS. However, their cyber space is either characterized by applications or conceptual models that abstract only from the technical aspects, thus not capturing the representation of business-like activities and decisions. Moreover, they are not concerned with the creation of DSMLs.

Conversely, other related work [23, 28–30] extended existing modelling languages for the creation of DSMLs for CPS in the transportation sector. For example, *SafeUML* [28] is an extension of UML to model safety-related concepts of aerospace systems, which only relates to certification information.

Aziz et al. [29] proposed a DSML as an extension of UML for CPS in which the rationale is to simplify the design models of cyber-physical systems while allowing the representation of their structure and behaviour in a unified way. The approach was validated through the implementation of two case studies: "Traffic Light" and "Arbiter". Although they can be related to the transportation domain, the DSML leaves out movements of means of transportation.

Similarly, *RCSD* [30] is another UML-based extension for the design of railway and tramway control systems, but is not reusable for mobility planning purposes in the business context.

More closely related to our approach, Graja et al. [23] describe the extension of BPMN to cover CPS components. The authors argue that the BPMN standard creates a standardized bridge for the gap between the business process design and the process implementation, thus addressing the business context too. Their DSML, however, is not expressive enough to cover the physical movements that are foreseen by means of transportation in a mobility plan. Moreover, the DSML has only design purposes, whereas our approach also aims to create execute models able to have a direct impact on the physical world.

27.3 Methodology

The artefact in this chapter was conceived by following the Design Science Research (DSR) methodology [31]. The three DSR cycles "Relevance Cycle", Design Cycle" and "Rigor Cycle" were employed to ensure that the designed artefact was relevant to the application mobility planning domain and theoretically grounded. The design cycle was further extended with the phases of the AMME methodology [32] to provide additional rigour to the creation of the modelling method BPMN4MoPla.

As shown in Fig. 27.2, the AMME methodology presents five iterative phases:

- The *Creation* phase is a mix of knowledge acquisition and requirements elicitation activities that capture and represent the modelling requirements.
- The *Design* phase specifies the metamodel, language grammar, notation and functionality.
- The *Formalize* phase aims to describe the outcome of the previous phase in non-ambiguous representations with the purpose of sharing results within a scientific community.
- The *Develop* phase produces concrete modelling prototypes.
- The *Deploy/Validate* phase involves the stakeholders in hands-on experience and the evaluation process [32].

In [34] the Deploy phase is further extended with an evaluation cycle consisting of "design models", "evaluate models" and "evaluate method". That is, the design of models in the deployed modelling tool serves as basis for testing the models and modelling method, which in turn triggers the generation of feedback to be accommodated back in the engineering cycle shown in Fig. 27.2.

For the creation of BPMN4MoPla each phase was instantiated but formalized as it was considered out of the scope of this chapter.

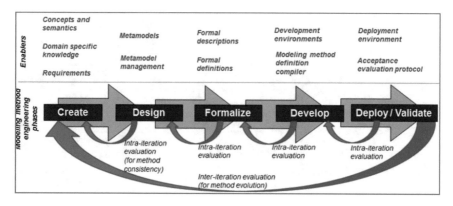

Fig. 27.2 The AMME methodology [33]

Figure 27.3 graphically depicts the instantiation of the AMME methodology (including the evaluation phase for the feedback loop) for the creation of BPMN4MoPla.

Specifically,

- In the *Creation* phase, a fictitious use case representing a mobility plan was first analysed (Domain analysis). From this, three categories of requirements were elicited: (1) one for the modelling extension, (2) one for the modelling tool and (3) one for the cyber-physical system infrastructure.
- In the *Design* phase, the meta-model was conceptualized by (1) identifying the standard language to extend, (2) identifying the modelling construct to extend, (3) extending the modelling construct with new concept and properties, and (4) the addition of constraints. An example of a constraint is the value LED that if chosen from the Movement Type attribute enables the property LED-Control to be assigned with a colour that comes in the form of an *enum* data type (see Sect. 27.5).
- In the *Develop* phase the meta-model extension was implemented in the ADOxx Development Toolkit. The graphical notations for the new modelling constructs were also implemented in this phase. The *Formalize* phase is skipped because the formalization of the meta-model does not contribute to achieving the goal of this work.
- In the *Deploy/Validate* phase the modelling method was evaluated with respect to (1) the extended modelling language BPMN4MoPla and (2) the execution behaviour of the models. While for the former the deployed ADOxx-based BPMN4MoPla tool was sufficient for the execution behaviour, the mobility planning use case was modelled and executed through BeeUp[1] and Camunda,[2] as both provide execution capabilities.

---

[1] https://www.omilab.org/activities/bee-up.html

[2] https://camunda.com/

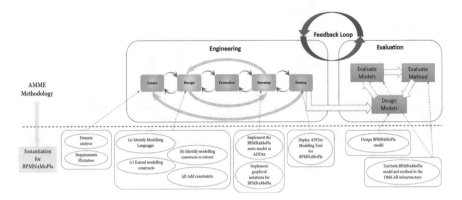

Fig. 27.3 Instantiation of the AMME methodology for BPMN4MoPla

27.4 Conceptualization of BPMN4MoPla

This section illustrates the main concepts of the addressed mobility planning application domain, which are derived from the analysis of a mobility planning scenario. Thus, first, the scenario is described and then the requirements are listed. The latter are then considered for the elaboration of the conceptualized BPMN4MoPla.

27.4.1 Mobility Plan Scenario

The scenario abstracts from a real-world situation of a citizen based in Switzerland who travels to the Zurich Airport from his home in the city of Olten. Such abstraction focuses on an early stage of a mobility plan where basic concepts are to be discussed and decided: pick-up and drop-off locations of means of transportation, types of means, routes and decision criteria for choosing a particular transportation means or route. For the sake of simplicity, decisions about transportation means and routes that are based on space and time are left out, e.g., decisions based on a particular distance between different locations or based on departure and arrival time of a transportation means. Such decision criteria would bring a higher level of detail that is more adequate for a later stage of mobility plan where additional stakeholders of the transportation ecosystem (e.g. railway companies, car- and bike-sharing platforms) are requested to be involved in the decision-making.

The scenario is sketched in Fig. 27.4 and consists of three main locations: citizen's house is the starting point, the train station is the intermediary location, and the airport is the final destination. From the starting point there are three ways to reach the intermediate location: by car, by bicycle or by foot.

Depending on the travelling conditions one route is chosen. Namely, for business trips the citizen travels to the airport by car, whereas for leisure trips it will be specified whether he or she has light or heavy luggage. In case of heavy luggage, the suggestion is to go by foot until the intermediate station (the train station) and then take the train until the airport. Otherwise, with light luggage the citizen is advised to go by bicycle until the train station and then change the transportation means into the train to reach the airport.

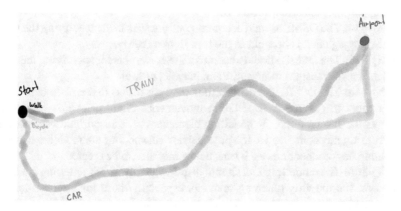

Fig. 27.4 A sketch of the mobility planning scenario

27.4.2 Requirements for BPMN4MoPla

The previously presented mobility planning scenario was analysed to derive requirements. These were grouped into the following three categories:

Requirements for the DSML
Requirements for the modelling tool
Requirements for the CPS infrastructure

Respectively, all requirements are described below with the convention: REQ-<n. of categories><n. of requirements>. The number of categories is consistent with the above-enumerated list while the number of requirements starts with 0, e.g., REQ-010 is the first requirement for the DSML.

- **REQ-010:** The DSML should accommodate constructs to model process logic and decision logic. Process logic refers to the prescribed flow of activities, e.g., sequence of movements of a transportation means to reach a location. Decision logic relates to how transportation decisions are made, e.g., riding a bicycle until the train station in case of light luggage.
- **REQ-011:** The DSML should accommodate constructs to model different transportation movements: drive straight, turn left, turn right, change means of transportation.

- **REQ-012:** The DSML should accommodate constructs to group transportation movements into a different level of abstraction, i.e., in a sub-model. Creating routes in sub-models ensures an adequate level of abstraction of the model elements and allows the reusability of the transportation movements (or routes) in other models.
- **REQ-013:** The DSML should accommodate constructs for specifying the travelling purpose: leisure or business.
- **REQ-014:** The DSML should accommodate constructs for specifying the weight of the luggage that is brought to the trip: light or heavy.
- **REQ-015:** The DSML should accommodate constructs for specifying the different means of transportation: car, train, bicycle, or foot.
- **REQ-016:** The DSML should accommodate constructs that embed connections to a robot to execute transportation movements. Addressing this requirement allows the instantiation of modelling elements (i.e. transportation movements) that are already connected to the physical device, and thus the modeller can avoid creating new connections each time a new model is to be created.
- **REQ-100:** The modelling tool should display the full set of modelling constructs used for the mobility planning scenario, especially those for the transportation movements. The availability of tailored graphical notations while modelling supports increasing the modelling productivity [35] and the perceived *ease-of-use* [36] of the DSML (see also [37]).
- **REQ-200:** The CPS environment should provide connectivity to the cyber-physical space and be able to execute robotic movements. After starting a movement task, the model needs to be informed that the task is either completed or aborted to continue.
- **REQ-201:** The CPS environment should foresee a robot with sensors capable of detecting the physical space and following predefined routes. A vehicle to fulfil the robotic actions is required.
- **REQ-202:** The CPS environments should provide indicators to differentiate among the means of transportation: car, train, bicycle and walking.

27.4.3 Conceptualization of BPMN4MoPla

The modelling standard BPMN 2.0 [38] was chosen to address REQ-010. This standard is the most widespread notation for modelling business processes and allows for the specification of both process and decision logic. The latter can also be further specified with the standard DMN [39] for future and more complex mobility plans. The expressivity of BPMN was adequate to address:

REQ-012, through the sub-process construct
REQ-13 and REQ-14, through the instantiation of the gateway construct as it allows the specification of conditions

Conversely, for requirements concerning the transportation movements such as REQ-11, REQ-15 and REQ-16 extension activities of the BPMN meta-model were required. The extension activity was supported by analysing the possible reflecting physical representation in the OMiLAB environment [40]. The injection of physical aspects into the language has the benefit of reducing the semantic gap between a model and its physical representation, thus facilitating the design and understanding of CPSs.

Hence, runtime transportation movement advocated by REQ-016 was captured through a new concept called *CarMovement*. The OMiLAB environment provides a robotic car as a transportation vehicle and therefore the class name starts with "Car". The control of physical devices is possible via the invocation of external services, such as web services or applications. In BPMN, a Service Task is a task that uses a web service, an automated application or other kinds of services to complete a task. Given the semantic equivalence, the new class *CarMovement* has been added as a sub-class of Service Task. Figure 27.5 shows the BPMN meta-model extended with the newly added modelling construct (in pink colour).

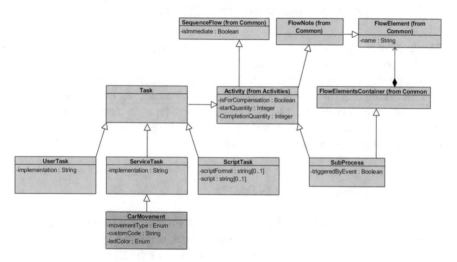

Fig. 27.5 Extension of the BPMN meta-model

The new class was specified with the following three attributes:

- A *movement type* (addressing REQ-011) specifies the type of movements, straight, left, right and jump gap, which refer to the change of means of transportation, e.g., from a bicycle to a train. The name "jump gap" originates from the street layouts of the OMiLAB environment, in which black lines are interrupted by white gaps.
- A *custom code* (addressing REQ-011) specifies the possibility to enter a (customized) script for each movement type, allowing change in the speed of the robotic vehicle that is available in the OMiLAB environment.

- *An LED colour* (addressing REQ-015) indicates the transportation means: car (yellow), train (blue), bicycle (green) and walk (red). The robotic vehicle in the OMiLAB environment is of one type only and it incorporates a LED. Therefore, the different colours were used to identify different transportation means.

27.5   Proof of Concept: The BPMN4MoPla Tool

The proof of concept for BPMN4MoPla in this chapter consisted of two parts: (1) the creation of a model in BPMN4MoPla reflecting the mobility plan scenario, which is introduced in Sect. 27.4.1, and (2) the execution of corresponding models through the two modelling environments BeeUp and Camunda. The following two sections present the two subsequent evaluations.

27.5.1   Meta-Model and Model for BPMN4MoPla

The implementation of the conceptualized BPMN4MoPla was done through the ADOxx meta-modelling environment [41]. The latter allows the creation of a modelling language and method, offering a deployment possibility for the creation of a modelling tool. Moreover, it provides existing modelling languages ready for extension, including BPMN 2.0. This contributes to an agile language engineering practice as one does not need to implement the whole meta-model from scratch but can incrementally extend the already implemented one.

27.5.1.1   Meta-Model for BPMN4MoPla

The way in which the BPMN 2.0 library is implemented in ADOxx is such that a change in the conceptualization of the language extension was required. That is, a new *CarMovement* task element was implemented as a sub-class of Task instead as a sub-class of Service Task. This is because the specializations of the BPMN Task element (e.g. Service Task) are implemented as attribute types in the given library.

The final list of attributes for the *CarMovement* element was implemented consistently for the conceptualization, and the respective graphical representations are depicted in Fig. 27.6. Each graphical notation is implemented in the ADOxx meta-modelling tool through a dedicated script on the built in AttrRep attribute. The additional and tailored graphical notations fulfil the requirement REQ-100.

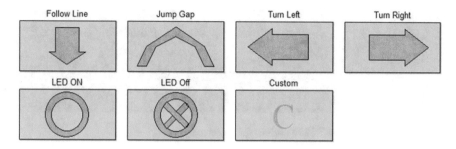

Fig. 27.6 Graphical notations for the class CarMovement

The implementation of all the attributes for the *CarMovement* element is visualized on the left-hand side of Fig. 27.7. The right-hand side of the figure shows the graphical depiction of a few attributes of a *CarMovement* model element in the ADOxx modelling tool, for example "Movement Type" and "LED-Control" for which a value shall be selected from a dropdown menu, respectively.

Given the inability of the meta-modelling tool to retain scripts, a work-around had to be found to fulfil REQ-016. As Fig. 27.7 indicates, the "External AdoScript" attribute allows the attachment of predefined ADOxx proprietary scripts while modelling. Hence, this requirement is partially fulfilled on the model layer instead of the meta-model.

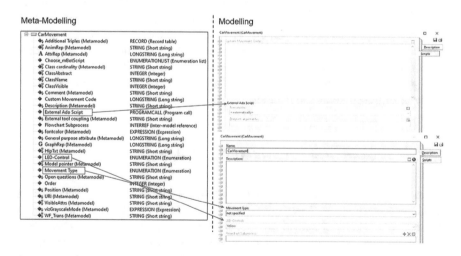

Fig. 27.7 Meta-modelling and modelling visualization for the attributes of CarMovement

An example of an external AdoScript is presented on Fig. 27.8. The script calls the REST API of the robotic car (i.e. the mBot) and lights the LED with both red and green, resulting in a yellow light. As conceptualized, the yellow light symbolizes the route that will be taken by car.

```
≡ 0-mBotYellowLED.asc ⟩ ...
1    SETL map_headers:({"Content-Type":"application/json"})
2    HTTP_SEND_REQUEST("http://10.0.6.59:8080/mBot/api/internalled/turnonled?red=100&green=100")
3    str_method:("GET")
4    map_reqheaders: (map_headers)
5    str_reqbody:("do")
6    val_respcode:val_httpcode
7    map_respheaders:map_respheaders
8    str_respbody:str_respbody
```

Fig. 27.8 AdoScript TurnON LED yellow for the route by car

As an alternative to the external scripts, the modeller can write and save a script directly by the instantiation of the *CarMovement* element through the Custom Movement Code attribute.

27.5.1.2   The Mobility Plan Model in BPMN4MoPla

The model in BPMN4MoPla that reflects the mobility plan scenario (see Sect. 27.4.1) is shown in Fig. 27.9. Each route is contained in a sub-process, i.e., Drive to Airport, Walk to Train Station, Cycle to Train Station, and Take Train to Airport.

Two sub-processes are expanded in the model: the "Drive to Airport" (from element "Switch Yellow LED On (Car)" to element "Switch Yellow LED Off") and the "Take Train to Airport" (from element "Switch Blue LED On (Train)" to element "Switch Blue Led Off"). Each model element in the respective sub-process reflects the sequential commands that are sent to the robotic car. Note that at the beginning of each route the corresponding LED colour is turned on whereas at the end of the route it is turned off. Moreover, "Take Train to Airport" also has the "Jump Gap" model element (i.e. named as "Catch Train") because of the transition of means of transportation to the train.

27.5.2   Execution of BPMN4MoPla Models

For the execution of the BPMN4MoPla models, we relied on the digital innovation OMiLAB infrastructure. Thereby, the BPMN4MoPla model presented in the previous section was transformed into an executable model to prove its correct execution behaviour. Next, to prove its executability in another modelling environment featuring a workflow engine, the model was transformed into a BPMN model using the Camunda modelling environment. Figure 27.10 depicts the two transformations.

In the following section the OMiLAB infrastructure is introduced and then the executable models implemented in BeeUp and Camunda are presented.

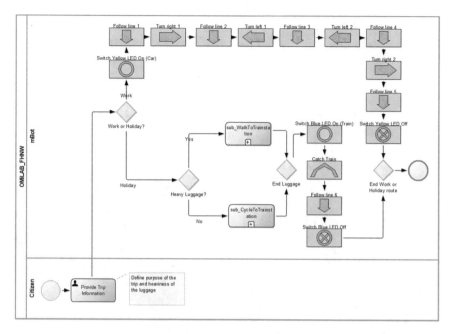

Fig. 27.9 The mobility plan scenario modelled in BPMN4MoPla with two expanded sub-processes

27.5.2.1 The OMiLAB Infrastructure for the Cyber-Physical System

The OMiLAB infrastructure enables the quick prototyping of cyber-physical systems [40] and fulfils the remaining requirements about the CPS, i.e., REQ-200 to REQ-202 (see Sect. 27.4.2). The following main hardware and software components were used for the quick prototyping of our CPS (details are left out for space reasons):

- A laptop, able to launch the modelling environment, BeeUp and the Camunda modeller.
- The modelling environment BeeUp is used in research and offers built in functions to send HTTP requests through the proprietary AdoScript language. In our case, it allowed the creation of executable models through the Flowchart modelling language.
- The modelling environment Camunda has a strong focus on process automation and is widely used across industries. It offers a Java-based workflow engine and a modelling environment through which it is possible to extend BPMN models with technical aspects, such as HTTPS requests and scripts in JavaScript.
- A robotic car mBot manufactured by Makeblock. The embedded *Me Line Follower Sensor* was used for the mBot to detect black stripes representing the routes (addressing REQ-201). Moreover, the robotic car incorporates an LED,

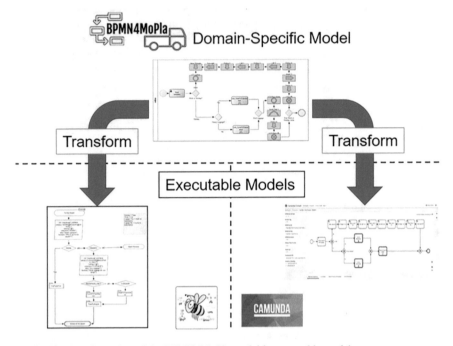

Fig. 27.10 Transformation of the BPMN4MoPla model in executable models

which can be turned on and off and can change colour. Hence, requirement REQ-202 is also fulfilled.

- Printed street layout containing the black stripes to be followed by the mBot.
- mBot API or a REST interface consists of a predefined list of HTTP commands to be consumed from the Flowchart model (via AdoScripts) to control mBot. The latter accesses the APIs by means of a Raspberry Pi.

The prerequisite for a cyber-physical system to work is to connect the physical devices (laptop and mBot) with a WIFI access point. Hence, REQ-200 is finally fulfilled.

27.5.2.2 Executable BPMN4MoPla Model in BeeUp

For the execution of the mobility plan scenario in BeeUp, the BPMN4MoPla model, discussed in Sect. 27.5.1, was transformed into a Flowchart model. The right-hand side of Fig. 27.11 depicts the complete model.

Each route (Drive to Airport, Walk to Train Station, Cycle to Train Station, and Take Train to Airport) was implemented as a main function (see the rectangles with double borders on the right-hand side of Fig. 27.11). In turn, each route is composed of atomic functions for the movement and the LED colour change of the robotic car. Such atomic functions were also implemented through Flowchart and can be used to create more routes. Similar to the shape of BPMN Gateways, Flowchart visualizes conditions in a diamond-like shape, e.g., see Work, Holiday, Backpack only and Luggage in Fig. 27.11. An AdoScript is executed before each main condition for the user input (see the two parallelepiped elements in Fig. 27.11), which is then used to automatically steer the workflow as a result of the evaluated conditions. The bottom right part of Fig. 27.11 shows the two pop-up windows that are triggered by the two AdoScripts, respectively.

The left-hand side of Fig. 27.11 depicts the physical environment in which the Flowchart model was executed. Each bubble contains a number for the logical order of the workflow and one alphabetic letter that represents one instance, i.e., a, b and c. Whenever the bubble is coloured, it means that the LED of the mBot is turned on; otherwise it is turned off.

To give a running example, let us follow the instance "a" from the top of Fig. 27.11: first the user clicks on the bubble "execute" of the Flowchart, which triggers the first script (see bubble 1a). Next, the user chooses "Work" from the pop-up window (see bubble 2a). Hence, the condition of driving by car evaluates to true and the function "Drive to Airport" is executed, which switches on the LED in yellow colour (the colour for the car) and lets the mBot move from home to the airport (see bubble 3a). Note the same bubble 3a also on the left-hand side of the figure to show the approximate position of the mBot at the time of the execution. Finally, once the mBot arrives to the airport (final destination) the LED is switched off (see bubble 4a).

Similarly, the execution of the remaining instances b and c can be followed by looking at the two threads from bubble 1b to 7b and from 1c to 7c, respectively in Fig. 27.11.

27.5.2.3 Executable BPMN4MoPla Model in Camunda

The BPMN4MoPla model (see Sect. 27.5.1) was transformed into an executable model where the model is compliant with the BPMN 2.0 standard. The built-in offered by the Camunda Modeller allows the technical configuration of the BPMN Service Tasks, i.e., HTTP-connector. Hence, the CarMovement model elements were all transformed in Service Tasks.

The transformed model is shown in Fig. 27.12. While elements in the first layer of abstraction are the same as for BPMN4MoPla, the elements in the three sub-processes are all service tasks that were configured to consume the mBot API. The first task is implemented as a User Task so as to collect the required data to be then evaluated in the out-going sequence flows of the two XOR Gateways. The left-hand side of Fig. 27.13 shows the specification of the condition on the out-going sequence flow named "Yes" of the first gateway. If the condition evaluates to true,

Execution of the model in the OMiLAB   Executable Flowchart model in BeeUp
physical environment

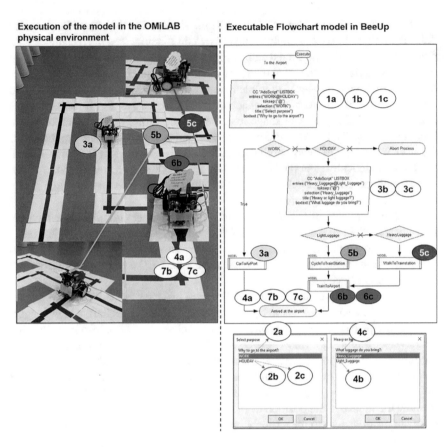

Fig. 27.11 The mobility plan model executed via BeeUp

the activity that is pointing to the sequence flow is executed, which according to the model shown in Fig. 27.12 is "Switch Yellow LED On". The specification of this service task in Camunda is shown on right-hand side of Fig. 27.13. Namely, after specifying the connector ID as an HTTP-connector, the input parameters of the HTTP call can be entered, i.e., method (GET), URL (it addresses the URL of the mBot API command that turns the LED colour to yellow), headers (it sets the content-type to application/json), and payload (it contains the script in JavaScript to convert all methods, URL and headers into a JSON format).

Once the entire model is deployed, it can be executed, and the workflow engine takes care of the sequential execution of the process. In our case the deployment was carried out locally through the Apache Tomcat web server environment and thus the execution environment of Camunda was accessible via *localhost:8080*.

The execution behaviour of the BPMN process model was the same as that through BeeUp. This proved that the BPMN4MoPla model can be executed in the OMiLAB environment for the quick prototyping of cyber-physical systems. Such a proof validates the conceived BPMN4MoPla method.

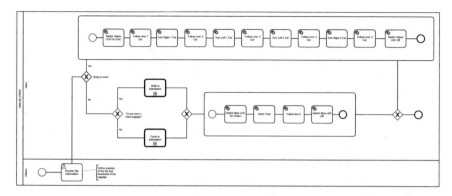

Fig. 27.12   The mobility plan model implemented in Camunda

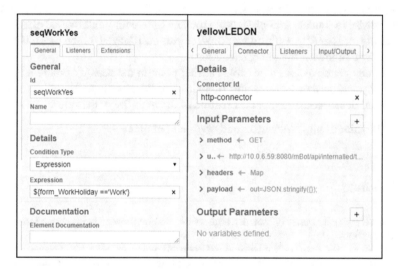

Fig. 27.13   Example of technical configurations in Camunda

27.6   Conclusion

This chapter presents the modelling method BPMN4MoPla. The modelling standard BPMN was extended to integrate physical car movements with business-like process and decision logic. This extension allows the creation of domain-specific models for mobility planning. Both the domain specificity of models and their execution support the decision-making in early stages of mobility planning by generating a feedback loop from both the design time and the runtime.

The modelling method was created by following the Design Science Research (DSR) methodology and was supplemented by the AMME methodology for its engineering.

A list of design requirements for both the DSML and the CPS was derived from the analysis of a mobility planning scenario. Next, the requirements were addressed for the conceptualization of the DSML and for the adoption of the CPS environment: the OMiLAB infrastructure for the quick prototyping of CPSs.

The DSML was implemented with the ADOxx Meta-Modelling Toolkit and deployed in a modelling tool, which enabled the design of a mobility planning scenario with BPMN4MoPla. The execution of the BPMN4MoPla model was performed by transforming the model into two executable workflows using two different modelling environments respectively: the research-based tool BeeUp and the industry-based modelling tool Camunda. Hence, the validation of the method was performed by modelling the mobility planning with the DSML and by proving that the two corresponding executable models output the expected result.

The goal of future work includes the integration of the design and runtime environments for the BPMN4MoPla by either (1) automatically transforming BPMN4MoPla models into executable models by creating interfaces between the modelling tools or (2) creating a workflow engine customized for the BPMN4MoPla modelling method for the direct execution.

This chapter advocates a possible starting point in the design of more advanced cyber-physical systems embracing domain-specific modelling languages for the support of decision-making in the creation of the mobility of the future.

Tool Download   https://www.omilab.org/bpmn4mopla.

References

1. WEF: Shaping the Future of Mobility, https://www.weforum.org/platforms/shaping-the-future-of-mobility
2. Krukle, Z., Biezina, L., Ernsteins, R.: Sustainable urban mobility planning development preconditions: governance system approach. In: Engineering for Rural Development. pp. 954–963. Latvia University of Life Sciences and Technologies (2019). https://doi.org/10.22616/ERDev2019.18.N528
3. Deka, L., Khan, S.M., Chowdhury, M., Ayres, N.: Transportation Cyber-Physical System and its importance for future mobility. In: Deka, L. and Chowdhury, M. (eds.) Transportation Cyber-Physical Systems. pp. 1–20. Elsevier (2018). https://doi.org/10.1016/B978-0-12-814295-0.00001-0
4. European Commision: Study to support an impact assessment of the urban mobility package - Final Report. 392 (2013)
5. EU: Integrated planning | CIVITAS, https://civitas.eu/TG/integrated-planning (2020)
6. Lah, O.: Sustainable urban mobility in action. In: Sustainable Urban Mobility Pathways: Policies, Institutions, and Coalitions for Low Carbon Transportation in Emerging Countries. pp. 133–282. Elsevier (2018). doi:https://doi.org/10.1016/B978-0-12-814897-6.00007-7
7. Okraszewska, R., Romanowska, A., Wołek, M., Oskarbski, J., Birr, K., Jamroz, K.: Integration of a multilevel transport system model into sustainable urban mobility planning. Sustainability. **10** (2018). https://doi.org/10.3390/su10020479
8. Benyon, D., Bental, D., Green, T.: Conceptual modeling for user interface development. Springer (1999)

9. Laurenzi, E.: An Agile and Ontology-Aided Approach for Domain-Specific Adaptations of Modelling Languages. https://repository.up.ac.za/handle/2263/73419
10. Kelly, S., Tolvanen, J.-P.: Domain-specific modeling: enabling full code generation. Wiley-Interscience (2008)
11. Hudak, P.: Paul: Building domain-specific embedded languages. ACM Comput. Surv. **28**, 196-es (1996). https://doi.org/10.1145/242224.242477
12. Hinkelmann, K., Laurenzi, E., Martin, A., Thönssen, B.: Ontology-based metamodeling. In: Dornberger, R. (ed.) Business Information Systems and Technology 4.0. Studies in Systems, Decision and Control, pp. 177–194. Springer, Cham (2018). https://doi.org/10.1007/978-3-319-74322-6_12
13. Atkinson, C., Gerbig, R., Fritzsche, M.: A multi-level approach to modeling language extension in the Enterprise Systems Domain. Inf. Syst. **54**, 289–307 (2015). https://doi.org/10.1016/j.is.2015.01.003
14. Braun, R.: Towards the state of the art of extending enterprise modeling languages. Model. 2015 – Proceedings of the 3rd International Conference on Model. Engineering and Software Development, pp. 394–402 (2015). doi:https://doi.org/10.5220/0005329703940402
15. Atkinson, C., Gerbig, R., Fritzsche, M.: Modeling language extension in the enterprise systems domain. In: 2013 17th IEEE International Enterprise Distributed Object Computing Conference, pp. 49–58. IEEE (2013). doi:https://doi.org/10.1109/EDOC.2013.15
16. Braun, R., Esswein, W.: Classification of domain-specific BPMN extensions. In: The Practice of Enterprise Modeling, pp. 42–57. Springer, Berlin (2014). https://doi.org/10.1007/978-3-662-45501-2_4
17. Reimer, U., Laurenzi, E.: Creating and maintaining a collaboration platform via domain-specific reference modelling. In: EChallenges e-2014 Conference: 29–30 October 2014, Belfast, pp. 1–9. IEEE (2014)
18. Völter, M., Stahl, T., Bettin, J., Haase, A., Helsen, S.: Model-Driven Software Development: Technology, Engineering, Management. Wiley, West-Sussex (2013)
19. Acatech: Cyber-Physical Systems - Driving force for innovations in mobility, health, energy and production. Springer, Berlin (2011)
20. Tao, F., Qi, Q., Wang, L., Nee, A.Y.C.: Digital twins and cyber–physical systems toward smart manufacturing and industry 4.0: correlation and comparison. Engineering. **5**, 653–661 (2019). https://doi.org/10.1016/j.eng.2019.01.014
21. Wan, K., Alagar, V.: Dependable context-sensitive services in cyber physical systems. In: 10th International Conference on Trust, Security and Privacy in Computing and Communicationsh Int. Conf. on FCST 2011. pp. 687–694. IEEE (2011). doi:https://doi.org/10.1109/TrustCom.2011.88
22. Huang, J., Bastani, F., Yen, I.L., Dong, J., Zhang, W., Wang, F.J., Hsu, H.J.: Extending service model to build an effective service composition framework for cyber-physical systems. In: IEEE International Conference on Service-Oriented Computing and Applications, SOCA' 09, pp. 130–137. IEEE (2009). doi:https://doi.org/10.1109/SOCA.2009.5410453
23. Graja, I., Kallel, S., Guermouche, N., Kacem, A.H.: BPMN4CPS: A BPMN extension for modeling cyber-physical systems. Proceedings - 25th IEEE International Conference Enabling Technologies: Infrastructure for Collaborative Enterprises. WETICE 2016. 152–157 (2016). doi:https://doi.org/10.1109/WETICE.2016.41
24. Lu, Y., Liu, C., Wang, K.I.K., Huang, H., Xu, X.: Digital Twin-driven smart manufacturing: Connotation, reference model, applications and research issues. Robot. Comput. Integr. Manuf. **61**, 101837 (2020). https://doi.org/10.1016/j.rcim.2019.101837
25. Negri, E., Fumagalli, L., Macchi, M.: A review of the roles of digital twin in CPS-based production systems. Procedia Manuf. **11**, 939–948 (2017). https://doi.org/10.1016/j.promfg.2017.07.198
26. Kumar, R., Chanchal, C., Apurva, A., Anjali, A.: Internet of Things (IOT). Proceedings of the International Conference on Innovative Computing & Communication (ICICC), April 23, 2021 (2021). Available at SSRN: https://ssrn.com/abstract=3832727 or http://dx.doi.org/10.2139/ssrn.3832727

27. Compagnucci, I., Corradini, F., Fornari, F., Polini, A., Re, B., Tiezzi, F.: Modelling Notations for IoT-Aware Business Processes: A Systematic Literature Review. 1–13 (2020)
28. Zoughbi, G., Briand, L., Labiche, Y.: Modeling safety and airworthiness (RTCA DO-178B) information: Conceptual model and UML profile. Softw. Syst. Model. **10**, 337–367 (2011). https://doi.org/10.1007/S10270-010-0164-X
29. Aziz, M.W., Rashid, M.: Domain Specific Modeling Language for Cyber Physical Systems. In: 2016 International Conference on Information Systems Engineering (ICISE), pp. 29–33. IEEE (2016). doi:https://doi.org/10.1109/ICISE.2016.12
30. Berkenkötter, K., Hannemann, U.: Modeling the Railway Control Domain Rigorously with a UML 2.0 Profile, https://link.springer.com/chapter/10.1007/11875567_30, (2006). https://doi.org/10.1007/11875567_30
31. Hevner, A.R., March, S.T., Park, J., Ram, S.: Design Science in Information Systems Research. MIS Q. **28**, 75–105 (2004)
32. Karagiannis, D.: Conceptual modelling methods: The AMME agile engineering approach. In: Silaghi, G., Buchmann, R., Boja, C. (eds.) Informatics in Economy, pp. 3–19. Springer, Cham (2018). https://doi.org/10.1007/978-3-319-73459-0_1
33. Karagiannis, D.: Agile modeling method engineering. ACM International Conference Proceeding Series, 01-03-Oct, 5–10 (2015). doi:https://doi.org/10.1145/2801948.2802040
34. Bork, D., Buchman, R.A., Karagiannis, D., Lee, M., Miron, E.-T.: An Open Platform for Modeling Method Conceptualization: The OMiLAB Digital Ecosystem. Communications of the Association for Information Systems (2019)
35. Frank, U.: Outline of a method for designing domain-specific modelling languages, http://hdl.handle.net/10419/58163, (2010)
36. Tullis, T. (Thomas), Albert, B. (William): Measuring the user experience: collecting, analyzing, and presenting usability metrics. Elsevier (2013)
37. Laurenzi, E., Hinkelmann, K., Reimer, U., Van Der Merwe, A., Sibold, P., Endl, R.: DSML4PTM: A domain-specific modelling language for patient transferal management. ICEIS 2017 – Proceedings of the 19th International Conference on Enterprise Information Systems 3, 520–531 (2017). doi:https://doi.org/10.5220/0006388505200531
38. OMG: Business Process Model and Notation (BPMN), Version 2.0. http://www.omg.org/spec/BPMN/20100501, http://www.omg.org/spec/BPMN/20100502, (2011)
39. OMG: Decision Model and Notation. (2016)
40. Karagiannis, D., Muck, C.: OMiLAB Physical Objects (OMiPOB). https://www.omilab.org/assets/docs/OMiROB_description_draft.pdf
41. Efendioglu, N., Woitsch, R., Utz, W., Falcioni, D.: ADOxx Modelling Method Conceptualization Environment. Astesj. (2017)

Chapter 28
BPMN Extension for Multi-Protocol Data Orchestration

Andrei Chis and Ana-Maria Ghiran

Abstract The Web of Things enriches Web development ecosystems with new kinds of data sources, complementing databases whose content used to be originated primarily from manual user input with data picked by sensors and physical devices. Consequently, the traditional notions of service orchestration or ETL data pipelines must be revisited to capture the technological specificity of digital ecosystems where workflow execution must combine traditional REST-based data APIs with data obtained through alternate protocols. CoAP is such a protocol introduced by the Web of Things for constrained devices—i.e., data sources where HTTP is not always adequate, or must be complemented with a lighter, UDP-based approach. We revisit the concept of model-driven data pipelines by extending BPMN with technology-specific concepts and properties that are able to trigger both HTTP and CoAP requests from a modeling environment. For this, a BPMN-centric modeling method was implemented, which may be used either as a design-time tool to maintain a Web API ecosystem or as a run-time dashboard to trigger the execution of API requests using either HTTP or CoAP, which makes it fit for testing data services in the Web of Things environment or to orchestrate them using BPMN as control flow. The implementation was built as an extension to the open-source BEE-UP modeling tool with the help of the ADOxx metamodeling platform.

Keywords REST API management · CoAP · API modeling · BPMN · Model-driven software engineering · Web of Things

28.1 Introduction

As a substantial number of business processes rely on the provision of data services from other companies, i.e., adopting a service-oriented architecture (SOA) [1] as a solution for their organizational needs, there are numerous challenges in managing

A. Chis · A.-M. Ghiran (✉)

Business Informatics Research Center, Babeş-Bolyai University, Cluj-Napoca, Romania

e-mail: andrei.chis@stud.ubbcluj.ro; anamaria.ghiran@econ.ubbcluj.ro

© The Author(s), under exclusive license to Springer Nature Switzerland AG 2022   639
D. Karagiannis et al. (eds.), *Domain-Specific Conceptual Modeling*,
https://doi.org/10.1007/978-3-030-93547-4_28

that architecture and having its technical view aligned with the process-centric business view as promoted by Business Process Management. Traditional approaches used to focus on designing the control flow while the data available or necessary at run time is neglected [2]. Certain design flaws could only be observed at a much later time, after system implementation. Therefore, there is a need to complement the design time business process with the run-time execution of data services, so that one can quickly test their performance and correct possible faults. From this point of view, we propose a modeling method that brings closer the run-time and design-time view on data APIs as resources for process execution. Moreover, we address the technology-specific context of the Web of Things, by incorporating in the modeling method not only concepts pertaining to generic REST-based APIs [3] but also the UDP-based alternative of CoAP, the Constrained Application Protocol [4], which is necessary for data services running on constrained devices that capture not only discrete values but also continuous data streams.

To this end, BPMN process diagrams are enriched with semantic links to new types of models describing API requests (both HTTP-based and CoAP-based), having API calls triggered directly from the modeling environment. Consequently, business process models that require interaction with APIs are completely documented and even tested for reliability. From another perspective, the modeling method can also be used to maintain a conceptual diagrammatic view, with features such as model queries for analysing BPMN models coupled with the Web of Things ecosystem in which they run.

The proposed modeling method is called MULTIPROTOCOL, as it extends the BPMN standard [3] to enable model-driven, process centric, multi-protocol API management—this is planned to evolve toward incorporating other protocols, but in the version presented here it covers HTTP and CoAP support.

The proposed method is the result of an iterative Design Science research effort [5] that had early partial iterations reported in [6, 7], with new improvements now added to extend its applicability toward the Web of Things. The initial draft reported in [8] was a typical case of a model-aware software product in the sense given by [9] where "model awareness" refers to run-time components that query model contents and act according to the diagrammatic information and its annotations. The new version progressed toward a "model-driven" software artifact, with certain components generated from models, complementing HTTP with CoAP, which is used to communicate with devices that have constrained resources—wireless sensors usually encountered in the Web of Things, gradually permeating enterprise information systems (according to a Gartner study, "senior executives regard IoT as a top-five game changing technology" [10]).

The functionality for launching API requests from the modeling environment is coupled with BPMN, which is part of the MULTIPROTOCOL implementation, as adopted from the BEE-UP tool [11]. Therefore, we extended BEE-UP's BPMN model type with aspects regarding API configuration and execution manifested at both conceptual level (by providing new concepts in the metamodel) and application level (by adding mechanisms for making requests to those APIs through HTTP and CoAP).

As a running example, a case from the area of a production company was selected in order to demonstrate the feasibility of the new features included in the modeling method. The envisioned situation is a manufacture that must use specific temperature and humidity in the products' packing process in order to meet the clients' quality requirements and to support quality control processes. Therefore, we exemplified a small process including as a prerequisite step checking the level of these sensors before product packaging tasks.

The remainder of this chapter is structured as follows. Section 28.2 provides the motivation, offers a high-level overview of the proposed method, and discusses other related works. Section 28.3 discusses design aspects for our modeling method and Sect. 28.4 presents the proof-of-concept implementation illustrated by the application case. The chapter ends with conclusions.

28.2 Method Description

Our work was driven by the new challenges regarding business operations management that must consider process improvement by assessing information available at run time (rather than reconsidering the design after the implementation phase). Supplementarily, an increased number of business activities rely on data services, as many organizations were inspired by the service-based architecture (SOA) [12]. Therefore, it is of paramount importance to ensure as early as possible that such a service is reliable as there could be multiple process activities which depend on it.

Even with the increased demand to ensure interoperability between the design phase and the execution time, business process descriptions and service configurations and executions evolved separately. BPM systems like Camunda [13] focus on creating workflow and decision models and deploying them but disregard the possibility to have service descriptions as modeling constructs. Interface description languages like Swagger [14] enable the description of a software's API in a language-independent way but are missing a visual interpretation and also a service execution engine. Robotic Process Automation (RPA) tools like UiPath [15] enable the specification and execution of a flow of activities but completely ignore business process modeling standards such as BPMN.

28.2.1 Problem Statement and Solution Overview

The above-mentioned shortcomings inspired the work at hand—a modeling method for designing API calls for both analysis and execution purposes. API descriptions like those enabled by Swagger are thus extensions to the BPMN modeling language and specific algorithms interpret the model semantics and achieve the intended execution (like in an RPA tool). This integration, on one hand, empowers the possibility to have the service descriptions in a diagrammatic modeling language also benefitting from existing BPMN analysis mechanisms, and on the other hand, to run and test service requests directly from the business process modeling environment, minimizing the time to incorporate feedback from the execution phase into the design phase.

Figure 28.1 provides an overview over the developed prototype and its processing flow. For fast prototyping of the method, we employed the ADOxx metamodeling platform [16], and Node.js [17] scripts which are required as an execution medium for our source code.

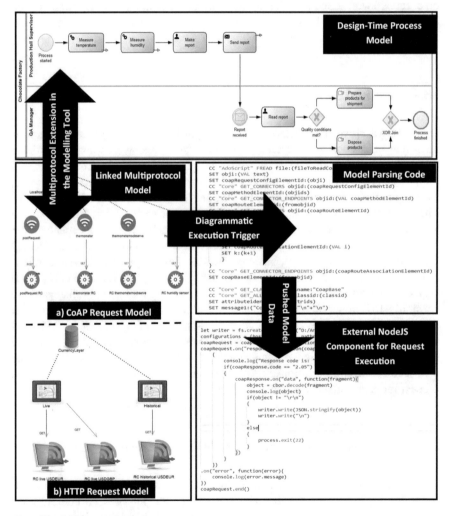

Fig. 28.1 Solution overview

The proposed solution can also evolve to integrate more diverse business modeling languages, facilitating its adoption by modelers that are familiar with other notations than BPMN.

There are three relevant stakeholders that could find beneficial our modeling method (depicted in Fig. 28.2), a distinction between such roles is not clear cut:

1. A business process modeler—in addition to her/his ability to describe how the business is done (as-is) or should be done (to-be), now there is also the possibility to document the execution for those activities that require integration of API calls.
2. A process automation expert—can have a high level overview of the configuration and execution of the API calls in a modeling environment.
3. A project manager—will have the ability to perform various analysis through ADOxx's model queries over the combination of the BPMN-API models.

Figure 28.2 suggests use cases that cover both System Automation Environments and Modeling.

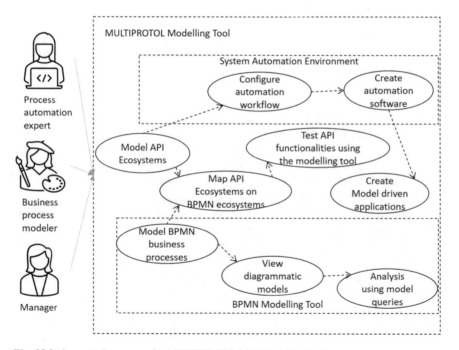

Fig. 28.2 Supported use cases for MULTIPROTOCOL Modeling Tool

28.2.2   Related Works

Closing the gap between the design phase and the run-time phase in business process management projects has been under consideration since the advent of Workflow Management Systems (WfMS) [18] that aim to automate business processes, by modeling and controlling their execution. With WfMS, the business process models are transformed into a formal language supported by a workflow engine (e.g., XML Process Definition Language—XPDL [19] or Web-Services Business Process Execution Language—WS-BPEL [20]) and then executed. If some unexpected situations or errors are identified at run time, the cycle must be reiterated. In dynamic environments, characterized by a high number of changes (as is the case of business settings that use numerous unreliable devices, with changing availability, e.g., sensors, third-party services), designing a business process should strive to anticipate all the possible changes and include various combinations of resources required for process activities or risk to include potential flaws in the model because of the unreliability of the data.

This problem has been identified by other researchers as well: Goldstein et al. [21] refer to this as "a strict separation between BPM lifecycle phases" and proposed an approach to include run-time data during design time by creating business process representations that are shared across all phases, using a meta-programming language called eXecutable Modeling Facility [22] to implement a business process modeling language, OrgML, part of the Multi-Perspective Modeling Framework (MEMO) [23].

Other studies tackled the problem of having an increased number of business activities that rely on service architecture, and identified the need to incorporate API management at model level [24]. They proposed a rule-based language that enables creation of models from API objects and, vice versa, generation of such API objects from models. For this, they created some mapping definitions between JAVA API specifications and the metamodel that is used to represent them.

Ivanchikj et al. [25] extended BPMN Choreography diagrams to create RESTalk, which allows API developers to represent the client–server interactions in diagrammatic form. Their goal was to improve the developers' understanding of the API structure that needs to be implemented and to make them employ better API-driven applications. Another work in the area of modeling RESTful conversations has been conducted by [26], which also extended the notation that is used in BPMN Choreography models.

Zalila et al. [27] devise OCCIWare, a model-driven tool for managing cloud service resources using the Open Cloud Computing Interface (OCCI) but their approach separates the design phase and the run-time phase into two components.

Our work is also related to studies in the area of domain-specific modeling languages for orchestrating the ETL process (as their main goal is to manage access to various data sources). From this perspective, we can point to the work of Biswas et al. [28] that used SysML, an UML extension, for modeling an ETL process from a conceptual point of view in order to have a high-level overview of the system activities. Akkaoui et al. [29] had been using BPMN to model the ETL process, while Grossmann et al. [30] created a domain-specific modeling method called DICE (Data Integration and Cleansing Environment) that allows specification of a data transformation workflow to support various phases in the business decision making.

28.3 Method Conceptualization

This section describes the MULTIPROTOCOL modeling method. On the conceptual level, it is an instance of the notion of a modeling method [31] with three building blocks: the modeling language, the modeling procedure, and the mechanisms and algorithms. The suggested conceptualization requires identifying the constructs of the modeling language, setting a flow in modeling activities, and relating constructs on the mechanisms and algorithms for processing purposes. Agile Modeling Method Engineering (AMME) [32] was selected as a methodological approach to be able to develop the method iteratively and in quick engineering cycles. AMME guides the development of domain-specific modeling tools or adapting them to match a situational purpose, following an iterative and incremental approach. In our case we extended the BPMN implementation included in the open-source BEE-UP tool [11] with concepts that can describe the Web of Things API ecosystems.

The extensions are reflected at both the conceptual level and the application level. At the conceptual level, the domain specificity manifests further on the notational level (new symbols for the added concepts), semantic level (several REST and HTTP/CoAP properties have been defined), and syntactic level (some cardinality restrictions and domain and range limitations were imposed). At the application level, specific mechanisms were defined to trigger the functionality of API requests in the modeling environment either through HTTP or through CoAP.

First, we will detail the proposed extension elements pertaining to the modeling language, and then we will proceed with describing the mechanisms and algorithms in delivering the functional requirements of our modeling method. We will describe the modeling procedure alongside the exemplified use case.

28.3.1 Proposed BPMN Extensions

The proposed extension to BPMN includes new concepts that are needed to describe API calls through the considered protocols—HTTP and CoAP. These are grouped in two different model types to achieve a separation of concerns.

For these changes, the metamodel included several new core classes and relation classes that can be observed in Fig. 28.3, where we used UML as one of the possible approaches to specify a metamodel out of the techniques suggested by [33].

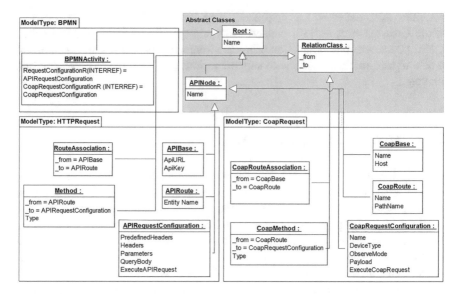

Fig. 28.3 MULTIPROTOCOL metamodel

Figure 28.3 depicts the metamodel of our extension, omitting almost all of the BPMN concepts, as they are not the subject of the current work.

The only BPMN construct that is depicted is the BPMNActivity for which two attributes have been added, RequestConfigurationReference and CoapRequestConfigurationReference, in order to connect it with the Configuration concept from the new model types. These attributes exclude each other: If the modeler sets a value for one of them, the other one becomes deactivated. This notational variability helps in reducing possible unintended errors of connecting activities with the wrong API calls.

We decided to group the proposed concepts in separate model types, thus allowing distinct descriptions of API services that can be reused by various business process activities that are linked to them.

The two model types, HTTPRequest and CoAPRequest, act as containers, grouping concepts that are related to trigger the API requests. HTTPRequest contains concept classes that deal with HTTP requests: APIBase, Route and RequestConfiguration grouped under a more general concept APINode and two relation classes, RouteAssociation and Method.

The second model type, CoAPRequest, includes similar concepts tailored for the CoAP protocol. A key difference is that the CoAP protocol is designed for machine-to-machine communication, which implies that when sending requests these should emerge from a backend server, and when receiving the results, some decoding must be performed (this is the reason for selecting Node.js to implement the functional component in our proposal). However, configuring a CoAP request similarly allows declarations for routes and methods (but limited to GET, POST, PUT, DELETE), and hence it can be depicted in the modeling environment similar to the other HTTP requests.

28.3.2   Semantic-Level Customizations

The proposed concepts are enriched with specific attributes in order to describe the API requests according to each protocol.

The *CoapBase* concept represents the request destination. Its attributes will include a name, which is just a more friendly way to refer to a request destination, and the APIURL attribute, which is used to store information regarding the base address of the request.

Various routes for the host are stored as *CoapRoute* concepts. Similar to the CoapBase concept, we included the name attribute and the PathName attribute, the latter to describe the path for a certain sensor of the host.

The *CoapRequestConfiguration* class stores all parameters needed to perform the request. These are tailored for the configuration details expected by the CoAP protocol. The most important attribute is DeviceType, which can take two values, Sensor or Actuator. Other attributes (ObserveMode and Payload) are enabled or disabled based on the chosen value for the DeviceType. The ObserveMode attribute is enabled if the request is for a Sensor and it can also take boolean values: True or False (True means that the requester can listen continuously to a response stream). The Payload attribute is activated only if the device type is Actuator and will be used to send a piece of information, a small string (e.g., setting a new threshold value or a command to the actuator). Besides these, CoapRequestConfiguration class also includes the ExecuteCoapRequest (of type Programcall in ADOxx terminology), which offers the possibility to launch into execution the API request with the established configuration.

28.3.3   Syntactic-Level Customization

Regarding the syntactic rules that should be defined for the proposed constructs, some of them, like domain and range constraints, must be set in ADOxx as soon as relations are created.

The relation class *CoapRouteAssociation* has the role to connect the CoapBase concept with its associated routes (i.e., CoapRoute). It does not include attributes as its role is just to link various possible routes to a host.

The relation class *CoapMethod* is used to link a specific CoapRoute to CoapRequestConfiguration. We decided to include within this construct an attribute (Type) to specify the type of request (GET, POST, PUT, DELETE).

Other syntactic restrictions can be set through cardinality rules. We imposed the existence of a single Base concept (either APIBase or CoapBase) for a model type instantiation. In this way, each diagrammatic model represents the description of a single API service.

Also, we imposed the maximum cardinality of 1 for the destination link Request-ConfigurationReference and CoapRequestConfigurationReference to address a single configuration concept (a one-to-one mapping between a BPMN task and a specific API request is achieved).

28.3.4   Notation-Level Customization

For all the proposed constructs, we aimed to correlate their graphical representation with their meaning, by selecting domain-specific symbols, guided by the semantic transparency principle discussed by [34].

Figure 28.4 shows the icons that we employed for all the proposed constructs (covering both HTTPRequest and CoapRequest model types).

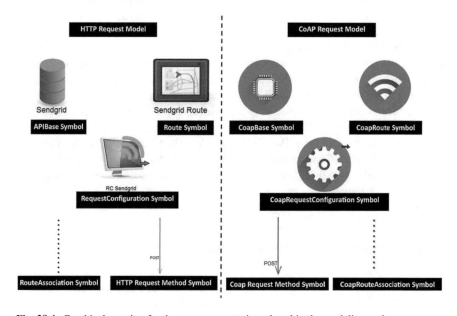

Fig. 28.4 Graphical notation for the new constructs introduced in the modeling tool

28.3.5   Functional Components

Even if a possible implementation could have been to use the built in ADOxx mechanisms for HTTP requests, we preferred to externalize this functionality to a

Node.js component for two reasons: first, support for handling JSON data structures is more intuitive, and second, we also tackle the alternative CoAP protocol which has no built in support in the metamodeling platform. CoAP actually requires exchanging data between devices, and hence a data access component had to be created to overcome this limitation. Nevertheless, we employed ADOxx's internal programming language (ADOScript [35]) to pass the information captured in diagrammatic models to the run time (e.g., all the configuration details for an API request).

There are two key algorithms that provide the run-time functionality of our API modeling method: one, in AdoScript, which reads the models' content (diagram path parsing algorithm) and another, in Node.js, which handles the API request execution (HTTP/CoAP Request execution algorithm). They interoperate in order to achieve the goal of supporting model-driven process automation based on APIs. The created API models (either HTTP or CoAP) can be considered as controllers for the execution of API requests as they dictate dynamic generation of scripts.

The CoapRequestConfiguration concept plays a central role by triggering the path parsing algorithm and by sending all the necessary data to the request execution algorithm. Launching the API request is handled by the Node.js component that reads a file with the API request's parameters created as an outcome of running the diagram path parsing algorithm. When the results are obtained from the API service, most of the time they are in a compressed format (e.g., CBOR [36] a binary alternative to JSON or EXI [37]—a binary alternative to XML), and therefore some decoding transformations should be performed. Similarly, if we send a request other than GET, the payload also needs to be encoded. Although JSON format can be used in some cases, we simplified the prototype by resorting to encoding and decoding to a single format, which is for our case the CBOR format. In the end, the results will be forwarded to the ADOxx modeling environment.

Figure 28.5 describes the involved processes in providing the API Requests functionality. The first two run in the modeling environment while the last one runs on Node.js.

The diagram path reconstruction process starts by obtaining the internal identifier for the concept from which the request is triggered, and then the connector ID corresponding to the Method concept is retrieved. Final steps in the process, likewise, are collecting the identifiers for the Route and Base concepts.

The data gathering process takes as input the identifiers list from the previous process and parses the attributes corresponding to each one. The combination of all these attributes is needed in order to define a full request—the URL is taken from the API Base or CoapBase, the full route is found in the PathName, the Type is an attribute of the Method connector, the RequestConfiguration concept contains Headers, Parameters, Body and CoapRequestConfiguration concept includes ObserveMode, Payload. All these attributes' values are stored in a file, whose content can be accessed by the external request execution script.

The Request Launching process (HTTP or CoAP) creates the necessary variables and reads the values of the request parameters from the file created in the previous step. According to the employed protocol, the script builds the request and launches it with the set configurations. The returned results are decoded, saved to another file and sent to the modeling environment.

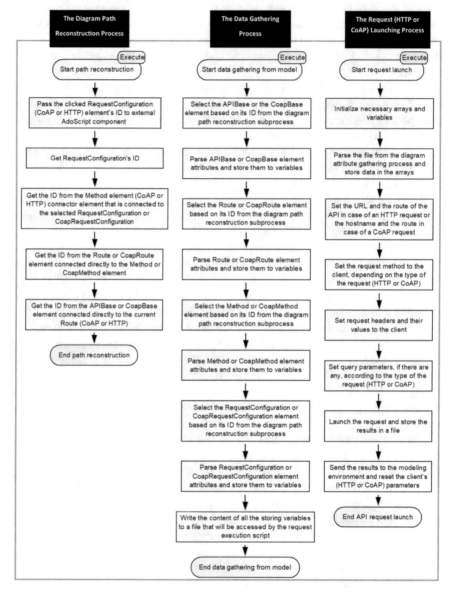

Fig. 28.5 Flowcharts describing the diagram path reconstruction process (left), the data gathering process (center) and the Request Launching process (right)

28.4 Proof-of-Concept: Multiprotocol Data Access Modeler

This section demonstrates the applicability of the MULTIPROTOCOL modeling method for complementing a business process model not only with a description of the required API calls it solicits, but also with the possibility to test them for better reliability.

The application scenario describes a business process that includes activities associated with IoT devices polling, for which CoAP protocol is suitable to complement HTTP calls for more traditional data. A straightforward example is a production company that should consider strict levels of temperature and humidity in the products' packaging process in order to ensure certain quality requirements. The production hall is equipped with various sensors to capture the values for temperature and humidity levels, and a production room Supervisor reports them to a Manager, who can decide if they will jeopardize the quality of the delivered products and consequently if the current packaging process should be disposed.

Figure 28.6 shows a BPMN model sample for such a situation.

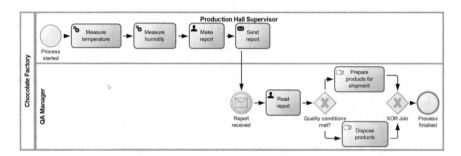

Fig. 28.6 Products' packaging process with data retrieval tasks

Considering that the sensors comprise capabilities to be remotely polled, the activities for reading their values can be further described in our modeling tool using our API model types.

For this reason, a second step in the modeling procedure is to model in a diagrammatic abstraction details pertaining to the data retrieval or changing their internal state (which will affect the environment they operate in). These models can be used as a repository that documents the adoption of smart devices across the organization and their capabilities. In other words, the models can be considered as digital twins of the physical objects, decoupling their digital representation from their concrete manifestation (in our models, the interface for accessing the device can have both sensors and actuators, and can receive both get and post requests, and correspondingly it will advance it to a specific widget).

The modeler can also describe a data service accessible via HTTP requests, having an overview of all the data dependencies.

Figure 28.7 shows on the left side a model describing the capabilities for a thermometer in terms of the base address to which it responds, the possible routes it can process, possible request types, and some request configurations it can interpret. On the right side, we can see details regarding the customization of the CoAP call that a modeler is able to set for a request sent to the same interface where the thermometer is also available. In this case, it is a post request with a small message (e.g., a message that sets a new threshold for temperature to the controlling component/actuator of the thermometer).

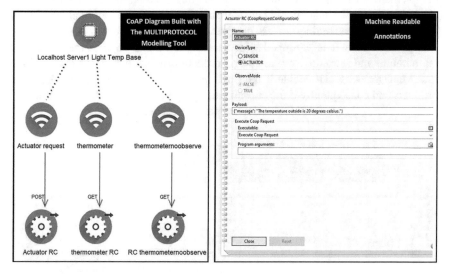

Fig. 28.7 Requests' capabilities description for a thermometer sensor (left) and customization of a CoAP Request addressed to this device (right)

Having both BPMN models and API request models, the next step in the modeling procedure is to map them, by associating activities from the business process with the required API calls. This is done by using semantic links between an element from a model and another element (possibly in another model, as shown here, where its destination is the RequestConfiguration concept either from HTTPRequest models or CoapRequest models) or to an entire other model. The links appear as hyperlinks in the modeling tool, allowing model navigation.

Figure 28.8 shows visual clues in the form of hotspots that enrich the BPMN activities once they are associated with an API request description.

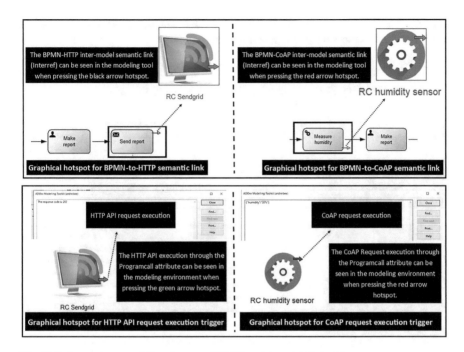

Fig. 28.8 Interactive associations between BPMN models and API models

In the next step in our modeling procedure, the modeler can execute the API requests by triggering an interactive visual hotspot built on a ProgramCall attribute. This operation will invoke the specific algorithms for launching the request, which creates the model-generated scripts that can fetch run-time data into the modeling tool. In this way, the process designer can quickly test the availability of a specific device needed in a business activity, and in case it is unresponsive, another one can be selected to ensure continuity.

In addition to testing the API requests in the modeling tool, our solution enables query-based analysis not only over the BPMN process models or API domain-specific models, but also over the combination of the BPMN-API models. ADOxx query Language, AQL [38], that is available in BEE-UP can also be used in our extended implementation.

First, an example of an AQL query to retrieve domain-specific information could be one that obtains the request parameters sent to devices of type actuators.

AQL code: < "CoapRequestConfiguration">[? "DeviceType" = "ACTUATOR"]

The result of the query is visible in the top part of Fig. 28.9.

Another example of an AQL query, this time one that combines information from both model types (BPMN and CoapRequest models), could be finding all the details (all the attributes) of an API request associated with a certain BPMN task, like "Measure humidity." By using these kinds of queries, users (e.g., managers) have the possibility to retrieve an IoT service's metadata and to understand how the IoT device can be employed (in which business activities).

AQL Code: ({"Measure humidity"}–> "CoapRequestConfigurationReference")

The result of this query is visible in the bottom part of Fig. 28.9.

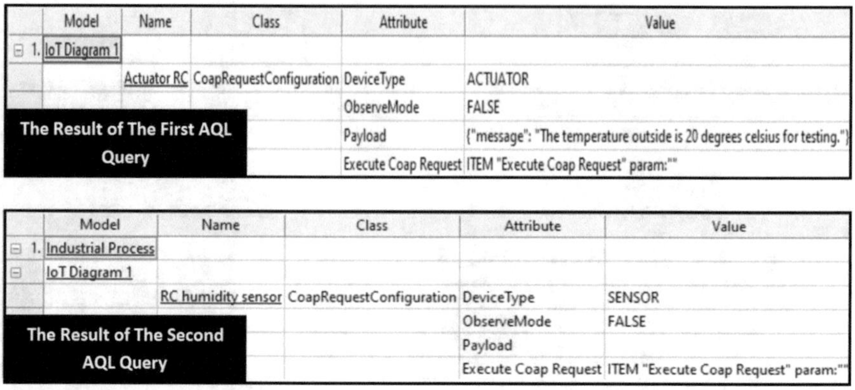

	Model	Name	Class	Attribute	Value
⊟ 1.	IoT Diagram 1				
		Actuator RC	CoapRequestConfiguration	DeviceType	ACTUATOR
				ObserveMode	FALSE
The Result of The First AQL				Payload	{"message": "The temperature outside is 20 degrees celsius for testing."}
Query				Execute Coap Request	ITEM "Execute Coap Request" param:""

	Model	Name	Class	Attribute	Value
⊟ 1.	Industrial Process				
⊟	IoT Diagram 1				
		RC humidity sensor	CoapRequestConfiguration	DeviceType	SENSOR
				ObserveMode	FALSE
The Result of The Second				Payload	
AQL Query				Execute Coap Request	ITEM "Execute Coap Request" param:""

Fig. 28.9 AQL query samples

28.5   Conclusions

This chapter presented a modeling method that aims to couple the design time business process activities with the execution time activities which require interaction with data APIs. In this way, information that is available at run time can be incorporated from an early design phase of business activities which improve the reliability of these operations. At the same time, having a model-based description of the API ecosystem facilitates a better understanding of the implications of the data services it is implementing while providing a multi-protocol client tool directly in the business process modeling environment. This actually moves into a BPMN environment functionality that is found in independent HTTP client tools (Postman [39]) while extending it to multi-protocol support by the addition of CoAP requests that are relevant for an IoT API ecosystem.

New model types were added to BPMN to capture the API domain-specific knowledge and to support testing, management and automation of APIs. Our motivation for adding CoAP was driven by the current trends in the organizations' initiatives to adopt IoT technology in their data architecture infrastructure, due to its ability to provide real-time performance indicators or environmental conditions on which certain business process tasks depend. Smart devices are affordable, and employing them in the operating structures can reshape an entire business process.

Tool Download   https://www.omilab.org/multiprotocol

References

1. The Open Group, SOA Source Book. http://www.opengroup.org/soa/source-book/intro/index.htm (2021). Accessed 01 Mar 2021
2. Garcia, M.O., Braghetto, K.R., Pu, C.: An implementation of a transaction model for business process systems. J. Inf. Data Manag. **3**(3), 271–271 (2012)
3. The RESTful API Modeling Language (RAML). https://www.raml.org/ (2021). Accessed 01 Mar 2021.
4. Shelby, Z., Hartke, K., Bormann, C.: The constrained application protocol (CoAP), IETF RFC 7252. https://tools.ietf.org/html/rfc7252 (2014). Accessed 01 Mar 2021
5. Wieringa, R.J.: Design Science Methodology for Information Systems and Software Engineering. Springer, New York (2014). https://doi.org/10.1007/978-3-662-43839-8
6. Chiş A.: Proof of concept for a BPMN-driven semantic orchestration of web APIs. In: Proceedings of the 18th International Conference on Informatics in Economy (IE 2019), pp. 193–198. https://doi.org/10.12948/ie2019.04.08 (2019)
7. Chiş, A.: A modeling method for model-driven API management. Complex Syst. Inf. Model. Q. **25**, 1–18 (2020)
8. OMG: The BPMN Specification Page. http://www.bpmn.org (2021). Accessed 01 Mar 2021
9. Buchmann, R.A., Cinpoeru, M., Harkai, A., Karagiannis, D.: Model-aware software engineering – a knowledge-based approach to model-driven software engineering. Proceedings of the 13th International Conference on Evaluation of Novel Approaches to Software Engineering. **1**, 233–240 (2018). https://doi.org/10.5220/0006694102330240
10. Gartner: IoT adoption trends: where your competitors are investing. https://www.gartner.com/en/innovation-strategy/trends/iot-adoption-trends (2020). Accessed 01 Mar 2021
11. OMiLAB: The metamodelling page for FCML and the bee-up tool. http://www.OMiLAB.org/bee-up (2016)
12. Demirkan, H., Kauffman, R.J., Vayghan, J.A., Fill, H.-G., Karagiannis, D., Maglio, P.P.: Service-oriented technology and management: perspectives on research and practice for the coming decade. Electron. Commerce Res. Appl. J. **7**(4), 356–376 (2008)
13. The Camunda Modeling Tool. https://camunda.com/. Accessed 01 Mar 2021
14. The SwaggerHub API Development Tool. https://swagger.io/tools/swaggerhub/. Accessed 01 Mar 2021
15. The UiPath RPA Solution Provider. https://www.uipath.com/. Accessed 01 Mar 2021
16. The ADOxx Toolkit: https://www.adoxx.org/live/home (2021). Accessed 01 Mar 2021
17. OpenJS Foundation, Node.js: https://nodejs.org/en/ (2021). Accessed 01 Mar 2021
18. WfMC Standards Framework - Workflow Management Coalition: http://www.wfmc.org/2 (2021). Accessed 01 Mar 2021
19. WfMC XPDL specification—official website: http://www.wfmc.org/53-standards/xpdl (2021). Accessed 01 Mar 2021
20. OASIS: BPEL—the official website: https://www.oasis-open.org/committees/tc_home.php?wg_abbrev=wsbpel (2021). Accessed 01 Mar 2021
21. Goldstein, A., Johanndeiter, T., Frank, U.: Business process runtime models: towards bridging the gap between design, enactment, and evaluation of business processes. Inf. Syst. e-Bus. Manag. **17**, 27–64 (2019). https://doi.org/10.1007/s10257-018-0374-2
22. Clark, T., Sammut, P., Willans, J.: Applied Metamodelling: A Foundation for Language Driven Development. Springer, New York (2008)

23. Frank U.: The MEMO meta modelling language (MML) and language architecture: ICB-Report 43 (2011)
24. Izquierdo, J.L.C., Jouault, F., Cabot, J., Molina, J.G.: API2MoL: automating the building of bridges between APIs and model-driven engineering. Inf. Softw. Technol. **54**(3), 257–273 (2012). https://doi.org/10.1016/j.infsof.2011.09.006
25. Ivanchikj, A., Pautasso, C., Schreier, S.: Visual modeling of RESTful conversations with RESTalk. Softw. Syst. Model. **17**, 1031–1051 (2018). https://doi.org/10.1007/s10270-016-0532-2
26. Pautasso, C., Ivanchikj, A., Schreier, S.: Modeling RESTful conversations with extended BPMN choreography diagrams. In: Software Architecture, ECSA (2015), Lecture notes in computer science, vol. 9278, pp. 87–94. Springer, New York (2015). https://doi.org/10.1007/978-3-319-23727-5_7
27. Zalila, F., Challita, S., Merle, P.: Model-driven cloud resource management with OCCIware. Future Gener. Comput. Syst. **99**, 260–277 (2019). https://doi.org/10.1016/j.future.2019.04.015
28. Biswas, N., Chattopadhyay, C., Mahapatra, G., Chatterjee, S., Mondal, K.C.: SysML based conceptual ETL process modeling. In: Computational Intelligence, Communications, and Business Analytics: First International Conference, pp. 242–255. CICBA, Kolkata, India (2017)
29. El Akkaoui, Z., Mazón, J.N., Vaisman, A., Zimányi, E.: BPMN-based conceptual modeling of ETL processes. In: Proceedings of International Conference on Data Warehousing and Knowledge Discovery, pp. 1–14. DaWaK, Vienna, Austria (2012)
30. Grossmann, W., Moser, C.: Big data integration and cleansing environment for business analytics with DICE. In: Domain-specific Conceptual Modeling, pp. 103–123. Springer, New York (2016)
31. Karagiannis, D., Kühn, H.: Metamodelling platforms. In: Bauknecht, K., Min Tjoa, A., Quirchmayer, G. (eds.) Proceedings of the Third International Conference EC-Web 2002—DEXA 2002, Aix-en-Provence, France. LNCS, vol. 2455, p. 182. Springer, Paris (2002)
32. Karagiannis, D.: Agile modeling method engineering. In: Proceedings the 19th Panhellenic Conference on Informatics (PCI 2015), pp. 5–10. ACM Press, Athens, Greece (2015)
33. Bork, D., Karagiannis, D., Pittl, B.: A survey of modeling language specification techniques. Inf. Syst. **87** (2020). https://doi.org/10.1016/j.is.2019.101425
34. Moody, D.: The "physics" of notations: towards a scientific basis for constructing visual notations in software engineering. IEEE Trans. Softw. Eng. **35**(5), 756–779 (2009). https://doi.org/10.1109/TSE.2009.67
35. The AdoScript Programming Language: https://www.adoxx.org/live/adoscript-language-constructs (2021). Accessed 01 Mar 2021
36. Bormann, C., Hoffman, P.: Concise Binary Object Representation, RFC 8949. https://www.rfc-editor.org/rfc/rfc8949.html (2020). Accessed 01 Mar 2021
37. Schneider J., Kamiya T., Peintner D. Kyusakov R.: Efficient XML Interchange (EXI) Format 1.0, W3C Recommendation. https://www.w3.org/TR/exi/ (2014). Accessed 01 Mar 2021
38. The AQL Query Language: https://www.adoxx.org/live/adoxx-query-language-aql. Accessed 01 Mar 2021
39. The Postman API Development Platform: https://www.postman.com/ (2021). Accessed 01 Mar 2021

Printed in the United States
by Baker & Taylor Publisher Services